Samuel Fitch Hotchkin

Ancient and Modern Germantown

Mount Airy and Chestnut Hill

Samuel Fitch Hotchkin

Ancient and Modern Germantown
Mount Airy and Chestnut Hill

ISBN/EAN: 9783742809681

Manufactured in Europe, USA, Canada, Australia, Japa

Cover: Foto ©ninafisch / pixelio.de

Manufactured and distributed by brebook publishing software (www.brebook.com)

Samuel Fitch Hotchkin

Ancient and Modern Germantown

ANCIENT AND MODERN

GERMANTOWN,

MOUNT AIRY

—AND—

CHESTNUT HILL

—BY—

Rev. S. F. HOTCHKIN, M.A.,

Author of The Mornings of the Bible, etc.

P. W. ZIEGLER & CO., Publishers,
No. 720 Chestnut Street,
Philadelphia, Pa.
1889.

COPYRIGHT, BY REV. S. F. HOTCHKIN, 1889.

GREEN'S HOUSE, FROM WATSON'S ANNALS, BY PERMISSION OF EDWIN S. STUART, PUBLISHER.

THIS BOOK IS

RESPECTFULLY DEDICATED

To my Friend,

H. H. HOUSTON,

WHO HAS DONE SO MUCH TO MAKE

<u>Ancient</u> Germantown <u>Modern</u> Germantown.

PREFACE.

This volume is an attempt to preserve the history of a delightful suburb of a pleasant city; and to increase the interest in those who have dwelt in the houses, and walked in the streets of Germantown in former days.

The lives of our fellow men here briefly recorded show that history is philosophy teaching by example; and may the Christian work, so often noted in these pages, encourage efforts to hand down religion and learning to those who are to dwell in Germantown in future years.

The author gladly acknowledges the constant kind courtesy of Henry W. Raymond, in furthering his work, as all the articles of the series appeared in the GERMANTOWN TELEGRAPH, edited by him, and his interest in local history stimulated the endeavor to disseminate information on the subject.

List of Illustrations.

NO.		PAGE.
* 1.	Seal of Germantown, ...	Frontispiece.
2.	Green's House, ...	2
* 3.	The Wister House, Main and Price Streets, .	12
4.	Stenton, former Residence of James Logan, .	20
* 5.	Loudon, Residence of Mrs. Anna A. Logan, .	26
* 6.	Royal's House, . . , . .	30
7.	Fishers Lane and Germantown Avenue,	34
8.	On the Road above Fishers Lane, . .	38
9.	Wister Homestead, . .	42
* 10.	Roberts Meadow, . . .	46
* 11.	Fleckenstein's House, . .	50
* 12.	The White Cottage, . .	54
* 13.	Ye Conyngham House, . . .	58
* 14.	The Friends' Meeting House, . .	62
* 15.	The Deshler-Washington-Morris House,	66
* 16.	Main and Manheim, .	70
17.	The Germantown Academy, .	72
18.	Shoemaker's First Farm, . . .	76
19.	St. Luke's Church, ...	80
20.	Chapel of Market Square Presbyterian Church,	84
21.	Market Square Presbyterian Church, .	86
22.	Market Square, . .	90
* 23.	The Old Ironsides, . .	96
24.	Matthias W. Baldwin, . .	98
* 25.	Main Street from School Lane,	102
* 26.	Main and Chelten Avenue, .	106
27.	First Presbyterian Church, .	114
* 28.	Shoemakers House, . .	122
29.	Residence of Mahlon Bryan, . . .	130
30.	The Young Men's Christian Association,	138
31.	E. H. Butler's Residence, .	142
32.	The Morris-Littell House, .	144

LIST OF ILLUSTRATIONS.

No.		Page.
33.	"Wyck",	148
34.	Friends' Free Library,	150
35.	The Daniel Pastorius Mansion,	152
36.	The Mennonite Church,	156
37.	St. Peter's Episcopal Church,	160
38.	Christ Church,	164
39.	The Rodney House,	180
40.	The Chew House,	192
41.	The Second Baptist Church,	214
42.	Carlton,	220
43.	John F. Watson,	244
44.	Keyser Coat of Arms,	266
45.	The Channon House,	268
46.	Samuel Keyser,	272
47.	Calvary Episcopal Church,	276
48.	Devonshire Place,	296
49.	National Bank of Germantown,	336
50.	Saving Fund,	338
51.	Mutual Fire Insurance Building,	340
52.	Scene on the Wissahickon,	346
53.	Grace Church,	354
54.	Mount Airy Presbyterian Church,	356
55.	Mount Airy College,	362
56.	Residence of James Gowen,	388
57.	The Gowen Homestead,	390
58.	Wissahickon Inn,	400
59.	Druim Moir,	420
60.	Druim Moir,	422
61.	St. Martin-in-the-Fields,	425
62.	Home for Consumptives,	438
63.	Rev. Samuel Durborow,	440
64.	St. Paul's Church,	444
65.	"Graystock" Country-Seat of George C. Thomas,	450
66.	Residence of Colonel George H. North,	452
67.	Norwood Hall,	458
68.	"Stonecliffe," Residence of Mrs. Charles Taylor,	464
69.	"The Evergreens," Residence of Mrs. Thomas Potter,	472
70.	"The Anglecot," Residence of Charles A. Potter,	480
71.	Residence of William Potter,	484
72.	"Edgcumbe," Residence of Charles B. Dunn,	488
73.	Residence of A. M. Collins,	492
74.	"Rauhala," Residence of A. Warren Kelsey,	498
75.	"Westleigh," Residence of Hon. Richard Vaux,	508
76.	"Roslyn Heights,",	514

LIST OF ILLUSTRATIONS.

NO.		PAGE.
77.	Churchill Hall,	528
78.	Franklin School,	534
79.	Residence of G. Ralston Ayers and S. Huckel,	536

* All the illustrations marked with an asterisk are inserted by the kind permission of Frederick D. Stone, editor of "The Pennsylvania Magazine of History and Biography," in which they appeared in connection with Townsend Ward's articles. Mr. H. W. Raymond, editor of the GERMANTOWN TELEGRAPH, was instrumental in introducing them into that paper.

Ancient and Modern Germantown.

> "Hail to posterity!
> Hail future men of Germanopolis!
> Let the young generations yet to be
> Look kindly upon this.
> Think how your fathers left their native land,—
> Dear German land! O sacred hearths and homes!!
> And where the wild beast roams
> In patience planned
> New forest homes beyond the mighty sea,
> There undisturbed and free
> To live as brothers of one family."
>
> *From the Latin of F. D. Pastorius—Whittier's translation.*

Townsend Ward furnished eight most interesting articles on "The Germantown Road and Its Associations" for the *Pennsylvania Magazine of History and Biography*, beginning with No. 1 of Vol. V, A. D. 1881, and ending in No. 4 of Vol. VI, A. D. 1882. He then stopped to solicit funds for the purchase of the new Historical Society rooms, formerly General Patterson's house, at the southwest corner of Thirteenth and Locust streets. His lamented death has made a final pause where he expected to make but a temporary one.

Mr. Ward had agreed with the editor of the GERMANTOWN TELEGRAPH, to continue the work in the columns of his paper, by request of the editor. It has fallen to the lot of the present writer to take up the task. He will receive some aid from the manuscripts of the late author, kindly placed in his hands by the courtesy of Frederick D. Stone, Librarian of the Historical Society of Pennsylvania.

Mr. Ward left a mass of notes on various topics, which show him to have been an indefatigable, as well as a wise, student of local history. In traveling he would pick up bits of information and jot them down, and his correspondence shows how he faithfully searched into details and was ready to correct errors. It also displays the great esteem in which he was held by persons of high station in the community. It is a source of much regret that the facile pen which lovingly described Second street and Darby road and Germantown road can work no more, and it would be desirable to print much of what he left in manuscript.

It now remains to do what the Germantown weavers described in the articles named would have done—that is, take up the broken thread and unite it and drive the loom ahead again. While young and old delight to read histories of Greece and Rome, why should they not look into the history of their own towns? The great English scholar, Lightfoot, was once writing on Jerusalem and had occasion to visit a piece of ground, in the sale of which he was interested, a mile or so from his own house, and could not locate the spot. While we look into that which is distant, let us not neglect what is near. On one of Ward's manuscript papers he has written that as Dr. Johnston said that the true history of a broom-stick would be interesting, much more "the history of a house with its various occupants, often similar, but often nevertheless, bringing together strange and startling juxtapositions."

In A. D. 1698, Gabriel Thomas's account of Philadelphia and the Province was printed in London. It reaches up to 1696. He resided here about fifteen years. Watson quotes the work in his Annals, Vol. I, p. 66, etc. He thus describes early Germantown: "All sorts of very good paper are made in the Germantown, as also very fine German linen, such as no person of quality need be ashamed to wear; and in several places they make very good druggets, crapes, camblets and serges, besides other woolen cloathes, the manufacture of all which daily improves; and in most parts of the country there are many and spacious buildings, which several of the gentry have erected for their country houses" (p. 72).

If the reader would look into the history of the settlement of Germantown, he can do so by examining Sam. W. Pennypacker's Historical and Biographical Sketches, published by R. A. Tripple, of Philadelphia. The interesting account in that volume is reprinted from the *Pennsylvania Magazine of History*, Vol. IV, p. 1, etc. The drawing of lots for locations took place in the cave of Pastorius, in Philadelphia, October, A. D. 1683.

North of Germantown proper lay Krisheim, Crefeld and Sommerhausen, perpetuating the names of the dear fatherland, to which the hearts of the settlers turned. Whittier's touch in "The Pennsylvania Pilgrim" of Up den Graff conversing with Pastorius of former days by the firelight is a natural one. Sommerhausen was the name of Pastorius's birthplace. The families of the first settlers, in addition to the agent of the Frankfort Land Company, Francis Daniel Pastorius, were as follows:—Dirck, Hermann and Abraham Up den Graff (now written Updegraff and Updegrove), three brothers from Crefeld, and Tones Kunders (that is, Dennis Conrad), from the same place; Lenart Arets, Reynier Tyson, Willem Streypers, Jan (English, John) Lensen, Peter Keurlis, Jan Seimens, Johannes (English, John) Bleikers, Abraham Tunes and Jan Lucken (now Lukens). These fourteen families, with their wives, children and servants, were the first inhabitants of Germantown, which was properly named as a German settlement.

Huts and caves were made as places of abode. There were fifty-five lots of fifty acres each on both sides of the Main street.—Pennypacker's Sketches, pp. 207-8. Germantown was sometimes styled Germanopolis by Pastorius.

Pennypacker regrets that the early history of the pious and faithful Germans lacked chroniclers, while the New England settlers had many. New England has abounded in authors from Cotton Mather and Joel Barlow to Mrs. Stowe, and naturally they have painted their ancestors, while Mrs. Hemans has given an English idea of the Pilgrim Fathers, and their governmental struggles made them famous. Let them have all due credit, but the noble Church of England Virginia Colony, with its good Parson Hunt, and the Friends and Mennonites and Moravians, of Pennsylvania, with Penn and Pastorius and Zinzendorf, must not be forgotten.

It has been said that in peaceful times there is no history, and the Germans and Friends lived such quiet and peaceful lives that little happened to strike the world or produce writings until the battle of Germantown shook their repose. They were as the man whom Saxe humorously describes, whose life ran so even that his neighbors thought him very odd. In later years, before Bryn Mawr and its surburban neighboring villages were known, Germantown was the great suburb of Philadelphia. Now the business of the Main street is driving the new country seats to the side lanes which have been opened on both sides of the Main avenue, and the suburb is really a city in itself; eventually the lanes may also feel the push of business as the busy hive of city life swarms upon them. Still even Main street, or Germantown road, has not lost its country aspect, though it has a patched appearance as new and old strike each other. As one enters Germantown from the city he is struck with a number of cameos set in the picture-frame of the street. The pretty country house of the Logans, at Loudon, with its rustic surroundings, and adjoining rural houses on the upper side forms a pleasant scene, while the Wakefield Presbyterian church and the Adamson residence grace the opposite side of the avenue. The Lower and Upper Burying Grounds, with the Mennonite graveyard, and the massive cross in the yard of Trinity Lutheran church to the memory of Henry Goodman and wife are fit reminders of the peaceful dead in Christ, and may they ever remain, like Trinity churchyard in New York, and Christ churchyard, Philadelphia, to teach the thoughtful a lesson of the end of life. As Bonar's lines express it, they may be a comfort to the patient toiler as he passes them in his daily walk:

> "Rest for the toiling hand,
> Rest for the thought-worn brow,
> Rest for the weary way-sore feet,
> Rest from all labor now.
>
> Rest for the fevered brain,
> Rest for the throbbing eye,
> Thro' these parched lips of thine no more
> Shall pass the moan or sigh."

St. Luke's Episcopal church and Parish building form a pretty view from the street, which will be much finer when the proposed tower is built. By the side of the church and in its rear repose those who loved its holy worship. The Roman Catholic dome meets us at Price street, and St. Stephen's Methodist church is an object of attraction.

The Henry and Butler and Duval properties, and Miss Haines's antique home, with the Chew mansion, and Mrs. Norton Johnson's house and grounds, at Upsal, must not be forgotten.

THE JOHN WISTER HOUSE.

One of these cameos is the John Wister estate, just north of Chelten avenue, on the west side of the street. Here Townsend Ward closed his printed account, and here we take up the thread of the narrative.

Germantown road was the backbone of the ancient village. Matthias Zimmerman's plan of Germantown was copied by Christian Lehman, and recopied by his grandson, Joseph, for his own father, Benjamin Lehman. This plan is invaluable in these researches, and it may be seen at the Pennsylvania Historical Society rooms.

The traveler is now requested to turn his back on the sunny south and look toward the frigid north, while on his right lies the rosy east and on his left the golden west, and start on his observant journey. We find ourselves on Section 14 of the plan. In this vicinity Peter Shoemaker, Sr., originally owned two and a half fifty acre lots. Later on Melchior Meng, Kreyter, Bockius, Kurtz and Peter Smith are the owners of two and a half lots running to "Rittenhouse Mill road."

Ward had treated of Melchior Meng, and closed his last article in the *Magazine* with a few words on the Wister place, while a fine picture of the mansion faced his final page. His manuscript states that James Matthews built the house about 1803, and adds: "He was of the firm of McAllister & Matthews, whipmakers. He also built the spring-house on the lawn, put a sun dial and post, and planted a willow switch alongside, which, however, soon grew so large that its shade obscured the dial." In one of his articles he refers to the fact that Peter Kalm, the Swedish traveler, noticed the picturesque and useful spring-houses of Pennsylvania in 1748. He visited Germantown, however, long before the building of this house.

In Delaware and Chester counties, the spring-house is indeed a pretty feature, and a tavern near Gwynedd is called "The Spring-house;" but it looks quaint to see one in a busy street, and it appears lonesome, like a ship on dry land. Still it is well that it remains as a touch of country life, and the willow over it may be a descendant of that first willow twig which Dr. Franklin gave to Deborah Norris, afterwards Deborah Logan. A little stream runs through the lawn. As the stream and spring-house occupy the front of the grounds the railing is unbroken by a drive, and the entrance is at the side. This helps the effect in leaving an unobstructed country grass plot.

By the upper side of the carriage way a board walk leads alongside a hedge to the mansion which lies some distance back from the street. The sun dial

still does duty in front of the main door of the house on the lawn. It is a pleasant relic of former days and old time customs. It has also its lesson of content, as it marks the shining hours and skips the cloudy ones, in accord with the inscription once placed on such an object, "I mark only the hours that shine." It rests sweetly at night. It also tells of the vast importance of time. A sun dial at the English University of Oxford has the Latin legend "*Horae pereunt et imputantur.*" "The hours perish and are laid to account." The house is of stone, two stories high, with basement. The stone shows in the front of the basement, but is whitened in the upper stories. A flight of stone steps leads to the front door. This door has a carved pillar on each side and is surrounded with an ornamented frame of woodwork, terminating in a square finish above, which, however, has an arched window underneath it. The roof is cut off at both ends so that the ridge is shortened. A triangular front containing a semi-circular window is also inserted in the roof above three of the front windows, while a dormer window projects on each side of it. Two high chimneys complete the variety. These old houses, while they lack the conveniences of modern ones, have an old-fashioned English dignity which is attractive and deserves to be preserved by pen and pencil, before the red brick dwellings drive them away. Perhaps a new fashion will yet reproduce them. There is a fine old hall which contains an antique upright clock, which may rival the sun-dial in duty, and works more constantly. The mansion boasts another ancient clock in a room adjoining the hall. One of these was made by the clock-maker, Augustine Neiser, spoken of by Ward. It is a chiming clock. The clock belonged to John Wister, the elder, the great-great grandfather of the author of the following lines. It was made by Augustine Neiser, about the year 1735, probably in Germany, for such excellent work could scarcely have been done at that early date in this country. Neiser emigrated to America, and was the first Germantown clock-maker. In the distribution of the *reliquiæ* of Vernon, after the death of Miss Ann Wister, the clock came into the possession of her nephew, the one who has commemorated it so feelingly.

THE VERNON CLOCK.

Tick, tock! tick, tock! a strange and solemn sound!
  Tick, tock! tick, tock! a tone akin to things beneath the ground.
To things beneath the ground which are to be,
  To things beneath the ground which are no more,
A murmur of the great engulfing sea,
  Which still grows clearer as we near the shore.

Tick, tock! tick, tock! the pendulum swings heavily and slow,
  The rustle of Time's garments, and the chime,
As stealthily the slender fingers climb,
  Is but his footfall. As the quarters go,
They speak the quarters of our lives with power,
  And hint of him who comes to strike the hour.

Even as a merchant counts us out our gold,
  Which we are free to spend in good or ill,
So the old clock, with neutral mien and cold,
  Counts us the moments we may waste at will.

Kind friends, I cannot waste them as of yore,
  The rush and fire and haste have passed away;
Ye took my gladness when ye went before—
  Could ye not leave it for my little day?
Nor can I freely spend them all alone,
  I can but sit, as nears the mid of night,
And question the old clock of hours flown,
  And ask of scenes that passed beneath his sight.

Kind friends, the clock beheld you one and all,
  First those of old, and then us gathered there,
Within your beautiful and stately hall,
  And still ticks on while you are less than air.

It saw the rush and revelry and glare,
    And hurrying feet,
    And eyes that meet,
And lips that long to kiss, half shy, half bold.
    Inscrutable,
    Immutable,
    Slow ringing,
    Still swinging,
It ticked each hush as they lay lifeless there,
It saw us bend o'er the last forehead cold;
Then saw the walls stripped, tenantless and bare.

Tick, tock! tick, tock! a strange and Solemn tone—
  An echo of the voices of the blest,
A sound which bears me on to those at rest,
  Who for an hour have left me here alone.
A sound both grim and grand, both stern and free,
  The whisper of the shell to time's eternal sea.

March 19th, 1889.   ALGERNON SYDNEY LOGAN.

The hall clock came from Edward Jones, of Merion, having a date of the year 1708 upon it. Edward Jones was the great-great grandfather of the Wister ladies. The former has been handed down from John Wister, the great grandfather of the present occupants of the house.

A spiral stairway, adorned with fine wood carving, leads from the hall to the top of the house. Indeed, this carved wood-work is one of the main features of the mansion. It is displayed on the ancient parlor mantel in figures and adorns the outside of the windows, even those in front of the attic, which project from the roof; the hall doors are tastefully carved. In the parlor the front windows are recessed and paneled below the glass. The fine carved mantels are continued through the house. On one of the first floor mantels two pillars are carved on each side, while on the other but one appears on each side. A wood fire-place is still in use. The old furniture in the parlor and the carved wood-work lose their interest as one gazes at a beautiful painting by Gilbert Stuart. It is a likeness of Miss Nancy Pennington, aunt of the Misses Wister, to whom the mansion belongs. The flesh color seems as bright and the appearance as life-like as if the artist had finished his work yesterday. The lovely lady died at twenty years of age, and the picture is supposed to represent her at the age of eighteen. An excellent portrait of Governor John Dickinson also hangs in the parlor.

A back hall runs through the house cross-wise, a section of which appears to be a later addition. Some of the partitions are of stone, solidly built, while the rear building is of stone, plastered. An extensive lawn behind the house, with a grass field adjoining, makes the place look like a quiet country retreat. On the lower side is the Sunday-school building of Chelten Avenue Presbyterian Church, while on the upper side, the rear of the Evangelical Church and graveyard on Rittenhouse street bound a part of this lawn, while the green-house and the barn complete the scene. The rear and upper view of the mansion is quaint, as the angles and chimneys become more prominent in that direction. There is a deep ravine on the upper side which has a wild look, near a busy thoroughfare. This sometimes contains a stream of water, but is dry in summer, as the gardener informs me. Dogwood trees make their home in it. A conservatory joins the mansion on the lower side, while the ancient trees and ample grounds give a very rural appearance both in the front and the rear.

The ground slopes from the house toward the street. The front wall of the house is beautified by the ivy and Virginia creeper which cling lovingly to it, and brighten the picture. There are double doors in the front, and each door contains its own brass knocker, so, like twins, they both stand side by side. John Wister, Senior, named this place Vernon in honor of Washington's home, Mount Vernon. Vernon Hall near by perpetuates the name.

Ward notes that the elder John Wister was never in the railway cars. It should be added that they ran to Philadelphia in 1832, and he lived until 1862. He never visited New York. His son, John Wister, died January 23, 1883. The following admirable lines were written on the occasion, by his nephew, Algernon Sydney Logan, great-grandson, by the by, of John Dickinson, whose portrait hangs in the same parlor as that of Miss Nancy Pennington at Vernon:—

> Slow came the morning, slow, with features pale,
> White robed, close muffled in a misty veil.
> She seemed to feel that Death was at her side,
> And thus like him all stealthily to glide,
> And emulate his footfall and his hue.
> She came; but yet unmarked of one who knew
> Fair Nature in her subtlest changing mood,
> Beloved companion of his solitude,
> Who could predict the aspects of her face,
> For whom her smiles and frowns had equal grace—
> She came unmarked—he slept, and slept for aye.
> What lesser sleep than an Eternity.

> Could balance that unrest beyond control,
> The life-long inner combat of a soul
> Born for the whirlwind, yet becalmed through life?
> Cast in mad times of tumult and of strife,
> Of popular uprisings and of rage,
> Strong in the storm within him, to assuage
> The tempest and to rule a surging sea.
> Of uncouth men had been his destiny.
> His mighty strength, his ready eloquence,
> His light and feathery fancy, solid sense,
> His tender heart (to him was childhood dear),
> His courage never tarnished by a fear,
> In other times and scenes had made his name
> Known of his kind, perchance of lasting fame.
> But now obscure, as glad of rest, he sleeps,
> And one who loved him well in silence weeps,
> Up to the dizzy verge of death we climb,
> And peer into the dark abysm of Time,
> Which has engulphed this strong Reality—
> Then sighing journey on, and pondering sigh.

John Wister Sr.'s two daughters now dwell in the paternal mansion, the number of which on the Main Street is 4916.

To complete this sketch I add a notice of John Wister, Sr., kindly placed in my hands. It is also fitting to say that Mr. Charles J. Wister has supervised this article, and it is deemed a favor to have had the aid of a scholar so well versed in the history of Germantown.

Mr. John Wister was born in Philadelphia in the Revolutionary days of 1776, and was the son of Daniel Wister of this city. He was a birthright member of the Society of Friends and brought up under the influence of their principles. He early entered into mercantile life in the counting-house of his Uncle, William Wister, and after his death continued the business in partnership with his brother Charles, under the title of John and Charles Wister. About the year 1812 Mr. Wister purchased the place known as Vernon, in Germantown, where he resided the remainder of his life. He was the head of a large, influential and wealthy family and his name and position was as familiar to the community in which he lived, though living in the closest retirement, as if his life had been the most ostentatious and prominent. He retired from a brief mercantile career, with a large fortune, to Germantown where he found those enjoyments at his own fireside which few so highly appreciated and with which few have been favored to the same extent. His home was his paradise—and all were made happy who came within his gates. He affected no display. There was not a grain of factitious pride in his nature. He possessed a firm and manly will, and had a decided opinion on all questions, but in it all there was an ever-flowing spring of geniality, extremely pleasing and at once putting every one at ease. If the acts of Mr. Wister are to be received as the best evidence of character, then there was no better Christian than he. Indeed his whole life was a beautiful model for example. To an austere uprightness he added an unchangeable consistency and a religious affluence that pervaded his well-balanced mind and illustrated his daily practices. No charity passed under his eyes unassisted, and no one deserving pity left him empty-handed. Thus while he shut himself up technically from society and the world, no one fulfilled his allotted duty more studiously, more usefully, and more in accordance with the truest dictates of a discriminating wisdom and humanity. His memory requires no eulogium at the hands of any one. Sufficient be it to say that no man has passed through this life more scatheless, so entirely unaffected by its worldliness and heresies, or when laid in the receptacle of all the living, was more devotedly regretted, than John Wister. He died on Wednesday, Dec. 10th, 1862, in the eighty-seventh year of his age.

TOWNSEND WARD'S NOTES.

In order to make the series more complete, this narrative will now condense Townsend Ward's interesting articles on the Germantown road in the *Pennsylvania Magazine of History and Biography*, beginning with No, 1 of Vol. 5, A. D. 1881, and ending with No. 4 of Vol. 6, A. D. 1882. This was a part of Mr. Ward's proposed plan with regard to the TELEGRAPH articles. The present writer will use his own words for the most part. If quotation marks are introduced they may be understood as embracing Mr. Ward's language, unless it is otherwise stated.

In entering Germantown from Philadelphia the first settlers are supposed to have used an Indian path. Watson says that A. Cook told Jacob Keyser that he could remember Germantown street as an Indian footpath through laurel bushes. Now Second Street and Germantown avenue may be considered as a fairly built up street and road for thirteen miles to Chestnut Hill, being "one of the greatest avenues of any city in the world."

In leaving the city the old Norris estate at Fair Hill is passed, and the Fox Chase Tavern, no longer an inn, near the connecting Railroad, and the Rising Sun Inn, and Nicetown, named from the Nice family. In Nicetown the avenue passes the old residence of Dr. Joseph Martin, brother of Mrs McKee, of Germantown, and of Prosper D. Martin and Mrs. Giles Dallet, of Philadelphia. He was a man of note. As I treated of Stenton in the TELEGRAPH of July 8th, the place will be passed by, except to say that the McClellan hospital, during the war, was on part of the estate.

The account of Louis Clapier, who owned Fern Hill, west of Wayne station, is interesting. When a poor woman's house was burned, he said, "Ah! gentlemen, I pity her $50, how much do you?" He led nine others to give the same amount.

On a map of 1750 two houses near here were marked Neglee and Dewalden, from the Dewald family.

We now pass under the railroad bridge at Wayne station and follow Germantown avenue up Neglee's hill, named, I presume, from the Neglee family just mentioned. General Henry M. Neglee is of this connection. The southern boundary of Germantown crosses Germantown avenue almost exactly at the railway bridge at Wayne Junction.

On the left lies Thones Kunder's "Side Lot, No. 2," of the ancient division. The name Kunder is now Conrad. Rev. Thomas K. Conrad, D. D., the first rector of Calvary church, Manheim street, is his descendant, as well as the broker of that name in Walnut street. Rev. Dr. Conrad's uncle, Robert T. Conrad, was the first Mayor of Philadelphia after the consolidation.

Sometimes the early travelers avoided the steep Neglee's hill by passing along about where Wayne street is now. In 1773 the Pennsylvania *Packet* records the highway robbery of Mr. John Lukens on this hill on a July evening. He was obliged to deliver his watch.

Before going further, let it be noted that Francis Daniel Pastorius, the agent of the Frankfort Land Company, in 1683 purchased 5700 acres of land, which was laid out by the Surveyor-General in 1684. The patent of 1689 begins its descriptions of the township thus: "Beginning at a corner hicquerie tree." William Penn, in the Germantown charter, August 12th, 1689, styles himself the "Proprietor of Pennsylvania in America under the Imperial crown of Great Britain."

Stenton avenue, formerly the Township line road, is the exact place of passing the southern boundary of Germantown. When LaFayette visited Chew's house, fifty years after the battle, an escort met him here. Ward here tells Dr. William H. Denny's story of LaFayette being introduced to men in the towns on the Ohio river, and, asking each man if he were married, if the reply was "Yes," the General would say, "Happy fellow," if "No," he would exclaim. "Lucky dog."

Ascending Neglee's hill, on the left, that is, the west side of the avenue, stands the old mansion with a Grecian portico styled Loudoun. It is the property of the Logan family. The number of the house is 4356. It was built at the end of the eighteenth century by Thomas Armat for his only child, Thomas Wright Armat, for a summer residence. Thomas Armat was from Dale-Head Hall, Cumberland, England. He settled in Loudoun county, Va. There his son was born in 1776. He became a merchant in Philadelphia, and during the yellow-fever removed to Germantown. He was a philanthropist and a religious man. He donated the ground on which St. Luke's Episcopal church stands, and assisted in building it. He promoted Sunday schools. He was one of the first to give plans for using coal for heating.—See Poulson's *Daily Advertiser*, February 15th, 1819. He got a patent for an improvement in hay scales. The old scales were opposite his house, now No. 4788, Dr. Ashmead's residence. Thomas Wright Armat died young.

STENTON, FORMER RESIDENCE OF JAMES LOGAN.

The author inserts the following article, among these notes, which he had written for the TELEGRAPH before this series began.

JAMES LOGAN AND HIS COUNTRY SEAT.

SONNET TO STENTON.

[By our beloved and Honored Friend, Deborah Logan. Written in 1815, for her affectionate relatives, W. Logan and Sarah L. Fisher.]

> "My peaceful home! amidst whose dark green shades
> And sylvan scenes my waning life is spent,
> Nor without blessings and desired content!
> Again the spring illumes thy verdant glades,
> And rose-crowned Flora calls the Æonian maids
> To grace with songs her revels, and prevent,
> By charmed spells, the nipping blasts which, bent
> From Eurus or the stormy North pervades
> Her treasures—still 'tis mine among thy groves
> Musing to rove, enamor'd of the fame
> Of him who reared these walls, whose classic lore
> For science brightly blazed, and left his name
> Indelible—by honor, too, approved,
> And virtue cherished by the Muses' flame."

A house like Stenton, which is supposed to have been finished in A. D. 1728, is an American antiquity, though it may not rival a castle on the Rhine, nor an English baronial mansion, in age. It seems hard to disturb such retreats, and the locomotives on the two railroads which pass Wayne Junction ought to be ashamed of themselves for shrieking loudly in a place where nothing more modern than a coach should be allowed. The cricket ground has a right there, as being a country sport.

As we draw near Stenton, James Logan's ancient mansion, we are struck with the quiet and dignified simplicity of the place, which was consonant with the character of its master. It was not an attempt at grandeur, but an effort to produce a spacious and comfortable residence, which should attract rather than awe the beholder. The building is two stories in height, with high attics, having dormer windows. The material of its construction is brick, said to have been burned in the neighborhood. The front door has its long glass windows at the sides to enhance its dignity, after the fashion of the day. The semi-circular stones which form the doorstep have done long service. On entering, the large hall greets one with a hearty welcome. Those old halls were a pleasant feature in ancient dwellings, and help to keep up the primitive idea of "the hall" in song and story, even if its capacity has somewhat diminished. The immense old key of the hall door is a curiosity in itself, and may rank with the key of the Bastile at Mount Vernon, though it has a pleasanter history. A large wooden bar also guards the door. On the first floor there are two parlors, one on either side of the hall. The antique closets in one of these rooms with rounded backs, built into the wall, are worthy of notice. One of them has a strange shell-like formation for its top, and they probably served to display the fine table ware of the mistress of the house. A picture of one of them may be seen in the book, "A Sylvan City" (p. 194). That picture also displays some of the ancient pottery, and one of the fireplaces. It states that Stenton was considered "a palace in its day" (p. 176). The same volume speaks of the dinners and suppers at Stenton, which have left a record of "white satin petticoats worked in flowers, pearl satin gowns, or peach colored satin cloaks; the white necks were covered with delicate lawn, and they wore gold chains, and seals engraven with their arms."

Let us again look around the rooms where these gay scenes occurred. The old fireplaces are of much interest, and where the hand of vandalism has spared the fine old Scriptural paintings on the tiles one is reminded how Dr. Doddridge learned his early religious lessons by his good mother's instructions based on such pictures. One of the fireplaces has a marble hearth and a fine marble facing.

The large amount of well-preserved wood-work in the interior of these old dwellings is remarkable. There is much wainscoting, and a wooden cornice and old inside wooden shutters with quaint openings for light cut out of the upper portion, and some queer fancy wood-work in the rear hall, while the builder thought it needful to cut even the attic closet doors with ornamental openings. The hands that did this work have lost their cunning, but the work abides.

The long and narrow windows, with their small panes, have beneath them cosy window seats, which in summer would afford a pleasant place to catch the cool air and view the pretty lawn and fine trees in front of the house. The wood of the mansion is said to have been brought from England.

In the rear of the two parlors there are two other rooms of somewhat similar style. Between the front and back hall is a door with a fine arch. In a passage-way, on the first floor, was an opening in the woodwork, apparently for escape in danger, and I noticed in the attic rooms doors leading into a cubby-hole. This passage is supposed to run around the upper part of the house just under the roof and communicate below, as there was an underground communication to the barn from the house, and it is thought also another to the vault in the family graveyard. These passages were escapes in danger. At the Potts house, in Valley Forge, there were secret doors for Washington to escape in sudden dangers. There was a trap-door in the floor of one of the rear rooms on the first story which communicated with the cellar, apparently for the same purpose, for we can hardly think of the ancient idea of raising tables covered with food from one story to another here. We may imagine in sudden surprises that the Stenton family used these retreats, though they stood very well with the Indians. There is a fine old stairway, and tradition avers that the Indians used to sleep on these stairs at night.

The Indian chief, Wingohocking, loved James Logan, and asked him to change names with him. Logan replied that the Indian might have his name, but that, instead of accepting the Indian's, he would give it to the creek which ran through the estate; so that became Wingohocking creek, though it was often called Logan's run. This is the chief whose name designates the Logan House, Altoona, and whom William Wirt uses to illustrate Indian oratory.

In the second story of Stenton, two rooms have been made of what was once a banqueting hall, extending the length of the house, but it became a place for feasting the mind when James Logan made it his library, and here were those books in Greek and Latin and other languages which now adorn the shelves of that literary palace, the Ridgway Library.

Outbuildings extend to the rear of the mansion. These were the servants' quarters. They adjoin the main building. There are two old-fashioned kitchens and a greenhouse beyond them. The outbuilding is a story and a half high and is prolonged by the addition of an extension. The outbuilding is of stone and its wall is adorned with pigeon houses, where the busy birds are carrying on their summer work with joy, careless of the past generations of men who have dwelt there.

The family graveyard lies on a pretty hillside near by, well walled in, and furnished with an ancient vault. It is a sweet spot and a fitting resting place for Deborah Logan and her relatives. Here assembled in February, A. D. 1839, that mourning throng of friends who accompanied the body of Deborah Logan to its resting place.

The means of following out the Penn and Logan history, which is the foundation of Pennsylvania history, have been largely afforded by the patient toil of years of this devoted intellectual woman, who is praised by her friend Watson, the annalist. She found the letters between William Penn and James Logan, with other epistles, neglected, mouldy and torn in an attic at Stenton and covered thousands of pages with her copies of them, adding scholarly notes. Her relations with the families of early settlers gave her much information, which she well knew how to use to good effect, and a natural enthusiasm encouraged her in her efforts. Few persons have done so much for American history as this most estimable lady. It was her custom to give the early morning to her task of copying and annotating, and she doubtless enjoyed the historic panorama which then passed before the eye of her mind. One of her poems is entitled, "The Hour of Prime."

Mrs. Deborah Logan was the granddaughter of William Penn's special friend and co-worker, Isaac Norris, Sr., whose letters appear in the Penn and Logan Correspondence, as he was a correspondent of James Logan. He was Chief Justice of Pennsylvania at the time of his death. He died at the Friends' Meeting House, in Germantown, and his body was carried to Stenton, where vain efforts were made to resuscitate it. Mrs. Logan was a pupil of Anthony Benezet, and, though full of glee, still her teacher, on leaving his place for a time, would call "Norris" to preside over the young flock. Even in old age, young and old loved this bright, intelligent woman, and the mourning at her death was general. She heard the Declaration of Independence read in the State House yard in Philadelphia, and entertained Washington at Stenton, and, with her husband, visited him at Mount Vernon.

During the Revolution the important letters which were to present the ancient Pennsylvanians to their descendants in their daily dress were near being lost. The British burned seventeen houses between Philadelphia and Germantown in retaliation for alleged aggressions from some of the houses. They ordered Stenton to be burned and two men came to burn it, and told the housekeeper, a colored woman, to take out her private property while they went to the barn for straw to set the house on fire. A British officer just then rode up, asking for deserters. The housekeeper, with quick wit, replied that they had gone to the barn to hide in the straw. He cried: "Come out! you rascals! and run before me into camp!" They protested and alleged their commissions, but the Logan house, with its important manuscripts, was saved.— Watson's Annals, Vol. II, p. 39, edition of 1857. The faithful colored woman is buried in the garden at Stenton. The old barn of stone still stands.

Mrs. Deborah Logan wrote an account of James Logan, which is printed in the Penn and Logan Correspondence, but a more extensive history of him is found at the Historical Society rooms in a volume published by Charles Gilpin, in Bishopsgate street, Without, London, A. D. 1851. It is entitled "Memoirs of James Logan, a Distinguished Scholar and Christian Legislator, Founder of the Loganian Library," etc. By William Armistead. As I find the author's family name mentioned among the early Friends in Pennsylvania, he may have an ancestral interest in this country. This sketch will combine the accounts of Mrs. Logan and Mr. Armistead, and those in the two volumes of the Penn and Logan Correspondence.

The name Logan, like that of Washington, came from a locality. The chief Logan was Baron of Restalrig, and the family was connected with the most noble families in Scotland, and one of them married a daughter of Robert II, who granted him the lands Grugar, by a charter addressed "Militi dilecto fratri suo"—(To his well-beloved soldier brother).

In 1329, when, in compliance with the dying request of Robert Bruce, an attempt was made to carry his heart to the Holy Sepulchre, "Sir Robert Logan and Sir Walter Logan were the chief associates of Sir James Douglas in that illustrious band which composed the flower of Scotch chivalry."

The Logans fell under the walls of Granada, battling with the Moors, in attempting to rescue Lord Sinclair. The heart of Bruce was brought back to Scotland, and buried in the Monastery of Melrose. In 1400, Sir Robert Logan, Lord Admiral of Scotland, defeated an English fleet.

James Logan was the son of Patrick and Isabel Logan and great-grandson to Sir Robert Logan, Baron of Restalrig. Isabel's maiden name was Hume. She was "of the Scotch family of Dundas and Panure." James was born in

Ireland, at Lurgan, A. D. 1684, but as his family were Scotch people, who had gone into Ireland after his father became a member of the Friends, he should be considered a Scotchman in early life, and after emigration a Scotch-American. The father taught his son, whose strong mind developed early. Before he was thirteen years old he knew Latin and Greek and some Hebrew, and afterward became a good mathematician. He was apprenticed to a linen draper in London, but the Prince of Orange landed and war came on in Ireland before he was bound, and so he returned to his parents and went with them to Edinburg, London and Bristol. At Bristol he taught and also studied Greek and Hebrew, French and Italian and some Spanish.

In A. D. 1699, Penn offered James Logan a position as his secretary and he accepted it, though he had opposition to encounter, in the advice of friends, against the step.

While Penn and Logan were three months at sea, in coming from England to America, they avoided the danger of yellow fever by the delay. It had been raging in Philadelphia, but ceased before their arrival.

Logan's public life began early. When only about twenty-five years old he was in the close confidence of Penn and had received several important offices from him.

In less than two years Penn returned to England, leaving his faithful secretary. He was Secretary of the Province, Commissioner of Property, President of Council and Chief Justice of Pennsylvania.

He married Sarah Read, whose sister was the wife of Israel Pemberton, Sr.

A touch of family life occurs in Hannah Penn's sending Mrs. James Logan two bottles of "convulsion water" as an extraordinary medicine for her little girl. Logan had "a true helpmate, children not undutiful," as he wrote Simon Clement, an uncle of Hannah Penn.

While Penn lived in this country during his second visit, James Logan, then a bachelor, resided in his family, and when Penn and his lady moved to the unfinished house at Pennsbury, on the Delaware, above Bristol, he remained at the town house, and so directions about family affairs are met with in the letters of the Penn and Logan Correspondence.

Mrs. Deborah Logan calls James Logan Penn's "most able and upright secretary." Well did he deserve this description. The correspondence with William and Hannah Penn showed great familiarity and confidence on both sides.

Hannah Penn takes an interest in Logan's love affairs, and Logan writes about Letitia Penn's proposed marriage to Mr. Aubrey.

Penn's business directions are particular and confidential, and show unlimited trust. He tells him how to treat the men with whom he comes in contact, and even asks him to send his leather stockings, and writes about "a fine new wig."

From shipboard Penn writes Logan: "I have left thee in an uncommon trust, with a singular dependence on thy justice and care, which I expect thou wilt faithfully employ in advancing my honest interest."—Penn and Logan Correspondence, p. 59, Vol. I. The trust was most honorably discharged in long years of service.

Penn left Logan the privilege of finishing the year in the Philadelphia slate-roof house he himself had occupied in Second street. Its location was the northwest corner of the Corn Exchange. It had a lot and garden.

Penn gives Logan minute instructions in business matters, and Logan provides a banquet for the Governor and others on Penn's behalf and in his name. In government matters there is much to write about, and there are clashing interests in forming a new Province, as was natural. The Three Lower Counties, now the State of Delaware, were tied to Pennsylvania in a way that caused much friction. The Three Upper Counties, which formed Pennsylvania proper, were Philadelphia, Bucks and Chester, and Delaware county was cut off from Chester county in after times.

Penn charges Logan to watch that too much wood is not cut about the Falls, which term then designated Trenton.

He commits his eldest son, William Penn, Jr., to his special care, when he sends him to Pennsylvania. We find Logan entertaining Lord Cornbury, both in Philadelphia and at Pennsbury. This nobleman was a first cousin of Queen Anne, and came to proclaim her accession.

During Penn's pecuniary troubles Logan worked bravely to collect and remit funds, and the letters contain much about quit rents. Logan did not work merely for reward, and for years deferred the receiving of his salary, but in latter life a moderate sum was given him for the accumulated debt, and by business he became wealthy. It is strange to read how land was sold in vast quantities at trifling prices. A square at Second and Market, exclusive of a burying ground in it, was offered by Penn to a friend for less than £30 and declined, though the person who refused the square afterward regretted it. Penn then told him that the village would be a great city.

Logan wrote Penn about William Penn Jr.'s coming over: "This is a place of ease, *though not to me*, compared to that buzzing theatre." I suppose that the reference is to London.

Logan tries to get a census and rent rolls, and the letters are enlivened by a discussion about hats which Penn ordered as choice beavers, and which Logan declared were not such when they reached this country.

Logan writes that he wishes that Penn could own William Trent's slated house in Second street, affectionately adding, "I would give £20 to £30 out of my own pocket that it were thine; nobody's but thine." Trent was a rich man who had interests at Trenton, N. J., and who gave name to that place.

Logan's letters are lengthy, minute and faithful. And among quit rents are sprinkled births, marriages and deaths, as the joys and sorrows of that generation passed into eternity.

LOUDON, THE RESIDENCE OF MRS. ANNA A. LOGAN.

Logan was President of the Province, with reputation to himself and satisfaction to the public, as Edward Armstrong notes from Proud's History of Pennsylvania, Vol. 2, p. 41, Penn and Logan Correspondence, Vol. 2, p. 399, *note*.

In 1710 Logan was in England, having gone there by way of Lisbon and France. He spent twenty months in and about London, in 1710 and 1711, on Penn's affairs.

For forty years Logan was Penn's secretary and principal agent, and when he wished to retire, the six years of sickness which fell on Penn served to call out his continued work.

Logan's influence over the Indians was good and he sometimes entertained 300 to 400 of them at Stenton for days at a time. The Chief Cannassetego, of the Onondagoes, styled him, in behalf of the Indians, "our old friend, James Logan," and when he "found him hid in the bushes," as he expressed it, in his retirement and bodily infirmity, he drew him to Philadelphia from Stenton to assist at a treaty in A. D. 1742. The Indians testified "their satisfaction for his services and sense of his work, calling him a wise and good man, and expressing the hope that when his soul ascended to God one just like him might be found for the good of the Province and their benefit."

It was a blessing of Providence that this toilsome man was allowed to retire from active life in advancing age. The scholar and lover of science found a congenial retreat at Stenton. He corresponded with foreign literati and entertained distinguished strangers at his country place. He patronized skillful men and encouraged merit. Dr. Franklin enjoyed his protection and friendship, and revered his memory.

In age he was crippled by a fall. He spent several years at his country place, and to use Mrs. Deborah Logan's words, " finished his useful and active life at his seat at Stenton, October 31, 1751, having just entered into the 77th year of his age." He was buried at the Friends' graveyard, Fourth and Arch streets.

There is a portrait of Logan at the Ridgway Library.

Makin addressed to him his Latin poem, "Descriptio Pennsylvaniæ," in which these lines occur:

> "On just and fairest terms the land was gained;
> No force of arms has any right obtained.
> 'Tis here, without the use of arms alone,
> The blest inhabitant enjoys his own ;
> Here many to their wish, in peace enjoy
> Their happy lots; and nothing doth annoy."

Logan contributed to this peaceful relation with the Indians. In New York the Seneca Indians adopted a similar man, Philip E. Thomas, into their nation, giving him the name Sougonan, meaning Benevolent.

In Day's Historical Collections of Pennsylvania, Stenton on Logan's Hill, is called the "favorite country residence of James Logan," and such it was.

Logan translated Cicero's "De Senectute" into English, with notes. Dr. Franklin wrote a preface, giving "his hearty wish that this first translation of a *classic* in this *western world*, may be followed with many others, and be a happy omen, that Philadelphia shall become the seat of the American Muses."

Logan Square, and the Loganian Society of Haverford College, perpetuate this great man's name, while his descendants still retain the ancient mansion.

When the Philadelphia Library was formed a committee asked Logan to select a list of books to send to England, judging him to be "a gentleman of universal learning and the best judge of books in his part." Logan built a building for a library and donated books and left a moderate endowment for a librarian, for which he deserves the thanks of Philadelphia. The old library building was at the northwest corner of Sixth and Walnut streets. A picture of it may be seen in Thompson Westcott's Historic Mansions of Philadelphia, p. 404. Watson in his Annals, describes Logan as "tall and well proportioned, with a graceful yet grave demeanor."

In Logan's 73d year he was asked to resume the Presidency of the Province, but declined.

Religion was the comfort of his old age. He believed that, as he said, "the true end of man is the union of his soul with God." He drew up a paper of Christian resolves, addressed "To Myself"; and wished to keep his Christian profession ever in mind, and to be active for good, and constant in prayer. He desired to rise early, and at night to examine himself, seeking God's forgiveness, and asking new strength from Him, watching against Satan, and praying to keep his heart right before God.

Is it a wonder that at his death Duponceau should say, "And art thou, too, gone, friend of man! friend of science! Thou whose persuasive accents could still the angry passions of the rulers of men, and dispose their minds to listen to the voice of reason and justice."

James Logan's son William was a member of the Provincial Council, and gave aged Indians a settlement on his land, called the Indian field. He also educated young Indians at his expense. He made a manuscript journal of travel from Philadelphia to Georgia.

Dr. George Logan, son of William Logan the second, and grandson of Sarah Emlen, the husband of Deborah Logan, was a grandson of James Logan, and was born at Stenton in 1755. He improved the farm, and was a member of the city and county Agricultural Societies, and of the Philosophical Society. He stood high in public life, and was United States Senator from 1801 to 1807. He visited France at his own expense in 1798 to strive to stop the threatened war between France and America, and met Talleyrand, and Merlin, Chief of the Directory. See Willis Hazard's Annals, a continuation of Watson, making Vol. 3, p. 446, where it is stated that his visit averted the war, which Thompson Westcott denies. See Historic Mansions of Philadelphia, "Stenton," p. 152. The visit stirred up much political excitement in this country, among the Federalists, and caused an act of Congress to be passed in 1799, "sometimes called the 'Logan Act.'" However, in 1810, he undertook another kindly voluntary mission to France, hoping to show English statesmen the poor policy of the conduct which induced the war of 1812. "Blessed are the peacemakers," said the Master; let us honor his good deeds. He was an acquaintance of Sir Samuel Romilly, Wilberforce, Thomas Clarkson, Mr. Coke, the Duke of Bedford, and the Marquis of Wellesley.

Deborah Logan survived her husband eighteen years, living through the Revolution. A very interesting account of her may be found, from the pen of Mrs. Owen J. Wister, in "Worthy Women of our First Century," edited by Mrs. Wister and Miss Agnes Irwin. "Sally Wister's Journal" was kept for the use of her "Dear Debby Norris" afterward Mrs. Logan. Conarroe painted her portrait when she was over seventy.

When Deborah Logan went to Stenton, the estate, though already divided, stretched from Fisher's to Nicetown Lane, and from the Germantown turnpike to the Old York Road. It lies in a beautiful country, and Washington was delighted with its fine grass and tasteful and beautiful improvements, while he kindly noticed the children there.

Stenton was for a time the headquarters of General Howe.

After Dr. George Logan died, Albanus C. Logan resided at Stenton with his mother, Deborah Logan.

If the reader would pursue the subject of the Stenton estate farther, let him consult the Pennsylvania Magazine, Vol. 5, p. 127, etc., A. D. 1881, No. 2, "Germantown Road, and Its Associations," By Townsend Ward. The article has a picture of the mansion, and one will be found in Historic Mansions of Philadelphia. Mrs. Rebecca Harding Davis notices Stenton in an article on "Old Philadelphia," in *Harper's Magazine*, and I believe that *The Continent* has published somewhat concerning it several years ago, though I have not been able to examine the last three papers named.

We now resume the synopsis of WARD'S NOTES.

The distinguished Madame Greland had a ladies' school in Philadelphia from 1808 to 1835 or later. She rented this house for several years for the summer months for her school.

The Logans at Loudoun are descendants of Mr. Armat. After the battle of Germantown the wounded Americans were carried to this hill and many were there buried.

The Toland family occupies No. 4418. The house was built about 1740. Eighty or ninety years ago this family rented it for a residence in summer, but they bought it in a short time. Congressman George W. Toland lived here. On the 22d of June, 1881, Elizabeth Toland died here in her eighty-fourth year. Her sister, Margaret, died January 1st, 1880, in her eighty-ninth year. Even in extreme old age they would walk a long distance to church. The end of the "large old rambling house" is toward the avenue. It is entered on the north side. The paving and grading here have exceeded the amount of the purchase money. On a window pane was an equestrian likeness of Frederick the Great, supposed to be the work of a Hessian officer, inscribed, "M. J. Ellinkhuysen, fecit, 1783, Philadelphia." Mr. Toland had it framed.

During the Revolution this was Colonel George Miller's house. His son Jacob was questioned by English officers quartered there with regard to "the rebels." His mother baked bread for the British, being paid in flour. The lad heard of no insult or violence. At the battle he crossed the road to where Mr. Lorain built afterwards, and now the late Mr. Adamson's fine, large, new house stands. From the cellar he and others saw the cannon balls flying, and heard the bullets whistling. He saw Sir William Howe.

There was a British hospital in the stable at Mechlin's house, now George Mechlin Wagner's, No. 4434, crowning the hill. Charles M. Wagner states that this property consists of seven and a half acres and has been held since 1764, having been bought of the executors of John Zachary. Zachary had bought different parts from John Theobald Ent and Baltes Reser. In 1747 he built the house and stone buildings in the meadow. There are still blood stains on the floors. The lands of Jan Streepers, Lenart Arets and Jacob Tellner are mingled in this tract. Tellner sold to the three Op den Graef brothers. The Shippen tract, through which Manheim street was opened, was anciently Op den Graef property.

Opposite Fisher's lane is a house built about 1760, but enlarged by John Gottfried Wachsmuth. He died about 1826. He was a German and a merchant of some eminence. He married Mrs. Dutihl. In 1828 John Bohlen and others, executors of Wachsmuth, sold this place to John Snowden Henry, son of Alexander Henry. John S. Henry was an active manager of the House of Refuge, a Director of the United States Bank, and with Reuben Haines, was one of the founders of the Germantown Infant School, which still exists. John S. Henry's widow died in 1881. Her son, Mayor Henry, lived here in his youth. On the east side is a public school and the beautiful Wakefield Presbyterian Church, built by a bequest of William Adamson. Rev. A. Wilson Clokey is its pastor. Lorain's house stood where Mr. Adamson's does. John Grigg occupied it several years. John Lorain had eight daughters, the youngest being named Octavia. One married Mr. Swift, of Easton. Mr. Charles J. Wister's painting of the Shoemaker mansion contains the two Misses Lorain who taught school in it. His father is speaking with them from the pavement.

No. 4429 was William Mehl's house, but its appearance has been changed by the present occupant, Mr. William Henson. Another of the old landmarks on Germantown avenue is the unpretentious stone and plastered double house, No. 4431, above Wakefield Church, built in 1776 by Christopher Ottinger, a soldier of the Pennsylvania line, who volunteered at the age of 17. His widow drew a pension for his service as 1st Sergeant. Capt. Douglass Ottinger, son of Christopher, was born in this old mansion Dec. 11, 1804, and still occupies the same bed-room in which he was born. The Captain made his first voyage in 1822 on the ship Thomas Jefferson, of Philadelphia, and was

commissioned a Lieutenant in the U. S. Revenue Cutter service in 1832, by President Andrew Jackson. By order of the U. S. Government he expended the first appropriation for the Life Saving Service, and invented and named the "Life Car." In 1849, he constructed and furnished with a complete and effective life-saving apparatus, eight stations on the New Jersey coast from Sandy Hook to Little Egg Harbor. He is still (1889) in service as Senior Captain in the U. S. Revenue Marine. In the parlor of the old house hangs a life-size portrait of the Captain, painted by an eminent artist of New York, over forty years ago. The Captain was then in the full vigor of manhood, and now, although in his 85th year, is still in the enjoyment of health, walks erect, and carries his years with a soldierly grace.

At the south-east corner of Fisher's lane, John Dedier built a hip-roofed house in 1773. In the wall at the corner of Fisher's lane and the avenue, is a piece of a tombstone, with skull and cross bones, and the words "Memendo Mory." Here is the

LOWER BURYING GROUND.

Jan Streepers, of Holland, gave a half acre for this graveyard, and afterward more ground was added. Here is one inscription:

Here
Lyeth the body
of Joseph Covlston,
Husband of
Margaret Covlston
And son of Capt. Thomas
Covlston, of Hartshorn,
In Darbyshire, in old
England, who departed
This life Vpon
The first day of
February, 1707-8,
Aged 38 years
And 8 months.

The stone is talcose slate. Samuel Coulston, "aged six week," has, also an ancient stone. John F. Watson piously placed here a tombstone for two British officers. The inscription runs:

"No more at War.
Gen. Agnew & Col. Bird
British Officers.
Wounded in the Battle of Germantown."

Their remains were removed to the de Benneville family burying ground, Milestown, as Mrs. Anne de Benneville Mears informs me. Rev. Christian Frederic Post, Missionary to aborigines of North and Central America (see Pa. Mag. of Hist. No. 1, of vol. 5, p. 119), was buried here in 1785, and has his tombstone near the gateway, to the right. He persuaded the Indians to leave their French allies and join the English.

Captain Robert Lee, a native of the English Northumberland, died in 1798, and a stone marks his grave. Another commemorates a lad of 18, named after Washington, and who had attained "a silver goblet for a literary production," as the epitaph states.

William Hood, of Germantown, who obtained wealth in Cuba, died at Paris in 1850. He is buried here. By will he provided for the massive marble front wall. His nephew, William H. Stewart, a member of the Historical Society, caused William Struthers to construct the wall with its fine balustrade. It has been called Hood's Cemetery. Fisher's lane bounds the burying ground on the south. It was laid out "to Busby's, late Morris's Mill, in June, 1747." It is spoken of as a public road "leading to the late Christian Kintzing's, now Charles Hay's Mill." The city ordinance styles it East Logan street. The lane, as far as the railway near Ruscombe street, has fine houses and grounds adorned with trees. Two primeval large oaks on the south side, between Stenton avenue and the railway, are remarkable. They are said to equal English oaks in beauty. An old stone house stood at the northeast corner of the lane and Wakefield street. It was built in 1743, as a farm house by John Wister, grandfather of the late Charles J. Wister, who facetiously called it the "Castle of Rosenheim." It was of one story, but high, with a large loft and a large cellar. "Mr. Wister has an ambrotype of it." When demolished, buttons found seemed to indicate British possession.

The lane descends, the Wingohocking creek soon crosses it. The old mill seat is now occupied by the Wakefield Mills. Between the Wingohocking and Mill Creek in 1777, the "First Battalion of British Guards" were located, where Little Wakefield stands. The posts on Fisher's lane protected Sir William Howe's headquarters at Stenton.

Joshua Fisher, before the Revolutionary war, had a line of packet ships between Philadelphia and London. In 1756 he made a chart of the Delaware bay and river. His children are noticed in Ward's Walks in Second street, in the *Historical Magazine*. His son Thomas is commemorated in Fisher's lane. He was born in Lewes, Delaware. He traveled abroad and was captured at sea in the war, in 1762-3, and carried a prisoner into Spain. He returned and joined his father and brother in the shipping business. He lived in Second street below Walnut. In 1771 he married Sarah, a daughter of William Logan. The yellow fever drove them to Germantown. They erected a small stone building "on the northernmost part of Stenton, which, as their portion, had fallen to them." In 1795, "or immediately afterwards, they built the house called Wakefield, named after the place of residence of his maternal ancestors, Joshua Maud, in Yorkshire, England." Seven generations have lived on this estate. "James Logan, his son William, William's daughter, Sarah, her son, William Logan Fisher, his son, Thomas R., his daughter, Mary, and her daughter Miss Letitia Carpenter," who married William Redwood Wright, "a great-grandson of Miers Fisher of Ury." "On the wedding day the digging of the cellar of their house, Waldheim, was begun by the bride, who was followed by Mr. Wright's great uncle, the venerable Mr. Eli K. Price, who threw out the second shovelful of earth."

BITS ABOUT THE CORNER
OF
FISHERS LANE
AND
GERMANTOWN
AVENUE.

William Logan Fisher established mills on his property. He was "an author of some note as well as a manufacturer." Pott's two water corn mills, also supposed to be called "Busby's, late Morris's," are thought to be the Wakefield Mills. About 1830 an English newspaper speaks of frame work knitters as going to Germantown. Hose, gloves and broadcloth were made. The early settlers also made "excellent linens." The seal of the Bank of Germantown contained a loom. The stocking industry is still important in Germantown, one mill producing 18,000 pairs in a day.

Wakefield meadow has been the scene of the meet of the "Hare and Hound Club," when the scattered bits of paper and the sounding horn have made a lively sport.

Belfield joins Wakefield. Charles Wilson Peale, the artist and founder of the Museum, resided here. He sold to William Logan Fisher. His daughter, William Wister's widow, now occupies the delightful place. William Wister was a genial man, some of whose pleasant sayings are noted by Ward. He lost his mills by fire. The goods of others were in them, but by years of economy he honorably paid his losses.

Danenhower's mill and Armstrong's mill, are thought to be the same, a little north of Duy's lane. A lane running to the mill is called on a chart the "Road to Shellebarger's Mill." "It appears to have been about where Armstrong street now is."

Thorp's Mill was north of Belfield. There were print works there. James, John and Issacher Thorp, three English brothers, gave name to the mill and lane.

Wister street now replaces the earlier names of Danenhower's and Duy's lane. No. 4473 Main street, is Miller's old house. In its rear a quaint stone house, with creeping vines, is ancient. On the corner of Mehl street, is the Episcopal Church of St. John the Baptist. Of its architect and architecture Ward quotes:

> "The solemn arches breathe in stone,
> Window and wall have lips to tell
> The mighty faith of days unknown."

Rev. Chas. H. Hibbard is rector, and Rev. Joseph Wood, assistant minister. No. 4511 was George Royal's house. His grandchildren dwell in it. Another Royal house is opposite. The double stone house No. 4515, belongs to the same family. Its front door is a half door.

The southern boundary of ancient Germantown was a little south of Duy's lane. Its northern boundary was Washington street. The distance was 1.27 miles. The land south of Neglee's Hill and north of Washington street was divided into "side lots" and numbered. The man who had a corresponding number on his Germantown lot obtained the side lot also. From Duy's lane to the foot of Neglee's Hill was called Schmiersburg.

The emigrants brought passports on parchment, written with golden ink, and began their first stone town in this country under William Penn's gentle sway. Some of them missed a navigable stream, but Oldmixon writes about 1700: "The whole street, about one mile in length, was lined with blooming peach trees."

Peter Kalm, the Swedish traveler, pleasantly describes the town in 1748. "Most of the houses," he says, "were built of the same stone which is mixed with glimmer. Several houses, however, were made of brick. The town had three churches, one for the Lutherans, another for the Reformed Protestants, and the third for the Quakers. The inhabitants were so numerous that the street was always full. The Baptists have likewise a meeting-house."

Alexander Wilson, the ornithologist, walking to Niagara passed Germantown, and thus writes in the poem, "The Foresters":

> "Till through old Germantown we lightly trod;
> That skirts for three long miles the narrow road,
> And rising Chestnut Hill around surveyed,
> Wide woods below in vast extent displayed."

A noted New York architect said that the masonry of Germantown was the best in the United States.

No. 4537, Christopher Kinzel's barber shop, is the site of Thones Kunder's house. This building was Lesher's Tavern. A part of the wall of the ancient house is still in this one. In Kunder's house in 1683 "the Friends held their first meeting for worship."

From Jefferson to Ashmead street were the grounds of Mr. Philip R. Freas. The printing office on the north side was long the place of printing the GERMANTOWN TELEGRAPH, which was under his editorship for over fifty years. Logan's run rises in a fish-pond on these grounds.

COLONEL PHILIP R. FREAS.
(Communicated.)

Philip R. Freas, was born at Marble Hall, Montgomery county, Pa., February 22, 1809. At the age of sixteen he began to learn the printing business in the office of the Norristown *Herald*, then the leading Democratic paper of Montgomery county. When he reached his twenty-first year, he was offered an interest in the Herald establishment at a reasonable price, but preferred to start a newspaper of his own, and with that intention came to Germantown on the day that he reached his majority, February 22, 1830, bringing with him the names of sixty-five citizens of Norristown subscribers to the proposed journal.

A few weeks after his arrival in Germantown, on Wednesday, March 17, the VILLAGE TELEGRAPH appeared. Although but a small sheet compared with newspapers of the present day, it was then one of the largest journals in Pennsylvania. Germantown at that time was a straggling village of a few hundred inhabitants; the sidewalks in a number of places along the main

*This statement is very questionable. I have a letter written by Gen. Agnew's orderly, who does not mention it, though describing his burial, and saying that he was buried in a church-yard. C. J. W.

street were not paved; a railroad was not yet contemplated and an old rattling four-horse stage took a few passengers to the city in the morning and brought them home in the evening, nearly three hours being consumed in the round trip, and this was the only source of communication with the city. In a short time, however, suggestions in regard to the construction of a railroad between Germantown and Philadelphia began to appear in the TELEGRAPH, and in 1832 the project had so far advanced that the stock subscription books were simultaneously opened in Germantown, Philadelphia and Norristown and the rush of people anxious to buy shares was so great, that windows were broken, iron railings demolished by the swaying crowds and a number of persons were carried home in a fainting condition.

When the "Native American" riot broke out in Philadelphia, in 1844, during which fifty people were killed or wounded, two Roman Catholic churches destroyed by incendiary fires and fifty houses burned or pillaged, the TELEGRAPH was the only journal that fearlessly upheld sheriff Morton McMichael in his efforts to promptly subdue the riot and although the office of the TELEGRAPH was threatened with destruction, Mr. Freas in his editorials declared that he would continue to fight for the immediate enforcement of the laws and suppression of the mob by the military, so long as he had a newspaper to command.

Mr. Freas did much to promote the best interests of Germantown at a time when public improvements of every kind met with great opposition from many of the older citizens, who preferred having the primitive condition of things undisturbed.

He was a strong adherent of the old Whig party and enjoyed a personal acquaintance with Henry Clay and Daniel Webster. He never occupied any public office, although several were offered him, the last and most important being that of Commissioner of Agriculture, tendered by President Grant, in 1870.

Mr. Freas continued to conduct the TELEGRAPH until August 1, 1883, a period of more than fifty-three years, when it was sold to Mr. Henry W. Raymond of New York. For two years and a half Mr. Freas lived in retirement and died on the first day of April, 1886, in his seventy-seventh year.

A sketch of Col. Freas appeared in the TELEGRAPH in April, 1886, a few days after his death.

Henry W. Raymond, a son of the former editor of the New York Times, became editor of the paper in 1883.

ST. STEPHEN'S METHODIST EPISCOPAL CHURCH is a building of English architecture and fine appearance. Rev. Wesley C. Best is the pastor.

On the south-east corner of Bringhurst and Main streets, was the Bringhurst Mansion, owned by Jabez Gates. John Keen Gamble states that the early Bringhursts were buried in the Lower Burying Ground. They were extensive carriage builders about the time of the Revolution and afterwards.

Near the Bringhurst house is the site of the noted publishing house of Christopher Saur. Prof. Oswald Seidensticker, of the University of Pennsylvania, and Abraham H. Cassell, a descendant of Saur, have afforded means of giving his history. He was born in 1693, in Laasphe, Wittgenstein, Westphalia. In 1724 he came to Germantown with wife and son. The son was born September 26, 1721. Saur was a Dunkard preacher. He was bred a tailor, but had many other pursuits, being called in deeds "a clock and mathematical instrument maker." He imported German Bibles. He built a large stone house where No. 4653 stands. In a room here the Dunkards worshipped. Saur became a printer and in 1739 put forth his first almanac. Then he printed the book, "The Hill of Incense," in the German tongue. In 1743 he printed the Bible in German forty years before it was printed here in English. In 1739 he began a newspaper, the "High German Pennsylvania Historian, or, A Collection of Important News from the Kingdom of Nature and of the Church." Saur pitied emigrants, and was the means of establishing the Lazaretto. He died September 25, 1758. His only son, Christopher, took up the business of his father. He married Catharine Sharpnack (Germantown has a Sharpnack street). "He issued a second edition of the Bible in 1763." He introduced ten-plate stoves, which Dr. Franklin improved. He sold medicines from Dr. DeBenneville's prescriptions. "In 1773 he built a paper mill on the Schuylkill." In 1775 the Convention of Pennsylvania "passed resolutions favorably commending his ingenuity." In 1776 he issued a third edition of the Bible. The paper was continued till 1770 by Billmeyer, and afterward by Samuel Saur. The family kept up the printing business, and the Philadelphia publisher Charles G. Sower is a descendant. Mr. William H. Sowers of Harvey street is another.

Squire Baynton lived in this same house. Dr. Owen J. Wister built on this site the fine house numbered 4653, and dwelt in it. Afterwards Moses Brown bought it and resided in it. Mr. Robert Pearsall Smith now lives there.

Next on the north is "WISTER'S BIG HOUSE." Hans Casper and Anna Katerina Wister (Wuster) of Hillspach near Heidelberg, Germany, were the progenitors of the Wisters and Wistars so well-known in Germantown and Philadelphia.

Casper reached Philadelphia in 1717, and established button and glass factories. When Casper took the oath of allegiance in 1721 the clerk wrongly spelt the name Wistar, and his descendants still write it so. Dr. Casper Wistar, founder of the Wistar parties was one.

John Wister, brother of Casper, was the father of Mrs. Dr. William Chancellor, from whom are descended the Chancellors and Twells. John Wister's second wife, a German lady was the mother of Mrs. (Col.) Samuel Miles, and the ancestress of the McKeans, of Washington, and the Bayards of Germantown. John Wister owned Wister's Wood, through which Wister street runs. He died in 1789. In 1744 he built "Wister's Big House," opposite Indian

"WISTER HOMESTEAD," GERMANTOWN, BUILT BY JOHN WISTER, 1744.

Queen Lane, "for a summer residence." It is marked No. 4661. Here General Agnew died.

The granddaughter of this gentleman wrote "Sallie Wister's Journal."

REVOLUTIONARY INCIDENTS ASSOCIATED WITH THE WISTER HOMESTEAD, MAIN STREET, OPPOSITE INDIAN QUEEN LANE, GERMANTOWN.

In the early part of the last century, there lived in Lancaster county, Pennsylvania, an old German and his only daughter, a child of tender years, Justina by name. The old man being prostrated by a fatal malady, and convinced that his days were numbered, was much disturbed by the reflection that his death would leave his daughter without friend or relation to protect her. In this strait he determined to send her to Philadelphia, and entrust her to the care of John Wister, the elder, whose charity and benevolence had reached his ears. Instructing her to this effect, when her father had been carried to his last resting place, she set out for the city, alone and on foot, and thus performed the whole journey of seventy weary miles. The confidence of her father was not misplaced, for Justina was kindly received and forthwith taken into the service of her benefactor, in whose family she remained, a most faithful servant, until her death at a very advanced age.

During the occupancy of Philadelphia by the British, in 1777–8, John Wister remained in the city, and was thus separated from his family, who, in order to escape the inconveniences they were likely to be subjected to by the hostile army, took up their abode at North Wales, Montgomery county. Germantown being too near to afford the security sought, the old mansion, meanwhile, was left in charge of Justina, who had by this time come to years of discretion, and proved her trustworthiness. When the British advanced to the village, the mansion being one of the largest in the place, was seized upon for the headquarters of Gen'l Agnew, a distinguished officer of the invading army.

On the day that the battle of Germantown was fought, October 4, 1777, Justina was observed by Agnew hard at work in the garden with a small, two-pronged German hoe—long preserved in the family as a relic. The kind-hearted man expostulated with her for exposing herself in this way, and recommended her, when the battle commenced, to retire to the cellar as the place of greatest safety. The old woman was obstinate, however, and continued working away throughout the fight, quite unharmed. After giving this humane advice, Agnew set out for the scene of action, but never to reach it; for, as is well-known, he was shot by a man named Boyer, concealed behind the Concord school-house. Mortally wounded he was carried back to his headquarters, and laid bleeding on the floor of the west parlor, where the stain of his blood is still visible, having resisted the scrubbings of a century. Some of the boards were so stained that they were removed. It is proverbial that the marks of blood cannot be washed out, and this goes far to confirm it.

Old Justina's exit was as mysterious as her introduction into the family in whose service she so long remained, and savored of the supernatural. In fact the respect that she entertained for her benefactors required that the announcement of her departure should not reach them by any less reliable agent than herself, consequently her wraith very properly assumed the responsibility of making the communication.

During the yellow fever summer of 1793, Justina was, as usual at that season, in charge of the city dwelling, whilst the family of John Wister were in their homestead at Germantown. Awaking at the early dawn, one morning, to their great surprise, two of its members perceived in the mysterious grey light, Justina standing at the door looking in at them. So distinct was the apparition that one expressed to the other great surprise, knowing that she was in the city. In the course of the day (for there were no telegraphs or express carriers to convey news, then) when the whole matter was dismissed from the minds of the incredulous persons to whom the vision was related, and who viewed it as a phantom of the imagination, the staggering intelligence arrived of the old woman's death, not only, but of its occurrence at the precise hour—that weird and ghostly hour when day and night seem to meet—in which she so mysteriously appeared in Germantown.

The Wister Homestead was the pioneer of its class, for it was the first house built in Germantown designed for a summer residence; it is an example that has had many followers in latter days. It was built to resist the ravages of time moreover, for the walls are of prodigious thickness, and the joists are of oak hewn in Wister's woods.

The garden, above referred to, connected with the house, is worthy of special mention, for there

> "No daintie flowre or herbe that growes on ground,
> No arborette with painted blossoms drest
> And smelling sweete, but there it may be found
> To bud out faire, and throwe her sweete smels al around."

This inclosure, in after years so exquisitely cultivated, and whose fragrance is such as belongs only to gardens mellowed by time, and filled with the sweet memories of many generations of fruits and flowers, had originally better claims to the title of orchard, for John Wister, the elder, brought with him from the Fatherland the German taste for cultivation of fruits, and a great variety of pears, plums, etc., were cultivated by him; several remnants of which old stock still flourish, and produce though they have witnessed at least a hundred and fifty returning summers.

The name of Wister was never spelled Wuster, as has been stated. The German *u*, with the *umlaut* (*ü*) having no equivalent in the English language, the letter *i* was substituted as that most nearly approximating it.

The PHILADELPHIA NEWS, gives this note on this place:

On the grounds of the old Physick mansion on Fourth street, which I have

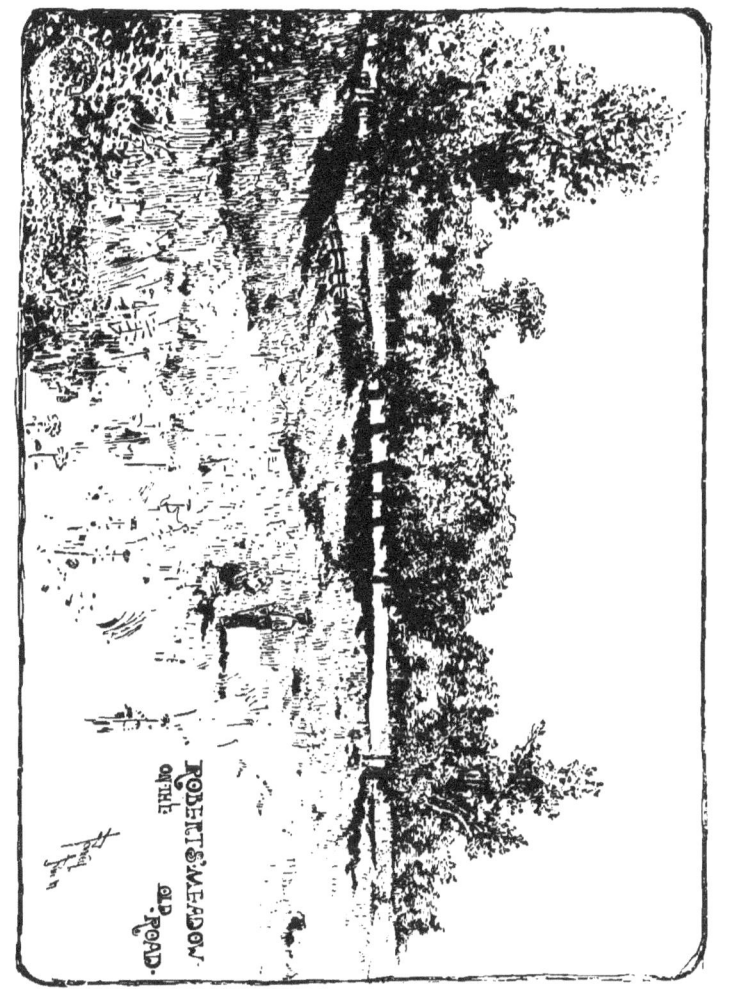

told you about, there grows a mighty elm, which, although not quite so handsome as the Dundas tree, is still an object of admiration and a great source of speculation as to its age to the hundreds of working people who daily pass up and down Fourth street. On the grounds of Mr. Charles J. Wister's place in Germantown there grows a specimen, probably of the rarest tree in America; it is called the Virgilla lutea, I believe. It is said to have been named after the poet Virgil. A few of these trees were transplanted to this part of the country from Kentucky, where they grow wild sparingly along the Kentucky river. This tree bears a white flower, which resembles that of the wisteria; the wood is extremely hard and has a yellow color; on this account the tree has been vulgarly called the "yellow wood." There is a story connected with it—that the shittim wood spoken of in the Scripture is one and the same thing as the Virgilla lutea.

In 1779, Major Lenox dwelt here briefly and was married to Miss Lukens in the west parlor, where also William Wister of Belfield was married. Here "Major Lenox was advised of the attack on Fort Wilson, at Third and Walnut streets." See Frederick D. Stone's excellent account of the matter, *Pennsylvania Magazine of History*, vol. 2, p. 392. Afterwards the Wister house was assaulted at night by nearly two hundred men; his cousin, a young lady, walked to the city and called the First City Troops to the rescue.

Daniel Wister, son of John, married Lowry, a daughter of Owen Jones, of Wynnewood. He is the father of John and of Charles J. Wister, deceased. He was very fond of animals. At Daniel Wister's house in Market street, Philadelphia, Dr. Franklin put up his first lightning rod. Daniel Wister died October 27, 1805.

Daniel's brother William with Owen Jones, Jr., and Col. Samuel Miles "signed much of the paper money of the province." He died in 1800. He was a bachelor, kind-hearted, and cared for the unfortunate, even keeping some poor at his own table. An Indian whom he supported was asked by him to pile some wood, and he received the reply "Do you think there's work enough for two, Billy? for if there ain't, you had better do it yourself."

Charles Jones Wister, was a son of Daniel, and a nephew of William, in whose counting-house he was employed. He traveled through Pennsylvania and Virginia to collect debts; there was much wilderness and few bridges. George Ashton, their clerk, warned him; "Charley beware of creeks; thee'd look very foolish if thee was to come home drownded." At Winchester, Va., he met the Duke de Rochefaucault, who wished to dine alone but was forced by the landlord to admit the other guests. Still the Duke's travels do justice to American innkeepers, one of whom was Baron Beaulieu. At Moundville, Ohio, Ward once found a refined landlady, and being mistaken for Charles Dickens was "taken on a fox hunt by the landlord."

Charles J. Wister was intimate "with Adam Seybert, a pupil of Wagner and Blumenbach, who had come here from Germany with the first cabinet of minerals known in this country, and he also in time formed for himself an extensive one." After his uncle died he was partner in the firm, "John & Charles J. Wister;" afterwards, John M. Price being introduced, it was "Wister, Price & Wister." The Germantown wool and farm and mansion on the avenue fell to him. He used the house "as a summer residence until 1812, after which he remained there permanently." He kept up active business till 1819, going daily to the city. Peters' stage made tri-weekly trips, slowly, over poor roads. He often started his drive by starlight. After business was over he and others went to James P. Park's store to converse. They formed the Twilight Club, some of whom aided in establishing "the world renowned Academy of Natural Sciences of Philadelphia."

Mr. Wister "led a retired life." He was thoroughly scientific, but very modest. John Jay Smith pronounced him "the greatest botanist living." He lectured on botany and mineralogy for the benefit of the Germantown Academy, and was Secretary of its Board of Trustees. In 1835 he built an observatory, which contained "a transit instrument and an astronomical clock made by his friend, Isaiah Lukens. He made daily observations, giving the villagers correct time. He read the English classics with care and could quote them freely. He had mechanical skill and left many admirable pieces of handicraft. He died July 23, 1865, in his eighty-fourth year. His son, Mr. Charles J. Wister, now occupies the house."

We continue the abridgment of Ward's Germantown Road. His fifth article begins by stating that the early makers of yarn worked so faithfully in the ancient village that "Germantown Wool" denoted "the best article of the kind, wherever made throughout the States." He ascertained that the vineclad house back of No. 4473 was a "bakehouse for troops during the Revolution." Mr. Justice Blair Linn, of Bellefonte, wrote Mr. Ward further information as to Ellinkhuysen, who made the equestrian statue of Frederick the Great on a window pane in the Toland house. His grave is in the Presbyterian churchyard at Lewisburg, Pa. The inscription runs:

> "Here lies the body of Mathias Joseph Ellinkhuysen,
> Who departed this life July 17, 1792,
> Aged thirty-eight years and three months.
> Since it is so we all must die,
> And death doth no one spare;
> So let us all to Jesus fly,
> And seek for refuge there."

James F. Linn, Esq., stated that Carl Ellinkhuysen, of Amsterdam, Holland, had the title to all the town lots in Lewisburg, except seventeen, derived from George Derr, son of Ludwig Derr, the proprietor. Carl sent his son to this country to look after his interest." He used to draw "striking likenesses of his companions." His wife Clara Helena was a great skater, which was natural in a Dutch lady.

The Wagner house is next to Toland's, and Mr. Justice W. Jordans's researches aided Ward here. In the *Magazine of History*, Vol. 5, p. 250, Mr. Ward said: John Zachary had purchased part in 1745 from John Theobald Ent,

Fleckenstein's House, Spring Lane.

and in 1747 he built the present house." Mr. Jordan adds the following information: Ent, or properly Endt, became an active Moravian. On January 12, 1742, a Synod was held at his house. Count Zinzendorf presided. Endt's children were pupils at the Moravian schools.

Next to Endt's house was that "of the Rev. John Bechtel, a Palatine from Franckenthal, whose daughter married the Indian Missionary, Buttner. Bechtel prepared for the Moravian Church a reformed catechism, which was printed by Franklin in 1742. John Stephen Benezet's house was near by." Zinzendorf came to Philadelphia in 1741. He boarded with Bechtel. In 1746 Justice Peter Muller, Englebert Lock, Jean de Dier, Peter Hoffman, Anthony Gilbert, Cornelius Weygand, Marcus Munzer and Hans Gerster requested the Moravians of Bethlehem to open a girls' school in Germantown. Justice Bechtel offered the use of his house. The boarding and day school opened in September. Rev. James Greening and wife supervised it. Two Indian girls attended the school. It was kept up until 1749. In 1747 Mr. Bechtel gave ground for a Moravian graveyard on his place.

West Logan street has been called Norris street and Terrace avenue and Abbotsford avenue.

Logan's run crosses the Henry property. Royal's charming meadow was near by, where sheep used to diversify the picture. The British built huts for cavalry around in it. They used rails covered with sod. In 1793 George Royal, supposed to be a son of a Royal who lived about the middle of the last century, married Mary Sommers. Peale painted her portrait. George Royal lived in a house on the east side of Main street, no longer standing. John Wagner's new houses are on its site.

No. 4506, west side, "is the house of George Royal's son, Edward, who bought the meadow." It is said to have been built in 1747. It is "modernized." Edward Royal, in driving, once met a wagon in a narrow place, the driver of which would not turn out; he waited until the driver yielded, when he said, "Do you know what I would have done if you had not turned out when you did?" "No," was the gruff reply. "Why then," said Royal, chuckling, "I should have turned out myself."

No. 4511 was the residence of George Royal's son, Jacob. "The children of these brothers continue to occupy these large buildings." No. 4515, before spoken of, "was bought by the Royals about twenty-five years ago. Previously it had been for two generations occupied by the Duys, who gave their name to the lane near by."

Spring Alley is named from a spring on it. North of it is the old house, numbered 4528. Samuel Fleckenstein lived in it, and later another bearing the same name, who used to tell of the battle of Germantown. Latterly Frederick, grandson of the first, lived here. They were fine mechanics. The eldest one did some of the iron work needed to aid the Sauers in printing. The two first Fleckensteins used to do jobs at 3 cents a piece, no matter how long they were occupied. Frederick tried this, but the war forced him up to

5 cents. With small gains they were contented, happy and respectable. Ward asks, "who, then, can say they were not wise?" The second Fleckenstein was with Miller in Lorain's cellar at the battle. He never went into the city, as he told Alexander Henry. Chickens and pigeons were at home in his little shop. The artist, George B. Wood painted the interior of the shop excellently. Fleckenstein was fond of botany and mineralogy, and took long walks with his friend, George Redles, botanizing. About nine years ago this simple-hearted student of nature died of pneumonia, when about eighty years old.

On the north side of Duy's lane, about a quarter of a mile east of Main street, is a house, which in 1837 was bought by the late Jeremiah Hacker, and where his family now live.

At the southwest corner of Main and Manheim streets is an old-fashioned inn with hipped roof. It has been tastefully enlarged. Pickus and Bockius afterward kept it. William K. Cox enlarged it and conducted it. The lane at the side has been called Pickus', Betton's and Bockius's, and Cox's. Jacques Marie Roset called it Manheim street, "in honor of the beauty of the ladies of Manheim, in Germany." Roset, a Frenchman, came as a young man from Austria to America, attracted by Washington's character. Having landed in Philadelphia in 1792, and walking up Chestnut street with some of his countrymen he met Washington, who saw that they were Frenchmen, and, as Watson says, thus greeted him: "*Bien venu en Amerique.*" This pleased Roset greatly. In 1821 he began to reside in the Toland property, on Main street, below Manheim, and remained there twelve years. He moved to a house on the corner of Spring Alley and Manheim street. He had a Sunday-school here and was a favorite with children. He was fond of flowers, and used to present Mrs. Butler (Fanny Kemble) a bouquet when she rode by his house. He died at the age of 86. He is buried in the Lutheran churchyard. John Roset, his eldest son, was a merchant in Philadelphia. His wife was Miss Mary Laning, a granddaughter of Judge Matthias Hollenback, of Wilkesbarre; one of his daughters married Dr. Justice L. Ludlow, another, Justice Broadhead, and a third, Anthony J. Drexel.

Dr. Samuel Betton came to Germantown from the Island of Jamaica, when Dr. Bensell was growing old. He married the daughter of Col. Thomas Forrest, "a Revolutionary character." He bought the rather striking, but agreeable looking house,

"WHITE COTTAGE,"

which yet stands on the north side of Manheim street, west of Greene, and is occupied by Theodore Justice. He added the octagon room. The Bettons were of the Bethune family, as was the Duke of Sully, the minister of Henry IV. His son, the late Dr. Thomas Forrest Betton, married Elizabeth, a daughter of Albanus Logan, of Stenton. These are now represented by Mr. Samuel Betton.

Opposite this cottage is Taggart's Field. A part of the house on it is said

to be prerevolutionary. Here the British infantry had huts. After they departed young Miller saw on the field " Count Pulaski's Legion of Cavalry, four hundred men in their uniform of nearly white. He said the Legion was formed mostly of prisoners of Burgoyne's Army, Germans and others."

Beyond Betton's is Thomas A. Newhall's place, originally Robert Toland's. In 1860 the Marquess of Chandos, afterward Duke of Buckingham, was a guest here. The Marquess saw William Penn's portrait in the Hall of the Historical Society, which had been presented by Granville Penn, his great-grandson. He told Ward that he remembered it, having seen it at Stoke-Poges, the English seat of the Penns.

No. 4558—This large double stone house was occupied by Commodore James Barron, forty or fifty years ago, when he was in command of the Philadelphia Navy Yard. This gentleman painted one of James Gowen's fine cattle; the painting is in Mr. Blake's parlor in London. The Commodore's grandson, Capt. James Barron Hope, who wrote the ode for the Yorktown Centennial was a schoolboy in Germantown. Count Miollis often dined at the Commodore's. He taught French at McClanagan's Academy. He was an officer under Napoleon the Great, and made the Pope a prisoner.

After Commodore Barron left his house, Capt. Henry A. Adams, of the Navy, occupied it, and afterwards Col. John G. Watmough, " who earned his laurels in the sortie at Fort Erie." He was Sheriff, and a Representative in Congress.

No. 4562 was the shop of Green the hatter. The long old building, Ward quaintly says, had nine parts of a proof of prosperity, and one of traffic. There used to be fifty martin boxes here.

Edward Shippen, a wealthy Boston merchant, whose nephew was a member of Parliament, " Honest Will Shippen," as Robert Walpole styled him, having been punished for being a Quaker in Boston came to Philadelphia. He was the first Mayor of Philadelphia, and built "Shippy's great house" in Second street above Spruce. The name was pronounced Shippy. It was called the Governors' House, as many Governors lived in it.

In 1709, Joseph Shippen, son of the Mayor, began to buy land in Germantown. He and his sons at length owned 100 acres. In 1716 he began to live there, perhaps in summer. Doubtless he built the house which was on the site of the one occupied by Mr. Heft, No. 4912. It is not known whether he or his family lived any length of time in it. In 1740 in Joseph's deed to his sons Edward, Joseph and William the house is called the " Roebuck Tavern." In 1819 William Shippen, great-grandson of Joseph's son William, together with his wife Mary, "conveyed the property to George Heft, with whom it became the well-known Buttonwood Tavern, marked by two stately trees of that variety standing before it, only one of which now remains. It is a large old gnarled tree, spectre-like, for its bark is gone, and altogether it is one of the most striking looking trees in Germantown." Caspar Heft, son of George, is now the owner of the property.

"Joseph Shippen's youngest son, Dr. William, was born in 1712." He was eminent as a physician. He died at ninety, being beloved by all who knew him. He was twice a member of the Continental Congress, and though aged, constantly attended its sessions. He married Susannah, daughter of Joseph Harrison, of Philadelphia. Prof. William Shippen, his son, was born in 1736. He studied with his father and " under the celebrated Hunters in England." In 1776 he was appointed " Chief Physician for the Flying Camp." He was elected " Director-General of all the Military Hospitals in the United States." He died in Germantown on the 11th of July, 1808. Thacher, in his Medical Biography, speaks of these Shippens, father and son, and in high but just terms. Dr. Wistar's graceful eulogy on the Professor was given in 1809. Prof. Shippen married Alice Lee, " daughter of Col. Thomas Lee, Governor of the Province of Virginia." Thomas Lee Shippen, his son, was born in 1765. He graduated at Princeton, studied law at Williamsburg, Va., with James Madison, and was afterward of the Inner Temple, London. He married in 1791 " Elizabeth Carter, daughter of Major James Parke Farley, and granddaughter of Col. William Byrd, 3d, of Westover, on the James. Their son was Dr. William Shippen, born at Farley, Bucks county, Penna., in 1792, married in 1817, Marie Louise Shore, of Petersburg, Va., and died in Philadelphia, June 5, 1867. He was a Vice-President of the Historical Society.

No. 4622 is the residence of Mr. William Wynne Wister. Gilbert Stuart, the artist, once resided here. The remaining walls of his studio still stand back of the house. There he painted the excellent portrait of Washington.

No. 4626 is Mr. Harlan's large house; first a summer residence, but now in continuous use.

No. 4630 was Squire Peter Baynton's daughter's residence. The Bayntons were a noble English family noted by Burke. They were related to the Budds, of New Jersey, and the Chevaliers, Markoes, Wisters and Camacs of Philadelphia, and the Morgan family near Pittsburg. Squire Baynton was Adjutant General of the Pennsylvania Militia. His son John was Mayor of Natchez. He died in Philadelphia, and his widow "is the only one now bearing the name."

No. 4634 is a large house standing back, nearly opposite to where the Bringhurst house stood. For more than thirty years " it has been owned and occupied by the late Isaiah Hacker and his family." It was built by Mr. Forbes. David Hayfield Conyngham, of Ireland, son of Redmond Conyngham, Esq., and Martha, daughter of Robert Ellis, of Philadelphia lived in it. Redmond Conyngham came here in 1756, and was one of the original members of the firm of J. M. Nesbit & Co. He returned to Ireland in 1767 and died in 1785. David married in 1779, " at Whitemarsh, Mary, daughter of William and Mary West. She died August 27, 1820." He was a partner in the house of J. M. Nesbit & Co., which was distinguished in the Revolution. After 1783 the firm was Conyngham, Nesbit & Co. David H. Conyngham was a descendant of William Conyngham, Bishop of Argyll, and a cousin of Baron

GERMANTOWN.

Plunket, Chief Justice of Ireland, and also a cousin of Capt. Gustavus Conyngham, U. S. Navy. David II. "was father of the Hon. John N. Conyngham of Wilkes-Barre. He died on the first of March, 1834, and was buried in the grounds of our Christ Church." His life was interesting, and Rev. Horace E. Hayden, of Wilkes-Barre, is to write his memoir. "After Mr. Conyngham left the house, and perhaps immediately, Miss Hannah, a maiden sister of John and Charles J. Wister, occupied it for a dozen years or more." In 1832 the house was sold by Samuel Taylor and William Rainey to Alexander Prevost. In 1835 he "sold to the Rev. William Neill, pastor of the old Presbyterian Church on the Main street below Haines." In 1844 he sold " to the late Isaiah Hacker." No. 4636 on the west side of the street, with its shaggy exterior, defies the storm, and promises comfort within. On a pane of glass in it was written, "Anna W. Morris, and Maria Abercrombie, 1807." Miss Abercrombie's father was assistant minister of Christ Church and St. Peter's. She was vivacious in age, as well as youth. She was a cousin of the Bayntons. Mrs Abigail Johnson Morris, wife of Justus Johnson, lived here long since; of late it has been the abode of the late William Howell's family.

No. 4838 is Handsberry's house. This was once Theobald Endt's house. Last autumn it was the theatre of a scene that always pleases—the ancient couple residing there celebrated their golden wedding in 1882.

Woltemate's greenhouse, No. 4646, is the site of the residence of the Van-Lauchets. Christian and John, grandsons of the long ago Barbara Van-Lanchet, have recently died. They were the last of a Holland family, who were early settlers in Germantown. Michael Riter's Indian Queen Inn is now a grocery store at the southwest corner of Indian Queen Lane. "Modernus," Mr. Ward says, "affect to call it Queen street." He thought that the change would not succeed. A fruitless attempt was made "to have it called Whittle's or Riter's lane. An earlier name, Bowman's, has also passed into oblivion.

"In the early part of this century the properties No. 4630 to 4638 inclusive, belonged to a well-known family named Forbes. William Forbes erected the house occupied by David H. Conyngham."

At Indian Queen Lane some American soldiers were about to arrest a British surgeon after the battle of Germantown, but learning that he had dressed the wounds of three American officers in the house of Widow Hess, he was allowed to go free; while a man who overset his chaise at Bowman's Lane and exposed some silver plate was captured.

On the northeast corner of old Bowman's lane and Knox street, Louis Rene Jacques Joseph Binel lived. He was an accomplished Frenchman. His grandfather was a friend of General Armand, whose picture adorns the Hall of the Historical Society. He met Mons. Gardel, the Philadelphia teacher, in Constantinople, and he spoke highly of Germantown. He became Legal Adviser to Maximilian, and when the Mexican Empire failed, engaged in teaching French in Germantown. He spoke of the quick apprehension of the poor Empress Carlotta.

Watson says all the British infantry were located about where Col. John Morgan Price's seat was, *i. e.* Manheim street, west of Wayne. "On the north side of Indian Queen Lane is a Potter's Field." It was bought in 1755 for £5, 10s. It contained 140 perches. It lies west of Wayne street, about where Pulaski crosses, and the region about it is called 'Pulaski Town.'" It was cut out of John Blicker's lot, No. 6. On the same lot on the Main street is a double house built by Christopher Sauer. It was Joseph Bullock's residence and afterward used by his son, Dr. Bullock. It is said that the solid foundations of a former house underlie this one, and that here Christopher Sauer did some of his work in preparing type. Trinity Lutheran church owns it. It is a parsonage, and the Rev. Luther E. Albert, D. D., the minister of the parish, dwells in it. Formerly Dr. Justus Fox's house was north of it. His son, Emmanuel, manufactured lampblack. Emmanuel's son George was in the same business, and was a bee fancier. Their conscientious work made" Germantown lamp-black " the highest grade in commerce.

Trinity Lutheran Church is the daughter of the church farther up Germantown avenue. It was founded in 1836, holding service in a brick building, corner of Main and Mill streets. Rev. Dr. Mayer installed its vestry. Rev. William Scholl was the first pastor; Rev. S. M. Finckle, D. D., and Rev. William F. Eyster followed. Rev. Dr. Albert became pastor in 1851. Prof. Martin L. Stoever is buried in the graveyard. The very tall man, of this church, James Reeside, was also interred here. He was called "Admiral," as he directed stage coaches. Mrs. Stellwagen buried here is thought to have been 101 years old.

Capt. Jno. Stadelman lived about the present No. 4718. He commanded the Germantown Blues. He was a great fisherman. Christophel Bockius lived at the N. W. corner of Coulter and Main streets. He was an aged farmer, and owned about 20 acres of land.

The Frankfort Land Company gave an acre of land near the Friends' Meeting House on Main street, west side, for "a Market, Town House, Burying Place, and other Public Buildings." This was the center of the town, and here Ward thinks that the Court was held till removed to Market Square. Its seal was a trefoil surrounded by the words "Sigillum Germanopolitanum."

THE FRIENDS' MEETING HOUSE.

The FRIENDS' MEETING HOUSE belongs to Frankford Monthly Meeting and Abington Quarterly Meeting. The Germantown Friends, while meeting at private houses in 1688, "issued their famous testimony against slavery." Jacob Shoemaker conveyed the land to the Friends. The first Meeting House is thought to have been of wood; and a part of its foundation was found a few years ago. In 1708 a new stone building on the same site arose. In this building the first Isaac Norris died, A. D. 1735. In 1812 a third meeting-house was built, west of the old site, near its location, and near the present school-house. In

THE FRIENDS' MEETING HOUSE, COULTER AND MAIN STREETS.

GERMANTOWN. 65

1871 it disappeared and a fourth meeting-house was erected, still further to the west. An old tablet from the 3d house is preserved in the committee room.

PENN	ANNO	GER
OLD	1705	MAN
NEW	1812	TOW.

A Friends' burying-ground joins the meeting-house. Perhaps fifty years ago the Friends had a library. Alfred Cope and others of late "began to build upon this foundation." They erected the fine stone building, and stored it with about 3000 valuable books. Alfred Cope endowed it. It has now about 11000 volumes. Novels are excluded. The library building, Ward believed to have been on a part of Lot No. 9, which was Jacob Isaacs van Bebber's. He soon left Germantown. One of the name was Judge in the Supreme Court of Delaware, and another a noted physician in Baltimore. The Maryland Van-Bebbers were a distinguished family. Van Bebber's Rock at Falls of the Kanawha commemorates a daring Indian fighter of that name.

"The library is under the charge of William Kite, a Friend. He is descended from James Kite, who preceded Penn. He held land in the present Park, and "paid the Indians what they deemed the value of it." He married Mary Warner, a daughter of William, supposed to be an ancestor of the one who owned the land occupied by the "Colony in Schuylkill," styled by the amateur fishers "Baron." On the 1st of June they paid him as rent, "three fresh sun perch."

There was an earlier "Germantown Library." The date of its seal was 1745. Baltus Reser was Treasurer and Christian Lehman, Secretary.

No. 4772 was Albert Ashmead's residence. His father was John, and grandfather William, "brother of Captain John Ashmead of the Revolution." He brought in cargoes of powder. The great nephew, Albert, was "Captain of the Troop of Germantown Cavalry." William Ashmead, an iron worker, originated "Germantown Waggons," in place of the heavy imported coaches. He built one, and his son John took up the business, "not long after the Revolution." Mr. Bringhurst also was a large carriage builder. William Ashmead invented wrought iron moulds for ploughs. La Fayette bought four of these ploughs for his estate, La Grange. Some one substituted cast iron for wrought iron. Jno. Ashmead, father of Albert, lived in No. 4774. He was a Friend, but fond of music. He saw the British army when a boy of twelve. He sat at his father's door as they passed down Main street, 20,000 strong. The order was complete. The Highlanders had kilts and plaids, the grenadiers were in scarlet and the loyal refugees in green. Cavalry and footmen and officers passed along with pomp; but there was no display of colors and no music. "There was no violence." Ashmead's father gave the soldiers milk and cider, at their request, until an officer placed a sentinel before the house to stop the demand. "Capt. J. C. perhaps Craig" saw the soldiers later, headed by Cornwallis. Some Grenadiers addressed the boy in a brotherly way, and shook his hand. Young Ashmead, at the battle, "took refuge in the cellar of Delaplaine's house, on the N. E. corner of Schoolhouse Lane." After the battle he secured an English and an American cannon-ball. Dr. William Ashmead has the English one. The Revolutionary boy lived to the age of 83 and his wife to 87.

THE DESHLER—WASHINGTON—MORRIS HOUSE.

No. 4782 was built in 1772-3 by David Deshler, who had come here from Heidelburg, where his father, whose wife was a sister of Casper and John Wister, was an aide-de-camp to the reigning Prince. He was in successful business in Philadelphia. "As honest as David Deshler" was "an old saying." Mrs. Deshler bought a salve from a butcher, which was called "Butcher's Salve" and afterward "Deshler's Salve." Dr. Wistar put the recipe in his Pharmacopœia. "Adam Deshler, perhaps a cousin of David, also came here, and has left descendants. One of these is Mr. William G. Deshler, a resident of Columbus, Ohio." David Deshler's wife, Mary, was a granddaughter of Madame Mary Ferree, a French Huguenot widow, who owned much land in Pequea Valley, where a Huguenot settlement arose, favored by the Indian King Tanawa. David Deshler's daughter, Mary, married Ellis Lewis in 1763. Owen Lewis, a Friend, in Wales, was the ancestor of Ellis Lewis. His residence was "Tyddyn y Gareg, near Dolegelle, in Merionethshire." The late Chief Justice Ellis Lewis is descended from Owen Lewis, "and the present Mr. David Lewis, so well known in Philadelphia, is of the same line." Rev. William P. Lewis, is a son of David Lewis. Sir William Howe was the occupant of Deshler's house for a time. David Deshler dressed in "olive-coloured silk velvet, with knee buckles and silk stockings, bright silver shoe buckles and the usual three-looped hat—a costume that well became his handsome face and manly form." His wife died in the Revolutionary days, but he lived until 1792. The wife never lived in the Germantown house, but Mrs. Moses Dillon, her granddaughter informs me that she died in Philadelphia before the house was finished. David Deshler occupied it as a summer residence with his daughters and granddaughters. His will requested its sale to settle the estate. Col. Isaac Franks, a Revolutionary officer, bought the house. He was cousin to the celebrated beauty, Miss Rebecca Franks, who married Sir Henry Johnson. Colonel Franks' wife was Mary Davidson. Judge Franks, of Reading, was his son. Col. Ffanks was ancestor of "some of the Jacobs of Lancaster county, and of a family named Davis, of Camden, N. J." During the yellow fever epidemic Washington rented the house of Col. Franks.

In 1804 Elliston and John Perot bought the house as a summer residence. It is a tradition that a persecuted Huguenot ancestor of this family was preserved alive in imprisonment by a hen laying an egg daily at the grated window of his French dungeon. The crest of the Perot coat of arms is a setting hen. The persecuted man came from the French Rochelle to New Rochelle, N. Y., where his son James was born. In 1710 James went to Bermuda and Elliston

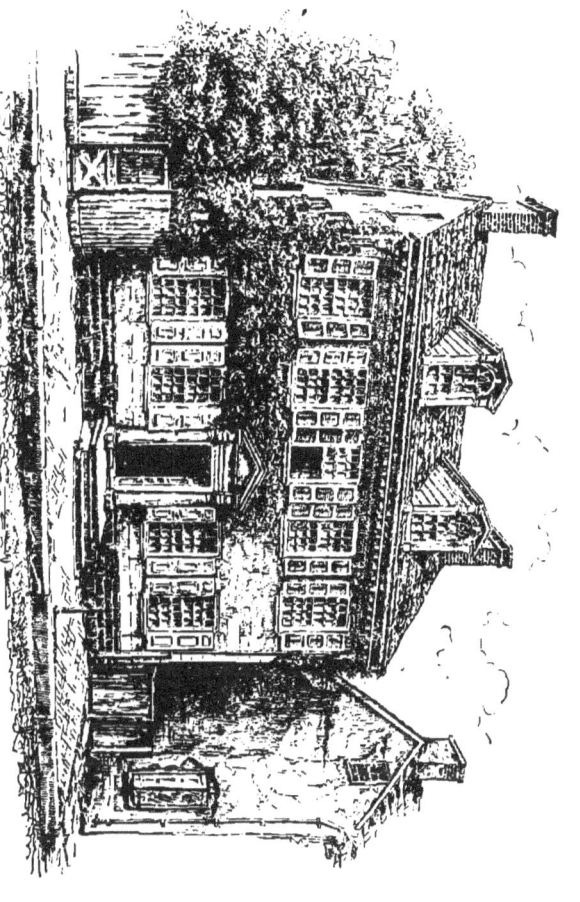

THE DESHLER—WASHINGTON—MORRIS HOUSE, MARKET SQUARE.

and John were born there, though they, after vicissitudes in the West Indies, settled in business in Philadelphia. Elliston's daughter, Hannah, "married Samuel B. Morris, of the old shipping firm of Waln & Morris, and he purchased the house in 1834." He was a descendant of Antony Morris. The present owner, Elliston Perot Morris, is a son of Samuel B. Morris.

The house is of stone, with extensive back buildings, The front would have been wider, but a plum tree moved Deshler's heart, and he could not cut it down. There is a beautiful garden containing box trees of more than a century's growth. Jesse Waln took tea in this house with his schoolfellow, George Washington Parke Custis, by Washington's invitation. The house contains Washington's letter of thanks to Capt. Samuel Morris for the services of the First City Troop, and the "pitcher likeness" of Washington, presented by Captain Dunlap to Captain Morris.

An informant writes:

"The Deshler who built this house had a son 'Adam,' who had a son 'David Wagoner,' who had a son 'William Green,' who had a son 'John Green.'"

The two last named are bankers in Columbus, Ohio. The "Manual of the Columbus Female Benevolent Society" for A. D. 1888, is a neatly-bound volume which indicates faithful Christian work to aid the needy. The Deshler family are well represented among its members. Mrs. Ann Eliza Sinks Deshler is in the list of "Names in Memorial." The President, Mrs. Mary J. Hubbard notes that Mr. William G. Deshler gave $33,000 to endow this Society as a memorial of a beloved daughter. The fund is styled, "The Kate Deshler Hunter Fund." Mrs. Hunter for many years lovingly taught in the Industrial School, showing practical charity. Mrs. John G. Deshler also willed $25,000 to this same good cause, and owing to legal complications about that will, Mr. William G. Deshler guaranteed the sum.

One fund bears the name, "The Betsey Green Deshler Fund." It consists of $100,000 donated by Wm. G. Deshler in memory of his mother. That mother, when her neighbors suffered from sickness, failure of harvests, and business troubles in a new country, sympathized and aided as a christian wife and mother, and left letters indicating her desire to do more. These letters stirred the gift of the son in after years, and the buried seed bore precious fruit, and will continue to bear it.

A portion of the income of this noble gift is to go to the "Hannah Neil Mission and Home of the Friendless," in Columbus. A very interesting Semi-Centennial address, by Mr. Deshler, reviewing the Christlike work of the Columbus Female Benevolent Society, is found at the close of the volume under review.

The old Germantown house has a new interest as we consider the good work of those descended from its builder, and hope that many Germantowners may imitate such noble deeds.

GERMANTOWN.

FROM "THE HOMEMAKER" MAGAZINE.

Historian, painter and poet have made familiar to us the story of the imprisoned Huguenot, condemned to die from starvation, who was kept alive by the seeming accident that a hen laid an egg daily on the sill of his grated window. From this French Perot descended Elliston Perot Morris, the present proprietor of the old house on the Germantown Road, which is the subject of this sketch. It was built in 1772 by a German, David Deshler, long and honorably known, as a Philadelphia merchant. A pleasant story goes that the facade of the solid stone mansion would have been broader by some feet had the sylvan tastes of the owner allowed him to fell a fine plum tree that grew to the left of the proposed site. The garden was the marvel of the region during his occupancy of the country seat, and was flanked by thrifty orchards and vineyards.

At Deshler's death in 1792, the Germantown estate passed into the hands of Colonel Isaac Franks, an officer who had served in the Revolutionary War. He had owned it but a year when the yellow fever broke out in Philadelphia, then the seat of the national government. Colonel Franks, with his family, retreated hurriedly to the higher ground and protecting mountain-barrier of Bethlehem, although Germantown was considered a safe refuge by the citizens of Philadelphia. On the eve of the Franks' flitting, the Colonel received a communication from President Washington's man of affairs, offering to rent the commodious residence on the Old Road for the use of the President and his family. The patriotic cordiality with which the retired officer granted the request did not carry him beyond the bounds of careful frugality. He made minute mention in his expense book of the cost of sweeping and garnishing the house for the reception of the distinguished guests, also of "cash paid for cleaning my house and putting it in the same condition the President received it in." This last bill was $2.30.

COST OF TRAVEL.

From this account book we learn what were the expenses of transportation of Col. Franks and family back and forth to Bethlehem, and what was paid for the hired furnished lodgings in the mountain village. There were lost during the Summer of exile (presumably under Lady Washington's administration) "one flatiron, valued 1s., one large fork, four plates, three ducks, four fowls," and consumed or wasted by the temporary tenants, "one bushel potatoes and one cwt. of hay." These items swelled the bill for removals, hire of Bethlehem quarters, and rent of Germantown premises, to $131.56.

The President, his wife, and their adopted children, George Washington Parke Custis and Nelly Custis, lived in health and peace in suburban quarters during the Summer of the pestilence. The boy went to school at the Old Academy, of which a cut is herewith given. A few days after the transfer of the executive party from town to country, a group of boys playing on the

pavement in front of the Academy parted to left and right, caps in hand, before a majestic figure that paused at the foot of the steps.

"Where is George Washington Parke Custis?" demanded the General.

Charles Wister, a Germantown boy, plucked up courage and voice and told where the great man's ward might be found.

Another boy of the town, Jesse Waln, went home from school with Parke Custis one afternoon and played with him in the garden, until General Washington came out of the back door and bade his adopted son "come into tea, and bring his young friend with him." Nearly three-quarters of a century afterward an old man asked permission, upon revisiting Germantown to go into the tea or breakfast-room, back of the parlors in the Morris house, and sitting down there, recalled each incident of the never-to-be-forgotten "afternoon out." The grave kindness of the head of the household, the sweet placidity of the mistress and the merry schoolfellow whose liking had won for him this distinguished honor—this is the picture for which we are indebted to Mr. Waln's reminiscences.

LADY WASHINGTON'S HYACINTHS.

The hegira from Philadelphia must have taken place early in the Spring, for Lady Washington pleased herself, and interested her neighbors, by raising hyacinths under globes of cut glass. There were six of these, and upon her return to Philadelphia she gave them to the young daughter of the deceased David Deshler, to whom she had taken an especial liking. A fragment of the glass is still treasured by a descendant of Catherine Deshler.

The occupation of the Morris house by the President and his family is the incident in the history of the homestead which abides most vividly with us as we pass from one to another of rooms which are scarcely altered from what they were in his day. The walls are wainscoted up to the ceiling; the central hall; the fine staircase at the right; the hinges mortised into the massive front door; the wrought-iron latch, eighteen inches long, that falls into a stout hasp over the portal; the partitions and low brows of the spacious chambers are the same as when the floors echoed to the tread of the Commander-in-Chief and ministers of state and finance discussed the weal of the infant nation with him who will never cease to be the nation's hero.

We linger longest in the tea-room, which is the cosiest of the suite. The wide-throated chimney is built diagonally across one corner; the fireplace is surrounded by tiles of exceeding beauty and great age. In another corner, on the same side of the room, with a garden-ward window between it and the chimney, is a cupboard which was also here in 1793. Behind the glass doors of this cabinet are the cup and saucer and plate of old India blue china which were used on the evening of Jesse Waln's visit, with other choice bits of bric-a-brac. "The rear window, opening now upon a small conservatory, then looked upon a long grape arbor, running far down the garden."

THE WASHINGTONS AT TEA.

Between the drawing-room door and this window—the fair, extensive pleasure grounds, sleeping in the afternoon sunshine, visible to all at the table —the Washingtons took their "dish of tea" in security, shadowed only by thoughts of the pleague-striken city, lying so near as to suggest sadder topics than the sweet-hearted hostess would willingly introduce. It is an idyllic domestic scene, and the lovelier for the cloudy background.

The "pitcher-portrait" of Washington in the possession of Mr. Morris was presented to his great-grandfather, Governor Samuel Morris, captain, during the War of the Revolution, of the First City Troop. These pitchers were made in France, and were tokens of the distinguished esteem of the General for those honored as the recipients. The likeness was considered so far superior to any other extant at that time that an order for duplicates was sent to Paris when the first supply was given away. Unfortunately, the model had been destroyed after the original requisition was filled, and the attempt to reproduce the design was unsatisfactory as to likeness and execution, a circumstance which enhances the value of the originals.

Mr. Morris justly reckons as scarcely second in worth to his beautiful relic an autograph letter from Washington to his great-grandfather, Governor Morris, thanking him for the gallant service rendered in the War of Independence by the First City Troop.   MARION HARLAND.

"No. 4784 was occupied by one of the Bringhurst family, related to the Ashmeads." Rev. Prof. Charles W. Schaeffer, formerly of St. Michael's Evangelical Lutheran Church, resides there. He married a sister of Dr. William Ashmead.

In No. 4788 Dr. William Ashmead lived many years. It is supposed that Mr. Morgan built it about the year 1790. Nathan Bunker often visited there. In 1806 Ann Morgan, Robert Wahn and others sold it. Thomas Armat lived there. He was generous and kind.

In A. D. 1742 Zinzendorf began the first Moravian school in this country in Germantown. (See Annals of Early Moravian Settlements in Georgia and Pennsylvania, p. 83.) He rented 4792, belonging to an Ashmead. Two Church Synods were held there. "Zinzendorf's fair daughter, the Countess Benigna," was a pupil. While in this house Zinzendorf gave up his title. The school opened in May and was moved to Bethlehem in June, where it yet flourishes.

No. 4792 was the residence of James Ashmead, John's brother. "The Ashmeads came from Cheltcham, England, in 1682." The first marriage in the family here was with a Sellers at Darby. They went to Cheltenham and thence to Germantown. A Jno. Ashmead built at 4790. The rear of the house stands, but the front was replaced about 1790. At present the occupant of Nos. 4790 and 4792 is a great-great-granddaughter of John Ashmead.

THE GERMANTOWN ACADEMY

WILLIAM KERSHAW Ph.D. PRINCIPAL.

FOUNDED 1760

GERMANTOWN

No. 4794, at the southern corner of School House Lane, was the site of a house pulled down by Dr. Bensell. In the old low frame house, lined with brick, Penn preached. It was built for Jacob Tellner, "one of the town magistrates." Dr. George Bensell built the building that stood here before the Saving Fund built its handsome home, about 1795. Charles W. Churchman and Dr. George Malin and the Workingmen's Club have at various times occupied it.

School House Lane was called Bensell's Lane.

Green street Ward attributes to the green sward before it was fully opened, and not to Green, the hatter, nor Gen. Greene.

THE GERMANTOWN ACADEMY

Was organized in 1760. Hilarius Becker was German teacher in 1761, and David James Dove, English teacher. Col. Graydon, in his Memoirs, relates how Dove, in Philadelphia, used to send boys with lighted lantern and bell in the day-time after late scholars. Pelatiah Webster taught after Dove. The British made the Academy a hospital. In the yellow fever of 1793 the Banks of North America and Pennsylvania used "the lower floor and cellar." The royal crown of England still surmounts the belfry vane. Rev. Mr. Travis and Horace Wemyss Smith have prepared a History of the Academy, which is printed. In the library is a spy-glass used by Washington. On the site of the next house west, David J. Dove strove to start his private school. In 1777 the Magistrate Jno. Miller lived there and kept a Revolutionary diary. William Chancellor became owner of the house and used it as a summer residence. His grandson, Henry Chancellor, as Jno. J. Smith wrote Ward, once took the Broad Axe stage, running from that place in Montgomery county to Philadelphia through Germantown, and found that it stopped at the Rising Sun Hotel for breakfast in merely going to the city. If one missed the Bethlehem or Broad Axe stage he had to defer his trip to the city to the next day. This was just before the railway was opened in 1832.

Dr. Frailey, a water-cure doctor, lived in an old stone house on School House Lane, beyond Chancellor's. On each side of the house were lines of German poetry, painted in oil colors. Beyond Dr. Frailey's in "Ashmead's Field near the woods," were the huts of the Hessians, being rails covered with straw and grass sod. Those of the officers "had wicker doors, with a glass light." The chimneys were of grass. "One of these Hessians afterwards became Washington's coachman."

"Jno. Coulter, an East India merchant, and a director of the United States Bank," owned one hundred acres east of Township Line Road, and south "from School House Lane to beyond Indian Queen Lane." At the southeast corner of School House Lane and the Township Line Road, on this property is now the handsome seat of Mr. E. W. Clark.

Returning to the avenue we pass along the northern side of the lane.

ERRATA.—In the last historical article on "Ancient Germantown," the following corrections are to be made: 'Squire Baynton did not live in the brick house next to Harlan's (No. 4630), but his daughter went there after his death. Mr. Conyngham did not build the Hacker house, but a Mr. Forbes, who owned property in that neighborhood. Christopher Sauer, and not Mr. Bullock, built Rev. Dr. Albert's house on the corner of Queen Lane. Mr. Binel never lived there, but at the corner of Knox and Queen Lane.

In continuing the abridgment of Mr. Ward, we note that the double house, No. 4651, east side of the street and "next south of the site of Sauer's ancient place, belongs to the estate of the late Charles Ashmead." The widow of Peter Grayson Washington, who was the Revolutionary Gen. William McPherson's daughter, once lived there with two daughters. The McPherson Blues were named after the General. Mr. Washington had been Assistant Secretary of the United States Treasury.

"About fifty years ago Anthony Gilbert, a village blacksmith, lived in the rugged looking stone house, No. 4665, belonging to the estate of the late Charles J. Wister, and next north of 'Wister's Big House.'"

No. 4667 is the site once occupied by "an antiquated low building." Here lived a family named Frey. Johannes Frey, a German, died in 1765 and was "buried in the 'Lower Burying Ground.'" The epitaph in German is thus Anglicised:

> "I was called Free, but now
> Have I become truly Free,
> Live free from sin, then will you be as I am Free indeed."

The double stone house, Nos. 4669 and 4671, was the Germantown Bank, and its cashier, Jno. F. Watson, "the noted Annalist of Philadelphia," lived in it. Watson says that Generals Washington, Knox and Greene slept in it "one or two nights." The British also occupied it and held a court martial in the parlor upstairs. William Gerhard de Braham, Surveyor General of His Majesty, dwelt here. He wrote the "American Military Pocket Atlas," and the "Atlantic Pilot." During the yellow fever epidemic of 1793 Thomas Jefferson and Edmund Randolph, Attorney General, occupied the house. Afterward Richard Bayley, an Englishman, owned and dwelt in it. Mr. Bayley was a fine singer. Watson did most of his difficult work in this house. He could not locate places as well as now, since the late Jno. McAllister, Jr.'s, system of numbering houses has been adopted.

Ward reminds us that Lieutenant Danenhower, of Arctic fame, was of the Germantown family.

On the site of No. 4677, southeast corner of Shoemaker's Lane, stood the residence of Miss Molly Donaldson, and her nieces, Sally Donaldson and Rosanna Roe. Miss Donaldson was the hospitable daughter of a Revolutionary officer. Her colored girl, "Lize," would often give the pleasant summons: Missis Donaldson sends her 'spects to Mr. Wister, and wants him to please

SHOEMAKER'S FIRST FARM, FROM WATSON'S ANNALS, BY PERMISSION OF EDWIN S. STUART, PUBLISHER.

come in and smoke a cigar with Dr. Bensell." Messrs. Charles J. and John Wister, Richard Bayley and William Chancellor used to be invited to her suppers.

"Sarah Schumacher, a widow, with several children, from Kresheim, in the Palatinate, came to Philadelphia on the 20th of March, 1686." She lived in Germantown, where her relatives were already settled. Her son, Isaac, married Gerhard Hendricks' only child, named Sarah. She was born in 1678. Hendricks drew Lot No. 8, "east side of the road, and David Sherkger the adjoining lot to the north, which for some reason bore the same number." In 1714 Isaac Shoemaker owned both lots.

It is probable that Gerhard Hendricks built the first house here, called " Rock House," or " Rock Hall," on " the north side of Shoemaker's Lane, just to the east of the railroad." It is seen in passing Wingohocking station. In that house, or on the rock near by, William Penn preached. Another very old house stood near this one till about 1835. It was a one-story stone house, and straw had been mixed with the mortar. It " had a very high, peaked roof," which itself " contained two stories and a loft." It was said that Penn was a guest and preached in this house. Perhaps this was Gerhard Hendricks' mansion. William Logan Fisher bought the property and called it "Shelbourne." Isaac Shoemaker may have built the large house which stood till 1843 on Main street, northeast corner of Shoemaker's Lane. It was a long two-story building of stone, with a main entrance from the rear, old country fashion, while the cellar was entered from the street.

"Isaac Shoemaker died in 1732, and his son, Benjamin, and grandson, Samuel, were successively Mayors of Philadelphia. A great-granddaughter was the wife of William Rawle." Samuel married Francis Rawle's widow, who received a place called Laurel Hill from her first husband. The cemetery is "a mile or so above it." Samuel owned the Duval place, now owned by Amos R. Little. Before the Revolution the Shoemaker's lane house " was for a time the country residence of Samuel Burge, whose daughter married William Rawle." The British used it as a hospital under Dr. Moore.

Samuel Shoemaker was loyal to England, and his property was confiscated, but he generously " exerted himself for the relief of Americans" held as British prisoners in New York, and " secured the liberation of numbers of them." In London he kept a diary. See *Pennsylvania Magazine of History*, Vol. 2, for "an account of his interview with George III. He returned to Philadelphia in 1789 and died in 1800." James Parr bought the life estate in the confiscated Laurel Hill and leased it to Chevalier de la Luzerne.

Benjamin Shoemaker, a son of Samuel, occupied the Germantown house. He died in 1808. " His only daughter, Anna, married Robert Morris, son of the Financier, and was therefore the mother of the present Dr. Robert Morris." One of her daughters was Mrs. Malsam, an intimate friend of Miss Ann Ridgway, who became Mrs. Dr. James Rush. Mrs. Wilkins, of Georgia, was another daughter. She and her husband and family were lost at sea when coming from Savannah, intending to take up their residence in the Shoemaker mansion, "a few years before it was sold to G. H. Thomson." After Robert Morris died Mrs. Morris married Mr. Bloodgood, of Albany. She was remarkable for her beauty, even in old age.

Benjamin Shoemaker had three sons who died childless, and the name is lost among Isaac's descendants. One of these sons, named Benjamin, was unusually intelligent and brave. He and Charles J. Wister walked to Philadelphia during the yellow fever period of 1798. The lads found barricaded streets; and the stillness and the dreadful dead cart made a deep impression on them.

In 1841 the Shoemaker house was occupied by the de la Roche family and a son-in-law by the name of Croskey. The Misses Lorain kept a school here, and "it is said that Miss Adele Sigoigne passed a summer there." She had a ladies' school "of great note, which her mother established on Washington Square. Madame Sigoigne, whose sister was the wife of the first Dr. La Roche, escaped with them from the massacre in St. Domingo." His son, Dr. Rene La Roche, was noted for a knowledge of music. He wrote a voluminous history of the yellow fever. "His daughter Susan married Dr. Wm. V. Keating, descended from an Irish family which adhered to James II."

Of late "the remnant of the Shoemaker property, some twenty-five acres, was known as the place of George H. Thomson." Mehl's beautiful meadow was a part of it. Some of the British cavalry had huts in it. "The glory of Wingohocking has now departed." Ward mourns for the beaver dams which a culvert now replaces. The old Shoemaker house is gone. Cottage Row is on a part of its site. The houses stand back and are numbered 4703 to 4717. "The first of these is the residence of Mr. Lloyd P. Smith, who succeeded his father as Librarian of the Philadelphia Library. The last is that of the aged and venerable Mr. Daniel B. Smith, now the oldest member of the historical Society."

Mr. Thomson built a handsome house on the Lane, and others arose. Lloyd Mifflin lived on the Lane. He died at the age of 93, and Miss Betsey Wistar succeeded him in the house. She died at the age of 92, and Mr. Marmaduke Cope occupies the house now. Mr. Mifflin invented a machine for weaving carpets, and "an ingeniously contrived sun-dial."

Mr. Robert P. Morton, son of Dr. Samuel George Morton, "craniologist," and William T. Richards, "the artist," reside on the Lane. Also Francis Rawle, who married Miss Aertsen, and George Willing, who married Miss Shippen, have erected houses on this lane. East of Hancock street is Thomas MacKellar's place. Here are ancient trees, fifteen feet in circumference, and over one hundred feet high, "topping all others in Germantown."

"On Shoemaker's lane stands the admirable GERMANTOWN HOSPITAL, which will preserve the name of Mrs. Pauline Henry better than any bronze that was ever cast." The present writer must add to Ward's words the good work of this benevolent lady in building the beautiful Episcopal Church named the Memorial Church of St. Luke, the Beloved Physician, Bustleton, as a memorial to her husband. It commemorates the dead and blesses the living. May many erect such useful monuments.

Across the country from the Germantown Hospital, "are the new JEWISH ORPHAN ASYLUM, and the large house of the 'LITTLE SISTERS of the POOR.' To the southeast, on Duy's lane, is to be seen on a prominence the rather striking looking house of Mr. William Rotch Wister."

A small old house stood on Main street, next north of the Shoemaker property. Leonard Nutz owned it and the tannery along side. Count Baldusky occupied this house. He "was a French Emigrant of the Reign of Terror." He was a starch maker, but retained some French elegance in his adversity. The Count became ill one night. Dr. Bensell was summoned. A silk counterpane covered the invalid. A small sword hung over his head. The Doctor advised bleeding. The Count told the Doctor if a drop of blood fell on the counterpane he would "run him through." A flickering candle held by a servant lighted the tremulous physician. The blood "spurting into the flame of the candle, extinguished it." The Doctor rushed down stairs and the Count followed him, sword in hand, with his servant. The Count "tripped and fell headlong, with the servant on top of him, in the entry. Dr. Bensell escaped, but he lost his patient—not, however, by death."

"Dr. Runkle, Captain of the Germantown Blues," lived in the Nutz house at a later date. His father was pastor of the Market Square Church. "Mr. William Wynne Wister remembers having seen him leading his redoubtable band on its way to Camp Dupont in the 'late war,' as that of 1812 is still called by aged persons."

About where Tarr's store is, No. 4733, southeast corner of East Coulter and Main streets, "was the residence of John Book," a preacher among the Friends. In preaching he quivered with excitement. His daughter, Louisa, had a children's school here, and made Quaker bonnets.

Next was Waterman's house, now gone. "It stood where East Coulter street now begins."

About here lived the widow, Granny Bische, "in her early years." She sold apples from trees on her own place, "about where Tulpehocken street now is, and to which she subsequently removed."

Then came the shoemaker, Ulrich Freihoffer's house. "The aged Handsberry," heretofore mentioned, "served his time" with him. James Jones's store is on the site, Nos. 4737 and 4739.

The double stone house, Nos. 4747 and 4749, next south of St. Luke's entrance, was owned and occupied by Dr. Runkle. Abraham Keyser, and his cousin, Charles Keyser, lived in it. Later it was the "King property." Mr. King married Jabez Gates's sister. St. Luke's Church now owns the house.

ST. LUKE'S EPISCOPAL CHURCH "is the parent of the five other Episcopal churches which are now in Germantown." It stands back, but has "ample grounds." St. Luke's was organized in 1811, though services were held long before. Rev. Mr. Neill, a Church of England missionary at Oxford and Whitemarsh, lost his "glebe house by fire in 1760, which led him to seek a temporary residence in Germantown." At the request of some "English people" he preached in the evenings in the Lutheran and Calvinist Churches. Germantown had but one Church of England family, but most of the young people understood English. The British army chaplains probably held services in some church or churches. The chaplains of the Hessians "preached in the Lutheran Church."

In 1793 the yellow fever brought many strangers to Germantown. Then the Episcopalians "held services in the Market Square Church, for Samuel Breck remembered that Dr. Smith, of the Falls of Schuylkill, went there to preach." It is supposed that Rev. Mr. Scott held services in that church on June 9, 1811. The church then contained about twelve families in and about Germantown. On June 28, A. D. 1811, "a meeting was held at the house of Thomas Armat. He was made President; Daniel Lammat, Secretary; and James Stokes, Treasurer, and the meeting resulted in the organization of the congregation of St. Luke's." For the first year Rev. Jackson Kemper, Assistant Rector of Christ Church and St. Peter's and St. James's Churches, chiefly performed the services. He afterward became our first Missionary Bishop, and after, by untiring labor, bringing several dioceses into union with the General Convention, was Bishop of Wisconsin. In 1812 Rev. Mr. Warren, of South Carolina, passed the summer in Germantown, and served the parish three months. Many South Carolinians then spent the summer in Philadelphia and owned houses. The north side of Spruce street, from Tenth almost to Ninth, was called South Carolina. Rev. Mr. Ward, in 1813, followed Mr. Warren, remaining five months and then going to Lexington, Ky. Rev. J. C. Clay held St. Luke's with Norristown from December, 1813, to February, 1817." The parish was organized under him in 1816 with sixteen communicants. Thomas Armat and James Stokes were its first representatives in the Diocesan Convention in 1818. Dr. Clay was afterward the faithful Rector of Gloria Dei Church. Before Rev. Mr. Ward's day the congregation met in the afternoons in the Market Square Church, but when a settled clergyman was secured the services were held in a house which James Stokes offered on Market Square, opposite School House Lane." This proving too small, he supplied the house which "stands at the northeast corner of Market Square and Church Lane. Rev. S. H. Turner, D. D., afterward an honored and beloved Professor in the General Theological Seminary was called. He then lived on the Eastern Shore of

Maryland. In 1817 the Rev. Charles M. Dupuy became the first Rector, and remained until 1824. In 1818 the sum of $5300 was subscribed for a building, and in that year, on ground which Thomas Armat presented, the first edifice of St. Luke's was erected." "It was enlarged in 1840," and again enlarged in 1851. Rev. Edward R. Lippitt succeeded Mr. Dupuy, having charge "from March, 1824, to September, 1825, when the Rev. John Rodney was elected Rector. The ministry of this acceptable and venerable gentleman was continued until 1867, when he became Emeritus Rector, which position he now holds at the age of eighty-nine years." Rev. Dr. C. F. Knight, of Lancaster (now Bishop of Wisconsin), was Assistant from October, 1854, to May, 1856. Rev. Dr. B. Wistar Morris, Bishop of Oregon, was Assistant from January, 1857, to November, 1867. "He married a niece of Mr. Rodney." Having declined a call to St. Peter's, Philadelphia, at Mr. Rodney's desire he was elected Rector, Mr. Rodney resigning. His rectorship ended in January, 1869. Rev. Albra Wadleigh, of Williamsport, Pa., succeeded him. He died in 1873, having in a short time won "the warmest love of all his people, as well as the universal respect of the community." In 1865 the parish bought ground north of the church, on which "a most commodious parish building" was built. The property was "The Rookery," or "Pine Place," as large pine trees grew on it. During Mr. Wadleigh's rectorship St. Luke's purchased the 'King property.'"

Rev. Dr. William R. Huntington, of Worcester, Mass., was elected Rector in August, 1873, but declining, on the 8th of October, following, the Rev. William H. Vibbert, then Professor of Hebrew at the Berkeley Divinity School, Middletown, Conn., was elected. In his rectorship the new church was built. The last services in the old church were on May 2, 1875. The corner stone of the new church was laid June 26th of that year, and the new church was consecrated by Bishop Stevens on June 8, 1876. "This building is a remarkably fine one, and all the workmanship is excellent. The windows are filled with stained glass, mostly memorials to John S. Littell, George H. Thomson, the Rev. Mr. Wadleigh, George W. Carpenter and others. The walls and ceilings are richly and tastefully decorated." It was finished without debt. Mr. James M. Aertsen, a warden, has collected materials for a history of the parish. The Rev. Samuel Upjohn, rector of St. Mark's Church, Augusta, Maine, entered upon the rectorship of St. Luke's Church, December 1, A. D. 1883. The aisles of the church have been tiled during the past year. A project is now on foot for securing a Rectory for the parish.

No. 4755 was George Wilson's shoemaker's shop. He was postmaster. Next to the north lived Samuel Butcher, "toll-gate keeper at Chestnut Hill." Between Wilson's and Butcher's is a court wherein lived two of the three generations of the now extinct name of Gravenstein, who were the hereditary sextons of St. Luke's. The family of the last one still lives there. The first one lived on Church Lane.

GERMANTOWN.

A double stone house, opposite the Friends' Meeting House, standing back, was the "Pine Place" or "The Rookery." The Masonic Hall stands there, numbered 4761 and 4763. The Post-office is on the first floor of 4763. Two ladies named Smart, formerly occupied "The Rookery." They were daughters of a British officer. One married Thomas Armat. "The other married the Rev. James Rooker, of Baltimore, pastor of the Presbyterian church in Germantown, on which he went to the house to live, which led to its being called 'The Rookery,' a name that had almost faded away." After Mr. Rooker died A. Bronson Alcott had a school here. "Miss Alcott, authoress of 'Little Women,' was born there." Miss Sarah Rooker had a school and Charles J. Wister was her pupil. "At first it was at Barr's near John Wister's, but afterwards at Stuckert's, which, at a later time, was Charles Relf's house, a brick one of three stories, next north of 'The Rookery.'" There was open ground from Relf's on the north to Mill street or Church lane. Freddy Axe had a little shop at the corner of the lane, where boys could supply their wants. He was a cripple on crutches.

Roberts' Mill was "on the north side of Church Lane, the present Mill street, or the 'Road to Luken's Mill,' as it was anciently called, just one mile northeast from Market Square. The mill jutted somewhat into the lane, and this together with its antique appearance, which is still remembered with delight, produced the most picturesque effect known in Germantown." This first grist mill, in this vicinity, was built "in 1683, by Richard Townsend, an English millwright, who came over in 1682 in the ship *Welcome*, along with William Penn, who aided in the enterprise by advances." Townsend in an address, speaks of his early difficulties in connection with this mill, and "the Providential aids extended to him at the place." It was the only grain mill hereabouts, and very useful. Grists were carried "on men's backs, save one man, who had a bull so tame as to perform the labour." Mr. Townsend died about 1714. He left only one child, Mrs. Cook. Richard's brother Joseph, "was the ancestor of Mr. Joseph B., Henry C. and J. Townsend." The beautiful and picturesque mill has departed, though Dr. Owen J. Wister strove to buy it for preservation. About the crossing of Mill street and Township Line Road is "Roberts' Schoolhouse," "a benefaction in whole or in part, of one of the family of that name. Spencer Roberts' farm was in the vicinity, and on it was the grave of Godfrey, whose name is imperishably associated with Germantown."

"Thomas Godfrey, inventor of the quadrant, was born in 1704, on the family farm, which lies somewhat to the east of the old mill." A book on mathematics, early in life, turned his studies that way. He learned Latin to read Newton's *Principia*. He studied optics and astronomy with pleasure, though "his trade was that of a painter and glazier." When working at Stenton "a piece of fallen glass suggested an idea, and he sought a volume of Newton in James Logan's library. Logan "was pleased with Godfrey's ingenuity." "The Quadrant was produced. As early as 1730 he lent it to Joshua Fisher, for his trial surveys of the Delaware Bay and River." In Fisher's survey with this instrument Cape Henlopen differs but ten miles from the results of the Coast Survey. "On the family farm the graves of the Godfreys were marked by headstones, one as early as 1705. About the year 1840 the remains of Godfrey were removed thence to Laurel Hill, where a monument with an appropriate inscription marks the place of their reinterment."

No. 4781 is a large two-story brick house. The upper story extends northward, and includes a part of the adjoining house, and there is or was a communicating door from the entry, so that the two houses have been occupied by one family. The United States Bank used it in the Yellow Fever of '93. "Massive vaults have been constructed in the cellar, to which the treasure was conveyed, escorted by a troop of cavalry. This is the house which was used by the congregation of St. Luke's for five years." Mr. Billings afterwards dwelt it it. He married a sister of Dr. Bensell. "Their daughter vied in beauty with Miss Roberdeau. Charles Biddle married a daughter of James Stokes, and had the house, for the summer only at first, for several years. He was a son of Charles Biddle, Vice President of Pennsylvania, while Franklin was President, and brother of Nicholas Biddle, President of the Second Bank of the United States. His son is the present James S. Biddle, formerly a Lieutenant in the Navy. Godfrey Twells married a daughter of James Stokes, and then lived there." Mr. John S. Twells was a son of Godfrey Twells. He resided here at one time, but now lives in Woodbury, N. J. The Misses Stevens and Aertsen had a school here. The Women's Christian Association now occupy the house.

No. 4783 belonged to James Stokes. "It was for a time the place of residence of the pastor of the Market Square Church. Mrs. Leonard, a granddaughter of Mr. Stokes, occupied it for a time."

We add to Ward's sketch a narrative from the GERMANTOWN DAILY INDEPENDENT, of July 31, 1889:

STOKES'S MILL.

Yesterday morning the workmen engaged in tearing down the cellar walls of the Seminole Hall, formerly known as Stokes' Hall, on Mill street, came across a sealed bottle, covered with tin foil, that had been walled in a brick pocket, about eighteen inches above the cellar floor. It was expected that there was a stone or receptacle of some kind, containing records of the erection of this old structure, which was built for a steam grist mill, by the late Wyndham H. Stokes, in 1838, but nothing was found until yesterday, and this was by the merest accident, as a small wine bottle, might easily have been crushed, and the papers, containing a history of the erection of the first steam grist mill in Pennsylvania would be buried beneath the debris.

When the bottle was found, everyone standing around was anxious to see what it contained. Orfa Jordan, the architect, who drew the plans for the new hall, to be erected on the site of the old structure, and who has had charge of the demolition of the old hall, broke open the glass receptacle and found several shinplasters such as were in circulation about the year 1838, and three pieces of parchment. On one was written the names of the Township officers of Germantown, the parties who worked on the Stokes mill, the wages paid in those days, the price of provisions, the value of land on the Main street and back lanes, and other matters that will prove quite interesting to our readers.

Ever since the workmen commenced razing the old building there has been considerable discussion as to the exact date of its erection, and the discovery of the bottle puts at rest all doubts in the matter. It was in this building, we believe that William N. Butcher, of the *Guide*, the first cadet of temperance, of Division No. 1, was initiated. Among the occupants of the building since its erection was the late Charles Spencer, where he carried on the hosiery business for some time prior to the erection of his first mill, on Cumberland street, in 1849.

Wyndham H. Stokes, whose push and enterprise is set forth in one of the parchments, died on April 1, 1870. He was one of Germantown's leading citizens and for many years was President of the Mutual Insurance Company. He lived and died on the Old Stokes homestead, Main street, below Chelten avenue, the site of the present Stokes block. The records and data contained in the several parchments follows:

RECORD OF THE OLD MILL.

"This record was made May 11, 1838. This is the first steam grist mill erected in the township of Germantown, owned by Wyndham H. Stokes. The carpenter, Jonathan Wolf; the mason, Isaac Glackens; the millwright, Joseph Randall; the miller, John K. Hellings; the superintendent, Jacob B. Bowman. The dimensions of this mill, 28 by 40, three stories high, with an engine of fifteen horse power. The vane, rod and ball were taken from the old German Reformed Church, and are one hundred and four years old. This new church now building is to have no spire, and as a relic this old vane is placed upon this mill. Journeymen who worked at this building: Millwrights—John Sheldrake, William Hartranft, William Coward. Masons—Philip Ditchy, John Shubert, George Fry, John Ruch, William Tuston. Laborers—Samuel Dove, John Harmon, William Kephart, David Charles, Peter Stroup, George Stroup, Jacob Stroup, Jr. Thomas Heap, plasterer; Charles Cox, lumberman; John Clark, burr builder. Wheat flour, $8 per barrel; rye flour, $5.25; corn, per bushel, 80 cents; oats, 45; wheat, $1.75; rye, 85; beef, 9 cents; mutton, 6c.; veal, 8c. Farm land in the immediate neighborhood $200 per acre. Supposed cost of mill, when finished $6,000. Anthracite coal, per ton, $6; building lots on the lanes, 50c. per foot; on the Main street, $1; average depth, 200 feet. Township officers are: Daniel Snyder, John Seibert, Jacob Peaver, Benjamin F. Topham. Justices of the Peace: William Sommers and Chas. Donat, Super-

CHAPEL OF MARKET SQUARE PRESBYTERIAN CHURCH.

visors; Benj. Lehman, Jr., Wm. Crout, Samuel Keyser, Charles Bonsall, Jacob Derr and Joseph Dickinson. Overseer of the Poor, G. F. Stuckert; John Smith, Daniel Billmeyer, Street Commissioners; Geo. Sommers, Jacob Haas, Constables. Population of the Township, five thousand five hundred. There is two Lutheran, one Episcopalian, one German Reformed, one Presbyterian, one Methodist, one Baptist, one Dunkard, one Orthodox and one Hicksite Church, a bank and four incorporated academies, seventeen taverns, four lines of stages daily, and railroad cars five times a day to and from the city. Fare in the stages twenty-five cents, in the cars twenty-five cents. Wages for laboring men, one dollar per day; carpenters, $1.50; masons, $1.75; millwrights, $1.62½; burr builders, $1.75; millers, $25 per month; farm hands, $12 per month.

There is quite a mania for raising silk in the township. How it will answer is unknown."

JOHN F. WATSON ON STEAM.

"This first steam mill in the county of Philadelphia, erected for the purpose of grinding grain, etc., done in this fruitful "age of experiments," awakens many thoughts. The mind is led out in wonder at the comtemplation of the *possible* future application of *steam* to the uses and benefits of man. In this same "Church lane," at Robert's mill, began the first grist mill (in 1683) in Philadelphia county; and now in 1838, we behold this new device of steam agency for the benefit of the adjacent country. Most amazing invention! from a cause now so obvious and familiar! It is only by applying the principle seen in every house, which lifts the lid of the tea kettle and "boils over,"—that machines have been devised which can pick up a pin, or rend an oak; which combines the power of many giants with the plasticity that belongs to a lady's fair fingers! Thanks to the names of Fitch, Evans and Fulton!

"Done at Germantown, this 11th day of May, 1838.

"JOHN F. WATSON."

W. H. STOKES'S ENTERPRISE.

"W. H. Stokes, Esq., who has caused this stone to be laid here, on this the 11th day of May, 1838, has gained for himself much credit through his enterprising spirit, not only for the erection of this the first steam grist mill in the place, which is more for the convenience of his neighbors than profit to himself.

"Possessed of a good and public spirit, he has ever been watchful in guarding against encroachments of corporations or of individuals upon their neighbors or the public, and instrumental in obtaining many praiseworthy enactments of the Legislature of this State, of which he has been a member, all of which tend for the general good and convenience of the inhabitants of this place, some of which are, viz.: Paving the footpaths from the 5 mile to the 7 mile stone, and preventing the turnpike company from piling loose stones along the sides of the road.

"And in short he has ever been awake for the interest of the place and the good of the people; a friend to the poor, though quite wealthy himself, and a prop to the Episcopal Church.

"By request of the undersigned who keeps store opposite the Market Square, this was permitted to be placed in this bottle by his friend.

CHARLES F. ASHMEAD."

SHINPLASTERS FOUND.

A shinplaster for 25 cents, of the Phoenix Manufacturing Company, of Philadelphia, bearing interest at the rate of one per cent per annum. On the back was the following, written in bold legible hand: "James Ashmead, storekeeper for forty years, Germantown opposite the Market House. Was present May 11, 1838." A five-cent shinplaster, of the Girard Loan Company, office 398 Market street, Girard Row, Philadelphia. Another of six and a quarter cents of the Girard Manufacturing Company; one of five cents, of the Village of Port Deposit, Md.; one of fifty cents, of the Tradesmen's and Mechanics' Loan Company, of Pennsylvania.

The PRESBYTERIAN CHURCH on Market Square was in care of the Rev. Mr. Cowan, its twentieth pastor, when Mr. Ward wrote. The church site was obtained in 1732 by the "High Dutch Reformed Congregation." They built a church in 1733. In 1762 they doubled the size of the building by a rear addition. The ancient bell in the steeple summoned the people to prayers for over seventy years. When the church was taken down in 1838 to erect the present brick building, the late Charles J. Wister bought the bell. In 1874 "his son of the same name" gave it to the church, "on the condition that it should be well taken care of, and not suffered to be lost, destroyed or sold. It was cast in 1725," bearing the German inscription, "Gott allein die Ehre"—"To God alone the Honour." The early dwellers in Germantown imagined that the old bell said:

"Injun Jake, drove a stake."

And also,

Beggar's town, is coming down."

The upper part of Germantown was called Beggar's town. The Dutch organ disappeared in the change of 1838, except the "Trumpet Angels in their golden glory," which the children thought made the music. John Minick, a member of the parish, preserved these relics. "In this church Count Zinzendorf preached his first sermon in America, on the 31st of December, 1741, and his last one, before his departure for Europe, on the 17th of June, 1742. The Moravians held a Synod there." The steeple of the old church had rifle bullets shot by the "Paxton Boys" at the "Weathercock." Mr. Charles J. Wister has the bullet-marked vane.

In the battle of Germantown, the battalion of *tall* Virginians under Colonel Mathews, having been taken prisoners, were lodged in the church. In the battle "these Virginians had just before captured a party of British in the

MARKET SQUARE PRESBYTERIAN CHURCH.
For Cut of Original Building, Built 1733. (See Page 90.)

A. D. 1839—1887.

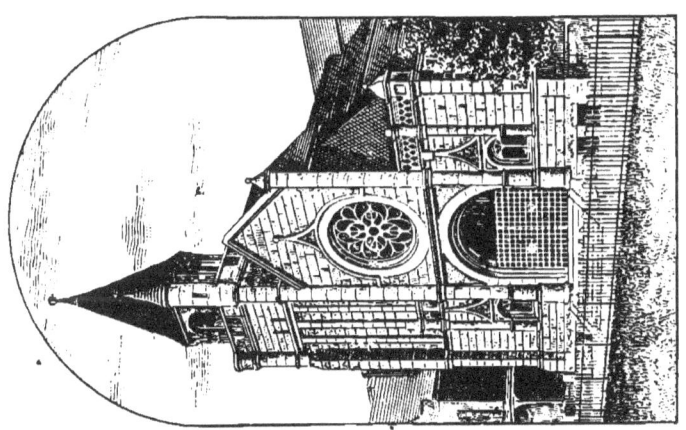

DEDICATED JUNE 17, 1888.

fog, and set up a great hurrah, which brought a greater force upon them, and caused their own capture." In this church, in the fever of '93, " Washington regularly worshiped, as often as there was English preaching, a service performed occasionally by Dr. Smith, an eminent Episcopal clergyman, Provost of the College of Philadelphia. It seems also to have been the practice of the General to attend the German service."

"It is probable the first building had no organ, and that the bell hung on a tree. The enlarged building had a steeple where a bell was hung, and certainly it had the organ and the angels." A sounding board was above the high, narrow pulpit. The present brick church was built in 1839. It was enlarged in 1857. "In 1882 a handsome parsonage on the north side was erected. Since Ward wrote this article Rev. J. Elliott Wright, D. D., has become the twenty-first pastor, having assumed charge of the parish in April, 1883. During his pastorate, in 1884, a beautiful chapel was built, costing $16,000, exclusive of the ground. It is pleasant to say it was dedicated free of debt, so that man could have no claim against the Lord's House. The style of the building corresponds to that of the pretty parsonage or manse.

The church was rebuilt and a beautiful stone front added, during the pastorate of Dr. Wright.

"John Bechtel, as a layman, preached from 1728, and regularly in this church, after it was built, until 1744. He prepared a catechism, beautifully printed by Franklin;—one of the gems of the early Pennsylvania press. In 1742 he was ordained by Bishop Niteshman, of the Moravian Church. In 1746 the Rev. Michael Schlatter, of St. Gall, Switzerland, was sent over by the Reformed Synod of Holland, to visit the 'Reformed Churches' here. He often preached in this one. His portrait and an engraving of his house at Chestnut Hill, may be seen in the Historical Society's copy of his life by Harbaugh. In 1753 the Rev. Conrad Steiner took charge of the church, and also of that in Philadelphia. He kept a record, but only remained three years. He was succeeded by the Rev. William Stoy, who remained only one year. The Rev. John George Alsantz became the pastor in 1758, and remained five years, bringing about the enlargement of the building. In 1763 the Rev. F. C. Faber came and staid not longer than six years. In 1769 the Rev. Frederick Foring takes charge, and two years afterward his name appears along with those of the trustees, etc., in an Act of Incorporation granted by Thomas and Richard Penn. In 1772 the records indicate a change, when the Rev. T. C. Albertus Helfelstein followed in the list of ministers, and remained until 1776. In the following year the Rev. Samuel Dabendorff began to make entries, and continued them until 1779. In this year the Rev. Mr. Helfelstein returns, and remains ten years. In 1790 the Rev. Frederick Hermann took the charge and continued it until 1801. In the following year the Rev. William Runkle, began his entries and continued them until 1806, followed by the Rev. Charles Helfelstein, who appears to have remained until October, 1810. About this time there was a movement to have the service in English.

GERMANTOWN.

This led to the withdrawal of those in favor of the change and to their formation of the First Presbyterian Church of Germantown. On the 6th of May, 1811, the Rev. Frederick William Van der Sloot makes his entries in the record, and continues them for a year or more, when the Rev. Casper Wach began his ministry, which lasted until 1824. In this latter year the Rev. John H. Smaltz became the pastor. He began to make entries in the record, in English, and as far as is known, he was the first to keep a record of the members. In 1830 the Rev. Albert Helfelstein, Jr., assumed charge of the church, and continued it until 1837, when he was succeeded by the Rev. Truman Osborn, who remained until 1841. It was during the time of the latter that the stone church was taken down. In 1842 the Rev. Jacob Helfelstein commenced his pastorate, which lasted twenty-seven years, until 1869." In 1852 the pastor and people became "Independent," and continued so for three years. In 1856 they became Presbyterians. In February, 1870, Rev. Edward Payson Cowan, of Missouri, " was installed as pastor."

COMMUNICATIONS.

PROPERTY VALUE.

[To the Editor of the TELEGRAPH.]

We, as old inhabitants of Germantown, have been much interested in the reminiscences of this old German settlement, and can not only look back to the time when our streets were lighted with such dim oil lamps as required a lantern to be carried when a visit to a neighbor was made, but to that also when property was to be bought at a marvelously reasonable price. For instance, in the year 1848 that tract of land which lies from the Main street to the Reading Railroad and from Shoemaker lane, now East Penn street, to Church lane, now Mill street, containing twenty-four acres, between 200 and 300 feet front on Main and 2000 feet to Reading Railroad, with the yellow brick house on the corner, mentioned in the reminiscences, and some of the finest trees in the neighborhood interspersed over the lot, was offered to two Philadelphia "Friends," who had just removed to these suburbs, for thirteen hundred dollars, but they being over-ruled by some of their friends who considered it would be a risk, and having the prudence of their sect, declined the offer. It was three years afterwards bought by George Thompson, for $15,000. In 1870 it was valued at $100,000, and in 1886 what do you think would be its value?   H.
Germantown.

AN APPARENT ERROR.—A gentleman who has lived in Germantown for 63 years points out an apparent error in a communication published last week and signed " H." The property in question extended probably from Penn to Coulter, as the streets are now called, and not to Mill street. The figures or the names are wrong and not knowing the address of the writer it is impossible to ask there for the proper correction.

MARKET SQUARE AND CHURCH, FROM WATSON'S ANNALS, BY PERMISSION OF EDWIN S. STUART, PUBLISHER.

GERMANTOWN.

The BOROUGH OF GERMANTOWN was incorporated in 1689. "In 1692 one-fourth of the acre reserved out of the front part of the Frankfort Company's lot was proposed to be exchanged with Paul Wulff for one whole acre," that is two half acres, one on the east and the other on the west side of the town.

On January 25th, 1694–5, an order was issued for the erection of stocks. In 1702, James De la Plaine was ordered to remove the old iron from the rotten frames of these stocks, and in 1703, it was thus ordered: "Peter Schumacher and Isaac Schumacher shall arrange with workmen that a prison house and stocks be put up as soon as possible." In 1699 Edward Shippen and Anthony Morris issued a writ of *quo warranto*, in William Penn's name, "against Germantown for refusing to levy a tax for the support of Government." In 1701, "a tax was laid for the building of a prison, erection of a market, etc." The same year, "it was found good to start a school here in Germantown." Pastorius was the first teacher. Anthony Benezet, a Huguenot, also taught the school. "Several members of his family lie in the Lower Burying Ground."

The half acre on the east side of Main street, procured by exchange from Wulff, is "Market Square," or "The Green," as it was formerly called. The whole acre was not secured. In 1703–4 the Bailiffs, etc., "for the common good and to purchase a place nearer the now midst or center of the said town, as also for and in consideration of four pounds current silver money of Pennsylvania, to them in hand paid," "sold the remaining three-quarters of an acre of the first seat of Government to Paul Wulff. And on the same day," "immediately for the £4 was purchased from James De la Plaine, one-half acre, to wit: on Main street fourteen perches and on the cross street five and three-quarters perches broad; this half acre is to be used as a Market Place and the Prison House, Stocks, Pound, etc., shall be built thereon."

"An agreement was made with Herman Van Bon and James De la Plaine to build the prison house and stocks, each of them shall have three shillings, six pence per day and find themselves. The Pound was at the southeast corner of the Square, and the prison of logs near it." Adam Hogermoed, when Germantown lost its charter, "bought the prison and 'moved it to where it now forms part of Joseph Green's group of houses.' Green was a hatter on the east side of Main street, above Market Square."

William Penn gave the Germantown people liberty "as a free gift, and so, of course," Ward says, "they did not value it." "They were averse to the duties of office to which they might be elected, and at last, about 1706, for want of a due election, the charter was lost."

Pastorius could not "get men to serve in the general Court on account of 'conscience sake,' but he trusted that an expected arrival of immigrants might remedy it." The Government lasted fifteen years.

In 1740 "Market Square was surveyed by Benjamin Eastburn, Surveyor General of the Province." In 1741 the Market House was built. 1762 was a troublous year, and there were Indian massacres. This was the era of the Paxton Boys' invasion.

Ward speaks of some Indians as yet in Pennsylvania, and says that where the Allegheny river enters our State, on the border of New York, " there is an Indian territory of the extent of one square mile, which is the home of a few of the Cornplanter tribe." " In my early days," he adds, " I have met troops of this or the New York tribes, hunting in the northern part of the State. When, however, Philadelphia was the capital of the Federal Government, Indians occupied a considerable part of Pennsylvania, and often came hither in large numbers. It was their custom to stop in Germantown, and to come to Market Square for their meals. A table, often used for their dinners, is preserved by Dr. William Ashmead. The old Market House remained till our day. An Act of Assembly, 16th of April, 1848, authorized its demolition, but this did not occur till some years afterwards; the same Act authorized the erection of the Town Hall."

A notice of Abraham Keyser now appears. His father was a Dennkr, Abraham owned a place on Main street, opposite the Friends' Meeting-House grounds. At Quarterly meetings his house was open to entertain distant Friends. His neice, Susan Douglas, was hostess.

Ward states that while he had spoken of John Stadelman, captain of the Germantown Blues, " in apparent connection with Camp Dupont and the War of 1812," that Dr. Runkle was then Captain, and Stadelman "attained that rank afterwards."

" There is an ancient family in Spain named Ashmede, as I believe the name is spelled there, which is thought to be of Moorish origin. Some one had said the names, possibly, came from Achmet." Mr. Ashmead, M. P., who married the Baroness Burdett-Coutts, is of the Germantown race. I would add that his brother is also a member of Parliament.

In leaving the old busiest part of the town, Ward gives pictures of the seals of the borough in 1691, and Germantown Library in 1745. The first is a three-leaved clover with " Sigillum Germanopolitanum " surrounding it. The second contains the sun above open volumes and other devices, and the inscription " Scientiae Literatura Resplendent."

When roads were poor the intercourse with the city was uncertain. Then there " were ' great stores' in Germantown, in Frankford and along the road to Lancaster." Farmers sold produce to Stoneburner, Fry or Miller, in Germantown, and could buy fish, seeds, groceries and dry goods. The stores were granaries and also cured pork and beef were sold, making money. Turnpikes hurt this trade.

James Stokes, before 1812, counted in one day more than 500 wagons on the road, many of them Conestogas, having sometimes six or eight horses. Ward describes the simplicity of the early days. The half-doors were on the houses, and the upper part would be kept open usually. At funerals a herald would pass along, and standing on each threshold cry, " Thyself and family are bidden to the funeral of Direk Hogermoed at three o'clock to-morrow." At the funeral the mounted procession moved along, the wives riding on pillions behind their husbands, " to the burying ground to see their ancient comrades,

* Each in his narrow cell forever laid.' "

Ward saw a reference to early funerals in Deborah Logan's Note Books, which showed that " at Dr. Franklin's burial the old custom of the body being carried to the grave by the 'watchmen' of the city was not observed. On account of his illustrious career it was borne by prominent citizens." He adds " I have been told of an instance in Germantown of girls carrying the body of a companion to the grave, as was the custom in the city. Miss Eve speaks of it as a 'foolish custom for girls to prance through the streets without hats or bonnets.'"

Our author finds romance in the ancient half-door: " When evening closed and night had come, some pretty Gretchen with her neat cap and short sleeves, leaned over the door at her accustomed place, and listened to the honey-vows of her lover Herman, who stole her heart as he sat upon the doorstep, his life divided between his love for her and for his pipe, a puff for the one and a sigh for the other."

The closing of the lower half of the door kept out animals, but the open upper half admitted the air of Heaven. The inmate of the house could find rest in standing at the door, leaning upon the lower half, while he conversed with those without.

An amusement of weighing pigs by placing stones in an opposite scale, and guessing at the weight of the stones is said to have been an ancient Germantown pastime. Beef was then rare, and pork was largely used, and hog-killing was an interesting time.

The lots numered 9 and 10 were owned by Direk Kolek and Wygert Levering. Soon James De la Plaine becomes their owner. They contain 66¼ acres. Market Square came from the western end of one lot.

No. 4801, N. E. corner of Germantown Road and School House Lane, is now fitted for business use. Originally it had a " strikingly antique and picturesque appearance." It was a stone house of two very low stories, " with a far-projecting belt-course or pent-house, dividing them, the roof is hipped." It was old and built " by, it can hardly be doubted, James De la Plaine." Mrs. William H. Fisher, " of New York, owns a portrait of Nicholas De la Plaine, painted in his advanced age. It is said he reached the term of one hundred and five years. A majestic face and vast and full-flowing beard reminds one of an ideal creation of Gustave Dore." He was a Huguenot. His son Nicholas "married Susanna Cresson, a Huguenot. of Ryswyck, in the New Netherlands." They are believed to be the parents of James, " who left New York for Germantown." Whitefield preached " from the gallery " of De la Plaine's house " to the people assembled in Market Square." A later De la Plaine, named Joseph, " together with John F. Watson, published some books, one of which in 1812, was *Epitome Historiae Sacrae*. Its preface contains a recommendation by J.

Thomas Carre, of Clermont College, which place afterwards became Jacob Ridgway's country seat, half-way between Germantown and Frankford." Let me add that the college was burned. The country house is seen from the connecting railroad near Potter's Oil Cloth Works, and on the same side of the railroad. There was also a recommendation by " F. H. Brosius of the college at Mount Airy. Professor John Sanderson, author of that charming book, 'The American in Paris' married a daughter of Mons. Carre, who came here from one of the West India Islands."

Joseph De la Plaine wrote the "Repository of the Lives and Portraits of Distinguished Americans." His wife was " Jane, granddaughter of William Livingston, Governor of New Jersey." John F. De la Plaine became Secretary of the American legation at Vienna. Geo. Patten De la Plaine of Madison, Wisconsin, belongs to the family. "The name is known in Wheeling," Nehemiah, a son of James, lived in Newport, Delaware. "His grandson, James, was collector of the Port at New Castle, and built a house in Wilmington, which he afterwards sold to James A. Bayard." Sophia De la Plaine was in Cuba when Lopez invaded it. She was imprisoned, "and published an account of her troubles " in 1852.

In the Revolution, Squire Ferree owned and occupied the house. He married a De la Plaine. He was a relative of Mrs. David Deshler. In 1776 the Pennsylvania Council of Safety ordered salt to be stored in Germantown. James Biddle and Owen Biddle were to attend to the storage. An order appears that calls on Joseph Ferree to deliver 25 bushels " to John Mitchell, commissary for victualing the Navy." Another order for salt occurs, so it appears to have been in his care. Also there is an order " to deliver to Henry Huber one ton of saltpetre."

Here is a noteworthy resolution : " Resolved, that Dr. Charles Bensel, Joseph Ferree and Leonard Stoneburner, be appointed to collect all the leaden window weights, clock weights, and other lead in Germantown and its neighborhood, for which the liberal price of six pence per pound will be allowed, and they are authorized to draw on this Board for the same." This is dated July 8th, 1776.

At the battle of Germantown John Ashmead, as a boy, " was, with the other children, placed by their father in the cellar of their house with a view to safety." John got the others to push him out. He went to Main street, and Squire Ferree saw him and took him to the cellar of his house, where he was kept till the battle closed. "After Squire Ferree's time the house was owned by a Fromberger." In his occupancy tea was handed to a cook for preparation, and she sent it to the table as boiled greens. James Stokes bought the place for a residence. He paid John Fromberger $6000 for the buildings and about three acres of ground, in 1799. In 1807 more purchases were made of joining lands. One entry in James Stokes's account shows that he sold Lorain's house and lot in 1803, to John Lorain, Sr., for $4000.

"THE OLD IRONSIDES" RAILWAY ENGINE.

(SEE APPENDIX No. 2.)

"John Stokes was born at Bexley, Kent, in England, on Michaelmas Day, 1724. He came to America in 1776, and to Philadelphia in 1780." He bought the "Old London Coffee House," still standing at the southwest corner of Front and Market streets." He became rich and retired to the Germantown house and died in 1781. North of the Stokes house there was a small stone house back from the street, with three hemlocks before it. Thomas Megargee, of the Bank of Germantown, lived in it. Then "some ladies of the Stokes family, who owned it, resided there. Joseph and Jacob Green, hatters, bought the property next to the north from Jacob Roset." "William Meredith, a baker, succeeded his father in the house next north, and then adjoining it, came Robert Thomas, a shoemaker. Here, in front of No. 4813, stood the old six-mile stone, planted in the year 1801, which, by reason of the city growing toward Germantown, was changed somewhere about the year 1840 to five miles. James McIlvaine, a well digger, and who met his death in one, lived in the next house, and it was followed by that of David Harmer, a shoemaker." Then came the old jail which was moved to Adam Hogermoed's lot. "The jail stood until about 1850." Armat's, afterwards Bensell's meadow, was next on the north, extending to Laurel street, which was Crout's lane. "On its north side was the coach-trimmer, Clement Bringhurst. And then came Mrs. Dungan, a widow, followed by George T. Stuckert, who was followed by Jacob Fry, a storekeeper and farmer." His property reached almost to the north side of the present Chelten avenue, joining Bowman's lot.

The old railroad station is on "the southeast corner of Germantown avenue and Price street." This railroad connecting the old village and the city, affected Germantown greatly. In May '74" the late Edward H. Bonsall, father of Mr. Spencer Bonsall, so long in the service of the Society (Historical) gave the Society reminiscences of the railroad and of Germantown. He was the second President of the railroad, and when he wrote "the last survivor of those engaged in the enterprise." "He lived in Germantown from 1819 to 1835, and more recently." He remembered the old town as "almost exclusively confined to the Main street, and he thought it probable that three-fourths of the inhabitants were descendants of the original German settlers." The majority of the older people spoke German—wrongly called "Pennsylvania Dutch"—as easily as English. In a circle of six miles, with Chew's House as a center, he thought, outside of Main street, there would not have been five houses superior to "an ordinary farm house." Probably there were not in the town "ten houses of genteel style less than thirty years old."

In those days the town was quiet and unprogressive and isolated. Two-horse stages ran to the city twice daily, except when "an opposition line was put on for a time. On special occasions a four-horse stage was run. The Philadelphia stage office was the 'Old Rotterdam Inn,' on the west side of Third street, a few doors above Race. The times named for starting were 9 A. M. and 3 P. M., but these hours were not rigidly adhered to. Four miles an hour, when they were going, was considered a good speed, but they made up for this haste by stopping, often half an hour, at that agreeable watering place, the Rising Sun Inn."

During this condition of things Edward H. Bonsall and "his friend, Joseph Leibert, a Moravian, of Bethlehem," with others, in 1827, visited Mauch Chunk and saw the marvelous Gravity Railroad, just built, the first railroad proper constructed "in the United States." On the return of the Germantowners "they soon became lions" with their wonderful accounts. A public meeting was held concerning a railroad to Germantown. John Edgar Thomson was engineer. The charter was given in 1830–31, and the company was organized in May, 1831. Jno. G. Watmough was President, and Edward H. Bonsall, Treasurer; David B. Douglass, of West Point, Chief Engineer. There was an excess of subscription for stock, so that "each of the five-share subscriptions had to be reduced to three shares." The intention was "not to cross the turnpike at the present Wayne Station, but to keep the road on the west side of the town." It is said that Thomas R. Fisher, of Wakefield, was the means of having the crossing effected and having the road on the east side. In August a contract was made for five miles of road from Poplar street and the work began. "In November, Edward H. Bonsall was elected President. On the 6th of June, 1832, the road was joyously opened, and with much ceremony." The Councils of New York were present, and there was great interest. The cars were from Baltimore. "They were drawn by horses, and made six trips a day between the city and the then terminus, which was just south of Shoemaker's lane," on the property of Mr. Charles J. Wister.

"On the 23d of November following the first locomotive manufactured in the United States, 'OLD IRONSIDES,' made by Matthias W. Baldwin, was placed on the road." It is still in existence, for its semi-centennial has just been celebrated. Mr. E. H. Kite, now a ticket agent, was a brakeman on the first train. The locomotive was a wonder, and the President used to go on the

---

COMMUNICATION.

ANCIENT GERMANTOWN.

[To the Editor of the TELEGRAPH.]

A letter I received to-day, tells me you are publishing things relating to the old inhabitants and to the houses they built in Germantown. The house No. 4431 Germantown avenue was built by Christopher Ottinger, my father, as I have been told, soon after he came out of the war of the Revolution, about 1781. I heard him tell of the battle of Germantown and the *whiz* of the bullets; he fought in that battle. For his services as a soldier, a Land Warrant No. 80,027, issued to his widow, my mother; in it he is ranked "non-commissioned officer." He volunteered before the age that would have subjected him to draft. My father afterwards was a master coachmaker, his shop was on the lot near by where our old house is.

Erie, Pa.   DOUGLASS OTTINGER.

MATTHIAS W. BALDWIN.
(See Appendix No. 2.)

train to guard against accidents. He said that "Ninth street, from Poplar to Green, appeared black from side to side with the dense mass of people gathered there to witness the action of the novel motive power." Farmers would come for miles to Germantown to see the train arrive. The late Daniel Smith, Jr., who lived considerably beyond ninety years, told Mr. Ward that he once went to the station at Ninth and Green streets to take the cars, but as the directors were to dine in Germantown the train had left a half hour before "the appointed time." This was probably an exception. The railway carriages were long coaches with seats along the sides, as in the present street cars. The stock once sold for 37½ cents a share, and it ran up to "considerably more than one hundred dollars." Price street is named after Eli K. Price. Dr. Samuel Betton lived in a house which stood on a part of the ground "occupied by the Railway Station."

Ward now asks his readers to return "to School House Lane, and walk along the western side of the avenue."

On the northwest corner of School House Lane and Germantown Avenue is the BANK OF GERMANTOWN. Here stood a stone hipped-roof house, "with pent-houses and low ceilings quaintly ornamented. It was erected early in the last century by Carl Benzelius, called here Charles Bensell." He was an educated man, being a son of a Swedish bishop at Upsal. Ward supposed that a tombstone in the Lower Burying Ground was his. "It is of Dr. Charles Bensell, born 11th of April, 1725; died 17th of March, 1795." About 1806 what was then "The Germantown Library" was kept in the Bensell house, and it "continued there until about forty years ago." "Boisbrun, a French emigrant," was librarian. His daughter succeeded him. With her the Library "seems to have ended." Cakes, candies and medicines were sold in the shop containing the Library. "The old house was taken down about the year 1867, when the bank erected the present building."

"As well as I have been able to make out, Carl Benzelius had a son, or perhaps a nephew, George, who died in 1765, leaving a widow, Anna Barbara. A son, Dr. Charles Bensell, built and lived in the large three-storied house of stone, No. 4804. It was perhaps he, or it may have been his father, who, on the entry of the British, left with his family for Horsham." His furniture and medicines were destroyed or removed by the invaders. Lieutenant George Bell, of the English man-of-war *Roebuck*, having been taken prisoner and paroled, Dr. Bensell was requested by the Council of Safety to "provide proper lodgings" for him.

Ward here corrects himself, as in quoting Watson he had "supposed that Nos 4669-71 was the house he referred to. It appears he (Watson) formerly lived at No. 4804, and that the bank was there. [The bank was moved from the Bensell house to No. 4669, so it was at both places at different times.— C. J. W.] Some time afterward Paschall Coulter dwelt here. Still later Miss H. K. Lehman owned it. The third floor was once a single room, where the

Odd Fellows met. The Workingmen's Club afterward used the building for several years. It had beautiful wainscoting and "ornamental woodwork," which "attracted much attention." Alterations destroyed this beauty. In the Lower Burying Ground is another grave marked "Dr. Charles Bensell, b. 14th August, 1752, d. 15th July, 1796." This is no doubt that of the person mentioned above. "Besides Dr. Charles Bensell there was Dr. George Bensell, born in 1757. He was a son of Carl."

"During the war, Dr. Bensell happened, one evening, to obtain early news of some American success. He went into the old church at Market Square, and seating himself at the organ he pealed forth therefrom a most triumphant air. The wondering neighbors quickly gathered at the place and soon heard the welcome news."

Dr. George Bensell of modern times was "bred to mercantile life, but on the death of his brother he studied medicine," and practised it. He was successful and built the large double house No. 4794, occupied by the Workingmen's Club when Ward wrote. He was highly intelligent, a genial companion and faithful friend, and an agreeable and beautiful man. "He married a woman noted for her horsemanship, Mary Robeson, daughter of Peter, of the Robeson Mills, at the mouth of the Wissahickon." The Doctor could not tell one horse from another and once bought back a horse "he had sold but a few hours before. He proudly paraded him before his wife as a superior animal, bought at a very moderate cost. Throwing open the window, Mrs. Bensell inquired, 'Why on earth had he brought the old pony back again; and what did he mean to do with him?' Mr. John Jordan's father-in-law, Mr. Bell, of Bell's Mill, near Chestnut Hill, used to tell of often having seen this lady riding across the country, following her father's pack of hounds." Her family entertained the First City Troop in 1794, after the campaign of the Whiskey Insurrection. They presented her a silver cup. In her youth she would break her father's colts on his farm on the Wissahickon. To the farm she returned after her husband's death. In her ninetieth year she took a ride on horseback. She died about 1856, aged ninety-six.

Dr. Bensell had a mulatto boy, known as "Copper Ike," from his complexion. He used to carry a lantern before his master at night, through the rough footways of the dark town. One stormy night the Doctor, on taking soundings, found that his guide had led him into the gutter.

The Doctor had a talent for drawing and poetry. He would send poetical invitations to dinner to Charles J. Wister, and receive like responses from him in verse. "He died in December, 1827, in the seventy-first year of his age. Two grandsons inherited the artistic talent spoken of, one of whom, George, is dead. The other, Edmund Birckhead Bensell, is a well-known artist, living at Mount Airy."

The double stone house, No. 4806, in the yellow fever of 1793, became the capitol of Pennsylvania. Gov. Mifflin and Alex. J. Dallas, Secretary of the Commonwealth, were then there daily. "Early in this century, Benjamin

Davis, a Friend, resided in the house and had a school there. He added to this occupation the sale of books, of which he had a fair supply." His girls' school was "an excellent one, for he was a good classical scholar, and all the girls there studied the Latin language." His pupils loved him. He had two daughters. The one who died last bequeathed her property "of several thousand dollars to the 'Germantown Infant School,' which is now situated in Haines street and has recently passed its fiftieth anniversary." She must have loved her profession. James R. Gates, owns the house once occupied by the Davis family. "It was just about here, but perhaps further to the north, that Jedediah Strong, a Justice of the Peace, once lived."

"The old 'King of Prussia Inn' extends its ample front along the avenue, and bears upon successive parts the numbers, 4812, 4814 and 4816." Ward remarks that Carlyle would have been pleased to see so many tavern signs around Philadelphia bearing his hero's portrait. "This house, no doubt, like all the others, dates from the time of Frederick the Great. The first stage coach with an awning was run from the King of Prussia Inn to the George Inn, Second and Arch streets, Philadelphia, and was started, three times a week, by one Coleman." Before this time Ward found a coach noted thus: "In 1726, the four-wheeled chaise formerly kept by David Evans was kept by Thomas Skelton, living on Chestnut street, near the Three Tuns Tavern. Mr. Skelton offered advantageous terms to those who were disposed to make adventurous excursions six miles from the city. Where four persons went together they were allowed the privilege of going to Germantown for twelve shillings and six pence."

Watson says that Gilbert Stuart painted an equestrian figure of Frederick the Great for this inn sign, desiring to be unknown in the matter, but afterwards the name of the inn was painted over the figure. "The sign is still preserved." Michael Riter left the Indian Queen Inn, at Indian Queen Lane, for a time and "kept the King of Prussia." The Masonic fraternity then met in it. There were other landlords after Riter. In 1823 Tripler kept it. About 1834 "it ceased to be used as an inn. Formerly, there was a large and very long barn in the rear of the inn, which, when the British were here, was used by them as a slaughter house."

No. 4818, north of the inn, standing back, is "an attractive looking old house, built of stone." Mr. Jones, a Friend, once lived here, "afterwards it was occupied by Christian Lehman, a man of considerable note in the affairs of Germantown. He was a son of Godfryd, grandson of George, and great-grandson of Henry Lehman. This latter was born about the year 1535, and became 'Steward of the Revenues' of the Manor of the Borough of Trebgen, eight English miles from Dresden. Christian Lehman was born in Germany in 1714, and in 1731, with his father, came here with a passport on parchment, elegantly engrossed with golden ink. In Germantown he became a Notary Public and Surveyor."

"In the year 1766 he copied in an excellent style the early plans of Germantown, which Matthias Zimmerman had made in 1746. By this work Lehman has earned the gratitude of all who may desire to explore the earlier times of the ancient village." I may add that a copy of this work may be seen at the rooms of the Pennsylvania Historical Society. The descendants of Christian Lehman's son, Benjamin, live in the house next to the north.

An advertisement in the Pennsylvania *Chronicle*, of April 12, 1768, shows that Germantown had good trees, and was proud of its climate. Christian Lehman advertises various trees, "Hyacinth roots and Tulip roots," in his nursery, and also his "house and place," which "would exceedingly well suit any West India or other gentleman for a pleasant, healthy and commodious country seat." He was ready also to prepare parcels of plants and seeds for transportation.

"Mr. Robert K. Wright lived in Christian Lehman's old house for a time. John Moyer lived north of Benjamin Lehman, and owned much ground, which he sold to Wyndham Stokes, whose family built upon his land a large double house far back from the Main street. On the north is a property of the Langstroths, relatives of Benjamin Lehman. This, years ago, was George Riter's who owned stages. Afterward Alexander Armor, a carpenter, owned it. At the northeast corner of the Germantown road and Chelten avenue was William K. Fry's tinsmith shop. From it all the people of the village obtained their supplies in this line, and no complaint was ever heard." His tinware was excellent. Mr. Fry was a grandson of the Frey family mentioned before in these articles. Chelten avenue was to be named Market street. Its plan was approved by the Burgesses in 1852, though the confirmation of final damages did not occur until 1857. "The western part of the avenue passed through Jesse Barr's farm."

"About the beginning of this century there was one large piece of ground with a front on Main street, extending from about where Langstroth's property is northwardly to that of the Wister's at Vernon, opposite the railroad station. Chelten avenue now divides that old front about equally." Kurtz, a German, owned it. There was an orchard with excellent apples. Kurtz usually wore small clothes and a cocked hat, which gave him somewhat of a military look. Six dogs attended him on his walks. He had a large collection of military books. He bequeathed them "to a church in Germantown, but their whereabouts is not now known. His house, situated on the Main street, was long, low, and with pent-house and porch. Back of it there stood one of the ancient houses of Germantown. No stone appeared in the structure. It was two stories in height, and was built of staves and clay. Another building, perhaps a tool-house, was where, at one time, Miss Rooker had her school. These buildings were removed when Chelten avenue was opened." There is a plate of the house in the *Magazine*, which Ward acknowledges to be made from "a sketch by Mr. Charles J. Wister, who has done very much to rescue from oblivion the picturesque views of the olden time of Germantown."

Kurtz delighted in horticulture and botany. He had rare trees and plants and shrubs, but in 1864, a writer says, only "a huge English horse-chestnut" remained on the sidewalk. His plants were set without order, and so it was difficult to find their owner, who daily worked among them. He was generous and never sold plants, but gave them freely. He died in 1816. He had many friends, among whom was Mathias Kin or Keen, who used to visit him. Mr. Thomas Meehan notices this man in the *Gardener's Monthly*, September, 1864. Some German horticulturists employed him to collect seeds. From the trees collected by him, which were decaying in 1864, Mr. Meehan thought him "contemporary with William Bartram and Marshall, possibly even with John Bartram." Germantown had many trees collected by him. There was a *Virgilia lutea* probably seven feet in circumference, and a large *Magnolia acuminata*, nine feet in circumference, and perhaps eighty feet high, and, as was thought, as fine a specimen as its better known comrade in Marshall or the Bartram gardens." Also "a Pecan Nut, probably eighty feet high and six feet in circumference. But what was regarded as about the choicest thing of all was a *Magnolia macrophylla*, a noble specimen, which Kin, as it was said, brought in his saddle-bag wrapped in damp moss, from North Carolina. A fine American Yew with "its beautiful coral berries set off by its sap-green leaves was believed to have been introduced by Kin."

Kin was fully six feet high, broad shouldered, with large bones, but thin and "the picture of Death." He dressed as an Indian and was called "The Wild Man." He loved the forest and spent years in exploring the North American wilds, acquiring the habits of wilderness life. He would send "seeds and plants" from Philadelphia to Europe and then resume his explorations. He died in 1825, having done much for his favorite Science. He bequeathed his effects to the Almshouse. His will speaks of his plants in the gardens of Peter Reyer in Sixth street, Mr. Lambert in Fifth street, and Mr. Wilkinson on the new Second street road, which were to be sold. It is thought that he owned a place "one mile from the city, where the Government road joins." He is described as "a man of great information," and "an original and honest, good man."

Next to Kurtz's place north was John Christopher Meng's property. He was "born in Manheim, Germany, in the year 1697; he married Anna Dorothea Baumannin von Elsten, on the 20th of June, 1723." Ward saw their good credentials brought from their native land. They reached "this country in 1728, in the ship *Mortonhouse*, Captain John Coultas." The house Meng lived in is now the tin shop, No. 4912. There was formerly a building north of, and connected with it, but back from the street. It was removed to make what is now the carriageway to Vernon. The meadow, or a part of it, and the old spring-house of Meng, are, however, still to be seen, for they have been preserved by the late John Wister and his family. The property reached west beyond Green street. Apple trees that were on it still stand on the part now owned by Mr. Reed A. Williams. John Christopher Meng and his son John

Melchior Meng " were members and trustees of the church in Market Square and both were trustees of the old Academy ; Melchior Meng's children, sons and daughters, were educated there." Some poet of the day was deeply impressed by this, for his song was,

> Melchior Meng! the bell doth ring,
> Melchior Meng, the school is in.

I may add that in Travis and Smith's History of the Academy one of the Mengs is named as a subscriber to its funds. There was a saying in old time that " whenever Melchior Meng mowed his meadow it rained."

Christopher had a son named John Meng, who died early. He was " an artist of more than ordinary promise," being a portrait painter. He was born February 6th, 1734, and " died at the age of only twenty-one years, in one of the West India Islands. A portrait of his father and one of himself, a kit-kat, nicely painted, are in the possession of his kinsman, Mr. Charles S. Ogden."

" Melchior Meng had 'a very fine garden,' and shared with Kurtz his friendship for Kin and his seeds. The immense Linden tree that stood in front of his place was certainly planted by him, as possibly were many others of the large trees which stood there. 'Meng's garden was much larger than Kurtz's, and while the latter paid the most attention to shrubs and plants, the former boasted of his very fine lot of trees, which at that time, was inferior to very few collections in the country.' Melchior Meng died on the 13th of October, 1812, in the eighty-seventh year of his age."

" There is one thing about Meng's garden that is particularly gratifying. While Kurtz's has entirely disappeared, and most of the specimens of rare trees in most other old arboretums in the country are fast being lost, with no friendly hand to replace them with younger ones, or to add new ones, this property has fallen into hands which know how to care for them. That part of Meng's property lying north of his house, which was nearly the whole of it, was purchased by the late John Wister, who added to and resided in the ample building there, and who called the place Vernon."

Here we close our abridgment of the " Walks on the Germantown Road " with our interesting leader, Townsend Ward, with a sigh for his unexpected death ; but some of his manuscripts will still help to guide us as we walk alone, and as the younger shrubs and trees have grown from the old ones above spoken of, so may our new Walks be pleasant, as the result of his work, though lacking his special printed guidance. Certainly we must thank him heartily for past help before we proceed further.

A CORRECTION.

[To the Editor of the TELEGRAPH.]

In reading your Historical Article on Ancient Germantown, in a late paper, I notice there are one or two mistakes, and being a grandson of Peter Robeson,

I take the liberty of telling you that Mary Robeson, wife of Dr. Bensell, was not a *daughter* of Peter Robesen, but was his *sister* and housekeeper at the time she married Dr. Bensell. JONATHAN ROBESON MOORE.
Philadelphia, Jan. 28, 1886.

In closing Ward's abridgment and resuming the narrative, it is but proper to acknowledge the kindly aid of Mr. Charles J. Wister in the revision of that work.

Among Ward's manuscripts was an extract in his handwriting from JOHN DAVID SCHOEPF's Travels in the United States of North America, East Florida and the Bahama Islands in A. D. 1783–4. The work is in German, and the interesting passage concerning Germantown, which will now be introduced, was translated by Miss Helen Bell. John D. Schoepf was Surgeon of the German Auxiliary troops in the service of England, 1776—1783. He was one of the most enlightened and unprejudiced of foreign travelers in the United States. His work was published at Erlangen in 1788.

"In the neighborhood of Philadelphia, in the direction of Germantown, there were still many sad traces of the war, in burned and ruined houses. The road to Germantown leads over a level, sandy, clayey soil, and through a pleasant, open and well-cultivated country, dotted by numerous houses. Here, as well as along the beautiful Schuylkill, there are many pretty, tasteful country houses, which, however, in design are neither large nor substantial. We met many wagons going to market, drawn by four or more splendid horses, which were driven without reins, and merely by the words and whips of their drivers.

"Germantown is only six English miles from Philadelphia; the place itself is between two and three miles long. All the houses stand off more or less from each other, and each one has around or near it its grounds, gardens and thrifty outbuildings. Most of the houses are well and substantially built of stone, and some indeed are really beautiful. One of the finest is the house at the northern end of the place, in which Col. Musgrove, in the autumn of 1776-77, with a company of British Light Infantry, defended himself so bravely against a large body of the American army. Germantown is indebted for its name and origin to a German colony, which was brought to Pennsylvania, by a Franz Daniel Pastorius, of Weinheim, in the year 1685 (1683). The inhabitants are almost all Germans, with the exception of a few Quakers who have settled among them. They are employed in farming, and also in linen and woollen weaving and other manufactures; in particular, many common woollen stockings were formerly made here; but not enough to supply even the fourth part of the country. It is asserted that America as yet does not produce as much wool as would supply each one of its inhabitants with a single pair of stockings. There are many well-to-do people among the inhabitants; and much property and many houses here are owned by Philadelphians, who make use of this place as a summer resort; and in general, on account of its nearness, frequent excursions are made hither. On Sundays the whole road is covered with the wagons and carriages of the pleasure-riding Philadelphians. There is a Lutheran and a Reformed Church, and a Quaker Meeting House here. Some families of another sect, called *Tumblers* (Dunkers), live here also; they wear beards and a simple dress, not, however, of the Quaker fashion. They are allied to the Anabaptists; but I cannot say in what especial dogmas or opinions they differ from the latter, for it is difficult to distinguish the peculiarities of the many American religious sects from each other.

"Beyond Germantown the ground becomes uneven and hilly, still consisting of the sandy clay, which now and then resembles the red earth of Jersey. A few loose pieces of rock along the road consisted of a sandy-slaty rock, in which was interspersed a great deal of mica. Similar rock occurs frequently in the neighborhood of Germantown and along the Schuylkill; most of the houses in Germantown are built of it.

"We staid over night on Chestnut Hill, two miles beyond Germantown, where there are two or three inns, besides some other dwellings. Chestnut Hill is one of a long ridge of hills, all of which are dry and barren, or at least require more labor and manuring in order to become productive than it is the custom of the country to bestow. The lower land around here brings in three and four times as much revenue as the barren acres of these limestone hills. On the other hand, from some places there is a beautiful view of the cultivated country, and of the ornament of the outstretched plain, the city of Philadelphia. These outlooks are sought in vain in many neighborhoods in the other parts of America. This view induced a Quaker, Mr. Elms, to erect a building here in the form of an ancient tall watch-tower. Such an uncommon building was so displeasing to the country people that, with one accord, they gave it the name of 'Elms' Folly;' but they frequently came to make use of the Folly, and to enjoy, by payment of a small fee, the rare view from the roof of this building. From here can be seen, at the distance of several miles, the surroundings of Whitemarsh, where, securely encamped on the heights, General Washington, in the winter of 1778, bade defiance to General Howe."

The death and burial of the Moravian Missionary spoken of as buried in the Lower Burying Ground is thus described in a note in the *Pennsylvania Magazine of History:*—

"Christian Frederic Post, a well known missionary to the aborigines of North and Central America, died in Germantown, April 29, 1785, and on the 1st of May his remains were interred in the Lower Graveyard of that place, the Rev. William White, then rector of Christ Church, conducting the funeral service." This was Bishop White.

For the following sketch I am indebted to Mr. William A. Ulmer, of Germantown. The house spoken of is seen from the railroad near Wayne Junction. Its modern roof makes it look like a very old man wearing a very new hat:

"There is, standing on the west side of Main street, at the extreme lower end of Germantown, a one and a half storied house, in which lived in Revolutionary times the maternal grandmother of William A. Ulmer—a life-long resident of Germantown—who distinctly remembers the old lady's descriptions of incidents connected with the battle which took place on the fourth of October, 1777.

"When the cannonading began she was out in the yard feeding her chickens. She heard the whizzing of the shot as they flew over her head, and, thinking 'discretion the better part of valor,' she quickly returned to the house, locked windows and doors, and, with her sister, took refuge in the cellar, which all people considered the proper thing to do while the storm of battle was raging.

"After the fight was over, and the British army had marched down to Philadelphia, two straggling 'Red Coats' entered the house and called for something to eat, which, of course, was given them. When they left they took all they could carry, regardless of the needs of the occupants of the house.

"One of the men asked Mr. Ulmer's grandmother if 'the army had gone down yet?' In answering him she said, 'which army, the American or the British?' which greatly enraged the questioner, who drew his bayonet from its scabbard, and, rushing towards her, using language much more emphatic than polite, would no doubt have killed her on the spot had it not been for her sister and the soldier who forced him to forego his murderous design. Had she said the 'Royal' army instead of the 'British' army he would have been better pleased.

"After the war was over this young woman married John Harchey, a German, who was a soldier in the American army. They took up their abode in the house still standing on the rock, on Shoemaker's lane (now Penn street), near the Wingohocking station, on the Germantown Railroad, and which, to this day, is known as the 'Rock House.'

"In 1765 or '66 she was a school girl at the old Germantown Academy, as was also her daughter Sarah, the mother of Mr. Ulmer, about the year 1794. Mr. Ulmer spent all his school days at the same place, and his son, G. Linn Ulmer, now of Lafayette College, Easton, Pa., graduated at the time-honored Academy in June, 1885, he being of the fourth generation, in a direct line, who attended the same school.

"In the year 1793, when Washington occupied the house now owned by Mr. Elliston P. Morris, Mrs. Harchey was his next door neighbor, and for some little act of kindness done him by her he put into her hand a whole (silver) dollar, which of course was highly prized by her, but it was finally lost, much to her regret.

"John Hachey was one of the party of Hessians, Brunswickers and Waldeckers who were made prisoners by Washington at Trenton.

"Mr. Ulmer distinctly remembers the old soldier telling the story of their capture. He said, 'We were put in an old church under a strong guard, and after a time were marched out, and drawn up in line close to a tavern post, minus the 'swinging sign,' which we took to be the gallows on which we were all to be hung. After an address from Washington, through an interpreter, we were taken to long tables filled with eatables, the principal dish being sauerkraut, which we enjoyed very much indeed. We then made up our minds never to fight against Gen. Washington.' At the battle of the 'Cowpens' he was one of the Cavalrymen that chased Colonel Tarlton 'through the woods.'"

FIRST PRESBYTERIAN CHURCH.

The article which introduced this series described "Vernon." The FIRST PRESBYTERIAN CHURCH, which adjoins this property, well deserves a notice. The fine architectural stone building faces Chelten avenue. A late pastor, Rev. Dr. J. F. Dripps, has carefully recorded the history of the parish in a printed volume, which gives us needed information. The elders at that time were T. Charlton Henry, Thomas Mackellar, Charles M. Lukens, Enoch Taylor, and Edward L. Wilson. The President of the Pastoral Aid Society was Mrs. Mary D. Westcott, while J. Addison Campbell was President of the Young Men's Society.

This used to be called "The English Church in Germantown." It is a daughter of the Market Square Church. Mr. Joseph Miller, Franklin B. Gowen's maternal grandfather, was "a chief mover in the new enterprise." Rev. Dr. Samuel Blair, son of an eminent divine of the same name, aided the work. One of the earliest services in the new building was for the benefit of a company of soldiers in the war of 1812. Rev. Thomas Dunn, an Englishman, was the first pastor. Services were held for two years in Dr. Blair's house, on the eastern corner of Main street and Walnut lane.

At Mr. Dunn's ordination Dr. Archibald Alexander, Dr. Ashbel Green, and Rev. Nathaniel Irwin officiated.

The site of the first church was that of the present Young Men's Christian Association building. John Detweiler received £800 for it in 1811. Mrs. Detweiler received $50 extra for signing the deed, being promised 100 cabbages to replace her growing cabbages, as the secretary of the Building Committee, Isaac Robardeau, records. On July 19th, 1812, the church was dedicated. Mr. Joseph Miller was for years the faithful organist, and aided the parish in other ways. Mr. Dunn was a faithful and successful leader, but ill-health forced him to resign his work. Rev. George Bourne, an Englishman by birth, followed him. In 1818 Rev. James Rooker, also of English birth, takes the parish as a licentiate, and afterwards receives ordination and is installed. Dr. Neill, Rev. Thomas H. Skinner and Rev. J. K. Burch officiated. Rev. Mr. Rooker, a faithful Christian pastor, died, and Rev. James Nourse was a supply in 1829 and part of 1830. Rev. Dr. George Junkin, principal of the Manual Labor Academy, served "several months," and under him twenty-two members were added. Dr. William Neill, in 1831, became pastor. He is yet "remem-

FIRST PRESBYTERIAN CHURCH, CHELTEN AVENUE.

bered with great interest." In 1842 he resigned. Rev. Thomas B. Bradford was pastor from 1842 to 1850. From October, 1850, to June, 1852, Dr. Septimus Tustin performed a good work here. He was chaplain in Congress for several years. He died in 1871.

The Chestnut Hill Church and the Second Church of Germantown were partly formed from this parish. Rev. Dr. Henry J. Van Dyke, Sr., now of Brooklyn, became pastor in 1852. From 1853 to 1867 Dr. James H. Mason Knox, now President of LaFayette College, had charge of the parish. In his day the church building was altered, and the church showed a new life. The people have been liberal givers to mission work. In 1870 Dr. J. Frederick Dripps became pastor. In his pastorship the beautiful new church was erected. The building committee were T. Charlton Henry, William Adamson, Thomas Mackellar, Enoch Taylor, Woodruff Jones, and Thomas H. Garrett. The finance committee were James Garrett, James Kinnier, Dr. G. H. Burgin, Jonathan Graham, Charles W. Henry and William B. Mackellar. The foundation of the building rests on solid rock. It was dedicated May 19th, A. D. 1872.

The old building was sold to the Young Men's Christian Association.

The payments for the new building were distributed over two or three years, and the poor, as well as the rich, aided liberally. The parish assigns seats, but allows each person to give by envelopes. The money matters for internal and external objects are arranged by an excellent and systematic plan. Various societies divide and energize the parish work. There are two chapels, one at Pulaskiville, and one at Somerville.

Dr. Dripps resigned this parish in 1879, leaving the new church to mark his work. Rev. W. J. Chichester succeeded him, remaining nearly six years. In October, 1885, he closed his relation with the church, much to the regret of his flock, and took up new duties in Los Angeles, California. Rev. Charles Wood, of Albany, New York, assumed charge in 1886.

ZION EVANGELICAL CHURCH.

Zion Evangelical Church stands in Rittenhouse street, and its graveyard touches the northern boundary of the Vernon estate. The pastor is Rev. S. T. Leopold. The parsonage stands on a lot adjoining the churchyard. The congregation is German and English, as was common in "Ancient Germantown." The first three Sunday mornings in the month the services are in German, and the last Sunday they are in English. The earliest services were held in A. D. 1835. The first church building is in the rear of the new one, and is now used as a chapel. The new building was erected about six years ago.

In the Lutheran Church on Herman street, near Morton, the German language is still used entirely; and that is thought to be the only place where this is the case in this old German town, where at first English services were unknown.

THE RITTENHOUSE FAMILY.

Passing up Main street we come to what is now called Rittenhouse street, but its first designation was Rittenhouse lane, and it extended west, crossing Township Line, then, near what is now known as McKinney's quarry, crossing Paper Mill run, and after ascending a steep hill going to the Wissahickon creek and crossing that, thence going over to the Ridge road. It no doubt derives its name from the early settlers in Roxborough who had there built a paper mill, of which and its founders I give the following account from the pen of Hon. Horatio Gates Jones, a resident and native of Roxborough, and a vice president of the Historical Society of Pennsylvania, to whose *Magazine* he has contributed several papers. Ex-Senator Jones writes thus:

"I do not know when Rittenhouse lane was first opened, but no doubt it was at an early day, for with the exception of School lane it was the nearest route to Germantown Main street. Among the earliest settlers of Germantown were the Mennonists who came from Holland. Their emigration has been portrayed in a very graphic style by Samuel W. Pennypacker, Esq., in the *Pennsylvania Magazine of History*, Vol. 4, pp. 1–58 ('The Settlement of Germantown,' etc.), and also in the *Penn Monthly* for September, 1875 (Abraham and Dirck Op Den Graeff). If these articles were read by the residents of Germantown, they would have occasion to feel proud of the early settlers. They are contained in the volume of Pennypacker's Historical Sketches. Time and space forbid me from going into details about the family named Rittenhouse. In Holland they were called *Rittinghuysen, Rittinghusius or Ritterhausen*, which signifies, so Barton says in his Memoirs of David Rittenhouse, *Knight's Houses*. For many years the old spelling was retained, as their autographs in my collection show, but as with other names so this name was changed and became thoroughly anglicised into Rittenhouse.

"It was in 1688 that Wilhelm (William) Rittenhouse, with his wife and two sons, Klaus (Nicholas) and Gerhard (Garrett), and a daughter, Elizabeth, arrived in Germantown from New York. How long they had been in New York is unknown, but my own belief is that they came directly to Pennsylvania, and very probably were so induced by Francis Daniel Pastorius, who knew the importance of having a paper mill in this colony. William Rittenhouse was a native of the principality of Broick, in Holland, where his ancestors for many generations had been papermakers, and was born in 1644. In Germantown proper there was not water enough for their purpose, but they soon found a small stream, now called *Paper Mill run*, in Roxborough, and there in a meadow they located their mill. This *run* empties into the Wissahickon about a mile above its junction with the Schuylkill. The mill was built in 1690 by a 'company,' composed of such men as William Bradford (the first printer in the Middle Colonies of British America, the Bi-Centenary of whose introduction of the Printing Press was celebrated by the Historical Society of Pennsylvania on the 11th and 12th of December, 1885), William Rittenhouse, Robert Turner,

Thomas Tresse and Samuel Carpenter. The land was owned by Carpenter and extended from Township Line to the Wissahickon. Mr. Thomas, in his History of Printing, says that 'there was neither dam nor race for this mill' (Vol. 1, p. 20), but my neighbor, Mr. Nicholas Rittenhouse, a lineal descendant of the first paper maker, informs me that this must be an error. His father, also named Nicholas Rittenhouse, who died in 1857, at the age of eighty-three years, told him that there was a dam and that it was located on the property now owned by Mr. H. H. Houston, in Germantown, adjoining the Township Line. From this dam there was a race, which crossed Township Line and carried the water to the mill. Had there been neither dam nor race the mill could not have been washed away by a freshet, as it was about ten years after its erection.

"The most active man next to the founder was his son Nicholas, who appears to have been a very intelligent person, and was a preacher among the Mennonists. As all students of Pennsylvania are aware, Bradford moved to New York in 1693, but he still retained an interest in the paper mill and no doubt got much of his paper from Rittenhouse. In 1697 he rented his share of the mill, the one-fourth, to the Rittenhouses. The original lease is in my collection, and it seems he was to receive as his rent '7 reams of printing paper, 2 reams of good writing paper, and 2 reams of blue paper yearly.' Bradford was a longheaded man, for he also provided in the lease that for ten years he should have the refusal of *all the printing paper they made* at 10 shilling per ream, and also 5 reams of writing paper at 20 shilling per ream, and 30 reams of brown paper at 6 shillings per ream.

"The Rittenhouses continued to carry on the mill very actively until the year 1700 or 1701, when a freshet carried away the whole of their valuable property. But they were not disheartened, although their copartners were, for I find that they bought from Robert Turner and Thomas Tresse their half of the mill about the date of the freshet, and they soon after bought Bradford's share and became the sole owners of the property. When the mill was destroyed William Penn was here, and Mr. Barton says he had before him, when writing his Memoirs (see Memoirs, pp. 83-4), a paper in Penn's handwriting, recommending that all persons should give the sufferers relief and encouragement. In that paper William Rittenhouse is called an old man and is said to have been 'decrepid' but he was not at that time sixty years of age. Although Bradford still retained his interest in the mill, he did not contribute to its reconstruction, but in 1704 he was induced to sell out and the Rittenhouses became the sole owners, and from that time until the present date the first paper mill in America—at least what remains of it—has been in the Rittenhouse family.

"The mill was rebuilt by the Rittenhouses and was carried on very successfully for many years by William and his son Klaus, and then by Jacob Rittenhouse, and then by the Markles. At last it was changed into a cotton factory.

"It was not, however, until February 9, 1705, that the Rittenhouses had any deed for the mill property. The land was owned by Samuel Carpenter, and on 'the ninth day of the Twelfth month, called February, in the fourth year of the reign of Queen Anne,' in 1705, Carpenter leased the premises, containing about 20 acres, to William Rittenhouse for the term of 975 years from the 29th of September, 1705, at a rent of five shillings sterling per annum. Such is a brief sketch of the first paper mill in America.

"Before closing, let me add that there is an interesting history connected with the *water mark* of this mill. My researches lead me to believe that the first mark used was the word '*Company*.' The next was the letters 'W. R.' (the initials of the founder), on one half of the sheet of paper, and on the other half the *Clover Leaf* in a shield surmounted by a kind of crown, while beneath was the word '*Pensilvania*.' The clover grass, or *Klee Blatt*, used by the Rittenhouses as part of the device was, according to Pastorius, the common Town Mark or Seal of Germantown, near which the mill was located. On some of the paper I have seen is simply the clover leaf. The next mark used was 'K. R.,' the initials of Klaus Rittenhouse, and this mark can be seen in Andrew Bradford's *Weekly Mercury*. The only other Rittenhouse mark that I have seen is that of the letters 'I. R.,' which stood for the initials of Jacob Rittenhouse, a great-grandson of the founder.

"As stated before the Rittenhouses were members of the Mennonite Church, as were most of the Hollanders who settled in Germantown, where they organized a Church as early as May 23, 1708, which still exists. In an article on "Mennonite Emigration to Pennsylvania," by Dr. J. G. De Hoop Schaeffer, of Amsterdam (translated by Mr. Pennypacker) and which appeared in the *Pennsylvania Magazine of History*, Vol. 2, p. 117, and sketches p. 177, etc., it is stated that the elder of their two preachers, Wilhelm Rittenhausen, died in 1708," but Morgan Edwards, in his History of Pennsylvania Baptists, Vol. 1, p. 97, only mentions Cleas Rittenhausen as one of their preachers. Dr. Schaeffer, no doubt, had good grounds for his statement, that William Rittinghausen was a Mennonite preacher, and as Mr. Pennypacker (now Judge Pennypacker) follows Mr. S., I have little doubt that William was also a preacher.

"William Rittenhouse, the founder of the first paper mill, died in 1708, aged 64 years. His son, Nicholas, who was born June 15, 1666, married Wilhelmain Dewees, a sister of William Dewees, also a papermaker, and died in 1734. He had three sons and four daughters. He left the paper mill to his son William, and when he died his son Jacob Rittenhouse became the owner and carried on the business until 1811, when a family by the name of Markle, also papermakers, occupied the mill. The above-named William Rittenhouse, had a son, named Matthias, who was born in 1703. He lived at the homestead in Roxborough, and in 1727 married Elizabeth Williams, a daughter of Evan Williams, a native of Wales. They resided in a house still standing, just back of the Rittenhouse Baptist Chapel. It was built in the year 1707, as appears from the date stone in the gable end. It was in this house that on the eighth of April, 1732, was born the celebrated American astronomer, David Rittenhouse. When David was a few years old his parents left the old homestead and went to Norriton Township, Montgomery County. Of his wonderful career I have not time now to speak."

I append a short sketch of the astronomer to Senator Jones's article. In Henry Simpson's "Lives of Eminent Philadelphians," a short account of David Rittenhouse occurs, but Samuel W. Pennypacker gave a longer sketch of him in *Harper's Monthly*, May, '82, which is re-printed in his "Historical Sketches," from which we make a few notes. The career of this farm lad seems to have started when an uncle who died left some mathematical books. His plough handles and the fences were soon covered with his calculations. When a mere child he made a miniature watermill, and in boyhood a wooden clock. In discovering the method of fluxions he rivalled Newton and Leibnitz, as Mr. Benjamin Rush declares. " In 1770 he completed his celebrated orrery." In 1769 his calculations and observations of the transit of Venus at Norriton so affected him that he swooned at their successful conclusion. He was a fine mechanic, and could construct the instruments needed for his astronomical calculations. Rittenhouse was prominent in the Revolutionary War, being vice-president of the Committee of Safety. For twelve years he was treasurer of the States of Pennsylvania, Virginia and New York. He was the first Director of the Mint. Rittenhouse wrote various scientific papers for the American Philosophical Society. After Franklin's death he became president of that Society in 1790. He received the high honor of an "election as a foreign member of the Royal Society of London in 1795." He died in 1794. A friend having given him "some slight attention," his last words of gratitude and Christian faith were: "You make the way to God easier." Ceracchi made a bust of him, and Peale painted his portrait. A Philadelphia square bears his name. He was a good linguist, ready and apt in imparting knowledge. In public affairs he was strictly honest. In person full, with a mild countenance, his sympathetic nature included Indians and negroes in its embrace. With simple tastes his own home was his happiest resting-place.

COMMUNICATIONS.

VALUABLE OLD PAPER.

[To the Editor of the TELEGRAPH.]

In the TELEGRAPH of March 13, reference is made to some paper made at the Rittenhouse Paper Mill, in Roxborough, by C. Rittenhouse in 1691. This person was no doubt meant to be Claus or Nicholas Rittenhouse. In 1691 he was not the owner of the paper mill referred to, but as you will see in one of Rev. S. F Hotchkin's articles, the *first* papermaker in British America was *William* Rittenhouse, who was the father of Claus. David Rittenhouse was not the *nephew* of Claus but his grandson. Mr. Childs of the *Ledger* is not endeavoring to have the papermakers meet in 1890, but has cordially seconded

the suggestion of Horatio Gates Jones, one of our citizens, who called upon him to obtain his opinion of the proper celebration of the bi-centennial of the Rittenhouse Paper Mill. The statement that authentic documents cannot be found to prove that the first mill was erected in 1690, is entirely wrong, for Mr. Jones has such proofs in his possession and will be happy to exhibit them at the bi-centennial, if it is ever held. BROICH.
Roxborough, March 23, 1889.

In the *Pennsylvania Magazine of History* (No. 1 of Vol. 5, pp. 118, 119), is a note which states that a MORAVIAN SYNOD was held in Engelbert Lock's house, May 10 to 14, 1747, and asks its location and adds, quoting from some source: —" It stands on the left of the road going down to Philadelphia, a little below the Cooper Vende. It is a bakery with rooms enough to lodge all the deputies, and a fine hall for sessions, with two doors for entrance."

In the annals of the Early Moravian Settlement in Georgia and Pennsylvania, p. 183, I find this record in 1742: " May 16 the Synod met for the sixth time, and in Lorenz Schweitzer's house in Germantown." On the same page the fifth meeting, on April 28, in the Reformed Church is noted.

The people could not always keep the time or even know when Sunday came. The first almanac of Sauer was published in 1738. In 1743 a picture of a flying angel was introduced with other pictures. Medical information was given as physicians were scarce and the people poor. He also treated on horology. Sauer's weather predictions at times failing he incurred the displeasure of some but met it with good nature. In 1748 he ingeniously printed the almanac in colors, imitating a fashion in Germany. He was very successful with his almanac, but the last one was issued in 1778, when the Revolution broke up his establishment. A printer, named Dunlap, in Philadelphia, continued the series. In No. 3 of Vol. 6, Jacob Fatzinger, Jr., gives the title of a German almanac, issued in 1831, by Andreas Bradford.

In the *Pennsylvania Magazine of History*, No. 1 of Vol. 6, it is stated by Charles G. Sower that William H. Sowers was not a descendant of Christopher Sauer. Rupp's " Thirty Thousand Names" of Pennsylvania immigrants before 1775 shows that Sauer, or Sower, was not an uncommon name among them. Chris. Sauer, " first," was a " Separatist," and " his son was a Tunker preacher and overseer." Six-plate stoves were his inventions, from which ten-plate stoves afterwards originated. " Mr. Fleckenstein did not 'forge' his types. They were *cast* by himself in *matrices,* said to have been forged under his (Sauer's) direction by Mr. F."

In the same Magazine W. P. Bagnall has a letter to Mr. Ward saying that Mr. Thomas R. Fisher's Hosiery Mills could not have been started before 1834, when Mr. Fisher bought his machinery from Thomas Jones and engaged him as superintendent. The Wakefield Mills had made woolen cloth or cloth of cotton and wool mixed. Thomas Jones died before the hosiery machinery was ready for action in the Wakefield Mills in 1834. His son Aaron became

Shoemakers House

superintendent, but went into business for himself in 1839. His brother John succeeded him in Mr. Fisher's employ. He lives in Philadelphia and gave Mr. Bagnall all the facts.

Thomas Jones and the late John Button began to make "hosiery at Germantown about the beginning of April, 1831." Mr. Jones moved from Nicetown and Mr. Button from South Third street, below Shippen street. They came "from Leicestershire, England, in April, 1830." The credit of introducing the hosiery business in Germantown is due to them, though stockings had been made on hand-frames in the Germantown homes from "the settlement of Germantown by the Mennonites in 1684." In 1809 Thorp, Siddall & Co., near Germantown, printed cotton on copper cylinders. The machinery was imported. Magazine No. 4 of Vol. 8, p. 383.—Samuel H. Needle's article on "Governor's Mill and the Globe Mills, Philadelphia."

In the Magazine No. 3 of Vol. 6, Ward has an article on Dr. Horace Evans's country place on Indian Queen Lane, west of Township line. The stone blacksmith shop there is said to have been used by the British. It has been enlarged and is a tenant house. In 1802 Archibald McCall obtained the property, and strove to improve there the breed of sheep. In 1818 Griffith Evans, Dr. E.'s father, became owner. The house has been changed, but has an old stone dated 1732. Griffith Evans was in the American Revolutionary army in the medical department. He was Secretary of the Commissioners to settle difficulties in Wyoming and went there with Timothy Pickering. He was also secretary to the Board of Commissioners for adjusting claims of British subjects under Jay's Treaty of 1794. The commissioners do not seem to have reached any practical result. Griffith Evans died in 1845, aged 85.

Near Dr. Evans's place lived the handsome Irishman, Col. Walter Stewart, a favorite of Washington. His beautiful wife was Blair McClanachan's daughter. He called his place Mount Stewart.

Robert Shoemaker, of Shoemakertown, writes that Sarah Schumacker's husband, George, died at sea, as she was coming to this country with her family of seven children. Benj. Hollowell, a well-known teacher in Alexandria, Va., who died in 1877, was a descendant of George Shoemaker. He wrote that George's son, George, lived at Criesheim, and being persecuted as a Friend, came, by Penn's invitation, to Pennsylvania. The family came on the ship "Jefferies," Arnold, master, Richard and his granddaughter, Sarah Waln, were fellow passengers. The ship landed at Chester, in 1685. In 1694 George Shoemaker and Sarah Waln were married at Richard Waln's house. George signed the certificate in German. The original is in the hands of Dr. Wm. L. Shoemaker, of Georgetown, D. C. The children of this marriage were "Abraham, Isaac, Jacob, Elizabeth, George and Richard." The children of the elder George were "George, Barbara, Abraham, Isaac, Susannah, Elizabeth, Benjamin."

Isaac Price married Susannah in 1696. These were ancestors of the late distinguished lawyer, Eli K. Price.

Robert Shoemaker, who writes the note, signs himself " of the sixth generation, from George and Sarah Waln."

As to Augustine Neisser, the Germantown clockmaker, John W. Jordan, in the Magazine (No 4 of Vol. 4), states that in 1736 he " was engaged to build ' ye great clock ' for the congregations of Moravians at Bethlehem ; 58½ lbs. of brass work costing £18 had been purchased before. He finished the clock in 1747, receiving £8 as compensation."

REV. JOHN COSENS OGDEN, an Episcopal clergyman, wrote a work called an " Excursion into Bethlehem and Nazareth in 1799," with an account of the Moravians. It was printed by Charles Cist, of Philadelphia, in 1805. Allibone's Dictionary of Authors states that this author was born in New Jersey. He was rector at Portsmouth, N. H., from 1786 to 1793, and died at Chestertown, Maryland, in 1800.

In going to Northampton county from Philadelphia, he says: "Germantown is the most considerable settlement. It begins about six miles from Philadelphia, and forms one continued and very compact street of stone houses for several miles. The road is muddy and dusty when rain or droughts prevail.

"The houses in Germantown are very universally shaded with weeping willows, the Lombardy poplar and other ornamental trees. The gardens are under excellent cultivation, with valuable fields in their rear. Their churches are strong—plain structures of stone, in good repair, as are the houses universally.

"No obscure cottages, the retreat of poverty and misfortune, or the haunts of vice and indolence are exhibited. The inhabitants are industrious, rich and happy. That elegant mansion, called Chew's house, a noble stone building, at a small distance in the rear of a large area in its front, and decorated with trees, cannot be passed without notice. It is more remarkable as it was a place, during the last war, where a very serious conflict took place between the British and Americans. Chestnut Hill and White Marsh also brought to recollection the events of part of the war when the American army possessed those places while they surrounded the enemy within the city. Some of the breast-works appear which were cast up at that time.

" As the German husbandmen seek the conveniences of meadow and water before they erect their homes, and then build in the most commodious places, where these can be obtained, the houses of the inhabitants do not appear so frequently on the roadside as in the northern States. These are skirted with woods and orchards, as soil and heights present for the preservation of the first and planting of the second" (pp. 5, 6).

The Rev. Israel Acrelius, Provost of the Swedish Churches in America, and rector of Old Swedes Church, of Wilmington, Delaware, in his " History of New Sweden," published by the Historical Society of Pennsylvania, says that Germantown " is three miles long. It has one principal street, which is a public wagon-road, and 350 houses. The inhabitants are generally German mechanics," p. 143.

In 1760, Rev. Mr. Neil, who lived in Germantown, but served as the Propagation Society's Missionary at Oxford and White Marsh, reported that Germantown contained 300 houses. He intended to officiate in the town on Sunday evenings.

"The inhabitants of Germantown are Dutch save two or three families of English, and they belong to the Church of England. There is a Lutheran Church and Calvinist Meeting in this town, one of the Quakers and one of the Minnists. German Town lies 6 miles northwest of Philadelphia, a place of considerable inland trade, situated about 3 miles from navigable water for small craft called the River Schuylkill. It stands upon a rising ground and contains 100 fair houses, and is in length 2 miles. There are houses scattered all along the road from German Town to W. Marsh (White Marsh), and the situation of the church (St. Thomas's White Marsh) on a high hill, is very agreeable from whence we may see it very plain at 3 miles distance riding on the great road." Report of Rev. Aeneles Ross, Missionary at Oxford and White Marsh, to the English Society for Propagating the Gospel in Foreign Parts, A. D. 1745.

SCHOOL HOUSE LANE.

As Ward said little about SCHOOL HOUSE LANE, only noticing it from Main street to Township line, we will now go backward a little, and take up that old thoroughfare. It is one of the finest avenues in this country. On Ward's written chart it is marked Ashmead's Road, Bensell's lane, School lane, and Robeson's Mill Road. It had yet another name, and was originally called King street to correspond with Queen street. The Revolution may have driven out that name, though Wilmington, Delaware, still has a King street.

In 1711 John Ashmead bought 500 acres of land on Main street and School lane. On the site of the Saving Fund building, southwest corner of School lane and Main street, was, as Watson says, the first stone house in Germantown. It was one story high, and is supposed to have been built by the great-great-grandfather of Dr. William Ashmead. The rear of the old house which stood here was more antique than the front. When the first house gave way, and Dr. Bensell put up a new building, a part of the original dwelling may have remained in the back-building.

The Boisbrun house occupied the site of the Bank of Germantown.

A piece of the cornice faced with lead of the old Bensell house was shown me at the Mutual Fire Insurance Office, while the front of Mr. Howell's residence on Main street is adorned with much of the same cornice, taken from the old house.

Dr. William Ashmead informs me that the original building on the site of the Saving Bank, was of logs, and that it ran farther into the street than the

Saving Fund edifice. The foundations encroached four to six feet upon the present pavement. Penn twiced preached there. Dr. Bensell bought the lot, and built a two-story stone house about 1793. The property afterwards fell back into the hands of the Ashmead family, and the Bensell house was torn down to make way for the benevolent institution and its good work.

A Revolutionary incident finds place here. A man who lived in Dr. Ashmead's house or one near by, in fleeing from the British received a shot in the leather of his boot, and knew not of it till he stopped his riding miles away.

In the little wooden house on the corner, east of the Academy, lived Betsy Dougherty, who was so weighty that after her death her coffin was passed through the second story window to the excitement of the neighborhood.

Ward having treated of the Academy, we will simply note that the chocolate colored house on the south, lying east of Wayne street occupied by John Wood, is the old Coulter mansion. The west end was removed and a neat modern addition of stone and wood took its place. The house is pebble-dashed with a hip-roof and dormer windows. John Coulter was a Philadelphia merchant, who owned and ran a line of vessels. His son Stephen was a sea-captain. He died two or three years ago. Another son, named David, was a sea-captain in the merchant service. The building which stands in the yard of the Coulter house was the engine house of the Fellowship Fire Company. They were located in Armat street. The old engine was called the Shag-Rag. It is still in Germantown. The side is marked, Germantown, 1764. The wheels are blocks of solid wood. The Dutihls formerly owned the Coulter estate.

We will however enter School lane at the other end. Riding along the beautiful Wissahickon drive, and passing Rittenhousetown while the snow-clad earth contrasts strikingly with the trees which are so abundant, and the Park assures the inhabitants of *rus in urbe*, we reflect on the goodly heritage of the Germantowner. A friend and companion remarks that this wild valley would in the western land, which he has traversed, be called a canon. The houses perched on the cliffs beyond the creek have a fine location.

The High Bridge Mansion opposite the creek, now a public house, was the old Robeson mansion. On the cliff above it was a Hessian redoubt. The dam, which has been tattling to the stones for so many years, and cannot be quiet day or night, may remind one of Southey's beautiful description to his child of the "sparkling" and "darkling water that comes down at Lodore." This is the old dam of the Robeson mill, and it used to work hard for a living, now it is only playing. There were originally two races which served the mill. In the Hon. Horatio Gates Jones's "Leverington family" we find that Andrew Robeson, who died in 1719–20 gave to his eldest son Andrew, by will, "All lands and tenements belonging to the *Roxborrow mill* and *Bolting mill*."

As this part of Roxborough is identified in the public mind with Germantown, the limits of the two places will not be noticed.

In the "Levering Family" eleven ancient mills are named, and their owners designated. Nine were on the Wissahickon, and eight were grist-mills. There was an oil-mill and a fulling-mill.

In Jones's History of Roxborough, the name of Sumac Park is given as the designation of the Robeson estate, which name is still retained. It is added that the mill was called the Wissahickon Mill, and may have been the first on the creek, and being on the King's Highway, near the city, it was prominently before the public. It was visited by the Duke de la Rochefoucault Liancourt and described by him. This was in 1795 when Peter Robeson owned and managed it. In the Revolution John Vandeeren occupied it; the despatches call it Vandeering's Mill. It was an important point by reason of the Hessian redoubt. Nathan L. Jones, a brother of the author named, had a board-yard a little above at Righter's Ferry, on the other side of the creek. The fine viaduct of the Reading Railroad, with its noble arches of gray stone, brings us back to modern days, and shows a sight which would have startled the eyes of the Revolutionary people. The stone abutment on the far side of the creek is a part of the old bridge.

We ride by School Mansion, another place of public resort, and leaving Ridge Avenue enter School Lane by a steep ascent. On a knob on the right are the earthworks of the late war.

The first property on the left, with its pretty rustic fence has been owned by Mr. Philip Guckes, on the right is Powers and Weightman's Laboratory, and near by a tract of land owned by James Dobson.

After crossing the Railroad at the corner of Gipsy Lane on the left is Chas. C. Harrison's property. On the right is the mansion built by the late Thomas A. Powers, with a fine large conservatory. The Weightman property joins this estate on the lower side. The Powers mansion is occupied in the summer. There is a beautiful hill view from it.

Opposite is Charles C. Harrison's fine house with woods in the rear, and its Queen Anne gardener's and coachman's double cottage. James C. Kempton built the original small house, and sold to Ellis Yarnall, who enlarged it and sold it to Mr. Harrison. There is an abundance of woods near Germantown, and the country is undulating, and affording good building sites.

The Weightman house, built by William Allison, with its pillared front porch and double bay windows at both ends, next draws the attention. This stone house is the oldest on the Lane, but has been modernized. It lies on the right hand side. Thomas Rea and Edward C. Pechin were former owners. Next to this comes William H. Merrick's place with its tasteful, variegated brick and stone wall at two stiles, with an iron railing between. The house is a pretty country residence of good size, with a conservatory on the lower side. It is of stone, plastered. Its hospitable owner has enriched his mansion with many foreign curiosities. He is a son of the late Samuel V. Merrick.

The house was built by Mr. Smith, a U. S. Marshall about sixty-five or seventy years ago. Messrs. Bowen, Hill and Spangenburg of New Orleans, and the Hagan family, also of New Orleans, possessed it. Thomas Dunlap, the last President of the Bank of the United States, was the next owner, and was followed by William H. Merrick.

The late ex-Mayor Henry's estate lies next on the same side of the way. The house is occupied by his widow. It is a pleasant cottage with fine trees in front. It was built by Dr. William M. Uhler, who sold to Mayor Henry.

On the other side of the road a square tower, like a Turkish minaret, now strikes the eye. This is the abode of Caleb F. Milne. Thomas W. Smith built a part of the present house, and Archibald Campbell, a manufacturer, of Manayunk, enlarged it. He died October 23, A. D. 1874, at fifty years of age. There is an extensive piazza attached to the house, which adds to its summer attractions. It is constructed of stone, and is one of the largest and finest residences in the vicinity. The property once belonged to Benjamin Morgan, a blacksmith, who married Amelia Sophia Levering, daughter of Wigard Levering, a pioneer settler of Roxborough. His old house is still standing.

On the right side next to Mayor Henry's, is the old-fashioned, stylish, white stone mansion, with its Grecian pillared porch, which was at one time owned and occupied by the late Aaron Doan, a much esteemed citizen. George Presbury sold to Mr. Doan. Charles J. Ingersoll once owned the place. The property next to Mayor Henry's was once owned by Abraham Martin. Old settlers called it "The Infants' Retreat." It was an Infants' Boarding School, under the care of Mr. and Mrs. Martin, where children were well cared for when parents were absent or traveling, or for any reason wished to have their children provided for. Mr. Martin was connected with the American Sunday School Union. He was well known and beloved in the Sunday schools of Philadelphia and its vicinity, and used to visit them, making touching and effective addresses. He was called Father Martin. Blindness came upon him, but he still attended the noonday prayer meeting, conducted by his faithful wife, who still survives him. The same place was occupied by Miss Spafford as a Ladies' Boarding and Day School.

Next to the Milne property is that of John Wagner. It is the old family homestead and lies on a private road east of the Milne house. The residence is in a valley, while the ground slopes upward to School lane. A tulip poplar on these grounds at the roadside, with a very large girth, is quite observable. Its great beauty is seen in the spring, when it is covered with tulip flowers. The bark is regularly divided into ridges. The Wagner estate has been long in the family. The fifth generation now dwell there. John Wagner's grandfather, also named John, bought the place in 1784, in yellow-fever times.

Adjoining the Doan property is the house of Mr. John F. Orne. It is large and adorned with Corinthian pillars. The entrance is on the side. A new stone wall has been built in front of the grounds by the present owner.

Two cottages in one inclosure on the right belong to Mr. Bell of Pittsburg.

The next property to Wagner's is that of the late George Leib Harrison. It formerly belonged to Dr. J. K. Mitchell, the father of Mrs. Harrison. It is a summer residence, and a neat porter's lodge introduces the way to it. The fence is similar to that on the old Merrick place. When John Walter, editor of the London *Times*, was in this country, he rode out from the city to Germantown with Mr. McKean, of the *Public Ledger*. His English insularity was unmoved until he saw the iron fence at S. V. Merrick's place, which struck him so much that he alighted and measured it as a pattern for use in his own country. When he came to the Milne place, the noble view of the hill country stirred him, and he called his son to him, crying out, as he pointed to the hills, "Barkshire," being reminded of the views in that English district. School lane is thought especially English by Englishmen, and the cricketers who visited us last summer so regarded it.

Next to George Leib Harrison's place, on the left is Samuel Welsh's house and grounds. Grand old oak trees, and chestnut and cedars mark it. A long low wall runs along the lane. The house lies well back and is occupied generally in the summer only.

The opposite house, on the right, was built about 1800 by Richard Hill Morris. In 1813 it belonged to the eminent Dr. Caspar Wistar, who founded the Wistar parties. It is a quaint frame building, with a low roof and peculiar dormer windows and two wings. Moses Brown, whose first wife was Dr. Wistar's niece, occupied it. His second wife was Miss Morris. Thomas Wistar Brown enlarged it. Moses Brown died lately over eighty years of age. The house of Jeremiah Brown was once rented by Dr. Tiedeman, a South Carolinian, who used to drive four in hand. Dr. Caspar Wistar called School House lane the Montpelier of America, as being the healthiest section, in his knowledge, about Philadelphia. The wings of the Moses Brown house were built by Dr. Wistar.

Next to this place, on the right, is that of the late Jeremiah Brown, who was of the firm of J. & M. Brown, commission merchants. He died at an advanced age. Mrs. Moses Brown, Jr., now dwells there. It is a white, rough-cast, stone house, with a semi-circular porch.

Opposite is J. Kimball's modern house. It is in Queen Anne style, and is constructed of stone, brick and wood, having a red-tiled roof. There is a conservatory on the west side and a fine stone gateway. Mr. Kimball was lately the President of the Shenandoah Valley Railroad. On this place is a cottage which was occupied by ex-Mayor Richard Vaux during his Mayoralty. He formerly owned the property. He informs me that he had six rooms built in one week in adding to this house to enable him to occupy it at once when cholera threatened the city. His family then lived on the S. Morris Waln place, which lies opposite the Treichel property. He married a sister of that gentleman. Mr. Waln's sisters now reside there. The house was built by James C. Kempton, who sold to Mr. Waln. Mr. Kempton was once surprised, as he sat in his house, by English burglars, while his family were absent visiting Judge J. Righter Jones. They locked him in a closet and also locked up the servants and ransacked at pleasure. The silver taken was afterwards recovered.

Continuing on School lane, the property covered by the places of Messrs. Sill and Dougherty and the Misses Waln was formerly owned by Mr. Craig, who had a fine driving track there for exercising his horses. He kept a fine stock of them. Mr. Craig resided in the mansion now occupied by Mrs. Cornelius Smith, at Falls lane, corner of Township line. Most of School lane has been built up since 1836.

Next to Jeremiah Brown's, on the right, Mr. Herbert Sill's fine large Queen Anne cottage is situated. The first story is of stone and the second of shingle work. The similar residence of Mr. Dougherty, Mr. Sill's brother-in-law, is adjacent. Opposite lies Redwood Warner's house and grounds. This is said to be the best-kept lawn, with the finest turf, in Germantown. The house commands a fine view in the rear across the valley of the Wissahickon. Its material is grey stone. It is of modern style, with a Mansard roof. The Frenchman, Mansard, who invented this style of roof, did much to make the upper story of a house pleasant and useful. The house is occupied by Mr. Warner, with whom reside his sister and brother-in-law, Mr. and Mrs. Lewis. The adjoining property belongs to Mr. William Allison, but is occupied by Mr. Almy.

The Treichel place comes next in order. It is now owned by Colonel George A. Woodward, on the retired list of the U. S. army, son of the late Judge Woodward, of the Supreme Court of Pennsylvania. The house, built by Dr. Treichel, was remodeled and enlarged by him, and a porte cochere added. It is a rough-cast stone building, with brick trimmings about the windows and doors. Two noble Norway firs in front ornament this pleasant country home. Colonel Woodward is a member of the publishing firm of L. R. Hamersly & Co. Dr. Charles Treichel was formerly connected with the Custom House. He was Deputy Collector of the Port of Philadelphia. He married a sister of Bishop Hopkins, of Vermont. Two of his sons served with distinction as officers of the late war. Colonel Charles Treichel is in the New York Custom House. His two sisters live in the same city.

The fine residence of Mr. Edward T. Steel, President of the Board of Education, next meets us on the same side of the Lane. The house was purchased by him from Mr. Justice, who erected it, and the present owner has modernized it. It is an elegant house, built of stone, rough-cast, with brick trimmings. A conservatory opens into the parlor and library. Here Mr. Steel gave a magnificent reception to President Hayes, during his Presidency. The grounds were illuminated with Chinese lanterns. The lawn is prettily wooded.

Next on the right appears Edward N. Wright's square frame mansion, built by his father, Peter Wright. In the same inclosure is the house of Mrs. S. Warner Johnson, a sister of Mr. Wright. It is a Gothic cottage, with the gable toward the road.

On the left hand side, after passing Mr. Steel's, is the Lovering house. The place is named "Taworth." It is a modern stone building, with a square tower. The grounds abound in fine evergreen trees. Mr. Joseph S. Lovering's

RESIDENCE OF MAHLON BRYAN, WEST WALNUT LANE.

widow and children reside here. The house was built by Lewis D. Senat, who sold to Stephen Morris, of Morris, Tasker & Co., who sold to Mr. Lovering. Next to this, on same side, is the well-known Merrick estate. The late Samuel V. Merrick bought it from Mr. Wharton Chancellor, whose mother lived next to the Academy, about 1864. Mr. Chancellor built the house for his sister, Mrs. Twells. Within a year or two Mr. Justice C. Strawbridge, of the firm of Strawbridge & Clothier, purchased it. He is enlarging the mansion. The grounds are extensive. The porte cochere is prominent. The front of the house is broken into various angles.

Opposite is Mr. James S. Mason's modern stone cottage, with its mullioned windows. Then comes the exceedingly large brick house of Mr. Warden, with its ample piazza, and its peaked roof and corner demi-tower, capped with an octagonal roof. The front is on Township Line. Sheriff Porter's house is on the northwest corner of the Lane and Township Line.

Mr. Ward had alluded to Mr. E. W. Clark's fine mansion.

On School Lane, on the lot adjoining E. W. Clark's property, on the east, on Dr. Ashmead's place, are three sassafras trees and some stones in a little hollow, where it is said that Indians were buried.

As late as 1856 there was but one small stone cottage on the Coulter estate, near Wayne street. The rest of the space, between Township Line and Captain Coulter's house and farm, was vacant.

The building opposite the Academy was a boarding house for the pupils. The side buildings were for the use of the teachers, though the one nearest Green street is said to have once accommodated sixteen persons as boarders. The Academy was used as a hospital in the Revolutionary war.

One of the Modern Houses in Germantown is that built in 1886, by Mr. William H. Scott on the corner of School Lane and Wayne Avenue. It possesses several attractive features among which is an Old English Walnut tree growing out of the stable porch. Mr. Scott preferred to build around it rather than cut the tree down.

In 1838 or 1839 the space from Moses Brown's house to the Coulter house was open, excepting a couple of small barns and a stone cottage. Peter Wright's house was the first one to break this gap.

In preparing this sketch of School Lane the writer has been kindly aided by Ex-Mayor Richard Vaux, Mr. John Wagner, Colonel G. A. Woodward, the Hon. Horatio Gates Jones, Mr. Jabez Gates and Mr. Wistar Brown.

GERMANTOWN, February 25, 1886,—In compliance with the request of Rev. Mr. Hotchkin, I contribute to his "Historical Sketches of Germantown" the following observations on the Chancellor houses and some other properties on Schoolhouse lane. The name of David James Dove is mentioned in a book entitled "Eminent Philadelphians," published in 1869, and edited by Henry Simpson. It is dedicated by him to Horace Binney, Esq. (a more eminent Philadelphian it would have been difficult for him to select), and it is therein stated that said David James Dove was an Englishman by birth, of some notoriety in his country as a satirical poet, and that, emigrating to America, he was, in the year 1759, appointed teacher in the Philadelphia Academy, now the University of Pennsylvania. On the fifth of February, 1761, this same Dove, having quarreled with the Trustees of the Philadelphia Academy, and resigned his position, was appointed master of English in the Germantown Academy, Schoolhouse lane; "to enter into the service as soon as the schoolhouse be ready." This irascible gentleman, between whose name and character there seemed to be no similarity, again, shortly, exhibited his undove-like disposition by quarreling with his new patrons; for, on the 24th of June, 1763, they resolved to dismiss him, the *casus belli* being that he had been heard by one of the Trustees to say that he would not "comply with the order of the Board" (limiting the number of his boarding scholars, which he probably found the most profitable of his pupils, to sixteen), "any longer than until he had the building finished that he was erecting contiguous to the schoolhouse." The building here referred to is the three-story mansion, adjoining the Academy property on the south-west, known, *par excellence*, as the Chancellor house. It will be seen therefore that this venerable mansion, now much altered however by an attempt to modernize it, was built in the year 1763, and is not less than one hundred and twenty-three years old; it will also be understood why the unusual addition of a third story was placed upon it; unusual at that time, especially so in a country house. Precisely how long Mr. Dove occupied or owned the house, which was evidently built for a rival to the Academy, and as a defiance to its Trustees, I do not know, for his history is lost in the abyss of time; but that it was purchased by Mr. William Chancellor, in the early part of the present century, is beyond question. Mr. Chancellor was the son of Dr. William and Salome Chancellor, the latter being a daughter of Mr. John Wister, the elder. He was the father of Messrs. William, Wharton and Henry Chancellor; the last of whom was the last of the family to occupy the house, his death occurring about the year 1865. Mr. William Chancellor was also the father of Mrs. Twells, whose country seat, on the west corner of School lane and Township line, will hereafter be mentioned.

Regarding properties on the lane, other than those of the Coulter and Ashmead, the holders of which, in former days, Mr. Hotchkin requests me to name, I would mention that Dr. George Bensell, besides the lot attached to his residence, on the south corner of the lane and the Main street of Germantown, owned a considerable tract on the southeast side, west of the present site of Wayne street, now, or lately, included in the Coulter property. On it, until within a few years, stood a small house or cottage, surrounded by many pear trees. To old Germantowners it was known as Dr. Bensell's pear orchard, and they no doubt, as would be the case at the present day, divided pretty evenly with the Doctor the produce of this small farm. Nearly opposite this, now bisected by the Chestnut Hill branch of the Pennsylvania Railroad, Mr. John Wister, Sr., of Vernon, owned a tract, still in possession of his descendants.

On the west corner of the lane and Township line road, Engle Bensell, a brother of Dr. Bensell, owned a large tract, purchased some forty years since Mr. Wharton Chancellor, son of Mr. William Chancellor, already mentioned, who built thereon a summer residence, a second Chancellor mansion, which he, with his brother, William, and sister, Mrs. Twells, occupied at that season for many years. This country mansion has been even more severely dealt with than its *confrere*, the Chancellor house hitherto mentioned, for not a vestige of it remains to tell its tale. A gentleman named Stockton, originally from New Jersey, and probably of the family of Commodore Stockton, owned a large tract of land on the southeast side of the lane, opposite to this latter Chancellor mansion, extending from the Township line road to, and perhaps including, the property now belonging to the Misses Wahn. He was a gentleman of elegant leisure, and the owner of fine horses, etc. Much of his property afterwards came into the hands of Mr. John Craig, and subsequently of Mr. Cornelius Smith. C. J. W.

The records of J. W. Jordan state that John Engelbert Lock, already spoken of, died July 9, A. D. 1769, aged 72. He was buried in the Moravian burying ground corner of Franklin and Vine streets.

As we proceed up Main street, let us take another look at the depot and reflect how many depots now give convenience to Germantown, while in the early days of railroading the passengers were deposited in the street. The Chelten avenue station, as well as several others, may be called luxurious. It is remarkable how Germantown delights in W's in her stations. She would not be, like Silas Wright, in the song, right without her W. Westmoreland and Wissahickon, on the Pennsylvania line, and Wayne, Wister, Wingohocking, Walnut Lane and Wyndmoor on the Reading, strain the printer's font of type and show a penchant for one letter. The Mixture of Indian, English and family names, and a queen and an American general, is however in good taste, and a help to perpetuate history.

John C. Channon was on the first locomotive which passed back and forth from Philadelphia to Germantown. William Green, who has just died, was another passenger. Mr. Channon describes the cars as being fine and like carriage bodies. The passengers were for some time landed in the road where Price street was afterwards opened. There was a little ticket office at the side of the road.

A railroad anecdote comes in here. Years ago a conductor of the Reading branch was going to New York as a passenger. He fell asleep and as the train slowed up at a station he awoke, and thinking himself at his customary work, jumped up and shouted "Tioga," much to the amusement of some gentlemen who knew him.

GERMANTOWN.
THE FIRST BAPTIST CHURCH.

Price street cut the land of the late Eli K. Price and bears his name. As we go up it with its Grecian front, meets us, and we subjoin a short sketch of its history. It stands on the right hand side of the street, on high ground, overlooking the Main street depot.

Steps looking to the organization of a Baptist Church in Germantown were taken as early as 1837, but with the closing of Haddington College, in 1841, the effort was abandoned. In 1851, the Rev. J. M. Richards, D. D., began to preach in Germantown, and in 1852 organized the First Baptist Church with a membership of seventy-three. The Second and Third Baptist Churches have since arisen, children of the mother, the First. Some thirteen hundred persons have been connected with the church, and the present membership is four hundred. The following gentlemen have served the church as pastors since the resignation of Dr. Richards: The Revs. C. W. Anable, D. D., Warren Randolph, D. D., A. H. Lung, Thomas A. Gill, M. C. Thwing, E. N. Harris, J. O. Critchlow, and J. S. James, who is the present incumbent. Although never pastor of the church, one of the most active and efficient of its founders was the Rev. J. Newton Brown, D. D., whose body rests at the west entrance of the church.

ST. VINCENT DE PAUL'S ROMAN CATHOLIC CHURCH.

A little above, on the other side, is St. Vincent de Paul's Roman Catholic Church. This parish is under the care of the Lazarist Fathers, an order noted as workers in Poland and Spain. They are named from the priory of St. Lazarus, in Paris, where they organized. Father Byrne is now in charge of the parish, and Fathers Walters and Henelly assist him. The parish was founded about forty years ago. The present incumbent is doing a noble work in erecting a splendid parochial building to cost between forty and fifty thousand dollars. It is an ornament to the town, being of fine architecture. It is of Germantown stone, plastered. There are two schools connected with the parish. The chapel on Chelten avenue, corner of Magnolia avenue, is under its care. Three Temperance Societies are connected with the parish. The various rooms of the parish building are convenient. I know of no better building of the kind in this city. The architect is Capt. Biand de Morainville, a Frenchman, formerly an engineer in the French army. The upper story is a Sunday school room and children's chapel, capable of seating 1800. In the basement are rooms for games and bath rooms and a gymnasium. Thus this good priest wishes to make the house a home for his people, and to guide their innocent amusements and recreations. Bishop Domenec, of Pittsburg, was formerly at the head of this parish. Some Germantowners doubtless remember the genial man. He was a native of Spain and returned to that country, where he died. The fine frescoes in the interior of the church, above the chancel and dome, represent scenes in the life of the good and benevolent

Frenchman, St. Vincent de Paul, who would have delighted to see his memory honored by such aid to the poor as the parish building will give.

Townsend Ward left the following note. Mr. Charles Weiss, shortly before his death, informed me that the person's name was John Ellison: "About half way between Price street and Rittenhouse, on the east side of the Main street, there lived some sixty or seventy years ago, a man, large in size and of an appearance so striking that one could see that he had been born to a better position than he then occupied. He never labored—it was easy to see that he could not. He was exceedingly well educated, but he was an inebriate, and this made it impossible that he could be entrusted with affairs of any importance. When lamps were established along the Main street, he was employed by the citizens to take charge of them. He did so tolerably well, and he cried the hours, when he could, and it is remembered that it was in a stentorian voice of a somewhat remarkable power. He was an attendant at the services of the Episcopal Church, but it was known that at times, perhaps Easter, he prepared the communion, and partook of it alone. He was thought to have been an English nobleman, but it is most probable that he was of a family of position, and that he had been a priest of the Established Church, degraded because of his unfortunate habit."

Numbers 5015 and 5017, east side of Main street, belong to the estate of Mrs. Caroline Potter. Her husband, William Potter, formerly made this house his residence. He died in 1869. The place has been in the Beck and Potter families over a century. Mrs. Potter's maiden name was Conrad, and that of her mother Beck.

There is a tradition that a British soldier, at the battle of Germantown, in retreating, demanded something at this house, which was refused, when he attempted to enter the doorway on horseback.

Formerly there was a half-door and pent-house here, but the building has been altered and modernized by William A. Potter. The original place had about two and a half acres of ground, extending directly in the rear to Jacob Floyd's garden, which was noted for its strawberries. The rear garden was adorned with boxwood and cedars, which have departed. The house is now divided into two stores, occupied by Miss Fannie Creighton and Mrs. Elkins and Mrs. Bryan. There was a vacant lot on the south, which belonged to the estate, on which five brick stores have been built. The toll gate rested on the curb of the vacant lot, almost directly opposite Rittenhouse street. Mr. W. F. Potter affords me this information.

TOLL GATE.

The toll gate of the Germantown and Perkiomen turnpike stood on Main street, opposite Poor House Lane, now Rittenhouse street. Ward preserved an anecdote concerning it. An early keeper, who felt a pride in Germantown, was asked by Judge Peters (or some say the Judge merely narrated the story), where Cliveden was, as he was to drive there. The keeper replied that Mr. Chew's house, " was sjoost above old Jake's," and on asking who was old Jake, the answer was received, " Why, don't you know old Jake? Then you don't know nothing." Old Jake was a renowned stocking-weaver. The direction was a little plainer than that of a Dutchman, who told a man that the house he sought stood by the side of "a leetle yaller dog."

The last keeper of the gate was the noted Enos Springer, a Pennsylvania German, whose broad face was full of good nature. He was shrewd and independent, and humorous, and his public life brought him in contact with many people; and his quaint sayings are yet reported. He was a worker in fancy wood-work, and an old Germantown boy has spoken to me of his famous sleds and jumpers. He owned several houses. He opened Springer street through his property.

Samuel Harvey was the first President of the Turnpike Company and Charles Nice and Jacob Rittenhouse were Superintendents for a long time.

As Temple Bar, between Fleet street and the Strand, in London, though built by Sir Christopher Wren, and adorned with royal statues has lately been removed on account of the pressure of city life, so the Germantown toll gate departed, and the driver is relieved of trouble as he passes along Main street, though the antiquarian may long for a sight of the old gate with its jolly keeper.

THE YOUNG MEN'S CHRISTIAN ASSOCIATION.

The building, numbered 5021, on the east side of Main street, is the home of the YOUNG MEN'S CHRISTIAN ASSOCIATION. It was formerly the First Presbyterian Church and the grave yard is yet in the rear. The foundation of this institute is chiefly due to the late William Adamson, the founder of the Wakefield Presbyterian Church. He was an elder in the Chelten avenue church when the work was established on a sure footing. He made himself responsible for its current expenses, and advanced much to purchase the present building, as Dr. Dripps notes in his " History of the First Presbyterian Church." He was the first president. The body was organized January 9, A. D. 1871. The association partially reimbursed Mr. Adamson, but he gave them a large donation. They took possession of the present building in 1873. Before that time they were located at No. 4767 Main street, having the upper stories of that building. The present building is free of debt, a mortgage having been paid during the past year.

Mr. William Brockie succeeded Mr. Adamson as president. He served for several years. He is the president of the Maritime Exchange. The present president is W. B. Whitney. Vice presidents: J. Bayard Henry, William Brockie, John T. Roberts, H. S. Rorer and W. G. Spencer; treasurer, Charles A. Spiegel; secretary, W. E. Wayte.

The successful work of the society still goes on. It strives to further the physical, intellectual, social and spiritual improvement of young men. The

THE YOUNG MEN'S CHRISTIAN ASSOCIATION, MAIN STREET.

membership is four hundred and fifty. There is a library and a large hall, where frequent entertainments take place. A gymnasium, lecture-room, chess and checker room and bath-room afford pleasure and comfort. There is a Boys' Branch with its separate library for their use. A Ladies' Auxiliary has aided in furnishing and embellishing the building. Such good work is needed in training and Christianizing the young, and it deserves high commendation.

The fine large house of E. H. Butler, the publisher, with its striking portico and conservatory and ample grounds, is a marked feature of the east side of Main street. Formerly John Rose owned the property, and a slaughter house stood on a portion of it. The Moravian records in Philadelphia contain the names of Peter Rose, who died at Germantown, A. D. 1740, and of his daughter, Mary M. Rose, who was born in South Carolina, September, 1737, and came to Germantown with her parents in November, 1739. The mother's name was Catharine. Another daughter was named Ann C. Rose. She was born in Germantown, January 1, 1740. This may be the same family.

In 1831 William Lehman and his wife Mary deeded the property to Thomas Seddon. The house occupied by Lehman and Seddon stood on the street, at the lower end of the lawn. This two-story stuccoed house was demolished by E. H. Butler, father of the present owner. It had a gable roof similar to that of 5041 Main street, which is owned by Edgar H. Butler, but was formerly Mrs. Harkinson's property.

After Seddon's ownership follows that of William Rose and wife in 1836. Frederick Seckel owned the place from 1845 to 1856, when the father of the present owner obtained it. Mr. Seckel built a house which E. H. Butler altered and enlarged, and in 1874 Edgar H. Butler, his son, reconstructed and again enlarged the mansion. In 1885 he improved and beautified it. Six houses have been built by him in the rear. He has increased the homestead by purchase from the Morris-Littell estate on the northwest, and the property now covers about four acres. He also purchased William Williams's property on Haines street. Mr. Butler deserves credit for the manner in which he has improved and kept in order the properties owned by him in Germantown. Such a man is a public benefactor.

We now cross the street and return to Chelten avenue. Near the shoe store on Chelten avenue was originally the Fountain Inn, owned by the Wister estate and occupied by H. B. Bruner.

North of this inn was the house of Mr. Ogilby, a carpenter and builder. It is now a tailor shop. The Ogilby property ran from the hotel to the Insurance Building, including that building. The shop is thought to be one hundred years old.

A frame building on the lower side of the alley was Conrad Carpenter's house. George W. Carpenter was born on this place in a house which has passed away.

John Smith built a house on the corner of Rittenhouse and Main streets, on the lower side of Rittenhouse. He was the son of Peter Smith, a Pennsylvania German. The house was three stories high. The place now belongs to the Daniel Keyser estate. John Smith was a skillful blacksmith and accumulated a property. His shop was where Engard's confectionery, formerly Harkinson's, now stands.

Matthias Adam Hogermoed owned the ground where the Town Hall stands. Ward states that an act of Assembly, April 10, 1848, authorized the erection of the Town Hall.—*Pennsylvania Magazine of History*, No. 3, of Vol. 6, p. 283.

The Town Hall is where Samuel Harvey's residence stood, from whom Harvey street takes its name. His son Samuel died about a year ago. His house was removed to make way for the Hall. It was a stone building, erected about 1800. He owned the land from Main street to Township line. He was one of the early Methodists who assisted the weak society, and was a local preacher. He belonged to the Haines Street Church. The Infant School, on Haines street, near Main, was the First Methodist Church in Germantown. The corner stone was laid by Mrs. Dorothy Reger, who also made a prayer at the service. Samuel Harvey was Burgess of Germantown.

THE ENGLE HOUSE.

The Engle house was built by Benjamin Engle in A. D. 1758. He willed this property to his son Charles, who willed it to his son George, who gave it by will to his son, Charles B. Engle, who now occupies it. It is an old-fashioned, pleasant, strongly-built double-house, of stone. The parlor has the old style window seats. The inner doors of yellow pine have panels of white cedar. The old stone out-buildings in the rear were a tannery. A rear room on the first floor has a wainscot over the fire-place and the hall is thus adorned likewise, while the door of the back hall is a double one. Woodwork covers a portion of the wall, but the windows have been modernized. The old iron-bound chests of the early emigrants of the family are still preserved.

The name of the ancestor, Paul Engle, is on the oldest-marked stone in the graveyard at Skippack, dated 1723. In 1703 Paul Engle declined to be a burgess in Germantown for conscientious reasons.

Elizabeth Engle, wife of Charles, saw the wounded General Agnew carried past her house on a door. One of the family's horses was taken by the English, and a poor one put in its place.

As one leaves this gray stone house, which has sheltered generations, he notes the water-shed which breaks the first and second story in front, which is curved into a slight canopy over the front door, while the old-fashioned cellar door serves as another mark of one of the ancient homes of Germantown.

THE MORRIS—LITTELL HOUSE.

The antique English looking house, with its latticed windows, at the southeast corner of Main and High streets, would draw the notice even of a passing

E. H. BUTLER'S RESIDENCE.

stranger. My friend, C. Willing Littell, Esq., kindly gives the following sketch of it:—

"This 'quaint house with its broken angles,' and grounds with the comparatively narrow frontage, but extended depth, characteristic of old Germantown, was, from 1812 until January 11, 1853, the date of her death, the residence of Mrs. Ann Willing Morris. Mrs. Morris was a daughter of Charles Willing, a merchant, and a member of a family prominent among the merchants of this city in the days of the mercantile pre-eminence of Philadelphia. He was a descendant paternally of Major General Thomas Harrison and Simon Mayne, two of the members of the Court, which condemned Charles I. His father, Charles Willing, was Mayor of Philadelphia in 1748 and in 1754, in which year he died from ship fever, contracted in the discharge of his official duties. His mother, Anne, née Shippen, was the sister of Chief Justice Edward Shippen. Through her he was descended from Edward Shippen, appointed the first Mayor of Philadelphia in its charter by William Penn, October 25, 1701, was the first named to the Provincial Council in 1701, and was President of the Council in 1702–4. His elder brother, Thomas Willing, occupied many positions of trust and honor. His signature was the first affixed to the non-importation resolutions of 1764. He was the first President of the Bank of North America, chartered by Congress in 1781, and afterwards the President of the first Bank of the United States, Mayor of Philadelphia, Secretary to the Congress of Delegates at Albany, President of the Provincial Congress, and delegate to the Congress of the Confederation. Mr. Charles Willing, the father of Mrs. Morris, lived for many years in Barbadoes, and died March 21, 1788, at Coventry Farm, Delaware county, Pa. His remains are interred in Christ Church burial ground, Philadelphia. His portrait, by Benjamin West, with those of his mother, Mrs. Anne Willing, by Charles Peale, and of his daughter, Mrs. Ann Willing Morris, by Eicholz, are in the possession of his great-grandson, Mr. Charles Willing Littell.

"Mrs. Morris was the widow of Luke Morris, a descendant of Anthony Morris, who came to America in 1683, and was second Mayor of the city of Philadelphia in 1703–4. Mr. Luke Morris died March 20, 1802, at his residence, Peckham, which then stood with its spacious grounds extending to the Delaware, and was included in the district of Southwark. He is interred in the Friends' burial ground, at the corner of Fourth and Arch streets, Philadelphia.

"Mrs. Morris was a lady of great mental energy and remarkable attainments. She never lost the vigor and freshness of her early and Revolutionary associations, predilections, and principles. One morning, soon after the occupancy of these premises, during the war of 1812–15, a company of troops from Montgomery county, on the march to join the American forces in Philadelphia, halted to rest in front of her house. It was at once thrown open, its supplies were all appropriated, as many of the men who could be accommodated were heartily invited within it, while the steps and curb were covered with refreshments for the defenders of what was to her a sacred cause. She was one of the originators of St. Luke's parish; her name appears in its first subscription list, in 1811. She was a kind friend and sympathetic neighbor. It is believed that no one in distress ever left her house, during her life or those of her daughters, the Misses Elizabeth Carrington and Margaretta Hare Morris, without relief. Such, at least, were the orders of this household.

"The garden, so protected by its trees and shrubbery as to retain the attractions of its original seclusion, was for many years the beautiful scene of the scientific researches of Miss Elizabeth Carrington Morris, who, retiring in disposition, was an accomplished botanist, and numbered among her many scientific correspondents Dr. William Huttall, Dr. William C. Darlington, of West Chester, and Dr. Asa Gray, of Cambridge, Massachusetts. Her collection of rare plants, cultivated and preserved, was celebrated among many, whose refined taste led them to pursue with her this course of study. Her garden was her Eden, and the greenhouses of Messrs. Thomas Meehan and Henry C. Waltemate, were her favorite resorts.

"In these grounds Miss Margaretta H. Morris pursued her investigations which led, among other results, to the discovery of the habits of that scourge of American agriculturists, the seventeen year locusts, enabled her to predict with accuracy their periodical appearance, and to direct effectual protection against their ravages. She was the first and for many years the only lady elected to membership of the Pennsylvania Academy of Natural Sciences.

"Time, which is transforming Germantown so rapidly, is fast obliterating the memories of its distinguished characteristics. On the premises, which form the subject of this sketch, before their occupation by Mrs. Morris, near the boundary line of Mr. E. H. Butler stood an old house, once the residence of Fraley, some of whose descendants yet remain in Germantown, who was a pupil of Dr. Christopher Witt. Although they cast nativities, used rods to discover proper localities for sinking wells, and were called conjurors, they should not be confounded, as they too often are by local tradition, with ordinary charlatans and soothsayers. Dr. Witt was a physician of no ordinary acquirement, although a believer in Rosicrucian philosophy. Fraley was an expert and valuable herb doctor. The simplicity of his practice will not be considered, in our day of discovery, an argument against it, or be condemned as empiric, because not understood. It is believed that he was interred in the old burial ground, on which, and on the adjoining lot given to St. Michael's parish, by Miss Elizabeth Carrington Morris, St. Michael's Church now stands. The east window of this church was inserted by Miss Margaret Hare Morris as a memorial to her brother. Both these ladies were among the founders of St. Michael's parish, and among its most liberal contributors.

"Miss Elizabeth Carrington died February 12th, 1865, and Miss Margaret Hare Morris, May 29th, 1867, in their old homestead. Their remains repose with those of their brother, in the family lot, in the cemetery of St. Luke's Church, Germantown.

THE MORRIS—LITTELL HOUSE, MAIN AND HIGH STREETS.

"After the death of Miss Margaretta Hare Morris, this house was occupied by Mr. John S. Littell, and his wife, Mrs. Susan S. Littell, the youngest daughter of Mrs. Morris, and from 1869 to 1879 by Mr. Charles Willing Littell, her grandson. It remains the property of her family.

"Mr. Littell's ancestors were, on his father's side, among the earliest settlers of East, and on his mother's, of West Jersey. He was a descendant of Captain Eliakim Littell, a partisan Artillery officer in New Jersey when this State was the battle ground of our Revolutionary War. The uniforms of his company, supplied by patriotic ladies of Newark, were blue, and thus originated the soubriquet "Jersey Blues." Mr. Littell was maternally descended from Anthony Elton, who came to New Jersey in 1697, and from Thomas Gardiner, who came to Burlington, New Jersey, in 1676. He was one of the founders of the city of Burlington, and for many years a member of the Provincial Governor's Council. His son, also named Thomas Gardiner, was Treasurer of the Western Division, and first Speaker of the Assembly after the union of East and West Jersey in 1703.

"Thomas Willing, the only son of Luke and Ann Willing Morris, was born in Philadelphia, October 25, 1792. He was a member of the Philadelphia bar. During the whiskey insurrection he served as an aid to General Cadwalader, for the short time the difficulties averted by the wisdom of President Washington, were impending. He married Miss Caroline M. Calvert, daughter of Mr. George Calvert, of Riversdale, Maryland. After his retirement from practice, Mr. Morris moved to Maryland, where he lived for many years. He died May 12, 1852, at his seat, Glenthorne, Howard county. His remains are interred in the family lot, Laurel Hill."

As to the Littell family it is but proper to add that they were long, faithful and laborious members of St. Luke's Church.

WYCK.

Before Germantown Road was opened, the oldest part of the present Haines residence was built. The ancient passage way through this section was an Indian track, running through low ground, near the present Adams street. The end of the house adjoining the street was probably built after the opening of the road, as formerly a door and windows opened upon it. The name "Wyck" comes from an English residence. It means white, and by a coincidence suits this very white house.

The casual passer-by cannot but be struck with the quaint beauty of the old white two-story rambling mansion. The house is a delightful antique, and the air of antiquity has been well preserved.

A peculiar opening in the front forms a recess by reason of certain alterations in the building. The house is entered by a door which faces the yard. The fact that the house stands endwise to the street gives it an individuality which was unstudied, but makes a picturesque idea for artists to imitate. The ancient brass knocker, which supplements the modern bell, is in keeping with the surroundings.

Within, the rooms are light and pleasant. The old fire-place yet does duty. The antique, dull-looking glass Wister goblet is yet in its old home. There is a pretty kitchen with its small window panes and brick floor. The fine old door, with its strap hinges, has been worn at the handle by the many who have opened and closed it in the years that are gone. The stone step is deeply indented where generations have trodden upon it. The ample yard with its shrubbery, and the projecting chimney with its vines, make a pretty picture. The property formerly included John Welsh's estate, which was called "The Wood Lot." I here add manuscript left by Townsend Ward:—

"Wyck. 'Lot No. 17, towards Schuylkill,' as laid down on Zimmerman's plan of Germantown, is a fine property extending along the avenue from No. 5056 to Walnut lane, and formerly reaching back as far as the Township Line. It has come down from the earliest proprietor by inheritance, and for a long time through the female line. And thus it was: Hans Millan took the property between 1683 and 1689. His daughter Margaret married Diedrick, called Dirck Jansen, now Johnson. Their daughter Catharine, born in 1703 married Caspar Wistar. Margaret, a daughter of the last, married Reuben Haines, born in 1728, at Enshom, N. J. His grandfather, John Haines, was settled in New Jersey as early as 1683. He had a large family and a number of sons, one of whom was Josiah, who died on the 28th of December, 1728, leaving an only son, the above Reuben, who, in 1760, married in Philadelphia the Margaret Wistar spoken of above. She was more than a true Wistar, for she wrote her name not only thus, but also at times Wister. Her father founded the first glass works in New Jersey, at Salem, in 1740. One of the products of these glass works is an old tumbler still preserved at Wyck. It has engraved on it 'Margareta Visterin, 1751,' showing that the maker must have been a German to have given the feminine termination to the name, as well as the V instead of W. The memory of her great worth and excellence is preserved in the 'Memorials of Rebecca Jones.' Their only son, Caspar Wistar Haines, was probably the first of the name to come to Germantown. He was one of the originators of the turnpike, and became its treasurer. He married Hannah, daughter of Benjamin and granddaughter of Christopher Marshall, whose memory will not fade away in this community, for he kept his famous 'Remembrancer,' in which he recorded the events of each day throughout the Revolutionary War, closing September 24, 1781. The only son of Caspar Wistar Haines was Reuben, who came down to nearly our own time. He married a daughter of Robert Boune, of New York, who was a grandson of Captain John Underhill, of Massachusetts, of fighting memory. Reuben Haines was a member of the Philosophical Society, and, in its first year, of the Academy of Natural Sciences. Of this latter he was secretary until his death.

"WYCK," THE RESIDENCE OF MRS. HAINES.

"There can be but little doubt that the house at Wyck was built by Dirck Jansen before 1700, and perhaps begun earlier by Hans Millan, and that it is, therefore, perhaps the oldest house in Germantown. Considerable additions were made to it in the last century, and some alterations about sixty years ago. At that time a huge chimney stack occupied the center of the older half of the building. When this was taken down two large ovens in it were also removed, one of which had been walled in, so that its existence was unknown to the residents. With the material of the chimney and ovens there was built an extensive wall at the foot of the lawn. It is a striking looking building, standing with the gable end to the avenue, its front of eighty feet facing southeastwardly. Its width varies from twenty feet to thirty. Of immaculate white, with a chimney stack outside, this house situated among the fine trees that ornament extensive grounds, is one of the many agreeable features of Germantown. Of course Wyck bore its part in the battle, and its floor is yet stained with the blood of the wounded soldiers who were carried into the house during the engagement.

"When General Lafayette revisited this country in the year 1824 he of course was invited to Germantown. In the latter part of September he was entertained by R. Haines, and held a reception in the old house, when he was introduced by Mr. C. J. Wister, to the ladies of the town. During part of the time the General sat in an arm chair that belonged to Dr. Franklin, and which he had brought from France on his return from his embassy there. This chair now belongs to Mr. John S. Haines. On the occasion of the reception it was placed in the Hall, which has large folding doors both front and back. The visitors passed into the grounds by the lower gate, then through the Hall to be presented, and out through the garden by the upper gate, which now is apparently closed to visitors.

"General La Fayette was a wonderfully popular man. Mr. John Armistead Carter, of Loudon county, Va., has told me that when on his way to Yale College, the General was traveling in that direction at the same time, and that the roads all the way from New York were literally crowded with people, horses and vehicles. Perhaps this unwonted popularity arose from a nice regard for the feelings of all who approached him."

On the seventh day of the Third month, 1691, Thomas Lloyd, Deputy Governor, granted naturalization to sixty-four of the first inhabitants of Germantown. By act of Assembly, 1708, these and some others were again declared naturalized.

North of Church lane, or Mill street, Ward's diagram gives the following ancient lot owners on the east side of Main street, going north : 10, James Delaplaine; a second lot, both opposite the Market, is marked 10 also and bears the name Dirck Kolk, and Wiggart Levering afterwards; 11, Herman Von Bown; 12, Hans Seller, Gerhard Levering; 13, John Henry Sprogel, Isaac Sheffer, Henry Buckholtz and Frankfort Company. Then comes Haines street. 14, Paul Kestner, Cornelius Bonn; 15, Daniel Geissler, Isaac Hilbeck; 16, Francis Daniel Pastorius, Euneke Klosterman, first owner; 17, John Doeden; 18, Christian Warner, Sr., Andreas Souplis; 19, Arnold Von Fossen, William Rittenhouse, Baptist Burying-ground, 1766; 20, Paul Engle, Claus Rittenhouse; 21, Hans Henry Lane, Claus Rittenhouse; 22, Dirck Keyser; 23, Paul Engle, William Streepers.

THE SPROGELL FAMILY.

From Public and Church Records, Communicated by George F. Lee.

Johanes Henrick Sprogell (first), born October 11, 1644, in Quedlinburg, Kingdom of Saxony, Germany, died February 25, 1722, at Stolpe, was married in 1674 to Susanna Margaretta Wagner, only daughter of Michael Wagner, a well-known musician of Quedlinburg. She died in 1730; they had six children—(First), Salome Margaretta, born August 17, 1675; (Second) Anna Sophia, born June 7, 1677; (Third) Johanes Heindrick, born February 12 1679; (Fourth) Anna Mariah, born March 27, 1681; (Fifth) Ludwig Christian, born July 16, 1683; died June 5, 1729, in Philadelphia; buried in the Quaker ground. (Sixth) Anna Elizabeth, born April 5, 1686; died December 20, 1760, as the widow Hoppin. All the children were born in Quedlinburg, except Anna Sophia, who was born in Lebus, on the Oder.

He was an eminent divine and man of culture, was instrumental in eradicating useless ceremonies from the Lutheran Church, prominent among which was having the hymns translated into the German, as the worshipers could not understand the Latin, and as he said would go to sleep.

He was first teacher of the Seminary at Quedlinburg and pastor at Werbin in the Altmark for seven years up to 1705, when he was called to the Marion Kirche (St. Mary's), at Stolpe, an important historical church of the Fourteenth Century; he remained in charge up to the time of his death, and was buried in the church aisle in front of the altar near the Baptismal Font.

In 1724 his widow and son, John Henry (second), had his remains removed to the chapel on the estate of Baron De Bandem. Salome Margarepha, the first child, married a Mr. Zeissing in Germany. Anna Sophia, second child, was born in Lebus on the Oder, and married Paster Fortreman.

Johanes Henrick (second), third child, came to Philadelphia about 1700, naturalized 1705; he was a man of great business enterprise, shipping merchant and large land owner. He had the historical law suit with Pastorius, which was settled by Pastorius taking the Germantown tract, and Sprogell a tract of some 22,000 on the Schuylkill, composing a large part of Hanover Township, and site of Pottstown, Montgomery County; he also had large tracts on the opposite side of the river. He donated fifty acres for a church, and the land for the Sprogell burial ground in Pottstown. His home was on the Schuylkill at the mouth of Sprogell Run.

FRIENDS' FREE LIBRARY.

GERMANTOWN.

He married Dorothea ———; she died in 1718. They had five children that we know of. Dorothea married Jas. Boyer, on June 5, 1732; they had a daughter Susanna, who married; they left decendants. Rebecca, it is supposed, married Thomas Graves. John Henry (third), married Johana Christiana ———; they had a daughter Susanna, who married Michael Bard; left descendants. Frederick and Margaret died young, and are buried with their mother in the Sprogell ground at Pottstown.

Anna Mariah, the fourth child, lived at Perlebery in the Altmark, as the widow of Godfreid Arnold; he was a poet, historian and theologian, and took an active part with his father-in-law, John H. Sprogell, the pastor, in the Church Reforms, and was author of German hymns. G. F. Lee has a copy of the memoir of his life Ludwig Christian, the fifth child, came to Philadelphia about 1700, with his brother, John Henry. They were naturalized 1705. He was prominent in colonial and municipal affairs of that early day. "See Colonial Records, Vol. 3, page 201. etc." He gave a number of volumes to Christ Church Library, and imported the old historical organ.

He married Catherine ———; they had two children, Susanna Catherine and John Lodowick. Susanna married Doctor Thomas Say, of Philadelphia, on June 15, 1734. She died in 1749; they had eight children who all died leaving no descendants.

John Lodowick, married Mary ———; we have her portrait in oil; she was a fine queenly looking person. He was an active citizen and business man. Muster Master General for Pennsylvania during the Revolutionary war. They had three children, Catherine, Lodowick and John. Catherine married Samuel Morgan, son of Rev. Abel Morgan; they had a daughter Mary, who married Erasmus Kelly, the pastor of the First Baptist Church at Newport, R. I., from 1771 to 1784. Left issue, John Callender.

Lodowick married Margaret Yorke, and left descendants.

John, married, first, Ann Crostin; second, Elizabeth Towne. By the first marriage had Edward, Mary, Eleanor, Charlotte and Ann. Edward married Elizabeth Marshall; had six children, John, David, Elizabeth, Ann, David Marshall, Edward Crostin.

Elizabeth married Stephen B. Lassalle; issue:

Ann married Commodore Thompson Shaw; descendants:

David Marshall married Matilda Bird; issue:

Edward Crostin married Rosanna Elkins; issue:

John Sprogell, son of John Lodowick Sprogell and his wife Mary, had five children by his second marrage to Elizabeth Towne, namely, John, Lodowick, Elizabeth, Ann and Benjamin.

John married; no descendants known. Lodowick married Margaret Jenkins; left issue one son, William and descendants.

Elizabeth married Franklin Lee; issue: Ann died unmarried. Benjamin died young.

Ann Elizabeth, the sixth child, married first to Pastor Christian Lippe at Stolpe, Germany, came to Pennsylvania and died as the widow Hoppin. Buried in the old Trappe ground, Montgomery County, Pennsylvania. She left descendants by name of Custer.

Franklin Lee and Elizabeth Sprogell were married, as above; they had eight children. Elizabeth died young. Geo. F. married first to Mary Gentry; issue all deceased. Married second to Mary H. Davis; descendants. Charlotte married Samuel T. Altemus; issue: Elizabeth Ann died young. John married Caroline Piper; issue: Rebecka married Lemuel H. Davis; had issue, all deceased. The above information was collected in Germany, by Lemuel H. Davis, of Riverton, New Jersey.

Old Germantown ended at Abington road, now called Washington lane. Engle's lot is also marked Anna Morris or Malson, Anna Reisler, Mary Morris last.

We now go back to School lane and return northward, noting lots on the west side: 10, Heinert Papen, Dr. Bensell: 11, Jacob Jansen Kleingen afterwards Tunis Conrad; 12, Cornelius Siverts (Shuard); 13, Hans Peter Umstad, George Adam Hogermoed, 1766, Peter Shoemaker. Next follows Rittenhouse road. Then 14, Jacob Tellner; 15, Jurian Hartsfelder, Hogermoed, 1766; 16, Claus Thompson; 17, Hans Milan, afterwards Dirck Johnson: this is the Haines place; 19, Henry Frey; 20, Abraham op den Graeff; a second 20, Aret Klinken; 21, John Stilpers.

Washington lane was called Abingdon road, as it led from Roxborough to Abingdon. The Keyser family owned a large tract below this road, on the east side, a century or more ago. The Johnsons also owned a large section on the west side of Main street.

The Rev. Dr. Murphy kindly contributes the following sketch of a High street parish and edifice:

ST. MICHAEL'S CHURCH.

"St. Michael's Church was the outgrowth of an effort in 1858 to establish a mission as the child of St. Luke's, called 'The Holy Cross.' When the parish of Calvary Church was started, the minister in charge of the mission of the Holy Cross moved with its members to the number of about thirty further up town, and began services at St. Michael's Church in the hall now on Lafayette street, December 5, 1858. The organization was effected in the house No. 5041, by the formation of a vestry and the election of the Rev. J. P. Hammond as rector. This house was afterwards leased to the parish for eight years as the residence of the present rector. A lot of ground was offered and accepted for a church building, on High street, beyond Hancock. The donor was Miss Elizabeth C. Morris, to whom the altar window in the church was afterwards a memorial. The condition of her gift was that the edifice to be erected on the site should be forever a 'free seated' church. It was 150 feet front by 125

THE DANIEL PASTORIUS MANSION, BUILT IN 1715, SUBSEQUENTLY THE GREEN TREE INN; NOW OCCUPIED BY DR. ALEXIS DU PONT SMITH.

in depth. There was a small private burial lot upon it in a sad condition of neglect, and the place was known in the neighborhood as 'Mount Misery.' The first sod on the site of the new church was turned over by the rector, April 18, 1859. Its corner stone was laid by the Rt. Rev. Bishop Bowman, Assistant of the Diocese, April 29, and five months after precisely, St. Michael's Day, September 29, 1859, it was opened for divine service. At that service the Rev. T. Gardiner Littell, a nephew of the lady who had given the ground for the church, was ordained deacon, and assumed for awhile the duties of an assistant minister. For nearly two years it had a very prosperous history, daily services, frequent eucharists, and its bell was rung at the beginning, the middle and the ending of each day. Mr. Littell left in April, 1861, and Mr. Hammond resigned the rectorship for a chaplaincy in the army, and a position elsewhere on the 5th of August, 1861. The Rev. Levi Ward Smith became the second rector, after a long interval of great depression, July 5, 1862. He ministered not only in the church, but as chaplain of the Cuyler General Hospital, U. S. A., stationed at Germantown. His health failed and he died, deeply regretted, at the house of his attached friend, Dr. Dunton, December 23, 1863. The congregation has placed a window in the church in his memory. Another year of lay reading and supplies occurred, and the Rev. Edward Hyde True accepted the rectorship, December 4, 1864. This third rector of the parish labored earnestly for three years, and resigned, December 31, 1867. The fourth and present rector, Rev. J. K. Murphy, began his ministry at St. Michael's, January 1, 1868, and after eighteen years still continues it. All indebtedness having been paid, the church was consecrated by the Rt. Rev. Bishop Stevens on September 29, 1876. A fine new organ of Hook & Hastings, Boston, was placed in the church that same year. A lot adjoining the church lot was secured by the vestry and an attractive and comfortable rectory built thereon during 1880-1, and occupied by the present rector since April, 1881. And a beautiful and convenient parish building has also been lately erected, finishing the handsome group of stone buildings which are now regarded as an ornament to the neighborhood."

The Rev. William Ely is the faithful assistant of the rector. The Rev. Dr. Littell is now the rector of St. John's Church, Wilmington, Delaware.

Dr. Dunton's House is on the Pastorius property. A part of the original house stood in High street before it was opened. Daniel Pastorius and his descendants lived here. This is an ample stone residence with a pleasant yard.

The Green Tree Tavern was famous in the days of Charles Mackinet. The house is now the residence of Dr. Alexis Du Pont Smith. Charles Mackinet bought it in 1797, though it is thought probable that he was renting it from Heath in 1777. The family tradition is very clear, that the American forces pushed down this far at the battle of Germantown. In 1775 John Livezey sells this property to Andrew Heath; in 1797 Heath sells to Mackinet, and in

1820 Mackinet deeds it to Charles Mackinet Pastorius. In 1838 the last named and wife deed to Jno. D. Wells; and in 1854 he and his wife deed to Jno. Longstreth. Two days afterward Longstreth and wife give a deed to Humphrey Atherton, and the next month Atherton and wife sign a deed to John D. Wells, who, with his wife, in 1850 sell to George W. Carpenter. In Mackinet's time the neighbors called the place the "Hornet's Nest," because the biggest nest known in this section of the country was kept there as a curiosity. Curiosities of the vicinity were collected here. The tavern was a resort of eminent Philadelphians in their drives, and sleighing parties patronized it. Mrs. Mackinet was noted for good cooking. She was a Pastorius, and a Pastorius afterwards owned it, and so the name of Pastorius House was given to it. The building was erected in 1743. The house was built by a Pastorius, a relative of Francis Daniel Pastorius. The letters D. S. P. are still on a stone under the eaves, initials of Daniel and Sarah Pastorius. Daniel is supposed to have been the builder. The date on the stone is 1748. Dr. Smith thinks that Mackinet married the widow of Daniel Pastorius. When La Fayette was in Germantown he dined here, and Miss Ann Chew, at the age of 16, presided at the feast. In repairing the old mansion, the present owner, Dr. Alexis Du Pont Smith, states that an antique slipper was found under the floor of the third story. It may have been worn by some belle of former days, and is a touching reminder of the flight of time. The bright young wearer has been forgotten for many a day. The slipper comes to a perfect point in front. It is sadly dilapidated. The old house with its pent roof has enormous joists, as the repairing workmen found. They brought to light nails of wrought iron, beaten out by hand. The old oak laths were split by hand. How our ancestors did toil over their work! General Washington is supposed to have stayed in this house. Dr. Smith is a son of the late Dr. Francis Gurney Smith, Professor in the University of Pennsylvania. The Professor's father, F. Gurney Smith, Sr., was the oldest living member of the First City Troop, of Philadelphia, in 1873. A testimonial, dated January 7th, of that year, hangs on the wall of the grandson's office. The standard of the Philadelphia Light Horse was presented to that corps by Captain Abraham Markoe, 1774-5. Watson tells how the sleighing used to continue two or three months in winter, and sleighing parties used to come out from the city to Macknett's old tavern, where his son afterwards lived. He adds that in summer sailors resorted to the country inns, and young men amused themselves with target shooting.

In the house next to the north of the Green Tree Tavern the Warner family lived. The grave-yard in St. Michael's church yard, in High street, was their family burying-ground. They were people of importance in their day. The original name was Werner.

THE MENNONITE CHURCH.

The Mennonite Church is on the east side of Main street just above Herman street. Funk's Mennonite Almanac, for 1875, published at Elkhart, Indiana,

THE MENNONITE CHURCH, AND THE OLD KEYSER HOUSE, THE RESIDENCE OF SAMUEL KEYSER'S FAMILY.

gives an account of this church from which we glean our facts. In A. D. 1683, a number of Mennonites, so called from Menno Simon, came to Germantown from Holland or Germany at the invitation of William Penn. Here they established the first Mennonite Church in America. They were on good terms with their Quaker neighbors in Philadelphia. They found the Indians kind on account of Penn's good treatment of them. At first, it is supposed, that they held service in private houses, or, in summer, under the shade of trees. A school was organized. The first meeting-house was built of logs in 1708. The building was small and plain. It was used as a school room, and Christopher Dock, the pious school master of the Skippack, so well described in Pennypacker's Sketches, taught for a long time. Watson says that he was teaching here in 1740. Jacob Funk, Andrew Ziegler, and John Minnich were among the oldest ministers of the church. Ziegler was a bishop, and Funk was a nephew of bishop Henry Funk, of Skippack. Jacob Funk was an able preacher and a devoted Christian. He often visited the churches in Bucks and Montgomery counties. He died March 11th, A. D. 1816, aged 86. He is buried near the church door. His father may have been a minister. Henry Seller gave the church lot September 6th, 1714. The present stone church was erected in 1770, as the date in front shows. Jacob Keyser, Sen., Nicholas Rittenhouse, Abraham Rittenhouse and Jacob Knorr were the building committee, appointed January 20th, 1770; the edifice was completed the same year at a cost of £202 and 5 shillings, Pennsylvania currency. In 1789 the list of communicants, in addition to some family names already given, notes the following: Kolb, Moyer, Schreiber, Merewine, Benner, Culp, also Kolp, Nice, Engle, Margaret Smith, David and Mary Getter, John Rife, and Hannes Schneider. In 1675 John Funk, aged 81, was living on a farm on Willow Grove avenue, several miles from the Meeting-house. It is probable that his grandfather Jacob, the minister, occupied the same farm. His father, John, was deacon in 1835, and is buried in the grave-yard. The oldest inscription reads thus:

ANNO 1736,
DEN 16. FEBR 11,
1ST HENRICH RITTENHOUSE
GEBOREN ;
GESTORBEN DEN 13. FEBR. 1760.

The building is well preserved, and in constant use. The interior has been modernized, but is still plain. The old grave-yard with its lowly mounds and simple stones, is interesting to the thoughtful mind. The 200th anniversary of this church was celebrated not long since. The first log building stood on the lower side of the burying-ground, where a building has now been erected.

No. 5216, Mrs. Hocker's residence, opposite the upper burying ground, was dwelt in by the daughters of Jacob Unrod. The Unrod family was large, mostly in the female line. The family name has disappeared from Germantown.

GERMANTOWN.

No. 5145, next below Mr. Channon's, was Henry Moyer's house. He was an old resident of Germantown. The Moyers were relatives of the Unrods. Next below Moyer's, on the east side, stood Francis Engle's house, now owned by Henry Freas.

No. 5149. This old stone house is the residence of JOHN C. CHANNON. It was a Keyser property a century or more ago. In the basement is a cellar door, which in warm weather exhibits a scene of beauty similar to that in the Baldwin conservatory in Chestnut street, though smaller in extent. This is a landmark, or rather a flowermark, of Germantown. It is a kindly act to give pleasure to so many in the street by thus displaying the glories of God. When Henry Ward Beecher began his Western ministry hotels were rare, and he selected private houses for spending the night in traveling where he saw flowers in the window, and in such found comfort. The writer is much indebted to John C. Channon for information about Germantown.

David Kelter lived where Freas's grocery store stands. The old house is gone. Michael Lippard resided in the house below. The building was destroyed some time ago. It stood on the site of Mr. Freas's residence.

No. 5177, the Washington tavern, was owned and kept for a long time by Daniel Hines, previously by Mr. Sellers, now by Matthew Ifill.

Nos. 5153 and 5155, being one house, next above Mr. Channon's and next below Nice's livery stable, was formerly the abode of Mrs. Hannah Keyser. It now belongs to Mrs. Hannah Nice. It was the celebrated old tavern called the Wigwam. It was kept for some time by Conrad Redheffer.

Below Lippard's are the houses of George and Frederick Axe. They were Revolutionary buildings of stone. They have departed. Gideon Keyser's house is on the site of Frederick's.

No. 5165 is Samuel Weaver's former home. It is now owned by Dr. Martin Weaver. Martin, the father of Samuel, lived there.

No. 5169, the present shoe store of William Buzzard, was the property of Jacob Bowman. It now belongs to Samuel Nice.

ST. PETER'S EPISCOPAL CHURCH.

In passing Harvey street the spire of St. Peter's Episcopal Church calls attention to its history. On April 8, in the year of our Lord, 1873, Messrs. H. H. Houston, E. A. Crenshaw, S. B. Kingston, E. Bedlock, J. B. Barry, M. S. Shapleigh, J. A. Schaeffer, A. B. Shipley, A. J. Denny and T. R. Ash met to form this parish. Mr. H. H. Houston kindly donated a fine plot of ground at the corner of Wayne and Harvey streets. Ground was broken, May 20th of this year, and Bishop Stevens laid the corner stone, June 30. On November 6, Rev. Theodore S. Rumney, D. D., was elected rector; he assumed charge of the parish on December 15. On December 21 (St. Thomas's Day), Bishop Stevens opened the new church. The foundations of the Sunday school buildings were laid in the fall of 1873. On March 1, 1874, the Bishop opened them-

ST. PETER'S EPISCOPAL CHURCH, PARISH BUILDING, AND RECTORY, WAYNE AND HARVEY STREETS.

and twenty persons received confirmation. The cost of the property is estimated at about $65,000. A rectory has been added at a cost of $10,000. The church was consecrated free of debt. While the parish is largely indebted to Mr. Houston for the gift of land, and assistance in the erection of the buildings, they have also done all in their power to further the work. The beautifully situated stone church, with its tower and bell; the commodious rectory and well-arranged school buildings, of the same material, show the interest and taste of the layman spoken of and of the congregation combined. Mr. E. A. Crenshaw has been Accounting Warden from the foundation of the parish, and still acts in that capacity. Mr. H. H. Houston is Rector's Warden. Messrs. Charles Bullock and Joseph A. Schaeffer have been Vestrymen from the beginning of the parish. Marshall S. Shapleigh and Stephen B. Kingston died during their vestryship, having done efficient service. On the death of Mr. Kingston, his son, H. H. Kingston, was elected vestryman. R. Singleton Peabody is a member of the vestry. Messrs. Edward Bedlock and Joseph B. Barry were also members of the vestry at the founding of the parish. The vacancies have been filled by the election of S. F. Champion and S. K. Kille. Mr. Bedlock, though not in the vestry, is an efficient aider in church work. St. Peter's is a live parish, with a large surpliced choir and a Guild, embracing many efficient chapters. It does good work at home and abroad, and Foreign Missions are not neglected under the plea of too much work at home. The new organization has been successful from its beginning, and a splendid future seems to lie before it by reason of the opening of the Germantown and Chestnut Hill branch of the Pennsylvania Railroad. The parish is growing largely, as the last large confirmation class in March, '86, indicated. Dr Rumney is the faithful rector, and the church has had but one rector. Rev. T. P. Ege was assistant for a time and Rev. H. B. Bryan now holds the position.

An ancient log house formerly stood about where Tulpehocken street breaks from Main street on the west side. It was occupied by the family of a colored shoemaker named John Douglass. At the time that he lived there, perhaps, there were not more than one or two colored families in Germantown.

CHRIST CHURCH.

In passing along Main street, northward, at Tulpohocken street, if the pedestrian turns his eyes westward, he will see the tower of CHRIST CHURCH. The rector, Rev. Dr. J. B. Falkner, gave a sketch of this church and parish in the preface of a sermon delivered by Rev. Dr. C. M. Butler, at the consecration of the church, after it had been rebuilt. We will glean from it. Prior to 1852 St. Luke's was the only Episcopal Church in Germantown. The northern population needed more accommodation, and the town had largely increased in number. A meeting was held in June, A. D. 1852, at Mr. Beekman Potter's house; an organization was effected. The Mennonites kindly offered the use of their church, on Main street, to the infant congregation, and on August 15 it was first used. The Rev. Kingston Goddard took the morning service and the Rev. Samuel Clark the evening. "Both these servants of God have since been called to the Church Triumphant." Services were held in this place until October, 1854. Various ministers officiated until July, 1854. At that time Rev. A. B. Atkins became rector. The eligible church lot, on the corner of Tulpohocken street, was obtained through the kindness of Messrs. C. and J. Fallon. More land was afterward bought, extending the lot to Washington lane. The building committee were Messrs. P. E. Hamm, T. H. Powers, Charles LeBoutillier, T. S. Williams, and John B. Champion, "all of whom except two, now rest from their labors. One of the survivors, Mr. LeBoutillier, was a member also of the building committee appointed to superintend the erection of the edifice just completed." On May 15, 1854, Bishop Alonzo Potter laid the corner stone. Chestnut Hill stone formed the material of the church building. It had a steeple 180 feet high. There was a lecture room and Sunday school building two stories in height, erected in the rear of the church. On the first Sunday in October, 1854, the congregation first used the basement of the church for worship. On the last Sunday in May, 1856, they entered the new church. The consecration took place on the tenth of July, 1857. The church has since been blessed temporally and spiritually. Rev. A. B. Atkins resigned the rectorship in 1869. Rev. I. Newton Stanger, now rector of Holy Trinity Church, Harlem, New York, had temporary charge until the spring of 1870. Rev. T. S. Rumney, D. D., was rector from May, 1870, until December, 1873. Rev. Dr. Falkner became rector on March 8, 1874. He is still in charge. In 1878 a hurricane prostrated the steeple, which fell on the roof and demolished the church. With laudable energy, on the same evening, a movement was made toward building a new church. One week brought out subscriptions to justify commencement. Charles Spencer, Charles W. Chandler and Charles LeBoutillier were the building committee. More money was needed than had been expected, but the congregation cheerfully, with self-denial, finished the work. The old stone was placed in the walls, and new stone added, so that they are massive. On February 10, 1880, Bishop William Bacon Stevens, assisted by Bishop Thomas H. Vail, of Kansas, consecrated the church. The rectors of the Germantown churches took part in the service, and the various congregations were well represented. Between sixty and seventy clergy from city and country were present. The Rev. Dr. Butler, the father-in-law of the rector, preached the sermon on the glory of the spiritual Jerusalem—the Church of God. He well described the manful way in which the demolition of the church was met by an immediate resolve to rebuild, and invoked peace on the sacred walls and prosperity in the homes of the people. A good rectory stands in the church lot.

THE JOHNSON HOMESTEAD.

THE JOHNSON HOMESTEAD, No. 5206, with its double door and knocker, stands at the southwest corner of Main street and Washington lane. Dirck

CHRIST CHURCH.

Jansen, the ancestor of the Johnson family, was one of the original lot owners of Germantown. The family came from the northern part of Holland, and the quaint house with its porch and pent roof is like the Dutch houses. John Johnson built the house for his son John. It was begun in 1765 and finished by 1768, which date is in the peak of the roof, when the younger John brought his bride here from the Quaker Meeting, immediately after their marriage He was the great-grandfather of the Misses Sarah P. and Elizabeth R. Johnson, who now dwell in the old mansion. The maiden name of the bride spoken of as the first mistress of the house was Rachel Livezy, and she was of the Wissahickon family of that name. The battle of Germantown was fought six weeks before the birth of the father of the Misses Johnson—Samuel Johnson. He received the house after his father's death, and married Jeannette Roland, of the vicinity of Lewes, Delaware There were twelve children as the fruit of this marriage. The house is very interesting as showing the results of the battle of Germantown. The bullet holes still remain, and the splintered doors of parlor, sitting room and hall tell a sad tale. During the battle the family wisely retreated to the cellar. After it closed the English soldiers cleared the house of eatables. The ancient furniture is lovingly preserved. The small spinning wheel of the mother of the ladies adorns one of the rooms. That mother came to her new home here in 1805, and lived to be 91, dying in January, A. D. 1876. The corner cupboard contains blue and variegated China ware from England and Canton, mostly one hundred years old. A pretty little conservatory brightens the lower side of the dwelling, and there is a fine yard on the upper side on Ellwood Johnson's place. There is a hall in the rear, and a double outer door in the parlor. The present building is of stone throughout. There is wainscoting over the parlor fireplace, and about the chimneys through the house.

ELLWOOD JOHNSON'S HOUSE.

The second house on the west side of Main street, above Washington lane, is the residence of ELLWOOD JOHNSON. It was formerly the abode of Rev. Peter Keyser, the Dunkard preacher. It is numbered 5214. The building is of stone throughout, rough-cast. It was erected by the father of Rev. Peter Keyser, who was also named Peter. It was built about A. D. 1765, and remodeled by its present owner in 1866, about a century afterward. The old window panes used to have the names of Peter Keyser's children cut in them. The house is pleasant and brightened with flowers in the little conservatory in the rear. The flowers in the yard at the side of the house also attract the toilers who pass by. Ellwood Johnson bought this dwelling of Mrs. Clementine Lynd, the mother of Judge Lynd, in 1857. The old hipped roof has given place to a modern Mansard one. In the rear a terrace diversifies the grounds. An old swamp cypress, nourished by Honey Run, which flows under its roots, is perhaps one hundred feet high and five feet in diameter. Other cypresses stand near as companions. One has been partially blown over, but lives leaning at an angle. Honey Run is now for the most part a covered drain. An old-fashioned spring house, built perhaps in 1760 to 1770, is a picturesque feature of the rear of the yard. The quaint building is large; its roof slopes in one direction. There is a circular window, lined with brick, over the door. The pretty spring is walled in. It is fuller in drought than at other times. The noted Friend, Israel Pemberton, of Philadelphia, when he had the yellow fever craved this water, but the physician's advice was against its use. However, he sent a colored servant out to the spring for water and drank a quantity of it and recovered. The Revolutionary fence, riddled with bullets, is one of the greatest curiosities among the relics of the battle of Germantown. It is preserved with very great care. Such antiquarian interest is commendable in this utilitarian age. The original boards may have been an inch thick, but time and weather have worn them very thin. The cross boards are ancient; the posts have been renewed. The boards are of white cedar and have lost perhaps half of their original thickness. An American in the old country, when he saw a stone a thousand years old, rubbed against it; so one feels like touching this fence.

The ancient stone buildings in the rear of the two Johnson places were parts of a tannery. There are two beam-houses. One of these outbuildings now serves as a cow-house on Mr. Ellwood Johnson's place. An old oak beam over the chimney of a fire-place in one of these buildings has the name of P. Keyser, 1784, cut in it, and plainly to be read, though the whitewash brush has been at work. The beam-houses were where the skins had the fleshy substance scraped off after they had been in lime. The stone bark house on Ellwood Johnson's place where bark was ground and stored is now a stable and carriage house.

The stone wall between this property and that of the Misses Johnson, next south of it, served as a breastwork at the battle of Germantown. The British were below the wall, and the Americans above it. The wall has been repaired and now awaits reconstruction. Two or three pear trees planted by Peter Keyser yet stand. They were placed by him at a point where he remarked that three American soldiers were killed, and are living monuments.

An old stone wheel leans against the bark-mill on the Misses Johnson's lot, which used to run its weary round by horse-power in grinding bark. Peter Keyser was a tanner as well as a Dunkard preacher, and Samuel Johnson was also a tanner. The tannery buildings at the Engle place next the Town Hall show that the occupation of Simon, mentioned in Scripture, was common in ancient Germantown.

The sons of Peter Keyser were Elhanan, Peter, Nathan and William. His daughter Clementine was Mrs. Lynd, the mother of Judge Lynd. Dr. Peter Keyser is a grandson of the preacher, and so becomes Peter the third.

Ellwood Johnson's land runs back almost to Adams street in the rear. An old chestnut tree on the Misses Johnson's place still fights manfully with time, though sadly broken and marred in the contest. An old box bush in the yard of Ellwood Johnson also indicates the age of the estate. An upright clock within the mansion was once the time-keeper of a Philadelphia Friend, who used kindly to feed the squirrel tribe. His name was Henry Pemberton.

The house also contains a curiosity in the shape of a little wine made by Thomas Livezy, who lived on the banks of the Wissahickon. It is dated 1760. It was a portion of some that was sunk in the mill race on Mr. Livezy's place, at the foot of Allen's lane, during the Revolution, to keep it out of the hands of the British.

Rev. Peter Keyser, the former owner of this mansion, used to preach in Philadelphia at Crown and Callowhill streets, and in Germantown, on alternate Sundays. His faithful old mare carried him back and forth in an old-fashioned chair, but he used to walk over the route also.

Some idea of the condition of roads in Ancient Germantown may be formed from the fact that when Reuben Haines wished to visit the Morris-Littel house, nearly opposite his own, he often had his horse saddled to cross the street. Mr. Haines was one of the founders of the Philadelphia Fire Department. The gentlemen of that day took a personal interest in that work; but in a city so large as our present town it is far better to have a paid force.

Mrs. Moses Dillon states that when her great-grand-father, David Deshler, who lived in the city, and who was described by Ward, used to go out to Germantown, to superintend the building of his summer residence, she thinks that she has heard that he was obliged to stay there all night, as the quagmires made returning difficult.

Horse cars and fifty daily trains on steam railways show a change; what will be the condition of things fifty years hence?

Another interesting feature of the old town was the location of buildings. They were stretched along Main street, and followed the fashion of German villages, where the people cluster together, and go out to work in their outlying farms. The farms here extended in long narrow strips back of the houses Such was the shape of the original lots.

Judge Samuel W. Pennypacker, in his address at the Bi-Centennial of the settlement of Germantown, speaks of the Dutch and German elements, which constituted the new town, and refers to the fact that the royal race of England is from Germany, and that William Penn's mother was from Rotterdam; so in this early village of the western world Englishman, Dutchman, and German were to meet and fuse into Americans, a type of what has been going on in the United States on a grander scale ever since.

THE POOR HOUSE.

Cross streets were rare in the early times. The old German would naturally object to the cutting of his little farm, and so people at] that time when

modern feverish haste was unknown quietly went around. The Turkish idea that haste was from the devil, and rest from Allah, would have suited them. Perhaps they have lived longer for their equanimity. Adam Hogermoed may have been thought enterprising when he opened Rittenhouse street (Poorhouse lane) through his own property. The old POOR HOUSE is said to have been his residence. It is an object of interest, as it may have contained many old residents who have seen better days. Here insane Ned Runkle was chained to the floor. Still the poor fellow played pleasantly on the flute, and attracted the boys of the neighborhood. There was a little old woman, who used to patch up her room with fancy-colored paper. I saw an insane woman on Blackwell's Island, New York, who imagined herself the wife of each successive President of the United States, and her gaily adorned walls indicated her grandeur. It is well when such fancies can amuse the diseased brain, and it is a pleasanter sight than
"Moody madness laughing wild amidst severest woe."

The old Poor House property extended from an alley a little west of Main street back to Green street. It was a strip of land perhaps 250 feet wide.

In 1832 a cholera building was put up at the corner of Green and Rittenhouse streets. It was constructed of wood and was torn down. There was a grave yard on Green street. The bodies were removed several years ago to the Potter's field, at the corner of Green and Pulaski streets.

Mattinger's grocery store, No. 36, was the residence of the steward of the Poor House. The old alley was styled Tull's court.

About seventeen years ago the old Poor House was abandoned, and the new one near Wayne street was occupied, and that is soon to be removed to the Unruh farm. The ground was divided and sold in lots. Osborne & Willihan bought the Poor House and made it into a tenement house.

Let us take a look at it. The old building is numbered thirty. It is of stone, being plastered outside the stone. The walls are solid. The building has been divided into five apartment houses. The gable stands toward the street, and the house is exactly on the street, having no front yard; though there is a yard above and below, and a fair amount of ground in the rear. The gable front on the street has been modernized, and the cornice of the roof has been adorned with brackets. Wooden steps project into the street. Green Venetian shutters are in the upper windows, while solid wooden ones are below, colored white. The glass windows of the cellar are partly below the pavement. A modern cucumber pump, painted green, in the yard, on the eastern side of the house, in its fine bravery of bright color, and its ornamentation of yellow paint to enliven the green, contrasts strongly with the old wall of the house. The house is of three stories on the east side, the lower story being a basement in part. There are but two stories on the west side, as the ground is higher there; so it is like some of the dwellings in Edinburg. Three dormer windows enlighten the attic on each side.

Joseph Scheetz, was for some time the steward of the poor house. He is now the sexton of the Dunkard church.

CONCORD SCHOOL HOUSE.

The record book of this old school is kept at Mr. Ellwood Johnson's, as he is the treasurer. Gideon Keyser is the president, and Romaine Keyser is secretary. The title of the book is, "Proceedings of the order and management of the school and building, the Concord school house at the upper end of Germantown, 1775." Then follows: "Be it hereby remembered that whereas a number of the inhabitants of the upper end of Germantown taking into consideration the distance and particular inconvenience through the winter seasons of sending their children to the lower school (i. e., the Academy), and seeing the number of children continually increasing, and the rooms rented for the school in that neighborhood mostly be to small and inconvenient. When the building of a school-house in that part of the town was proposed by the way of subscription: In consequence whereof a meeting was appointed in order to obtain the voice of the people in that part of the town for the purpose aforesaid. When agreeably to appointment a number of the inhabitants met on the twenty-fourth day of March, 1775, in order to promote the building and erecting a convenient school house and establishing an English school in that part of the town. When the plan of the house and spot of ground was unanimously agreed upon being that part of the burying-ground lot at the upper end of Germantown formerly intended for that purpose by one Paul Wolf the original grantor of the said burying ground lot and in order therefore that the said building might be carried on expeditiously. Jacob Engle, Peter Keyser, Peter Leibert and Jacob Knorr were unanimously chosen to be the managers of the said building, by whom it was carried on, and nearly completed by the latter end of October the same year fit for school, which was first opened and kept by John Grimes, schoolmaster."

A list of contributors follows. I add a few of the names of old Germantowners interested in education. John Bowman and John Knorr, executors of Catharine Rife, are credited with 50 pounds, paid from discretionary part of estate; John Bowman, 10; John Johnson, Sr., 12; Jacob Engle, 11; Peter Keyser, 12; John Johnson, 10; John Knorr, 10. A subscriber named Fred'k Smith is marked minister. The total was 245 pounds one shilling and two pence. A note after this reads "the Continental that came to nothing 2 pounds. Real amount 243 pounds 1 shilling 2 pence."

April 13th, 1806, Martin Hocker takes charge of the school. There are accounts of expenses for fire-wood which read strangely in these coal-burning days. A black boy's tuition is noted. April 15th, 1783, meeting to choose trustees. Voters must have subscribed fifteen shillings at least. Number of trustees at least five, and not over seven, to be chosen on Whitsuntide Monday. Jacob Engle, Peter Keyser, Peter Leibert, Jacob Knorr, John Johnson, Jr., and

Winard Nice were chosen trustees. The deaths of Daniel L. Keyser, William Berkner, and Samuel Johnson are worthily noted at the close of the book. Samuel Nice, Dr. Robert S. Woodrop, David C. King and Jacob Keyser were the last trustees chosen. Dr. Woodrop has since died. The date in the gable of the school house, which stands toward the street, is 1775. The house is stone, rough-cast. It has been enlarged. It has a cupola and bell. There is a half-door on the lower side, the number is 5213. It is now a private school, kept by Miss Anne McMurtrie. A high stone wall guards the lower side of the property. The first story contains the school room and the rooms of Mrs. Dillon, the janitress; the upper story is the Charter Oak Library. The Upper Burying Ground joins the property on the north.

THE UPPER GERMANTOWN BURYING GROUND.

Dr. Peter D. Keyser, of Philadelphia, a descendant of the Germantown Keysers, has an article on this subject in the *Pennsylvania Magazine of History*, No. 4 of Vol. 8. From it we cull the following information, simply adding that the inscription on the marble slab in the front of the wall reads 1724, 1776, 1843:

When Germantown was settled (1683–1695), the Mennonites and Quakers were the two religious bodies of the town. At first their meetings were held in private houses, and it is supposed that at times they worshiped together in the same house till the building of their meeting houses. It is not known that they had a special burying place, and the dead were probably buried in their own grounds. When the Friends' Meeting House was built in 1705, and the Mennonite Church in 1706, each building had its graveyard adjoining it for the "burial of members of each body."

"After 1700, Dunkers, Lutherans, etc., began to settle in the town and vicinity, and as there was no place in the upper part of Germantown as an open ground for any one of different religious views who wished to be buried in a regular graveyard, Paul Wulff, in 1724, granted one half of an acre of ground, situated at the upper end of Germantown, on the Main street, above the road to Abington, or Keyser's lane, to the corporation for a burying ground."

A stone wall was needed in front of this ground. The people subscribed for this "money, labor, stone, etc." All subscribers were to have the right of burial. The place was styled the "Upper Germantown Burying Ground."

"The front wall, on the main road, was begun in May, 1724, by Dirck Johnson and John Frederick Ax." A list of those who aided the work is added, which should interest ancient Germantowners. We find the names of Paul Engel, Garret Rittenghausen, Hans Reyner, John Strepers, Johannes Jansen, Dennis Cunrads (Tunis Cunders), Peter Keyser, John Gorgas, Peter Shoemaker, Christopher Witt, Frantz Neff, and many others. The work cost £40 8s. 6d.

No record of burials is found till 1756, when a record book was opened. On seven tombstones before this date are found the names Catherine Machinetin,

A. M.——, geboren, 1679; gestorben, 1735; William Dewees; Mary, daughter of Catherine and Godfrey Lehman; William Palmer, Elizabeth Palmer, Christiana, wife of William Dewees.

In 1753 the land was properly surveyed and bounded, Dirck Keyser owning the land above and below. A post and rail fence was placed on the back of the lot. John Frederick Ax remained in charge, having had the care of the ground since 1724. When he became too feeble by age for this service, the subscribers appointed Ludwig Engelhardt and Richard Robb to the charge. The spot was called Ax's Burying Ground from its superintendent. In 1758, George Schreiber and Engelhardt are in charge.

In 1760 it was determined to inclose the whole yard with a stone wall, and subscriptions were made. Another long list of names helps the antiquary. Amount raised, £29 13s. 0d. The wall cost £33 4s. 10d. Strangers who were able could pay for graves; if poverty applied there could be no free burial. In 1776 a new front wall was built, as the old one needed repair. Jno. Knorr and Justus Fox were appointed collectors for it. George Schreiber and Peter Keyser were "overseers and managers of the Burying Ground," etc. They oversaw the building of the wall. So it has stood from 1777, when it was finished.

When Dr. Keyser wrote, Samuel Nice and Joseph Channon, "descendants from the old line," were in charge.

"In the latter part of the eighteenth century a stone school-house was built in a triangular lot adjoining this ground on the southwest line, which was called the Concord School-house. From the proximity of this house to the ground it came to be called the Concord Burial Ground, which name it popularly bore for many years."

In 1756 George Schreiber begins his record of burials with a child of Jacob Traut, June 28th. "During that year ten bodies were buried therein, all children but one, the wife of George Palmer." Many a Rachel then wept for her children.

Wives and children were entered as such a person's wife or child. "For instance, June 20, 1751, The Catholic man's son."

"Up to about 1800 the erection of tombs was not frequent." In 1757 the record which Dr. Keyser gives, read, "The Catholic Man from Chestnut Hill." This year John Freddrick Ax, "the first superintendent," is recorded. The long list shows German names, and in two cases the record is in German. Here is one in 1761, "Ist der alte Knor begraben." The other is in 1772, "Ist der alte Kraut begraben." Indeed George Schreiber wrote the record in German, but the list only retains these two specimens of German. Schreiber died two years after he gave up his post, and "his co-overseer for so many years, Ludwig Engelhard died the same year." Both were buried in this ground.

In 1781 the record becomes English and a change comes over the spelling of the German names. The record in the Magazine stops in 1799.

UPSAL.

The pleasant mansion of Mrs. Norton Johnson, on the west side of Main street, bears this Swedish name, given by Mrs. Johnson, grandmother of Dr. William N. Johnson. It is numbered 5234. The old trees and shrubbery give it a spacious and comfortable appearance. There are several monarchs of the forest, which have withstood many a winter storm. The square and solid stones of the mansion give it an air of stability.

The house was erected by Norton Johnson's father, in 1798. Here he brought his newly-wedded wife, Sarah Wheeler. Here both husband and wife died, and now their nine children are also dead. One son died in the city. The others died here, so that the old house is full of the history of the joys and the sorrows of family life.

The grandfather of Norton Johnson was named Joseph. His wife was an English lady, Elizabeth Norton. They were married in 1773.

Dirck and his wife Katrina Jansen were one of the thirteen families who settled Germantown. They were the ancestors of this family, as well as of the other Johnsons already noted.

In the house we meet again the pretty old wainscoting, which speaks so well for the skill of the ancient carpenters. The mansion is well constructed, having been built by day's labor, and not by contract. It was three years in building, and people from the country around came during that time to see the wonderful house-building.

The division walls are of stone, and run all the way up, so that the weak lath and plaster are avoided.

The ceilings are high. The wood carvings of the mantels are of the Queen Anne style. The original mouldings at the top of the ceilings are still excellent, though colored. The original fire-places have been preserved.

The old conservatory in the rear of the back parlor is of the same age as the house. The extensive stone servants' buildings, with sloping roof, stand in the rear, and remind one of a Southern residence.

The gabled front and back of the house present an antique and dignified look.

Ample and beautiful grounds surround the ancient mansion. An orchard gives a country touch to the scene, while a greenhouse among the shrubbery and an old stone barn complete the picture. A stone wall bounds the lower part of the estate.

In front the pines and the oaks stand as sentinels before the old door, under its arched window. The porch and dormer windows, and the stone strip reaching along the front of the house give it an individuality. The street in front is adorned with trees.

The grounds are opposite the Chew House.

The following is from the *Philadelphia News:*

Upon "Upsala," the Johnston country place, in Germantown, opposite the Chew house, grows a large silver fir tree, which is now unfortunately, fast going to decay. For many years it has been one of the sights of the neighborhood on account of its remarkable beauty. There was a tradition that this tree was planted by Washington, but this story has been proved to be without foundation, as it was planted in 1800 by the grandfather of the present owner of the property. It grew very rapidly, and twenty-five years ago it was ninety-six feet high. At the present time it is over a hundred feet. It is of the same species as the trees which compose the famous Black Forest in Germany, the name of which is derived from the dark color of the foliage. Recently, to commemorate the marriage of Dr. William N. Johnson, there was planted near this old fir tree an Apolinian silver fir. It is one of the rarest evergreens in cultivation. There are a number of other choice trees on the Johnson grounds, many of which were planted by Doctor Johnson, the original owner of the place, who was a well-known botanist and one of the early members of the Academy of Natural Sciences.

WILLIAM N. JOHNSON, M. D. (Contributed).

WILLIAM N. JOHNSON, M. D. was born in the Johnson homestead, Upsal, on the 10th of May, 1807. The rudiments of his education were obtained at home from his accomplished mother, and, when about 9 years of age he attended the Germantown Academy. Here he remained until 1823, when he entered Dickinson College. After attaining honors there in 1826, he matriculated at the University of Pennsylvania, Medical Department, graduating in 1829. In 1830 he went to Paris, at that time the greatest seat of medical learning in the world, where he applied himself assiduously to the continuance of his medical education. It was while here in the pursuit of his studies and investigations, that he contracted a most serious and almost fatal illness—septicaemia resulting from a dissection wound. He was attended most faithfully by his life-long friend, Dr. William Ashmead, lately deceased, to whose great skill and accurate judgment he owed his life. After completing his studies he extended his travels through Europe, and his admirable letters were copied by his mother in three volumes and preserved among his other papers. Upon his return after an absence of three years, he began his practice of medicine, which he successfully continued until within a few years of his death, when his poor health prohibited very active work. Courteous and courtly in manner, and grave and dignified in his demeanor, he endeared himself to his large circle of friends and patients. It may not be amiss to call attention to the fact, that he enjoyed his chief success in the practice of obstetrics. In 1836 he was elected to the Board of Directors of the Germantown Bank, where he remained an active member until his death, which occurred on June 22, 1870.

A two-story concrete house being torn down at Main and Johnson streets to make way for extensive improvements was erected prior to 1762, and the land is part of a tract conveyed through Francis Daniel Pastorius, to a Mr. Sprogel, in 1683.

Dr. James Mease's "Picture of Philadelphia," published by B. & T. Kite, No. 20 North Third street, A. D. 1811, has the following notice as to the Germantown drive:

NORTH ROUTE.

"The most direct way to Germantown, is to pass up Third street, at the extremity of which you meet the turnpike road, and at the distance of six miles from the city reach that healthful village. There are to be had the well-known woolen hosiery, which bear the name of the town, manufactured in the families of the German settlers. Germantown is a summer retreat for a number of citizens, and, except its airy and elevated situation, being on the first ridge after you leave Philadelphia, it has little to interest or detain strangers. From this town you may pass by several roads in a westwardly direction into what is called the Township line road, and thus vary the ride back to the city, which exhibits a fine view from the heights. Previously to leaving the Township line road and resuming the turnpike, into which it conducts you about two miles from Philadelphia, you may be gratified by visiting Upsal botanic garden, established and conducted by Bernard McMahon. This garden is near the junction of the Township line and Turnpike roads. When you have reached the city your ride will have been thirteen miles. If, when at Germantown, you wish to extend your excursion you may pass up the turnpike, through the village of Cresham, ascending as you proceed to Chestnut Hill, thence to the Perkiomen creek. A short distance from the bridge which crosses that stream, are the celebrated lead mines, well worth visiting. The mineralogist will be amply repaid by his visit to this place."

[Note as to Chestnut Hill: "From this place the view is extensive and picturesque."]

Mease speaks of Robeson's flour mills, and says of the Wissahickon: "The scenery up this creek is very romantic; the creek passes in a serpentine course among majestic hills, from the sides of which rocks in rude disorder impend over the stream."

He also mentions the oil mill at Falls Tavern, on the east side of the Schuylkill, as of interest, as well as the Spring Mill and the vineyard of the Pennsylvania Vine Company near it.

One of the most interesting points in Germantown is the southern corner of East Walnut Lane and Main street. Here lived the famous Dr. Christopher Witt. In the Leary edition of Watson's Annals there is a short account of him. (Vol. 1. p. 267, and Vol. 11, p. 22.) The references are to the 3 Vols. with Willis P. Hazard's additions. He was born in England in 1675, and came to America in 1704; and died in Germantown, 1765, aged 90 years. He was religious, but esteemed a diviner, as he cast nativities. But the Germans of that day, and many of the English did the same.

DR. WITT.

In Dr. J. J. Levick's addresses on the Early Physicians of Philadelphia, p. 16, Dr. Witt is named. Dr. Levick kindly referred me to Dr. Joseph H. Toner's Annals of Medical Science for further information. The pamphlet is in a volume of pamphlets in the Philadelphia Library, entitled "Orations, Addresses, etc." It speaks of him as being eccentric, and states his age to have been 99 years. The number of the book is 20,197. In Charles S. Keyser's book on Fairmount Park, p. 160, Bartram is referred to as saying as Mr. Jones has noted, that when Dr. Witt was in his garden he could not distinguish a leaf from a flower. He was then 86, and as the time named was 1761, and he died in 1769, the age of 99 above mentioned must be an error. A note in Mr. Keyser's book says that he was buried at the feet of Kelpius, at his own request, but this can not be, as Kelpius is said to have been buried on the Prowattain place, near his abode in Roxborough. Watson says that Dr. Witt translated Kelpius's German hymns into English poetry, line for line. (Vol. 1, p. 22.) He also states that he left his property to strangers who had been kind to him on his arrival in giving him a hat in place of one that he had lost on shipboard. (Vol. 2, p. 36.) He calls the family Warner.

Near the chancel of St. Michael's church in High street is the grave of Dr. Witt. I am indebted to Rev. Dr. Murphy, the rector, for information about this old burial place. The Warner family, as the name was spelled afterward, are buried here. The low rough stone which marks Dr. Witt's resting place shows no inscription now. One stone reads thus:

In Memory of
Doctr
Christopher Warner
Who departed this life
February 17th 1783
Aged 39 years &
4 months.

Here is another:

Memory
Doctor
Jonathan Warner
Who departed this life
December 24th 1793.
Aged 22 years & 1 month.

This is thought to be a son of the former. The stone supposed to mark Dr. Witt's grave is between Dr. Christopher Warner's grave and the rectory. The Warner name was also spelled Wermer and Werner. Two friends of Dr. Witt are thought to lie by his side; they are supposed also to have been disciples of Kelpius. They are now in the land where their mystic queries are answered. Those men give a poetic touch to the history of the quiet old town where they dwelt. Several members of the Warner family lie in the rear of

St. Michael's chancel. The reputation of magicians attached to them in the common mind. Two of the Warners we have seen bore the title of Doctor. Tacitus declared that everything unknown was esteemed magnificent, and while in some things these men may have been superstitious, as men are at all times, in other matters they may have been ahead of their times in knowledge. The Bible of Dr. Witt is in the possession of Louis D. Vail. It once contained a loose slip of old yellow paper with a record of the burial of the Warner family at St. Michael's church. Miss Clare owned the Bible for a long time. It was given to her by Mr. Lybrand, who bought it at the sale of the effects of the Warner family. She was a member of the Society of Friends. She and her sister lived next door to the Friends' Meeting-House on School Lane.

The Hon. Horatio Gates Jones takes a deep interest in the history of Germantown, which is near his home, and has contributed the following most valuable paper on

DR. CHRISTOPHER WITT.

ROXBOROUGH, May 8, 1886.

Dear Sir:—When I promised to give you some memoranda about Dr. Witt, I had no idea it would require so much research. This fact must explain my delay in the preparation of this paper. There is no doubt that Dr. Witt often visited Roxborough, especially to see his friend, John Kelpius, the Hermit of the Ridge, whose portrait, it is said, he painted, and which is now in the Historical Society of Pennsylvania, prefixed to the small volume containing the Latin Journal and several letters of Kelpius.* It is also probable that he visited "the last of the Hermits"—John Seligius, alias John Schlee, who lived on the farm of William Levering, a lineal ancestor of myself. His association with Roxborough leads me to feel that what I now am writing is part of the history of my native place.

This distinguished man was a native of Wiltshire, England, and came to America in the early part of the Eighteenth Century, and having imbibed the ideas of the Mystics became associated with John Kelpius, the famous "Hermit of the Ridge," and his associates. Of his early life and pursuits, nothing is known. As a believer in the Rosicrucian philosophy of his day, in which he indulged to a great extent, he became noted in Germantown as a Magus or Diviner, and taught Christopher Lehman and Fraley the mysteries of horoscopes, which made all of them noted in their day, giving to Dr. Witt the name of a "conjuror," because he "cast nativities," as Watson, the great annalist, tells us in his works. Be that as it may, Dr. Witt was a skillful physician, a man of science, a lover of Nature, while he lived in an age when learning was confined to the few, and the learned were regarded with great

---

* Mr. C. J. Wister is in possession of Kelpius's Journal, presented to his great-grandfather by Seligius. It is written in four languages—Latin, German, French and English.

awe. Dr. Witt was associated with many of the learned and scientific men both in America and England.

There is no doubt that he was a naturalist of no mean powers, as he corresponded with the well-known Peter Collinson, and was also an intimate friend of our early botanist, the celebrated John Bartram. Like many of the great men of the present day, Dr. Witt was exceedingly credulous, and dealt much in the marvelous, and, as we shall see, he anticipated some of the wonderful beliefs of the so-called "spiritualists" of the Nineteenth Century.

Mr. Watson says that Dr. Witt owned and dwelt in the three-story stone house in Germantown, now situated at the northeast corner of East Walnut lane and Main street. There is no doubt that he lived there and had in the rear of his house a garden which he cultivated and devoted to trees and plants of every variety and to which he made his friends welcome at all times.

As early as June 11, 1743, John Bartram, when writing to Peter Collinson, and after describing his visit to Dr. Witt's garden, which was filled with flowers and plants, says, "We went into his study, which was furnished with books containing different kinds of learning, as Philosophy, Natural Magic, Divinity, nay, even Mystic Divinity, all of which were the subjects of our discourse within doors, which alternately gave way to botany every time we walked in the garden. I could have wished thee the enjoyment of so much diversion, as to have heard our discourse, provided thee had been swathed from hips to armpits. But it happened that a little of our spiritual discourse was interrupted by a material object within doors; for the Doctor had lately purchased of a great traveller in Spain or Italy, a sample of what was imposed upon him for *Snake Stones*, which took me up a little time, besides laughing at him, to convince the Doctor that they were nothing but *calcined horse bones*. Indeed, to give the Doctor his due, he is pleasant, facetious and pliant."

Between Mr. Bartram and Dr. Witt there was no doubt a very warm friendship, as both were devoted to botany at a time when few persons in America understood the importance and value of plants, trees and flowers. On the 10th of December, 1745, Mr. Bartram, who had again been to Germantown to visit Dr. Witt, writes to Peter Collinson, and in his letter says, "Now though oracles be ceased, and thee hath not the spirit of divination, yet according to our friend Doctor Witt, we friends that love one another sincerely may, by an extraordinary spirit of sympathy, not only know each other's desires, but *may have a spiritual conversation at great distances one from another.*"

If Dr. Witt, one hundred and forty-one years since, proclaimed such peculiar views, there is no wonder that he was regarded even by John Bartram as a conjuror or wizard! But at this age of the world, when telegraphs, cables and telephones are drawing the whole world together and the remotest portions of the habitable globe seem close by us, we are more charitable and are apt to ascribe such a belief to the peculiar mental organization of Dr. Witt, and we are prone to believe that he may have had in his mind some of the grand discoveries of the present day.

About the year 1758, when he had reached the age of 83 years, Dr. Witt, was so unfortunate as to lose his eyesight, and in 1761 Bartram, who was warmly attached to his learned friend, visited Germantown and ministered to him as best he could, cheering him by his reports of news from Collinson and Fothergill and telling him of new plants which he may have lately discovered. About the same time Dr Witt made a visit to Bartram and no doubt the old philosopher's heart was full of quiet love and sympathy as he experienced the friendly act of a heart like that of John Bartram. His steps were slow and he needed the aid of a cane and perhaps the arm of his friend as they walked through the beautiful grounds. In a letter written by Bartram July 9, 1761, to Collinson, he says: "Poor old man! He was lately in my garden, but could not distinguish a leaf from a flower." He was then 86 years of age, and had outlived all or nearly all of his contemporaries who were here when he arrived. Among the first to die was the learned mystic, John Kelpius, the famous "Hermit of the Ridge," of whom it is said Dr. Witt was a devout follower and whose portrait he painted, as may be seen in a manuscript volume now in the Historical Society of Pennsylvania, and a lithograph I had made for my book entitled "The Levering Family" in 1858. Of Kelpius I have not time now to write, but may at some future time. Of him even the gentle Whittier, in his poem entitled "The Pennsylvania Pilgrim," speaks as

> "Painful Kelpius from his hermit's den,
> By Wissahickon, maddest of good men."

Then followed Matthias and last Johannes Seligius, or John Sehlee, better known as John Selig, who died on the farm of my great-great-grandfather, William Levering, of Roxborough, April 26, 1745. This hermit was, like his friend Dr. Witt a, "diviner," and Mr. Watson says there was a tradition about him to this effect that he directed that when he died his "divining rod" should be cast into water. This was done and the rod exploded with a loud noise! *Credat Judæus Appella.*

Among his effects, he had 25 shirts, 54 glass bottles, 5 Bibles, 10 of Jacob Boehman's books and 150 Latin, Dutch and Greek books, all of which, I regret to say, have disappeared.

As Dr. Witt felt the feebleness of age, like a sensible man, who had no relatives to inherit his property, he made his will, while in the possession of all his faculties, at the age of 86 years. It bears date, November 7, 1761, and extracts therefrom should be of interest to the citizens of Germantown, where he was once such a prominent character. He describes himself as a "Practitioner of Physick." He gives to the Pennsylvania Hospital £60. He manumits from "slavery and servitude" his mulatto servant "commonly known as Robert Claymer, and also gives to him a certain tract of land in Germantown on the north side of Keyser's lane, which I bought of Adam Holt." "Also to said mulatto Robert, all my tools, instruments and utensils belonging to or appertaining to the making of watches and also my great clock which strikes every quarter. Also all household goods belonging to me which shall be found at the time of my decease, in my old house where I formerly lived next door above Andrew Keyser's (alias Pistorias)." The rest of my estate real and personal he gives to "my well beloved friend Christian Warner of Germantown with whom I now live." He appoints as his executors his "loving friends Richard Johnson and Christian Warner."

From the inventory of his personal property filed in the office of the Register of Wills at Philadelphia, I give a few items, which show very plainly that the learned Doctor in addition to his profession as a physician, followed other occupations, as was often done in early times, and that he possessed a taste for music and for the making of clocks. In this particular however he did not equal his old neighbor and acquaintance, Christopher Sauer, who, it is said by Mr. Townsend Ward in one of his "Walks to Germantown," followed from fifteen to twenty occupations." *

In the list of Dr. Witt's goods I find a *Telescope, an Organ,* † *Virginals, Mathematical Instruments, Library and Prospect Glasses, Drugs, Medicines and Utensils belonging to the Apothecary and Doctor's way, Two Clocks, a Clock and Clockmaker's tools.* The value of his personalty was £314 5s. 6d., which at that time was no small sum.

Dr. Witt died in January, 1765, at the advanced age of ninety years and was buried on his own ground in Germantown, according to the statement of Mr. Watson, and tradition points out the house and grounds at the northeast corner of Main street and East Walnut lane as the place where he lived and died. A recent visit to this spot naturally recalled the famous man. It was easy to imagine him as walking in his once beautiful garden, leaning on the arm of his "loving friend," Christian Warner, or attended by his faithful servitor, Robert Claymer, the mulatto, whom he remembered so generously in his will, and who no doubt was constantly with him during his seven years of blindness. As I looked at the old trees still standing there, some of which were most likely planted by the Doctor I tried to see if any of his garden walks were visible, but alas they had disappeared. No longer are heard the solemn notes of his organ, nor the weird sounds of the Virginals, but all was silent as the grave and only memory could attach to the place any special interest. Pity indeed that there are no traces of his organ, or virginals, or the telescope, or the "great clock that strikes the quarters." Master and loving friends and devoted servant have gone to their heavenly rest, and there no doubt the great and learned man is surrounded by his loved ones, by the devout Kelpius and Seligius and Matthias and Pastorius and Bartram, where all that was so dim and obscure here has been made clear. Peace be to his memory.

Watson's reference to the Blair House is in Vol. 2, p. 32, but I think the chronicler was mistaken, unless there was a previous building on the site,

---

* Pennsylvania Historical Magazine, Vol. 5, p. 369, Ward says that Sauer was bred a tailor in Germany, and acquired proficiency in thirty other pursuits.

† A Virginal was a keyed instrument of one string, jack and quill to each note like a spinet, but in shape resembling the piano forte.

though Mr. Jones's remarks on the garden may not be wide of the mark if his garden was near the Warner houses. In Watson's Appendix to Vol. 2, p. 554, after the battle of Germantown, Lieutenant Whitman, of Reading, who was wounded, is spoken of as a patient of Dr. Witt.

POMONA GROVE.

I am indebted to JAS. DUVAL RODNEY, ESQ., for the following sketch:

Next to the Ax burying ground (formerly the Upper Burying Ground) and the Concord school house is POMONA GROVE, owned now by Amos R. Little, and rented by the Misses Davis. This place is best known as Duval's place and as such is referred to, in Watson's Annals. It was owned at the time of the Battle of Germantown by Christopher Huber and formed part of the battle-field. Many an unsung hero of either side was quietly buried within its limits. The old springhouse at the fish pond now replaced by a modern grotto (the spring remains the best water of the neighborhood) was the rallying point of some of the Virginia troops. Watson mentions that in 1832 Captain George Blackmore, of the Virginia Line, made his acquaintance and desired to go over the battle field where he had fought side by side with his brother who was killed and left at that spring-house. Mr. Watson says: "He wanted to find the place again and shed a tear. He had some difficulty to find the places and positions in his memory, so changed since by elegant improvements. It was a feeling concern to travel once more with his eyes and explanations over the tented field to book the dead." I gave him a leaden bullet picked out of Chew's door and introduced him to Mr. Jacob Keyser, who had helped to bury his brother and four other soldiers in one hole near the spring-house; they were buried in their uniforms. The house was occupied at one time by army tailors making up clothing. The shoemakers and smiths would go in squads to the shops of the town and use the tools found there for their work, in which the owners would readily join, not always from generous motives, but for the sake of keeping an eye on their tools and materials. From the Hubers the place passed into the hands of William Shoemaker, hatter, a son of the Councillor and a brother of the Mayor (Samuel), who was so conspicuous a figure in Revolutionary history. Mr. Watson speaks of Samuel as the owner of the place, but the legal title was certainly in William, for he and his wife Martha (she was a Brown, of Moreland) conveyed to Col. Forrest. Possibly William held it for Samuel's beneficial interest, as Samuel's relations about that time with the State prevented his holding property. Col. Forrest purchased it in 1788 of William, aforesaid. Colonel F. was a well-known citizen and altogether a remarkable man. There is no particular interest attached to this country place. It has been owned for more than a century by retired merchants, gentlemen of leisure, who, being without political aspirations or scientific tendencies, have left no mark on the social landscape, with the single exception of Col. Forrest, who purchased it after he

THE RODNEY HOUSE, AT ONE TIME OCCUPIED BY JOHN KEYSER.

resigned from the Army of the United States. He was always a prominent man and must have possessed a superior mind, for although all we know of him (he had no biographer) we get from anecdotes, yet his character, veiled as it often was in eccentricity of dress and apparent frivolity, exhibits a basis of shrewd wisdom and clever methods of expression. The nearest point he reached to memorial notice was to have his autograph affixed to what is claimed, on the best authority, to be a bogus portrait in the Pennsylvania Archives. It may not be out of place in this article to relate a few anecdotes, which, taken together, give a good idea of the man, and may of themselves interest many who read them in this shape for the first time, as illustrating that era.

The first mention made of Forrest as a soldier is as raising in 1775-6 a company dressed as Indians, with painted faces, leggings and plumes. This eccentric episode must have lasted only a short time, for we learn that on the fourteenth of August, 1776, Captain Thos. Forrest was made Captain of the Second Company, of Captain Thomas Proctor's Company of Pennsylvania Artillery. On the fourth of the next December he was detailed by Major Proctor to start from Philadelphia and go to Trenton to place himself and company at George Washington's disposal. On the 26th we find him in close companionship with Washington, for we have the following anecdote: The column, headed by Washington, reached the enemy's outposts exactly at eight o'clock, and within three minutes he heard the firing from Sullivan's division. "Which way is the Hessian picket?" asked Washington of a man chopping wood at his door. The surly reply came back: "I don't know." "You may tell, cried out Captain Forrest, of the artillery, for this is General Washington." The aspect of the man at once changed, and raising his hands toward Heaven, he exclaimed: "God bless and prosper your Excellency, the picket is in that house there, the sentinel under that tree there."

The good service performed by Captain Forrest's Company is described in a letter written by one of his Lieutenants, Patrick Duffey, to the Mayor, under date of December 28, he says: "I have the pleasure to inform you that yesterday we arrived in Trenton, after a fatiguing engagement, in which the artillery gets applause. I had the honor of being detached up the Main street in front of the savages, without any other piece, and sustained the fire of several guns from the houses on each side of the street, without the least loss. Captain Forrest reports on the same date that "the artillery captured a complete band of music and that they expected to go on another expedition across the river." (What a boon he would be in these days, this excellent extinguisher of German bands.) Forrest reached the rank of Lieutenant Colonel and resigned as such May 9, 1783.

After he purchased this place from William Shoemaker, he added to the buildings and started the cultivation of trees and fruit. He astonished the world by his indifference to social claims. His carelessness in dress and manners appeared to have no limit. He sometimes took his produce to market himself, though under no necessity to do so. Sometimes he drove a four-in-hand team of bulls. Perhaps this was on one occasion only, when Chestnut street was filled with his fellow members of Congress for some reason, and he selected that day with care. Once he had advertised for a gardener, and whilst walking about his grounds in the simplest attire, even to being barefoot, he saw a stranger approach, who asked: "Where is Colonel Forrest?" "What do you want with him?" he replied. "I wish to be engaged as gardener, he needs one I hear. I have excellent credentials from some of the highest gentlemen in England, where I have lived in the best places." "What is that under your arm?" "An umbrella." "How do you use it?" It was raised. "What is it for?" "To keep off the sun and rain." The Colonel moved the applicant gently out of the gate, saying, "You have seen Col. Forrest; he does not need a gardener who is afraid of sun and rain." (It may be remembered that up to the end of the Eighteenth Century umbrellas were looked upon as dudish and their use quite uncommon.)

Colonel Forrest attacked in his peculiar manner a prevailing tendency to belief in divination and witchcraft, and the following extract from Watson's Annuals, Vol. 1. p. 268, states *inter alia:* "Colonel Thomas Forrest had been, in his early days, a youth of much frolic and fun, always well disposed to give time and application to forward a joke. He found much to amuse himself with, in the credulity of the German families. When he was about twenty-one years of age, a tailor, who was measuring him for a suit of clothes, happened to say, "Ah, Thomas, if we could only find some of the money of the sea robbers we could drive our coach for life." The sincerity and simplicity with which he uttered this caught the attention of young Forrest, and when he went home he began to devise some scheme to derive amusement from it. There was then a prevailing belief that the pirates had hidden many sums of money about the banks of the Delaware. Forrest got an old parchment on which he wrote the dying testimony of one John Hendricks, executed at Tyburn for piracy, in which he stated he had deposited a chest and pot of money at Cooper's Point, in the Jersies. This parchment he smoked and gave to it the appearance of antiquity; and calling on his German tailor, he told him he had found it among his father's papers, who had gotten it in England from the prisoner whom he had visited in prison. This he showed to the tailor as a precious paper which he could not let go from his hand. This had the desired effect. Soon after the tailor called on Forrest with one Ambruster, a printer, whom he introduced as capable of "printing any spirit out of hell," by his knowledge of the black art. He asked to show him the parchment; he was delighted with it and confidently said he could conjure Hendricks to give up the money. A time was appointed to meet in an upper room of a public house, in Philadelphia, by night, and the innkeeper was let into the secret by Forrest. By the night appointed they had had prepared, by a closet, a communication with a room above their sitting room, so as to lower down, by a pulley, the invoked ghost, who was represented by a young man entirely sewed up in a close white dress, on which were painted black-eyed sockets, mouth and bare ribs, with dashes of black between them, the outside and inside of the legs and thighs blackened so as to make white bones conspicuous there. About twelve persons in all were there around a table. Ambruster shuffled and read out cards, on which were inscribed the names of the New Testament Saints, telling them he should bring Hendricks to encompass the table, visible or invisible he could not tell. At the words, "*John Hendricks du verfluctcr cum herans,*" the pulley was heard to reel, the closet door to fly open and John Hendricks with ghastly appearance stood forth. The whole party were dismayed and fled, save Forrest, the brave. After this Ambruster, on whom they all depended, declared that he had by spells got permission to take up the money. A time was fixed when they were to go to the Jersey shore and there dig by night for the treasure. The parchment said it lay between two great stones. Forrest prepared two black men entirely naked, except white petticoat breeches, and these were to jump each on a stone when they came in digging near the pot, which had been previously put there. These frightened off the company for a little while. When they next assayed they were assailed by cats tied two and two, to whose tails were tied spiral papers of gunpowder, which illuminated and whizzed, while the cats wauled. The pot was at last got up and brought in great triumph to Philadelphia wharf; but oh, sad disaster! while helping it out of the boat Forrest, who managed it and was handing it up to the tailor, trod upon the gunwale and filled the boat, and holding on to the pot, dragged the tailor into the river and it was lost! For years afterwards they reproached Forrest with its loss and declared he had got the treasure himself and was enriched thereby. He favored the conceit until at last they actually sued him in a writ of treasure trove, but their lawyer was persuaded to give up the case.

Some years afterward Forrest wrote a play in two acts called "Disappointment; or the Force of Credulity," which was published in New York over the nom de plume of "Antony Barker, Esq." It was quite clever but gave offense for various causes and was not represented on the stage. For many years he kept up his reputation for hexing (conjuring). He always kept a hazel rod scraped and smoked with which to divine where money was hid. Once he lent it to a man, who for its use gave a cartload of potatoes to the poor house. A decent storekeeper got him to hex his wife, who fancied she had been bewitched and had swallowed a piece of linsey-woolsey. He cured her by strong emetics and showing her a wet piece of linsey-woolsey. He touched a thief with cow-itch and by contemporaneous remarks induced, as the itching began, a full confession. These circumstances got about and made him quite famous. It will be seen that Forrest carried on a well-regulated crusade against a prevailing superstition. In strong contrast to practical jokes, we have the following exhibitions of sentiment; the first is this: When the Army was encamped at Valley Forge it was joined by a New Jersey regiment, mostly farmers, who were, as Forrest discovered, in deadly fear of smallpox. Forrest rose one morning early and wrote with a piece of chalk upon the doors of all the huts which faced the Jerseymen, "Smallpox here!" The consequence was that each Jerseyman as he came out of his hut in the morning read the inscription, and without communicating with his fellows at once put on his hat and deserted. By roll-call the whole regiment was gone. Washington discovered that Forrest was the joker, and at parade gave him a very severe public reprimand from which Forrest never recovered, and hated Washington until his death; but it is said that after Washington died Forrest often showed great emotion at the sight of the likeness of his quondam friend, and his regret over the occurrence greatly contributed to the cause of his retirement first from military, then from social life.

The second occurred at a reception given to the Marquis Lafayette during his last visit to this country. Col. Forrest, one of the Revolutionary officers, upon being presented, burst into tears, when Judge Peters, who was standing by the Marquis, dryly observed: "Why, Tom, I thought you were a forest tree, but you turn out to be a weeping willow." In 1811, Col. Forrest sold his place to Mr. Duval and moved to a property near Branchtown, which he owned. His life was saddened by the death of his only son, and his retirement was caused by that and the marriage of his only daughter to Dr. Samuel Betton, the father of Dr. Thomas Forrest Betton and grandfather of Samuel Betton, Esq., all of White Cottage, Manheim street. Col. Forrest was elected to the XVIth Congress, was defeated by Henry Baldwin for the XVIIth, but was afterward elected to fill a vacancy in the same. He was a regular attendant upon Friends' Meeting and used their dress. His footsteps were not by any means noiseless on his entrance; he had a habit of making all the noise he could, so that they might know he had come. He died in 1825. He was a citizen of the State in Schuylkill (member of the Fish House) from 1790 until 1800.

In 1811, Col. Forrest sold his place to Mr. James S. Duval, a retired French merchant of Philadelphia, who added greatly to the mansion and built other out buildings for various purposes, and upon the already good basis of fruit and tree culture, he constructed a veritable Pomona Grove, as he called it. His taste lay in the direction of trees and fruit of all kinds. His constant intercourse with France and his ability to pay for a fancy permitted him to lay the French Pomona under constant contribution, and for years scarcely a vessel arrived, from France or her colonies which did not bring something to beautify his home. His gardens and lawns were stocked with the rarest fruits and trees. Many varieties remained for years almost unique. A few memorials of Forrest and Duval remain, but "with the new masters came the new men." In this instance they came as landscape gardening fiends, and most of the natural and fostered beauty of the place has been sacrificed to achieve a result in symmetry which is, at best, only suggestive of an ordinary inter-mural park.

Next is the residence of the Rev. John Rodney, rector Emeritus of St. Luke's Church. Mr. Rodney married Mr. Duval's daughter, and has lived with his wife here since 1829, with the exception of a few years when they resided at Pomona Grove. They celebrated their golden wedding in 1879, and continue in good health, he in his ninetieth and she in her eighty-sixth year. The first occupant of the present house was Mr. Samuel Wagner, who married another daughter of Mr. Duval. They also lived to celebrate their golden wedding. The upper end of the house was the John Keyser house, and is old. The new house was built into it, as it were, and the old part from the upper wall to the new house is unchanged and the peculiarities of its internal architecture remain. The old double shop door forms part of the partition in the same position as formerly, when it was ready to be used on the approach of a customer. Mr. Watson says of this house: "Jacob Keyser, now an aged citizen of about eighty-nine years, was then a lad (Battle of Germantown). He with his father's family lived where is now the house of Rev. Mr. Rodney. Its high position above the street enabled them by placing an apple under the cellar door to peep abroad and see the battle in the opposite field distinctly." The march of municipal improvements has made the cellar higher than ever, but the door and the apple are things of the past.

THE MANUAL LABOR SCHOOL.

The Rev. Dr. Blair, a Presbyterian clergyman, who aided in the founding of the First Presbyterian Church, though he was not its pastor, lived in the historic house at East Walnut lane already spoken of in our last article. Services were held in his house at the beginning of the enterprise. He is buried in the graveyard in the rear of the Young Men's Christian Association Building, which was the edifice of that church before the new building was erected on Chelten avenue.

The Manual Labor School afterward occupied the house in which Dr. Blair had lived. The Rev. Dr. J. P. Tustin, who was a pupil there, has given me some information on the subject. Rev. Dr. George Junkin, afterward President of Washington and Lee University, was the head of the institution. Mrs. Prescott, the authoress and poet, was his daughter. Another daughter was Mrs. Hannah Jackson. George Junkin, Esq., of Walnut street, is his son. The school was under the Old School Presbyterians. There was a number of wooden buildings for its use, which have disappeared. There were as many as one hundred and fifty students at one time, and the corner must have presented a busy scene in those days when so many young and earnest hearts enlivened it. Some of the students became eminent, and doubtless in after life threw many a glance backward at the scene of toil of head and hands. The school merged into Lafayette College, at Easton, Pa. It was conducted in Germantown from 1830 to 1833. The Rev. Dr. McCay, afterward President of the University of South Carolina, was a professor. Rev. David X. Junkin was another professor. He was a pastor in Chicago afterward. The pupils taught Sunday school classes where they could find such good work. Some taught in the Baptist Church in Roxborough, three miles distant. Thirty years afterward the Hon. Horatio Gates Jones had the pleasure of meeting his former Sunday school teacher, the Rev. Charles F. McCay, just mentioned. The scholar recognized the teacher's name on a hotel record.

The Manual Labor School system has not generally succeeded in this country. It was tried at Lane Theological Seminary, near Cincinnati, and at Bristol College, but the plan did not work, though adverse circumstances may have helped to obstruct it. The system succeeded well in Mt. Holyoke Female School, under the indefatigable Miss Lyon. Manual Labor Schools have lately been introduced in connection with the public school system in Chicago, Toledo, Philadelphia and Baltimore. See article in *Harper's Monthly*, February, 1886. In France the system has been a success. There is need that head and hands should work together to make a fair equipoise, and it is sinful to strain the poor brain by constant effort. I know a clergyman who is an amateur wood carver, and he must find pleasant relief from professional toil in such work, while his house is beautified as the result. There is a foolish idea for a republic that labor is degrading, as if an idle man could be more respectable than a busy one. The Jews were right in teaching their children trades so that they might be in condition to support themselves if need arose. The biography of Rev. George Junkin, D. D., LL. D., by D. X. Junkin, D. D., gives an account of the present school.

Some philanthropic gentlemen in and around Philadelphia, who were Presbyterians, inaugurated this institution to aid in educating young men for the ministry. Manual labor was introduced for health and economy. Dr. Junkin had tried the system in a small way in his last parish in Milton, Pa., and had much heart in the scheme. He was qualified for a leader in the work as combining two rare qualifications, those of a literary scholar and of a man skillful in mechanics and agriculture. After Dr. Junkin took charge of the school an abundance of students came until accommodations failed. The Doctor showed energy and decision in his laborious position. Many young men followed him from the region of the Susquehanna, whence he had come. Still the fearful question of needed funds stared him in the face, and the institution was in debt. It is easier to raise money when a good per cent is expected than when benevolence calls and the reward is to wait until the next world. There was a farm and workshops, and the responsibility fell on the Doctor of carrying on the whole concern when the school alone was enough to tax his powers. He continued the drag for twenty months, and helped to educate many who have since stood high in learned professions and State and National councils.

There were literary societies and other aids, which gave the school the nature of a college. Prof. McCay was a fine scholar and a philosopher, and was the efficient coadjutor of Dr. Junkin in instruction. He became Professor of Natural History in the University of Georgia, and President of the College of South Carolina. Dr. Junkin's brother, the writer of the biography, was also an instructor.

A year's experiment showed that Germantown was not the place for the work. Living was as dear as in the city. The materials for the workshop must be bought at city prices, and brought out over the turnpike at heavy tolls with great cost, and the manufactures must be returned to the city at similar cost to compete with the products of city workmen. Packing boxes were made as at Bristol College. These, with trunks, constituted the principal articles of industry. The students were paid by the hour, and the loss fell on the school. A site on the Delaware, above Philadelphia, was selected for removal, where there would be water transportation. That plan, however, was not carried out, but the result was the founding of Lafayette College.

In addition to his heavy school work Dr. Junkin preached in Germantown, or Philadelphia, or elsewhere, on Sundays, and held a Bible class and weekly prayer meeting at the school, and was ready to aid in Christian work. His Bible classes were very instructive, and he gave theological information in them. The Rev. Dr. William Neill was then pastor of the Germantown Presbyterian Church, and their intercourse was fraternal.

Lafayette College was chartered in 1826. Through the influence of Dr. Steel, of Abington, who was an influential clergyman, Dr. Junkin was elected President in 1832. In April of this year Dr. Junkin removed to Easton to enter upon his new duties. The professors and nearly all of the students of the Manual Labor Academy went with him. He tried the manual labor system at Lafayette at first, earnestly believing that mind, body and spirit should all be educated. He gave money and toil to carry it out, but when he went from that college to take the presidency of Miami University the system was abandoned.

In Easton temporary buildings were erected by the hands of the students for increasing the number of pupils till more permanent edifices arose. So the manual labor did practical good, and those who occupy the fine buildings that now crown the hill at Easton, and who enjoy the fruits of Mr. Pardee's liberality, should sometimes think of "the day of small things" and remember good Dr. Junkin. His biographer gives the secret of his success in these words: "Dr. Junkin was a man of strong faith in Christ and of much prayer."

A bronze tablet to the memory of Dr. Junkin has been placed in Lafayette College. Prof. Thos. C. Porter, LL. D., delivered an address at its unveiling in May. A. D. '87. Rev. Chas. Elliott, D. D., made the presentation, and Rev. President Knox received it on behalf of the College. Dr. Junkin was the father-in-law of General "Stonewall" Jackson.

The three-story house at the lower corner of East Walnut lane and Main street, occupied by the Misses Burkhart, and owned by the heirs of George W. Carpenter, stands on ground as high as the steeple of the State House. It was built by the Rev. Dr. Blair. The academy farm extended in the rear of the house and covered many acres.

Let us step into Squire Thomas's office and learn from him the history of this most interesting corner. On September 12, 1749, Christain Warmer (so the name is there spelled), makes a will which is proved November 4, A. D. 1768. His wife was named Lydia. The will shows that Christopher Witt formerly granted the property to him. It refers to the former owner, John Doeden, who owned lot seventeen, east side, as marked on Ward's copy of the old draught of Germantown, while on that Wermer (so written) and Andreas Souplis owned lot eighteen just north of it. Dr. Witt appears to have owned where two Warmer houses stood, though his line may have been below the site of the Blair house. The old shoe shop, lately demolished, was one of the Warmer houses. Warmer also owned land above East Walnut lane. Elizabeth Warmer married John Leibert. Christian willed the old shoe shop to his daughter. The house below, occupied by John Kerrigan and owned by Miss Haines, was also her property. A deed marked April 1, 1775, conveyed the corner to Dr. William Shippen. Dr. Blair buys of Leibert and other administrators, who represent the Warmer estate. The Warmer will referred to speaks of the wall of the graveyard at St. Michael's Church, which was a family burial place. Rev. Dr. Blair married Dr. William Shippen's daughter Susanna. Her father gives her a house and fifty-seven acres of land at this point. She conveys this to her husband. He wills everything to his wife, who survives him. Mrs. Frances Pierce, daughter of Dr. Blair, afterward lives here. This house is styled, "The Mansion House." Dr. Shippen was buried from this house. There was a famous funeral. A Warmer house stood on the site of Dr. Deaver's residence, No. 5075. I believe that it is thought that Dr. Witt lived with the Warmers.

The Pierces sell to Samuel Bucknell, a manufacturing jeweler, in 1827. In 1829 he conveyes the property to the Manual Labor Academy Association. The school had forty-two acres. On May 5, 1832, the Association conveys to James Ogilbe. The same year he orders by will that it shall be sold within a year of his death. The intention was that it should be Congress Hall Hotel. It was afterward called "Our House," and was kept by Col. Alexander as a branch of his city hotel for summer use. The executors sell at public sale and Samuel Bucknell buys the property the second time. He sells again this year, '32, to Wm. E. & Zenas Wells. It afterwards falls into Col. Alexander's hands. Chas. Harlan became owner in 1850 and in 1851 sold to Charlotte Cushman with sixty acres more belonging to Dr. Philip Physic's estate, which fronted on Washington lane. Streets were opened in 1852 by 'Squire Thomas, by direction of Miss Cushman.

The following letter finishes the account of the famous Blair House, although it should be added that it was once used as a Ladies' School. It certainly has had many vicissitudes:

GEORGETOWN, D. C.

TOWNSEND WARD, ESQ.—*Dear Sir:*—My aunt Miss Susan Shippen Roberdeau has written what she could recall of the Blair house, which I transcribe as follows:

"The Blair house was purchased by Dr. Wm. Shippen the elder, as a farm of many acres. [Watson in his Annals says, p. 32 of Vol. II., this house was once the residence of a Dr. Witt, a sort of conjurer. Witt is mentioned also on pages 22 and also I, 267.—R. B.] When the British entered Philadelphia [1777] the family fled to Jersey, where my great-grandfather had large possessions. [One large tract called Oxford Furnace was in 1809 or thereabouts sold to Judge Morris Robeson and has been the home of that family ever since. Judge Robeson was the father of Secretary of Navy, George M. Robeson.] A skirmish was fought in the Blair house, during the battle of Germantown, and the building used as a hospital. The room I slept in had the mark of bullets in the wall, and the print of a man's foot in blood on the floor. My grandmother [Mrs. Dr. Blair] would not have it removed. After the battle Lord Cornwallis told my grandmother he preserved the sofa and used it for his bed when his soldiers were destroying everything [this must have been not at the Battle of Germantown where Lord Howe commanded, but at the entrance of the English Army into Philadelphia for Lord Cornwallis was in command there].

"Dr. Shippen's town house [Dr. Shippen *the elder*], my grandfather's, was at the corner of Fourth and Market Streets, where he practiced his profession. The Blair house in Germantown is now a boarding house [it having passed out of the family many years ago]. The "bow room" at the side was built by Dr. Shippen but an extension has since been built to accommodate the boarders. The garden extended towards Philadelphia filled with rare plants and trees. The grounds also extended back a long distance to the township line. [My mother, Mrs. F. Selina Buchanan adds this last clause. I do not know the distance of the township line, but Miss Elizabeth C. Morris, an old resident, deceased some 15 years ago, told me the grounds extended back to a creek, pointing it out to me. It must have been half a mile off.—R. B] The house on the other side [northwest] was built by Dr. Blair for his son, Samuel Blair, Jr. [Walnut street, which runs between these two houses and close to the Blair house has been cut through of late years.] In the house beyond, Andrew Heath lived, whose name was coupled with that of Melchior Meng, 'For old times,' as the song goes.

"The church on Main street, now the Y. M. C. A., was built on ground given by my grandfather [Dr. Blair]. My father [Isaac Roberdeau afterward Lieut. Col. U. S. A., and chief of the Bureau of Topographical Engineers, was the architect. The Bureau was organized under his supervision in 1818. He was placed at the head of it where he remained until his death in 1829.] The organ which was imported from England, had two angels with wings extended one on each side, as large as life. One holding a trumpet, the other a lyre. My childish imaginations thought the music came from them. They were indeed beautiful.

"I wish I could distinctly remember the stories told me of the Blair house; it was always said to be haunted. [The belief in haunted houses was common in those days according to Watson. *I think* I have read in his Annals a confirmatory statement that the Blair house was thought to be haunted, but a search recently has failed to find the passage.] Ghosts were seen, servants were always talking of the ghosts they had seen in the cellar; soldiers with swords walking round. Myself and sisters were born in that house. Mrs. Washington who was a friend of the family used to visit at this house."

The above is my aunt's own writing save the portions in brackets which I have added myself.

The relationships may be more clear to you from the following pedigree:

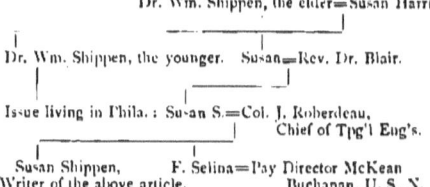

Biographies of these will be found in my genealogies of the Roberdeau and of the Shippen families which you have in the Library.

Of Dr. Blair, I may say, he was an exceedingly talented and learned man, and a fine Greek and Latin scholar. In fact all of the Blair family have been talented. To this family belong the Montgomery Blair, Postmaster General under Lincoln, and his brother the late Gen. F. P. Blair. Also Vice President John C. Breckenridge, who is a grandson of Rev. Dr. Samuel Stanhope Smith; besides others of less note.

Dr. Shippen was wealthy, and said his daughter should not marry any one who could not lay down "guinea for guinea." His daughter however was not of the same mind, but preferred the talented young divine who could not lay down a copper farthing to his father-in-law's guineas. The marriage proved a very happy one, and they lived to celebrate their golden wedding, and to reach the ages of 77 and 78 respectively.

I remain, yours very truly,

ROBERDEAU BUCHANAN.

P. S.—The stone house, the first or second [on Main street, S. W. side] below Tulpehocken, Mrs. Roberdeau lived in for about a year after her husband's death.

Among Ward's papers was this note:

PHILADELPHIA, March 30, 1758.

"Last Wednesday, the 22d instant between 10 and 11 o'clock P. M. a slight earthquake was noticed here.

"At the same time the earthquake was felt at Germantown; some say, they felt a shock twice within two minutes. Some were enough shaken to get awake and know at once it was an earthquake. It has not yet been heard how far it extended. Also the following:

"Those of my readers who may have perused George Ordi's delightful life of Alexander Wilson, will be interested in the fact that the great Naturalist was once in love with a Miss Rittenhouse, who lived on this ancient lane. Neither of them ever married, and at his death, Wilson left her a chest of papers and drawings. In time she too passed away, and many years afterwards, one of her family parted with what remained in the chest to Mr. Wm. Redwood Wright. Among the scraps was an account of an early immigrant, Michael Hinego, written in the year 1811, by an appreciative acquaintance. Fortunately the account is accompanied with a water-color drawing of the subject, who was clad in a blue coat. By the engraving, we have a veritable representation of the costume of at least one of the men of Pennsylvania's earlier days. The brief preface is, "Mr. Wilson may make an interesting picture of these barren incidents which we have collected from the old man, as he is congenially disposed in some things. His memory begins to fail him, and it is not easy to communicate with him." I have thought it would not be proper to take any liberty with the quite creditable production of an unknown author:

"Michael Hinego was born in the year 1726, in the county of Hanau in the Circle of the Lower Rhine, Germany. He received a tolerable education, but the death of his parents before his sixteenth year blasted his hopes and expectations, the political convulsions which then agitated Germany, having extended their fatal influence to the place of his nativity. Persecuted and oppressed by the hand of despotism, with that regret which characterizes a feeling heart, in his twentieth year, he forever relinquished the scenes ' where in early life he sported,' and from the desolation and distraction of wars sought an asylum in the peaceful and far distant wilds of America; poor, friendless and unenterprising, he avoided society and resided for some years after his arrival on the banks of the Delaware near Trenton;—his subsistence there was chiefly ' the fortune of the chase.' Sometime after he chose for his residence a small spot of ground in York county, Pennsylvania, which he purchased and where he now resides.

"His residence is on the sloping side of a rich valley open to the morning sun surrounded by wastes and barrens. Remote from man he passed his days in converse with the warblers of the wood and field. During the summer months, the wild retired situation of his little farm renders it the retreat of thousands of the feathered tribes. By the help of curiously constructed traps he can make himself master of any bird that passes him. His house is quite an aviary. He is a man of observation, intelligent, honest and well disposed. He is pleased with those who occasionally visit him and is extremely hospitable and generous. He is well acquainted with the history and habits of most of the birds that frequent the country around. A scanty gleaning from the little farm, with some fine fruits, constitute his subsistence.

He is now in his eighty-fifth year, and from his temperate habits and hardy constitution may survive many years. Once or twice in a year he visits the town of York dressed in an antiquated, fanciful manner. He brought his dress from Germany and sets high value on it.

"Beginning to feel the infirmities of old age, some years ago he was persuaded to take to himself a partner who, like himself, had had little intercourse with the world. (Mr. Wilson has seen her, and the power of her charms he would be fully sensible of.) His singularities consist chiefly in his solitary habits—cut off from the world—in his hermitage only he feels happy and independent. The reasons (for this) one could not learn from him. He is a man of reflection, and possibly becoming disgusted with the bustle, care and strife attending a connection with society, he sought a peaceful retreat 'where every grove is melody and every gale is peace.' He delights in the healthier air of uncultivated nature, particularly in the music of birds. In his morning walks he is saluted with the wild warbles of the wood robin and his evening retreat is cheered with the mellow notes of the thrush and mocking bird.

"A few years ago a singular circumstance induced his claiming the assistance of social institutions. He is expert in snaring foxes and other noxious animals that disturb his musical retreat. He had placed a large fox-trap in a retired place in the wood. An ill-disposed person who lived near him, whom he suspected for having frequently pilfered his fruits and robbed his traps, was caught in the trap. He carried it home with him, and Hinego, having some presumption against him, sued him. Not being able to make out his case fully, judgment was however against him. His presumptions afterwards proved to be right, and his opponent, greatly to the old man's satisfaction, left the country."

THE CHEW HOUSE AND THE BATTLE OF GERMANTOWN.

> "Down the dark future, through long generations,
>   The echoing sounds grow fainter and then cease;
> And, like a bell, with solemn, sweet vibrations,
>   I hear once more the voice of Christ say, 'Peace!'"
>
> "Peace! and no longer from its brazen portals
>   The blast of war's great organ shakes the skies!
> But beautiful as songs of the immortals,
>   The holy melodies of love arise."
>
> —*Longfellow*.

For more than a century the Chew house has been an object of curious interest to visitors to Germantown. Watson tells us that Penington's country house occupied the site before the Chews obtained it, and that "the present kitchen wings of Chew's house sufficed for the simplicity of gentlemen of those days." The present dwelling is familiar from the various pictures of it which have appeared, so that those who have never visited it have been made

THE CHEW HOUSE, FROM "THOMPSON WESTCOTT'S HISTORIC MANSIONS OF PHILADELPHIA," PUBLISHED BY PORTER & COATES.

acquainted with its outer aspect. The cut which illustrates this article is obtained by the courtesy of Mr. Henry Coates, of Porter & Coates, Publishers. The Chew family are ancient and of high standing. A lengthy account of them is given in *The Provincial Councillors of Pennsylvania*, by Charles P. Keith, and a short sketch in Willis P. Hazard's third additional volume of *Watson's Annals*. Col. Samuel Chew came from Chewton, Somersetshire, England, to this country in 1671, with Lord Baltimore, and settled on West river, in Anne Arundel county, Maryland. John Chew had emigrated to Virginia still earlier, in the reign of James I. He was a member of Assembly. He is said to have been the father of Samuel Chew, of Maryland, who was great-grandfather of the Councillor. Larkin Chew, a relative of Samuel, lived in Virginia, and married the great-aunt of President Madison, and was an ancestor of President Taylor. The Chew family were longer settled in America than any other family represented in the Provincial Council.

Samuel Chew was a judge. A second one of the same name, being the father of Councillor Chew, was known as Samuel Chew, of Maidstone, an estate near Annapolis. He was a doctor. He moved to Delaware and had a house in Dover. He was Chief Justice of the three Lower Counties, which now form the State of Delaware. He was a Friend, but learned in the law. He gave a charge declaring defensive war lawful when the French threatened the Colonies in 1745. Benjamin Chew, the Councillor, was the son of this gentleman. He was bred a Friend, but became an adherent of the Church of England. About 1761 he built Cliveden, as the Germantown house is called, for a country seat. There were about sixty acres of land in the property. Benjamin Chew was fond of study. He was a student in the law office of Andrew Hamilton, in Philadelphia, and was highly esteemed by his preceptor for his talents and diligence. When the distinguished Hamilton died he continued his studies in the Middle Temple, London. On his return he secured extensive practice. He became Attorney General of the Province and held other important offices. He owned an elegant house in Third street, below Walnut, near Willing's alley, which Charles Willing built for his son-in-law, Col. Byrd, of Virginia, and which Governor John Penn and wife once occupied. Here he entertained Washington and Adams and leading members of the Continental Congress of 1774. John Adams notes a banquet at Judge Chew's in his diary, and describes the dinner in detail, as if giving a bill of fare.

Judge Chew was speaker of the Assembly of the Lower Counties in 1756. He was a faithful and laborious officer. Miers Fisher declared that the Chief Justice told the Grand Jury boldly, in reply to a query during his charge, that when the King, or his Ministers, exceeded their constitutional authority submission to their mandate became treason. His official positions ceased with the loss of royal authority, though he acted as Register General for a time. Judge Chew was arrested, as he had held office under English rule. Governor John Penn and several Friends were also arrested. Many Friends opposed the war on peace principles. Chew signed a parole and went to the Union Iron Works, in Hunterdon county, New Jersey, where he remained ten months. After his release he remained quiet during the rest of the war. He was upright and honorable, and was the friend of Washington both before and after the war. Governor Mifflin appointed him President Judge of the High Court of Errors and Appeals. He died in Third street, January 20th, A. D. 1810, at the age of eighty-seven years. He was buried in St. Peter's churchyard. Judge Chew married, in 1747, Mary Galloway, daughter of John Galloway. She died in 1755. In 1757 he married Elizabeth Oswald, niece of Joseph Turner, the Councillor. She died in 1819. He had a large family. One daughter married Alexander Wilcocks. His daughter Harriet married Charles Carrol, of Carrolton. Sophia, who was at the Meschianza, married Henry Phillips. Peggy, whose champion was Major Andre at the Meschianza, became the wife of John Eager Howard, of Baltimore. He was a Revolutionary officer, and Lee said that he turned the fortune of the day at the battle of Cowpens. He was Governor of Maryland and a United States Senator, as well as a member of the Continental Congress. Washington attended his wedding.

In 1779 Judge Chew sold Cliveden to Blair McClenachan for £2500, but repurchased it in 1797 for £8500. The Judge was attorney for the Penns, with Tench Francis, after John Penn went to England. Benjamin Chew, Jr., was the Judge's successor in the Cliveden estate. He was born in Philadelphia in 1758. He studied law finishing his course at the Middle Temple, London. In 1788 he married Catharine Banning. He entertained Lafayette in 1825. A painting in the family of the event keeps up its memory. Benjamin Chew died at Cliveden, April 30th, 1844, at the age of eighty-six years. Two of his sons, Benjamin Chew, Jr., and Samuel Chew, became lawyers, and occupied high positions. Miss Ann Sophia Penn Chew, daughter of Benjamin Chew and granddaughter of Chief Justice Chew, the Councillor, still possesses Cliveden and resides in the old mansion.

The brave old house is interesting because it really became a fort, and in its resistance showed the honest work of the masons of a former day, and the excellent lime which bound its stones together in the firm wall. The house is of ample dimensions. It is two stories in height, with an attic, and there is a pent roof. There is a door on the north side, as well as in front. The window above the north door is in a line lower than the second story windows which are its companions, to make a little variety in the plan of the building. There are wings on the upper and lower side. A vine on the rear wall of the north wing gives a rustic look. A projection of woodwork surmounts the front door, which faces on the Main street. The wings are plastered in part, while two dormer windows, semi-circular at the top, break the front of the roof. The house stands lengthwise with Main street. Three wooden urns stand on brick pediments, and there is one on each end of the roof. It is pleasant sometimes to see the remains of an old fashion on an ancient house. The main house is plastered on the south end. There is a quiet and dignified simplicity about the antique mansion that makes it look as if it had a history, both as to family and governmental life, and was proud of it. The ancient lawn, embracing ample grounds, adorns the old place; and its natural beauties exceed all architectural displays. The mansion stands very far back from the street, which adds to the picturesqueness of the view in front.

On entering, a large hall greets the incomer. These halls were a pleasant characteristic of old-time mansions. Two pillars stand in its midst, and two others against the side walls, with wood-carving about them. The wood-work in the interior is fine. The frame work and carving over the doors, and the cornice is the result of hand labor. Machinery now usurps much of this work. There is a wainscot in the parlor, which room deserves special remembrance, because the brave and good Lafayette breakfasted in it. There is more woodwork over the fire-place, which is ceiled. An inner door has the old-fashioned ornamental frame-work around and above it, which is so pleasant a reminder of former days, though old fashions in building are again reviving. The marks of the battle are still seen both within and without the house. The outer wall was broken by bullets, and the bullet marks still remain in the plaster of the hall, and are seen on the wall. A small room opens from the hall on each side, in the front of the house. The panes of the windows are small and the divisions of wood-work between them are broad. The rear hall is newer than the front hall, and it contains the staircase with its wooden railing. The front doors are heavy. There are yet marks on the floor made by muskets when they were struck there in emptying their charges. An engraving of Col. Musgrave adorns the hall, the Chew House being represented in the back-ground. H. L. Abbot was the artist, and the date is 1796. It was engraved in England by G. S. Facius in 1797. It is inscribed, "Lieut. John Thomas Musgrave, Governor of Gravesend and Tilbury Fort. Colonel of 76th Regiment of Foot. Engraved from a picture painted 1786, with a view of Mr. Chew's house near Germantown in Pennsylvania, 1777." Wm. Penn in treaty with the Indians in 1681 is another appropriate engraving in the old hall. There is a painting of Joseph Turner, an Englishman, the uncle of Miss Ann Chew's grandmother. The effort has been to keep everything in its ancient condition as far as possible. There are some quaint mirror frames of open wood-work, which came from the Penn family, being a part of their drawing-room furniture. Two large and two small mirrors of this antique cast ornament the parlor walls. Mr. E. L. Henry, the New York artist, has a picture in the school-room of the firing at the battle. A rear building has been added to the house. There is a circular connection between the main house and the kitchen which is open, with pillars. An American gentleman told Washington that he could show him an unprotected door, but they found the columns here and thought it a British barricade. Now the colonnade is built into the addition. The stone steps in front of the house are antiques. The dining-room, with its wood-fire in the fire-place, was found cheerful on the wintry day of my visit. The long sticks of wood were such as warmed the worthies of Revolutionary times, while the wood-work around the fire-place and a quaint closet, kept up the idea of antiquity. The stone of the outer wall of the house is in its original condition, except where the broken part has been re-plastered. In the ancient barn, in the rear of the house, is an old coach of the Chew family, like that of Washington. The lower half is colored yellow and the upper half black. It has large glass windows, and the early "Germantown wagons" of which Ward speaks, were light in comparison with it. The springs are of leather, and there is a fifth wheel under the front, as coach-makers style it. The body is semi-circular. The drivers who guided that coach are long since dead, and the box is lonely. The faces which gazed out of those windows no longer look on earthly scenes. Will the relic stand until it goes to pieces of itself, like Oliver Wendell Holmes' "One Hoss Shay?" The Chew grounds were increased by purchase. The Clements property was bought by Benj. Chew, Jr. The very extensive lawn used to be still larger. It has a quiet country appearance. Quiet as the old house and lawn look under the spring sun, or the winter snow, this was once the scene of mad rage, and murderous strife when a young nation contended for life, struggling against its unnatural mother; and men of the same speech and lineage were seeking to destroy each other's lives. The door, lately entered so easily, was then barred and defended, so that entrance was impossible. The windows blazed with the fire of musketry, and the dead and dying were on the court-yard.

But let us consider the circumstances which made this a centre of an important contest. More than a year had passed since the Declaration of Independence had been read in Philadelphia. The patriots could not foresee the weary days which were to follow, but there was much disaffection among the Americans themselves, and those who dwelt around Germantown were by no means unanimously in favor of the war. The intrepid Washington was lying with his poorly clad army, on the Metuchen Hills, on the Skippack creek, about twenty miles from Germantown. It is said that he believed that a withdrawal of some of Howe's forces to operate against the forts on the Delaware river would weaken him temporarily, and afford a good opportunity for attack, but that by a change in Howe's plans this advantage was lost. Howe, with a large force was camped in Germantown, his line running at right angles to Main street, the central point being the Old Market-House square, where the Presbyterian Church and the Soldiers' Monument now stand. The Market House appears in the picture in Watson's Annals. Washington determined to attempt a surprise, and to do this by sending various detachments by various routes, in such a manner that they should meet at a given time, and the Market-House seems to have been the central point of attack. The move was well planned, Washington, having been defeated at the Brandywine in the preceding month, and the massacre at Paoli having lately occurred, both officers and men were ready to strive to regain a good reputation for bravery. The large force of Howe in Philadelphia, the Capital of the new Republic, was a standing disgrace to the cause of freedom. While Washington had been lying at Pennypacker's Mill, between the Perkiomen and Skippack creeks, new troops had rejoined him and they could be put in action.

The plan of surprise was as follows: Generals Sullivan and Wayne, flanked by the brigade of the Frenchman, Conway, were to advance by Chestnut Hill, General Armstrong, with the Pennsylvania militia, was to pass along the Manatawny, or Ridge road, by Van Deering's mill, afterwards, Robinson's mill on the Wissahickon, and strike the enemy on their left and rear. Generals Greene and Stephens flanked by McDougall's brigade, were to come by the Limekiln road and attack the right wing of the enemy. The Maryland and New Jersey militia, led by General Smallwood and Forman, were ordered to take the Old York Road and fall on the rear of the right wing of the British.

On October 3, 1777, in the early evening, Washington and his army quietly left their camp, and proceeded toward Germantown. Washington was in the division of Sullivan and Wayne. Tear away the gaudy trappings of war for a moment, and on this dark night see what a dim monster presents himself. A crowd of poorly clad, and poorly shod men have left loving homes to steal in the darkness upon their fellow Englishmen, who have come thousands of miles across the sea to coerce, and if need be, slay them. Many are marching to certain death, and thoughts of father and mother, wife and child, are painful, as the terrible uncertainty of the coming day stares them in the face. God hasten the time foretold by the prophet, when swords shall be beaten into plow-shares, and spears into pruning hooks. While we behold the smiling fields and beautiful residences of Germantown may we never forget the great cost at which our present prosperity was obtained.

Parties were sent out in advance of the American army, to secure any one who might give notice to the English of their approach. The effort was to reach the British pickets before daylight. The roads were rough, and it was nearly sunrise when the army came out of the woods at Chestnut Hill. At dawn the British patrols detected the approach of the enemy and gave an alarm. Judge Allen's house then occupied the site of the late James Gowen's fine residence, and that house afterwards became Mount Airy College. English soldiers were stationed in it, and here was the beginning of the eventful day's contest. Here the surprised British soldiers were at once put under arms. At 7 o'clock the advance force of Sullivan, led by Conway, and mainly from his brigade, attacked the pickets at Allen's house. The British had two six pounders, but they were driven back to the main body, which was constituted mainly of the 40th Regiment, and a battalion of light infantry. Sullivan's main body left the roads and took the fields at the right and formed in a lane, which led to the Schuylkill, and attacked in such numbers, and so vigorously, that the enemy gave way, after a spirited defense. The Americans pursued. Col. Musgrave, the commander of the British center, and five companies of the 40th Regiment, entered Judge Chew's house, then occupied by the servants of the family. Musgrave had been encamped east of the house, and may have observed its strong walls with a soldier's eye before he found a needed refuge in it. From his retreat he fired on Woodford's brigade and checked its advance. The Americans attacked the extemporized castle in vain.

Though most of the generals were with their various commands, a hasty council was held by the officers at hand. Gen. Knox was much esteemed as an adviser by Washington. His verdict was to stick to the military rule, which forbade leaving a castle in the rear, and it was followed. The rule is generally a good one, and a professor in college once gave it me as a maxim for studies. In the present case Col. Pickering's advice to press on and leave a regiment to watch the Chew house would probably have secured a better chance of success. Old warfare did not adapt itself to emergencies as well as that of the present day. It went by iron rule.

Lieutenant Matthew Smith, of Virginia, was assisting Adjutant General Pickering in the duties of his office. A flag of truce with summons to surrender was suggested, Pickering asserting that the flag would be fired on, but Smith bravely volunteered to carry it. He was wounded, and died a few days afterwards.

Maxwell's brigade cannonaded the house, but they struck it obliquely, instead of in front, and the strong walls mocked their assault, and the brave English soldiers within were akin to those described in Tennyson's "Charge of the Light Brigade." So the attempt failed. Major White, of Virginia, an aid of Sullivan, strove to set the house on fire, but was shot from the cellar and killed. Years after his son was much moved in visiting the scene of his father's death. De Chastellux (Vol. I, p. 213), quoted by Lossing, says that M. Mauduit also made an effort to set the brave house on fire with burning straw.

Many Americans were slain at this point, and it may well be called the turning-point of the Battle of Germantown. The inmates of the house were so well protected that they suffered scarcely any loss. Wayne's divison was brought back to the Chew house, and this uncovered the left flank of Sullivan, and broke the plans of the Americans.

The advanced post of the British had been below Allen's house at Mount Airy. The next outpost on the Main road was the 40th Regiment, under Col. Thomas Musgrave, which entered the Chew house. On the Limekiln road the First Battalion Light Infantry was stationed at the northwest corner of Keyser's lane. The Queen's Rangers, a Tory corps of moderate numbers, was on the York road. The British main body was on Lucan's mill lane. The right wing was commanded by Generals Grant and Matthews. The left wing reached from the market house to the Schuylkill on School house lane, under General Knyphausen; Generals Grey and Agnew were subordinate to him, as well as General Von Stirn and his Hessians, while the Chasseurs, mounted and on foot, under Col. Von Wurmbs, were in the same division of the army. The dismounted Chasseurs were at the Wissahickon, at Ridge road and the Schuylkill. In the first attack Wayne and Sullivan drove the English down Main street as far as the Green Tree Tavern, kept by the Mackinett family, now the residence of Dr. Alexis du Pont Smith. On a late visit there the doctor informed me that tradition was clear that this house was reached. The rear of their force was however detained at the Chew house. General Greene's division, with Muhlenberg's, and Scott's, and McDougall's brigades, which composed Stephen's division, added to it, marched down Limekiln road and the adjacent fields and struck the British infantry at Keyser's lane, attacked and routed them. The veteran local historian, Thomas Westcott, in an interesting article in the Philadelphia *Public Ledger*, March 4, 1885, from which I have drawn the position of the British troops, shows that the new National Soldiers' Cemetery is on a spot where a part of this spirited contest occurred. Col. George Matthews, of Virginia, followed by Col. Walter Stewart, of the 13th Pennsylvania Regiment, pressed on. Another British force was met at Lucan's mill and Col. Stewart routed them, and captured a small redoubt, but he found that Matthews had been overpowered and had surrendered; and so was obliged to turn and flee. Stephens was drawn from the work assigned him in Washington's plan by hearing the firing at the Chew house and started toward it. Maxwell's brigade there, in the fog, mistook his men for those of the enemy and fired into them. The fire was returned, and thus the Americans ignorantly fought each other. Gen. Wayne wrote his wife that this blunder caused a retreat of nearly two miles when the Americans were in possession of the British encampment.

When Greene had routed the British on their right wing he strove to enter the village, expecting help from Armstrong, Smallwood and Forman, but in this he was disappointed. Armstrong did not attack the German Chasseurs, and Smallwood and Forman arrived too late to aid Greene. The British were struck by the bravery of the Americans, and, ignorant of their numbers, were about to retreat, but Generals Grey and Knyphausen marched to the help of the centre of the army, which was pressed by the Americans. The contest in this battle was a severe one and the victory was almost in the hands of the Americans. The dense fog had much to do with the defeat. The sun, which had scarcely showed itself in the morning, soon hid its face from the shocking spectacle, and a poet well called the fog "the Shroud of Death," for it cost the death of these brave men. Washington wrote his chagrin to Congress, and attributed the loss of the battle to the fog. Col. Forrest stated that when a drummer beat a parley at Chew's house, the Americans made a mistake and thought their comrade was sounding for a retreat, and hence a panic arose and helped lose the day. It had been ordered that each American soldier and officer should wear a piece of white paper in his cap. If this was done it did not distinguish friend from foe in the dense fog. The American army had a rough country to pass over in making an advance on the enemy, and fences and stone walls and marshes added to the difficulty. Still the stone wall at Ellwood Johnson's place served as a breastwork, and may remind us of Stonewall Jackson's tactics.

I have found Lossing's Field Book of the Revolution, as well as his History of the United States, useful in this review. He visited the Chew House on November 1, A. D. 1848, and All Saint's Day was a proper one on which to behold a scene consecrated by the blood of patriots. The picturesque features of the strongly built Germantown houses strike him. He calls Chew's house "the most noted and attractive relic of the Revolution now in Germantown." He says, as does Watson, that four or five carpenters were employed a whole winter in repairing the house. Watson adds that the front door was full of shot holes, and that it was removed and preserved. The cannon which assailed the house were on the grounds of Mrs. Norton Johnson, but the present mansion was not then built. When Watson wrote it was known as John Johnson's house. In the description of the Misses Johnson's house at Washington Lane and Main street, it should have been noted that the upper corner yet displays the mark of a cannon ball. John Johnson's house is described in a previous article of this series, under its name "Upsal." At the time that Lossing visited the Chew house, which is called Cliveden, the widow of a son of Chief Justice Chew gave him the needed information.

Washington computed the American loss at the Battle of Germantown at about 1000 killed, wounded and missing. Lossing places the English loss in killed at 100. General Howe reported officially that 535 were killed, wounded and missing. Gordon says that a British manuscript, left at Germantown showed the English loss to be about 800 killed. General James Agnew was slain as he rode by the Mennonite grave yard by some one from behind the wall. He was carried to the Wister mansion, opposite Queen street, his headquarters, where his blood still stains the floor. Lieutenant Colonel Bird was an other distinguished English officer who was killed. Watson had a monumental stone placed over the remains of Agnew and Bird in the Lower Burying ground, and another over Captain Turner, of North Carolina, and Major Irvine, and six American soldiers in the Upper Burying ground. Thus did this kindly man show honor to bravery on both sides, after years had destroyed the rancor of contest; as the blue and gray are now learning, in this land, to give the due meed to bravery, on whichever side it was exhibited. General Nash, of North Carolina, and Major Sherburne, Major White, aids to General Sullivan, were also among the slain on the American side. Congress voted thanks to Washington for his attack on the enemy, and to the officers and men for their "brave exertions." The farmers who had heard the feet of the passing host as they went to battle on the night of the 3d of October, on the 4th saw the American army retreating to the Skippack. From this point Washington soon returned with his command to White Marsh, but after a short stay there he made his winter encampment at Valley Forge, and that fearful winter of pain and trouble has ever left its impression on the mind of Americans. When Washington afterward visited that spot how many sad memories must have filled his mind, as well as brighter thoughts of hope for a country bought with blood, as he looked on the scene of former misery.

Dr. Alfred C. Lambdin gave an address at the 100th anniversary of the Battle of Germantown, which has been of assistance to the writer of this article. It appeared in the Pennsylvania Historical Magazine, Vol. I, p. 368, etc. The

Doctor had the valuable aid of the officers of the Historical Society of Pennsylvania, and had access to important documents at the Rooms. He follows Sullivan through the fog and the smoke of the artillery to Washington Lane, and Wayne to the Widow Mackinett's Green Tree Tavern. We will follow his leading on a path no longer dangerous. The New Jersey regiments lost 46 officers and men. They belonged to Maxwell's brigade. Chevalier Duplessis and John Laurens are to be added to the volunteers I have named as being ready to set fire to the Chew house. We find Chief Justice Marshall an officer in Woolford's brigade. I once walked by this great man's house in Richmond, Va., in company with Dr Haight, of Trinity Church, New York, and he lifted his hat in token of regard for the memory of the good man, and thus should we ever remember one who was so useful in his judicial position, and also a faithful upholder of the Christian faith.

Col. Von Wurmb, commanding the Hessian Yagers, is said to have expected the attack and to have kept a watch on the eventful night " in the horrenduous hills of the Wissahickon." Cornwallis reached Germantown from Philadelphia after the Americans had been driven from the town, and joined Grey in their pursuit. General Howe said that he pursued the enemy four or five miles. Gen. Greene's retreat was difficult and with some loss. Gen. Knox observed that the battle lasted two hours and forty minutes. It was at the doors of the people, and in their gardens and orchards and fields. When the fog and smoke cleared away the old Germantowners saw a scene of destruction. Watson says that hundreds from Philadelphia visited the place the day after the battle.—[*Annals*, Vol. II, p. 66.] The Friends sent a deputation to protest against war to the Commander of each army. Washington was visited on October 7th.

The American General Nash was attended by Dr. Craik, who was Washington's own physician and the father of the late celebrated Rev. Dr. Craik, of Louisville, Kentucky. The General was buried at Kulpsville. Major Witherspoon, the beloved son of Parson Witherspoon, of Princeton, was slain in this battle. The Haines house was made a field hospital. The boards stained with blood on the first floor were afterwards taken up and replaced in a floor in the upper story. The wounded were afterwards carried to hospitals in the city. Major Witherspoon was buried in front of Phillip Weaver's house near Beggarstown.

The English retired from Germantown to the city soon after this battle. While they themselves fought bravely, they had found that the Americans were of the same stock and were not to be despised. The brave Washington endangered himself, though the Americans entreated him not to do so. His sublime character shone out in victory or defeat, in its patience, courage, dignity and trust in God. When this noble man resorted in prayer to the "God of battles" he was indeed "strong in the Lord of hosts."

I find in Christopher Marshall's Journal a statement (p. 132) that on September 25th a number of Tories, said to amount to four or five hundred, paraded Germantown and triumphed all night through the streets, seizing and sending prisoners those who were thought friends to the "Free States of America." We can see in this Journal the same kinds of rumors and excitements as occurred in the time of the Southern war. On October 22d, 1777, Marshall notes that Thirty English and five Hessian prisoners, taken in a skirmish in Germantown, were brought to the city via Reading and lodged in jail; also, three light-horse and four yagers, who were out on a scout, and were taken and confined with the other prisoners. At one time cannonading is heard in the distance. When Marshall is at Lancaster, on November 6th, he notes that Mary Brown's son came the night before from Germantown. He had seen his mother and Mrs. Owen there, who had gone out from the city on parole to procure provisions, as they were dear in the city. Mrs. Owen told him to tell Mr. Marshall that the enemy had destroyed the fence around his garden, at his country seat, and put soldiers into his house in town as well as his house in the country.

In Edward J. Lowell's *Hessians in the Revolutionary War*, a fact of interest appears. It is stated that the Hessians were warned of their approaching danger by a man whose property Captain Ewald, of their body, had protected on one occasion, though he was not a Tory. In glancing over this volume we may see how the word Wissahickon looks in the German language. Here it is: "Vishigging." The Indian name is prettier.

In retreating to the Skippack, Washington made use of churches and other public buildings as hospitals, between Perkiomen and Reading, beyond his camp. Col. Pickering's letter in Theo. W. Bean's "Washington at Valley Forge" is useful in the details it gives concerning our subject.

A number of Hessians were buried in a trench at the Upper Burying Ground. Some American sharpshooters attacked the burying party, but were driven to the Wissahickon by the British cavalry.

Hessian and English soldiers were both fed at the same houses. The wounded Americans were conveyed by their fellow soldiers as far as the western part of Moreland, and Upper Dublin, and even against the will of the people, were left in their houses.

In considering the causes of the loss of this noted battle, we see several events combined. The fog, failure of Washington's men to come together at the neighborhood of the market house, as the plan required, the detention at Chew's house, and the panic and attack of American troops on each other. Still Gen. Wilkinson, as is seen in the Appendix of Watson's 2d volume, thought it a kind dispensation of Providence that the battle was lost, as he believed that if the Americans had gone on to the city at that time they would have been overpowered by Howe. History is "God's footsteps marching through time;" so let us believe that all was for the best, and that, as the infant must use its muscles to become strong, so the infant nation may have needed exercise to develop its powers. War has its amusing side. Goodrich's History says that in the battle the cue of Maj. Burnet, the aid-de-camp of Gen.

Greene was shot off. His general told him to dismount and get it, which he did. Soon a shot took a powdered curl from the head of the General, while the British were in hot pursuit; the major advised him to dismount and secure it, which the General would not do.

If the reader would follow an exuberant fancy, in reviewing this history, let him read George Lippard's "Battle of Germantown." There he will see, as in a picture, the crimson and green uniforms of the English soldiers. He will behold the quiet town going to its rest the night before the battle, little thinking of the awfulness of the coming morning, when the houses should be closed in the great danger, and the inhabitants would hide in the cellars, as the missiles of death were hurled through the air, while struggles went on in the streets of the astonished town. He narrates the burial of American officers at the Mennonite graveyard at Towamensing, twenty-six miles from Philadelphia. He gives a tradition that Gen. Agnew had a presentiment of his death, and another, that a kind Quaker was seen relieving the wounded in the thick of the fight at the Chew house, according to the well-known benevolence of his body, and that the name of this well-doer was unknown. For a quieter work of imagination see "The Quaker Soldier," by Judge J. Righter Jones. The representation of good Mrs. Jacob Keyser, reading the Scriptures to the wounded American Colonel Lynnford, whom she is caring for, and the good effects of the simple piety of the Mennonites as shown in herself, her husband, and her pastor on the invalid's mind are well described, while the faithful colored servant of the Colonel gives amusing variety to the picture. Dr. Bensell is introduced as the Colonel's physician. The late Rev. John Rodney's residence is the house mentioned as the abode of the Keysers.

Lord Stirling, who was thought by many the rightful heir to a Scotch title, and the brave Pulaski, who loved a foreign nation in its trouble must not be forgotten as we number the worthies of Germantown. We have the letter which announced Agnew's death: How many such missives carried sad news to homes on both sides of the Atlantic. Let us pray for the time when

"They hang the trumpet in the hall,
And study war no more."

The Centennial of the battle was observed as the following programme shows. The GERMANTOWN TELEGRAPH of the next day, contained valuable Revolutionary information. I think the account of the fireworks was in the GERMANTOWN GUIDE.

1777.  1877.

OCTOBER FOURTH.
:o:
CENTENNIAL CELEBRATION, BATTLE OF GERMANTOWN.
:o:
ORDER OF EXERCISES:

. I. *Salute of* 100 *Guns at sunrise, by the Keystone Battery, N. G., of Pa.* Lieut. James O. Winchester, commanding—on the Battle Ground.

II. 100 strokes on the Bell at 9 o'clock a. m., by Mr. W. F. Gamble. Clock will be set in motion by Mr. G. Wilbur Russell.

AT 12 O'CLOCK, NOON.

III. Parade as per orders of General Louis Wagner, Chief Marshal.
IV. Mass Meeting of Citizens at Town Hall, at 2 o'clock, P. M.

1. Introductory Remarks, - by Washington Pastorius, Esq., President.
2. Prayer, - - - - - - - Rev. C. W. Schaeffer, D. D.
3. Historical Address, - - - - - - Dr. A. C. Lambdin.
4. Oration, - - - - - - - Hon. M. Russell Thayer.
5. Presentation of Clock and Bell, - - Thomas A. Gummey, Esq.
on behalf of the Committee.
6. Reception of Clock and Bell, - - - Mr. Norton Johnson,
for the Citizens of Germantown.
7. Benediction, - - - - - Rev. Jacob Helffenstein, D. D.

The exercises of the meeting will be interspersed with Music by McClurg's Band.

V. Display of Fireworks by Professor Samuel Jackson, at the corner of Coulter street and Wayne avenue.

HEADQUARTERS

COMMITTEE OF ARRANGEMENTS

———:o:———

Centennial Celebration of the Battle of Germantown.

———:o:———

General Orders, }
    No. 1.   }   *Germantown, Pa., Sept.* 26, 1877.

I. GENERAL LOUIS WAGNER having been appointed Chief Marshal of the parade to be held on Thursday, October 4, 1877, hereby assumes command.

II. MAJOR GALLOWAY C. MORRIS is appointed Chief of Staff, and the following gentlemen as Aides de Camp:

COL. HENRY W. GRAY,	COL. ROBERT L. ORR,	COL. EMLEN CARPENTER,
MAJ. ALBERT J. RORER,	CAPT. ISAAC R. MARTINDELL,	CAPT. OSCAR BOLTON,
LIEUT. HENRY D. HIRST,	LIEUT. HOWARD A. BUZBY,	WILLIAM GLADDING,
EDWARD T. STEEL,	CHARLES WEISS,	JOHN C. MILLER,
WILLIAM H. MCCALLUM,	WARREN INGERSOLL,	SAMUEL LOEB,
IRVING MCCALLUM,	ROBERT S. SMITH,	REED A. WILLIAMS, JR.

Additional appointments will be announced in future orders.

III. The column will form in three Divisions. The first Division will consist of the First Division, National Guard of Pennsylvania, Girard College Cadet Corps, and other military organizations under command of Major General Robert M. Brinton, and of the National, State and Municipal authorities, in carriages.

The second Division will consist of the Grand Army of the Republic and the organized secret civic societies in regalia, with Col. Daniel W. Bussinger, as Marshal.

The third Division will consist of citizens mounted, delegations from the manufacturing establishments of the ward, with such teams as they may need to display the processes of their establishments, the delegation of German citizens, other citizens on foot and in carriages, with Ellicott Fisher, Esq., as Marshal.

IV. The line will form at 11.30 a. m., on the lower side of Chelten avenue, the right of the First Division resting on the Rail Road Depot, and its left extending if necessary, south on Main street. The right of the second Division will rest on Main street, extending if necessary, south on Green street. The right of the third Division will rest on Green street, extending if necessary, south on Wayne street.

The column will move at 12 m. *precisely* over the following route: Countermarch on Chelten avenue to Wayne, Wayne to Coulter, Coulter to Green, Green to Manheim, Manheim to Main, Main to East Walnut lane, East Walnut lane to Morton, Morton to Cliveden or Battle Ground, Cliveden to Main, Main to Johnson, Johnson to Adams, Adams to Tulpohocken, Tulpohocken to Main, Main to Town Hall, to be reviewed by General John F. Hartranft, Governor of Pennsylvania, and the civil authorities, and there dismiss.

Property owners and residents on the route of parade are requested to clear the streets in front of their respective properties, of all obstructions, and all citizens are requested to close their places of business and to decorate their houses.

V. The Head Quarters of the Chief Marshal will be at No. 341 Walnut street, Philadelphia, during business hours, and at the Town Hall, Germantown, at 8 p. m. daily, until the day of parade.

VI. Organizations and societies desiring to participate in the parade will report the name of their organization, their probable strength, &c., not later than 8 p. m., on Tuesday, October 2, 1877.

By order of
LOUIS WAGNER.
Chief Marshall.

GALLOWAY C. MORRIS,
Chief of Staff.

{ HEADQUARTERS CENTENNIAL CELEBRATION,
BATTLE OF GERMANTOWN.

General Orders,
No. 2.
Germantown, Oct. 2nd, 1877.

I. The Head quarters of the Chief Marshal, on October 4th, will be at No. 134 East Chelten Avenue. Marshals of Divisions and Aides de Camp will report for duty properly mounted and equipped, at 10 o'clock, a. m.

GERMANTOWN.

II. The column will move at 12 m., PRECISELY, in the following order:
1. Reserve Corps, City Police, Lieut. C. D. Crout, Commanding.
2. Gen'l Louis Wagner, Chief Marshal and Staff.
3. FIRST DIVISION, commanded by Maj. C. W. Karsner, 6th Regt. N. G. Pa.

Keystone Battery, Capt. S. B. Poulterer, Commanding.
Detachment of 6th Regt. N. G. Pa., Capt. T. B. Chadwick, Commanding.
Battalion, under command of Capt. John W. Ryan, consisting of State Fencibles, N. G. Pa., 1st Lieut. E. A. Packer, Commanding, and the Girard College Cadet Corps.

Company A, Capt. Rob't Hayward.
" B, " John D. Thomas.
" C, 1st Lieut. W. S. Burr.
" D, Capt. James Anderson.

With Cadet Corps Band under Thomas Dobson, Bandmaster.
"Continental" Company, of Princeton, N. G. New Jersey, Capt. Aaron L. Green, Commanding.

Company H 3rd Regiment, N. G. of Pa., Capt. Thomas Furey, Commanding.

Gray Invincibles, Capt. A. Oscar Jones, Commanding.

Artillery Corps, Washington Grays, N. G. Pa., Capt. W. C. Zane, Commanding as escort to His Excellency, John F. Hartranft, Governor of Pennsylvania, accompanied by his Staff, in carriages.

Hon. W. S. Stokley, Mayor of Philadelphia, and State and Municipal Authorities in carriages.

4. SECOND DIVISION, Col. Daniel W. Bussinger, Marshal, John D. Bowen, Chief of Staff. Aids:

George Trumbore,	Elwood Bevans,	Michael Oatis,
Acis Jenkinson,	George Trout,	Charles Mansfield,
William F. Keyser,	Edward Paramore,	Joseph Channon,
Edward Insinger,	James Shields,	J. B. Goslin.

The several Societies forming this Division will be in line (avoiding Main street) by 11.30 a. m. Aids will be detailed to conduct the Societies to their position as soon as they arrive.

The Headquarters of this Division will be at Parker's Hall, corner of Main and Price streets.

Grand Army of the Republic, Department of Pennsylvania.
S. Irvin Givin, Post 5, Department Commander.
J. M. Vanderslice, Post 2, Ass't Adjt. Gen'l.
David T. Davies, Post 24, Ass't Quartermaster Gen'l.
A. J. Hamilton, Post 8, Aide de Camp.
W. J. Mackey, Post 8, Council of Administration.
W. J. Kramer, Post 46, Council of Administration.
John Taylor, Post 51, Council of Administration.

GERMANTOWN.

Post. No. 1. Geo. W. Devinney, Post Commander.
" " 2. Chas F. Kennedy, "
" " 5. Andrew Jackson, "
" " 6. C. Bettenhauser, "
" " 7. Jacob F. Simon, "
" " 8. Wm. Letourneau, "
" " 10. George W. Young, "
" " 12. Thomas Wyatt, Jr., "
" " 14. W. J. Caskey, "
" " 46. J. A. Mather, "
" " 51. Geo. W. Lenoir, "
" " 55. Jno. B. Major, "
" " 63. Wm. H. Rightly, "
" " 71. Lewis R. Robinson, "
" " 77. H. J. Stager, "
" " 94. John R. Bignell "
Logan Lodge, Good Fellows, Tobias Sibel,   Marshal.
Germantown Lodge, K. P., Charles D. Gentry,   "

Herman Lodge, Uniform Knights, Harry Reif, Marshal.
Seminole Tribe, Red Men, and kindred Societies from Philadelphia, Robert Howat, "
Mt. Airy Lodge, I. O. O. F., James Wine, "
Walker Lodge, I. O. O. F., William Ployd, "
Mt. Pleasant Encampment, I. O. O. F., Jacob Fisher, "
Phila. Battalion of Patriarchs, I. O. O. F., J. B. Nicholson, "
Germantown Lodge, A. P. A., John Ware, "
Reliance Council, O. U. A. M., George W. Baxter, "
Washington Council, Jr. O. U. A. M. Lewis Harmer, "
State Council, Jr. O. U. A. M. C. M. Berry, "
St. Vincent de Paul Beneficial Society, and kindred Societies of Philadelphia, Sullivan, "
St. Vincent de Paul T. A. B., Patrick Lamb, "
Star of Promise Division, S. of T., John Harleigh, "
Cadets of Temperance, Chas. Evans, "
Independent Mounted Club. Wm. H. Chandler, "

5. THIRD DIVISION, Ellicott Fisher, Esq., Marshal, Major E. H. Butler, Chief of Staff. Aids:

Geo. W. Carpenter,	Conyers Button,	John Lund,
Harry Thurman,	John Axford,	Hamilton Boyer,
Wm. Hirst, Jr.,	Daniel Bray, M. D.,	James Logan Fisher,
Stephens Crothers,	O. M. Boyer,	Harry Moore,
Justice Coxe, Jr.,	F. S. Stallman,	H. H. Kingston.
Richard Hume,	Gillieum Aertson,	

GERMANTOWN.

This Division will form as follows:
1. Hosiery Mills, Conyers Button, Marshal.—Dr. Mahlon M. Walker, Aid.
2. Workingmen's Club, J. Topliff Johnson, Marshal.
3. D. Pooley & Co., Limited.
4. Schomacker's Piano Manufacturing Co., Harry C. Schomacker, Marshal.
5. The Old Volunteer Fire Department, Edw. R. Whiteman, Marshal. With engine 110 years old and a first-class Steam Fire Engine, of the present day.
6. German societies, Fred'k May, Marshal.
7. C. C. Baker, Pioneer Corps, Bridesburg, Capt. Henry.
8. Waterhouse, Printer, wagon drawn by four horses containing printing press.
9. Orphans Home of Germantown, Chas. F. Kuhnle, Superintendent.
10. Midvale Steel works, Nicetown, G. Aertson, Superintendent.
11. Snuffers, Indians, Geo. W. Wolfe, Marshal.
12. Agricultural Department, J. Paramore.
13. Peerless Brick Co., of Nicetown.
14. Henry Smith, Printer, wagon and presses.
15. Watchmaker's Association, wagon drawn by two horses.
16. Citizens on foot.
17. Citizens in carriages.
18. Citizens Mounted.

III. While countermarching on Chelten avenue, Division Marshals will see that no bands play while moving *east;* the column taking time from bands marching west.

IV. In addition to the Aides de Camp announced by General Orders, No. 1, the following are hereby appointed:

Col. Charles A. Newhall,
Col. Sylvester Bonnaffon, Jr.,
Col. T. F. Betton Tapper,
Maj. W. S. Darling,
Maj. W. F. Muller, M. D.,
Capt. Robt. Johnstone,
Lieut. J. George Henvis,
Thos. H. Shoemaker,
Wm. H. Cope,
Thomas Carroll,
S. Worthington Williams.

Saml. Heebner,
George B. Edwards,
George Willing,
Chas A. Graver,
Wm. H. H. Cline,
Henry B. Bruner,
Wm. H. Roop, M. D.,
Sidney L. Wright,
Wm. H. Schively,
Theodore Ashmead.

Lieut. Chris. Shortwell,
John Bardsley,
Andrew Zell,

Edwin A. Woolston,
Chas. B. Edwards,
Albanus C. Logan,

Maurice A. Hoyt,
Edward T. Johnson,
James Neiler,

James Kating,
Chas. Millman, Jr.,
Robt. Barr,
Owen McGinnis,
John Riley,
Edw. D. Page,
E. M. Snodgrass,
Robt. Dunmore,
Jacob C. Bockius,
James F. Young,

Clement N. Williams,
Jos. W. Johnson,
Alex'r Kinnier,
Chas. Millman,
Isaac Russell,
George Sholler,
Sylvester Banner,
William Hinkle,
Christian Jordan,

M. Fisher Wright,
W. H. Livezey,
Wm. Morrell,
Henry Buckner,
Wm. Smith,
George Crowder,
Thos. McCafferty,
Morris P. Livezey,
C. H. Royal.

V. At 4 o'clock, p. m., the battalion of State Fencibles, N. G. Pa., and the Corps of Cadets, Girard College, under command of Capt. J. W. Ryan, will hold a dress parade on Chelten avenue, between Main and Green streets.

By order of
LOUIS WAGNER,
GALLOWAY C. MORRIS, *Chief Marshal.*
Chief of Staff.

COMMITTEE OF ARRANGEMENTS.—James R. Gates, Chairman.

Charles H. Spencer,
Daniel L. Keyser,
Isaac R. Martindell,
Norton Johnson,

Gen'l Louis Wagner,
Robert Bolling, M. D.,
C. Willing Littell,
Charles W. Henry,

Gen'l James Starr,
John K. Gamble,
Col. Henry W. Gray,
Wm. H. Emhardt, Sec.

COMMITTEE ON FINANCE.—Jabez Gates, Chairman.

Benjamin Allen,
Abraham Engard,
Spencer Roberts,
W. Wynne Wister, Jr.,
Col. E. H. Butler,
L. P. Thompson,
E. H. Howell,
John Shingle,
William Brockie,
Charles L. Eberle,

James S. Young,
Howard A. Buzby,
John T. Roberts,
John J. Kenney,
Charles Weiss,
W. A. Ulmer,
Edward Keyser,
George W. Russell,
Charles W. Henry,

James Neilor,
Washington F. Gamble,
Robert Thomas,
Daniel Freas,
George Heft,
Ellwood Johnson,
J. C. Channon,
Daniel L. Keyser,
Charles W. Otto, Treas.

COMMITTEE ON CLOCK AND BELL.

Edwin R. Cope, Pres't.
Charles Spencer, Treas.
Charles W. Henry, Sec.
Thomas A. Gummey,
George L. Ashmead,

C. Willing Littell,
James R. Gates,
Jabez Gates,
Abraham Engard,
Thomas Hobson,

John T. Roberts,
Charles L. Eberle,
Elliston P. Morris,
Charles Williams,
Lucius P. Thompson.

210   GERMANTOWN.

BUILDING COMMITTEE.

Thomas A. Gummey, Ch. George W. Russell,   Enoch Taylor.
Edwin R. Cope,   Jesse Lightfoot,

It should be added that Thos. A. Gummey, Edwin R. Cope, Charles Spencer, T. Charlton Henry, Enoch Taylor and Jabez Gates were appointed a committee to prepare the steeple on the City Hall to hold the bell and the clock made by Lukens, of Montgomery County, which were to be moved from the State House to Germantown, to fit the Centennial Celebration. The clock was removed in 1876. It was running on Oct. 4th, A. D. 1878. Henry Seybert had given a new clock. The bell was the second one in the history of the State House, and was cast in Philadelphia. It is said to contain 1000 Spanish dollars which give it its fine clear tone. The Swiss bell-ringers are said to have pronounced it the finest toned bell they had heard in this country. Thos. A. Gummey who obtained the bell from Councils presented the bell to the people of Germantown in a speech and Norton Johnson accepted it in behalf of the people. Between two and three thousand dollars were spent by Germantowners in building the new steeple.

"The largest crowd of persons that ever gathered together at night in Germantown, was doubtless that attracted to witness the grand pyrotechnic display on Garret's lot, bounded by Wayne, Coulter, Linden and Knox streets, in the lower part of the town, last Saturday. It is impossible to more than approximate numbers on such occasions, but to say that from 5000 to 8000 men, women and children were present is no exaggeration. This exhibition, in consequence of its postponement on account of the weather on the day of the celebration, was regarded as a part of the unfinished programme of that occasion, and it really looked as if the people had determined to go through the whole thing if it took them a half week to finish their patriotic resolves. Never was a night more favorable for a display of fireworks; never an exhibition of the pyric art received with greater satisfaction and delight. The pieces prepared by Professor Jackson were simply grand. The programme opened by illuminating the grounds with red and green colored lights. Then followed a flight of some six dozen rockets. Next the Star of Washington, a beautiful piece with crimson centre amidst scrolls of fire. A fairy magic circle was then given, inclosing the silver serpent's dance,' a novel and skillfully contrived affair. The Liberty Tree, composed of gold and silver coruscating fires, with rotating centre of emerald and ruby, gave great satisfaction. The Soldier's Glory, flaming with colors and coruscations of every hue was a fitting companion of the former. A bouquet of pyric roses, in fret-work of scintillating coruscations; then a Battery of Bombshells, which gave a fair idea of the terrors of war. The Pyric Gem of rubies and emeralds was followed by the Son of Freedom, with coruscating wreaths of jessamine fire and a Harlequinade of shells, a trio of noble pieces. A Cascade of Fire, representing fallen water, was a grand and successful design. But last, and better than all the others, was the Grand Battle Piece, beginning with a fierce engagement, and as it progressed, in silver letters of fire the word 'Germantown' appeared in a curved line, with '1777—Oct. 4—1877' underneath, while the American flag gracefully waved aloft in the national colors, in fiery jets, and revolving globes on either side were made to play eccentric movements. During the exhibition of the closing scene mortars were brought into requisition, shells filled the air, telling the thousands of spectators that 'Our flag was still there,' and the heavens above seemed full of every grand and terrible device the pyric art could suggest. The admiration and enthusiasm of the great crowd broke out in clapping of hands and appreciative compliments to Prof. Jackson and the Committee of Arrangements, to whom they were indebted for the sublime spectacle presented. On this occasion $570 worth of fireworks was displayed by the great American Pyrotechnist, and it were unjust to his patriotism and liberality to suppress the fact, that half the fireworks were contributed by him towards making the Centennial Celebration of the Battle of Germantown the great success it proved to be, in spite of the angry elements."

Aubrey H. Smith, Esq., writes me that one of the guns in the Soldiers' Monument, at Germantown, is a cannon from "the British frigate, Augusta" which was burned and exploded in the Delaware river, a few miles above Tinicum. Several of the large guns of this ship were recovered by dredgers who were deepening the channel.

When we try to represent to ourselves the condition of things at the Battle of Germantown, we must remember that the town presented a very different appearance from the crowded suburb of to-day. "Venable's History of the United States" well calls the ancient town "a straggling village near Philadelphia." Many incidents were kept in memory long after the battle. The barn, with its four stone corners, on Rev. Peter Keyser's place (now Ellwood Johnson's), was the scene of a tragedy. A bullet passed through the woodwork of this barn and struck an officer, who was carried to the rear of the bark-shed of the tannery, where he died near an apple tree which is now gone.

Germantown traditions are of more than usual value, because some of the old families still live in the houses of their great ancestors, and the spots of historical interest have been pointed out to present residents, we may well suppose, by those that are now gone to the great majority of the silent dead. The date in a stone in the peak of the roof at the house of the Misses Johnson, next below Ellwood Johnson's, is 1768. The present owners are lineal descendants of the first occupants. This is also the case with regard to the house of Mrs. Norton Johnson and that of Miss Haines.

In John Miller's diary, given by Watson, we find that Mt. Airy had some interest after the Battle of Germantown. On June 10, 1778, the English came out "by different routes and joined forces at Allen's lane (now Mt. Airy) and returned before nine o'clock in the morning, effecting nothing but the plundering of gardens, etc. The English commissioners came up strongly guarded as far as Chew's house and returned just after the above force."

"June 13. The army marched up for *the last time* and got as far as Mt. Airy. They returned in two hours."

"June 16 and 17. They are embarking and making all preparations for a departure from Philadelphia, and on the 18th, the *Americans* again took possession of the city. *Laus Deo!*" The praise to God naturally rises from a heart worn and weary with this long war.

The diary states that in January of '78, in severely cold weather, the English army went into winter quarters, but often sent foraging parties out to rob the surrounding country, and to guard the country people bringing them produce on market days.

On May 19, a large British force marched up the Old York road, and the next day a second party passed through Germantown, where they had a skirmish. They returned "in some haste," bearing dead and wounded in wagons. "The Indians killed seven British horsemen on the banks of the Schuylkill."

"May 28. A large detachment of the enemy came up and returned, without permission to do any harm."

"June 3. The British army came up and went through the town by break of day and returned by nine o'clock, A. M. They rob gardens and steal fowls as they pass along."

"June 6. They came up again in force and returned by nine o'clock, A. M., having with them a few wounded in a skirmish."

As Watson observes, this account says "more of the predatory aggressions of the enemy than was generally complained of by others."

Watson gives an interesting fact concerning the battle of Germantown in stating the following: "The daughter of Benjamin Marshal, Esq., at whose house General Washington stopped after the battle, told me he reached there in the evening and would only take a dish of tea, and, pulling out the *half* of a biscuit, assured the family the other half was all the food he had taken since the preceding day."

Watson takes us far beyond the date of the Battle of Germantown in his notice of Anthony Johnson, who died in 1823, at the age of seventy-eight. When he was a boy Chew's ground was a wood, and he saw a large bear in the daytime come from this wood and cross the road. The battle showed a fiercer strife than occurred among the animals in those days of early wildness. Watson gives a touching reminiscence of the battle in the visit of the Virginia captain, George Blackmore, to the battlefield where he had fought by the side of his brother, who was killed and left near a springhouse at Duval's fish pond. He went with the annalist "o'er the tented field to book the dead," and to seek the mournful and fatal spot. Watson gave him a battered bullet from Chew's door, which he said "he should incase in silver and hang to his watch chain and bequeath to his heirs." Jacob Keyser buried the captain's brother with four other soldiers in one grave. The annalist adds: "Alas, poor *undistin-*

guished, yet meritorious sufferers for their country!" The following letter to Mr. Ward is interesting:

"I met, some time since, Mr. John Bayne, who was born and resided on the old family homestead on Mill street, near Chew, who related to me the following interesting incident of the Battle of Germantown: 'Col. Thomas Forrest was stationed in the field east of Kelley's dam (now northwest corner of Chew and Chelten avenues) when he observed a company of Hessians approaching. He ordered them to halt. Still they advanced and were in the act of mounting the fence dividing the field when he ordered his men to fire, killing them all. He had them buried on the spot, which is now marked by a clump of cherry trees, and has remained undisturbed up to the present time. It was always known as the Forrest burial ground by the family. In speaking of the occurrence, Col. Forrest always made the remark that he only helped them the sooner over the fence.'"

I add another MS. from Ward:

"William Phillips, of Philadelphia, was bred a merchant in the counting-house of George Mead, grandfather of the late general of that name. As not unfrequently was the custom in that day, he went, in the year 1794, with two of his own vessels laden with flour to Bordeaux. His arrival there was at a time of such extreme scarcity that rations were issued to the inhabitants, and invitations to dinner contained a request that the guest should bring his own bread. This flour was sold at the almost famine price of fifty crowns the barrel. Investing the proceeds in brandy, he sailed to the free port of Guernsey to land it, and then repairing to London he sold the whole shipment to the Admiralty, to his great advantage. Gratified with an unusual success young Phillips with other American youth, obtained court-dresses and went in sedan chairs to a drawing-room. The apartment, as he said, was something like our old St. Peter's Church, with galleries around it, from which one had a good view. Taking his place there he saw George the Third and his Queen seat themselves on the throne, and the princes and princesses, of whom there were very many, ranged along side. He remembered that the Prince of Wales and his brothers would take out their sisters—the elder brother with the elder sister, and the next with the next and so on—and dance minuets in the stately manner which in that day was supposed to enforce, as it were, a propriety of demeanor not otherwise to be secured. What a Frenchman once said, "that the world is so small that one cannot get out of the way of people," was on this occasion realized by Phillips. Observing a person evidently of note enter, he inquired as to whom he was of a gentleman seated along side. "It is Mr. Pitt," was the reply. "And surely you must be a stranger to London not to recognize his person." "Yes," said Phillips, "I am an American, from Philadelphia, visiting here." "Ah!" said the strange gentleman, "I am acquainted in Philadelphia, I once passed some months there. I am Sir William Howe, and would be glad if you would tell me of my acquaintances there." He then inquired after a number by name, and particularly after the "Misses Chew of Germantown."

Ward has another record as follows:

"In 1777 one of the Keysers lived at or about the Rising Sun on the Germantown road. He was absent, but had told his wife that the British would surely come there, and that she must do the best she could to protect their property. This she effected by laying in a stock of wine and other essentials and directing the servants to pay every attention to the wants of the enemy. She then told one of her men that a pair of saddle-bags, filled with plate, was in a certain part of the stable and directed him to place, during the dinner, her side-saddle with bags on the best horse he could find among those belonging to the officers. Thus prepared, she mounted and fled, and while saving her silver acquired a fine horse. The silver was buried and lay so long a time that when taken up it was quite black. It has been seen by a descendant, Dr. Martin Coryell, of Lambertville, N. J., but was lost in 1833 by a robbery. Mrs. Coryell and her sister, Mrs. John Anderson, are descendants also of Mr. Duy, from whom Duy's lane takes its name."

Ward adds the following interesting note from Mr. Coryell, which is of interest, though it pertains to another subject. All of Ward's manuscripts deserve print. Would that some one would give them to the public. They are on various topics and refer to different sections of our country:

"Ann Hilborn (daughter of Ichabod and Sarah Wilkinson) was the wife of William Hilborn, who moved to Stockport, Wayne county, with Samuel Preston, and subsequently to the River Susquehanna near the Great Bend. Their daughter married Joe Smith, the founder of Mormons. I have been at their house and saw the knoll of a hill in which Joe pretended to have discovered the Mormon Bible with gilt leaves and binding unsullied. Joe was a raftman of lumber, and so misbehaved toward his wife that she returned to her father's. But after he founded the Mormon sect and became surrounded by proselytes she returned to his embraces as one of his wives, and became a fanatic.

    (Signed)   "LEWIS S. CORYELL."

It is said that Jemima Wilkinson was of the same family with Ann Wilkinson.

In reviewing ancient Germantown, the intensely German names of early settlers with the abundance of rough consonants in them is striking. Melchior Meng, Hans Milan and Arents Klinken are in point.

Mention has been made of the condition of the old roads. Watson says (Vol. II, p. 54): "The British army were covered with dust when they first passed through Germantown; they were at other times kept very clean. Their horses were heavy, clumsy and large. Horsemen of both armies would occasionally pass rattling through the streets of Germantown by night, and in the morning it was clearly designated of which side the horsemen were by the

THE SECOND BAPTIST CHURCH, MAIN AND UPSAL STREETS.

English horse being so very much larger in the hoof. The Hessian cavalry were gay ponies, much decorated with leather trappings."

I have seen an English horse shoe which indicated the vast size of the feet of some English horses, but in the present stone pavement of the old Germantown road the inhabitants could hardly trace hoof-prints in the morning to tell what manner of steeds had rattled along in the night.

As to properties, the following met my eye in an old law book. In the Laws of Pennsylvania, Vol. I, pp. 504–5, an act is recorded as passed February 18, 1769, enabling the Recorder of Deeds of Philadelphia city and county to receive in custody the ancient books and records of the corporation of Germantown.

In the PENNSYLVANIA EVENING Post, July 11, 1775, is the following advertisement:

GERMANTOWN BLEACHFIELD.

John Hunter, at the above Bleachfield, continues to whiten all sorts of plain Linen, Yard wide and under, not exceeding a 900 Reed, at 4d. per Yard, 1000 Reed, at 5d. per Yard, and all above at 6d. per Yard. Huckabacks and coarse Diapers at 4d. per Yard, fine Diapers at 5d. per yard. Twills, sheeting and plain Linen will be bleached for Merchants at 4d. per Yard, and dressed equal to any imported at 6d. per Piece. Cotton Thread whitened at 10d. per Pound, and Cotton Stockings at 4d. per Pair.

Families who have Table Linens stained or discolored may have them cleaned at a moderate Price.

Goods for said Bleachfield are received by the following Gentlemen in Philadelphia, viz: Mr. Francis Gurney, Merchant, in Front street, below the Draw Bridge; Mr. William Shute, Tallow Chandler, at the New Market; Mr. John Green, Merchant, near the upper end of Second street, and by John Hunter, at the Bleachfield. At all which Places Receipts will be given.

N. B.—The Advertiser presents his grateful Thanks to those who have favoured him with their custom; and the general Satisfaction he has given, he hopes will recommend him to their future Favours, and the Public in general; and as he has, at a considerable Expence, erected a Bleachfield suitable for carrying on a very extensive Business, he hopes the Public will give him such Encouragement as to enable him to prosecute so useful a Branch of the Linen Manufactory.

It is hoped that Mr. Hunter met with success. I have been told of some private persons in Germantown who followed this industry years ago, so it must be added to the Germantown manufactures. The New Market named ran from Second and Pine streets southward. The old Market of the city was at Second and Market streets—[Watson I, p. 301.]

SECOND BAPTIST CHURCH.

The following sketch of the Second Baptist Church has been contributed by Rev. John Love, Jr., the pastor:

"About twenty-seven years ago it became evident to careful observers that an inviting field for Christian work was presented in the vicinity of the present edifice of the Second Baptist Church. A Mission School was accordingly started in Franklin Hall, May 8, 1859. Seven teachers and sixteen scholars were present, and the little school was placed under the care of Mr. Joseph H. Harley, of the First Baptist Church. He was succeeded in a few months by Mr. William E. Burk. In the fall of 1861 Mr. C. H. Cummings was elected to the same office and has continued therein honored and beloved till the present time. Sabbath evening services were begun in the Hall, November 26, 1865, the pulpit being regularly supplied by city pastors and others. With the design of establishing a regular Baptist Church, Messrs. George Nugent and C. H. Cummings, in the early part of 1866, purchased in their individual capacity a portion of the Chew estate—a section of the old battleground—containing considerably more than an acre. The corner-stone of the chapel was laid May 12, 1866, and dedication services were held December 4. In October, 1871, Messrs. Nugent and Cummings made a proposition to the Church involving a surrender, on certain easy conditions, of all their claims against the Church, amounting to about $15,000, over and above their original subscriptions. Through this munificent offer the Church, after an existence of about five years, became possessed of a property free from all incumbrance which had cost about $40,000. The regular church organization was effected in September, 1866, with a constituency of thirty-two members, which within a year was increased to ninety-two. The first pastor was Rev. W. P. Hellings (now of Milwaukee, Wis.) who was called in February, 1867. Terminating his service in 1869, he was succeeded in the spring of 1870 by Rev. James Lisk. During his successful and eventful pastorate of thirteen years a commodious and attractive parsonage was built and the main edifice, an imposing structure, was reared. Dr. Lisk resigned his charge in June, 1883, to accept a secretaryship. The present pastor, Rev. John Love, Jr., began his relations in November, 1883. The Church is well organized and very prosperous. The Sunday School has grown to large proportions and has enjoyed remarkable prosperity. The property of the Church has been much improved of late.

In June, 1885, Mr. John Love, Sr., of New York, was by an unanimous vote elected to the offices of Associate Pastor and Sabbath-school visitor. It is believed that the relationship thus formed is entirely unique, no other instance being known of a father becoming an associate of his son. In the September following, Mr. Love was ordained to the full work of the ministry, which he had been exercising since 1853, under the limitations of a license. After a successful service of 18 months, in response to a call to become the Associate

GERMANTOWN. 219

Pastor of Rev. H. M. Sanders, in the Central Baptist Church, of New York City, he returned thither.

At the time of its organization, the Second Baptist Church numbered 32 members; 500 have since been baptized, 201 have joined by letter and 26 by experience, making a total of 727 names which have been enrolled on the membership of the church during its history.

The present membership (October, 1889) is 427. During the 23 years of its existence the church has raised for all purposes, about $173,000. The property of which it is now possessed is valued at $83,000, and is free of all encumbrance.

The growth and success of the church have been largely due to the Bible-school, which for upwards of a quarter of a century has been under the superintendency of Deacon Charles H. Cummings. In the summer of 1889, extensive improvements were made in the chapel. Galleries were erected at either end, and so divided as to provide 9 class-rooms, a library and Pastor's study. The platform was placed on one side of the room and chairs substituted for pews. Tasteful frescoing and attractive furnishings have rendered the chapel a model of beauty and convenience.

The re-opening services were held on the afternoon of October 6. Addresses were delivered by the Pastor, Rev. John Love, Jr., and Revs. James Lisk, D. D., John S. James, Wm. E. Needham, and others. Special services were also observed on the evening of that day, when an address was delivered by Rev. H. L. Wayland, D. D., editor of the NATIONAL BAPTIST.

QUEEN STREET.

About fifty-four years ago Queen street contained only Isaac Lackin's house, next west of the saw mill of Watson & Co., and an old-fashioned yellow frame house belonging to John Coulter, on Queen, west of Wayne, which is now demolished. A small story and a half house on the east side of Queen street, belonging to Mr. Disston, formerly was the property of the Brownhulse family. A lean-to adjoins it. The building is plastered and whitewashed.

Mr. Keifer's house, next to the house mentioned, is old, but modernized. It is now a grocery. The Jungurth house is near these buildings and has high steps. It is of stone, pointed. John Shingle's house, on the same side, is an old stone building. Mrs. Rittenhouse had a stone dwelling near. The place belongs to Mrs. Tilghman. The original dwelling has recently been demolished. It was an old landmark of stone. The Jungurths were carriage builders, and their place of business was below Jabez Gates's grocery, on same side, opposite Mr. William Wynne Wister's residence.

The frame house on the opposite side of the street, corner of Queen and Wayne streets, is the old Widdis property. Mrs. Widdis was a Miss Jungurth and her children still dwell there. The Shingle family are stone masons and builders of known reputation. The Jungurth house is owned by Samuel Bradbury, who bought it on the death of Miss Susan Jungurth, the last of the immediate family. The Littell estate runs through from Manheim street, having a large front on Queen street, adjoining the Rittenhouse property.

CARLTON.

On the west side of Queen lane, after crossing Township Line, we come to the estate of Cornelius S. Smith, called "Carlton," which name was taken from a castle of Queen Elizabeth. A stone in the foundation of the porch of the mansion has the date 1780. In a window pane in the stairway of the hall is the name M. R. Lee, 1827, Roxborough, written with a diamond ring. This was Mary, a sister of the Presiding Bishop of the Protestant Episcopal Church. This estate is a portion of a tract which contained 5000 acres which Wm. Penn, as Proprietary, deeded to John Lowther, and Ann Charlotte Lowther. He sells to Jos. Turner in 1731, who sells to John Ashmead. The Cornelius Smith estate was at one time over 100 acres. A part was sold to Mr. James C. Kempton, and is now owned by the Misses Waln, and Messrs. Sill and Dougherty, on School lane. The properties of Miss Emma Taylor, and Mr. H. L. Duhring, on the opposite side of Indian Queen lane, were also a part of it. Mr. James Vaux at one time held the property, and sold it to Mr. Wm. T. Stockton. The plantation was then called Roxborough.

The next owner of "Carlton" was Thomas Lee, father of Bishop Lee. Thomas Lee was followed in the ownership by John C. Craig, who married Miss Jane Josephine Biddle. He was a man of great wealth, and fond of horses, and kept a large stud of race horses for his amusement. He had a race course on the property. He died when traveling abroad, and the estate was sold to Mr. Cornelius S. Smith by Mr. Thomas Dunlap, executor, and guardian of the only child, a son, who died in youth. The large dwelling is built of stone and plastered and whitened, so that the exterior resembles the whiteness of the Haines house, on Main street. The partitions are of solid stone, plastered without lathing. The central part contains two stories and an attic, with a dormer window on each side. A fine old wide hall with an old stair case with antique woodwork is a pleasant point in the architecture, and the lawn on each side affords a pretty picture from the doors with the shrubbery and grass, in natural condition. The east doors of the hall are of remarkable width, and studded with brass nails, as a help against burglars. A stove pipe hole was cut in an upper panel perhaps before the days of hard coal and furnaces. In front there is a fine piazza with a stone floor and Grecian pillars. The rear of the hall, which contains the entrance from the carriage drive, in old English fashion, has a porch for admittance with a triangular front, containing a window on each side of the door. The parlor is furnished with chairs of the claw foot pattern or ancient style, which were a part of the furniture of the grandparents of the present occupants of the house, and stood on the first carpet used in Philadelphia at Fifth and Spruce

"CARLTON," QUEEN LANE, RESIDENCE OF CORNELIUS S. SMITH'S FAMILY.

streets, according to Watson's Annals. Mr. Craig built the two wings of the house, which he did not live to occupy. Under the main building are cellar kitchens and a sub-cellar. Under the front piazza is a wine cellar, and under the porch a vault for meat.

Cornelius S. Smith purchased the property in May, A. D. 1840. His two sons and two daughters (Robert L. and Cornelius S., and Rolanda S. Smith and Elizabeth S. Newhall), still occupy the old mansion. Since the purchase of the estate, it has been increased by purchase and diminished by sale. Mr. Smith purchased eighty-four acres in the original tract. A stone which used to be in a tenant house, which is now a ruin, reads thus: "Ruined by the war of 1777, rebuilt more firmly 1780 by the trusty Isaac Tustin." A number of Indian arrowheads, and several pennies of George the Fourth's day have been dug up on the property; the pennies had been taken up within four or five years. The Hessians were encamped on this place. The tradition is that Washington dined here. Some distance from the house Craig had his stables, which were of frame, and have since been removed.

The SCHUTZEN PARK is situated farther down the lane, as the music now heard reminds us, on the opposite side from Carlton, and joins Mr. H. L. Duhring's place.

Adjoining Carlton on the same side is a handsome stone house belonging to Mr. Samuel Bradbury. The estate contains some twenty acres. Mr. Bradbury is now opening streets, and building houses upon it.

At the corner of Queen lane and Township line was situated an old stone house and barn, belonging to the John Coulter estate. The stone barn was destroyed by fire several years ago. The mansion was removed on completion of the new railroad. It was occupied by Italian laborers during the building of the new railroad. One of the pretty stations called Queen Lane was built on the grounds.

THE SHIP HOUSE.

It is supposed that a sea captain had the ship placed which is formed of plaster of Paris on the lower gable of this house. The house is of stone plastered. The street has been raised thus lowering the house. The rear of the building was the first hall in Germantown, which was used for prayer meetings and singing-schools. It would hold 250 persons. The front part of the house is one hundred and twenty years old. The hall was built afterwards. George Peters kept a hotel here. The sign was the Indian's Treaty with Penn. Famous was this hotel in its day, and the Ship House is yet a noted spot. Sleighing parties used to come from the city, especially students. Mrs. Peters was a Miss Bender and was noted as a landlady, and as a helper among the sick. The Chestnut Hill stages used to stop here. The Bockius family, to whom I am indebted for information, think that stages first ran direct from here to the city. A little fire-engine called the Bulldog was kept in a small triangular room on the north side of the house. The roof joins the next house diagonally. In the days of the hotel it was the dependence of the town with its little leather buckets. The company was composed of volunteers. Mr. Josiah Woods owned and kept the hotel after Mr. Peters. The American army horses were accommodated here. Mr. James Ford bought the property and started a Ladies' Boarding School in it.

James Ford's Boarding and Day School for Young Ladies was in this place, about 1836, and afterward. The daughters of Watson, the annalist, attended it. Mr. Ford was a Scotchman. His wife was Miss Sutherland, of Scotland. Miss Isabella Sutherland, her sister, assisted in the instruction. Mrs. Sutherland, the mother of Mrs. Ford, an aged Scotch lady, made her home with them. The teachers were polished and well educated. The school was select and many young ladies of Philadelphia were educated there. The pupils were treated as members of the family. The place is just above Washington lane on the west side of Main street. The lot is large and the grounds are deep. The Fords went to California, and their descendants are there. The Chamberlain House, San Francisco, is kept by one of the family.

Charles Bockius bought the Ship House of the Fords about forty-five years ago, having previously owned and occupied the house below, which is No. 5226. Jacob Unrod, the grandfather of the Bockius family owned the land below the Ship House to Ellwood Johnson's house, together with the buildings there standing. He used to make horse collars, and his shop still stands, on the street below the Ship House, but partially destroyed.

The second house above Washington lane, on Main street, was owned by Wm. Keyser, who was a tanner and a brother of the Dunkard preacher, Peter Keyser. There was a tannery on the place in the rear of the house.

John Knorr was a noted town chronicler of Germantown. He died in a little stone house on the upper corner of West Walnut lane. The building has disappeared. He lived previously in a long house with small windows, which was called Noah's Ark from its appearance.

Rev. PETER KEYSER, Jr.

Abraham H. Cassel, of Harleysville, Pa., prepared a sketch of this good man for "The Brethren's Almanac," of 1884, which I will condense. The Keyser family were noted in Europe as followers of the eminent Menno Simon. Leonard Keyser was burned at the stake in Bavaria in 1527, on account of his religion. The family settled in Amsterdam. Hence Peter Dirck Keyser, the great-grandfather of the preacher, came to America, and in 1688 was one of the first settlers of Germantown. The preacher's grandfather, Dirck Keyser, was born here September 26, 1701; and Peter, his father, in 1732, on the 8th of August, and the preacher himself on November 9, 1766. The father was a tanner. He became a member of the "Church of the Brethren," sometimes called "German Baptists," and familiarly "Dunkards."

He was buried in the Concord graveyard, where most of the brethren were buried before they had a graveyard of their own. Rev. Peter Keyser, Jr., was baptized in his eighteenth year by Martin Urner, in 1784. He was a youth of quick conception and wonderful memory. He could readily commit chapters of Scripture. When grinding bark he had a shelf placed where he could see the open Bible while at work, and he memorized the New Testament and the greater part of the Old. The pious man was called to the ministry in 1785, and having proved a good laborer in Christ's vineyard, was installed Bishop or Elder in 1802, on the 2d of August. He died in the house in which he used to say that he was twice born, that is naturally and spiritually, on May 21, 1849, in his eighty-third year. The house is the one on Main street, near Washington lane, owned and occupied by Ellwood Johnson. Peter Keyser, Jr., was pastor of the Germantown and Philadelphia churches for sixty-three years. He was elder for forty-seven of these years. He was a very efficient preacher in English and German. He was profoundly learned in Scripture and was an eloquent orator. Crowds of hearers, including Roman Catholics and all denominations, attended his services. He used to rise at four o'clock to study before business, and this may have injured his sight, as he became blind. He preached, although blind. He would name a chapter and then repeat it from memory without missing a word. He would correct those who made a mistake in reading Scripture, as did the blind Saint Didymus, of Alexandria. Mr. Cassel says that, like Saul, he was "higher than any of the people," being six feet and three inches in height. He was "rather spare in form, but very athletic." In 1794 he gave up the tanning business, in which he had been engaged with his father, and removed to Philadelphia and entered into a large lumber business. In 1828 he retired and returned to Germantown. In his extensive business he never resorted to law suits. He was very tall and wore a Dunker suit of drab with a long coat and drab hat. Mr. Simpson, the author of "Eminent Philadelphians," speaks of his intimate knowledge of Holy Scripture in German and English. He seemed to remember the words of the whole Bible and the chapter and the verse which contained them. Rev. Dr. Phillip F. Mayer said that if the Scriptures were destroyed by accident he thought that Peter Keyser could replace them from memory. Mr. Keyser was a member of the Board of Health, and held office in the Prison Society and Public School Board. Dr. Peter D. Keyser has kindly added the following particulars to Mr. Cassel's interesting narrative:

"Peter Keyser resided in Germantown in the house now occupied by Ellwood Johnson, Main street, above Washington avenue, until 1794, when he moved to the city to embark in the lumber business with his brother-in-law, George Gorgas, on Front street, above Callowhill. He then purchased the homestead of Mr. Hare, the brewer (father of Robert Hare and John Hare Powell), on Callowhill street, below Second, where he resided until 1828, when he moved back into the old homestead of his father, where he lived until his death in May, 1849. He died in the same house in which he was born. He married, March 30, 1790, Catherine Clemens, of Horsham, Montgomery county. She was the daughter of Garret and Keturah Clemens. He left three sons—Elhanan W., Nathan Levering and Peter A.,—and six daughters. Mary, married to Christopher L. Langstroth; Elizabeth, to Benjamin Urner, of Cincinnati, Ohio; Hannah, to John Riehle; Clementine, to Michael K. Lynd (mother of Judge Lynd of this city); Susannah, to Frederick R. Backus, of New York; Margaret, to Cipriano Canedo, of Mexico."

The Rev. Mr. Keyser was a peace man in the Revolution, on account of his religious principles. In those stirring times his house was mobbed and stoned at night. He found a written paper belonging to a neighbor the next morning, and took it to him and said, "You paid me a visit last night."

The Keysers were long lived. They came from Holland, having left Germany previously on account of religious persecution. One branch of the family went to Baltimore. When Rev. Peter Keyser, Jr., was a boy he assisted in burying several soldiers after the battle of Germantown; one was a British officer. In the Upper Burying Ground, in the present generation, in digging a grave, buttons and clothing were unearthed, being relics of Revolutionary times. Peter Keyser lived in Callowhill street in the winter. He left his city house on account of yellow fever, and placed it in charge of a trusted servant, a redemptionist. This man died in the owner's absence, and was buried in some place unknown to Mr. Keyser, who was anxious to ascertain his burial place. In walking with his wife on a moonlight evening they both saw the figure of the dead man sitting above a grave in Franklin Square, and the figure vanished as they spoke about him. They found that this was his grave.

THE DUNKARD CHURCH.

On the east side of the Main street, a little above Sharpnack street, lies the old Dunkard Church. This is the first church of this denomination in the United States. It is now under the charge of Rev. Mr. Fry, of Philadelphia. The church was founded in the year of our Lord 1745. In approaching the church the sexton's house draws the attention. Owing to the raising of the grade of the street the building has been depressed. It has a quaint look, with its pent-roof, and the dormer windows make a second story in appearance. It is entered by a descent. Joseph Scheetz, the present sexton, occupies it. The angles into which the upper side is broken add to its picturesqueness. Mr. Scheetz informs me that the house is over 200 years old, and that forty deeds represent the property belonging to the church grounds. Christopher Saur, the printer, was a preacher in this place. There is a neat yard in front of the church. The edifice is simple. There is a porch before the door. Flag-stones cover its floor. Some ladies who have relatives buried in the grave yard have had an excellent flag-stone walk laid to the burying-ground in the rear. A circular window surmounts the porch and an arched window is on each side of the door. Formerly the ceiling was low, but the upper floor has been removed, and the ceiling has been raised and arches introduced. There are two arches on each side of the pulpit. John Mack was the first preacher and founder of the parish. His German epitaph reads: "Born 1712, died 1805." His wife Elizabeth is buried at his side. As we stand in this beautiful cemetery on this pleasant hill-slope, under the November sun, the sexton gives the striking information that about 2060 are buried in this city of the dead. They are quiet neighbors. A good wall surrounds the inclosure, which has stood about 50 years. Judge James Lynd was buried here in 1875. Here is the tomb stone of Godfried Lehman, which has been brought here from his place of burial when his body was removed. He was born in Putzkau, in the city of Dresden, Saxony, in Europe. Departed this life here in Germantown, October 4, A. D. 1756, aged 67 years, 11 months and 26 days. Peter Keyser was a preacher here. He lived for many years in Ellwood Johnson's present residence. He lies among his old flock. Here is his epitaph:

"PETER KEYSER.

Born November 19th, 1766. For more than sixty years a follower of the religion of Jesus, and for fifty years pastor of the German Baptist Church of this place. Died May 21st, 1849, aged 83 years. Finally brethren farewell; be perfect, be of good comfort, be of one mind, live in peace; and the God of love and peace shall be with you."

By his side is his wife. Her epitaph reads: "Catherine Clemens, wife of Peter Keyser, Born May 14th, 1770, Died June 6th, 1855, Aged 84 years."

This cemetery is kept in excellent order, and on this fall day there is a pleasure "akin to pain" in thus consorting with the dead, among whom we shall so shortly be numbered. The polite sexton and my antiquarian friend, J. Duval Rodney, Esq., assist my researches. A number of the Keyser family sleep peacefully beneath us. The Foxes, the Langstroths, and the Lehmans are also interred here. The Gorgas family have made this a place of sepulture. The epitaph of a former preacher is as follows: "In memory of my Grandfather, Charles Hubbs. Born June 16th, 1761. Died April 27th, 1847, in his 87th year. At the age of twenty he united with the German Baptists, preaching many years in this Meeting House, giving his services free in the cause of Christ. Erected by Virginia Hubbs." The cemetery grounds were enlarged by purchase not long since. The old horse-sheds are about to be removed to give more space for burials. The simple ancient brown building which faces the street on this narrow entrance to the deep lot dates from 1745. It is mentioned by the Swedish traveler Kalm.

Watson gives 1709 as the date when Tunkards from Germany and Holland came to Germantown, their first settlement in Pennsylvania. He speaks of a log house used for worship which stood in front of the present stone one. Alex. Mack was a leader. He was a rich miller from Cresheim, who gave his property into the common stock and in 1708 came, with eight or ten others, to Germantown. In 1719 others followed. Mack died at an advanced age. His son Alexander lived beyond the age of ninety. John Bettikoffer built the log house named above in 1731 for his dwelling. Alexander Mack, Jr., succeeded his father in the ministry of this parish. As early as 1723 Peter Baker was the minister. The Ephrata Tunkards dressed uniformly, their heads being covered with the hoods of their gray surtouts, like Dominican friars. Watson adds that old people living when he wrote remembered seeing forty or fifty of them on religious visits to Germantown, with long beards and girdles and barefoot, or with sandals, in Indian file, silently walking along.

Ward gives this anecdote about Dunkards, which may find its niche here:

"Mrs. Innes Randolph's grandfather, Robert Rutherford, was a member of the House of Burgesses of Virginia for about thirty years and of the Federal Congress of 1793. Early in life, in attempting to cross a swollen ford, he came near being drowned, a fate from which he was saved by one of the people called Dunkards. Filled with gratitude, Rutherford expressed his hearty thanks and promised to do anything his preserver would request. The simple-minded Dunkard said he would be pleased if Rutherford would assume the plain garb of the sect, and if he would wear his beard untrimmed as they did. This was somewhat more serious then than at this time when beards are so common. Adorned in this unusual manner, Rutherford made his appearance in Philadelphia, where, with other members of Congress, he was often invited out to dine. On one of these occasions he repaired to the house of his host somewhat before the hour named, and that hour in the age when so much devolved upon the hostess often required a considerable grace. Under the supposition that the visitor was a Pennsylvania Dunkard farmer, he was ushered into the kitchen, where he was at once requested to aid in peeling potatoes, after which he was invited to remain there. The dinner soon was ready and all the guests but one were assembled. The remarks usual on such occasions were made, and of course there was one concerning the untrimmed beard of the tardy member. This opened the eyes of the hostess, who at once exclaimed: 'He must be the man whom I requested to peel potatoes.' He was now soon seated at a table that proved all the merrier for a mishap which he enjoyed as much as any one there."

The following incident, narrated by Ward, has reference to the locality of the Dunkard Church:

"On Monday, June 28, 1885, I entered a passenger car at Wayne Station to go along the Germantown road to Cliveden, and I witnessed in it one of those little exhibitions of life that adds to its charm. In the car there were two men whose remarks attracted my attention. I gathered that they had left Germantown a quarter of a century ago to enter the army. Since then they had lived in Illinois, as well as I could make out. As we passed along the road they pointed out many a place they recognized, and occasionally they would call to some one they knew. One or two had been fellow soldiers, judging from their replies. When opposite the Dunker's Church, filled with enthusiasm, inspired by the glories of their native place, they spoke of the great age of the building, for it stood there, they said, at the time of the Revolution. This they addressed to a companion, a young man of about twenty-five, who was visiting the East for the first time. 'What was the Revolution?' inquired he. 'Revolution! Why, that was when the Americans fought for their liberties.' 'When was it?' 'In 1776.' The young man, whose remembrance did not carry him back so far, relapsed into a silence so profound that it was evident the matter was beyond his comprehension."

I gladly acknowledge aid from J. Duval Rodney, Esq., in tracing the history of upper Main street. In the account of the Manual Labor School a distinguished professor was called McCoy by mistake. The name should be Charles F. McCay, LL. D. Roberdeau Buchanan writes Ward that his genealogies of the Roberdeau family and "Descendants of Dr. William Shippen, the Elder" will give an account of some of the old inmates of the Blair House. They can be seen at the rooms of the Historical Society of Pennsylvania. The same gentleman writes me that there is a discrepancy in Watson who speaks of Lieut. Whitman as a patient of Dr. Witt after the battle, while he gives the date of the Doctor's death as 1765. He adds that Vice President Breckenridge should have been described as the grandson of Rev. Samuel Stanhope Smith, President of Princeton College.

For notice of Hessians on Mrs. Cornelius S. Smith's place, mentioned in a previous number, see J. J. Smith's Life of Henry Hill, and Ed. J. Lowell's Hessians in the Revolution.

One of the English weavers who came over with John Button said that Manheim street was originally a cart track to the farms in the rear. A part of it was called Shinbone Alley. Haines street was the first one opened as a street rather than a road and it was quite an event when that occurred.

The Upper Burying Ground contains some inscriptions which show the gradual change from the use of the German language to the English. First there is the name Schneider, then Snyder, and afterward Taylor follows in consecutive order, which is a translation of the German, as in old English this is the same as our word tailor. There is this remarkable epitaph: "A. Snyder, aged 969." The age was 69 and the first 9 was put in by mistake. The number was filled with cement, which fell out and left the strange record.

While the early purchasers of Germantown were styled the Frankfort Land Company, the patent given by Penn to the German and Dutch through his secretary, Markham, authorizing survey and location, is worded respectively to each ; so that they must have acted individually, though in concert. The Frankfort association should be called a combination rather than a company. Each separate foreign owner gave his power of attorney to the American agent. Carpenter street was nearly the line between Ancient Germantown and Cresheim.

The residence of John Stephen Benezet was spoken of by Ward but not exactly located. I have learned that he lived nearly opposite the Adamson mansion on Main street. His house has disappeared.

The Mennonite graveyard figured in the battle of Germantown. A later incident gives it a mournful history. In firing cannon here on the 4th of July, seventy or eighty years ago, one of the Unruh family was killed and two were maimed for life.

I have had the pleasure of seeing a picture of the old Mennonite church, drawn by Richards, which gives Samuel Keyser's house, which used to stand on the upper side. He was the father of Gideon, Reuben and Daniel Keyser. It was customary for the family to gather under the old roof-tree on Sundays. A frame shoe shop stood back of the stone house and a court yard in the rear contained several houses. The marble yard was a part of the property before Pastorius street was opened. The double house of Mrs. Washington Pastorius is now just above the site of the old mansion. Samuel Keyser had a number of young apprentices.

Bishop Benjamin Ely, in his History of the Mennonites, states that Herman Opden Graeff was a delegate to the Mennonite Conference, held in the city of Dortrecht on April 21st, A. D. 1632; and signed the eighteen Articles of Faith of the Mennonite Church. He was the father of eighteen children, one of whom, named Isaac, had four children, three sons and one daughter named Margaretta. This is the family that settled early in Germantown. My attention has been drawn to this interesting fact by Mr. Daniel Kulp Cassel, of Nicetown, a descendant in the sixth generation of Rev. Martin Kulp, the noted preacher at the Skippack Mennonite church. He is preparing a History of the Mennonites which he purposes to publish in book form, and which will be interesting to Germantown people, as treating of the early inhabitants.

Below the late Charles Megargee's residence was Mary Moyer's shop with this sign:

> "I, Mary Moyer, keep cakes and beer;
> I make my sign a little wider to let you know I sell good cider."

About where Pastorious street is was the property of Mr. Keisel. There was a house there which has disappeared. It was used as a tenement house, and several families occupied it.

On Morton street, between Hermon and the point where Tulpohocken would cut through, if it were opened, stands an old mansion long known as the COCOONERY. It was built by Philip Syng Physick, son of Dr. Physick, for the purpose of propagating silk-worms, about 1840, during the Multicaulis fever. Germantown was at that time covered with trees, planted for the food of the silk-worms. One of them still stands in St. Michael's churchyard, in High street, but improvements have largely swept them away. The trees were spread broadcast by Mr. Physick and his friends, but the venture did not result in much profit. A similar building, also yet called the

Cocoonery, now stands on the West Chester turnpike, a little beyond the Burd Asylum, and is a relic of those wild days of speculation. The Germantown Cocoonery was originally a one-story building. A second-story was afterward added some years ago, the present owner, Samuel Eastburn, adding a Mansard roof. The house was formerly like a great hall. For at least twenty years this large wooden building has been a boarding-house. The mulberry tree and the silk industry have had a wonderful history, as they have traveled together through the ages from their home in China, to Persia and Turkey and Greece and Italy. The white and red berries of the trees, which had shone under the sunlight in France and Spain, enlivened the streets of Germantown for a time, and then departed.

The property of HENRY FREAS lies on the west side of Main street, separated by one house intervening from the residence of Gideon Keyser. The three-story building there is on land formerly owned by Mr. Raser, and afterward by Joseph Baisch. Two stone houses, which have disappeared formerly stood on the ground. Matthias Raser was a tanner, as Gideon Keyser informs me. The white house numbered 5166 belonged to him and afterward to Baisch. Caspar Heft's grandfather—paternal grandfather—lived opposite Mr. Engle's present residence, in the Revolution. The land between Vernon Hall and the Wister estate once belonged to the Channon family. No. 5073, which has been demolished while these papers were appearing, was a quaint little building on the Carpenter estate, opposite the Haines place, used by John Francis, as a shoe shop. Its polite occupant showed me the structure before its demolition. It was the Germantown Post-Office during Andrew Jackson's administration. The walls are thick and solid. A closet cut into the wall was like the firm book-cases of a room in an English university. The ancient hinges and time-worn ceiling and inner wall had done duty for many a day. Several inches of accumulated lime wash were once taken from the walls on the first floor. The room yielded fifty-six baskets of scrapings. The old whitewashers did their duty well. It is said that Dr. Witt once lived in this house. Nos. 5159 and 5163 belonged to Christopher Hergesheimer. The building is the same, but it has been altered. Frederick Johnson has his livery stable there. No. 5216 is Mrs. Hocker's residence. It is made interesting by the fact that James E. Murdock, the elocutionist, once lived there and practiced his art. The old stone house marked No. 5218 belonged anciently to the Unrod family. It also belonged to Anthony Johnson, the father of Justus Johnson. Enoch Taylor now lives in it. The Main street depot of the Reading Railroad is on the Wunder property. The first ticket agent was Major Matthias Holstein, of a Swedish family, of Norristown. He had held stock in the railway, which collapsed, and so he got this berth. Messrs. Brooks and Krickbaum followed him in this position.

At the upper corner of East Walnut Lane, on Main street, the Rev. Dr. Blair built a house for his son-in-law, Major Roberdeau. Mr. Perot now resides there. John Button, the manufacturer, lived and died here. The house belongs to his grandson, Priestly Button. The next house above Mr. Button's house, marked 5105, was formerly owned by John Leibert. It afterwards fell into the hands of Conyers Button. Mr. Button owns the next double house. The Washington bakery is on the site of the house of George Ax. Frederick Ax was a militia officer in the Revolution, and a prominent early Methodist. The picturesque house of John Knorr, which stood at the upper corner of West Walnut lane and Main street, must not be forgotten. It was torn down a few years ago. An allusion to it has already been made, but it was of such interest that it deserves another word.

[Germantowners will see at the close of this sketch the name of a fellow citizen long noted in business, as well as in poetry and hymnody. He kindly aids our work.]

My earliest recollections of Germantown date back about fifty years, a short time after the railroad was put in operation. My first visit was on a summer afternoon with a friend, and most of the route was beautifully rural, as the city had made but little progress northerly at that day, fields with post-and-rail fences being then undefaced by the multitudes of houses seen by present travelers on the road. We were landed on an open space facing the Main street, and we started out to view the borough. We went up and down the long thoroughfare, and found it intersected by a few green lanes. All was slumberously quiet, with an occasional sleepy-looking inn. Few people were seen. The staunch stone houses with closed blinds seemed to be asleep, and the trees also. Everything indicated that the inhabitants were given to contemplative ease. We were strangers, without an acquaintance there, and we found no place of rest for our feet, no public garden, no ice-cream saloon nor spruce-beer nor peanut stand—nothing but a tavern or two, which we did not care to enter. The pavements were uneven, with frequent driveways across at the side of the houses. Well, we grew weary, and as no fitting place offered to us opportunity to join the burghers in their slumberous proclivities, we returned to the starting place and re-entered a car, and awaited the departure of the train.

The cars were composed of three compartments, as if three coach-bodies had been fastened together. Each compartment was entered by side doors, and contained two seats as broad as the car-body and facing each other, so that eight or ten persons would fill a compartment. The conductor in collecting tickets walked along a strip or platform on the side. Afterward cars of the present shape were added, except that the seats ran lengthwise, from the front to the rear, two of them back to back in the centre, with one on each side against the windows. I remember riding at another time in a Manayunk car, with cross-seats as now, but with leather curtains, fastened by buckles in bad weather, instead of glass sashes. I have a lively recollection of this car, for after I had unloosed a curtain to look out for my getting-off place, a conductor came along, and crying out "What fool opened this curtain?" at once refastened it. This was the only discourtesy I have ever experienced in a railroad car; and this, I am glad to say, was not on the Germantown branch.

In the early days of the Germantown Railroad the conductors did not hesitate to stop and pick up passengers along the way. Once, while returning to town from a visit to a friend who resided in the old borough, I saw a man running swiftly over the field where the Glen Echo Carpet Mills now stand; and as he ran he lustily bellowed out, "S-t-o-p! S-t-o-p! S-t-o-p!" The engine not coming to a standstill at once, the man continued to shout as he drew nearer. The engineer, becoming angry, let out a curse and exclaimed, "Do you think I can stop a locomotive like a wheelbarrow?" The man got aboard and the train went on. Railroads, like bad watches, did not keep exact time in that day. A daughter tells me that during a trip to Florida years ago the conductor halted his train for half an hour to give the passengers an opportunity to witness a horse-race. Another time he stopped to gather wild flowers for the lady passengers, and further on he waited awhile near a house by the roadside to allow a young woman to run over and kiss her mother, who resided there.

The Wingohocken, famed as a beaver haunt in the olden days of the borough, now glided ripplingly beside the embankment between Church lane and Shoemaker lane stations, and shone in the sunlight like a diamond studded ribbon. Before reaching the latter station, however, its course was deflected to the east by a massive rock. In the far-away ages the brook had cut its way into the side of the rock until a canopy of stone hung over it. On this rock Mr. Shoemaker erected a small stone house, now known as the Rock House and reputed to be the oldest building in Philadelphia; and the rocky projection formed the platform from which William Penn is said to have preached to the people gathered in the meadow below. Some iconoclastic agent of the Reading Railroad, devoid of antiquarian proclivities, a year or two ago had its ancient and venerable stone walls smeared over with mortar. Ugh!

The Wingohocken seemed to be an innocent little stream, with nothing to do but sing on its way to the delight of maiden and of poet, until some practical economic folk put it to use in turning round and round certain mill-wheels as far down its course as Fisher's Lane; and yet the quiet stream once in awhile broke out in sudden rages, even to the destruction of life of man and beast. These, however, came on rare occasions only, when a vast and sudden rainfall deluged its extensive water-shed. Phew! how it rushed at the old stone bridge over Church lane! and when the arched openings under it were not able to give the waters passage way, how it piled itself up and backed over the meadow till it became a lake! The bridge at Shoemaker lane formed a second obstacle, and the field between the two lanes became a second lake. Only a few years ago, the Armat street bridge was carried off just after night-fall, and the waters swept across the street and bore away a carriage in which an indiscreet coachman had attempted to stem the stream, and amid the darkness and thunder and lightning, the horse and the driver and his master's son all perished.

The stream silently subsided in the night time, and the bodies were found in the morning.

Honey Run, a little tributary to the Wingohocken, passes under the Main street above Chelten avenue. Once when that street was flooded by a furious rain, an aquatic dog leaped into the water and to the surprise of some on-lookers, suddenly disappeared. He had been sucked into an inlet opening into the Run and his fate was thought to be sealed. Not so, for after being swiftly carried for nearly a quarter of a mile, he had been shot out into the Wingohocken, and swimming to land, he returned from his subterrene excursion a wet and wiser dog.

In early times the Wingohocken valley was most beautiful. I have been told that a fine grove of trees studded the hillside above the present gas works, and down the declivity danced a silvery streamlet; and lovers were wont to wander here—and, no doubt, soberer folk too—to enjoy the mellow moonlight of summer eves.

Notwithstanding the somnolent characteristics of our first visit to Germantown, the beauties of her surroundings and the railroad thitherward more than rewarded us, and awakened within us a burning longing for an abiding place in her bosom. Some twenty years passed before an opportunity came for gratifying the passion. Hard work began to show its legitimate effect, and mind and body grew worn and weary. "Ride daily on horseback, or remove to Germantown," this was the doctor's dictum. The latter alternative was taken; and a red brick house next to Isaiah Hacker's place on the Main street was the only place of refuge available.

During our first winter a heavy snow storm visited the place. It began on Sunday at one o'clock P. M., the thermometer marking zero, and continued through most of the night. A furious wind prevailed and the snow was drifted into great heaps; and Germantown was shut off from the rest of mankind. The railroad was blocked. On Tuesday morning a large sleigh, with four horses and crammed with passengers, started from the hotel at Price street corner; but on reaching Negley's hill it came to a stand-still, for the wind had swept it bare. Two of us started ahead to walk until the sleigh should overtake us. We got along well enough till we reached Nicetown, where the snow was deep, and the traveling became toilsome. The sleigh did not overtake us, and we arrived in the city weary and wet with perspiration, notwithstanding the coldness of the morning. The train got through on Tuesday afternoon, though Manayunk remained still blockaded.

The Main street and Mill street continuation of a turnpike were the only macadamized avenues. There was no horse railroad on Germantown road; but a decaying plank road began on Wayne avenue at Queen street crossing and ran thence to Manheim street, thence to Pulaski avenue, and down this avenue cityward. A toll-gate stood at its entrance into Pulaski avenue, whence the planks were laid on both sides of a magnificent row of trees that then adorned the middle of that avenue; and very picturesque was the spot.

After the horse-road had been laid along the Main street, a rival road was constructed on Wayne avenue, but it did not become popular and its route was changed to run along Manheim and up Green street. An injunction was prayed for by the Main street line, and the court decided that the change of route was illegal and the new road was abandoned. Afterward a new steam road was projected, the route to be down Wayne avenue and under the old steam line at what is now known as Wayne Junction and thence to the city, coming in on Broad street. This was vigorously opposed and the scheme came to grief, but not till after a large amount had been expended in grading and quarrying through Wayne avenue, to the detriment of some of the properties along the route, which were left some thirty or forty feet high above the avenue.

Not a few of the streets were notable for numerous ruts and clayey holes in early spring; and if some of them could have been paved with the curses of teamsters whose wagons stuck fast in the holes, they would have been model roadways, Green street and Shoemaker lane especially. The sidewalk of Green street and some other streets were from two to four feet above the roadway and unpaved. Chelten avenue was opened only as far as Green street westerly, and apple trees adorned its predestined roadway several feet above its level.

Only a single track lay between Tioga street and Germantown, and the up-going train was compelled to await the down-coming one before it could leave Tioga. The Eclipse and the Fort Erie are the only locomotives that I now remember; and they were small but sturdy. Duy's lane was the Cape Hatteras of the railroad, and many a hard tussle did the little engines have before they were able to round that ascending point, and this they could not accomplish until the engineer spilled sand on the rails. One night when a heavy train was behind, even this last resort failed, and the train was divided and one-half was left on the road and brought up afterward. I got out and footed my way up to Shoemaker lane. These little engines perhaps still have a place in the Company's Museum, alongside the first locomotive built by Baldwin. The station at Germantown being 225 feet above tide water, a gravity car used to be started at 6 A. M. to find its way to town unaided by an engine. It was an exhilarating ride in the early summer morning, the speed of the car being kept under control by means of a brake. The only stopping place was at the bridge over the Main street. A bell hung on the front platform gave warning when approaching cross-roads and to stragglers on the track.

Of the early conductors in memory's gallery three are distinctly in my view: Hilary Krickbaum, Joseph Kite and Daniel Dungan, all capable men and veterans on the road and all now "gone over to the majority." Dungan was the lady-travelers' favorite, and they once complimented him with a gold watch. He was mild-spoken and of gentle manners, slim-built and medium height, and yet what a veritable Hercules he was when a rowdy misbehaved in a car! Some roughs once beset him at a station on the Germantown Railroad. Daniel was a proficient in the "noble art of self defense;" and he struck out right and left, and after laying several of the rowdies on the ground, he quietly stepped aboard his train and passed on. Dungan's gentle words and cheerful aspect seem to have been inherited by most of his successors even to the present.

While rambling near the Wissahickon about thirty years ago, I rested awhile on the trunk of a tree that had fallen beside the stream. A venerable man came along and sat down beside me, and we soon began to talk. Pointing to the hill opposite, then covered with trees, he said: "In 1796, when I was twenty-one years old, I cut down all the trees on that hill, and sold the wood for six dollars a cord." "Was not that a high price?" "Well, we wondered then where fuel was to come from after awhile. No one dreamed that an abundance of coal would be found in our own State." He told me that his name was Rittenhouse.

Most of the grand trees that bordered the railroad have disappeared. Some still remain in the improved grounds on the west of the railroad above Shoemaker lane, now Penn street. One, a tulip tree, was measured a month ago, which proved to be a few inches short of one hundred and twenty feet in height. They measure from eleven to fourteen feet in girth. Time is gradually diminishing their number. This place was known as Thomson's woods, and I remember participating long ago in a Sunday School picnic held therein, when it was bounded by a post-and-rail fence in the rear and by a fine arborvitæ hedge along the lane as far as John Jay Smith's villa. Fine oaks were in the Logan grounds, with chestnuts, on the west of the road. A band of Indians were wont to camp under these large chestnuts in pleasant weather, and sell their wares, even until within a dozen years or so. They may have been remnants of a tribe who still had traditions of the time when the old Governor was the friend of the Chief Wingohocken, and who gave his name to the beautiful stream soon to be entirely buried from human sight within the murky confines of a sewer. Just above Nicetown, to the east of the road was a fine grove of trees with an eye pleasing sward beneath them. The brickmaker has since been there, and nothing but clay-holes now mark the spot where once all was sylvan beauty.

A row of majestic and venerable willows adorned both sides of Church lane east of the railroad. Gnarled, warty and weather-beaten, with long branches, sleepily pendant or gracefully swinging at the back of the breeze, they seemed to be mementoes of the days when the men of unruffled lives and tempers dignified the borough. One tree stood in the middle of the road, at the intersection of Willow avenue. Tradition says that General Washington was wont to enjoy an evening hour under its pleasant summer shade; and the tree was allowed to remain untouched by the ax until a windy blast laid it low a few years ago. More fortunate was it than a large hickory tree—the finest I ever saw—that stood not long ago on the verge of the gutterway in Hancock street, west of Church lane. I always looked upon it with admiration, and as it would not interfere materially with the future curving of the sidewalk it seemed a long and honored life would be its destiny. But, on approaching it one morning, I saw a number of laborers standing around it with axes in hand, and to my consternation and horror I discovered that a deep gash had been cut clean around the tree, through the bark and far into the wood. I was dumfounded when I saw that nothing could now be done to save the tree. There was no necessity for its destruction and I could see no apology for the barbaric act. My wrathful indignation was intense, and the old feeling stirs within my heart even to this day.

What a pleasure-ground for the rambler was rural old Germantown! How many delightful spots for a stroll with wife and children! And were not sundry such rambles duly recorded in the GERMANTOWN TELEGRAPH a score and a half of years ago? And were they not modestly signed Query? Verily! What could surpass the scene around and about Roberts's quaint old mill, with its overshot wheel, its crystal brook, its mossy rocks with mint growing in the damp and shady places, and behind it on the upper level a beautiful lakelet and park-like acres? Did we not often get on a great rock beside the mill and quietly watch the mice hop about the window sills, and listen to the sweet trickling music of the brook as it danced around the slippery rocks? Ah me! how its glory has departed, the ugly abominations of mis-called dwellings that now deform the scene bear eloquent witness.

Another charming and romantic place was the old water-works dam, through which Paper Mill Run found its sinuous way toward the Wissahickon. This is a lovely spot yet, and will doubtless long remain such, with the admirable frontage of St. Peter's Church, and the embellishment of the beautiful houses lately erected near it by Mr. Houston.

What a lovely and romantic spot was the country surrounding Kelly's dam before the Chestnut Hill Railroad ran right straight through it and destroyed it. On the west side the ground sloped gently, diversified by evergreen's growing amid shelving rocks, to the water's edge. On the opposite side the land rose more boldly, and groups of trees hung over the banks or spread themselves about picturesquely up to and beyond an old red house now adjoining the Catholic College on Chelten avenue, then unopened and ungraded. It was my wont to wander there on summer afternoons in days lang syne, before I removed to Germantown, and muse a quiet hour while wandering around or reposing on the grand old rocks. A strong dam had been built here, and the Wingohocken, " cribbed, cabined and confined," spread itself out until it formed a beautiful lake, and sang merrily as its surplus water fell over the high dam into an abyss below. Well, well; the beauty has vanished to the eye; but the delightsome picture is fresh in my memory, "a thing of joy forever."

THOMAS MACKELLAR.

REV. PETER KEYSER, the faithful parson, who was described in a former article, said that one of the soldiers shot at the battle of Germantown was wounded in such a way that his leg was drawn up, and when the body was disinterred in later years the sinew was found to be contracted. This clergyman was a boy nearly eleven years of age at the time of the battle, and was concealed in the cellar of the Mennonite Church when General Agnew's gold lace attracted his attention and led him to believe that his position in the British army was high. The boy gathered bullets and cartridges as mementoes of the battle, but some British officers compelled him to give them up.

Much was said by Ward of the Saurs as Germantown printers, but as I find a Jansen mentioned as a printer in one of Samuel Pennypacker's sketches, perhaps the Johnson family may trace back to one who helped to enlighten the world by the printing press.

As to the yellow fever, a daughter of Mr. Johnson and the wife or daughter of Mr. Hubbs died of it, about the beginning of the plague, and an aged resident thinks that those were the only cases in Germantown. Watson says that six or eight persons died of it in Germantown, who "had derived it from Philadelphia."

A pebble-dashed house above Duval street, on the west side of Main, is now in the hands of the Thomas family. Formerly it was the property of William Keyser, who was a brother of the Dunkard preacher. He was a tanner.

On the northwest corner of Main and Upsal streets, stands an antique and picturesque cottage, which was the residence of John Bardsley. He was called "Sparrow Jack." The City Councils sent him to England to bring over sparrows to destroy the measuring worms, which troubled the trees as well as those who passed under them. The cry soon was, "Deliver us from our friends," for the sparrows proved more troublesome than the worms. Bardsley went to England through the influence of William F. Smith, who was a Councilman, and who resided in Germantown at that time.

An ancient stone house stood at the northwest corner of Main and Johnson streets, a story and a half high, with hipped roof. It belonged to the Johnson estate. A tablet in the gable on Johnson street had the date 1698.

Some fifty years ago there was a stone house above the Buck tavern on the same side. It has now disappeared. Mrs. Catharine Rittenhouse, when a young woman, at the battle of Germantown, took refuge in its cellar, opposite her own place of abode, and saw two British officers on the other side of the street from her position, heard the report of cannon and saw both knocked over and killed.

The passer-by in Haines street cannot help noticing a quaint, old-fashioned house on the lower side of the street. This is the old Germantown Infant School. It was founded in 1829 by John Snowden, Henry and Reuben Haines, with the aid of a board of ladies, and has been carried on in Haines street for many years. A small fee was charged for those who could pay, and the very poor came free. It is now to be given up, because the public schools supply the want. Mrs. William Wister and Mrs. John S. Haines are directresses; Miss A. M. Johnson is secretary, and Miss J. H. Bacon, treasurer. A late sketch of the worthy institution states that in olden times the children were provided with bread and molasses for dinner, and the little ones had a bed ready if they dropped asleep. The girls were taught to sew and to spin flax. The tuition was ten cents per week. Subscriptions paid what was lacking in the expenses.

TULPOHOCKEN STREET.

The name of this street is said to have been given in honor of an Indian chief.

Paper Mill Run, called so from Rittenhouse's paper mill, formerly ran along this street, but the Pennsylvania Railroad has cut it off.

Walnut lane derived its name from an immense black walnut tree, which was allowed to stand in the street after it was opened. It was near the barn on the Haines property.

Highland avenue was formerly called Thomas's lane. It was densely wooded fifty years ago.

Harvey street was called Roop's lane from the Roop family, who lived in it.

The old road of Germantown ran by the old Poor House, as Watson notes.—Annals, Vol. II, p. 35. It went in by the first (old) bank of Germantown and came out by Concord School House.

Chew street was Division street, as it divided the town lots from the side lots which extended back from this line.

At B. W. Beesley's, Coulter street, is the marriage certificate in fac-simile of Casper Wister and Katharine H. Johnson, in Friends' Meeting, at "Abbington," on March 25th, A. D. 1726. The Shoemaker and Jones and Bringhurst and Johnson families are among the signers, as well as Anthony Klincken and two females of that name. It is an interesting scrap of history. The Friends' Record Books, or their copies in the Historical Library of Pennsylvania, would afford many such. The Friends had so many signing witnesses that they made history.

ROADS.

" February 12th, 1801, the Germantown and Perkiomen Turnpike Company was incorporated. The road was to begin at the corner of Third and Vine streets. Benjamin Chew was chosen president, and John Johnson, treasurer. This improvement had become necessary. The old road to Germantown ' was called the worst road in the United States,' and travelers often went around by the way of Frankford, or across the open fields to escape its deep ruts."—Scharf & Westcott's History of Philadelphia, Vol. I, p. 509.

" It took Isaac Norris's team all day to carry a load from Fair Hill to Philadelphia and back, yet the Germantown road was one of the earliest laid out."—Scharf & Westcott's Philadelphia, Vol. I, p. 148.

At Penn's creek, Watson speaks of a "fearful quicksand." Teams used to be joined together to aid each other in pulling loads out of mires; horses were injured and sometimes killed. Rail stakes were set up in bad places to warn

people to avoid them. "A ride to the city" was thought "a serious affair."—
Annals, Vol. II, p. 33.

HOUSES.

In his oration at the Centennial of the Germantown Academy, Sidney George Fisher well said: "German thrift, morality, steadiness and good feeling prevailed also, and their impress on the neighborhood is yet visible in the manners of the people and the substantial, comfortable and prosperous look of the houses of the old time, many of which remain. Their rich gables, projecting eaves and cornices, hipped roofs, and pleasant sheltered porches, are similar to those now to be seen in the cities and villages on the Rhine, and whilst they recall a respectable and interesting past, might give also, if properly studied, some hints in architecture to builders of what Mr. Downing calls the 'cocked-hat school.' No art has made more rapid progress among us of late years than domestic, and specially rural architecture; yet there are houses in Germantown and its neighborhood, a century old, which in picturesque effect and the expression of solid respectability and home comfort and refinement, are at least equal to any of their modern rivals."

WASHINGTON TAVERN.

This very old tavern was owned and kept by Winfrid Nice some ninety years ago. After his death his widow acted as hostess for many years. John Nice, a brother of Winfrid, was a married man with two children when the Revolutionary War broke out. He raised a company and went to the war and served throughout it. He was captain of the company. He lived on Main street a little below John Channon's house on the same side.

After the war closed he became a Justice of the Peace. 'Squire Nice bound out many children, according to the custom of that day. He was also a referee in business matters and was highly respected. "His word was his bond." He was a tall and slender man, of a pleasant countenance and good looking. He rented a farm belonging to the Thomas family, near Thomas's Mill near the Bethlehem pike on Wissahickon creek where he farmed for several years. This was the place of his death. He was buried in the Lower Burying Ground at Germantown. I am obliged to the courtesy of his granddaughter, Mrs. Amanda James, for this information. Capt. Nice was paid in Continental money for his war services, and the depreciation in the value of that currency made the payment slight. The wife removed to the city after her husband's death and died at the residence of her daughter, Mrs. Mary Dugan. Mr. Sellers once was the host of the Washington Inn. Daniel Hines owned and conducted it for a long time. It is now kept by Matthias Hil and owned by Henry Freas, who lived on the opposite side of Main street.

GERMANTOWN. 241

UPPER BURYING GROUND.

At John B. Channon's the record book of this ancient cemetery is preserved. Its title reads: "Regulations & Ancient Original as well as subsequent proceedings from time to time Relating to the Burying-Ground at the upper end of German-Town, in the city of Philadelphia in the province of Pennsylvania. Entered the First day of January Anno Domini 1761. Christian Lehman." The excellent black ink has done its duty nobly in preserving the record and the penmanship is good. The cemetery is now under the care of Mr. John C. Channon. Watson says that some Indians of the Delaware tribe are buried here. [Annals, Vol. II, p. 34.]

JEREMIAH HACKER'S HOUSE.

Duy's lane is now styled Wister street. On the upper side of this street, a little above the Reading Railroad, near Wister station, stands an old-time mansion of stone, which Ward mentions and hoped to describe, but the Magazine contains no further account of it, though Isaiah Hacker's house on Main street has its place in the history. This ancient building stands among old trees, which are its fitting companions. Formerly a wood stretched behind it, but the rapid march of improvement and the axes impelled by American Gladstones have destroyed its glory. A hedge with an iron railing on its outer side bounds the street in front of the dwelling, and a fence stretches along the front of the lawn. The lawn extends both above and below the mansion, and is, on an autumn day, covered with the pretty fallen leaves. The grounds slope toward the railroad, while there is a pleasant view of the rolling country beyond, and the resting cattle on the sward give a pretty touch to the picture. The massive walls of the old house show themselves in the interior, where a later addition in the rear makes the back wall of the house a partition, and its doors betray the thickness, which shows how strongly the forefathers built the houses which were to stand alone, and did not need to be in a modern row for mutual support. The wall is so thick that a closet has been constructed in what was formerly a window. The old furniture within the hall and parlor is in unison with the walls which protect it. The Hacker family came from Salem, Mass., Isaiah leaving that place about A. D. 1825, and Jeremiah about 1830. They had country seats in Germantown. Finally they became permanent residents. Jeremiah lived at Fourth and Spruce streets in the city, and Isaiah in Third street, between Walnut and Spruce. Mr. William Hacker has furnished the following account of the property in Wister street:

" The house No. 170 Wister street stands on a part of the tract originally granted by William Penn to Lenhart Arets, in 1683. From him it passed through various hands until 1795. The present house was built upon it by Peter Unrickhouse, who sold to Martin Godfred Dorfenille in 1797, from whom it was bought by George Kutz 1808, then by William Taylor, then by Daniel

Zeller 1828, who in 1837, conveyed the property to the late Jeremiah Hacker, in whose family it still remains. Although the house has been added to at various times the original front remains and is almost unchanged. At the time of the last purchase, the house was surrounded by fields extending to the Main street with only one house intervening and giving no promise of the present built-up condition of the vicinity. For many years it was held only as a country place but lately has been occupied all the year.

"List of various owners of the land:
1683, William Penn to Lenhart Arets, 1000 acres.
1683, Lenhart Arets to Dennis Kunder, 300 acres.
1733, Executor of Dennis and Conard Kunder to John Janson.
1734, John Janson to Jacob Weiss, 7 acres.
1765, Executors of Jacob Weiss to Joseph Swift.
1795, Christian Duy, et al, Executor, 2 to George Danenhower.
1795, to Peter Unrickhouse, who built the house.
1797, to Martin Godfred Dorfenille.
1808, to George Kutz.
1808, to William Taylor.
1828, Daniel Zeller.
1837, Jeremiah Hacker."

BUCK HOTEL, No. 5474.

Mrs. Barbara Roop, who had charge of this old stone hotel kept it for forty-seven years. Her husband's name was George, but she did not assume the hotel until she was a widow. She died in October of 1886, aged 84, and is buried in St. Michael's churchyard. She was kind and esteemed in the neighborhood. There were several who kept this hotel before it came into the hands of Mrs. Roop. John Amy was one of these. George Hocker owned the property years ago, but it now belongs to the Carpenter estate. Years before Mrs. Roop's entrance on her duties, Mrs. Madeline Hesser, a widow, was the hostess for fifty years; so that the combined occupancy of Mrs. Hesser and Mrs. Roop covered nearly 100 years.

In this vicinity there are a number of two-story stone houses plastered, and for some reason the rears of several of them seem to run diagonally away from Main street, as if they were afraid of it.

ST. VINCENT SEMINARY.

The following has been contributed:—The large group of buildings on Chelten avenue, east of Magnolia, is occupied by a Catholic Educational Institution known as St. Vincent Seminary. It was founded in the West in 1818, and, in 1868, transferred to Germantown. It is the "House of Studies" for young men who aspire to become members of "The Congregation of the Mission" in the United States. This Congregation or Society was first established in the city of Paris in 1625 by St. Vincent De Paul. The Society is composed chiefly of Ecclesiastics whose work in the ministry is two fold—to evangelize the poor and to educate young men for the Priesthood. Hence, candidates for membership are required to undergo a special course of training and to study to qualify themselves for the work of the Society. An indispensable prerequisite for admission to the Seminary as a Student is to have completed the course of studies required in colleges of well-known standing. After admission to the Seminary the student finds himself only on the threshold of his scholastic labors. The course of study upon which he is entering requires eight years for its completion. It is divided as follows: Two years are devoted to an exhaustive revision of his previous studies in English, Mathematics, Greek, Latin, French and German. Following this period of revision come two years devoted to the study of Logic, Metaphysics, and, in accordance with the wants of the student, the study of Mathematics pure and applied. Next comes a four years course of Dogmatic and Moral Theology together with Sacred Scripture, Canon Law and Church History. During six years of the course Latin is the language of the class in Logic, Metaphysics, Theology, Sacred Scripture and Canon Law. The reason for adhering to the Latin is that by far the greater number of authors, who have written on the above subjects, use that language as a clearer and better medium for conveying their thoughts than is found in any of our modern languages with their constant mutations. It is, besides, the language of the Roman Church in her Ritual. The scholastic year consists of ten months, during which ten hours a day are devoted to study and recitations. To secure necessary relaxation and time for general reading two days of each week have neither fixed studies nor classes. Although the prescribed studies and duties occupy much time, yet many students find opportunity for branches of special study. Students, who have completed the course and passed the final examination, are presented for ordination to the priesthood. They are then assigned to one of the special works of the Society, and devote both their abilities and their time without any personal pecuniary recompense. The Seminary has a large library of Literary and Historical and Scientific works in both ancient and modern languages. Among the collection are many old folios dating from the infancy of the art of printing.

Mr. Editor: Some remarks about Bentz's bakery in Mr. Hotchkin's last article on Old Germantown, having been suppressed on account of its being erroneously located, I beg leave to offer the subjoined brief sketch of the Bentz family as a substitute:

Upon the arrival of a ship at the wharf in Philadelphia about the year 1810, hailing from the Fatherland, and freighted with German emigrants, Mr. C. J. Wister and Mr. Joseph Bullock, opposite neighbors and friends, went together to the city and selected two youths, Jacob and John Bentz by name, to serve them at their homes in Germantown. Mr. Wister took Jacob, aged fourteen years, whilst Mr. Bullock took John aged seven. The boys served their masters most faithfully for many years, and Jacob upon coming of age apprenticed himself to Adam Keppel the bread and cake baker *par excellence* of the village at that day. His shop was situated on the Main street nearly opposite Bockius's lane—the present Manheim street—and not more than a door or two from the spot where Kaupp's confectionery now stands. In course of time, Jacob, having served his apprenticeship, married Esther Donne, who was likewise a domestic in Mr. Wister's family, and established a bakery for himself at the upper end of the town, above the house occupied by John Knorr (better known to his fellow townsmen as Johnny K-ner) and near the present Tulpehocken street. Being honest and industrious he did a flourishing business at this stand during the remainder of his life. He died, leaving a son Jacob, who continued the business of his father. I do not know of any of his descendants now living. John Bentz remained with Mr. Bullock until the latter's death and then entered Mr. Wister's service with whom he remained until the year 1827, when he left Germantown and was lost sight of by his old employer. Both of these boys, selected from a shipload of their countrymen proved admirable in their positions, and grew to be worthy and respected citizens. Jacob, being the elder, retained perfectly the use of his native tongue, whilst John, having left the Fatherland so young, lost his altogether. The name of Bentz has long since disappeared from Germantown as a surname, as far as my knowledge extends. John Bentz was remarkable for his gastronomic powers, which, having been observed, were tested when it was found that he had consumed at one meal half a loaf of bread, half a shad, a shoulder of mutton and nine potatoes; and yet he was slight in form, much slighter than his brother Jacob who was by no means omnivorous. John was but a youth when this extraordinary consumption of food was effected; to what extent his capacity developed in after years is left to conjecture, for we have no record.

First month, Twelfth, 1887.   C. J. W.

In the account of ANCIENT GERMANTOWN, it seems best to give some of the main points in Watson's Annals, which have not been before mentioned in these papers, to complete the narrative. This is done by the courteous permission of Edwin S. Stuart, the publisher of the Annals.

In the third volume of the Annals, being Willis P. Hazard's Continuation, there is a memoir of John Fanning Watson. He was an honest and attentive man in business with good judgment. His historical work was his recreation. He was born in 1779. His mother showed him the Flag of Peace, hoisted on Market street hill, when he was a babe. His father was named William, and his mother's maiden name was Lucy Fanning. She was a noble and accomplished woman. His father was a volunteer in the sea service in the Revolution and also served in a land expedition. J. F. Watson was born, in Batsto, N. J. He became a clerk in Philadelphia and afterward was a clerk in the War Department at Washington. He was also a commissary in the army in

JOHN F. WATSON, THE ANNALIST,
BY PERMISSION OF EDWIN S. STUART,
PUBLISHER.

Louisiana. Then he embarked in publishing in Philadelphia, being publisher of Dr. Adam Clark's Commentaries on the Bible. In 1812, he married Miss Crowell, a descendant of Oliver Cromwell. The name was changed by her emigrant ancestors, because of Cromwell's unpopularity in this country. Watson was the faithful cashier of the Bank of Germantown for thirty-three years. Samuel Hazard printed some of Watson's notes in the REGISTER OF PENNSYLVANIA. The Annalist delighted to collect the reminiscences of the aged. The Annals were first published in 1830. In the beginning of the second volume will be found an interesting description of the author's love of antiquity and of his toil in collecting material and references to various sources as to the great value and importance of such work. Watson also prepared a history of New York.

The Historical Society was due to Watson. The Annalist consulted old newspapers and court records, interviewed old soldiers and pioneer settlers. He collected pictures and autographs. Watson was temperate and fond of exercise and gardening, strongly religious and patriotic. He was the originator of the First Episcopal Church in New Orleans, and was for 30 years a communicant of St. Luke's, Germantown. He died in 1860, in his 82d year. Rev. Dr. Dorr, at the request of the Historical Society, prepared a memoir of him, from which Mr. Hazard drew the materials for his sketch. The Hon. Horatio Gates Jones gave him "a touching eulogy." Mr. Lossing honored him with a memoir in EMINENT AMERICANS.

Mr. Ferdinand J. Dreer, has permitted me to inspect a large volume, part manuscript and part scrap-book, in his possession, which shows the patience of Watson in accumulating matter. He wrote a clear hand. The Historical Society has another volume.

In the Annals Watson gives the original price of Germantown land as one shilling per acre. He describes most of the old homes as plastered inside with clay and straw and a finishing coat of lime. Some frames were of logs and wattles; river rushes and clay filled the interstices. In an old house which was taken down the grass still preserved its greenness. The houses were one story high with gables to the street. Sometimes the front room would be of stone and the back one of logs. Hipped roofs were common, forming "a low bed chamber." The ends of the houses above the first story were formed of boards or shingles and contained "a small chamber window." Many of the roofs were tiled. Some log houses were in later times lathed and plastered outside. There were half doors and sometimes the upper door had folds. The windows formed two doors, opening within, and were originally "set in leaden frames with outside frames of wood." As to age, Wishert Levering, "a first settler," died at Roxborough, in 1744, aged 109. "Jacob Snyder lived to be 97."

The first meetings of the Friends were in Dennis Conrad's (Tennis Kundert) in A. D. 1683. The place was near an inn kept by Lesher. Penn preached in a house which stood on the site of Dr. George Bensell's residence, and also in Schumaker's house, built in 1686, in Mehl's meadow. When the Friends' Meeting House was built, the Abington contribution was chiefly in wheat at 4 shillings a bushel. "Byberry meeting gave forty bushels of wheat £8, 3s." Labor was 3s., 6d., "boards 10s. per thousand, timber 6s. per ton, sawing 10s. per hundred."

The Tunkers from Ephrata, dressed in gray surtouts to which were attached hoods for head coverings, looking like Dominican friars, used to make religious visits to Germantown "walking silently in Indian file, and with long beards; also girt about the waist, and bare-footed, or with sandals." Old persons in Watson's day remembered seeing forty or fifty of these people in such a procession.

Richard Townsend, who built Roberts's mill in Church lane, was once mowing and a young deer came near, and when he stumbled by accident the deer being frightened ran against a sapling and was stunned, taken and killed to the relief of the family who were sometimes straitened for meat in their secluded home in the woods.

There was a tradition that Courts were held in Germantown earlier than in Philadelphia, but the original patent of Penn is dated in London, 1689. It "passed under the great seal of the province of Pennsylvania" in 1691. A market was to be kept "every sixth day, in such places as the *provincial charter doth direct!*" The government of Germantown began in 1691, and lasted fifteen years. About 1720 Mr. John Wister bought 500 acres of land at two shillings per acre. He afterward sold part of it at £3 per acre, which he thought wonderful. In Watson's time it was "worth $200 to $300 per acre." Labor sixty years before the annalist wrote was 3s. per day in summer, and 2s., 6d. in winter. Hickory wood cost 10s. to 11s. a cord; oak, 8s. to 9s. In Watson's day hickory was $8, and oak $6. "and has been $2 higher."

In 1738 a tax of 1½d. per pound was laid on Philadelphia county for "wolves and crows destroyed, and for Assemblymen's wages." The Assemblymen got 5s. per day.

An aged man told Watson of Indian colonies, of twenty to thirty persons, which he had seen in Logan's woods, or on a "field southeast of Grigg's place." They would make huts and abide a year, selling baskets, ladles and fiddles. They shot birds and squirrels with bows and arrows. The huts were made "of four upright saplings, with crotch limbs at top." Cedar bushes and branches formed sides and tops. In winter the fire was on the ground in the middle of the hut. In Reuben Haines's house, "built by Dirk Johnson, a chief and his twenty Indians have been sheltered and entertained." Anthony Johnson, when a boy, saw near two hundred Indians on Jno. Johnson's place in a wood near the wheelwright's shop. He saw them jump fences almost in a horizontal position and yet alight on their feet. They shot at marks. Edward Keimer imitated their exploits closely. Johnson often saw beaver and beaver dams. Some of the early Indians were buried in the Concord graveyard. Wild pigeons were abundant in early times.

The people had their superstitions. "Old Shrunk," the conjuror, told fortunes and instructed people where to dig for money. It was thought that the pirates of Black Beard's time had hidden treasure near the Delaware and Schuylkill.

Women rode horses with two panniers to market. Women also "carried baskets on their heads and the men wheeled wheelbarrows, being six miles to market!" Man and wife would ride on one horse "to church, funerals and visits. The woman sat on a pillion behind the man." The better houses had balconies in front. At the close of day women could be seen sewing and knitting. The women generally attended church "in short gowns and petticoats and with check or white flaxen aprons. The young men had their heads shaved and wore white caps; in summer they went without coats, wearing striped trousers and barefooted; the old Friends wore wigs." Jamb stoves were used, but were not very good heaters.

There was formerly "a thick woods on the southwest side of the turnpike below Naglee's hill, where Skerrett's house now stands, called Logan's swamp and woods." "After James Logan's house was built, in 1728, at Stenton, a bear of large size came and leaped over the fence."

It has been said heretofore that Washington and General Howe both dwelt in the celebrated Morris house, opposite Market Square. King William IV, of England, then a Prince, made his home there when General Howe resided in it.

"The French West India residents" made gay times in Germantown. They dressed in St. Domingo style and the streets heard much French conversation, and at night music abounded. There was much shooting of game.

Pastorius states that there were but four known lawyers of the province in his day, and as his opponent in a suit had secured them he was unable to bring lawyers from New York, and prayed the Governor and Council to stop proceedings and wait "action from the principals in Germany." This was the small seed of the great tree of "Philadelphia lawyers," which has borne abundant and notable fruit. At first the city had no lawyers.

WAR TIMES.

"Gen. Agnew showed great kindness to old Mrs. Sommers. Col. Bird died in Bringhurst's big house, and said to the woman there, 'woman, pray for me, I leave a widow and four children.'" The British took up fences and made huts, cutting down buckwheat and putting it on the rails, with ground above it. B. Lehman goes to the city and sells "his old hen for 1 dollar!" He sees men come stealthily from Skippack with butter in boxes on their backs, which they sold at 5s. They worked their way through the woods, which ran near the city. Lehman was out in the militia. When paid $200 in paper money for two months' services, he gave $100 for a sleigh ride, and $100 for a pair of shoes. During the war business was prostrated. "Not a house was roofed or mended in Germantown in five or six years." People often had to borrow money, if they had substance to secure a loan.

In 1841, a "very curiously wrought powder-horn" was found in digging in the lot of the new Lutheran Church. It was lost at the battle of Germantown by Elijah Lincoln, of Windham, Conn. The owner's name (E. Gray) was engraved on it, and the GERMANTOWN TELEGRAPH published an account of the finding of it. It contained a sketch of Boston, Bunker Hill, the British fleet, etc. Ebenezer Gray and William Hovey, the maker of the horn, and Elijah Lincoln, were volunteers, and while encamped near Bunker Hill, the horn was engraved. Gray became a Colonel, and gave the horn to Lincoln, who promised to use it faithfully, and did so. In Germantown it was pulled from him by the grasp of a dying comrade, who was drawing a load from it. The publisher of *The Democrat*, in Columbia county, Pa., had been engaged in a pension claim for Lincoln and knew the facts. Col. Gray's widow and son and daughter, were then living in Windham. His grandson received the horn.

In the battle, fathers placed children with the women in cellars. In C. M. Stokes's house, which belonged to 'Squire Ferree, two dozen terrified and weeping women were gathered. George Knorr, with other boys, went toward the city but stopped on meeting Hessians at Nicetown. A "cannon ball struck a tree at Haines's brewery, as they passed, and then went before them down the street." Some boys went to the tops of the houses, and into the streets to see the battle. They saw the tall Virginians, under Col. Matthews, brought as prisoners, from Kelley's place, and put in the Market Square Church. The mouths of prisoners and guards were blackened with powder in biting off cartridges. The Virginians had captured some British in the fog, and their glad hurrah brought a larger British force on them and resulted in their own capture.

Dr. George de Benneville, of Branchtown, was 16 years old at the time of the battle, and saw much of it. Highlanders and British cavalry were quartered near him. "They were always cheerful, and always seemed to go gaily and confidently into expected fights." The "kilted Scots" kept up with the trot of the cavalry. After the battle a wounded British officer met a surgeon and said, "I believe it is all over with me, doctor. I have got a mortal wound!" The doctor examined him in the street and replied, "Don't fear, I shall save you—go on." He passed on renovated. The surgeon's work at such times was important and praiseworthy.

After the British left Germantown a troop of Americans following overtook a British surgeon who had dressed the wounds of three American officers in Widow Hess's house. They intended to arrest him, but W. Fryhoffer told of his good work, and he was permitted to walk to the city, while the officers were liberated.

John Ashmead, aged 12, saw various groups of the dead. At Chew's house there were about thirty dead soldiers whom citizens were beginning to bury. There was blood in every room of the house. A six pounder had come in at a front window and passed through four partitions and out of the back of the house.

A boy told Watson that he brought flour from the mill to a person in Germantown, who sold it at high prices to women who came from the city. They carried it home in small quantities, concealing it about their persons. Watson thinks that they probably sold it again. They "returned with salt, etc." Flour brought $8 per hundredweight in Philadelphia. Boys would carry it in by by-roads for fear of losing the precious burden.

On a secret invasion by the British at midnight, Mr. Lush, acting wagoner for the American gunpowder train was warned, and had his team ready. He rode down to reconnoitre, and was caught, but his wagoner saw the approach of the enemy, and dashed along the streets waking the people, and exposing the British.

John Ashmead saw the British army pass along Main street "at their first entry." He sat in the porch. The order of the army was good, with its officers, and red coated soldiers, and refugees in green, and Highlanders and Grenadiers with burnished arms. Colors were not displayed and there was no music. There was no violence. Some asked for milk or cider, and his father gave it, until the cider grew low, and a young officer asked for some, and when told the acts of the soldiers he had a succession of sentinels placed to guard the house.

Isaac Wood, on John Andrews's place, on Lime Kiln road, was killed while looking at the battle from his cellar door. The fight was on the side of Dr. Betton's woods.

Watson gives the case of William Dolbey, who had a soldier killed beside him on the Duval place, and became disgusted with war and left the army and joined the Friends, as did Watson's friend, John Baylie, at Trois rivers. Hearing a soldier as he entered battle pray for the salvation of those who should fall he felt unprepared for death, and made up his mind to kill no one, and fired above the mark.

John Smith saw an American trooper with his horse pursued by a troop, who hid himself and horse in a cider mill on John Wister's place, and escaped his pursuers.

The Hessian officers had wicker doors in their huts, "with a glass light, and interwoven with plaited straw; they had also chimneys made of grass sod." A Hessian became Washington's coachman, having abandoned the British army.

Germantown boys played war, "making three forts (upper, middle and lower), along the town." They had "embankments, and fought with stones, under a show of wooden guns." An American officer once called out in passing, "who commands there?" The reply was "Proctor," which was the officer's name.

An eye witness thus described the British Army: "The trim and graceful Grenadier, the careless and half savage Highlander, with his flowing tartaned robes and naked knees; then the immovably still German—here a regiment of Hessians,—and there slaves of Anspach and Waldeck, the first sombre as night, the second as gaudy as noon. Here dashed a party of dragoons and there scampered a party of *Yagers*. The British officers gay in spirit and action and the German officers still in motion and embroidery; the whole forming a moving kaleidoscope of colors and scenery."

Jacob Miller, when a boy of sixteen, saw General Howe ride up from Stenton at the beginning of the battle and stop near Lorain's and heard him say, "What shall we do? We are certainly surrounded." He and his officers then rode on up town. Miller used to get into the city to procure family necessities by following the rear of British parties which came out. He would return "by by-paths and back roads." The boys used to collect handfuls of bullets. Miller used to see Captain Allen, who acted as a scout, as did the officers Dover and Howard. On Taggart's ground he saw Pulaski's cavalry in "whitish uniform" in a grand display in a mock battle.

After the battle of Germantown the English followed "the Americans eight miles on the Skippack road, fifteen and a half miles from Philadelphia, into Whitpaine township, as far as the Blue Bell." There was much confusion there among the Americans. The dead and dying were there and women and children ran to learn the fate of fathers, husbands and brothers, hoping to meet them alive. General Nash, Colonel Boyd, Major White and another officer died in the retreat and were buried in the Mennonite burying ground, at their church "in Towamensing township, a place beautifully shaded with forest trees." Watson visited the spot and says, "We have since given them a monument there." The annalist deserves the highest praise for his constant efforts to honor the tombs of the patriotic dead.

Washington's quarters on the Skippack road were at Norris's, which place was afterward the country seat of Dr. James, of Philadelphia. He also had his quarters at the farm-house of Jacob Wampole, father of "Isaac Wampole, the eminent city scrivener," three-quarters of a mile from the Mennonite burying ground. "That family had known that the General was in the practice of retiring to pray." General Cobb stated that, "throughout the war it was understood in his military family that he gave a part of every day to private prayer and devotion." The General was precise and punctual at breakfast, and expected his aids, Cobb, Hamilton and Humphreys to be awaiting him. He left the papers he wished prepared by them and rode to visit the troops. He was not familiar in his intercourse with the officers. General Cobb enjoyed a laugh, but knew but one officer, Colonel Scammel, who could awake Washington's laughter. The General rode about with a black servant and a guard, and was attended by some officers.

GENERAL REMINISCENCES.

Thomas Jefferson once occupied the house in which Watson dwelt. John De Braine, a French-German astronomer, had lived there still earlier.

The German language was in old time used by Germantown boys in their plays. In Watson's day, Mr. Richards preached in German once a month. The Methodists first started preaching in English in the school-house. During the British occupation, Hessian chaplains preached in the German churches.

General Washington used to walk the town, and ride in his phaeton and on horseback. He and his family attended English preaching in the Market Square Church, sitting in the first pew. He also attended the German services. His house was closed on Sunday till the door opened and he came out of it on his way to church. In leaving for Carlisle, he rode out quietly to avoid ostentation. He was civil to all and was free to converse at Henry Fraley's carpenter shop, and Bringhurst's blacksmith shop. These men had been his soldiers. Lady Washington was beloved by the people.

Watson recalls the sombre houses with little windows of old Germantown and thought it improved in his memory. Pavements and trees were new benefits. He states that Newark workmen drew the coach business from Germantown by lesser prices.

Plaster of Paris which stimulated the growth of clover, was introduced for sale about 1780, by Abraham Rex, of Chestnut Hill, and Leonard Stoneburner, of Germantown.

The Germantown turnpike was largely due to the energy of Casper Haines. Wagon loads of hay sometimes passing on a trot showed good locomotion when a turnpike came.

By a spy-glass the bombarding of the river forts was seen from Germantown, as John Miller's journal, quoted by Watson shows. The following entry of Miller evinces natural, as well as unnatural disturbance: Nov. 27th, 1877. "There appeared a great and surprising northern light, as red as blood." The passage of the British army from Philadelphia to Whitemarsh to surprise Washington, and its return, is noted in the journal. They went out on the night of the 4th of December and returned on the 8th. On December 6th it is remarked that the enemy and the American light horse alternately patroled the streets of Germantown.

Those who fled to New Jersey from Philadelphia under the alarm of war were sometimes glad to sleep in barns there. Some who went "to Delaware and along the Chesapeake" were the next summer driven out by fresh alarms.

John F. Watson presented his manuscript book of "Annals and Recollections" to the Historical Society of Pennsylvania in 1830. A part of this volume appears in the printed volumes of the Annals. The handwriting is small and neat. The author gathered together such miscellaneous facts on all topics as came within his observation. Sometimes the full page boils over in a writing up and down the margin of the book crossways with the main writing. It is striking to read the heading: "Facts communicated by Doct. B. Franklin." The manuscript book at times becomes a scrap book, and thus information was accumulated. The picture of an Egyptian mummy from a newspaper is a startling contrast to the written pages. A pen and ink picture of Billy Brown, a colored man of Frankford, who was ninety-three years old, also helps the miscellany. Watson's mind was receptive, and he was very anxious to give information in every possible way. A medal or coin is outlined on the page, as well as William Penn's old bookcase. Continental money is pasted in, and also a specimen of the silk made by the remarkable poetess, business woman and legal arbiter, Susannah Wright, of Columbia, Pa. Dr. Franklin, when in the old country, corresponded with her about the silk which she sent abroad to be woven and which caused an interest in Europe. A piece of Dr. Franklin's velvet coat is also pasted into this wondrous book. Some pearl-colored silk made by a daughter of Reuben Haines, of Germantown, and sent to England to be woven, is here. There is a piece of red "Garden Sattin," which was presented to some one by the Bishop of Worcester. There are also two bits of white silk which shone at the Meschianza—one as the cuff of Mrs. Hamilton. There is a letter from Whitefield to Dr. William Shippen, the elder, which is yellow with age, and another from J. Wesley, and another from Lafayette, and one from Joseph Bonaparte. Bonaparte wrote in French. Lafayette's letter is in English, and written from New York.

OUR PICTURE EXPLAINED.

[To the Editor of the TELEGRAPH.]

I am at length able to locate, unquestionably, the picture introduced in connection with Mr. Hotchkin's article on "Old Germantown" in the TELEGRAPH of March 30th ult., the whole scene, though long since radically changed, distinctly presenting itself to my mind's eye. The point of view selected by the artist (probably William Brittain, drawing teacher at the Germantown Academy in 1832-3, to whom we are indebted for nearly all the surviving sketches of Old Germantown) is the north corner of the present Laurel street and Germantown road, the former then known as Bringhurst's alley, a family of that name living there. The field inclosed by the board fence, a low piece of ground, was called Bensell's meadow. Dr. Bensell, whose residence at the south corner of Schoolhouse lane and Main street is seen in the distance, being its owner. The old house with its gable facing the road, adjoining the meadow on the southeast, was occupied by old Peggy Wolf for a candy store. The large house on the same side, whose gable is seen above the surrounding community of buildings, in the distance, is the De la Plain house, afterwards owned by Mr. Charles Stokes, and recently removed to make way for the office of the Germantown Mutual Fire Insurance Company. To the left of this the low steeple of the old Market Square Church appears just above the tops of the trees, surmounted by the weathercock made a target of by the "Paxton boys" in 1764. This venerable building is supplanted by the unsightly brick church now used as a place of worship by a Presbyterian congregation.

GERMANTOWN. 253

The Germantown road, when converted into a turnpike, was necessarily regraded, and at certain points was very much raised. Bensell's meadow was one of these points, in consequence of which two steps were required to descend from the sidewalk (there were no pavements at that day) to the floor of Peggy Wolf's shop. This accounts for its sunken appearance. No vestige of the objects which this picture represents remains to tell its tale at the present day. All has been swept away by the ruthless hand of innovation, miscalled, improvement. C. J. W.
Germantown, 4th mo. 3d, 1887.

REVOLUTIONARY REMINISCENCES.

In Robert Morton's Diary in the Pennsylvania Magazine of History, Vol. I, No. 1, 1877, it is stated that Major Balfour, Aid-de-camp of General Howe, was much enraged that the people about Germantown did not warn the British army of the approach of Washington's army. Under October 18th, 1777, he notes: "A smart platoon firing this ev'g about Germantown." "Nov. 24th. People in expectation that Germantown will be shortly burnt." On December 4th, the evening march of Howe and his army through Germantown to Chestnut Hill is recorded. In William Black's Journal, in the same volume, Mr. Strettel is spoken of as taking Mr. Black to Germantown where he had a little country summer residence. He describes the place in 1744 as "a continued row of houses on each side of a public road, for more than a mile and a half the inhabitants are chiefly Dutch, and has a very good church with organs in the Town." There is an interesting account of his taking tea with James Logan and the Indian Commissioners at Stenton, and a notice of Logan's fine library. Black was secretary of the Commissioners, appointed by Governor Gooch, of Virginia, to unite with those of Pennsylvania and Maryland, in treating with the Iroquois about the lands west of the Alleghenies.

THE GERMANS.

Lawrence Hendricks, a German, says of his fellow Germans, that they were rugged, and could endure hardships. They wore heavy shoes with iron nails, and were zealous in serving God with prayer and readings, and innocent as lambs and doves. This description of Swiss Germans in the Rev. Edward McMinn's Life of Henry Antes, as he says, may have answered in the case of some of the American-German settlers. For this writer's account of the Germans and Germantown, see Chapter 3, of the Life of Antes. Mr. McMinn states that one chimney in the center of the building was a characteristic of the German architecture. For an interesting description of a simple Dunker Church and its service, and love-feast, and feet-washing, the reader may turn to a volume entitled "Katy of Catoctin," by George Alfred Townsend, Chapters 8 and 9, pp. 67–88.

In Rev. Henry Melchior Muhlenberg's Journal, translated by Dr. H. H. Muhlenberg, we find an account of the visit of the Paxton Boys, in 1764, to Germantown. See collections of the Historical Society of Pennsylvania, Vol. I, p. 73, etc. The butchers and other mechanics organized a troop of horses in the emergency, and marched through the town with a trumpet. Even the Quakers took up arms. The Rev. Dr. Wrangel, Provost of the Swedish Churches, reasoned with the Paxton Boys, and an amnesty finally took place, and the Bethlehem Indians in Germantown, who were the object of the hostile expedition, were spared.

In the volume above referred to, Deborah Logan writes a letter to Major Alex. Gordon, in which she speaks of a visit Col. Thomas Forrest made to her, and mentions his bravery and his service to the American cause at the Battle of Trenton. She also tells of Col. Pickering's visit to Germantown, to review the battle-field, and of the kindness of the Philadelphia women to the wounded Americans, who were carried to the lobbies of the State House. Sometime after she counted seventeen burning houses from the roof of her mother's house in Chestnut street. She knew that one of these houses was Fairhill, built by her Grandfather Norris, and occupied by "the excellent John Dickinson, who married her cousin." The houses were fired by the British.

Watson says in the same volume that Mrs. D. Logan saw George Washington's mother at Fredericksburg when she was eighty-five years old. She told her of her care in forming the minds of her children, and that she had sent George forty miles from home to the best school she could. "She lived in a one-story cottage, and declined to live at Mount Vernon."

Watson says that Mrs. Rev. Dr. Blair, of Germantown, once made the quiet Washington laugh heartily. Mrs. Powell and Mrs. Washington were present. The wife said: "General, surely you are no longer yourself." "True," said he, "I am now indeed Mrs. Blair."

When Watson wrote Washington's door was "in James Stokes's bank house in Germantown." On October 5th Dr. Muhlenberg notes that at night a party from the Germantown battle knocked and asked admittance, but were persuaded by the "widow Z." to go on.

Germantown Court Records are given in the same volume. The first Court of Record was held in 1691 in the public meeting house. Pastorius was bailiff. The indenture of a "servante girle" and an apprenticeship and a promise, under complaint, to finish a barn, enliven the records of 1692. In 1694 a warning is given against those who pull off papers which give notices of intended marriages and things lost and found. Charges of menacing a constable, beating a hog, and assault, and questions about roads and fences, and neglecting jury duty, and hogs (spelled hoggs) at large, and work on roads, are spread on the records. In 1701 the sheriff takes up two sows and three pigs with no apparent owner. The Court orders that he shall have them cried on the next public fair day, and if an owner appears the sheriff is to have half and the owner half, "otherwise to yoke the first half, according to law, and let them run for the owner." The Sheriff also took up a horse and an old mare, for which the Court declared that he should be paid. Here is a Coroner's verdict: "We, the jury, find that through carelessness the cart and the lime killed the man; the wheel wounded his back and head and killed him." One case is deferred because the plaintiff urges that it is Holy Innocents' Day, and his conscience demands the change in time, and that the witnesses will not come. In a sale the striking name Cathalintje Vande Woestjine appears. In 1706 a petition of the Oil Mill Company on Walter Simens's land is noted.

THE PAUL HOUSE.

On the southeast corner of Main and Gorgas streets is the house of the Paul family. This stone, pebble-dashed house, with its porch, is antique. The door-jamb contained bullet marks of the Revolutionary times, while a tree in the rear was once pierced with a cannon ball. In plowing leaden bullets were often unearthed here. The stump of an ancient tree stands inside the fence adorned with flowers. The date 1707 marks the time of its planting by a Gorgas.

An old carpenter shop riddled with bullets once occupied a portion of the lawn of the Carpenter place.

Henry Rittenhouse owned the Paul House before the last-named family bought it in 1812. The Gorgas family built it. Henry K. Paul, who bought the house, was a saddler. His shop was in the hardware store. He was one of the early subscribers to the GERMANTOWN TELEGRAPH.

Mr. Henry C. Paul, opposite Carpenter's place, was, when a boy, in front of Chew's house in 1824 when Lafayette made his visit and shook hands with the military company of Germantown Blues in the street.

THE BAYARD HOUSE, at No. 5519 Main street, is a long stone mansion opposite the Carpenter property. The Bayards, who are relatives of the Bayards of Delaware, one of whom is now a Cabinet officer, bought this property from Marshal Slocum, who purchased it of John Johnson, who bought it of George Hesser, who built the pleasant old house just after the battle of Germantown. He had dug the cellar before the battle, but as there was a sharp skirmish around the spot and several were killed, they placed the dead in the newly dug cellar and filled it up as a general grave. This was about where the carriage gate now stands.

Mr. Hesser's son, then an old man, gave this account to the Bayards some twenty-five or thirty years ago, when he came east from his home in Minnesota on a visit and called to see the ancestral place. The barn has the date 1777 upon it. I am indebted to C. M. Bayard, the present occupant of the house, for its history.

GERMANTOWN.

FRANCIS DANIEL PASTORIUS.

> "The German Town of which I spoke before,
> Which is at least in length one mile and more,
> Where lives High German people and Low Dutch,
> Whose trade in weaving linnen cloth is much,
> Here grows the Flax, as also you may know,
> That from the same they do divide the tow."
>
> [*From Richard Frame's Poem on Pennsylvania, printed by Wm. Bradford in 1692.*]

Watson calls Francis Daniel Pastorius "a chief among the first settlers," and speaks of his scholarship and his writing Latin in a good hand. He styles the manuscript book of writings and selections which he left, "The Bee;" it should be "The Bee-Hive." He once owned all Chestnut Hill. In 1687 he was a member of the Assembly; he died about 1720. James Haywood gave an explanation to Watson of the German pamphlet by Pastorius in the Cambridge Library called "A Description of Pennsylvania." It was printed in Holland.

Holm, in his history of New Sweden, faults Pastorius for his account of the motives of the Swedes in their settlement of the Delaware river. In the fourth volume of the Memoirs of the Historical Society of Pennsylvania, Pastorius's account of this State is given with this title: "A Peculiar Geographical Description of the lately Discovered Province of Pennsylvania, Situated on the Frontiers of This Western World, America." Lewis H. Weiss translated this description from the German. This old book makes the aborigines giants ten feet high. New England is styled *Nova Anglia*, and the city of Cambridge is noted as the place where the Bible was printed in the Indian language.

The river Delaware is spelled Delavarra, and Maryland, Marieland. He describes the city lots of the Frankford Company and speaks of the scarcity of money in the Province and the lack of goods for trade or exportation to Europe. He asks that an iron stove be sent him. Here is the account of Germantown: "As relating to our newly laid out town, *Germanopolis* or Germantown: it is situated on a deep and very fertile soil, and is blessed with an abundance of fine springs and fountains of fresh water. The main street is sixty and the cross streets forty feet in width. Every family has a plot of ground for yard and garden three acres in size." "The river Delavarra," he writes, "is so beautiful a stream as not to have its equal among all the rivers of Europe." Of this section he adds: "The springs and fountains of water are innumerable." "The woods and copse are filled with beautiful birds of great variety, which proclaim their Creator's praises in their pleasantest manner. There is, besides, a great abundance of wild geese, ducks, turkeys, quails, pigeons, partridges and many other sorts of game." Frankford already had "several good mills, a glass house, pottery, and some stores and trading houses." Pastorius says that the windows of his town house were made of oiled paper, as glass was wanting.

The late John William Wallace, President of the Historical Society of Pennsylvania, in an article on "Early Printing in Philadelphia," in the Society's

Magazine (Vol. IV, p. 434), gives from the late Nathan Kite, a record from Friends' Philadelphia Meeting in 1696, showing that Daniel Pastorius was willing to manage a printing press, which it was proposed to bring from England, but the arrangement was not carried out, as he engaged in school teaching.

Writing of the climate, Pastorius says: "The air is pure and serene, the summer is longer and warmer than it is in Germany, and we are cultivating many kinds of fruits and vegetables, and our labors meet with rich reward."

On the other hand, Dr. Rush said of the climate of Philadelphia, that it had the humidity of Great Britain in Spring, the heat of Africa in Summer, the temperature of Italy in June, the sky of Egypt in Autumn, the snows of Norway, and ice of Holland during Winter, the tempests to a certain degree of the West Indies in each season, and the variable winds of Great Britain in every month.— See Brissot de Warville's Travels in the United States.

The truth is that men estimate a climate according to their disposition and by comparison with their experience of other places.

In Penn's Account of the Province of Pennsylvania for emigrants, he says: "The place lies six hundred miles nearer the sun than England." In a letter, he says: "As to outward things, we are satisfied, the land is good, the air clear and sweet, the springs plentiful, and provision good and easy to come at, an innumerable quantity of wild fowl and fish, in fine, here is what an Abraham, Isaac and Jacob would be well contented with, and service enough for God, for the fields are white for the harvest. Oh, how sweet is the quiet of these parts, freed from the anxious troublesome solicitations, hurries and perplexities of woeful Europe." Scharf and Westcott's Philadelphia, Vol. I, p. 105.

Dr. Nicholas More writes to William Penn from Green Spring, his estate near Somerton, above Bustleton, that enemies of the new Colony have made evil reports: "As if we were ready to famish, and that the land is so barren, the climate so hot, that English grain, roots and herbs do not come to maturity, and what grows, to be little worth." He says that Penn knows the untruth of this, and that since Penn's departure, God has further blessed their "handy work."

As to live stock, we read "of cattle we have great abundance, but for want of proper accommodations they roam at large for the present."

The Indians preferred wampum strings in trade to silver coin, as they could not well detect counterfeits or calculate its value in relation to wampum.

Spanish and English coin circulated among the new settlers. Precious stones were lacking and were not desired, as they had been abused in other places for pride and ostentation.

At first, provisions were obtained from the Jerseys at high prices, later on, Pennsylvania had enough to use and a considerable surplus to sell. There were mills, brick-kilns and tile ovens. Manufactures were starting, and fairs were held to encourage barter and keep money from going abroad."

Pastorius thought that the Indians anointed their children with the fat of bears and other animals to make them dark. He describes the Indians as honest and faithful in promises and hospitable to strangers and faithful to death to friends.

He once saw four Indians enjoying a feast of boiled pumpkin sitting on the ground, with sea-shells for spoons, and the leaves of a tree for plates and was struck with their content with simple fare. The Indians listened to teaching concerning the blessed Saviour's life and death, with emotion, and behaved respectfully at church service. Pastorius and his fellow colonists wished aid to further their eternal welfare and the pious German prays for God's blessing on his undertaking.

Pastorius says that the Germans built a little chapel in Germantown in 1686.

In directing emigrants as to the mode of reaching this land the work in review stated that from April to the fall vessels sailed from England to Pennsylvania frequently, "principally from the port of Deal." The day of sailing was not fixed and the emigrant had to watch his opportunity. When thirty-five or forty passengers were collected a vessel was sent out. A grown man paid £6 passage money. Pastorius sailed from Deal on June 7th, A. D. 1683, with four male and two female servants. There were eighty passengers. The food given was poor. Pastorius thought it well to advise passengers to withhold a part of the fare till America was reached to force a fulfillment of contract. He advised persons to sail for Philadelphia direct and not for Upland (i. e., Chester), to avoid "many and grievous molestations." On August 16th the American continent was sighted, and the capes of Delaware entered on the 18th. New-Castle and Upland were passed on the 20th and Philadelphia reached that evening. William Penn and his secretary welcomed the new comers, and Penn made Pastorius "his confidential friend." Pastorius adds: "I am frequently requested to dine with him, where I can enjoy his good counsel and edifying conversations." Penn asked him to dine with him twice weekly, and declared his love and friendship to him and the German nation.

Pastorius wished that he could have some stalwart Tyrolians to throw down the gigantic forest trees. He declares labor is needful in the colony, as well as money. The Indians were used as laborers, but were not desirous of steady toil.

Samuel W. Pennypacker, Esq., sent to "Notes and Queries" in the Pennsylvania Magazine of History, Vol. IV, p. 253, a birthday ode to John Penn, signed by those believed to be the scholars of Pastorius in Philadelphia. It is in Pastorius's manuscript book, entitled "The Bee-Hive." I give an extract:

> "God bless the child (we young ones cry)
> And add from time to time
> To William Penn's posterity
> The like! Here ends our Rime,
> But fervent prayers will not end

"Of honest men for thee
And for thy happy government
With whom we all agree."

(Signed.) Zechariah Whitpaine, Israel Pemberton, Robert Francis, John White, Samuel Carpenter, Jr., Joh. Sam. Pastorius, for themselves and in the behalf of their schoolfellows.

When Samuel Shoemaker, a country resident of Germantown, had an interview with George the Third at Windsor, under the guidance of his friend, Benjamin West, the King asked him why the Province of Pennsylvania improved more than neighboring provinces, some of which had been earlier settled. Mr. Shoemaker politely replied to this German King that it was due to the Germans, and the King as politely answered that the improvement was principally due to the Quakers. (See Shoemaker's Diary, Pennsylvania Magazine of History, Vol. II, p. 38.) Both these classes were good and reliable settlers. The King was pleased that Mr. Shoemaker could speak German. The Queen wept when he spoke of the death of his children, showing a warm heart. Shoemaker thought that so kind a husband and so good a father as George the Third could not be a tyrant.

Governor Thomas, a deputy of the Penns to the Assembly in 1738, speaks strongly of the benefit Pennsylvania derived from her German settlers.

For an account of the effect of William Penn's travels in Holland and Germany in bringing emigrants to Pennsylvania, though that was not the object of the tour, see "William Penn's Travels in Holland and Germany in 1677," by Professor Oswald Seidensticker, of the University of Pennsylvania, Pennsylvania Magazine of History, Vol. II, p. 237, etc.

Dr. Rush quotes Tacitus concerning German villages to the effect that spaces were left between buildings either on account of danger in fire or "unskillfulness in architecture." He refers to the fact that few houses in Germantown are connected with each other.

The Doctor in his "Manners of the Germans of Pennsylvania," says that our State "is indebted to the Germans for the principal part of her knowledge in horticulture."—[Scharf & Westcott's Philadelphia, Vol. 2, p. 896.]

A friend furnishes the following information:

"In the German work of Seidensticker, which I obtained from the Philadelphia Library, which is a most excellent history of the early settlers of Germantown, and particularly of the noted man, Franz Daniel Pastorius, I find in reference as to his house the first mention on page 39, where it is said: ' His first temporary home in Philadelphia was of the following dimensions, namely, thirty feet long and fifteen feet wide, the window panes, in consequence of the scarcity of glass, he pasted over with oil paper, and over the front door he wrote these lines: *Parva domus sed amica bonis procul este prophani.*' All of which on the occasion of a visit from the Governor was a source of great amusement to him; and he encouraged him in the further construction of a building.

"I take it on page 49, that the settlement of Germantown is described as follows: 'Through the middle of the town a street sixty feet wide was laid out, planted on both sides with peach trees. Each house had a vegetable and flower garden to the extent of three acres, and the street intersecting at right angles was forty feet wide, and at the crossing of the sixty-feet-wide street was the market place. The fields for the cultivation of the crops laid to the North and South of the town, and the length of this settlement on this sixty-feet street was supposed to be one mile.'

"Pastorius was elected burgomaster of Germantown the first year when it was declared a town in 1691, and continued till 1692; then again in 1696 to 1697.

"Pastorius was married on the 16th of November, 1688, to Ennecke Klostermann, the daughter of Dr. Johann Klostermann, of Mulheim, on the ruhr (river). By this marriage he had two sons, Johann Samuel, born March 30, 1690, and Heinrich, born April 1, 1692.

"In the year 1698 Pastorius was elected master of the Quaker school in Philadelphia, which position he held till the year 1700. From letters which are still in existence we must conclude that he ruled his regiment of boys with great discipline. During that time he lived with his family in Philadelphia, and a letter addressed by the two sons to their grandfather in Germany gives us the fact that Pastorius must have had a house in Germantown. They express a wish that their grandfather would 'come over to this country and inhabit their house in Germantown, which has been standing empty, and has a vegetable and fruit garden, and prettily planted with flowers.' They also state that they 'attend school eight hours every day during the week excepting Saturday, when they are permitted to remain home in the afternoon.' Not the least interesting account of Pastorius is given on page 80, where it states that he died early in January 1720, and that his will dated 26th of December, 1719, was opened on the 13th of January, 1720. In it he bequeaths to his oldest son, Samuel (the weaver), his fifty acres of land in Germantown, two hundred acres on Perkiomen, an English quarto Bible, a gun, and the loom. The youngest son, Heinrich, who was a shoemaker, was to receive three hundred acres on Perkiomen, an English Bible, a silver watch and all his manuscripts, and the tools and appurtenances belonging to his trade. To both sons he bequeathed his printed books. To his wife Anna he bequeathed the rest of the land on Perkiomen, three hundred and ninety-three acres; also a disputed title to one hundred and three acres in Germantown; further, all the personal effects and the debts due him.

"On page 81 it is said 'that no stone or monument marks his burial place, and it is supposed that the founder and pioneer of the German settlers was interred in the old Quaker burial ground in Germantown.'"

ANDREAS HARTEL.

Whittier thus describes Pastorius:

> "So with his rustic neighbors sitting down,
> The homespun frock beside the scholar's gown,
> Pastorius to the manners of the town
> Added the freedom of the woods, and sought
> The bookless wisdom by experience taught,
> And learned to love his new found home while not
> Forgetful of the old.
>
> * * * * * * * *
>
> Where still the Friends their place of burial keep,
> And century-rooted mosses o'er it creep,
> The Nuremberg scholar and his helpmeet sleep."
>
> *Whittier's Pennsylvania Pilgrim Poems, pp. 346 and 347.*

THERE is no tombstone or record of Pastorius's burial, but his grave is supposed to be in the Friends' graveyard. See quotation from Prof. Oswold Seidensticker on page 358 of the Poems of Whittier. Prof. S. had one article in "*The Penn Monthly*," and another in "*Der Deutsche Pioneer*," on Pastorius. Pastorius was a rising young lawyer when he laid out Germantown. Samuel W. Pennypacker, Esq., in his "Historical and Biographical Sketches," in the article on "The Settlement of Germantown," p. 10, says: Pastorius possessed probably more literary attainments, and produced more literary work than any other of the early emigrants to this province, and he alone, of them all, through the appreciative delineation of a New England poet, has a permanent place in the literature of our own time." Pennypacker states that Pastorius first heard of the Frankfort Company in November, A. D. 1682, and bought the lands as agent in May and June of the next year. He refers to the Pastorius MSS. in the Historical Society of Pennsylvania.

Francis Daniel Pastorius was the son of Melchior and Magdalena Pastorius. His birth-place was Somerhausen, and the date of his birth, September 26, 1651. When he was seven years of age his father moved to Windsheim, where the boy attended school. He was later in the University of Strasburg and the High School at Basle, and studied law at Jena. When twenty-two years old he disputed publicly on law and philosophy in different languages. He practiced law in Frankfort, and traveled for over two years through various countries with "a noble young spark, named Von Rodeck." On his coming back to Frankfort, in 1681, the Pietists, who were his friends told him of the expected emigration to Pennsylvania, and he enthusiastically joined in the movement. He says: "A strong desire came upon me to cross the seas with them, and there, after having seen and experienced too much of European idleness to lead with them a quiet and Christian life." His education and social standing gave him the highest position in Germantown. In 1688 he married Ennecke Klosterman. He had two sons, John Samuel and Henry. He declares that he was "of a melancholy cholerick complexion, and therefore gentle, given to sobriety, solitary, studious, doubtful, shamefaced, timorous, pensive, constant and true in actions, of a slow wit, with obliviousness," etc.

> "If any one does him wrong
> He can't remember long."

He wrote various books. A few were printed and many were lost. He wrote to his sons that he was naturalized and therefore they were Englishmen, and that he prepared his manuscript book that they might repeatedly study it and become expert in the English language. He advises industry. Pastorius died September 27, 1719. Pastorius was the first school teacher in Germantown. His account book notes the payments of four pence per week for the school charges of Samuel Richardson's grandchildren. His influence brought over some of the colonists, but when he had persuaded his acquaintance Dotzen at Cologne to join him his wife declined, saying that at home she could ride in her carriage but in America she might have to milk the cows. So that family did not colonize. Mr. Pennypacker gives the above particulars. Pastorius was the only one of the Frankfort Company who came across the sea.

Dr. J. J. Levick, in his pamphlet on Early Physicians of Philadelphia, refers to the scholarship of Pastorius. Watson's Annals contain notices of Pastorius which we will summarize. He came from England in the ship America, Captain Joseph Wasey, a courteous and skillful man, and the ship was supposed to be chased by the Turks, but the suspected vessel was a French merchantman. He was as glad to land in Philadelphia in 1683 as Paul's shipmates to go on shore at Melita. The town had three or four small cottages. One was that of Edward Drinker, and another that of Sven Sener. Woods and underbrush were around, covering ground which is now a magnificent city. Pastorius got lost several times in going from his cave on the water side to the house of his friend William Hudson, which then was allotted to Cornelius Bom, a Dutch baker. He had lately been in London, Paris and Amsterdam and the new city did not look very grand in comparison with those places. Still, in 1718, he writes in the account: "That God has made of a desert an enclosed garden, and the plantations about it a beautiful field." In speaking of Pastorius's German pamphlet describing Pennsylvania, Watson styles him "a sensible man and a scholar."

John Johnson's family had a paper dated 1683 concerning a division of lands, "executed and witnessed in the cave of Francis Daniel Pastorius, Esq."
—Watson's Annals, Vol. I, p. 171. In this cave the division of Germantown lands was made.

Isaac Norris's garden at Fairhill pleased Pastorius, who was himself distinguished in agriculture. He writes to Mrs. Norris and her sisters, daughters of Governor Thomas Lloyd, concerning an article of his on gardening, flowers and trees, and says that the garden at Fairhill is the finest that he had then seen in the country, filled with rarities, and that the other ladies had a "pretty little garden much like his own, containing chiefly cordial, stomachic and culinary herbs." Of his own garden he writes:

> "What wonder you then
> That F. D. P. likewise here many hours spend,
> And, having no money, on usury lends
> To 's garden and orchard and vineyard such times,

> Wherein he helps nature and nature his rhymes,
> Because they produce him both victuals and drink,
> Both med'cine and nosegays, both paper and ink."

The poetry was written in red and green colors, which the poet says were formed of "tamarack and elder leaves." Watson, Vol. I, p. 493. In the same volume, pp. 516–518, we have a sketch of Pastorius, which ranks him with the "very fine scholars" of early days, Thomas Lloyd, Thomas Story, James Logan and John Kelpius. He lived 36 years in the colony. He wrote letters, acrostics and poems to the three daughters of Thomas Lloyd—Mrs. Rachel Preston, Mrs. Hannah Hill and Mrs. Mary Norris. These ladies were very religious and his writings include many pious thoughts. The articles were intended to be of interest to the parties concerned and their descendants. In a poem he recalls how on shipboard in the voyage to this country he, being a German, could talk with the Englishman, Thomas Lloyd, in Latin as a common tongue. They had a like love of "God's sacred truth." William Penn had much influence in keeping Pastorius in America. He conversed with him in French, when they were in Philadelphia. Afterward Pastorius became a good English scholar, and wrote in that language. He was eight weeks at sea. He makes a pun on the word America, using two Arabic words meaning bitter and sweet to represent the character of the new country at that time.

Pastorius once owned all of Chestnut Hill. "He was a member of Assembly in 1687." Watson, Vol. II, p. 19.

Pastorius had a little vineyard in Germantown where he made experiments in grape culture. Watson, Vol. II, p. 431.

On October 24, 1685, Pastorius, with the Governor's concurrence, laid out and planned Germantown or Germanopolis. He speaks of a fertile district, with its fresh water springs, and oak, walnut and chestnut trees and abundant pasturage. He made the principal street 60 feet wide, and the cross street 40 feet. He allotted 3 acres for each house and garden; allowing, however, 6 acres for his own dwelling house.

The Bee Hive of Francis Daniel Pastorius begins with an index written in his own clear fine hand. The ink is well preserved. The work was composed for the instruction of his sons. It is now in the possession of Mrs. Washington Pastorius, who resides next the Mennonite church, below Pastorius street. Seven different languages are used in this wonderful book. The languages are German, French, English, Latin, Greek, Italian and perhaps Dutch. It consists partly of his own ideas, and partly of quotations, including proverbs. There are several hundred pages in the volume. One section on its title page says: "A Bee may gather honey and a Spider poison from the same flower." The date on this heading is 1696. It also quotes Horace's Latin expression about mingling the useful and the agreeable. He calls it his alphabetical hive. His own poetry is scattered through the book, which has a religious tendency throughout, both in prose and poetry. It contains a genealogy of his family. He disclaims mere pride of birth, and speaks of the need of personal character, but he notes for his two sons their relatives in High Germany, with a prayer that they may attain heavenly bliss by the Holy Spirit's aid, and glorify God forever.

Here is a sample of his humor:

> "In times of old pipes were made of gold,
> (A picture of a flageolet follows.)
> But now, this day, they're made of clay."
> (A picture of a tobacco pipe follows.)

A warning against trusting on the PUBLIC LEDGER bills of to-day is a quotation from Pastorius.

The Bee Hive had various sheets stitched into it at different times, and was begun for the extracts of good thoughts from various writers. It is evidently the work of a scholar. He writes thus:

> "In these seven languages, I this my book do own;
> Friend, if thou find it, send the same to Germantown.
> The recompense shall be the half of half a crown.
> But tho' 't be no more than half the half of this,
> Pray be content therewith, and think it not amiss;
> Yea, and if when thou comest my cash perhaps is gone,
> For money is thus scarce, that often I have none.
> A 'cup of drink may do', or else, alas, thou must
> Trust unto me awhile, as I to others trust,
> Who failing, make me fail—a thing extreme unjust;
> To which I have no lust, but must perforce poor trust."

The manuscript book, in a time when books were rare, was a sort of encyclopedia, in which Pastorius accumulated useful knowledge from others and also stored his own thoughts. The sons of Mrs. Washington Pastorius, one of whom bears the name of his great ancestor, kindly displayed to me the striking points in the vast mass of manuscript, which must have cost the author many an hour of hard toil. The free use of the printing press to-day saves much of this kind of labor, and the typewriter adds its aid.

The PHILADELPHIA INQUIRER of October 7, A. D. 1889, gives this as to a German Annual Commemoration in Philadelphia:

HOW THE DAY ORIGINATED.

Dr. Ferdinand H. Gross opened the proceedings with a brief speech. He said the occasion was one worthy of commemoration. He referred to the Bi-Centennial Jubilee of the Germans in Germantown in 1883, and spoke of the extraordinary splendor and enthusiasm with which it was celebrated. At that time the desire manifested itself to celebrate the 6th of October annually as a German-American memorial day in memory of the co-operation of the German element in the development of the progress, greatness, wealth and liberty of our republic during the two centuries of its existence and in memory of those Pilgrim Fathers whose motto was: Freedom of mind, religion and labor and a liberal mode of life.

GERMANTOWN. 265

Dr. Oswald Seidensticker made an address in German, giving a history of German immigration and its influence on the development of the State and nation.

City Solicitor Charles F. Warwick delivered the address in English. He said that it was a red letter day not only in the history of the German race, but a red letter day in the history of America. When the thirteen men left their native homes to come to the New World they had a long and weary journey over a trackless waste of dreary waters. They came to find a new home in a new land, and he for one thanked God for the day they made up their minds to settle among us.

THREE GERMAN CHARACTERISTICS.

There were, he said, three things for which the German character was particularly noted. One was love of country; the second was love of domestic life, and the third was love of freedom. He honored them for all three of these characteristics, but particularly for the last. The love they bore for their old homes, he said, had now been transferred to the new home. They had stood by their adopted country in every hour of trial; during the Revolution, during the war of 1812 and finally during the war of the rebellion. It was just, therefore, that having taken part in its sorrows and its troubles, they should share in its peace and its prosperity.

The celebration concluded with an address in German by Dr. G. Kellner.

THE NORTHERN LIBERTIES.

The Northern Liberties was formerly styled North End. Near Cohocksinc creek, the road was in poor condition, and in 1701 country inhabitants of Germantown, Abington, etc., made petition to the Governor and Council for a settled road. The petition speaks of the Germantown road as being more traveled than the Frankford road, as it receives "much lime and meal from three mills, with much malt and a great deal of wood, timber," etc.

As to the group of houses, the picture of which was explained by C. J. W., in the GERMANTOWN TELEGRAPH of April 6, Watson, in the Appendix of Vol. II, p. 617, speaks of them as the *last* of the oldest houses remaining. The picturesque group of buildings then belonged to the family of John Green, and contrasted with the modern houses about them. They appeared to have been built at various periods. The front house, on the right in the picture, was faced with white mortar, and was the original log house used as a dwelling by John Adam Hogermoed. It had been the prison on Market Square. It was sold and Hogermoed bought it, and it was removed from the Square. "One of the higher houses in the rear, it may be seen, is diagonally boarded. The whole group seems to be found of *four* different constructions—a part is of stone. All such *remains* of the primitive times are fast fading from the things that be!"

In 1791 the Governor and Council received a petition from the corporation of Germantown, through Pastorius, for exemption "from county charges for Court, taxes, etc." They "proposed to pay all their own public charges; and they curiously added, 'they had seated themselves so close together, that they had scarce room to live.' They also at this time established the market-house, on the Main street, where the road 'goes to the Schuylkill.'" W. P. Hazzard's continuation of Watson's Annals, Vol. III, p. 66.

In Vol. I, p. 19, Watson says, "The Germans from Cresheim, near Worms, were nearly all of them Friends, and all of them made their settlement at Germantown. By this emigration, says Sewall, they providentially avoided the desolation of a French war, which soon after laid waste their former possessions."

Watson influenced "many to plaster the fronts of their houses," and stirred up the lot owners with regard "to paving the foot ways." Hes ays that Robert H. Thomas gave the first impulse to the increase of houses and population. He succeeded in opening streets, and selling lots and building cottages, and drawing persons into the country. He began on Centre street and then laid out lots on Kelly's farm. Eli and Philip Price, following his example, bought land of Wunder and laid out Price street, where Watson lived. The old Germantown faded out and the new came in, and the newer yet still drives out what preceded it.

Germantown was once selected as the capital of the United States, but a postponement to a following session killed the matter. This was in 1789. It is said that the influence of the financier, Robert Morris, brought Congress to Philadelphia. Watson's Annals, Vol. II, p. 605.

Watson names Jesse Torrey as the originator of the Germantown Railroad. I have given Townsend Ward's account of the matter in these articles. Mr. Torrey resided temporarily in Germantown. Various essays in Major Freas's GERMANTOWN TELEGRAPH sustain the work. The fluctuations of the value of the railway shares are described as well as its rise above par. Vol. II, p. 606. In Vol. II, p. 180, Watson gives from Heckewelder some meanings of Indian names: Wissahickon, catfish creek; Wisauchsican, a stream of yellowish color; Wingohocking (Wingehacking) fine land for planting, favorite spot; Tulpehoccon (Tulpewihacki) the land of turtles. This was the name of an Indian town at or about Womelsdorf. Vol. II, p. 255, and note. There was a Tulpehacka creek, p. 257. Says an observer, quoted in the Appendix of Vol. II, p. 529: "As I rode through the Tulpahocken, much I thought of the former Indian owners:

> 'Whose hundred bands
> Ranged freely o'er those shaded lands,
> Where now there's scarcely left a trace,
> To mind one of that tawny race.'"

WAPEN VAN DIRCK EYTHER, VERVAARDIGD IN HET GENEALOGISCH
EN HERALDISCH ARCHIEF TE 'S GRAVENHAGE, (NEDERLAND.)

Col. Jehu Eyre, a noted and patriotic ship builder of Kensington, was under command of General Armstrong, on the right, in the battle of Germantown and marched to the mouth of the Wissahickon " where he placed his cannon and opened the attack on the Hessians stationed opposite." Col. Peter D. Keyser's Memorials of Col. Eyre, Penna. Mag. of Hist., A. D. 1879, and pamphlet. While the danger of the collisions of war vessels sailing in a fog is great, so a fog on land, as at the Battle of Germantown, perplexes the combatants. Captain John Montresor's Journal in the Pennsylvania Magazine of History, No. IV, of Vol. 5, says that as the English marched to the battle of the Brandywine a thick fog contributed greatly to favor the march, p. 416.

To the notice of Mr. Alcott's school should have been added that Mr. Russell's Ladies' Boarding School in a yellow house, near Church Lane station, on Church lane, was contemporaneous with the school of Mr. Alcott. Mr. Jenks was at that time at the head of the Germantown Academy. These three gentlemen left Germantown, as I am informed, at about the same time.

GERMANS.

As to early German influence in Philadelphia it may be noted that in the Duke of Saxe Weimar's Travels, copied by Charles A. Poulson in his painstaking MSS. book of Extracts from Travelers as to Philadelphia, we find that the German Society, which had aided poor Germans reaching this country, gave a splendid banquet to that nobleman in the Masonic Hall. The travels were in 1825 and 1826. In returning from Bethlehem by stage the Duke says : "The last part of the road was particularly interesting to me. In the flourishing villages of Germantown and Nicetown there are handsome gardens and country seats of Philadelphians." He speaks of Washington's headquarters at Whitemarsh, and somebody had given him a story about a contest of the British for the possession of the well on the Chew place, which, as Mr. Poulson notes, is an error. Mr. Poulson deserved credit for the hard task in collecting so much matter about Philadelphia from native and foreign authors who had visited the city. The manuscript book shows what were the "lions" of early days and how "ithers see us." If a collection from it could be printed it would be interesting. The volume is in the Ridgway Library. In it Tyrone Power, the famous Irish comedian, who was lost on the ship *President*, speaks of the German farmers about Philadelphia who encircled the soil and clung to the customs of " Faderland." In 1833–35 he notes their dress and manners as still peculiarly German as well as their language. He remarks that there were German magistrates and a German interpreter in court. He also tells of a ride to Germantown and the ravine of the " Wisihissing." The wild ravines and bridle paths please the stranger. He thought that the first glance of the country about Philadelphia would not warrant an expectation of the pleasant surprises which a broken country does afford to one " of an errant habit and much given to exploration."

I have a copy of Joel Barlow's "Columbiad." The volume is magnificently printed by Fry & Kammerer for C. & A. Conrad & Co., Philadelphia, Conrad, Lucas & Co., Baltimore, and published in Philadelphia in A. D. 1807. As to the mechanical execution of this book, Dr. James Mease, in his "Picture (History) of Philadelphia," speaks of this and Wilson's Ornithology as "specimens of truly superb work," done in Philadelphia, p. 86. On page 250, Book VII, of this epic poem is a reference to the death of Nash which occurred at the Battle of Germantown.

> "But still Columbus, on his war-beat shore,
> Sees Albion's fleets her new battalions pour;
> The States unconquer'd still their terrors wield,
> And stain with mingled gore the embattled field.
> On Pennsylvania's various plains they move,
> And adverse armies equal slaughter prove;
> Columbia mourns her Nash in combat slain,
> Britons around him press the gory plain;
> Skirmish and cannonade and distant fire
> Each power diminish and each nation tire,
> Till Howe from fruitless toil demands repose,
> And leaves despairing in a land of foes
> His wearied host; who now, to reach their fleet,
> O'er Jersey hills commenced their long retreat,
> Tread back the steps their chief had led before,
> And ask in vain the late abandon'd shore,
> Where Hudson meets the main; for on their rear
> Columbia moves, and checks their swift career."

In book VIII, p. 309, a name familiar to Germantown is duly honored.:

> "And see sage Rittenhouse with ardent eye,
> Lift the long tube and pierce the starry sky;
> Clear in his view the circling planets roll,
> And suns and satellites their course control.
> He marks what laws the widest wanderers bind,
> Copies creation in his forming mind,
> Sees in his hall the total semblance rise,
> And mimics there the labors of the skies.
> There student youths without their tubes behold
> The spangled heavens their mystic maze unfold,
> And crowded schools their cheerful chambers grace
> With all the spheres that cleave the vast of space."

Another notable man whose history is connected with Stenton and Germantown, as described in these articles, is thus noticed on the same page:

> "To guide the sailor in his wandering way,
> See Godfrey's glass reverse the beams of day.
> His lifted quadrant to the eye displays
> From adverse skies the counteracting rays;
> And marks, as devious sails bewilder'd roll,
> Each nice gradation from the steadfast pole."

Another Germantown character appears in the "Columbiad," book VIII, p. 312, in a reference to Stuart.:

> "Stuart & Brown the moving portrait raise,
> Each rival stroke the force of life conveys;
> Heroes and beauties round their tablets stand,

THE CHANNON HOUSE, ONCE OCCUPIED BY DIRCK KEYSER;
ALSO THE RESIDENCE OF JACOB KEYSER, ELDEST
SON OF JOHN KEYSER.

"And rise unfading from their plastic hand;
Each breathing form preserves its wonted grace,
And all the soul stands speaking in the face."

DIRK KEYSER.

In almost every article under this heading, and particularly those written of Upper Germantown, the name of Keyser appears as inseparably woven into the early history of the place. It may therefore be appropriate in this connection to trace the history of this family from the year 1527. For the following sketch I am indebted to Mr. Romaine Keyser.

The earliest authentic history of the Keyser family appears in "Der Martyr's Spiegel," or "Het Blootige Toornal," "The Martyr's Mirror," or "The Bloody Journal," in which Leonard Keyser is spoken of as a Priest of the Mass in Bavaria, who, after a long series of persecutions, was burned at the stake, in Scharding, Germany, in 1527. The same year his family took refuge in Holland. According to Ten Cate, a Dutch historian, Leonard Keyser was one of the Waldenses, some of whose communities are said to have existed from the earliest Christian times. The first Keysers in America were Mennonites. "The origin of this sect is somewhat involved in obscurity. Their opponents, following Sleidanus and other writers of the 16th century have reproached them with being an outgrowth of the Anabaptists of Munster. On the contrary, their own historians, Mehring, Van Braght and Roosen, trace their theological and lineal descent from the Waldenses (Historical and Biographical sketches. Pennypacker). This then accounts for the religious belief of the family, previous to their appearance in America.

In the fall of 1688, Dirk Keyser, a silk merchant of Amsterdam, with his son Peter, and Dirk Jr., arrived in Germantown, by way of New York. Having left Holland, which had established on a firm foundation the true principles of religious liberty, they doubtless sought a new home where they could, with even greater freedom, develop this God given heritage, bringing with them love of liberty, some property and habits of frugality and industry. In the family Bible, now in the possession of Mr. Gideon Keyser, is written by Dirk Keyser: "September, 1688, died, my little daughter Joanna, and was buried upon a plantation called Cogenaw, between New York and Philadelphia." The family have still in their possession many papers and documents brought from Holland. Among these are marriage certificates, funeral notices and certificates of baptism, some of which, from their singularity or oddness at the present day, we present in this sketch:

CERTIFICATES OF MARRIAGE.

"This is to certify that Dirk Keyser and Elizabeth ter Himpel, upon their desire, after three Sundays having been published at Amsterdam, in all the churches, on the undermentioned date, in the church at Buicksloot, lawfully and in the presence of the Lord's congregation, are married: declare I, the undersigned secretary, at Buicksloot, the 22d day of November, 1668.

"Signed, B. VREDENHUIS,
"Secretary."

The following is the certificate of marriage of Pieter Dirk Keyser, who was born in Amsterdam, 25th November, 1676, and accompanied his father to America in 1688:

"This is to certify that on the 4th of September, 1700, I married Margareth Sieplie, aged eighteen years. May the Lord grant us his blessing, and all which will be necessary for us in this world and in the world to come, and we will praise his holy name, now and forever. Amen.

"PIETER DIRK KEYSER,
"Germantown."

INVITATIONS TO FUNERALS.

"On Monday, 5th July, 1655, you are desired to follow to the grave, the deceased youngest son of Dirk Gerritz Keyser, brother-in-law to Tobias Govertz, Van den Wyngaert, in Eland street, near the Resting Hart, at one o'clock, to come as near friend to the house. The corpse to be buried in the Wester Church."

"On Sunday, 14th October, 1657, you are desired to follow to the grave Elizabeth Van Singhel, wife of Pieter ter Himpel, in the house called 'ter Himpel,' to come as a friend to the house. The corpse to be buried in the South Church."

"On Saturday, 27th, 1676, you are desired to follow to the grave Josntye Van Gestel, late wife of Gerret Dirk Keyser, daughter of Jan Van Gestel, in Eland street, near the Resting Hart, to come as a friend in the house. The corpse to be buried in the Leydse Church, by desire of Dirk Keyser and wife."

Quite a number of notices such as the above, printed in the Dutch language, in bold type, upon heavy paper, and showing very little the effect of the two hundred years which have rolled over them, are still resting under the heavy lids of the old family Bible.

On the 4th of April, 1689, the first settlers in Germantown drew lots for choice of location in the town then about to be incorporated by William Penn. The Keysers drew lot No. 22, and shortly afterward purchased the adjoining property of William Streypers.

Dirk Keyser died 30th November, 1714, and was buried at Germantown, leaving his estate to his son, Pieter Dirk Keyser, who died 12th September, 1724. Tracing the descent into the eighteenth century the record continues. Dirk Keyser, son of Pieter Dirk Keyser, the first American of the family, was born in Germantown, 26th September, 1701; died 8th January, 1756. The stone marking his last resting place is still in an excellent state of preservation in the old Mennonite graveyard. His eldest son, John Keyser, was born 23d

SAMUEL KEYSER, PROGENITOR OF
THE PRESENT GERMANTOWN
BRANCH.

May, 1730, and died 2d May, 1813. He lived in the house now occupied by the family of the late Rev. John Rodney, 5233 Germantown Avenue. John Keyser's eldest son, Jacob, was born 18th September, 1754. After a well-spent life he died at his home, now occupied by Mr. John C. Channon, 5149 Germantown Avenue, 17th December, 1846. The names of these two ancestors of the family appear frequently in the old books of the Germantown Academy, Concord School and Mennonite Church, both as contributors and officers. They did that which is most worthy of notice—they gave of their time, their talents and their money for the advancement of the best interests of the town, and the gratitude of future generations should preserve their names from oblivion. Mr. John F. Watson, in his "Annals of Philadelphia," makes this mention of Jacob Keyser: "An aged gentleman, who has been a contributor of many of the facts of Germantown, and to whom I have submitted the perusal of the preceding pages, has commended them for their accuracy, and has furnished some additional illustrations." With the death of Jacob Keyser, in his 92d year, we come to the generation in which Samuel Keyser, born 25th January, 1783, was the eldest son, and standing as he does in the family record, midway between the past and the present, he may well be taken as a type of the hardy pioneers, who were plain, matter-of-fact, intelligent men, not easily discouraged and without the quality of fear. His tall person and stern features will be remembered by many of the citizens of the present day. He was a Director of the Bank of Germantown from 1837 to 1858, and a Manager of the Poor from 1830 to 1845. President of the Board of Trustees of Concord School from 1834 to 1866.

He was exacting, almost Puritanical, in his bearing, yet possessing a charity which made the man worthy of the highest regard. He was liberal to his church; in all her enterprises he was cordially enlisted; so far from laying burdens upon others which he was unwilling to assume himself, he usually took the lead in the work to be done. He dealt his bread to the hungry, and brought the poor that were cast out, to his house, not rashly, but considerately measuring his alms, remembering the law of the Universe, which decrees that if any man will not work, neither shall he eat. On the 9th July, 1868, he died, and of his six sons Gideon, Naaman, Reuben, Jacob, John S., and Daniel L., but two survive—Gideon, who is enjoying excellent health in his 80th year, and Reuben.* Naaman died at Germantown, August 9th, 1867. He was a Director of the Bank of Germantown from 1841 to 1843. Jacob died in San Jago de Cuba, whither he had gone in search of health, November 28th, 1839. He traveled to the West Indies with a school friend, Pedro Ferrer Landa, whose father, a wealthy planter, had sent him to Philadelphia to be educated. John S. Keyser died in Philadelphia, April 15th, 1862. It was thought his courageous efforts, while Chief Marshal of Philadelphia from 1850 to 1853, that order and quiet of the Quaker City was brought out of the chaos of rough rule. Daniel L. Keyser, the father of the author of this sketch,

* Gideon died 3 Dec., 1888. Reuben died 22 July, 1888,

died March 27th, 1884. He was a member of the town Councils from 1835 to 1852. Town Commissioner in 1844. In 1853–54 Chairman of Committee to build Town Hall. From 1855 to 1875 he filled the positions of auditor, treasurer, secretary and president of the Board of Managers of the Poor. In 1862 he enlisted in Company G, Eighth Regiment, Penna. Militia. He was elected school director for 22d Section in 1876, and remained its most active member until the day of his death, since which time a new school has been given his name. He was president and director of the Masonic Hall Association, and for nearly fifty years was the moving spirit in the religious work carried forward by the Methodists in Germantown. His life was one of ceaseless activity, devoted to measures for the public good, the care of the sick and the distressed in the church, and in the world, than whom there was, there is, no nobler, manlier man, for all men knew him to be temperate, reverent and pure. No man ever knew better than he how to forgive, or more frequently exercised the forgiveness of injury, "the noblest virtue of humanity, the highest excellence of Christianity." Appropriate it is, indeed, that this history of the family, opened by the martyrdom of the first Keyser, should close with the record of the heroic death of two of its youngest generation: Lieutenant Charles P. Keyser, son of Naaman, of Company B, 150th Regiment, Pennsylvania Volunteers, and Samuel Keyser, son of Reuben, killed at Gettysburg, Pa., July 1st, 1863. The same spirit of holy courage which prompted Leonard Keyser to suffer death at the stake, and the same love of Liberty that brought their ancestors to America, led these young men to lay down their lives upon the soil of the State their forefathers helped to make strong and great.

This family has already been noticed in these articles but the author of this work adds that "the fair women and brave men," who assembled at the Mennonite Church in Germantown on October 10th, 1888, to celebrate the Bi-Centennial, of the arrival in America, of the extensive and worthy Keyser family deserve a few words. I have seldom looked on a goodlier company, and Dirck Keyser might be proud of his descendants. Gideon Keyser, who presided, has just died. The addresses by the historian of the family, Charles S. Keyser, Esq., and Dr. Peter Dirck Keyser, and Miss Julia A. Orum's reading of the martyrdom of Leonnard Keyser, written by Chas. S. Keyser, and the addresses of Hon. Horatio Gates Jones, Samuel W. Pennypacker, Esq., LL. D. (now a Judge), and Prof. Seidensticker, and Prof. Adrian Van Helden, of Holland, and the foreign Consul Lars Westergard were all very instructive, and the godly family were traced in their wanderings and struggles and successes from Holland to Germantown.

CALVARY CHURCH.

The Rev. Dr. Perry has placed in my hands a sketch of the history of this parish which he prepared for *The Episcopal Register*, now called *The Church*, of

CALVARY EPISCOPAL CHURCH, MANHEIM STREET.

January 21st, A. D. 1882. A picture of the beautiful rustic church, with its cross-crowned porches and buttresses and bell tower, surmounted by a cross, adorned the narrative. This church in Manheim street was built in expectation of the growth of the town in that quarter. It was the fourth Episcopal parish in Germantown. Mr. James S. Huber offered the lot in a good location. Those interested in the enterprise met at the Episcopal rooms, No. 524 Walnut street, on November, A. D. 1858. The late Rev. Kingston Goddard, D. D., rector of the Church of the Atonement, Philadelphia, lived in Germantown and was deeply interested in this work. In a month the funds for a church building were raised and the contract for the erection made. J. C. Sidney was the architect. Ground was broken November 22d, 1858. Mr. Benjamin G. Godfrey was chairman of the Building Committee and was elected warden. The Vestry were Messrs. B. G. Godfrey, Harry Conrad, John Welsh, H. P. McKean, Edward Ingersoll, Wm. P. Cresson, Wm. B. Johns, P. E. Hamm, Thomas H. Powers, Edmund Smith, James Magee and Gilbert H. Newhall. Rev. T. K. Conrad, D. D., was elected the first rector and took charge of the parish on February 14th, 1859. He had been rector of All Saints' Church, Philadelphia.

The earnest chairman of the building committee pushed the building to completion on the 29th of April, and on the 30th it was consecrated by Assistant Bishop Samuel Bowman, who had encouraged the enterprise. Dr. Goddard preached from I Tim. 3:15, "That thou mightest know how to behave thyself in the house of God." The day following being Sunday Bishop Hopkins, of Vermont, preached in the morning from Col. 3:23, "And whatsoever ye do, do it heartily, as to the Lord, and not unto men." Bishop Stevens, who was then rector of St. Andrew's, Philadelphia, preached in the afternoon from Ps. XC. 17, "And let the beauty of the Lord our God be upon us; and establish thou the work of our hands upon us; yea the work of our hands establish thou it." In the evening Rev. Dr. Alex. Vinton, rector of Holy Trinity Church, Philadelphia, preached. The next Sunday several children came to the Church seeking a Sunday School. The rector and warden were there and promptly started one on the occasion. The school met in the church till a two-story building was erected for it in the rear. Dr. Conrad's rectorship closed in 1863. A parochial school has been formed and the playground was the place of training the famous Young America Cricket Club. The school building was enlarged. Rev. John A. Childs, D. D., was in charge of the parish for several months. Rev. George A. Strong, became the second rector on August 30th, 1863, and resigned November 1st, 1865. Under his rectorship the church prospered financially.

Rev. J. DeWolf Perry, D. D., from Rhode Island, became the third rector on the second Sunday of May, 1866. A volunteer choir was formed by the young members of the congregation. The church was enlarged and the chancel newly furnished. The school building was again enlarged by adding two rooms for parish uses. One contained the parish library. A parish Guild was formed in 1867 and has done good work. A Mothers' Meeting was added and night school for both sexes. A fine stone rectory has been built and lately enlarged.

The rector has done outside work at Kenderton and Nicetown. Rev. J. W. Ashton, when a candidate for Holy Orders, assisted zealously in the Nicetown undertaking. He is now in charge of a church in Olean, N. Y. The services at Nicetown, near the steel works, were discontinued, but the Sunday School and Sewing School continued successfully. The services at Nicetown were held in the railway station and afterward in an old building kindly loaned for the purpose. In 1869 the Church of the Resurrection in Rising Sun was prostrated by the wind. At this juncture Mr. Davis, then rector at Rising Sun, held services in the Railroad Hall at Tioga. A Sunday School was formed and St. George's Church was organized and called Rev. Joseph R. Moore to its rectorship. He has since become the rector of the Church of the Resurrection.

The organ of Calvary Church was the workmanship of Knauff & Sons. It was put in the Church in 1872. This year the wall of the chancel was re-illuminated as the work of the Sunday School. The stone wall in front of the Church gave place to an iron railing. In 1881, at Easter, the Church was freed from debt, according to St. Paul's injunction, "Owe no man anything, but to love one another." The Children's Mite Society has improved the Church grounds by laying stone pavements, etc. Dr. Perry is the Dean of the Convocation of Germantown. The members of the present vestry of the Church are as follows: Col. George A. Woodward, William Mellor, George M. Russell, David Hinkle, Jabez Gates, Henry M. Brown, J. Robert Maury, Charles C. Harrison, George S. Strawbridge, A. E. Brecht, Dr. Benjamin Lee, Robert S. Newhall.

GEORGE LIPPARD.

The pedestrian who looks into the gate of the Upper Burying Ground in passing will see a number of stones with the name of Lippard on them. These were relatives of the noted novelist. His grandfather and father and his maternal grandfather, John Cook, are buried in this old yard. The novelist is interred in the Odd Fellows' Cemetery in this city, and a monument has lately been erected to him by the "Brotherhood of the Union," which was founded by him. The chief officer of this body is styled Washington, and the names of Franklin and other famous men of revolutionary days are used to designate other officers.

George Lippard was the author of a number of novels, which were published by Peterson, and were successful in their day. "Washington and His Generals," "The Quaker City, or the Monk of Monk Hall," "Paul Ardenheim, or the Monk of Wissahickon," "Legends of Mexico," "The Nazarene," "Blanche of Brandywine," "The Belle of Prarie Eden, or A Romance of Mexico," and other volumes fell from his fertile pen. He published "The White Banner Quarterly," himself. Mr. Lippard was the cousin of John Cook Channon, of

Germantown, and his picture is at his residence, and his clear signature is in a book presented by him to the sisters of Mr. Channon. The long-haired bright looking youth with turned down collar and white vest, holds a scroll of paper in his hand and looks the personification of the poet. He was brought up a Methodist and in early life thought of becoming a Methodist preacher. He spent part of his youth with his mother's sister at Rising Sun, and took a deep interest in Germantown and wrote much about it. He was passionately fond of the country about the Wissahickon, and, with a poet's fancy, was married on the banks of the Wissahickon at sunrise. His wife and child died before him. He died in early mid-life of consumption. His imagination was strong and his picturing vivid. A reference to his description of the battle of Germantown, with his poetical additions was given in these articles. He was a prose poet.

He was an eloquent speaker, as well as an impressive writer. He wrote much concerning the legends of the beautiful Wissahickon. The mother of George Lippard was Jemima Ford, who lived on the Brandywine creek in Delaware. One of his books related to the Brandywine. His grandfather, David Ford, was one of the early Methodists of Delaware. His father, Daniel B. Lippard, was once County Treasurer. The author, in boyhood, spent some time in the office of Ovid F. Johnson, Esq., Attorney General of the State, which was located in Philadelphia.

THE OLD WELL AT THE CHEW HOUSE.

There is something very interesting in an old well, which has refreshed generations. In Genesis we read of the twelve wells of water at Elim, and the seventy palm trees, where the encampment was naturally made. Isaac and Rebecca at the well is a familiar picture from childhood, and our Lord's discourse on spiritual worship to the woman at the well of Jacob, was one of the most important contained in the Gospels. Woodworth, in his famous poem, has well given voice to the sentiment that clings around an old well, thus:

> "And now, far removed from that loved situation,
> The tear of regret will intrusively swell,
> As fancy reverts to my father's plantation,
> And sighs for the bucket which hangs in the well;
> The old oaken bucket!—the iron-bound bucket—
> The moss-covered bucket, which hangs in the well."

The Chew well was no doubt an object of great interest in its day. In winter the half frozen urchins in the early morning filled their pails, and hastened from the icy surroundings to the warm stove, and the comfortable breakfast. In the warm summer mornings there was more lingering for a word of gossip. The noon day found the tired laborer stopping to quench his thirst, and the evening perhaps heard its tale of love. But the barefooted children did not like to tarry here at night, but hurried by with quivering hearts. The old tradition ran that dead soldiers were cast into this well at the time of the battle, and their ghosts were naturally expected to appear. Women, as well as children, were afraid of the ghosts which were supposed to visit Chew's stone wall at night. A man once tried to play the ghost there, wrapped in a sheet or blanket, but men caught and flogged him. There must have been a strong feeling among children when those who lived at the time of the battle could tell them the tales of blood which their own eyes had seen. Southey represents this in his poem on "The Battle of Blenheim." The summer evening with old Kaspar telling little Peterkin and Wilhelmine about the fearful battle of long ago is a vivid scene:

> "'It was the English,' Kaspar cried,
> 'Who put the French to rout;
> But what they killed each other for
> I could not well make out.
> But everybody said,' quoth he,
> 'That t'was for a famous victory!'"

Would that such satires might help to prevent famous victories, and famous defeats alike, and banish the demon of war from the earth.

The old well at the Chew House had more history and romance connected with it than the modern fountains which adorn our city. Still these fountains are a very pretty feature, and justify the Hebrew usage, which called the fountain the eye, for they give life to the landscapes, as the human eye enlivens the countenance. The well stood in what is now Johnson street, where the board walk is. A wooden roof surmounted it, and buckets emptying and filling in ascending and descending, were worked by a cord and rope. Mr. J. Heyl Raser, the artist, whose studio is in West Walnut lane, near Main street, in Germantown, has taken great pains to get an exact idea of the well, and has painted a beautiful picture of it within the wall of the lawn, in oil, and its surroundings, including the Chew House and grounds, which adorns the wall of the Library Association at Market Square and Main street. The readers should go there and view it. An ancient Friends' marriage certificate of Baltas Reser and Mary Lucken, A. D. 1743, with the Germantown witnesses, having the old family names of Naglee, Shoemaker and Mackinet, shows that the artist's ancestors were Germantowners, and that he has a natural right to take a deep interest in the antiquities of the place. He has kindly aided my inquiries. One person has spoken to me of a pole being in use to work the bucket of the Chew well; if it was used, it may have been previous to the cord arrangement described.

I have elsewhere given the mistaken idea of a foreign traveler, who was wrongly informed that the possession of the well was an important point in the battle. A low stone wall used to run along the front of the Chew House and grounds, before the grading of the street caused the present ha-ha to be built. The well stood just within the wall, and the neighborhood was kindly allowed to use it, so that the chain or cord and pulley were in frequent demand. The land where the well stood and the well itself, are said to have belonged to

Leonard Stoneburner, before the Chews owned it. He is buried in the Upper Burying Ground. His house is now divided into stores. It is the last main building before striking the Chew property. It fell into the hands of Jacob Clemens, who married a granddaughter of Mr. Stoneburner. The old well and its companions in the town, the old toll-gate and market-house, have disappeared. They belonged to a day when peach trees bloomed and orchards of apple trees stood where the citizens have now built their fine cottages. While we admire the new lanes we can but mourn the loss of the picturesqueness of the early times. Thompson Westcott has called my attention to another antiquity at the Chew House. It is the old-fashioned iron-plate in the kitchen at Cliveden. I noticed a very fine one at Graeme Park, but they are a *rara avis* now.

The SHARPNACK FAMILY lived below Sharpnack street. The house is gone. The street, which perpetuates their name, runs through their property. Benjamin Sharpnack had been a Philadelphia merchant, and lived on this place with his sisters. The original members of this family are dead, but some descendants still remain in Germantown.

An interesting note relating to the Johnsons has fallen under my notice. Mr. Wallace was shown by Mr. Henry Phillips an almanack of 1763 with the imprint of Tiberius Johnson, who was a son of Reynier Johnson, Pennsylvania Magazine of History, Vol. V, p. 117, "Notes and Queries."

The reverend Israel Acrelius was the Provost of the Swedish Churches, and rector of Old Swedes' Church, Wilmington, Delaware. He wrote the History of New Sweden, and thus describes Germantown: "Germantown, six miles north of Philadelphia, is three miles long. It has one principal street, which is a public wagon road, and 350 houses. The inhabitants are generally German mechanics."

ROBERT P. McCULLAGH'S RESIDENCE, "LONGFIELD."

After passing the horse-car depot, on Main street, the residence of Mr. Robert P. McCullagh, "Longfield," meets us at No. 5511. The present owner informs me that this house was built by a carpenter, named Ideil. Some of the family live in Sharpnack street. It was next owned by the family of General Michael W. Ash, at one time sheriff of the county. Then Mr. Rodney King, who afterward lived in Roxborough, became the owner of the property. He sold it to the widow of Thomas Fassitt. Mr. McCullagh purchased of her heir or heirs. Rev. James Patterson had a school in Mr. McCullagh's house for two or three years. This was about A. D. 1823–4.

In Vol. III, p. 457 of Watson's Annals we find the following about the original Johnson House: "*The Johnson or Jansen House.*—The JOHNSON HOUSE which was on the corner of Germantown avenue, opposite the Chew property, was on the corner of Germantown avenue, opposite the Chew property, was built by Heivert Papen, one of the old German settlers of Germantown, in the year 1698. The Johnson (originally Jansen) family is also descended from old Germantown settlers, who formerly also owned ground on the west side of Main street and a portion of the ground on which Cliveden—afterward the Chew house—was built. A remarkable tree stood in the grounds near this mansion on Main street. It is the noblest tree of the kind—the silver fir (*Picea Pectinata*). Downing, in his *Landscape Gardening*, gives an illustration of it as a specimen tree—fig. 37—entitled 'The Silver Fir, at the residence of Dr. Johnson of Germantown: age fifty-seven years; height, one hundred feet.' This was thirty years ago, but, like all trees when too much crowded and shaded, it lost its majestic appearance. Immediately in front of the mansion is the finest specimen of the dwarf spruce (*Abies pumilla*) to be found in this vicinity." Willis P. Hazard here appears to give Watson's own emendation of Vol. II. The Fir tree still stands in the lower part of the lawn at Upsal, but shows its age. The lines which Watson quotes from Cowper's poem, "Yardley Oak," concerning old city trees in Vol. II, p. 491, well apply to this aged tree.

> "Survivor sole of all that once lived here!
> A shatter'd veteran,—couldst thou speak
> And tell who lived when thou wast young,
> By thee I might correct the clock of history—
> Recover facts,—misstated things set right;
> But since no spirit dwells in thee to speak,
> I will perform myself, in my own ear,
> Such matters as I may."

THE BILLMEYER HOUSE.

On the northwest corner of Main and Upsal streets (numbers 5344 and 5347), stands the ancient stone house of the Billmeyer family. The grading of the street has destroyed the old appearance of the property, but a photograph shows the grand trees which once adorned its front, while a side yard still holds some natural beauties which have escaped the ruthless hand of the highwaymen of modern times. The old stone steps which introduce the visitor to the mansion are antiques indeed, and the brass knocker has responded to the touch of various generations. The half-doors still retain their place, and have a quaint and simple air that is refreshing. Mr. George Billmeyer and family reside in the lower dwelling, and in the upper one the Misses Elizabeth M., Wilhelmina G., and Susanna C. Billmeyer. A part of the furniture is of the beautiful and strong patterns which delighted our ancestors, and which was honestly made for use and not for mere show. It has given comfort to many for about a century. An old high clock in all its dignity still ticks away solemnly under the moon which beautifies its face. A water-shed divides the upper and lower stories in front, and an old stone which formerly was placed on the lower side of the house on which Washington is said to have stood in commanding his Generals at the battle of Germantown, has wisely been placed within the yard, and I had the pleasure of standing upon it. The house was bought by Michael Billmeyer. His father wrote the name Billmayer. He was a native of Germany.

The American officers had a conference in front of this house, when the Chew House was in possession of the British, and Watson speaks of Colonel Pickering as being here. The British are said to have fired the house. There is a closet on the first floor which still retains the marks of the burning. A Mr. Haverstick built this old mansion for his two daughters, and a grandson of his named Henry was afterwards a tenant in the house.

In Theo. W. Bean's " Washington at Valley Forge, or Footprints of the Revolution," p. 24, it is stated in Lieut. Col. T. Pickering's letter that General Washington, General Knox and other officers were in front of a stone house north of Chew's house, which was apparently the Billmeyer house. There were then " open fields " above Chew's. There was a discussion whether the American troops should advance into the town or summon the garrison in the Chew house to surrender. There were British tents around the building.

Major Freas suggested in the GERMANTOWN TELEGRAPH of September 26th, 1877, that with modern firearms Washington could not have stood long on the stone. A bank then partially covered his body and the English were too busy with near foes to attack distant ones. A musket ball pierced the stoop and the remains are still there. A ball also pierced a second story window, and the woodwork still shows its mark.

Michael Billmeyer lived here at the battle, and used to speak of Washington. He was married by Rev. Michael Schlatter, ninety-nine years before Major Freas's visit to the house, to Mary Leipert (now spelled Leibert). The Gorgas and Leibert families in after years had a board yard at Gorgas and Main streets. Indian relics have been found on the place. The arrowheads are of stone from a distance. I had the pleasure of handling some stone hatchets. The family has a religious book published in 1617 in German. Jacob Billmeyer's name and the date 1777 is in the book. A Bible published in German in 1762 by Christopher Sower is in possession of this family. Michael Billmeyer succeeded Christopher Sower in the printing business in Germantown, and in partnership with Peter Leibert continued the work for years. He did printing for Congress.

Peter Leibert lived in the old stone plastered house on Main street, opposite Sharpnack street. The house once had a pent roof and porch, which have disappeared. It is an antique and perhaps as old as the Billmeyer house. John Crowson now owns and occupies it.

The stone house next below was owned by Christopher Mason, who dwelt in it. It belongs to the Carpenter estate. Mr. George Demuth occupies it.

The double stone house next below on the same side was built for Daniel L. Billmeyer by order of his father, Michael Billmeyer. His daughter, Miss Sophia Billmeyer, now resides in it. She is the only survivor of the family, which was quite a large one.

I am indebted to the Misses Billmeyer for the above information. The family has a coat of arms of German origin with an inscription referring to the printer's art, which would seem to indicate that the Emperor Frederick gave the honor for typographical reasons

It should have been noted that Christopher Sower lived in the present sexton's house of the Dunkard Church. There was an upper story to the church, where he did printing and kept his papers.

In front of the previous church building stood the old house which gave the traditional name to Beggarstown. The house was of log and frame. It was built for a dwelling and a church, but the new church arose in its rear. It was used as a house for the residence of the church poor. The present sexton, Mr. Scheetz, assisted in demolishing the house. The tradition is that this house was built by begging, at least in part, and so the tale is often told; but Townsend Ward believed that the term "Beggarstown," which was supposed thus to have started, was corrupted from Bebberstown from the Van Bebbers.

ST. MICHAEL'S LUTHERAN CHURCH.

This ancient parish lately celebrated its 150th anniversary, and the reminiscences of that occasion afford means for a short sketch of its history. In 1742 Rev. H. Melchior Muhlenberg, whose descendants are noted people, came from Europe and took charge of the church in Philadelphia, and at times preached in Germantown on week days. In 1745 Rev. Mr. Brownholz became pastor of St. Michael's Church. In 1746 the corner stone of a new church was laid. In 1751 Rev. Mr. Handschuh, a learned man, became pastor. The consecration of the new church took place in 1752. Rev. G. D. M. Heintzelman assisted Mr. Handschuh. In 1763 the Rev. Mr. Kurtz, of Tulpehocken, took the pastorship. Rev. John Ludwig Voight followed him in 1764. In 1765 Rev. Jacob Van Buskirk was pastor. Dr. Charles Magnus Wrangel was one of his examiners. Next comes Rev. John Frederick Schmidt in 1769. His pastorship covered the Revolutionary era. The parishioners were loyal Americans and the British seized the parsonage and used it as a fort for a time. They destroyed the church organ. A new one was procured. Germans love music and their church services are enlivened by it. Mr. Schmidt went into the city in 1786. Rev. Frederick Weinland succeeded him and held the post for three years. The church was incorporated in 1785, under Pastor Schmidt, Wichard Miller, Christian Schneider, Charles Hay, Samuel Mechlin, John Frey and George Hacker, as Trustees. John George Graefly, Henry Beck, Bernard Bisbing, John Altemus, Jacob Nees and Sebastian Reiber were elders. William Sommerlat, John Eggensdorf, Philip Kelsy and John Dowman were deacons. There was a parish school. In 1786 the Rev. Mr. Weinland gave up his charge, and in 1790 Rev. Dr. Frederick David Schaeffer, from Germany, became pastor. He had been a theological student under Rev. Jacob Goerring, of York, Pa. Four of his five sons became clergymen. Dr. Schaeffer came to this country in youth and taught school before studying theology. The church needed enlargement. The young desired English preaching, but the ancients preferred German speech. At times two of Mr. Schaeffer's sons preached in English. In 1812 their father took St. Michael's and Zion churches in Philadelphia. Rev. John C. Baker succeeded him. In 1813 this pastor was allowed to preach in English every other Sunday morning. In 1817 the Sunday school was started, though a portion of the church had been allotted to the children before that time and they had used it with regularity. The laying of the corner-stone of the church, which now stands among the graves of the dead in Christ, took place on March 25th, A. D. 1819. The next month the old church was taken away. The new church was dedicated in 1819 on the 21st of November. In 1828 Rev. Benjamin Keller succeeded Mr. Baker. The statistics show much pastoral work in his eight years of service. He started the idea of founding St. Thomas's German Church, which was finally built at Herman and Morton streets. At the age of seventy he gave up earthly work for the reward of Paradise, and was buried in St. Michael's churchyard, being the only pastor who sleeps among this flock. Rev. W. Richards, grandson of Muhlenberg, succeeded Mr. Keller in 1836 and remained till 1845. In 1846 Rev. S. Mosheim Schmucker became pastor and the German language was abandoned in preaching. In 1849 Rev. Charles W. Schaeffer gave up his post in Harrisburg to become pastor of St. Michael's. His work was appreciated by his people until in 1875, when the veteran withdrew, though still retaining an interest in his former parish. He is a professor in the Lutheran Theological Seminary in Philadelphia and resides on Main street in Germantown. Having married a Miss Ashmead, of one of the old families of Germantown, his interest in the place has been long continued and constant. In the Civil War, the parishioners of St. Michael's were prominent, and a number of the brave returned to rest in death where they had worshiped in life. The successor of Prof. Schaeffer was Rev. F. A. Kaehler, who resigned in 1884. Rev. J. P. Deck, a faithful and successful pastor, continues the work. The position of the old church building in the rear of the graveyard gives it a picturesque look from the street.

Watson says that of course the first Lutheran services were performed by the schoolmaster before they had an ordained minister, as is their custom in such cases. In Willis P. Hazard's continuation of Watson it is stated that "Rev. John Dylander, of the Swedish Church," laid the corner-stone of the first Lutheran Church in Germantown, in A. D. 1737. "He served for a few years and was succeeded by Mr. Kraft for one year, Rev. H. M. Muhlenberg, succeeding him on his arrival in 1742, and at the same time serving the Philadelphia congregation on Fifth street. After him came Rev. Peter Brownholtz, or Brownholz, in 1745, assisted occasionally by two schoolmasters, Mr. Vigero and Mr. Schaum."

There is a tradition that the British, after the retreat of the Americans at the Battle of Germantown, when they took possession of St. Michael's Church, tore out the pipes of the organ and ran along the street blowing in them and making confusion instead of the heavenly music which they had heretofore rendered under devout players on the instrument. A number of Union soldiers, as well as Major Lightfoot, who fell in the Battle of Germantown, are buried in St. Michael's churchyard.

As the residents of Germantown look on their monument to Soldiers and Sailors at Market Square and think of the brave dead who lie within their borders, let them recall the lines of Thomas MacKellar's Memorial Ode, read by Rev. Dr. Thomas T. Everett, when the monument was unveiled on July 4, A. D. 1883:—

> "Not they who shout are conquerors alone,
> For they who fall before the day is won
> Are also victors, and the laurel'd crown
> Fitly adorns the warrior smitten down,
>   No martyr dies
>   A fruitless sacrifice:—
>   Heroic deeds
>   Are the Immortal seeds—
> Nourished by blood and tears—
>   That grow the fruit of liberty
>   And conscience free
> Through time's unresting years."

CHRISTOPHER LUDWIG.

In St. Michael's churchyard is the tomb of Christopher Ludwig and his wife Catharine. A granite top stone is sustained by pillars of granite. The wife died in Germantown, in 1796, at the age of 80. Christopher Ludwig died in Philadelphia, in 1801, aged 80. The remarkably long epitaph gives a *resume* of his history, with the striking application at its close: "Reader, such was Ludwig. Art thou poor? venerate his character. Art thou rich? imitate his example." Dr. Rush wrote a memoir of this remarkable man. Watson describes him in the Annals. He was "an exemplary and valuable citizen." He was born in 1720, "at Geissen, in Hesse-Darmstadt, in Germany," to quote the monumental inscription. He was a baker. He had been a soldier in the Austrian army and had been in service against the Turks. He was in the hard siege at Prague. When the French conquered it in 1741, he entered the Prussian army. When peace came he went to India under Boscawen. As a sailor, he voyaged to Holland, Ireland, and the West Indies. In 1753, he visited Philadelphia, and made a large profit in a sale of clothing. Watson says he came again to this city, in 1754, as a gingerbread baker; the monument gives the date of his arrival as 1755. He began work in Letitia court, and money came in rapidly. He was industrious and honest and neighborly, and so influential that he was styled the "governor of Letitia court." When the Revolution approached, he was rich, and his money and influence were gladly given to his adopted country. He was put on committees and served in conventions. When General Mifflin wished to get arms by private subscriptions, and some held back, he called out "let the poor gingerbread baker be put down for £200," and overcame the opposition. He was for a time a member of the flying camp without pay. He encouraged the soldiers to patience, and once on his knees begged them to endure their insufficient ration and be hopeful. He asked to have eight captured Hessians given him, and took them to Philadelphia, and showed them the five churches of the Germans and the comfortable way in which humble Germans lived, and then they were sent back to encourage desertions, which frequently occurred. He went to the camp of the Hessians on Staten Island as a pretended deserter, to prove to the Germans the happy state of their countrymen settled in Pennsylvania. Congress made him baker-general of the army. They expected him to give a pound of bread for a pound of flour. He could have had a profit in the increase weight, which is the result of bread baking, but he would not grow rich by the war, and gave back one hundred and thirty-five pounds of bread for each one hundred pounds of flour. He often dined with Washington in company with others, and used to confer with him alone as to the supplies of bread. The General valued him and styled him "his honest friend." He was blunt without offense. The "German accent," originality and wit of this man made him popular and privileged in the army.

In the return of peace he dwelt on his farm which was near Germantown. Washington wrote "a certificate of his good conduct," which was framed, and hung in his parlor, and gave him much satisfaction. He once owned eight houses in Philadelphia, and had £3000 loaned. He left much to "public charities especially," a fund for educated poor children. He delighted to find out objects of charity, and to relieve their wants. In the time of the yellow fever of 1793, he went into Fraley's bakery, in Philadelphia, and worked at bread baking, gratuitously, to relieve the wants of the poor. He had a great respect for religion and its duties, which he said he inherited from his father, who had given him, in early life, a silver medal, on which was inscribed, among other devices, "The Blood of Christ cleanseth from all Sin." This he always carried with him as a kind of talisman; and with a view to enforce its remembrance and its precepts, when he left it to his family, he had it affixed to the lid of a silver tankard, and on the front he inscribed a device of a Bible, a plough and a sword, with the motto, "May the religious industry and courage of a German parent be the inheritance of his issue!" Well does Watson add to the account above quoted of him: "Such a man leaves the savor of a good name and a good example, to posterity. His remains now rest beneath an expensive monument, where the reader may read of his worth, and go, if he can, *and do likewise!*" His last house of residence in Philadelphia was No. 174 North Fifth street. He had two wives, but left no children to survive him. Their relations became his heirs. Christopher Ludwig was generally called the General. At one time he owned the plantation which in Watson's day belonged to John Haines. Watson says, that Ludwig lived in the house next to that of Mrs. Sarah Johnson. I find a note in Townsend Ward's MSS., stating that his residence was next to Dr. Wm. N. Johnson's "directly opposite the historic battle ground." He was of a very social character, talking freely along the street with all he met, and in so loud and strong a voice, as everywhere to announce his vicinity; so much so that it was usual in families, in doors, to say, "There goes the General!" The frankness which characterized him encouraged the woman who became his second wife, to say to him, in meeting him in the street, that as she felt concerned for his loneliness as a widower, she would offer herself to him for a companion, in case he thought it might conduce to their mutual happiness. He took it, as he said, into a short consideration, and they became man and wife; she being a good wife, and both of them a happy couple, in the opinion of all! He had but one eye." The war injured his property affairs, but he afterward acquired money. He left his receipt for gingerbread to those who succeeded him. The inscription on the monument states that "he bequeathed the greater part of his estate for the education of the children of the poor of all denominations gratis," and adds, "He lived and died, respected for his integrity and public spirit by all who knew him." This bequest founded two schools called the Ludwig Schools. They were on Walnut street, and under the care of the Friends. He gave to Zion Lutheran Church, in Franklin street, a bequest which still furnishes bread for the poor in winter. Ludwick Buildings, on Walnut street, above Sixth (No. 617), north side, has a stone tablet above its arch marked "Ludwick Buildings." "Ludwick's Building" is the original school building altered for offices. Charity scholars are still supported by the income of the good man's bounty. The Friends yet have charge of the schools, which are on the north side of Catharine street, above Fifth.

In Dr. Rush's Life of Christopher Ludwick, p. 20, there is a striking description of his death as follows: " In the last two years of his life he was frequently indisposed; he spent the intervals of his sickness in reading his Bible and religious books and in visiting his friends. He spoke often and now and then pleasantly of his approaching dissolution. Soon after the death of General Washington he was called upon to subscribe for a copy of his life. ' No,' said he, 'I will not, I am traveling fast to meet him, I will then hear all about it from his own mouth.' On Sunday the 14th of June, 1801, he begged his wife to read a sermon to him. When she had finished it he said, 'you will never read to me again on a Sunday; before next Sunday I shall be no more.' On the Monday following he was attacked with an inflammation of his breast, accompanied with a high fever. He had held his life for a year or two by the tenure of a small and single thread; it broke on Wednesday, the 17th of the month. There appeared to be a revival of the languid powers of reason in his last illness; he ceased to speak with a prayer upon his lips." Mr. Ludwick's second wife was a widow lady, named Mrs. Binder. Rush's Life of Ludwick is in the Library of the Historical Society of Pennsylvania.

ST. MICHAEL'S PARSONAGES AND CHURCH.

The quaint old stone cottage at the northeast corner of Springer and Main streets with its half-doors and pent roof is another of the lovable relics which still retain an air of former days, and keep up the flavor of the foreign in ancient Germantown. The cottage looks as if, like the holy house of Loretto, according to the legend, "It had been carried in the air from the old country." This was the old parsonage of St. Michael's church, which was invaded by British soldiers. It is still owned by the church. The number is 5465.

The pleasant double stone house just above it on the same side, marked No. 5467 is now the parsonage. It was built in the pastorate of Rev. Professor C. W. Schaeffer. There was a wooden building on the same site before this was built. A side yard joins the graveyard. In the burial ground, which has a quiet country look, are a number of graves of the Rex family and the Fry family and the Ashmeads and Roots and a large monument to the memory of Christopher Mason, who died in 1851, in the 62d year of his age. Anna Gottlieben Schneidern lies under an old flat tombstone on brick pillars. She died in 1727. An adjoining stone may be that of her husband. The inscription is blurred. Union soldiers lie in the yard. A shaft near the church door commemorates Frederick Hass. The tomb of John Sentz has a design of an angel bearing a cross. The church has been modernized and has a neat chancel surmounted with the text, "The Lord is in His Holy Temple, let all the earth keep silence before Him." An antique gallery remains to tell of olden times. The organ is in the gallery. A cross surmounts the chancel arch above the altar.

A large vestry room, used by the Dorcas Society, and former infant classroom, are attached to the rear of the church. The second story was formerly used by the Sunday School. An excellent and beautiful new gray stone Sunday school building, trimmed with brick, now stands near the church. It contains four rooms besides the library, and is adorned with stained glass windows. It is finished in natural woods. The cost was about $9000. The Rev. J. P. Deck, the present pastor, has kindly guided me through the buildings and given me information about them. The Sunday school library room has a fine case for the books, which contains a special wooden division for each book, so that the volumes are like Monks in their cells. They cannot fall on one another and cause disorder.

Two females, Solone Becher and Susanna Sorber, are commemorated by one stone in this graveyard. Jacob Butcher is on the next stone. Laura May Hetzel's cradle tomb, with its adornment of daisies plucked to brighten it, shows the more recent work of death. Michael Billmeyer's family vault is near the front gate. On entering the yard the shaft of the Lyle family meets the eye.

No. 5464 is an old stone plastered building next above the Franklin Inn. It was formerly owned by Mrs. Elizabeth Starr. No. 5466 adjoins this and belonged to the same person. No. 5468 is a part of the same building. Mrs. Starr owned this building for many years and lived in a part of it. She died over a half century ago. It belongs to the Carpenter estate. The stone house at the northwest corner of Westview avenue and Main street belonged to Philip Weaver. After his death George W. Carpenter bought it. It is now occupied by Mr. Wood.

TRINITY LUTHERAN CHURCH.

In abridging Ward's work a few lines were given to this parish. It deserves a longer notice. The position of the church building, far back from Main street, with its massive stone cross and other monumental stones in its graveyard before it, strikes the passer-by. Rev. Luther E. Albert, D. D., the present pastor, gave an historical sketch of this parish not long since. In 1836 some of the parishioners of St. Michael's Church colonized under Rev. W. N. School, Rev. Philip F. Meyer, of St. John's Church, Philadelphia, installed the vestry, as Ward stated. They were Thomas Haddon, Henry Goodman, Michael Trumbauer, David Heist, Henry Nicholas, Jacob Mehl, John Felton, George Heist, Jacob Geysel, Charles Heist, George Geysel and Joseph Heist. The congregation used the building now occupied by the Women's Christian Association, at the corner of Main and Mill streets. They bought the lot at the corner of Main and Queen streets and built a church on it. George Wallis, of Philadelphia, was the only one of the first communicants living when Dr. Albert delivered his historical sermon. Henry Earnest, son of Henry and Maria Goodman, was the first one baptized in the church. The first marriage was that of Reuben G. Tomlinson and Hannah K. Shepherd. The first burial was of William Saunders. Dr. School was living in Canajoharie, New York, when Dr. Albert's discourse was delivered. Rev. Samuel Finckel succeeded Dr. School in 1840. He first celebrated the Communion on the 7th of June in that year. He resigned in 1844. He was a gifted speaker and kind and popular in social life. He died in Washington in 1873. Rev. William F. Eyster succeeded Dr. Finckel in 1844. In 1848 many were received into the church. A Sunday school and parish building was erected on Queen street. In 1851 Mr. Eyster resigned. He is now a professor in the Augustina Seminary in Rock Island. Dr. Albert entered on his work in 1851 and has served the parish with fidelity and success over thirty-five years. This is his first and only parish. The new church was built in his pastorate. The Sunday school building on Queen street was sold. The new Church was dedicated in 1857. Rev. Dr. John G. Morris officiated. Henry Goodman was Sunday school superintendent for thirty-five years and died in the office. Theophilus H. Smith is now superintendent. There is a Young People's Lyceum with a very large membership. The trustees of this parish are: President, M. L. Finckel; Secretary, E. R. Pritchard; Treasurer, E. T. Coxe; Associates, Theophilus H. Smith, Samuel Goodman, Charles L. Eberle, William Broom,

John T. Monroe, William Garvin and A. Taylor Rittenhouse. The Snyder family, who lived near the Chew House, are interred here. There are German inscriptions on their flat tombstones in front of the church. An adopted child of this family was knitting stockings when the English officers were quartered on the household, and feared to lose her precious work, but they proved to be kind. She was eight or ten years old.

"S. W. P.," in Notes and Queries of the Pennsylvania Magazine of History, Vol. IX, p. 481, gives Howell Powell's quaint poem on Pastorius. It runs thus:

> "What Francis Daniel Pastorius
> Hath tane his flight from hence to Olympus
> Lost to his Posterity, ye Germantown specially.
> Loss (tho' great gains to him) it was to many.
> The Hermes, Glory, Crown, and Linguist's gone.
> * * * * * *
> Lowly, Lovely, Learn'd, Lively, still content,
> Now free from cares, dire troubles that attend
> This brittle case, the Heavenly quire befriend
> Him still; joyes in the glorious Lamb, alone
> Seeth the beatific vision.
> * * * * * *
> Tho dead to his corporal form, that sleep, he
> In immortality needs no reprieve."

The poem styles him "Scribe and Live Tutor," and "German's Polar Guide."

> "An antiquarian that was far from pride,
> Religious, zealous amanuensis;
> An universal man in arts, sciences,
> Who loved his friends, the Britains; yea all nations,
> Zealous for the truth, full of compations."

The poem commends his good example to his descendants.

Mention was made in a former article in reference to Pastorius, of the education of the grandchildren of Samuel Richardson. The reader who would know more of him may peruse in Pennypacker's volume of "Historical Sketches" (pp. 243-256), the memoir entitled, "Samuel Richardson, a Councillor, Judge and Legislator of the Olden Time." It appeared in *Lippincott's Magazine* in April, 1874. Richardson had a plantation of 500 acres near Germantown, where he had horses, cattle and sheep. His wife Ellinor died in 1703, and probably in 1705 he removed to the city. He married again, and lived somewhere about the intersection of Third and Chestnut streets. He was an alderman. "The Friends' records tell us that several grandchildren were born in his house, near Germantown."

The readers of Watson's Annals have noticed his quotations from a writer who used the signature "Lang Syne." This was Benjamin J. Leedom, according to Scharf & Westcott's History of Philadelphia, Vol. II, p. 953, column 2, Mr. Willis P. Hazard's 3d Vol. in continuation of Watson's Annals

(p. 219), gives the name of this writer as William McKay. This is probably a misprint, as in Watson's Annals (Vol. I, p. 182, and Vol. II, p. 548), the name is given by Watson as William McKoy. He was a teller in the Bank of North America, and his interesting articles were printed in *Poulson's Advertiser* in 1828–9. In the appendix of Vol. II (p. 548), Watson commends this writer as a model for those who would narrate incidents of old times. In Vol. I, (p. 182), he speaks of him as a thinker and reader, with "poetic associations and metaphorical imagery." Watson stimulated some of his work. He wrote two manuscript books of "characteristics" of his contemporaries. He was a man of humor.

Thompson Westcott, the local historian *par eminence* of Philadelphia, writes me as follows in reply to a query concerning this matter: "'Lang Syne' quoted in Watson's Annals was William McKoy, teller in the Bank of North America. He wrote originally for Poulson's paper about 1828–'29–'30. You will find several of his most interesting articles in Hazard's Register. Benjamin J. Leedom wrote a series of articles signed 'Lang Syne' of which I have a collection, for one of the Germantown papers. I have quoted him in my history, and endeavored to distinguish, whenever I wrote about them, between McKoy the old 'Old Lang Syne' and Leedom the *modern* article." This letter accounts for the two Dromios.

Watson refers to the Dusimitiere Manuscripts. The marvelous collection of the patient Frenchman, covers several volumes which contain the works of himself and of others, and they relate to various parts of this country, and also to foreign places. In No. 1413, "Y" "I" of the Ridgway Library (papers relating to Pennsylvania, New England, etc.), on page 5 we find the following note as to the Paxton Boys, who are connected with the history of Germantown. It is in an "Essay of a Chronology of Pennsylvania." "1764, Feby., 4, the alarm caused by the Paxtonians rioters marching in a great body towards Philadelphia to murder the Indians that were in the barracks." A note in red ink refers to *Parker's New York Gazette*, No. 1102. The Ridgway Library contains a history of this affair, for such as may wish to follow its details.

In Samuel Hazard's Register of Pennsylvania, Vol. I, pp. 279 to 284, and pp. 289–292, 43 and 335 there are notes concerning Germantown. Watson's manuscript is the basis of the information, and Mr. Hazard commends his patient toil. Germantown is here described as Springetbury Manor. On p. 49, etc., the Hon. Timothy Pickering's account of the Battle of Germantown is given from the *North American Review*. On p. 335, "A Church Member" notes that the Methodists preached in a coachmaker's shop which belonged to Jacob Sommers, in the Union School House, and occasionally in the Upper School House many years before 1798. A society was formed in 1793, and for "several years" there was "regular preaching," by itinerants and "the local ministry, in the house afterwards purchased by Mr. Lorain, at the south end of the town." This is taken from the "*Philadelphia Gazette.*"

Most, if not all, of Watson's notes here given appear in his Annals. For General Wayne's account of Affairs at Germantown, see Hazard's Register, Vol. III, p. 375. For an extended report of the History of the Lutheran Congregation, in Germantown, and the Lutheran Church at Barren Hill, the reader may turn to the above work, Vol. V, p. 193, etc.

On the 2d day of the 6th month, A. D. 1701, the "Bailif, Burgesses and Commonalty of Germantown" petition the Council in Philadelphia to hold a public market, as the Proprietary had previously allowed, by charter on the 6th day of the week "in the road or highway where the road or cross street of Germantown goes down toward the Schuylkill. This they think "would redound to the benefit both of the inhabitants and neighbors." This petition was granted. Vol. VI, p. 34.

In Vol. VII, p. 192, the GERMANTOWN TELEGRAPH is quoted to the effect that the first gun discharged at the Battle of Germantown was in the hands of a British soldier at Mt. Airy. The picket was in a building which was where William Cooper's public house afterward stood. The American Army had nearly reached the public house of Mr. Mason when the picket discovered it in the fog two hundred yards away. One shot his musket, and the ball cut off the small branch of a tree, and dreadfully shattered the wrist of an American soldier. He was conveyed into a house on the southwest side of the turnpike, a little above Mason's tavern, and the hand was amputated. In the same volume, p. 16, under date of December 29, 1830, it is noted that Saturday and Sunday were like spring by a remarkable change of weather, and "on Sunday morning, the plaintive notes of the blue-bird were quite numerous."

Vol. IX, p. 48, contains "Statistics of Germantown Township," giving the occupations of the people at length in a catalogue from the GERMANTOWN TELEGRAPH. Tallow chandlers, scriveners and button makers are not forgotten, and one is marked a saddle-tree maker. The horses, cows and dogs are noted. The account of the opening of the Germantown & Norristown R. R., in the same volume, p. 367, shows that the cars were named "The Germantown, Benjamin Franklin, Robert Morris, Penn Township, Madison, Jefferson, Philadelphia, William Penn and President." There was a car for the band. The president and directors were in the "President." These cars were drawn by horses. There was a banquet in Germantown, and much enthusiasm was shown. In Vol. X, p. 60, it is stated that Baldwin's engine ran a short distance on this road at a rate of forty miles an hour, and this was exceeded on the subsequent day and over sixty miles an hour was made.

The bringing in of stone on the new railroad is given as a notable matter from *Poulson* on p. 112. On p. 275, a quotation from the *American Sentinel* tells of a "new engine built by the West Point Foundry Association at New York" which was a complete success. On p. 320, the reference to the death of William Severn on the railroad, which had taken place some time before, shows how that awful list of accidents had already begun. The committee appointed to investigate, reported that "no earthly power, person or persons could have prevented." He rode a "young and unbridlewise horse which became frightened by the approach of the engine, and backing upon the track, both rider and horse were almost instantaneously killed."

In Vol. XII, p. 416, the GERMANTOWN TELEGRAPH is quoted to the effect that wood and "marketable produce" are higher priced in Germantown than in Philadelphia. This was in December, 1833. The number of May 24th, '34, quotes from the same paper that probably no such cold has been experienced in Germantown for 20 years so late in the spring. There had been frost. A farmer had seen ice a quarter of an inch thick. The same paper is quoted on p. 412, Vol. XIII, as to a night fire in McLehman's lumber yard, when thirteen engine and hose companies, from Philadelphia, kindly rushed out in an hour and fifteen minutes. Between four and five hundred firemen came. Hundreds of the citizens were on hand to help.

For an account of the opening of the Germantown R. R. to Manayunk, see Vol. XIV, A. D. 1834, pp. 276-7.

In Vol. XV, pp. 383, 4, the GERMANTOWN TELEGRAPH is once more quoted concerning a stalk of rye grown on the place of Mr. Jesse Bockius, measuring within half an inch of eight feet. Mr. Green and Mr. Botton also had some nearly seven feet high. Mr. Botton had a stalk of clover three feet high.

DEVONSHIRE PLACE.

Early in this century this beautiful property came into the possession of Mr. Blight's family. In 1793 and shortly after that period, when the yellow fever prevailed in Philadelphia, those who could seek a residence beyond the limits of the city did so.

The grandfather of the present owner, Peter Blight, was an extensive merchant, actively engaged in the tea trade with China. It was necessary to be near his place of business. This motive induced him to purchase a temporary residence on Nicetown lane, where he opened his "counting-house" during the prevalence of the fever. During the years 1808 to 1812 his numerous vessels were upon the ocean, and when the War of 1812 was declared, these vessels were captured and destroyed. The large claims his descendants have against the Government show how extended was his business. This brought great distress upon the family and caused them to make this counting-house (Harmony Hall), their permanent residence.

During these years of trouble, George Blight, Sr., was in Canton, and upon the death of Peter Blight, returned to this country, and desiring to live near the family residence, purchased what is now known as Devonshire Place, in 1816.

The former owner of this place was Captain Cochran, engaged in the merchant service and retired here for the balance of his days. George Blight, Sr., was born in Devonshire, England, and had all the tastes for country life so prevalent there. At this period this land was considered strictly fit only for agricultural purposes, his object was to cultivate, improve

DEVONSHIRE PLACE, THE PROPERTY OF MR. GEORGE BLIGHT.

and adorn it by planting choice varieties of trees, to which he added the raising of fine cattle. The present owner can well recall the herds of Shorthorn, Jersey and Holstein cattle that pastured on his lawn in those early days. In 1834, George Blight, Sr., died, and upon the division of his estate this property passed into the possession of his son George, who has endeavored to carry out the design of his father in keeping up the character of the property. In 1842 the present mansion was erected on the site of the old house, whose date of erection was in 1797. The former house was large and spacious and it was not the intention of Mr. Blight to rebuild, but it was found that so many repairs were necessary that the outlay would almost equal the cost of a new house and therefore he determined to reconstruct the whole. Increase of population and the value of land, induced Mr. Blight to dispose of certain portions suitable for building purposes. Mr. Blight has devoted his life to the cause of agriculture; its promotion in all branches; the raising of fine cattle and the production of large crops. In 1847 the Farmers' Club had its origin at Devonshire Place. This organization still exists, a long period for one of a social character. During Mr. Blight's prolonged absence in Europe, the house was occupied by different families until 1881, when he returned to the old homestead.

In chapter 422 of Westcott's History of Philadelphia, it is stated that Dr. Witt built the first three-story house in Germantown at East Walnut lane and Main street, which has been described in these articles as the Blair House and the Manual Labor Academy. John George Noer's house was nearly opposite. In chapter 516 is an account of the artist, Gilbert Stuart, in which occurs the following: "Some of his portraits of the first President—copies from the head—were painted by Stuart at Germantown, at which place he had a little building erected for a studio and painting room. He also painted a portrait of Mrs. Washington at that place." This was at William Wynne Wister's place.

In "A History of Education in Pennsylvania," reaching back to Swedish times, by James Pyle Wickersham, LL. D., on p. 81, we find a notice of Germantown as follows: "A school was established by the Dutch and German Friends at Germantown in 1701. Arent Klincken, Paul Wolff, and Peter Schumacher, Jr., were the 'overseers,' who collected the subscriptions and provided for opening the school. Francis Daniel Pastorius was the first schoolmaster, and Germantown has probably never since had one so learned."

His knowledge in languages and science is highly spoken of. On pages 142 and 143, it is noted that in the founding of Germantown Academy the Germans were prominent among the Trustees and "among the most liberal contributors." "A German department was organized, of which Hilarious Becker was master." On page 482, it is stated that "the three oldest schools of a secondary grade in Philadelphia, are the William Penn Charter School, the Germantown Academy, and the Protestant Episcopal Academy, the first

GERMANTOWN.

dating 1689, the second from 1760, and the last from 1785." An account of the Germantown Academy follows and a picture of the building. Dr. Egle, in his History of Pennsylvania, has also given a picture of the ancient Academy. On page 429, the Rev. John Monteith is mentioned as the head of the Manual Labor Academy in Germantown. This was described heretofore in these articles, and an account of Rev. Dr. Junkin's good work was there given.

In the first series of Colonial Records of Pennsylvania, Vol. X, p. 517, there is an order of the Council of Safety in May, 1716, that salt shall be moved to Germantown, "and stored under the care of the Committee of that town." On pages 596–7 of the same volume, James and Owen Biddle are authorized to secure store houses for salt, "saltpetre and other articles belonging to the Province," which might be sent to Germantown for safety. On page 660, we find Joseph Ferre requested to deliver salt to "John Mitchell, Commissionary for Victualing the Navy."

The Nice family are old residents of Germantown. In the Colonial Records, Vol. XIV, p. 671, we find this note: "John Nice's resignation of his office of Justice of the Peace for Germantown and Roxborough townships, in the county of Philadelphia, was read and accepted." The date is April 3d, 1786. In Vol. XV, p. 432, the following occurs: "A letter from John Nice, Esq., enclosing his commission as major of the second battalion of the militia of the county of Philadelphia, informing Council of his intention to remove himself and family to the Susquehanna river and praying leave to resign his said commission, was read and his resignation accepted." The date is "Saturday, April 12th, 1788." Samuel Hazard deserves great credit for his toil in preparing an index to the Colonial Records and Archives, which guides the seeker after historical details.

The "charter granted to the inhabitants of Germantown in 1691" is in the Pennsylvania Archives, selected and arranged by Samuel Hazard, Vol. I, pp. 111–115. The following quaintly spelled expression follows William Penn's signature: "Signed by the within named William Penn, and sealed with the Lesser Seale of the within menconed Province."

In Vol. IV, p. 731, the committee of safety writes to Peter De Haven thus: "Sir, the State of this Province is such at this time with respect to arms, that the Committee of Safety think it very improper to suffer any arms to be sold to go out of this Province, and being informed that a certain Mr. Frailey, of Germantown, has a number of arms for sale, which he has offer'd to Mr. Johnson Smith for the Virginians, we do therefore request you would apply to Mr. Frailey, and acquaint him with the opinion of this board, and also to purchase all the said arms which can be made fit for service, allowing a reasonable price for the same."

In Vol. V, pp. 206 and 225, General Gates orders Col. Melcher to appoint "a proper person to quarter the troops that are to march to Germantown." The date is January 31, 1777.

A letter of General Washington to President Wharton, written at the "Head Quarters, Germantown," is given in the same volume, pp. 617-618. Thomas Wharton, was President of the State of Pennsylvania, when the capital of the State was at Lancaster, in 1777. General John Armstrong's letter to President Wharton, about the defeat at Germantown, is on pages 645 and 647, and a letter from him to Council on military operations near Germantown in Vol. VI, pp. 70-72. It notes that General Irwin had three fingers shot off, and "fell from his horse." General Read had his horse shot, but escaped himself. On page 128, John Morgan, Jr., writes to V. P. Bryan thus: "I understand that all the stocking weavers are still at Germantown with their looms, and out of work, supposed to be about one hundred, also six or seven tanners, who have large tanyards full of leather, part of which is nearly tanned; they might easily be removed. Query, are they not objects worthy of notice of Council. Should the enemy determine to stay or leave Philadelphia this winter they will probably destroy them, which would be a great loss to this State." The letter is dated Reading, December 23d, 1777.

The last notice is in Vol. VII, p. 94, of John Delary, a private, wounded at the Battle of Germantown, who had been in "the hospital in Readingtown," who asked the Committee of Safety for back pay. He had lost one of his legs. How many of these wounded, maimed men remembered this sad battle all their lives!

Lambert Lare, of Haines street, informs me that when he came to Germantown about fifty years ago there was much wood cut in the surrounding country, and before the days of coal firewood was an important trade in the place. It was often sawed in the street. Some sixty years ago, David Moyer lived at Roxborough, on the Ridge pike near the nine-mile stone. He made a stove to burn coal in his house for heating, which was considered a wonderful thing in that day. Mr. Lare thinks he was the inventor of the process of cutting nails, as he was a blacksmith, and made wrought nails, and sold them in the city, and constructed a machine to cut the nails. He was a very skillful mechanic, but never took a patent for nail cutting. He constructed a gun from old horse shoe nails. A cut nail factory was established afterward about the mouth of the Wissahickon. The early cooking stoves were those of Beach, and afterward Finehower (?).

Thomas W. Evans, Esq., the father-in-law of General Huidekoper, has a pleasant stone mansion with a lawn before it just above the Chew House on the same side of the Main street. The ground is very high here, and Mr. Evans has been building some good dwellings in this location.

Miss Elizabeth Richards has a country place opposite, which she uses as a summer residence. The mansion is of stone, and has a roomy and comfortable appearance. It is just above the Johnson place named Upsal, on the same side of the way.

Among the older residents of Germantown, Mr. Joseph Green, opposite Major Freas's former residence, deserves mention. The family have long lived in the town, and been known as hatters. Townsend Ward speaks of this family. Mr. Joseph Green's son now conducts the ancestral business. It is an English way to hand down an occupation from father to son, and it is pleasant to see it in this country, as it indicates satisfaction and contentment when one continues in his father's line of business. Miss Myers, at Mrs. Kulp's, on Centre street, is another person whose age has permitted her to see many changes in Germantown. Her father owned property on Chelten avenue. Some aged persons have died during the collection of these notes before I have been able to see them. So the graves from the Upper and Lower Burying Grounds, and the soldiers' unmarked resting places teach us of mortality, and warn us to prepare in Christian faith for another and abiding city when our earthly record is closed.

As to improvements, in all these passing years, an old resident informs me that formerly lanterns were carried in the streets at night by those who were obliged to be out. Now the electric light scorns such devices of "Ancient Germantown." Still, London once had her link-boys to guide her citizens at night with their torches.

"THE CORVY," THE RESIDENCE OF WILLIAM WYNNE WISTER.

(Contributed.)

The quaint old-fashioned house situated on the southwest side of the Main street of Germantown, about half-way between Bockius's and Indian Queen lanes (by modern nomenclature, Manheim and Queen streets), was originally owned by Dr. William Shippen, formerly a large land-holder in the town and its vicinity. He owned the adjoining tract now part of the estate of the late Casper Heft, as well as "Carnaervon," the summer residence of Mr. Wister Price, and much other property on Manheim street. *En passant*, it may not be out of place here to mention that the lot adjoining "Carnaervon," at the corner of Manheim street and the Township line road, was rented by Mr. Shippen, a successor to Dr. William Shippen, to Col. John M. Price, the father of Mr. Wister Price, for agricultural purposes at a rental of *one ear of corn per annum*, on condition that the lessee should plant forest trees thereon—Mr. Shippen holding native trees in high esteem—which condition was conscientiously observed. This is the only instance of paying rent in kind within my experience. The property referred to passed from the hands of Dr. Shippen into the ownership of James Logan, of Stenton, by whom, in the year 1750, it was devised to his daughter, Hannah, the grandmother of the late Mr. John J. Smith, of Shoemaker lane. Later in its history it came into possession of Samuel Bringhurst, who, having had two daughters, one of whom married William Lehman, son of Benjamin Lehman, well known to old Germantown residents, and the other Samuel Ashmead, son of Capt. John Ashmead, officer in the Revolutionary army, Messrs. Lehman and Ashmead became joint owners. From the descendants of these it was, in the year 1849, purchased by the gentleman whose name stands at the head of this brief sketch.

The historical interest in "The Corvy" centres in its having been occupied, between the years 1790 and 1795, by the great artist, Gilbert Stuart, rendered forever famous by having put upon canvas the best likeness ever made of the immortal Washington. A small stone building in the rear of the dwelling was appropriated by Stuart for his studio or atelier, and here, within its ivy-covered walls, did the father of his country sit to him. Probably there is no precedent in history of an event of similar importance having been consummated in so humble an apartment. The date of the sitting is the summer of 1793, when Washington, in order to escape the yellow fever epidemic, then at its height in Philadelphia, took up his abode in Germantown, occupying the Perot house, opposite Market Square, now the residence of Mr. Elliston Perot Morris. All of this is confirmed by the daughter of Gilbert Stuart in her Memoirs of her father, as well as by local tradition. "The Corvy" stands retired from the Main street of the town, having a lawn in front shaded by gigantic maple trees, which add greatly to the attractiveness of its appearance. Since 1849, being the home of a gentleman of retired habits, its history has been uneventful.

THE FOUNTAIN INN.

The hotel thus designated (already referred to in one of Mr. Hotchkin's papers) was situated on the Main street of Germantown, nearly opposite to the Germantown and Norristown Railroad depot, and adjoined "Vernon" on the northwest. It was the scene of the following incident of village life about three-fourths of a century ago: During the war with England, in 1814, the military spirit was as enthusiastic in Germantown as it was in the memorable days of 1861-2, to the predominance of which we can most of us bear testimony. Since it was as desirable at the former as at the latter period that this spirit should be encouraged and moulded into some practical form in which it might be serviceable to a suffering country, it was resolved by the patriots of the town that a company of volunteers be raised who should hold themselves prepared to fly to her defense at a moment's notice. Accordingly, this enterprise was set on foot, and chiefly by the energy of one man, William Ent (Endt in the old records), a company of seventy-five recruits was raised, ardent for the fray, mustering under the title of "The Germantown Blues," to which Ent was appointed orderly sergeant, his modesty having prevented his acceptance of the captaincy.

A military organization in the village having become a reality, it was meet that some public demonstration be made, and the presentation of a flag of the most approved style was determined upon. Here again was the energy of the orderly conspicuous, for he, together with the lieutenant of the company, Wilson (landlord of the Fountain Inn), constituted a committee empowered to act as they thought most desirable in order to secure funds necessary to carry the proposition into effect. The lieutenant and orderly, therefore, determined to set out on a begging expedition, and forthwith commenced the unwelcome task.

The next question to decide was to whom to apply to head the list in order to secure a liberal contribution, well knowing the force of example in such cases. The lieutenant suggested that they had as well begin with the nearest house. This happening to be Mr. W.'s, the orderly remonstrated, reminding him that the well-known Quaker principles of the proprietor would leave them little hope from such an application. The lieutenant prevailed, however, and back the long carriageway they trudged, though with the discouraging prospect of an unsuccessful attempt before them. Their modest tap was promptly answered, when they were informed that Mr. W. was not at home, but that Mrs. W. would see them, who immediately presented herself. The object of the visit was stated and the subscription book presented. After reading the title page Mrs. W. retired, but soon reappeared with a bank note, which she handed them. This, though not examined in her presence, was nevertheless received with profound gratitude, but when its true denomination was ascertained the applicants were so convinced that it had been given them by mistake that their honesty would not permit them to keep it, and they accordingly retraced their steps and returned it. Mrs. W., upon receiving it, admitted that she had indeed made a mistake and withdrew, soon returning, however, with one exactly double the amount, which she handed them with the remark that their high sense of honor fully entitled them to the additional contribution, and that she wished to make this acknowledgment of her appreciation of it. The collectors took their leave, not only with a high respect for the generosity of the donor, but with much elation at the success of their first application. A sufficient sum being soon collected to warrant the ordering of the flag, it was resolved that when completed it should be handed over to the ladies of the town, and that the presentation should be made from the steps of Mr. Blair's house (afterwards Col. Alexander's, now Miss Burkhart's, corner of East Walnut lane and Main street), being a central situation, and that the honor of presenting it should devolve upon Miss M. R—— (Miss Mary Roberdeau, daughter of Major Roberdeau, who married Rev. Dr. Blair's daughter), celebrated for her beauty. Mr. C. J. W. was requested to compose the address, which Miss M. R. committed to memory, and the twenty-second of February was selected as a suitable day for the ceremonies to take place. Much solicitude was entertained on the part of the "Blues" on account of their ensign, Barwell, upon whom devolved the duty of receiving the flag, lest when confronted by so handsome and dignified a lady as Miss R. his embarrassment should so far get the better of him as to render him incapable of performing his part of the programme. As the event proved, however, their anxiety was superfluous, for the presentation as well as the reception addresses were delivered in excellent taste,

and the whole affair, which was witnessed by a large portion of the inhabitants of the village, passed off in the most satisfactory manner.   C. J. W.
Germantown, 6th Mo. 25, 1887.

In Rev. Andrew Burnaby's "Travels through the Middle Settlements in North America" in 1759 and 1760, we read: "Carlisle, Lancaster and Germantown, consist each of near five hundred houses; there are several other (towns) which have from one to two hundred." The writer also says: "The Germantown thread-stockings are in high estimation, and the year before last, I have been credibly informed, there were manufactured in that town alone, above 60,000 dozen pair. Their common retail price is a dollar per pair." The Rev. Mr. Burnaby was a Church of England clergyman and Vicar of Greenwich, England, and two editions of his book were published in London in 1775, and "printed for T. Payne, at the Mews-Gate." An edition was published in Dublin and a third edition in London in 1798. This shows a great interest in North America at that time.

As to the German influence in the advancement of the infant colony of Pennsylvania, Governor George Thomas of the Province, wrote to the English Bishop of Exeter, in 1747, that he believed that the Germans constituted three-fifths of the population. The whole population was 200,000. He says: "They have by their industry, been the principal instruments of raising the State to its present flourishing condition, beyond any of his Majesty's Colonies in North America." Bishop Perry, of Iowa, quotes this in "Papers Relating to the History of the Episcopal Church in Pennsylvania": "The late Prof. T. Daniel Rupp, in his edition of Dr. Benjamin Rush's "Manners of the Germans in Pennsylvania," adds in a note, that Pennsylvania led the Colonial States as to agriculture, because of her "many German settlers." He adds: "In 1751, there were exported 86,000 bushels of wheat, 129,960 barrels of flour, 90,743 bushels of Indian corn. The total exports of 1751 exceeded in value one million of dollars." Prof. Rupp also quotes Proud's "History of Pennsylvania" to the effect that the Germans seemed better adapted to agriculture and the Irish to trade. Proud states that Germans got estates as soon as industry and economy would procure them. Dr. Rush states that when they came in large bodies a clergyman came with them. They did not leave their religion at home. Rev. George Michael Weis, V. D. M., and Rev. Johann Casper Stoever were among the clergy who thus emigrated. Schoepf says that the German built his chimney in the middle of the house to economize in stove-pipes. An Englishman might build a chimney at each gable end. The Germans had smoke-houses or a loft to keep apples above their milk-houses. Trego declares that the Germans "wisely chose some of the best land in the State." The Germans were noted for their desire for good schools. The large German barns are spoken of by Dr. Rush. The kindness and hospitality of these people is noteworthy.

Dr. Rush quotes Tacitus to the effect that the Germans in ancient times left a space between the houses in their villages, either to guard against fire or from lack of skill in architecture. He adds: "Many of the German villages in Pennsylvania are constructed in the same manner. The small houses are composed of wood, brick and clay, neatly united. The large houses are built of stone, and many of them after the English fashion. Very few of the houses in Germantown are connected together. Where the Germans connect their houses in their villages, they appear to have deviated from one of the customs they imported from Germany."

Dr. Rush extols the agriculture and manufactures of the Germans, and holds them up for examples of imitation to the other inhabitants of Pennsylvania, and appeals to the Legislatures of the United States and the Legislators of Pennsylvania to learn lessons from them.

In the Reverend Morgan Edwards's "Materials towards a History of the American Baptists," pp. 68-71, will be found a history of the church at "Beggarstown." The abundant labors of the first minister of this Dunkard congregation, Rev. Peter Baker, are noted. He was a German. Mr. Edwards's book was published in A. D. 1770.

Rev. Alexander Mack succeeded Mr. Baker. He was a German by birth. He came to America, "with many of his congregation, in 1729, and became a minister of Beggarstown the same year. He married Anna Margareta Kling by whom he had children, Valentine, John, Alexander (now minister of Beggarstown), who married into the Hildebrand, Sneider and Nise families, and have raised him many grandchildren. His fourth child was Anna, now a single sister at Ephrata (there was a religious sisterhood among the Tunkers at Ephrata). Mr. Mack was a man of real piety. He had a handsome patrimony at Schrisheim, Germany, with a profitable mill and vineyards thereon, but spent all in raising and maintaining his church at Schwardzenau whereof he was father and the father of all the Tunkers." Rev. Alexander Mack bearing the same name as his father, succeeded him as minister of this parish. He married Elizabeth Nise. He was "a sincere good man."

Rev. Christopher Sower was born in 1721 at Lasphe, in Wingeinstein. He assisted the last-named Mr. Mack. "He married Catharine Sharpneck." His children were Christopher, Daniel, Peter, Catharine, Esther, David and Samuel. Mr. Edwards's description of the religious life at Ephrata among the Tunkers is interesting. Their simple dress and meekness and grace and soft tone in conversation and gentle and obliging deportment are described. "Their singing," he writes, "is charming; partly owing to the pleasantness of their voices, the variety of parts they carry on together and the devout manner of performance." There was a Brotherhood here, then numbering fourteen, while the Sisterhood had eighteen members. The chapel of the sisters was called Sharon, and that of the brethren, Bethany. The brethren and sisters worshiped "morning and evening, and sometimes in the night."

There was "a common church called Zion, built on the summit of a little hill. Here the single brethren and single sisters and the married people and their children meet once a week for public worship. The brethren have adopted the dress of the White Friars with some alteration; and the sisters that of the nuns; and both, like them, have taken the vow of celibacy. But some break through the vow. Then they quit their cells and go to the neighborhood among the married people. All the fraternity wear their beards. Their livelihood they get by cultivating the land, by a printing office (the Ephrata printing press is at the rooms of the Historical Society of Pennsylvania), by a grist mill, a paper mill, an oil mill, etc., and the sisters by spinning, weaving, sewing, etc. They slept at first on board couches with blocks for pillows, but now sleep on beds, and have otherwise abated much of the severity of their order."

Mr. Edwards's book (pp. 96–97) notices the Germantown Mennonites thus: "May 23, 1708, there was a church settled at Germantown consisting of fifty-two members which exists to this day, and is not only the first in the province but in some sort the mother of all the rest." The minister was Rev. Jacob Godtschalk. "In about sixteen years after, this church had branched out to Skippack, Conestogo, Greatswamp and Monatony, and become five churches; to which appertained sixteen ministers." The Tunkers of Ephrata, who have been here described, sometimes visited their brethren in Germantown.

The Annals and Archives of Pennsylvania may be found in the Friends' Library, Germantown, and those who can read the language of Holland may also find in Pieter Kalm's Travels, published in Utrecht, in 1772, an account of Germantown as that traveler saw it. William Kite has secured the volume for that Library which is under his care. The Library contains two volumes of the Journals of the Moravian Missionary to the Christian Indians, Frederic Post, who is buried in the Lower Burying Ground of Germantown. The first volume has also an "Enquiry into the Causes of the Alienation of the Delaware and Shawnese Indians from the British Interest, and into the Measures taken for Recovering their Friendship," from Treaties, etc. On the title page is the autograph of the celebrated Charles Thomson.

James Logan appears as one of those treating with the Indians. There is an account of the Indian Walk in the first volume. William J. Buck has lately issued a book on that subject. The fact that the good Charles Thomson was the secretary of the noted Indian chief Tedyuscung in nogotiations, makes the volume in the Germantown Library doubly interesting.

THE INDIAN MISSIONARY, REV. FREDERIC POST.

As to Mr. Post, he was selected to pacify the Ohio Indians. The book thus describes him: "He was a plain, honest, religiously disposed Man, who, from a conscientious opinion of Duty, formerly went to live among the *Mohican*

Indians, in order to convert them to *Christianity*. He married twice among them, and lived with them seventeen years, whereby he attained a perfect knowlege of their Language and Customs. Both his wives being dead, he had returned to live among the white People; but at the Request of the Governor he readily undertook this hazardous Journey. How he executed his Trust his *Journal* will show." He started from Philadelphia. He was successful in inducing the Indians not to join the French in attacking General Forbes. The journey was a matter of danger and difficulty, and reflects honor on this devoted man.

An extract on a printed slip in a fly leaf of the first volume states that Rev. Dr. William Smith attended Mr. Post's funeral at Germantown on May 5th, 1785. He returned to Philadelphia "with Dr. (afterward Bishop) White, in his chair." The article states that Post had worked among the Moravian Indians in New York and Connecticut. His first wife was Rachel, of the Wampanoag tribe. After she died, Agnes, a Delaware Indian became his second wife. She died, and in 1751 he "returned to Europe." In 1752 he went to Labrador, striving unsuccessfully to carry the Gospel to the Esquimaux. In 1754 he was back in Bethlehem, Pa., and was sent thence to Wyoming to preach to the Indians. In 1758 he performed the embassy described in the *Journal* to the Delawares and Shawanese in the Ohio country. Its result was "the evacuation of Fort Duquesne by the French and the restoration of peace." In 1761 he had an independent mission among those Indians, and built "a hut on the Tuscarawas, near Bolivar, in Stark county, Ohio." John Heckewelder went to him in 1762. The Pontiac war drove away the missionaries. In 1764 this indomitable man went to the Musquito coast and preached to the natives more than two years. In 1767 he made a visit to Bethlehem, returned to Musquito, and "was in Bethlehem, for the last time, in 1784. At this date he was residing with his third wife, who was an Episcopalian, in Germantown. Here he died, May 1st, 1785. On the 5th of May his remains were interred in the Lower Graveyard of that place, Rev. William White, D. D., of Christ Church, saying the funeral service." He had labored "in the Gospel forty-five years with distinguished Zeal, Prudence and Fidelity," as the inscription on his tombstone states. He died at the age of seventy-five years. Germantown is honored in holding the body of such a Christian hero in one of her ancient cemeteries.

Post made a second journey to the Indians of the Ohio to complete his peaceable mission, and the second volume of the work described contains the second journal, with its new fatigues and difficulties and dangers, as the French were regaining their influence. The "Advertisement to the Reader" in "The Second Journal," says: "These Journals also afford us a fresh Instance of the Power of RELIGION, and a SENSE OF DUTY, above SELF INTEREST, in inducing Men to undertake, and supporting the Mind in the most dangerous Enterprises for the Public Service; and also, of the Power of HONESTY above ART, in influencing the Minds of others, calming their savage Passions, and ruducing them to Reason, and to Peace." Post's conduct was so upright that the Indians gave him " the character of an *honest Man*, whose Word they might *safely rely on*." As a result of this good man's embassies the French were forced " to abandon the whole *Ohio* Country to General *Forbes*, after destroying with their own Hands their strong Fort of *Duquesne*.

Both of the volumes under review were published in London, the first, in 1759, was printed for I. Wilkie, at the Bible in St. Paul's Churchyard. The second volume, in the same year, is marked " at the Bible and Sun," which seems to indicate a double sign. The volumes are now very rare.

One article of Dr. Peter D. Keyser's on the Upper Burying Ground has been treated of. A second one in the Pennsylvania Magazine of History, Vol. IX, p. 62, etc., gives the names and dates of the tombstones yet standing. The task of preparation was commendable, though laborious. The change of names by the passage of time is noticeable. Schreiber, becomes Shriver and Shryber, and Bauman, Bowman, and Steinbuener, Stoneburner. Zachariah Poulson, editor of Poulson's *American Daily Advertiser*, and his wife and some children were buried in this yard.

Marquis de Chastellux, in his " Travels in North America," Vol. I, 206, says of Germantown, " Germantown is a long town, or village, consisting of a single street, not unlike La Villitre, or Vauginard, near Paris. From the first house at the south, to the last, at the north end of the town, it is near two miles and a half." He spent a pleasant day at the Chew House. He saw the marks of cannon balls on the house and three mutilated statues in front of it. It should be mentioned that the Chews did not receive remuneration for their loss. See Scharf and Westcott's Philadelphia, Vol. I, p. 386. De Chastellux was an aid of General Lafayette, and the same volume, p. 290, gives an account of another visit to Germantown with Lafayette and the Vicomte de Noailles, and the Comte de Damas. The two last named had never been there before. A visit was also made to Whitemarsh and Barren Hill.

In Townsend Ward's MS. notes, a reference to Joseph Reed's life by William B. Reed, Vol. I, p. 380, leads me to look up the point, which he makes of a visit to Cliveden by the Earl of Carlisle. The Earl writes about it to George Selwyn, and there is a reference to " George Selwyn and his Contemporaries," by John Heneage Jesse. The Earl describes the heat of Philadelphia, in June, as greater than that of Italy, as far as his memory of Italy goes. But let us quote his account of an early ride : " I have this morning at 5 o'clock been taking a ride into the country about ten miles, grieved am I to say, eight miles beyond our possessions. Our lines extend only two, and the provincial army is posted very strongly about six and twenty miles distant. This is a market day, and to protect the people bringing in provisions which otherwise they should not dare to do, large detachments, to the amount of about two thousand men, are sent forward into the country. We also profited by this safe guard, and I attended the General, Sir Henry Clinton, as far as Germantown, a place as remarkable and as much an object of curiosity to those who have any respect for the present times, as Edge Hill or Naseby Field, is to those whose veneration is only excited by their great-grandfathers."

Lord Carlisle was one of the commissioners from England, but Congress refused to treat with them. Chapter 16 of Reed's life has an account of the Battle of Germantown. An account of this battle, by an English officer, will appear in the October number of the "Pennsylvania Magazine of History."

At the corner of Limekiln road and Haines street, was the country seat of John Andrews for many years. He was the son of Rev. Dr. John Andrews, formerly Provost of the University of Pennsylvania. The mansion afterwards fell into the possession of Mr. Steel, who owns the stock farm near.

The graveyard on the north side of Haines street, at the junction of the Limekiln road, belonged to the Betton-Forrest estate, and passed into the possession of Mr. Tryon, and was afterwards sold for a Soldiers' Cemetery. The little old graveyard whose wall bounds the south side of Haines street, near Stenton avenue, was surrounded on three sides by the Abraham Kulp property.

The following is from Townsend Ward's manuscripts:

Mrs. Fishell, in Duval street, in the insurrection of St. Domingo, was an infant. To secure her escape, opiates were administered that she might utter no cry to betray her, and placed in a basket, she was thus smuggled aboard a vessel. She was brought to Germantown. In time she grew up; others joined her, perhaps a niece. They executed beautiful needlework. They lived in poverty almost, but their rooms were kept with the utmost nicety and even elegance. They had, long ago, a little shop on the avenue above Poor House lane.

In the Pennsylvania Magazine of History and Biography, Vol. VI, pp. 342-343, Townsend Ward gave a bit of Germantown history which I will here quote: "On Indian Queen lane, to the west of Township line road, is a structure of stone, which, long ago, was used as a blacksmith's shop. It is said of it that when the British were at Germantown in the Revolution, their farriers used it as a smithery for their cavalry. In recent years the building has been enlarged, and is now a tenant's dwelling house. It is on a place of some forty acres, in what in Colonial times was called 'liberty lands.' The property lies about half a mile north of 'Devon,' Blight's place. In 1702, it was owned by Henry Hill, a Philadelphian, long engaged in business in the Island of Madeira. Returning here, he built for a residence that fine old house on the east side of Fourth street, north of Union. He died of yellow fever in 1798. In 1802, Archibald McCall acquired the place, and made efforts there to improve the breed of sheep. He had imported Merinos, and dogs to protect them, but it is remembered that some of the dogs played the part of their cousin, the wolf. In 1808, the place passed from McCall to Griffith Evans, whose son, Dr. Horace Evans, now has it for his country residence. By these successive owners the mansion house has been enlarged, but its identity is established by the preservation in the building of one of the original stones of the house. This bears upon it the chiseled mark of '1732,' the date of erection of the oldest portion of the house.

"When the American Army was at Yellow Springs, Chester county, the youthful Griffith Evans, born the third of September, 1760, in Warwick, Chester county, went into the service and became attached to the Medical Department. In his long after years of peace, a campaigning story he used to tell to his compatriots, was of one McKaraher, who was also in the Medical Department. A number of the young men connected therewith were riding out one day during the War, when, on coming near a field where hemp was growing, their Hibernian friend, McKaraher, hurriedly rode away. Of course he was questioned as to the cause of this sudden movement, and his humorous answer was, pointing to the field of hemp: 'Do you see yon? Irishmen do not like yon!' In 1787, Griffith Evans was Secretary of the Commissioners to settle the difficulties in Wyoming, and accompanied Timothy Pickering to the troubled region. Afterwards he was appointed Secretary to the Board of Commissioners to whom was entrusted the adjustment of claims of British subjects, under Article Sixth of what is known as Jay's Treaty of 1794. The Commissioners' office was in a building belonging to Kearney Wharton, No. 3 South Sixth street. No practical result seems to have been reached by the Commissioners, whose labors in the course of a year or two ceased. Griffith Evans died in 1845, in the eighty-sixth year of his age.

"Near to Dr. Evans's place, only one lot intervening, was that of the handsome Irishman, Washington's favorite, Colonel Walter Stewart. He called his place 'Mount Stewart,' and there he lived with his beautiful wife, Blair McClanachan's daughter. The Colonel's house in the city was in Market street, below Sixth, the next house east of Washington's place of residence."

For a picture of an old house near Germantown, where tradition says that Penn preached, see Thompson Westcott's History of Philadelphia, in Scrap Book form, in the Pennsylvania Historical Society Rooms, Vol. I, chapter 35. There are two dwellings in the quaint, old-fashioned picture. For an account of the foundation of Germantown, see chapter 38. Crefelt, north of Chestnut Hill, is here also spelled Creveld. We will quote the boundaries:

"Germantown began fourteen perches four feet below Dannenhower's, now Shoemaker's lane, and ended at Abington road, now called Washington lane, and had 2750 acres. Cresheim began at Washington lane and went to Limekiln road, near the Mermaid Inn, 884 acres. Summerhousen extended from Limekiln road to about one-eighth of a mile above Chestnut Hill gate, 900 acres. Crefelt from thence to Streper's mill where the turnpike crosses the

Wissahickon to Germantown township line, 1166 acres. Total acres in Germantown township, 5700."

"Cresheim road ran an irregular course, tending to the northeast, beginning at Millner's road, west of the Main street, and finally entering into the Main street some distance above the limekiln road."

"The Germantown market place, containing half an acre, was granted by James Delaplaine to the bailiff, burgesses and commonalty of Germantown and their successors forever, January 11, 1704."

Townsend's "old grist mill, on Mill street or Church lane, * * * now known as 'Roberts' mill," is the subject of an illustration in chapter 39.

The old house built by Heivert Papen, in 1698, at the northwest corner of Main and Johnson streets, has its antique picture, with its hipped roof, and lean-to and dormer windows and projecting roof over the door in chapter 43.

The old Friends' Meeting House, at Fair Hill, Germantown road, built in 1707, has its picture in chapter 73, and Trinity Church, Oxford, is shown in chapter 74.

For an account of St. Michael's Lutheran Church, Germantown, see chapter 188. It states that the Rev. John Louis Voigt, had been a preceptor and an inspector in the Orphan House at Halle.

In chapter 196, Vol. II, we find the following, which place was noted by Ward in his manuscript, as well as other points here spoken of.

"In January, 1764, citizens of Germantown held a meeting at the Town Hall, in order to consult together in regard to the means of protecting themselves from the ravages of fire. They were situated at a considerable distance from the fire apparatus of Philadelphia, and the roads at that time were frequently so bad that no assistance could have been derived from the city fire companies. It was, therefore, resolved to form three separate fire divisions in Germantown and its neighborhood, and the fire companies which were formed were called the 'Fellowship of the Upper Ward,' 'Fellowship of the Middle Ward' and 'Fellowship of the Lower Ward.' Subscriptions were taken up to purchase apparatus, and money enough was collected to send to England for three Land fire engines, but by some misfortune the order was not fully completed. When the engines arrived one was sent to Germantown; but of two others, one went to Bethlehem and the other to Frankford. The companies afterwards received their apparatus, however. In subsequent years the names of the three companies were changed as follows: That of the Upper Ward, instituted March 1st, 1764, was named the Franklin Fire Company; that of the Middle Ward, instituted March 5th, 1764, was named the Washington Fire Company; and that of the Lower Ward, instituted February 20th, 1764, was named the Columbia Fire Company."

In chapters 202 and 203 David James Dove, the Germantown Academy teacher, is noted, and his fugitive pieces are mentioned. They were "satirical and political poems." "Mr. Fisher speaks of one, 'Washing the Black Moor

White,' as being the only known production of Dove's satire which has been preserved."

The poet, Thomas Godfrey, Jr., son of the inventor of the quadrant, is noticed in the same chapter, and his works are mentioned by name.

In chapter 215 John Meng, the young Germantown artist, who died at the age of twenty, receives due notice.

In chapter 217 Cliveden is noted. These five large volumes of newspaper articles show an immense amount of labor on the part of Thompson Westcott, for which he deserves great honor, as his work will always be helpful to local historians.

ROCHEFOUCAULT.

The Duke de la Rochefoucault Liancourt was a virtuous and philosophic French nobleman who visited this country. His travels were translated into English and published in two large volumes in London by R. Phillips. H. Neuman was the translator. The book was issued in 1799. In the second volume, p. 390, etc., the Duke pays his respects to Germantown. The heat in Philadelphia rendered the place oppressive, and Congress ceased to awake his curiosity. In leaving the city he pays a parting visit to Mr. Nicklen, a good Englishman, who had given him much attention, and who had married a Miss Chew. He lived in the summer on a handsome country seat on the Schuylkill, called Hill, and having a delightful prospect. We will quote his narrative: "The road to Germantown is upon the ascent, the summit of the hill on which that little town is built being two hundred feet higher than the bed of the Delaware, although the distance is only seven miles. The lands, though not of the first quality, are sufficiently productive; the vicinity to Philadelphia making it easy to get manure, while the high price of provisions in that city encourages the farmer to lay out such expenses as may insure the best and most abundant returns.

"All the way to Germantown the houses are close together, the properties being so valuable as to prevent them from being very extensive; there are a few of the farms which exceed two hundred acres. Stone abounds in this district and is found at a very small depth; it is uniformly micacious free stone. Of this all the houses are built. Those buildings would not be reckoned handsome in Europe. They are good small houses, without elegance and without ornament; but in the point of size, as well as distribution of the apartments, they afford their proprietors everything that comes under the denomination of convenience and comfort. Most of them are country houses for the relaxation of the inhabitants of Philadelphia.

"Germantown is a long village near two miles and a half in extent. The houses to the number of about three hundred, are all built on the side of the highway, and are erected pretty close to each other. The lands in all this district cost from an hundred and sixty to two hundred dollars the acre in whole farms; some particular acres, situated on the roadside, sell for from four to five hundred dollars. I was even told that it is not easy to procure it at that price, and I was shown a field of a dozen of acres, the proprietor of which estimates it at eight hundred dollars the acre. The culture of this part of the country is better attended to than in those parts which are at a distance from large towns, but it is far from being in that state of cultivation which it would be in Europe, near so good a market as that of Philadelphia. They raise a good deal of wheat, and still more Indian-corn, but very little rye or oats. All the produce which is not consumed in the farmer's family, is carried to the market at Philadelphia in consequence of which provisions are as dear at Germantown as in the city, to those who are obliged to purchase them. Nay, they are often even dearer; as the farmers who go to Philadelphia, where they are sure of getting quit of all their commodities, frequently refuse to sell any part of them on the road. Beef, for example, which is seldom higher at Philadelphia than eleven pence, costs fifteen pence at Germantown. All this country, and for a considerable way further is inhabited principally by Germans, and descendants of Germans."

The Duke speaks of the aversion of Germans to change their customs, even for better ones, but acknowledges their industry and their laboriousness. He goes on thus:

"They manufacture in their families at Germantown a great quantity of woolen, cotton, and thread stockings, which the farmers carry to market at Philadelphia with their provisions and which are reckoned very durable. There are also some tan works at Germantown. We find here a Lutheran and a Presbyterian Church, besides a third for the Quakers; an Academy, and two other schools of considerable repute. I stopped at the house of my excellent and respected friend, Mr. Chew. This house is celebrated as an important scene of action in the battle of Germantown in 1777."

Here follows a notice of the contest at the house, and the effect of the skirmish on the building, and the sale and repurchase of the property by Mr. Chew. The Duke proceeds as follows:

"Labourers receive, in the environs of Germantown, a dollar a day of wages during hay making and harvest. The women employed to turn the hay are paid half a dollar a day, all besides their diet, which is equal to half a dollar more. This diet consists of coffee or chocolate, with ham, to breakfast; fresh meat and vegetables to dinner; tea and ham for supper, and a pint of rum during the day. This is the manner in which labourers are fed in America, and if this diet appears expensive to those who employ them, if this expense prevent them from being able to employ a great number, it is gratifying to see how well a class of men, reckoned the lowest in Europe, is treated in this country, the only one where a man, whatever be his profession, is treated with respect; where all ranks are considered as men. We may be told that were our European labourers fed with coffee and fresh meat they would not work better, or be better content. It is, in the first place, not true that they would not work better and be more happy if they were better fed; and it is still more certain that were they treated with more respect and more attention they would consider themselves less debased; they would become better; they would feel with pride that they were a more noble branch of society, and consequently would be more interested in its preservation. Let us hope that the French revolution may, in this respect, operate a happy change in the lot of the laborious class of mankind. Without this liberty would be only a word without meaning, a pretext for disorder. A cord of oak wood costs six, and a cord of hickory from eight to ten dollars, at Germantown. Thus the lands covered with wood, which in the more distant parts are of much less value than other grounds, are here the most valuable. The wood from hence is carried to Philadelphia principally in the winter time; the river not being navigable, it could not be conveyed by it."

The Duke continues his notes on the road to Bethlehem. It is remarkable how much information Rochefoucault gathered in passing through Germantown, whether by stage or private carriage. If by stage, we may imagine his queries to driver and passengers. If the reader wishes to know more of this remarkable man let him turn to Disraeli's Curiosities of Literature, Vol. I, pp. 172-3.

An interesting account of the battle of Germantown may be found in John Hamilton's Republic, Vol. I.

THE MENG FAMILY.

I am indebted to Miss Hanna Ann Zell for the following information: She is the great-granddaughter of John Christopher Meng, who was born in Manheim, Germany, September 22, 1697, and came to this country and settled in Germantown, and on August 24, 1728, took the oath of allegiance as the Colonial Records of Pennsylvania show. He married Anna Dorothea Baumann (born Baroness Von Ebsten, 29th of June, 1723, and died October 17, 1785).

Samuel Michael Dorgabe, "Preacher of the Reformation," gave a certificate that Mr. Meng, "Burgher and Master Mason," and "his honorable housewife," were faithful in their religion and "in the use of the Holy Sacrament of the last Supper." John Christopher Meng had seven children. Franklin B. Gowen, Esq., is a direct descendant of this family, through his mother. John Meng, the son of John Christopher Meng, was a limner in the term of the day. He went to the West Indies to get colors, which could not be procured here. He was but 19 years old when he made this voyage. He painted a picture of himself, and of a lady to whom he was engaged, which was unfinished, and one of his father. The forefinger of the artist's left hand is extended, as an old lady declared that having been stung by a wasp it could not be bent. He was an artist of skill. Copies of these pictures of the father and son may be seen at the rooms of the Germantown Library Association.

John Melchior Meng used to ask his children the text of the sermon on Sundays, and if they failed to give it, they lost their dinner. He was a brother of the artist. John Melchior Meng married Mary Magdaline Colladay (in German Maria Jullendin). Anna Dorothea was a daughter of this marriage. She married Hugh Ogden. John Melchior Ogden was a son of this family. He was a Manager of the Spring Garden Institute and of the Northern Dispensary, and of the Grandom Institution and of other benevolent organizations. He was a member of the Friends, and stood high in the community. He died in 1882. A memorial volume was published to honor his memory. He was one of the originators of the House of Refuge.

Mrs. Hugh Ogden, when a child living next to Vernon, was brought up to sit on a stool with no back. Hence she was very erect all her life, and her age exceeded 90 years. Her straight-backed chair is in Miss Zell's residence. In extreme age she would sit so erect in it that she would not touch its back. Hannah Ogden, daughter of this lady, married Thomas Zell, a member of the Friends. He was a hardware merchant, whose word was his bond. He was one of the originators of the meeting-house at Spruce and Ninth streets. His Christian character was of a high order. His memoir has been published. His son is Col. Elwood Zell, the publisher, who resides in Church lane, Germantown.

A most interesting heirloom in possession of the decendants of the Mengs is an old German Bible, in clear print, bound in pig's skin, with brass corners and clasps. It is in excellent preservation. On the outside of the cover the letters J. C. M. and A. D. M. are stamped, indicating the first owners, John Christopher and Anna Dorothea Meng. The Bible was printed in Nuremburg, A. D. 1725. A written note in German on a fly leaf in front reads: "This book have I bought in Manheim of Mr. ——— (name not clear), bookbinder, upon the market for five guilders, May 12, 1727." Signed "John Christopher Meng." Underneath this is written another note saying that "this Holy Bible was inherited by John Melchior Meng from his father, John Christopher Meng." The son signs this, and so the Good Book did its work from generation to generation.

Dorothea Ogden had a son named Jesse, who died unmarried. He was a literary person, and belonged to the Philosophical Society of Philadelphia and kindred societies. He was a manager of the Apprentices' Library and of other organizations. The Ogdens throughout the country are largely connected with this family.

The coat of arms of the Ogden family was given by Charles the Second, to the family as a reward for sheltering him in the oak tree. The tree is a part of it and the Latin motto is *Et si ostendo non jacto*, that is, "And if I make a show I do not boast." Another Ogden coat of arms is marked in writing "Oak den or Oak-Dale, Ogden." Of Mrs. Dorothea Ogden, a motto was given, "the kind sister and the good housewife," in a society of which she was a member, and she deserved it.

Mr. Charles E. Smith, the former President of the Reading Railroad, and a distinguished botanist, is a descendant of the Meng family, and rightly inherits his ancestor's love for horticulture, described by "M," in the *Gardeners' Monthly* of September, 1884, which treats of Mr. Meng who lived next to Vernon.

Mr. Rittenhouse Fraley, telegraph operator of Lafayette Street Police Station, was born in William Wynne Wister's house. He says that the walks of the town were very uneven before the bricks were laid, and the people were some time in learning to use them. In walking over the bricks they would imagine that they were trying to escape the former holes, and step like persons uncertainly, leaving a ship. Mr. Fraley has spent his life in this town. He says that Christopher Jungkurth was the first maker of the Germantown wagons, though another has been named in these papers as having that honor. Mr. Fraley is the grandson of Henry Fraley named in Watson's Annals, as known familiarly by General Washington, who used to spend much time in his carpenter shop. Mr. Henry Fraley, made drums and other materials for the Government. Mr. Rittenhouse Fraley has two ancient chairs which belonged to his grandfather. His impression is that Manheim street took its name from his grandfather's farm which was called Manheim Farm. The grandfather was from Germany. The old farm-house has disappeared. Mr. Sellers bought the small farm of Henry Fraley's estate. Coleman Fisher next purchased it, and erected the comfortable mansion which is now occupied by Dr. Lee. This was long the abode of the late John S. Littell, Esq., and is yet in the hands of the family. Dr. Hewson occupied a house which stood on the site or forms a part of the mansion built by Mr. Fisher. He was only a summer resident of Germantown. The Fraley family never resided on this farm, but Henry Fraley lived where St. Stephen's Methodist Church stands on Main street. His carpenter shop stood where the parsonage is now located. A private wagon-road ran between the carpenter shop and Jungkurth's carriage shop, which was just above. The parsonage also covers the road as well as the site of the carpenter shop. The carriage shop still stands. The chairs named are said to have been used by General Washington in his visits. They look cosy as they stand on the piazza in their old age.

Mr. Henry Freas, the grocer, at the corner of Washington lane and Main street, has been longer engaged in the grocery business than any one else in this city, having pursued it for fifty-nine years, as clerk and principal. He is a brother of P. R. Freas, the founder of the Germantown Telegraph. Four years were passed by him in apprenticeship to Daniel Pastorius, who once owned Dr. Dunton's place, which had belonged to his father who was also named Daniel. The son went into the grocery business as a clerk in Philadelphia in 1827, on Market street, above Tenth. Mr. Freas was born at Marble Hall, in Montgomery county, Pennsylvania. He came to Germantown in the summer of 1832, and opened a store for himself in July of that year, one month before he was twenty-one years of age. This was the cholera year in Germantown. Mr. Freas says that for forty years, before his coming to the town, no house had been built in the town, and the buildings were not kept well painted. A carpenter named Curry, who was a journeyman, and who helped Charles Pastorius in putting up the shelves of Mr. Freas's store, died within twenty-four hours after finishing his work, of cholera. There was a larger proportion of deaths in Germantown from cholera, according to the population, than in the city. There were over thirty cases, and about half resulted in death. The streets were so muddy that the people used to walk single file in the middle of the turnpike. Mr. Freas's first store was where Guyer's cigar shop is, a little below his present location. He afterward moved to a house opposite, on Main street, at the end of Tulpohocken street, and afterward, in 1846, to his present store.

Property was very low at that time, and a thousand dollars would purchase a large amount. The side pavements were resisted on account of the expense at first, but Wyndham H. Stokes was influential in getting an act through the Legislature to effect this work, and he made the first improvements of consequence in forty years in Germantown. He lived near Main street where Maplewood avenue now is. He built a stone house with pillars on rising ground, which has now disappeared. Real estate improved rapidly after the railroad was opened in 1832, and the pavements were laid.

Mr. W. J. Buck informs me that in the Southern War, about 1861, he drove from Willow Grove to Germantown, and noticed a block of brick buildings being erected by a Mr. Langstroth, three stories in height or more. He expressed surprise that such an undertaking should be entered on in such dull times, and received the reply that it was no more strange than the means which enabled Mr. Langstroth to build them. It was then told him that this gentleman's father had discovered a special process to bleach beeswax white, so that it might be used properly for making candles, but he kept his discovery a secret and acquired wealth by it, though he took out no patent. Mr. James F. Langstroth, of Main street, informs me that his father, Piscator Langstroth, was once in business with Mr. Elliot. He adds that the wax was put into a kettle with water. The water was added to keep the wax from burning. Wax is more inflammable than oil. The melted wax was put into a tin box, which had holes in the bottom, which allowed it to fall on a roller which revolved in water. It was then placed on cloths and exposed to the sun. Three meltings were necessary before the operation was complete. It was broken up in the morning before the sun arose to heat it. The dirt would fall into the water. The work was conducted on the York road, just below Fisher's lane. About two acres were fenced in, the fence being about twelve feet high. Mr. Langstroth improved the business by a use of water after separating from Mr. Elliot. The wax was largely sent to Mexico for making church candles. Mexico was at war with Spain and had trouble as to the procuring of candles. It is Mr. Langstroth's impression that the yellow wax was sent from Mexico and bleached here and then returned in cakes. When the war ceased the traffic died away.

Piscator Langstroth was a paper maker, when paper was made by hand. He was engaged at McDowell's Mills, on the Pennypack, on the Newtown Railroad. He afterwards came to Livezy's Mill, on the Wissahickon, and carried on the business in connection with his brother John. Piscator Langstroth was like Charles Sumner, a man of extraordinary strength, having lifted seven fifty-sixes and a twenty-eight pound weight with one hand. He could have lifted more had the weights been at hand. He could lift a full barrel of cider and drink from the bung hole. Piscator Langstroth died in 1861, at the age of 71, in the house now occupied by the Workingmen's Club, on Chelten avenue. He married Eliza Lehman, daughter of Benjamin Lehman, Sr., who lived in the old stone house on Main street, near School lane, occupied by Dr. Topley, as a dentist's office. Mrs. Langstroth died at the age of 83, in the year 1876. They were both members of the Dunker Church.

The houses noticed by Mr. Buck were, we think, being erected by Benjamin L. Langstroth, a son of Piscator Langstroth. It is supposed that these houses were Vernon Hall and those adjoining. They were built on the Hocker estate. George Barr was a tenant of a building which stood on a part of this ground. He was well known in Germantown.

One of Piscator Langstroth's family married a Drexel, and another Count Fortunata J. Fouguera.

THE FIRST PRESBYTERIAN CHURCH, on Chelten avenue, is on the site of what is known as George Barr's spring, which was enlarged to a fish pond by Piscator Langstroth. On what is now Chelten avenue, in front of the location of the church, was an old barn, the mortar of which was made of clay and straw, showing antiquity.

"In 1876, the old and well-known State House Bell was removed to make room for the great bell presented by Henry Seybert. It was taken with the clock and placed in the station house at Germantown. Occasionally the inhabitant of other parts of the city visiting Germantown is startled by the sound of the bell when striking the hours. The tone was so peculiar and well known that it could not be forgotten by those who were accustomed to hear it before 1876, and it brings to mind the sounds of other days." Thompson Westcott's History of Philadelphia.

In Baily's Life of the famous English divine, Dr. Thomas Fuller (p. 23), I find a remark which may be applied to the stocking industry, long famous in Germantown. As the English City of Northampton made good shoes and stockings, or "stockens," as it was spelled by him, Dr. Fuller remarked, "it may be said to stand on other men's legs," but as he was very fond of a pun, the old and the newer town must excuse the jest. Fuller's remarks on the great trouble which he underwent in gathering the materials for his famous history of the English church may find an echo in the mind of any one who strives to write historical details.

TULPOHOCKEN STREET.

The following is from Townsend Ward's manuscripts:—"When Mr. John Fallon brought about the Water Works of Germantown, he opened Tulpohocken street and planted trees along it, and others on the back part of the lots. These latter are now, although thirty years old, hardly larger than those on the street were when but three or four years had passed after their planting. At this time those on the street have the appearance of trees of the original forest. This fine growth was the result of two causes. Along the street the pits for the roots were dug deep and wide. Besides this a lead pipe, connected with the water supply, was laid along the street, and where any tree was, a puncture with a pin was made in the pipe, and twice a day the water was turned on to nourish the trees."

The following is also from Mr. Ward:—"Arent Klincken's house stood on the west side where Tulpohocken street now is, and was removed that the street might be opened. It was two stories in height and of brick. One of these is preserved by Mrs. John Fallon, and has cut upon it, 'A. K., 16.' This was done in the clay before the brick was burned, as is evident from a critical examination. The bricks would seem, therefore, to have been made here. They are of a large size. William Penn attended the raising of this house."

It should be added that Watson speaks of this as a stone house, and the oldest Germantown houses were generally of stone.

About where Mr. Bolton lives the worthy colored shoemaker, Jno. Douglass, lived in an old log house, which has disappeared.

The property spoken of in this note of Mr. Ward came into the possession of Justus Johnson. The old house is said to have been the first two-story one built in Germantown. Penn dined at the raising of it.—See Watson's Annals, Vol. II, p. 20. An old house which stood some distance back of the present one may have been the house of Penn's day. The stone house in which Mrs. Peterson now resides, which has been tastefully modernized, was the abode of Justus Johnson, who married a Miss Morris, the sister of Mrs. John S. Littell, and of the Misses Morris who lived at the corner of Main and High streets. The house of Justus Johnson is on the west side of Main street, and south side of Tulpohocken street. There was a farm of seventy acres here. Tulpohocken street was cut through by the Fallon brothers, who bought the property and opened the street and established the water-works. John Fallon married a daughter of Justus Johnson. He died not long since.

Watson says that "Arents Klincken came from Holland with William Penn in his first voyage in 1682. He died at the age of 80." His son Antony

was a great hunter and had a house next to that of his father. Vol. II, p. 20.
Watson speaks of the bodies in the rear of Justus Johnson's house after the
Battle of Germantown. Vol. II, p. 38.

Next below this is the house of Enoch Taylor, which Anthony Johnson
built for his daughter, Mrs. Agnes Thomas. Anthony Johnson married Susan
Rubicam. The land once belonged to Martin Weaver. Mr. Thomas MacKellar has sent me the NORRISTOWN WEEKLY HERALD, of October 10, '87, published by Morgan R. Wills. It contains a history of that paper which was
established in 1799. Charles G. Sower, a grandson of the founder of THE
HERALD, and Robert Iredell write the sketches. Charles G. Sower's narrative
pertains to our subject. David Sower, Sr., a younger son of Christopher Sower,
the Germantown preacher, writer, printer and publisher commenced to issue
the paper then known as THE GAZETTE. In 1808 Charles Sower, the oldest
son of David Sower, Sr., and an able and genial man, took charge of THE
HERALD. He afterward moved to Uniontown, Maryland, where he started a
paper called THE ENGINE OF LIBERTY. He died in that place. David Sower,
Jr., brother of Charles, had possession of the paper after a time, and also published books.

The present large stone mansion, above the Franklin School, is a fine building, with a pretty lawn below it. The Franklin school is also a massive stone
building. This property is owned by a company, and Mr. George A. Perry is
the principal of the institution.

In closing the history of Germantown proper, various pictures rise before the mind as this magnificent suburb is contemplated; first the wilderness, and the beast and the savage, next the honest German, raising his stone
house to shield his household. The early traveler then saw an extended line
of such dwellings, with their strips of tillable land. Penn beheld the beginnings of the town. Afterward came the glory of Stenton, the noted country
place of James Logan, yet dignified in its old age. Loudoun afterward arose
to keep it company. The Tolands and Loraines meet us as we pass along
Main street, and the Henry house, and that of Mr. Hacker and the Wister
house, opposite Queen street, and Vernon at Chelten avenue, and the Duval
place and the Chew house and Upsal, and now the Germans and their successors are crowded on by a host of pretty cottages and stately mansions. The
old Mennonite and Dunkard churches are plain by the side of the grander
buildings which have risen to honor Christ. May the German faith and
industry not be forgotten in "modern" Germantown!

In closing a work like the History of Ancient Germantown some postscripts
are needed to complete the notes. Count Rochefoucault has been spoken of;
more can be learned of him in the Hon. Horatio Gates Jones's History of Roxborough, in scrap-book form, at the Historical Society rooms, in Philadelphia.

George Lippard, the author, died on the 9th of February, A. D. 1854.

Samuel Harvey's place ran from Main street back to Township line.

Rev. Prof. Charles W. Schaeffer informs me that Major Witherspoon, of the New Jersey Brigade, slain in the Battle of Germantown, is buried in St. Michael's Lutheran churchyard.

The village of Manheim was laid out at the southeast corner of the present Manheim street. It included "Caernarvon" (the residence of the late Mr. Wistar Price), and other properties in that neighborhood.

The Littell place on Manheim street, occupied by Dr. Benjamin Lee, son of the late Bishop Alfred Lee, of Delaware, is named Elton, after Anthony Elton, a former resident of Burlington, New Jersey, who was an ancestor of the Littell family. Anthony Elton married Susan, the daughter of Thomas Gardiner, who was the first Speaker of the House after the provinces of East and West Jersey were united. The mother of John S. Littell, Mrs. Susan Littell, is buried in St Mary's churchyard, Burlington, near the grave of her son's best and truest friend, Bishop Doane. It is a pleasant coincidence.

Justus Johnson lived in the store recently altered, near the south corner of Main street and Tulpohocken. The latter street was opened through his farm. Justus Johnson had three children living, a daughter named Ann, in Baltimore, Mrs. John Fallon, in Philadelphia, and Anthony, who married Miss Dorsey, and lives on a plantation in Maryland.

The following copy of family genealogy which has been kindly sent me, is very interesting:—

JUSTUS RUBICAM and wife, *nee* Susanna Rittenhouse, owned and lived on a farm on Washington lane, Germantown, which farm afterwards and probably still belongs to the Unruh family. They left six daughters and one son.—Ann or Nancy married Christian Donat, an extensive lime burner of White Marsh or that neighborhood.—Catherine married ——Sheetz, of White Marsh. Gen. Henry Scheetz and Ann Scheetz, wife of Jacob Rex, of Chestnut Hill, were their children. Margaret married John Gorgas, of Wissahickon. The late Samuel Gorgas, of Roxborough, was their son. Julia married Peter Gorgas, of Wissahickon. Their descendants are the Gorgases, of Mt. Airy. The above Gorgases were brothers. Sarah married Nathan Levering of Roxborough, and had two children, Deborah and Susan; the former married Rev. Horatio Gates Jones, the latter, Dr. Riter, of Roxborough. Susannah married Anthony Johnson, of Germantown. Their children were Agness, married to Daniel Thomas, of Wissahickon; Klineken, married to Lydia Tybout, of Delaware; Justus, married to Abby Willing Morris, of Philadelphia. Justus Rubicam, the son, married Elizabeth Dull, of Spring Mill. They had one child, Justus, and he one child, Daniel Rubicam, now living.

It is worthy of being added to this genealogy that the Rubicam family are commemorated in the name of an avenue in Germantown, and a station on the Newtown Railway.

KLINCKENS.

Arents Klincken was convinced of the Friends' principles by the ministry of George Fox, Robert Barclay and William Penn, when they were traveling in Holland on a religious visit. He emigrated from Holland to America about the year 1696 and settled in Germantown. He had one son and two daughters. His son Anthony and his wife Bilke (or Abigail) had one daughter, named Agnes Klincken, who married John Johnson. One of Arentz's daughters married Mr. Tunis and the other Mr. Williams.

THE JOHNSONS.

Dirk (in English Richard) and Margaret Johnson (originally Jansen) came from Holland about 1700 and settled in Germantown. Of their children, Ann first married Matthias Lukens, afterward Thomas Pedro. Katharine married Caspar Wistar. Their daughter married a Haines. John married Agness Klincken. Rebecca married Henry Benakin. Richard married Ann Binckley. Children of John Johnson, Agness Klincken, Abigail and Dirk died young. Anthony married Susanna Rubicam. John married Rachel Livezey (Washington lane and Main street branch). Joseph married Elizabeth Norton (Dr. Wm. N. Johnson's branch).

Mr. Joshua R. Johnson kindly contributes the following pleasant reminiscences:

"In my early days, dating back to 1812, there were three houses in Justus Johnson's yard, now Tulpohocken street. Two of them were 50 feet, more or less, west of the water company's office. The third, a mere hut, fronted on the Main street at the upper corner of the yard. It was of logs, plastered between, and was a comfortable dwelling. The other two were of stone, and had very high pointed roofs.

"The one in front was the largest, the back one being probably used for a kitchen, by the first owner. They were of dark stone, irregularly laid, and pointed with white. Some of us old residents regretted their destruction, as we did that of the old house at Johnson street, with its nearly two centuries of hallowed years. It could have been made a very neat residence without changing its outlines. May we hope that others of its age will meet a better fate! The house now owned and occupied by Enoch Taylor was built early in the present century by Anthony Johnson for his daughter Agnes, who married Daniel Thomas Miller, of Wissahickon. Anthony was the father of Justus and Klincken Johnson, for the latter of whom the Carpenter place, with its wealth of forest trees, was planted. The house was never built, and in course of time, from the vicissitudes of fortune, it passed into other hands. He held the meadows in the rear nearly to the township line, living with his interesting family in a pleasant cottage west of Green street, south of Carpenter street. It now belongs to the estate of John Welsh, deceased, and is being rapidly built up, with fine improvements.

To return to the old houses on Justus Johnson's place: the log-house was a cooper shop, Charles Shuster being the occupant. His wife was a Miss Mysinger, of Chestnut Hill. They were industrious people, and raised a large family. Then a colored man, John Douglas, and his wife Lucy, lived there many years. John made and mended shoes. Many is the time the writer sat and listened to his yarns while he pegged away at his shoes. John was a warm Abolitionist, and took and read the LIBERATOR, an ardent admirer of Garrison, Phillips and all the earnest anti-slavery men who started the ball that eventually rolled over and crushed the life out of slavery. John left Germantown, and I think lived to see the fruition of his hopes and prayers. Peace to his ashes. The other houses had laborers' families in them, who earned a living at work on the adjacent farms, for there were several quite large farms' in Germantown fifty years ago, and where stood apple trees, corn and wheat fields, we now see city rows of red brick houses, huge factories and stores, churches and halls, with all the variety of a great and growing city. The reader of this may admire the change; the writer does not, and would rejoice to see the old apple orchards and corn fields in their rustic beauty and usefulness restored, but that may never be. So with the quiet resignation of philosophy, and the consolations of religion, we submit to the inevitable.

ANOTHER VETERAN PLEASED.

A subscriber in Columbia county writes us, in regard to the TELEGRAPH: " It is a most interesting and valuable paper, especially the ' History of Ancient Germantown.' It brings me back to my boyhood days over sixty years ago, when I used to go from my native birth-place, Philadelphia, to Germantown as it was then. What a change has taken place there in that time. It is now over fifty years since I have seen that old, ancient town. It almost makes me feel young again when I think of the times I used to walk there and ride in the old-fashioned leather spring stage coaches, before railroad days. I think my first ride by rail to your beautiful town was in 1833. I am an old man now, in my seventy-third year, yet it does me good to think of the surroundings of Philadelphia as they were when I was quite a small boy. Wishing you success with so valuable and interesting a paper, I remain,

Yours, etc.,"
CHAS. H. MASON.

Canby, Columbia Co., Pa., Dec. 1, 1887.

THE UNRUH HOUSES.

Directly back of the Chew place lies the farm of the late William and Esther Unruh. The Reading Railroad crosses the property. Mrs. Unruh died not long since at her daughter's house on Church street. The house is an ante-revolutionary stone building, with a frame addition made in the early part of the century. There was a bake-oven and a quaint old-fashioned spring-house in front. Another Unruh farm had an entrance on Gorgas lane, and lay on the lower side of the lane. Another ancient ante-revolutionary stone house is on this place. It was occupied by English soldiery. I am indebted to William U. Butcher, long a worker in the press of Germantown, for the following notes:

The Bockius family married into Nicholas Unruh's family, who lived at the last-named mansion. The Rev. Mosely H. Williams married a daughter of Charles Bockius. He is connected with the American Sunday School Union in Philadelphia. Jacob Bockius is a son of Charles, and in business with his father. Many cannon ball and shot were ploughed up on the first-named Unruh place, and years ago were piled up in heaps in the yard. But we must now introduce Mr. Butcher's narrative.

THE UNRUH FAMILY.

The Unruhs came from Germany, from what particular part of Fatherland is not clear. Sebastian and Nicholas, brothers, were the first of the family to settle in Germantown. They were sturdy, well-to-do farmers, and came here with strong religious convictions to cast their lot with its first settlers, in the hope of assisting, by industry and moral example, the work begun by Penn and Pastorius. Sebastian and Nicholas at once gave an earnest of their convictions, their faith in the venture made, and the high purpose prompting their coming, by at once purchasing a large tract of the primitive soil on Washington lane, north of Chew street, and afterward extending their domain until, with but few intervening spaces, it reached beyond the present city line northward, including Ivy Hill cemetery.

The children of Sebastian were John, William, George, Abraham, Michael and Elizabeth, the last-named becoming the wife of the late William Hergesheimer, who lived on Gorgas lane, northeast of the railroad.

The children of Nicholas were John, Philip, Abraham, and others, doubtless, whose names cannot now be recalled.

The tract of land bounded by Washington lane, Township line and Chew street, was afterward occupied by John and William, the latter the husband of the late aged Esther Unruh, of Germantown.

John (or John Nicholas) Unruh sold all his lands, 240 acres, and started west in 1816, taking all his children save Sebastian, who was killed by the discharge of a cannon, with him to Warren county, Ohio.

The children of John Nicholas Unruh were Sebastian (above referred to), Elizabeth, John, Nicholas, Catharine, Sally, Joseph, Ellen and Polly.

Joseph returned soon after going west with his father to Germantown, and settled on Allen's lane after becoming married. Rev. John Nicholas Unruh, now engaged in the active ministry of the Lutheran Church at Wilmore, Cambria county, Pa., is a son of the aforesaid Joseph.

The westward enterprise by John Nicholas was not a success, and his new home, near Lebanon, on the Big Miami river, was the scene of hard deprivations and irreparable losses, his noble wife having died broken hearted in consequence thereof.

An incident in connection with the family may be here related: On a militia training day after the mustering had been answered and the companies dismissed, two Unruh brothers, William and John, sons of Sebastian Unruh, and Sebastian, a son of John, having charge of the cannon, on their way home with the gun halted on Church street (then called Bone lane), at the rear of St. Michael's Lutheran churchyard, to fire a parting salute, one of them remarking in a jestingly way, it was said, that "now we will raise the dead." While ramming home the cartridge, the vent became so hot that the thumb of the holder was taken therefrom and a premature discharge of the cannon resulted. William's left arm was blown off, John lost his right arm and Sebastian was killed outright, his head having been blown off. William lived to rear a family of eight children, all of whom, save one, are still living within a few miles of each other in Germantown and vicinity.

Rev. John N. Unruh, now of Wilmore, Cambria county, Pa., is a son of Joseph, who was a son of John Nicholas Unruh, who was a son of Nicholas, one of the two original Unruh brothers.

Francis Glass, residing at Knightstown, Henry county, Ind., is a son of Professor Francis Glass, formerly of Germantown, and teacher of astronomy and natural philosophy, who married Catharine, daughter of the aforesaid John Nicholas Unruh, who was a son of one of the original Unruh brothers.

William Unruh Butcher, residing in Germantown, is a son of John Hall Butcher, who married Harriet, eldest daughter of William Unruh, who was a son of Sebastian Unruh, one of the two original Unruh brothers settling in Germantown. William Unruh, of Edge Hill, and John R. Unruh, of Fitzwatertown, Montgomery county, are the only sons of William Unruh above and grandsons of the original Sebastian Unruh.

There is a tradition that Christopher Ludwick, described in one of these articles, was the original of Harvey Birch in Cooper's "Spy." While he was a pretended deserter in a Hessian camp to influence the Germans in favor of the Colonies, Cooper says in his introduction to "The Spy," that the Congressman who told Congress of the spy's noble work did not give his name, and Cooper did not know it, so that I cannot speak positively about it, though it may be true. One of Darley's beautiful pictures in Hurd and Houghton's edition of the book represents the faithful "spy" as refusing the money offered him by a grateful country, though Cooper had an impression that he received a remuneration afterward when the country was able to bestow it.

As to Germantown printing, a "Book of Prayer," was printed by Peter Leibert in 1788, and Michael Billmeyer issued a "Book of Lutheran Hymns," in 1795. In 1790 he published a weekly paper.

The family spoken of near the Chew House where a little girl was knitting stockings in war time, should have been called Schneider, instead of Snyder, and their burial place was in St. Michael's Lutheran graveyard, and not Trinity Lutheran graveyard.

Dr. James Rhoads, president of Bryn Mawr Female College, writes me that he has a cane made from the wood of Arents Klincker's house, which he bought of William Crout, who had a shop on Main street, between Chelten avenue and Armat street. When Watson says that William Penn was at the raising of this house, he may refer to the raising of the roof, as the walls were of brick or stone. A carpenter informed me that such an expression was allowable.

The house which was arranged as a Dunkard meeting-house before the present one was built was the donation of Elder Peter Schilbert. The place of Hon. John Welsh is in the district popularly known as Germantown, though geographically it is in Roxborough.

Mr. Morrell kindly furnishes the following interesting paper:

HISTORY OF WATER WORKS FOR SUPPLYING THE BOROUGH OF GERMANTOWN IN THE COUNTY OF PHILADELPHIA (now city) BUILT IN 1851 AND 1852.

It was first contemplated to put in a hydraulic ram of eight inches to supply Tulpohocken street and vicinity, as Mr. J. C. Fallon was owner of the greater portion of the property on Tulpohocken street, and extending northwest to Washington lane from Adams street and Tulpohocken southeast to Harvey street, including Green and Wayne streets, and from Wayne southwest to Wissahickon avenue or Township line, northwest to Washington lane.

The first plan of works was to build a small dam on Papermill run, a short distance southeast of Washington lane, and put in the eight-inch water ram, as mentioned previously, build a tank at a suitable elevation to give a supply of water to the property previously described. But upon searching for and finding a number of springs adjacent to the run in the valley between Washington lane and Walnut lane, after ascertaining the number of gallons by measurement the run flowed in twenty-four hours and estimating the amount of water to be collected by rainfall, it was determined to form a company to be called the Germantown Water Company. A company was then formed by making Mr. John C. Fallon president, and Christopher Fallon and others stockholders. In anticipation of obtaining a charter from the Legislature the works were commenced by digging a well at the southwestern terminus of Tulpohocken street, twenty-five feet in diameter, sixteen feet deep. A hole four inches in diameter and sixteen feet deep was drilled through a rock in the bottom of the well which furnished a considerable amount of water. The well was walled up by building an outer and an inner wall (dry) with stone, leaving a space between of four feet to be filled with coarse gravel or sand that the water might filter from the dam. The tops of the walls were furnished with coping which was procured from the quarry on opposite sides of the dam, drains were made and walled up on either side with stone and covered with flat stone, then the trench was filled in with broken stone and covered with coarse gravel or sand for the purpose of filtering the water from the dam and conveying it from these drains and from springs into the well, a dam breast was built at the northwest side of Walnut lane twenty-one feet deep at the breast of the dam and about eighty feet wide at that point; that level was the level of the creek or run at Washington lane. An engine house was built at the southwest terminus of Tulpohocken street, containing two horizontal high-pressure engines of three feet stroke, and of fifteen horse power, each working two six-inch horizontal pumps. Two cylinder boilers were placed therein, thirty feet long by thirty inches in diameter, for the purpose of supplying steam for the engines. The upper part of the engine house was used as a dwelling for the engineer, but owing to the heat from the boilers it did not answer the purpose intended. The company built a separate dwelling for the engineer on Tulpohocken street. A ten-inch main was laid through the engine house on Tulpohocken street to Germantown avenue with a twelve-inch outlet two hundred and fifty feet northeast of Wayne street. On the southeast side of Tulpohocken street (for stand pipe) an eight-inch main was laid on Germantown avenue northwest to Washington lane, and a six-inch main southeast to Mill street, and a four-inch main southeast to Duy's lane, or Wister street, and three and four-inch main in other streets at that time (1852). A stand pipe was erected on the southeast side of Tulpohocken street, two hundred and fifty feet northeast of the northeast house line of Wayne street, one hundred and twenty feet high and five feet in diameter, holding 14,000 ale gallons, made of boiler iron in three sections of forty feet each together with a funnel-shaped top or cap of seven feet high, as a finish to the pipe; the first section was seven-sixteenths inches thick, the second three-eighths, and the third section five sixteenths, and the top three-sixteenths, in thickness. The top or cap was not intended to be water tight but only to make a finish, as 120' was intended to be the level of a contemplated reservoir to be built on Allen's lane northwest of Germantown avenue, and was built by the company in 1854; and a four-inch main laid up to Allen's lane and Germantown avenue, and a ten-inch main in Allen's lane into this reservoir, preparatory to supplying a large reservoir which was built in 1885; and a ten-inch main laid on Germantown avenue connecting with the ten-inch main on Allen's lane. The four-inch main is now used as a high service main, as also the ten-inch main that is high service or direct pumpage to Tulpohocken street; below that point is supplied by gravity.

The stand pipe was set up on a cast iron base two inches thick; the base was bolted fast by eight two-inch bolts, drilled in the solid rock six feet deep, and filled around with melted lead, and caulked tight. The stand pipe had a corresponding plate which was bolted fast to the bed plate by sixteen one and one-half inch bolts, four in each corner. The pipe was put together on the ground and raised and set on the bed plate by means of a derrick and capstan, on August 13th, 1852.

The distribution was purchased from the Water Company by the city of Philadelphia in May, 1866. The use of works to supply Germantown distribution, and rented by the city, was abandoned September 30th, 1872; connections were removed from the stand pipe on June, 1873. The stand pipe was sold and taken down, by the parties purchasing it, on December 22nd, 1873, at 4 o'clock P. M.

November 15th, 1870, the twenty-inch main was laid by the city for supplying Germantown, being completed from Roxborough to the Mount Airy reservoir, the water was passed over in three hours and thirty minutes, a distance of about four miles. From that time to the present, 1888, the water has been supplied from Roxborough from the Schuylkill River above Flat Rock dam. The contractors for the original works and laying of mains were Messrs. Biskinline, Martin and Trotter, and Mr. D. E. Morrell, General Superintendent, all of Philadelphia.

The water from Roxborough passes over the Wissahickon creek at an elevation of one hundred and seven feet above the level of the creek, the pipe forms the bridge supported by invested arches of flat iron, and consists of four spans of one hundred and sixty-five feet each, erected in 1870.

Mr. J. W. Jordan, of the Historical Society of Pennsylvania, kindly gives the following correction of a statement quoted from another source in a recent article as to an early fire engine; it is from a communication which he wrote for *The Moravian*.

Being unable to obtain freight for Europe, Captain Jacobsen secured a cargo for the Island of Jamaica, and he sailed in December. The following spring she proceeded to England. During the year 1763, the *Hope* made the following voyages. January 31, arrived at New York, and sailed for London April 24. On the evening of October 21, she arrived from thence with Brother Frommelt, who was to be Economus of the Single Brethren in America; Brother Tiersch, co-Director of the Paedagogium at Nazareth; Sister Wernwig Laboress of the Widows' Choir; Susel von Gersdorf, Laboress of the Single Sisters at Bethlehem; and Sisters Justina Erd, M. Barbara Horn, Dorothea Leller, Frederica Peltscher, Elizabeth Seidlitz and Agalome Steinman, who were to enter the Sisters' House at Bethlehem. The first fire engine for Bethlehem was brought over on this voyage. On November 23, the *Hope* sailed for London.

Some remarks have been made in these notes with regard to the roads of Germantown. It is worthy of remark that about 1845, when Joshua R. Johnson and Abraham Kulp were Commissioners of the borough of Germantown, the roads were well cared for, at an expense of seven hundred dollars per annum, from the railroad bridge at Wayne Station to the County line at Chestnut Hill. Samuel Harvey was then Burgess, and Samuel Johnson, Samuel Keyser and others were Councilmen.

The Rev. Dr. Andrews, vice-Provost of the University of Pennsylvania, once resided in Germantown. In a note to a sermon of Rev. Samuel Magaw on the death of Andrew Brown and family by the burning of their house, I find that a chamber in the house of Dr. Andrews was burned and his youngest son, Edward, was so burned that he died afterward. A month after this the house was totally consumed. The sermon is in the Library of the Historical Society of Pennsylvania.

JOHN WELSH.

Spring Bank was the residence of the late Hon. John Welsh, our former Minister to England. The place derives its name from numerous springs upon it. It lies on the south side of Township line, now called Wissahickon avenue, at the east corner of Knight's lane, now called Germantown lane, it being a continuation of Carpenter's lane to the Wissahickon.

A private lunatic asylum kept by the late Samuel Mason, a member of the Friends' Society was here for a time. The oldest part of the building, which is of stone, was a farm house owned by Mr. Wilson.

Dr. Edward Lowber, John Welsh's father-in-law, bought this property about 1840 and used it as a country seat, in connection with Mr. Welsh. Both of these gentlemen had boarded at the place before buying it. About 30 acres were in the farm, which reached to the Wissahickon, including Molly Wicker's Rock. Mr. Welsh donated several acres to the park to perfect the park line on the north side of the Wissahickon. He also placed the stone statue of William Penn, inscribed "Toleration," on this ground, on a height which is very observable to those passing along the Wissahickon drive.

At the death of Dr. Edward Lowber, Mr. Welsh had purchased the property of his heirs. He had previously bought several acres of land to the east of this place and adjoining it, which is occupied by his son, Samuel Welsh, Jr., and is called "Kenilworth." He has enlarged a house which was upon the property, and spends the year there. Samuel Welsh, Jr., is a director of Germantown Academy.

Mr. John Welsh owned a good deal more land in this vicinity. His three daughters, Mrs. James B. Young, Mrs. Dr. George Strawbridge and Mrs. Thomas P. C. Stokes, live on a part of their father's estate, opposite Spring Bank, in architectural cottages.

Herbert Welsh resides near Wingohocking station, Germantown. He is the youngest son of John Welsh, and has been noted for his interest in the Indian question, and has done much good in lay preaching in St. Mark's Episcopal Church, in Frankford, where his uncle, the late William Welsh and family, have done such faithful work.

The Hon. John Welsh died at his city residence, at the southeast corner of Eleventh and Spruce streets, on April 10th, 1886. He was a member of St. Peter's Episcopal Church, in the city of Philadelphia, for over fifty years.

Mr. Welsh's daughter, Mrs. James Somers Smith, and family, now occupy Spring Bank. John Lowber Welsh lives at Chestnut Hill, William Lowber

Welsh resides abroad, and was recently United States Consul at Florence. The Hon. John Welsh was a man of national reputation, of whom Germantown may be proud as a Christian citizen.

The Franklin Fire Company's stone plastered building (No. 5428 Main street) was sold by the Company to William McCallum about five years ago. The Company was originally independent, but is now merged into the paid Fire Department of the city, which built a new stone edifice on Main street, opposite Carpenter street. The old building is about to be torn down to open Franklin street, and the store occupied by Jacob Peterman, on the Pullinger estate, next this building, must also be demolished for the same reason. The "Red Men" now use the old fire company's hall. The Franklin Fire Company may have caused this section to bear the name Franklinville, and so the Pennsylvania phlosopher's honor is perpetuated.

MEEHAN'S NURSERY.

On Chew street, at the end of Church street, lies the Nursery of Thomas Meehan. Mr. Meehan began business opposite the Carpenter place, where Meehan avenue, bearing his name, has now been opened. He continued there from 1852 to 1870, when he sold to William C. Royal, who opened the street through the place, which is now built upon. Mr. Meehan bought a part of this property of George Carpenter, Sr. The Burt family owned it previously, and Mr. Carpenter bought it of Mrs. Burt. The stone mansion has been remodeled, and is occupied by Mr. Royal, on the southeastern corner of Meehan avenue and Main street. The upper part of Meehan avenue belonged to the Hortter estate. The stone house is now Johnson's grocery store. It has been altered somewhat. The stone stable and barn still stand.

The present Commissioner of Highways, Joseph McDonald, began business in this house, having a drug store there. After about a year he started the express business, being one of the earliest, if not the earliest one, in Germantown to undertake this employment.

Mr. Meehan bought the property of the Hortter estate, which contained some of the largest pear trees in Germantown before Mr. Meehan bought it, and there was a great variety of fine kinds. Mr. Eberly, who was connected by marriage with the Hortter family, took much interest in the culture and grafting of these trees. Many of them were nine feet in circumference at the trunk. Mr. Charles Weiss, who lately died in Germantown, was also connected with the Hortter family by marriage.

In 1870 Mr. Meehan bought the Hong farm, so called from a previous owner, of Archibald McIntyre, for some time connected with the United States Mint. A portion of the property was bought of Jacob Hortter. The yellow plastered stone mansion on the hill side, occupied by Mr. Meehan, was built by Mr. Hortter for his own use, but he never occupied it. The brown ferruginous tint appears to come from the oxydization of the iron contained in the sand; as may be seen in other dashed houses in Germantown.

A fine unfailing spring is on the McIntyre tract. It is said to have been an Indian camping-place. A stream from it pours into the south fork of the Wingohocking, and is one of the important tributaries to that stream.

Many Indian relics, as arrowheads and stone axes, have been dug up here, and revolutionary bullets and grape shot have also been found. Mr. Edward Meehan, brother to James Meehan, has quite a collection of these curiosities.

Mr. Thomas Meehan's business extends over the world, including shipments to New Zealand, Australia, and elsewhere. He edits the *Gardener's Monthly*.

The rolling hills clad with trees present a beautiful scene even in winter.

A walk over the boards, wisely laid by the Reading Railroad Company on Gorgas lane, brings us to the quaint and pretty brick waiting room, and after the worthy flagman has given us some local information and mounted the ladder to place his signal light for the night we take our departing train. While we do not speed away from "Ancient Germantown" on the wings of the wind, Scott's lines are appropriate:

> "They'll have fleet steeds that follow,
> Quoth young Lochinvar."

In marking the short distance between the Gorgas lane station and that of Mount Pleasant above it, the remark of a friend as to another railway is appropriate, that if the stations were a little nearer together one would do for the front part of a train, and another for the rear portion of the same train. Still these frequent stations are a sensible arrangement in building up a suburb, and have helped to modernize the old town.

GERMANTOWN SOCIETIES.

Mr. Edwin R. Stevens, Secretary of Mitchell Lodge, kindly furnishes the following sketch:

MITCHELL LODGE, NO. 296, F. & A. M.

It appeared, during the years 1853-55, to many members of Hiram Lodge, No. 81, that a change of their place of meeting was so desirable that they had the question of removal several times debated, but without success; finally, they determined to peacefully separate, and with the aid of some of the members from other lodges, form a new one. With this object in view several preliminary meetings were held in the office of Dr. William H. Squire, the result of which was the formation of Mitchell Lodge, No. 296, F. & A. M., which was named in honor of Past Grand John K. Mitchell, M. D., and was dedicated on December 22, 1855, in the Grand Lodge room, Masonic Hall, Chestnut street, below Eighth, by R. W. Grand Master James Hutchinson, and the following officers were installed: P. M. William H. Squire, from Hiram Lodge,

GERMANTOWN.

No. 81, W. M.; John J. Griffith, from Phœnix Lodge, No. 230, S. W.; Daniel K. Harper, from Hiram Lodge, No. 81, J. W.; George Fling, from Hiram Lodge, No. 81, Treasurer; John A. Flynn, from Hiram Lodge, No. 81, Secretary.

There were twenty-two charter members, at that time the following familiar names in Germantown: Thomas M. Brooks, William K. Cox, Frederick Emhardt, E. M. Firth, George Fling. John A. Flynn, John J. Griffith, Daniel R. Harper, Thomas B. Henderson, Samuel B. Henry, M. D., William Hopkin, Thomas Jones, Theodore A. Mehl, John Roberts, Thomas J. Roberts, William H. Squire, John H. Tingley, Clement Tingley and William Wright. Some of the charter members are still living.

The first meeting was held in Philomathean Hall, December 27, 1855. For some time they met in Town Hall. They then fitted up a lodge room on Main street, below Price, over William Hopkins's property, where they met for a number of years, until in December, 1874, they took possession of the present quarters (Masonic Hall), Main, below Mill street, which was built at a cost of nearly $40,000.

The Lodge now has upon its rolls 170 members, among them some of the most enterprising business men of the town.

The affairs of the Lodge are in a very prosperous condition.

The present officers are William H. Brooks, W. M.; Alexander Kinnier, S. W.; Harlan Page, J. W.; Thomas W. Wright, Treasurer; Edwin R. Stevens, Secretary.

RELIANCE COUNCIL, No. 40, O. U. A. M.

Reliance Council, No. 40, Order of United American Mechanics, was instituted March 26, 1847. The names on the charter are: F. Augustus Ent, Charles Miller, William Dewees, Sylvester Handsberry, John Jackson, John R. Detwiler, John Holmes, Isaiah Shriver, William Deal, David Harmer, Jr., Joseph Shriver, John Shriver, Lewis Emery, Peter Shriver, Solomon Loverige, William P. Conyers, David Harmer, Sr., Daniel D. George, Joseph G. Beine, Rittenhouse Fraley and Alexander Niblack.

During the whole period of its existence this beneficial organization has never ceased paying benefits. Its stability is shown in the fact that some of its chief officials have been retained in office for more than twenty-five consecutive years.

In years gone by such men as Congressman Harmer, the late ex-Recorder of Deeds William Marshall Taylor, E. H. Butler the book publisher, and others of note were embraced in the membership of Reliance Council. During the war for the Union it took the lead in vacating Town Hall to Government Hospital purposes and contributed toward the cause in both blood and treasure. It still retains a fair membership which includes citizens prominent in business, politics and the professions.

KNIGHTS OF PYTHIAS OF PENNSYLVANIA RELIEF FUND.

BY WASHINGTON ROOP.

Germantown Lodge, No. 38, K. of P. Relief Fund, meets every Tuesday evening in Town Hall. It was organized December 1, 1885, with sixteen members, on No. 2 assessment, the object thereof being to secure to the family of a deceased member the sum of $250 by paying the sum of 25 cents per month. Its management and funds are placed in the hands of faithful members of the Grand Lodge, and its laws provide for the inspection of all books and accounts whenever those whose special duty it is may deem it necessary or advisable.

Assessments are called the first of each month closing with the end of the month, thus enabling the members to pay the assessment sometime during the month. Assessments must be paid each month in order to preserve a continuous claim on the benefits of the fund. There are 207 Lodges, a portion of whose members belong to the Relief Fund. There are 5783 members of the fund. The membership of Germantown Lodge, at assessment No. 22, was 93 members. There have been 64 deaths and the Grand Lodge has paid $16,000.00 in twenty-one months to its Lodges connected with the fund. Members paying the assessment for the first time are beneficial after the time within it was called and the receipt of the assessment by the Secretary of the Relief Fund. A member of any Lodge, K. P., of Pennsylvania, can become a member of said Fund, the requirements being normal good health. The officers of Germantown Lodge, No. 38, K. of P. Relief Fund, are: Jacob Pullinger, President, and Washington Roop, Secretary.

GERMANTOWN COUNCIL, No. 21, SONS AND DAUGHTERS OF AMERICA,

Meets on Friday evenings, at Axford's Hall, Rittenhouse street. It was instituted May 5, 1871. Worthy Grand President John D. Bayne, assisted by the Grand Officers, installed Worthy President Simeon McCowan, vice-President Emma Edney; Chaplain George Mitchell; Treasurer Samuel Rittenhouse; Recording Secretary William H. Livezey; Financial Secretary Charles H. Weiss; I. S. Kate Dooley; O. S. Charles Markley; S. G. James Pullinger. There were twenty-six initiated the same evening. Up to the present time over 600 have signed the constitution and become members of the Council; a number of these have been dropped. Among those active in the Order, having died are Simeon McCowan, Samuel Rittenhouse, James Pullinger, Susan Pullinger, William Dewees, Martha Wolf, Lizzie Flue, John Fortin, and others. Its present membership is 235. They have invested over $4,000 in bonds and building association stock, and have paid out a great sum for benefits to its members and other relief. Their object is: 1st, To establish a sick and funeral fund; 2d, To establish a fund for the relief of widows and orphans of deceased members; 3d, To assist each other in obtaining employment, and to encourage each other in business. Its present officers are W. P. Sallie Harrington; V. P. William Lester; R. S. Washington Roop; L. S. George Mitchell; Treasurer George Trumbore; Chaplain C. F. McCarthur; O. S. Joseph Morgan; I. S. Charles West, S. G. E. Todd.

PHILOMATHEAN LODGE OF ODD FELLOWS.

Mr. Robert K. Duffield, the Secretary of this lodge, has placed in my hands a sketch of its history, which I will condense.

He states that Germantown has about twenty benevolent Orders, embracing forty separate societies. They work for a common purpose—the good of humanity. The Odd Fellows are one of the leading bodies. The lodge here described is No. 10. It celebrated its forty-ninth anniversary on March 16th, A. D. 1887. It is the oldest lodge in Germantown, and in the State, as those previously organized did not keep up a continuous existence, as the Philomathean did.

Thomas Wildey, an Englishman, founded Odd Fellowship in Baltimore in 1819. He had belonged to the Order in England, and had advanced in position in it, and had been instrumental in founding Morning Star Lodge in London. He was the first presiding officer of that Lodge. After emigrating to this country he met another Englishman named John Welch, who was an English Odd Fellow, and in 1819 they, with John Duncan, John Cheatham and Richard Rusworth, organized Washington Lodge, No. 1, in Baltimore. These five working men had prejudices to meet and difficulties to face, but Wildey proved a good, hearty and loving leader, and English pluck buoyed him up in his undertaking. The work which he started is now known over the world. There are thousands of lodges in various lands, and hundreds of thousands of members. The revenue counts up to millions, and the disbursements aid the needy and the suffering.

In 1821 the first lodge was started in Philadelphia, and Philomathean Lodge was organized in 1828, on the 29th of December, in a building next the National Bank, now in the occupancy of E. B. Paramore. The bank then used the first floor.

For several years prejudices against this secret order choked its growth, but in time it advanced in strength. In 1830 a procession in Germantown, in which several city lodges joined, made an impression.

In 1835 Jacob Rosett, Sr., was building some houses on Manheim street, and made a third story room over two houses a lodge room, where the meetings were held for twelve years. In 1844 the Lodge bought its present property, on Wister street, and not long after built the building now used, at a cost of about five thousand dollars. The edifice was well constructed. The dedication of the hall took place in A. D. 1847, on the 15th of April. P. G. Thomas F. Betton, M. D., made the oration. He was a physician of high standing. There was a parade of lodges. This was the first Lodge, which, without embarrassment, finished the undertaking of building a hall for its own property.

This Lodge presented a block of white marble, properly inscribed, to the Washington Monument, at Washington. At the Philadelphia parade of 1869 this Lodge was under the Marshals Casper Miller and Joseph Mansfield. This was the fifteenth anniversary of the Order in America. The ladies presented the lodge with a beautiful white silk banner containing a picture of a female caring gently for two children, as an emblem of the benevolence of the Order. This Lodge has done much to relieve sick members.

Among the founders of Odd Fellowship in Germantown were strong men who practiced the virtues which their Order inculcated. This has been one of the most prosperous Lodges in the State, according to the statement of the late James L. Ridgely, Secretary of the Sovereign Grand Lodge. In the Chicago fire this Lodge sent a good donation to the sufferers.

In 1876, on the 20th day of September, the Order had its largest parade in Philadelphia. The Philomathean, Walker and Germantown Lodges, of Germantown, paraded on Main street before going to the city.

The fiftieth anniversary of Philomathean Lodge took place on February 14th, A. D. 1879. Grand Secretary James B. Nicholson made the address. Past Grands James Platt, John Waterhouse and John Platt were at this anniversary. They were the three oldest members. John Platt gave a history of the lodge. An address was made by P. G. Master George Fling. These gentlemen have all died.

The fifty-ninth anniversary was an enjoyable social gathering, enlivened by music and recitations by ladies and gentlemen. The committee were John J. Waterhouse, Thomas T. North, William Homiller, Frank A. Wheeler, David H. Barrows, Edward Mengert, Edward Wilson, S. W. Kephart and John W. Brooks.

I append some further statements in the words of Mr. Duffield:

The charter members were: Charles L. Rowand, Henry Birchall, John Hart, James Gifford, William Witworth, Robinson Lawton, William Botton, Ebenezer Forsyth.

The first officers were: Noble Grand William Botton; Vice Grand Robinson Lawton; Secretary Charles L. Rowand; Assistant Secretary Charles Saxton; Treasurer Ebenezer Forsyth.

The present officers are: Noble Grand Harry D. Graig; Vice Grand Thomas T. North; Secretary Robert K. Duffield; Assistant Secretary Edward Mengart; Treasurer Reuben Jagger.

Space is too limited to enumerate all the prominent citizens of Germantown who have been members of this Lodge, but among the leading ones may be mentioned: Martin Landenburger, William Ent, Hillary Krickbaum, Elias Birchall, Aaron Jones, Henry Woltemate, William K. Cox, William Allen, George Fling, Joseph L. Sykes, Thomas Brooks, Hon. William H. Brooks, Captain John Waterhouse, F. William Bockius, John Platt.

NATIONAL BANK OF GERMANTOWN.

At the present time the past officers vote for the Grand Lodge officers on the last meeting night in March, in their Lodge rooms. Formerly the practice was to vote at the Grand Lodge headquarters in the city. The Past Grands of No. 10 would go to the city in an omnibus, and the saying was: "As goes Germantown, so goes the election." And it generally proved correct.

WALKER LODGE, No. 306, I. O. O. F.

In the early part of the year 1848, several Odd Fellows residing in Germantown conceived the idea of forming a new Odd Fellows Lodge in Germantown, there being at that time but one organization of like character here. Several meetings were held at private residences and after overcoming many obstacles, on the 20th of March, 1848, Casper Guyer, William T. Hunt, Peter K. Shriver, Gideon D. Harmer, Alfred Van Horn, George W. Emerick, Chas. Miller, Allen Gill and William Fisher applied to the Grand Lodge of Pennsylvania for a charter, which was duly granted. Officers were elected and on the 24th of March, 1848, they were duly installed by the Grand Lodge Officers in the hall of Philomathean Lodge, on Wister street. The new Lodge was named Walker, in consideration of the valuable assistance rendered by George Walker, of Spring Lodge. Of the charter members, Casper Guyer, who was elected the first Noble Grand of the Lodge, is the only survivor. The meetings were held in the Hall of Philomathean Lodge until 1856, when Town Hall was selected as the place for the meetings and continued for some six years; then the Lodge removed to Langstroth's (now Vernon) Hall, and met there until March, 1869, when it removed to its new and commodious Hall, on Main street, near Chelten avenue, which is considered one of the finest Odd Fellows' Halls in Pennsylvania. The Lodge has had continued success and prosperity ever since its organization. By careful management of its funds it has faithfully and promptly met every obligation. The present membership is 395. Since its organization it has expended for relief of sick members, funeral benefits, etc., about $60,000. Besides owning its Hall, which is entirely free from debt, the Lodge has an invested fund of about $10,000. The present officers are John Cave, N. G.; Samuel A. Sibson, V. G.; C. K. Channon, Secretary, and William Ployd, Treasurer.

GERMANTOWN NATIONAL BANK.

The following account of the History of the Bank of Germantown was contributed to Scharf & Westcott's History of Philadelphia, by Charles W. Otto, the present vice-President: "The Bank of Germantown was chartered by the Legislature of the State in 1813, and went into operation July, 1814, with a paid-in capital of $55,000; Samuel Harvey, President, and John F. Watson (author of 'Watson's Annals of Philadelphia'), cashier. The first board of directors was composed of Samuel Harvey, Charles J. Wister, Richard Bayley,

Peter Robeson, Michael Riter, George Bensell, John Johnson, Edward Russell, William Rodman, Robert Adams, Samuel Johnson, Conrad Carpenter, John Rogers. Capital, January, 1815, $91,000; July, 1815, $150,000; January, 1816, 152,000; and in 1853, $200,000.

"From the minutes of the Bank of July, 1814, it appears that 'the committee for procuring and fitting out a banking house report that they have leased from Dr. George Bensell, for the term of six years and six months from the 15th of June last, at a rent of $300 per annum, payable quarterly, a three-story stone house opposite the sixth milestone, in the village of Germantown, and that they have purchased from Mr. James Stokes, the iron doors, etc., belonging to the vault of the late Bank of the United States, in Germantown; that they have employed masons and carpenters to make the necessary alterations, which they expect will be completed by the 23d inst.' The location was changed from the above place (which is the second house above School lane on the Main street) to Main street, below Shoemaker lane, in 1825, and again in 1868 to Main street and School lane, next door to the original location.

"Samuel Harvey died in 1848, and was succeeded by Charles Magarge as President. John F. Watson resigned the cashiership in 1848, and was succeeded by Lloyd Mifflin, who resigned in 1850, and was succeeded by Samuel Harvey, Jr. He resigned in 1860, and Charles W. Otto, the present cashier of the bank, was elected in his place. Mr. Magarge resigned in 1866, and William Wynne Wister, the present President, was elected to fill the vacancy."

To this must be added that Mr. Charles W. Otto, retiring from the cashiership, was elected vice-President, May 8th, A. D. 1885, and on June 23d of the same year, Canby S. Tyson was elected Cashier.

THE SAVING FUND SOCIETY OF GERMANTOWN AND ITS VICINITY.

This Society is not a purely money-making or money-lending institution, but it partakes largely of a benevolent character. It was projected by men who were kindly disposed to the poor and the working classes, and whose chief object was to furnish facilities and inducements for the laying up of small sums, which, accumulating year by year, should aggregate a fund by which homes could be purchased, or otherwise drawn upon in special times of need. The society has steadily adhered to these principles during its long and prosperous career. The managers give their time and influence without pecuniary consideration, and are prohibited by the charter from borrowing any money or moneys directly or indirectly, or in any way becoming indebted to the institution.

The first meetings of organization were prompted by the late Samuel B. Morris, a member of the Society of Friends.

On the 8th of May, 1854, the Society was formally organized and business was commenced May 24, 1854, in a back room of the building at the corner of

SAVING FUND.

GERMANTOWN. 339

Main and Armat streets, and $629.17 was received from sixteen depositors. At the end of the first year the deposits amounted to $12,788.84, representing 273 depositors. In 1855 the office was removed to the adjoining building, which it occupied until June, 1869, when temporary quarters were taken in one of the stores of Walker Hall Building until October, 1869, when their new building, No. 4908 Main street, was occupied, having been erected upon the site of the Channon property, adjoining Langstroth's Hall, now Vernon Hall. In this building the Society's assets increased from 190,000 to 1,400,000. After making changes from time to time in the interior, in order to gain more room, it became a matter of necessity to have a larger building, which want was met in the purchase of the property, corner of Main and School streets, from Mrs. Charles W. Schaeffer, and the present noble edifice was built and occupied April 1, 1883.

The institution has had a steady growth, increasing in deposits and accounts every year, with the exception of 1860 and '61 and 1878. The following table will show the growth of the institution in periods of ten years:

Date.	Deposits.	No. of Depositors.
June 1, 1856	523,325.20	368
January 1, 1866	115,638.20	1146
January 1, 1876	581,990.50	3543
January 1, 1886	1,745,305.36	8696
January 1, 1887	2,018,429.71	9849

The following have been the officers:—

Presidents—Abraham Martin, elected May 8, 1854, resigned May, 1867; T. C. Henry, elected May, 1867.

Vice-Presidents—T. C. Henry, elected May 8, 1854, resigned May, 1867; Franklin Shoemaker, elected May, 1867, deceased September, 1878; James M. Aertsen, elected September, 1878, resigned February, 1882; Isaac C. Jones, Jr., elected February, 1882.

Secretary—E. P. Morris, elected May 8, 1854.

Treasurers—William T. Ulmer, elected May 8, 1854, resigned July, 16, 1855; Theo. B. Butcher, elected July 16, 1855, resigned June 1, 1869; George A. Warder, elected June 1, 1869, deceased September 30, 1881; Charles A. Spiegel, elected October 1, 1881.

Solicitors—Alexander Henry, elected May 8, 1854, deceased December, 1883 J. Bayard Henry, elected February 2, 1884.

MUTUAL FIRE INSURANCE COMPANY.

The Managers of this Company met at Germantown Hall, on the eleventh of May, A. D. 1843, and organized, electing Henry S. Mallery, President; Wyndham H. Stokes, Secretary; and John Stallman, Treasurer. The incorporators, besides the officers named, were Matthias Haas, John Purcell, Jacob Derr, George M. Smick, Michael Snyder, John Felton, John L. Williams, Benjamin Lehman, Henry K. Paul, and Charles Treichel. The last two declined and Samuel Harvey and George Moyer were elected to fill these vacancies. Business was transacted at the house of the Secretary for several years. In 1843 John Stallman resigned the Treasurership, and Wyndham H. Stokes was elected to that position. On the fourth of September, 1843, the following Managers were elected: Henry S. Mallery, Benjamin Lehman, John Felton, Samuel Harvey, Theodore Ashmead, Alfred Creas, John Stallman, Joseph Handsberry, H. G. Jones, Matthias Haas, Samuel S. Ritchie, George W. Davis, Wyndham H. Stokes. In 1846, the Company rented a room of Benjamin Lehman. In 1847, Mr. Mallery gave up the Presidency, and Benjamin Lehman became his successor. In 1853, a lot was purchased at Germantown avenue and Armat street, being the north corner. An office was built here and used until the new building at 4801 Germantown avenue was entered in February, A. D. 1885. Benjamin Lehman died in 1867. Spencer Roberts was then chosen as President. In 1870, Wyndham H. Stokes, who founded the Company and had been Secretary and Treasurer from the time it was organized, died. Charles H. Stokes, his son, became the successor of his father. In 1871, he resigned, and Henry G. Stelwagon was chosen to succeed him. In 1872, Edward B. Clark became Secretary and Treasurer. He resigned in 1874, and William H. Emhardt was elected as his successor and has held the office by annual election to this time.

In 1885, the Company bought a lot on the northeast corner of Germantown avenue and School street. Charles W. Otto, Charles Spencer, Charles Weiss, Jabez Gates and Spencer Roberts, as a committee, commended the plans of the architect, George T. Pearson, for a new building. The plan was accepted, and this committee, in 1884, gave the contract for the building to James Kinnier's Sons, who did the work satisfactorily. In 1885, Spencer Roberts, who had been President since 1867, died, and Jabez Gates received the election to that position, and is still in that post. The present managers are: Jabez Gates, John Stallman, Nicholas Rittenhouse, William Ashmead, M. D., Joseph Boucher, Charles W. Otto, Charles Spencer, Edward T. Tyson, Enoch Taylor, Horatio G. Jones, John Allen, Reuben V. Sallada, Frederic A. Hoyt, Henry B. Brumer.

The building of the Company is an architectural one, and in its commanding position on the corner of Main street and Market Square is an ornament to the town. The offices are light and airy and furnished with taste.

In the second story the Library has its collection of books and carries on its good work. If an ancient Germantowner could view the change that has passed over this corner since the old house which served as a jail stood near it, he could hardly believe his eyes.

The Soldiers and Sailors' monument is a credit to the town, and commemorates the noble dead; and now the Market Square Presbyterian Church has remodeled its building, which will further ornament the Square. The pretty parsonage will then be in keeping with its surroundings. It is well that in the erection of a new building the congregation has not been tempted to leave the

MUTUAL FIRE INSURANCE BUILDING, GERMANTOWN.

historic place, which has been rendered sacred by the worship of so many generations, and the coming race can do reverence to their God and Saviour on the very spot where their ancestors offered Him their prayers and praises.

THE WOMEN'S CHRISTIAN ASSOCIATION.

In 1874, Mrs. E. L. Linnard was the President and Mrs. Charles Megargc, Mrs. L. P. Smith, Mrs. George W. Carpenter, and Mrs. F. B. Reeves, vice-Presidents; Mrs. Elizabeth P. Smith, Secretary, and Mrs. W. L. Corse, Treasurer. The third annual report (1873-4) states that a house had been bought at the northwest corner of Mill and Main streets and partly paid for. The object was to shelter young girls and give them a home, with moral and religious instruction. There were evening classes of study and sewing for those who toiled in the mills through the day, which accomplished much good.

THE GERMANTOWN LIBRARY ASSOCIATION,

Under the Presidency of Miss Hannah Ann Zell, is a useful institution. Its pleasant reading room above the Insurance building and facing Main street and Market Square, is attractive. Mrs. Weygant is Secretary and Mrs. Frank Taylor, Treasurer. There is a Board of Directors.

THE WORKINGMEN'S CLUB

Gave its first annual report in 1878. Its formal opening was in Parker's Hall, May 10, 1877, though the Club House was opened a few days before that date. It has a library and reading room and gives entertainments, including lectures, readings and concerts. In the report a Coal Club and a Beneficial Society are noted. In 1877 and 1878, G. W. Russell is marked as President, Samuel W. Wray, Treasurer, and R. H. Shoemaker, Secretary. In 1878, J. Topliff Johnson was vice-President. The report of 1883 notes the purchase of the pleasant Club House in West Chelten avenue, next to the Presbyterian Church, in a central location, and expresses a desire to build a hall. The Club had been located on the corner of School lane and Main street. A permanent Library Fund was started, and "Messrs. Charles Spencer and H. H. Houston were elected Trustees, Nov. 6, 1882." A fair had been held to aid the Fund. The library had 2119 volumes.

The Literary Society had Sheldon Potter, Esq., as its President. Herbert Welsh was vice-President and John F. Perot, Secretary. In appealing for co-operation in its literary work the wise couplet is aptly given:

> "Not what we give, but what we share;
> For the gift without the giver is bare."

The faithful aid of the President of the Club, Charles H. Spencer, is mentioned, and regret at his resignation by reason of his removal from Germantown.

The Apollo Singing Society has done good work.

Mr. Charles W. Schwartz has held the office of vice-President of the Club, and Dr. R. H. Shoemaker and G. W. Wills that of Secretary.

In 1884 the erection of the brick hall is reported. The first floor was for games and the second floor for a hall.

A class in penmanship and arithmetic had been under the charge of Rev. Thompson P. Ege, and had afterward given its time to bookkeeping. A class in German was taught by John H. Westcott, Esq., and had succeeded in its work. The board thanked the teachers. A semi-monthly journal had been started by the Literary Association.

In 1885 the report shows the club to be prosperous. Drawing and writing were taught. H. F. Lennig superintended mechanical drawing and Stewart A. Jellett freehand drawing, and D. H. Forsyth writing. Henry S. Pancoast, Esq., was President of the Literary Society.

The present officers of the club, are, George W. Russell, President; Charles W. Schwartz, vice-President; E. R. Sorber, Secretary; Alfred C. Watson, Treasurer.

This institution does much good. Would that every town had a like one.

THE GERMANTOWN DISPENSARY.

The report of 1868 gives James M. Aertsen as President; Elliston P. Morris, Secretary, and Charles J. Wister, Jr., Treasurer, and T. S. Leavitt, M. D., as house physican. In addition, Drs. O. J. Wister, J. Darrach and W. Darrach, and J. M. Leedom and A. C. Lambdin were out-door physicians. This was the fourth report. Many interesting cases of relief are spoken of in Dr. Leavitt's report. The rooms were then at No. 2, Town Hall.

In 1879 the hospital building is marked in the report as in Shoemaker's lane near Chew street. This was the ninth report of the dispensary and hospital, and the fifteenth of the dispensary, which was now at the hospital building. Dr. James E. Rhoads was then President; Thomas Stewardson, Secretary, and S. Harvey Thomas, Treasurer. Drs. W. Darrach, Miller, Leavitt, Downs, Deaver, D. Hayes Agnew, W. Hunt, J. Darrach and William R. Dunton were the physicians, and Mrs. Mary E. Booth the matron. The removal of the dispensary to the hospital gave it needed conveniences.

The Donation Day, under the care of the lady visitors, had now brought about $600 in money, besides a large supply of useful articles. Kind words are given in the report to the late President, Dr. H. R. Wharton, whose term of service had ended and who had devoted himself to the good work and had been a very valuable officer. The death of the useful and benevolent Franklin Shoemaker, a member of the Board, is properly noticed. He was the first member of the Board who died during service in that body.

The hospital has forty beds, and in addition to treating common cases has a special surgeon for diseases of the eye and ear.

The hospital was instituted for the aid of the sick poor of Germantown and Chestnut Hill.

THE PENNSYLVANIA INSTITUTION FOR FEEBLE MINDED CHILDREN

Was incorporated April 7th, 1853, and opened at Germantown. It has done much good in physically and morally benefiting the unfortunate class it treats, and its fine stone buildings at Elwyn, near Media, where it was removed are noticeable from the railroad. Dr. Alfred L. Elwyn was the originator of this institution. [See Scharf & Westcott's History of Philadelphia, Vol. II, pp. 1457-8 and p. 1462.]

THE FRIENDS' HOME FOR CHILDREN,

Organized A. D. 1881, and incorporated February, 1882, No. 3401 Germantown road. The good object is to protect orphans, and others who need care-takers, and find them homes. President, Jesse Cleaver; vice-President, Dr. Sarah T. Rogers; Secretary, Edwin L. Peirce; Corresponding Secretary, Mary F. L. Connard; Treasurer, Thomas J. Whitney.

THE ELLEN BUTLER MEMORIAL.

This Home was founded in 1882 by Edgar H. Butler, Esq., as a memorial to his deceased wife. It is in charge of a Board of Directors, and informally connected with St. Luke's (Episcopal) Church, Germantown. Its object is to provide a home for gentlewomen who, from sickness, reduced circumstances or want of employment, shall be in need of such a home, either temporarily or permanently.

THE GERMANTOWN HORTICULTURAL SOCIETY

Was instituted to encourage the cultivation of flowers. At its exhibitions premiums are given, and the town shows that it is a flower-loving community. In 1874, the late John Jay Smith was President and Charles H. Miller, Galloway C. Miller and Alfred C. Lambdin, vice-Presidents; George C. Lambdin, Secretary; T. L. Leavitt, M. D., Treasurer.

The following from the GERMANTOWN TELEGRAPH of October 16, 1889, gives further information on this Society.

At the regular monthly meeting of the Germantown Horticultural Society last Thursday evening, Prof. Thomas Meehan delivered a lecture on the plants on exhibition. The following premiums were awarded: For the best specimen plant, Maranta macoyana, first premium to Henry Nelson, gardener to Mrs. Chandler; second, Diffenbachia, to Michael Sammon, gardener to J.

M. Shoemaker. For the best collection of vegetables, twelve distinct varieties, first to William S. Beesley, gardener to Benjamin Homer. For the best collection of pears, three varieties of six each, to Henry Nelson. For the best hanging basket, to Robert Morrison, gardener to B. Ketchum. Special premiums were awarded to Robert Morrison for a Platycemum Alcicorne and an Acalphya; to Mrs. Hopkins, for a Sedum; special mention to William Beesley, for a collection of sixteen vegetables; to Meehan & Son for a Callicarpa purpurea and a Berberis thunbergia, and to Mr. Benjamin Shoemaker for a fruited branch of Gink-go.

Professor Meehan, in referring to the yew family of trees, spoke of the great English yew tree now standing at Hancock street and Pomona Terrace, on the Amos. R. Little property. He said that he understood that the ground on which it stood had been sold for building purposes, and that there was a chance that it might be destroyed to make room for improvements. He thought that it was unfortunate that such a noble tree with the historical record which it had must be cut down. He suggested that a subscription should be raised for the purchase of and the transplanting of it to some public grounds. The following extract from the *Public Ledger* of July 25th contains a history of this remarkable tree, and shows the propriety of the Professor's suggestions: "At one corner of the Little mansion is a venerable specimen of the English yew, the divided trunks of which measure 14 feet 10 inches in girth in the aggregate, while the branches cover a radius of 129 feet. Its height is over 20 feet. The tree many years ago was struck by lightning, when the trunk was divided and a portion of the tree was killed. New growth, however, soon filled up the spaces, and the tree to-day is a marvel of symmetry and beauty. It is claimed that this tree is the largest, oldest and handsomest of the kind in this country, and quite as large as some of the most famous ones in the churchyards of England, some of which are over two thousand years old. The latter were planted for the purpose of making bows, it being considered the best wood for that purpose, and the churchyards were selected as the place of growth, because it was thought that there they were less liable to be cut down. Just who planted this local specimen in its present location is unknown, although it is claimed, with some show of reason, that it was done through Colonel Forrest, a former owner of the place, in 1758, and that it was an aged tree when it was planted there. One hundred and fifty years is considered a low estimate of its age."

The old officers were renominated for another year. The next meeting of the Society will be the Annual Chrysanthemum Exhibition, which will be held on November 6th, 7th and 8th, in St. Vincent's Hall.

The following extracts are from the GERMANTOWN TELEGRAPH of November 6th, A. D. 1889:

The Germantown Flower Mission during the summer sent 1321 bouquets to the City Mission; 322 to the Germantown Hospital, also a quantity of fruit and loose flowers; thirty-eight bunches of flowers to the Jewish Hospital. One hundred and forty-five visits were made to sick people, who in all cases received ice-cream, fruit and vegetables.

The report of the Germantown Relief Society for the quarter ending September 30th, just issued, shows: 184 applications for assistance, seven new applicants, forty-six old ones, two cases not needing relief, forty-nine grants allowed to the amount of $152 and 118 visits paid.

The fifth annual donation day of the Pennsylvania Society for the Prevention of Cruelty to Animals, on Monday, resulted in the receipt of $433.

The new building for the Germantown Electric Light Company, now being erected, will contain power sufficient for 20,000 incandescent lights and 120 arc lights of the Edison system.

GERMANTOWN ORCHESTRAL SOCIETY.

The first concert of the season given by the Germantown Orchestral Society took place last evening in Association Hall, Germantown, under the direction of Mr. Otto L. Kehrwieder. The audience was quite large, and a creditable performance was given. The soloists were Mrs. Bell Dixon, soprano; Mr. William Geiger, violinist; Mr. Harry J. Dahl, cornetist. Zither quartette: Messrs. C. and H. Faltermayer, E. Oswald and O. Koch. John Dyson was the accompanist. The second concert will be given next February.

PHILADELPHIA INQUIRER, November 22d, 1889.

In closing "Ancient Germantown" the reflection arises that every house and individual is an interesting study; and if one hereafter writes of "Modern Germantown," he may find much more of interest.

"SCENE ON THE WISSAHICKON."
FROM WATSON'S ANNALS, BY PERMISSION OF EDWIN S. STUART, PUBLISHER.

MOUNT AIRY.

Mount Airy.

Mount Airy is an indefinite name, and has, perhaps, in olden time extended as far down into Germantown as Washington lane, as that was the northern border of the old town; but it seems proper to refer it to the tract which begins at Carpenter street and Gorgas lane, which are on opposite sides of Germantown road, and ends at Mermaid lane, and I shall so use it. This was the limit of the new borough. Mermaid lane is the upper boundary of Mount Airy. The southern boundary of "Ancient Germantown" was a little below Duy's lane; the northern boundary was the road to Abington, now Washington street. This covered about 1¼ miles, for the length of the old town, which was divided into 52 *pieces* of land of about equal size. [Townsend Ward's "Germantown Road," *Pa. Mag. of Hist.*, No. 4, Vol. V, p. 373.]

The name is said to come from the airy position of the district, and the ground rises as we leave Carpenter street. It is believed to have been given by Chief Justice Allen to his country-seat, and to have been widened out to embrace the district. The Judge bought his place about A. D. 1750. Scull's first map at the Historical Society of Pennsylvania Library is dated 1759, and the name Mount Airy is marked on it, as well as on a subsequent map of his, dated 1775. The date shows that the Judge might have been the father of the name. It is natural to allow some fancy in the use of the term "Mount."

A little child of my acquaintance once defined a mountain as "a velly high hill indeed," but Mount Airy hardly answers that description, though it is a high and airy position. Camp and Militia Hill, at White Marsh, and the higher hills beyond them, and the Welsh mountains in Berks county, and the noble Allegheny and other ranges show that Pennsylvania is blessed with an abundance of hills; it is believed that hills are an aid to freedom, and Mount Airy saw a conflict which may be named with the struggles of Swiss heroes among the Alps.

Across the road from the depot at Gorgas lane, on the Reading R. R., lies a mansion and farm belonging to the Unruh family, who were old settlers in this region, and two of whose places have been described by Mr. Butcher in these sketches.

Gorgas lane derives its name from another old family of note.

Watson says: "All the settlers in Cresheim built on the Cresheim road before settling a house on the Germantown road through Cresheim. There is an old map, made in 1700, in which all their residences and barns at that time are marked." Annals Vol. II, p. 18. The old term Cresheim is still somewhat used for the section along Cresheim road, which runs from Allen's lane to Wissahickon avenue. Gorgas lane, near Main street, has an old stone on the south side with the initials of the names of the original land owners marked on it. Cresheim lay between Roxborough and Bristol townships. In old sales of land in this tract, the division was made in long strips, as in Germantown, as can be seen in a plot in E. V. Lansdale's office, at 210 South Fourth street, which was kindly submitted to my inspection. I will add some notes taken from it as to early owners. Cornelius Tyson had seventy-five acres running from Bristol township line to Cresheim road. Reice Potts had fifty acres below him. Henry Sellen's strip from Bristol to Roxborough township came next, containing one hundred acres. Then follows William Strepers with fifty acres, Johannes Bleikers with one hundred acres, reaching the Limekiln road as a lower boundary. Crossing that road Gerrard Rittinghousen held fifty acres, and Derrick Sellen fifty acres.

Judge Allen bought a portion of his land of Conrad Widner, and it is supposed that he constructed the mansion. Andrew Allen, Jr., received from Judge Allen, his grandfather, by a will made 1769, the property. He sold to Lewis Anastosius Tarascon, a Frenchman. Blondin Constant, a well-known French refugee, afterwards acquired it. Aug. Lewis Rumford afterward owned it and conveyed it to William E. Rogers, brother-in-law of Gen. Meigs, the celebrated engineer. His widow, Harriette P., sold it to Jas. Gowen in 1846.

The first building on the left in going beyond Carpenter street on Germantown avenue is an old inn called "The Farmers and Drovers' Hotel, at the corner of Main and Carpenter streets, now kept by Mr. Scull. It is a narrow four-story building, jutting high into the air, with its dormer-windowed attic, making a fifth story. It is rare to see such a high, lofty building in the country. On the upper side a one-story addition with a high chimney gives a quaint appearance to the house. About sixty years ago Andrew Trellinger owned the place and kept the hotel. He also possessed considerable property in Mount Airy. There was once a private school in the upper wing. Daniel Heilig was the teacher. Mr. John Bishop, living in Mechan avenue, was a pupil. He has given me valuable information as to this region. Charles Neil occupied the hotel for several years. Matthias Craig and Henry Barnett were two who succeeded him, though not directly, after his departure. It belongs to George W. Carpenter's estate. Mr. Carpenter raised the building. It used to be styled the "Shot Factory" by boys, from its height. The original building runs back in its history to the Revolution. It was once the election place for both the upper and lower wards of German township, which then included Chestnut Hill. This has long been a favorite stopping place with farmers.

William Leibert, son of Peter Leibert, erected the house opposite Gorgas lane, and lived there until his death. The house is now the residence of his great-grandson, William Leibert. This is one of the old families of Germantown.

Anthony Johnson lived in an old-fashioned double stone house opposite the tavern. He used to wear breeches and buckles. He died over fifty years ago. He owned much property in this vicinity. Samuel Welsh is building new cottages on a part of his old farm in Carpenter street. Johnson had, perhaps, over 100 acres of land. He was one of the old settlers.

Opposite the Lutheran Orphanage is a field which belonged to Anthony Thomas. It was called "The Ten-Acre Field," and ran from Leibert's boardyard to Rush's. It was for years used as a place of review for the volunteer militia soldiers of Germantown and vicinity, about forty years ago, which was a delight to the boys. Tents were placed at hand where eatables were sold. Colonel Roumfort, President of Mount Airy College, used to conduct the review, and inspected the regiments every spring. Sometimes a sham battle enlivened the scene. Captain Huston, of the Lafayette Guards, and Lieutenant Frederick Fleming were among the officers. The Germantown Blues were present, and a Holmesburg Horse Company. The various companies formed a battalion.

Those passing the Lutheran Orphanage and the Home for the Aged have noticed these fine buildings conveniently connected by piazzas. The Home is of red brick, diversified with black stripes. The Superintendent, Mr. C. F. Kuhnle, kindly gives the following sketch:

LUTHERAN HOME.

Philadelphia has been justly noted for its many charitable and benevolent institutions. Among these the "Orphans' Home and Asylum for the Aged and Infirm of the Evangelical Lutheran Church at Germantown" holds a conspicuous place.

The design of founding a Home in Germantown dates back to 1852, but nothing definite was done until 1858, and on the 18th of March, 1859, the first child was received into a small house on Main street, which, however, soon proved too small and inconvenient. In October of the same year the property on Main street above Carpenter, where the institution now stands, was purchased. It has a front on Main street of 138 feet, and extends back 1075 feet to Cresheim road. The design from the first was to provide a home for destitute orphan children, without regard to creed or country. The first charter is dated June 4, 1860, and was subsequently amended by an Act of Legislature, and the institution exempted from taxation. In 1862 a building was put up for a school and dormitory for the boys.

When so many children were made orphans during the late war, this institution was among the first to open its doors for these soldiers' orphans, and 98 were admitted up to the time when the State provided homes for them. In 1865 the corner stone was laid for a large and suitable building to accommodate at least 80 children, which was finished in 1866 at a cost of $30,000. Although at times under clouds, the institution has prospered and grown more in favor with the Lutheran Church and community at large. In 1879 a building 140 feet long and 40 feet wide, with wings at the ends of 60 feet, was erected for the accommodation of the old and infirm, and was occupied May 1, 1880, after its cost of $20,000 had been raised by voluntary contributions, so that no debt remained. The grounds and buildings have been much improved during late years. Fronting on Main street is about an acre of well-kept lawn, dotted with flower-beds and planted with fruit trees. In the rear is a kitchen garden of about 2 acres, where all the vegetables needed for the institution are raised, with the exception of potatoes. The garden, with the help of one hired man and the assistance of the older boys under the management of the superintendent, is one of the best-cultivated gardens in Germantown.

The asylum for the old people is of brick with basement, two stories and mansard roof and is heated throughout by steam. It contains a large dining-room, chapel, parlor, two sitting-rooms, and thirty-five bed-rooms. Each inmate has a room to himself. A special feature are two porches, each one hundred feet long and twelve wide, sheltered for east, west, and north, and facing the lawn.

The orphanage is a stone building sixty feet square with a basement, three stories and attic. The basement contains the children's dining-room, playroom, kitchen, laundry and bath-room. The latter is so arranged that the children can learn to swim. The first floor is occupied by the main schoolroom, superintendent's dining-room and office, and the parlor; the next has the kindergarten, superintendent's and assistant's bed-room, and the sewing-room, and on the third are the children's dormitories. The building has three separate stairways from the basement to the dormitories, and in addition is provided with a regular fire escape on the outside. The play ground is large where the children enjoy themselves when they are not at work or in the schoolroom. Of the five hundred and forty-six children received into the Home from the beginning many are now engaged in the various occupations of life. Three of the boys are now pursuing their studies to prepare for the ministry. There are now in the Home fifty-five boys and twenty-five girls. In the Asylum thirty-one have a home, some of whom have nearly reached four score and ten. Thus from a small beginning this institution has grown to a considerable magnitude, and is in a prosperous condition and deserves the support of all kind-hearted and generous people.

The Hon. Horatio Gates Jones, in his History of the Levering Family, p. 186, mentions a MS. volume of the poetry of the hermit Kelpius, translated into English verse by Dr. Christopher Witt, who was Kelpius's friend, which was owned by John Leibert, of Mt Airy. A portrait of Kelpius, painted by Dr. Witt, is prefixed to the volume. The Latin Journal of Kelpius is in the possession of C. J. Wister. Kelpius died at the early age of thirty-five, in

MOUNT AIRY.

A. D. 1708, according to one of his followers, John Schlee (called Selig), in Latin Seeligius.

It should be stated that the property on which the Lutheran Orphans' Home and Asylum for the Aged stands, formerly belonged to Jacob Derr.

Next above the Lutheran Home, on the same side of the way, is the residence of Mr. Thomas Garrett, who is a manufacturing chemist. Just above this house lies the pleasant abode of his mother, Mrs. Garrett, with its ample lawn and hedge.

THE STEAMBOAT HOUSE.

It is a coincidence that as there used to be in the Great Valley, in Chester county, a public house called The Ship, and another near it styled The Steamboat, so Germantown boasts a Ship House and Mt. Airy a Steamboat House. It sounded strange in former years to hear the conductor on the Pennsylvania Railroad call out the station "Steamboat," in a hilly district, at a distance from any navigable stream, but modern civilization has changed the old name of the Chester county depot to Glen Loch. The Mount Airy Steamboat House is on the right in leaving Germantown, between Mount Pleasant avenue and Sedgwick street. It is owned by Mrs. Bostwick, who resides in it. The Grecian pillared front of the mansion faces toward Germantown. There is a fine lawn in front of it. Mrs. Bostwick has altered the quaint roof into a Mansard one. There is a bay window at the side of the porch and a back building with a piazza. The construction is peculiar. Mrs. Admiral Breese, a sister of Mrs. Bostwick, has a modern gray stone residence on the same lawn, just south of the Steamboat House. A fine natural terrace is in front. There is quite an elevation of the lawn above the street. The Steamboat House was formerly owned by Mr. Erasmus James Pierce. He had been a sea captain. The top of the house formerly had a flat roof, framed into the appearance of the hurricane deck of a steamer. This part, at least, was built by Mr. Pierce. He was a manufacturer of umbrellas in the city and lost his health, and sought this pleasant country home. He tried to establish the silk business here, and many mulberry trees still remain on the old farm as relics of those days. He had large cocooneries and raised many silk worms, but did not find the business profitable. He lost tens of thousands of dollars in this speculation. He employed a great many men in his different undertakings. His son, the Rev. E. J. Pierce, a Presbyterian clergyman in Farmingdale, New Jersey, writes me that in his own boyhood there was no church in the neighborhood, and that when he returned from Dartmouth College he "turned his father's old cocooneries into Sabbath schools, and now I rejoice in the thought that on the old farm there is an active, live Presbyterian church." The reference is to the parish of which Rev. Mr. White is the energetic pastor. The city residence of Mr. Pierce was in Sansom street, between Seventh and Eighth streets, on the south side, near the house of the artist, John Sartain. One of Mr. Pierce's daughters married Mr. Drown and another married Captain Landis.

Mr. Pierce was above medium height and of a cheerful and sociable disposition. He was quick in movement. He owned quite a tract of land, which is now cut up, on which Mr. Tourison is erecting a double cottage of modern design.

The Steamboat House became the property of a gentleman named Miller, who owned it about thirty years ago. At that time the flower beds were elevated and walled around with brick or stone, so that the lady who had the oversight of them was not required to stoop while performing her pleasant duties.

Mr. Pierce probably introduced the umbrella business into Philadelphia, having perhaps noticed their general use in China. The umbrella had long been carried in London, but was not common in this country, though probably many were imported. The business was profitable, as there was little competition.

No. 5635, east side, may be marked by a quaint old iron foot scraper, which naturally drew the attention of a friend of mind in passing, and led to a query about a house which could boast so antique an appendage. The worthy and useful scraper has held its position for over sixty years, and has cleaned the shoes made by two generations of shoemakers. The shoes, and many of their wearers have departed. "Still stands the scraper primeval," if Longfellow will pardon the adaptation. May it scrape coming generations of feet for many a day. The house spoken of is the residence of the Derr family. They are carriage makers. In 1810, Abraham Deavs and Martha Cadwallader, executors of Abraham Deavs, the elder, deeded the place to Samuel Deavs. It passed into the hands of Benjamin Lehman and wife in 1813. They sold to Thomas Arthur in 1814. Thomas Arthur sold to John Smith, and in 1824, John Smith conveyed the property to Jacob Derr. His son, Jacob F. Derr, inherited it, and it now belongs to his children. Carriagemaking has been carried on by this family for over sixty years in the present shop, and in the building used as A. Haas's Gentlemen's Furnishing Store, which was formerly a shop.

GRACE CHURCH.

On the 18th of May, 1858, several gentlemen met at Christ Church Rectory to take steps toward forming a parish in Mt. Airy. Mr. W. E. Stone was made Secretary, and the following persons were nominated as the first Vestrymen: C. S. Carstairs, Henry Berry, Thomas H. Powers, A. S. Robinson, S. L. Crentzborg, W. E. Stone, P. E. Hamm, Clem Tingley, Jr., Eli Burrhouse and Beekman Potter. "The Church of the Messiah" was first selected as the name, but finally changed to "Grace." A charter was procured, steps were taken to erect a chapel, and by the aid of the ladies through a fair held in the Town Hall of Germantown, and subscriptions amounting to $900, they were able to accomplish that object. Rev. Thomas Yocum, who was assisting at Christ Church, supplied services on Sunday afternoons. By November, 1864, it was

GRACE CHURCH, MOUNT AIRY, ON GOWEN AVENUE.

MOUNT AIRY. 355

necessary to enlarge the building, which was done at a cost of $2255.47. At this time Rev. Mr. Yocum resigned, and the Rev. J. Saunders Reed was elected rector, at a salary of seven hundred dollars, Christ Church furnishing three hundred of the amount. Rev. Mr. Reed having declined, Rev. J. R. Moore was elected and declined, then the Rev. Dr. Shiras was elected. Dr. Shiras apparently declined and so did Rev. John E. Ames. Finally the Rev. Edward Hale, in May, 1866, accepted the rectorship, salary one thousand dollars, but remained only two months. August 12, 1866, Rev. R. A. Edwards was elected rector. February 6, 1874, the resignation of Mr. Edwards was accepted, he having been called to Holy Trinity Memorial Chapel. Rev. S. C. Hill was elected to fill the vacancy on February 24, 1874, but declined. March 14, 1874, Rev. E. A. Reddles was elected rector and resigned February, 1875. Rev. E. H. Kettle was elected, but declined. April 15, 1875, the Rev. S. C. Hill was elected and accepted, and took charge the first Sunday in June, 1875.

The parish needs a larger church building, and desires another location, and is to erect a new church on a lot on the Gowen estate, at the southwest corner of Gowen avenue and Main street. The building will be built of stone from the vicinity and will be 100x78 feet in size. It will have a nave, aisles and baptistery, also a tower 90 feet high. The vestibule will be under the tower. The interior will be diversified by colored bricks. Steam heat will be used. Charles M. Burns is the architect. The cost will be about $18,000. The old church will be utilized for the Sunday school, until a year after the new church is completed, when it is expected that a parish building will be built in the new location. The lot is 90 by 120. The rector is to be congratulated on this advancement in parish life.

The Rev. S. C. Hill has contributed the above sketch of the history of this parish.

The following account of the consecration of the new Grace Church is from the "STANDARD OF THE CROSS AND THE CHURCH," of November 29, A. D. 1889. Rev. Dr. Atkins, and Rev. Mr. Edwards were former rectors of the church.

CONSECRATION OF THE NEW GRACE CHURCH, MT. AIRY.

On Wednesday, November 13th, Bishop Whitaker consecrated the new, substantial and symmetrical edifice of Grace Church at Gowen and Ardleigh avenues, Mt. Airy. Rev. S. C. Hill is rector of the parish. More than sixty clergymen in surplices attended the service, those to whom parts of the service were assigned being the Rev. Drs. Atkins, Upjohn, Harris, Perry, Watson, Murphy and Falkner and Rev. R. A. Edwards. The sermon was by Rt. Rev. Dr. Whitehead, Bishop of Pittsburg. After thanking his seminary classmate, the rector, for the invitation to preach, and congratulating him and the Bishop of the Diocese, upon the erection of this and so many noble churches which are rising in this region, he announced the text, Esther 5 : 2 : "And it was so, when the king saw Esther the queen standing in the court, that she obtained favor in his sight; and the king held out to Esther the golden scepter that was in his hand. So Esther drew near and touched the top of the scepter." Picturing the timid approach of the queen, forfeiting thereby, under custom, her life, but being graciously received, the Right Reverend preacher used the event as illustrative of the Doctrine of God's Grace, a subject suggested by the name of the church. Our thought of God determines what kind of worship we offer Him. St. Peter declares him to be the God of all grace, and we recognize it as the language of experience and penitence. The Church has never narrowed the message of God's grace. She ever stands bidding men reach out the hand to touch the Incarnation. Observation shows that men will naturally believe anything rather than the abundance of God's grace. The bearing of the message fully has its effect on the worship of the Church. Each church building becomes a witness of grace. The sacraments assume the chief place in worship, and their celebration becomes even gorgeous. Those who minimize Christian doctrine are most afraid of what they call externals of worship. The Church is not merely the messenger, but the very body of Christ, herself filled with His grace. In conclusion, the Bishop invoked the richest blessings upon rector and congregation in the use of this church, saying: "The Lord hear thee in the day of trouble; the Name of the God of Jacob defend thee, send thee help from the sanctuary, and strengthen thee out of Zion; remember all thy offerings and accept thy sacrifice; grant thee thy heart's desire and fulfill all thy mind." After the service the clergy were invited to luncheon at the residence of Mr. Franklin B. Gowen.

MT. AIRY PRESBYTERIAN CHURCH.

The Rev. Mr. White sends me the following history, which he prepared for *The Chronicle*. Mr. Wm. H. Scott kindly loans the plate which represents the church in this article.

During the latter part of the year 1879, there was inaugurated a movement in the interests of Presbyterianism in Mount Airy.

Sabbath preaching was instituted by Rev. William Travis, and a Sabbath School organized in the church edifice built by the United Brethren denomination, on Mount Airy avenue.

The Presbyterian churches of Germantown were early aroused to the importance of the locality as a mission station, and appointed the following committee to have charge of it: John T. Roberts of the Market Square Church, George F. Wiggan of the Second Church, F. B. Reeves of the Wakefield Church, and John Johnson, James Lorimer, and E. G. James of the mission. The first meeting of the above committee was held January 27th, 1880, at which time it was resolved to lease for one year the building temporarily occupied by the mission on Mount Airy avenue.

February 26th, 1880, Rev. John Rutherford was employed by the committee, as stated supply for the mission.

THE MOUNT AIRY PRESBYTERIAN CHURCH.

MOUNT AIRY.

On the 5th of October, 1880, the Presbytery of Philadelphia North, in answer to a petition presented by Elder Wiggan, appointed Revs. Drs. Knox, Owen, Cowan, McFetridge, and Elders Henry, Van Horn and Wiggan, a committee to visit Mount Airy, and, if the way be clear, to organize a Presbyterian church in that place.

This was accordingly done, November 9th, 1880. Twenty-four persons united in the organization—nineteen by letter from other churches, and five on confession of faith.

Rev. John Rutherford resigned as stated supply, October 4th, 1880. For the next seven months, the church had no regular supply.

At the fall meeting (1882) of the Presbytery the propriety of abandoning the field and dissolving the church was considered. Finally Rev. J. W. Kirk, Elders John T. Roberts, Francis B. Reeves and William H. Scott were appointed a committee to look after the church and complete the organization.

Up to December 24th, 1880, at which time Mr. John Lunn was ordained Ruling Elder, there was no regular session of the church, and hence it was but imperfectly organized. A few persons were admitted to membership, in connection with Elders from churches of Germantown, commissioned by Presbytery.

April 4th, 1883, Rev. W. P. White was elected pastor of the church.

He removed to Mount Airy, May 19th, and took charge of the church, preaching his first sermon May 20th, 1883. He was not installed pastor, however, until December 4th.

BUILDING THE CHAPEL.

The Church entered upon its most vigorous career when, having obtained a pastor, it began the construction of a house of worship for itself.

The lot on the corner of Germantown avenue and Mount Pleasant street, being one of the most beautiful for location in the Twenty-second Ward, was purchased in February, 1883. Plans for a chapel on the rear of the lot were designed by George T. Pearson, architect.

The corner-stone being ready to be laid, religious exercises were held on the site of the chapel, Sabbath afternoon, May 27. The pastor-elect presided. Addresses were made by Rev. J. W. Bain, pastor of the Alexander Church, Philadelphia, and General Louis Wagner. Prayer was offered by Rev. J. E. Wright, of Market Square Church, Germantown.

The chapel was dedicated September 30th, 1883.

At the morning service, the sermon was preached by Rev. A. A. Hodge, D. D., LL. D., of Princeton Theological Seminary.

In the afternoon, addresses were made by Revs. W. J. Chichester, J. W. Teal, and N. S. McFetridge, D. D., of Germantown, and Rev. Alfred Nevin, D. D., of Philadelphia. The prayer of dedication was offered by Rev. J. E. Wright, pastor of Market Square Church.

In the evening a sermon was preached by Rev. S. A. Mutchmore, D. D., of Philadelphia.

At the afternoon service, it was announced that still there was needed $784.34, in order to dedicate the chapel free of debt.

In a very few moments a note was read by Dr. McFetridge, signed "Incognito," in which the writer agreed to assume the entire amount.

There was remaining the cost of the lot, amounting to $3250, and the indications of Providence were that effort should be made to raise it. Before the evening service was held, a warm friend and faithful helper of the Mount Airy Church agreed to contribute $1000 of the entire amount. Two others agreed to assume $500 each. The balance was guaranteed, during the evening, by friends present.

The Installation of Rev. W. P. White, as pastor of the Mount Airy Presbyterian Church, took place December 4th, 1883. Owing to the illness of Rev. W. J. Chichester, some change was necessary in the programme. As carried out, Rev. J. W. Teal presided, proposed the constitutional questions, and made the installing prayer. Rev. S. C. Logan, D. D., of Scranton, preached the sermon; Rev. J. E. Wright, of Germantown, charged the pastor, and Rev. J. H. M. Knox, D. D., president of Lafayette College, charged the people.

The additional facts which follow show that Mr. White has had a successful ministry. The church is a pretty edifice of wood.

The following is the report of the Presbytery for the second year (1885)—Total number of communicants, 56; added on examination, 5; added by letter, 4; adults baptised, 1; contributed to Home Missions, $71; Foreign Missions, $46; Education, $24; Relief Fund, $26; Publication, $5; Freedmen, $15; Presbyterial Assessment and Mileage Fund, $7.64; Congregational, $5,650.

During the second year of Mr. White's ministry (1885) he built and paid for a parsonage and the following is what the Board of Trustees said of it.

Early in last year it was resolved to undertake the building of a parsonage and, with the exception of providing the lot, the whole burden of the undertaking was thrown upon the Pastor of the congregation, and your Board cannot speak too highly of his energy and zeal. We have only been able in this report to present a partial statement of the Parsonage Fund as the accounts are still open, but we can say that the cost of the building independent of the lot is over $4000, and that this amount, with the exception of about $100, has already been secured by your faithful Pastor.

MOUNT PLEASANT AVENUE M. E. CHURCH, MOUNT AIRY.

On the third of April, A. D. 1887, this parish celebrated its tenth anniversary, and Robert Thomas, Esq., read a history, and the Rev. G. M. Broadhead has kindly loaned me the manuscript. In 1854, Rev. Newton Heston was in charge of the Methodist Church in Germantown, and had a class and Sunday School at Mount Pleasant, which met in the upper story of a building belonging to Erasmus James Pierce, Esq., next to the property of Jacob Derr. Sunday afternoon services, and a week day evening service were held, generally by some local preacher or exhorter from Germantown, and the congregations were good.

In 1856 the church in Germantown was divided, and Mr. Heston assumed charge of the new congregation, called St. Stephen's. In 1857 he left Germantown, the Mt. Airy mission grew weaker, and when the building used by it was sold, the work was given up.

In 1874 Rev. Joseph Mason became pastor of the Haines Street Church, Germantown, and a number of his parishioners lived about Mt. Airy, belonging to the class of Mr. Neilson which had its place of meeting at the leader's house, in Franklin street. In 1875 this class met on the second floor of the Odd Fellows' Hall corner of Germantown and Mt. Airy avenues. A Sunday School was begun here, being a branch, or mission school of the Haines street parish. Charles M. Dungan was the superintendent, and Christian Smith became class leader. Sunday services were resumed by local preachers and exhorters. The hall was used for about two years.

In the summer of 1876 a committee of seven of the Christian brethren and sisters was appointed to endeavor to secure the lot on the west corner of Mt. Pleasant avenue and Bryan street, and to raise a thousand dollars for a chapel. The committee were: Gavin Neilson, Edward Savage, Henry Smith, Enos F. Hesser, Mrs. Charles M. Dungan, Mrs. Christian Smith and Mrs. Hesser. They added to their number Thomas B. Cope, R. S. Woddropp, William McCarthur, John T. Walker. The committee were successful, and Gavin Neilson took the title for the lot in his name, with a ground rent. A chapel was built and dedicated to the worship of Almighty God on Sunday, March 25th, 1877, when the bell called the waiting people together to the Lord's House. The building committee were John Sowden, William Benner, Gavin Neilson, Charles M. Dungan, and Robert Thomas. The Reverend Messrs. Joseph Mason, J. B. McCullough, and Andrew Longacre, of the Philadelphia Conference, and Rev. Dr. E. H. Stokes, of the New Jersey Conference, assisted in the dedication services. The next Sunday, April 1st, Rev. A. F. Dotterer, junior pastor of the Haines Street Church, took charge of the mission. A debt which was incurred in building was afterward paid. Edward Savage, in manhood, and Enos T. Hesser, in youth, who had been active in church work, were called to their heavenly reward before the chapel was finished. In 1880 the congregation bought an additional piece of land on Mt. Pleasant avenue, and in 1881 the ground rent which had stood against the church property, was extinguished, making the parish free of debt. In 1885 the congregation was incorporated with the following trustees: Thomas B. Cope, Robert Thomas, Robert T. Laughlin, Richard W. P. Goff, John T. Walker, Gavin Neilson, Charles K. Lippincott, Charles C. Crawford, and David Cliffe.

The list of pastors is as follows: Rev. Messrs. A. F. Dotterer, F. H. Moore, H. R. Robinson, and G. M. Broadhead, who is now in charge. The present trustees are Thomas B. Cope, John T. Walker, Charles T. Crawford, Francis Vogel, George H. Wilson, Gavin Neilson, Robert T. Laughlin, Robert Thomas, and George L. Taggart, Robert Thomas, Esq., is Secretary.

The *Philadelphia Methodist*, of April 9th, 1887, gives a pleasant account of the tenth anniversary of the parish. " The music and flowers and the large congregations made the fine spring day joyous. The pastor and John T. Walker, superintendent of the Sunday School, supervised the arrangement. Rev. Messrs. J. F. Meredith, A. F. Dotterer, J. B. McCullough, Rev. Mr. White, of the Presbyterian Church of Mt. Airy, and Rev. J. H. Hargis, of Germantown, and Hargis Dotterer made addresses at the three services which were held during the day." This account makes the establishment of the first regular service in 1851, by Rev. A. Longacre, before Rev. Newton Heston organized a class.

Squire Thomas informs me that in the early days of Methodism in Germantown, Bishop Asbury visited the place and preached in it. Mr. Thomas has made a study of Methodist local history, and is well informed concerning it. Services were sometimes held by the Methodists in the Germantown Academy.

OLD MOUNT PLEASANT INN.

The lower depot of Mount Airy and the surrounding section bears the name Mount Pleasant, I presume, from the pleasant position, and this comfortable and neat boarding house which has refreshed Philadelphians in the summer for years has adopted the name. The position is high, and the grounds commodious, and adorned with trees. In 1824 Edward Bonsall had a drug store in this building. John Miller enlarged the house and kept a store in it. He was an uncle of Franklin B. Gowen, Esq. He and his wife died at this place. For years the Gorgas family kept a boarding house here. The house is roughcast and has a neat and pleasant appearance.

The second house above Mount Pleasant avenue on the east side of Germantown avenue is an old stone building with this inscription in front, 17 W. Hottenstein 95. It was built by William Hottenstein, in 1795. He was the grandfather of Miss Mary Hottenstein, residing on Rex avenue, Chestnut Hill. He was a saddler, and his shop was next door below, and was moved to a point a little above Dr. Gilbert's by Martin Painter, who used it as a dwelling. It was afterward enlarged. William's son Isaac owned an old stone house which faced Germantown avenue, and the side was on Pleasant street. Pleasant street was cut through what was Isaac Hottenstein's property, but at that time it belonged to Erasmus J. Pierce, the umbrella manufacturer. Isaac Hottenstein moved to Chestnut Hill in 1831. The old house has been altered and improved. Isaac Hottenstein kept a store in the house. He invented a machine to make carter's lashes, and made quantities of them. His only brother Jacob was drowned in the Wissahickon. In crossing the stream, on a moonlight night in 1808, he made a mistake, and fell into the creek. It was New Year's night and several were with him. His burial place was at St. Michael's. The boys were born in Reading. William Hottenstein went west to secure western land, and died at Columbus, Ohio, on his homeward road.

Next above the Hottenstein house, with its ancient date, is a nice stone house which belonged to Mr. Schugard. It is a double house which he rented to tenants. The dwelling next above this house was Mr. Schugard's own residence. Both houses are standing. The son of the proprietor, named Henry, was a saddler. He lived and died at this abode. Mr. E. J. Pierce bought these houses. Afterward the larger house was purchased by Mr. Robert Thomas and the smaller one by Mr. Samuel Graver who lives in it.

Below Mount Airy College, on the left, was the Keyser family, who owned a frame and brick house but the road to Ivy Hill is on their site. Next below Keyser's was Adam Breish's old tavern, which is demolished. Thomas's Lumber Yard was a part of Mr. Hoffman's property. Two sons were brushmakers and had a shop there. One named George went out west, another named Jacob moved to Manayunk and kept a hotel and died there. An old pupil, whom I have met went to school on Allen's lane, on the upper side at the top of the hill. The present school house is on the opposite side. Mr. McDonald was the teacher about 69 years ago. Mrs. McDonald taught the girls to sew. An Englishman named Mr. Thomas was afterward the teacher and afterward Jacob Bockius held the position. The present school house is the third one. This pupil lived on the lower corner of Main street and Gowen avenue, on the left side. Garret Rittenhouse used to be seen by the younger generation sitting on his porch, next to Mr. Jos. Miller's place.

Adam Bickert had a double stone house on the left near the store. Mr. Hoffman's house joined the wall of Mr. Bickert's mansion.

The old house on the east side of Germantown avenue occupied by Joseph Casper Weiss has been in his possession over sixty years. It formerly belonged to the Nice family. A part of it has been removed. The old stone house on the hillside below the Mt. Airy Boarding House, belonged to a family named Lightcap. It is now owned by Franklin B. Gowen, and occupied by the Hamilton family. The ancient pretty stone dwelling opposite the end of Gowen avenue, occupied by Mr. Church, belonged to the Wolf estate. It is the oldest house on the Wolf property. The house is a part of the nursery property, belonging to Miller & Yates, which gives beauty to the Germantown road, and carries the seeds of beauty to many distant places.

Mt. Airy Nurseries were founded by Miller & Yates in 1870. The ivy-covered lower end of Mr. Church's residence is used as a bouquet room. Two aged sisters, named the Misses Oram, dwelt in this section of the house for a great many years. One died here and the other no longer resides in this neighborhood. In the carriage road, within the inclosure, is a well which is used in irrigating the plants. The drivers from up-country used to stop to quench their thirst with this delicious water. A house belonging to Mr. Wolf once stood at this point, and this was its well. Mr. Wolf, for many years kept the grocery store on the upper corner of Gowen avenue and Germantown avenue.

The Mt. Airy Boarding House was formerly a hotel called the "Golden Swan." It is an old structure well known to Philadelphians. It is a roomy building with a piazza.

The Golden Swan Hotel, on what was called the Germantown, Chestnut Hill and Reading turnpike, was kept by John Maison, who was a Frenchman, and a relative of General Maison, of France. He was one of those Huguenots driven out of France in the days of the Du Ponts. The building now in its cheerful yellow color justifies the ancient name of the Golden Swan. The boarding house is kept by Miss Errickson, and belongs to the estate of James Gowen, the father of Franklin B. Gowen, Esq.

No. 4754, opposite the proposed Lutheran Theological Seminary, is the dwelling place of the Misses Ketz. It was built by Jacob Ketz, who owned the property on Allen's lane. Jacob Ketz bought land of Judge Allen.

On the southwest corner of Allen's lane and Germantown road is the Gorgas House, with its stores, marked 5728 and 5730. The house was built by Benjamin Gorgas, Sr., the great-grandfather of the present occupants. Benjamin Gorgas, Jr., lived here with his son Charles, who had bought the property and started a grocery store, which is still carried on, but not by the family. He was a noted and highly respected business man in the neighborhood. At his death the place fell into the hands of his daughter, Miss Julia Gorgas. Mr. Charles Gorgas acted as a useful citizen in improving Allen's lane by constructing several houses on it. He was a man of spirit and enterprise in business. He was appointed Postmaster of Mt. Airy by President Lincoln in 1861, but died in the same year, and Miss Julia Gorgas became Postmistress afterward, and held the office until it ceased to exist on the coming of the letter carriers. Gorgas lane takes its name from Joseph Gorgas, one of the older relatives of this family who held property on that lane. Samuel Gorgas, a son of Charles, kept the Mt. Pleasant Inn, a boarding house, at the corner of Mt. Pleasant avenue and Main street. The Gorgas family are ancient settlers in this neighborhood and are of German stock.

Rev. Peter Keyser was in the lumber business in Philadelphia with one of the Gorgas family. The firm was Keyser & Gorgas. Mr. Keyser used to walk to the city and back from his residence, now occupied by Ellwood Johnson, on Main street, Germantown, near Washington lane.

An old mill in Roxborough, on the Wissahickon creek, was owned by John Gorgas, who lived near Allen's lane. Boone & Carman's factory is on the site. John Gorgas was a tanner and ran the old mill.

Bechtel's Paper Mills were two large stone buildings on the south side of Cresheim creek, about a quarter of a mile above its mouth. The lower mill years ago was used as a woolen spinning mill by Joseph Hill and afterward as a cotton spinning mill by his son, Milton Hill. It has since been unoccupied. It is owned by H. H. Houston. The upper mill, about sixty-five years ago,

MOUNT AIRY COLLEGE.

was owned by Joseph Carr, who made cotton laps. He rented it afterward to Thomas Randall & Son for spinning woolen yarn. It is now unoccupied and owned by Mr. Houston. Above the last mill, on the north side, is a mill, which, about seventy years ago, was owned by David Hinkle and used as a grist mill. His son Jesse continued this business. J. and E. France bought it and used it as a shoddy mill. They sold to David Hey who used it for the same purpose. A fire destroyed it during his ownership and it has been in ruins ever since. Mr. Hey still owns the property. Still further up, on the south side, is a mill, which, forty years since, was owned by J. and E. France, and used as a carpet mill. They sold it to David Hey, who utilized it as a shoddy mill and still uses it for the same purpose. These are all the mills on Cresheim creek and are all between the turnpike bridge and the Wissahickon.

I am indebted to Mr. David Hinkle, of Germantown, for this information:

The lower Bechtel's Paper Mill stood on the Cresheim creek where it empties into the Wissahickon, on the south bank, near Allen's lane railroad station. There was another Bechtel's Paper Mill on the same side of the Cresheim creek about a mile above. The family were papermakers. Peter Bechtel, grandfather of William Bechtel, bought both of these mills about the year 1800. They both fell into the hands of his son Peter, and were worked as paper mills up to 1833. Peter Bechtel, Sr., came from Germany.

Mr. Hill tore down the old lower mill and erected a new one. He purchased Patterson's flour mill, just above, for his work. Colonel Kester was the next owner. There was another flour mill above the upper mill, owned by Mr. Jesse Hinkle. Still above this was a comb factory, afterward used by John and Irwin France as a carpet factory. These proprietors are both dead.

Mr. Bechtel, who has a stationery store in the Post Office building in Germantown, is of the family named. His mother, whose maiden name was Horter, is living at an advanced age. He has kindly given me information as to this matter.

MOUNT AIRY COLLEGE.

[Written for the GERMANTOWN TELEGRAPH.]

> "Ah, happy hills! ah, pleasing shade!
> Ah, fields beloved in vain!
> Where once my careless childhood stray'd,
> A stranger yet to pain!
> I feel the gales that from ye blow,
> A momentary bliss bestow,
> As waving fresh their gladsome wing
> My weary soul they seem to sooth,
> And redolent of joy and youth,
> To breathe a second spring."
> —*Gray's Ode "On a Distant Prospect of Eton College."*

I am indebted to the courtesy of Franklin B. Gowen, Esq., for the preparation of the accompanying valuable engraving of Mount Airy College, once the residence of Judge Allen. The square building of stone, surmounted by the flag, was the Judge's country abode before the Revolution. The long buildings left of it were added when the property became a college under Mr. Constant, a Frenchman. The building farther to the left was the home of Sebastian Miller, the great-grandfather of Franklin B. Gowen. It was torn down by his father, James Gowen, about 1845. The sketch from which the above picture was made was taken in 1828, when the institution was under A. L. Roumfort and called "The American Classical and Military Lyceum." This was demolished by James Gowen in 1848 or 1849, who bought the place in 1846 from the estate of William Rogers, who had made it his country residence for several years.

"In 1750 William Allen, afterwards Chief Justice of Pennsylvania, bought of Matthias Milnes and wife, a lot of ground containing twelve acres, to which he added two years afterward by purchase from William Rittinghausen and wife, twenty-one acres more. The situation was on the east side of the main road from Germantown, above the village, and in Cresheim. Upon that portion of the tract bought from Rittinghausen, a fine large stone house was built by Allen, which was somewhat remarkable in contra-distinction to the country houses of the time, from the fact that it came out to the extreme limit of the main road and even went beyond it, having a porch upon the road in the manner of an arcade, through which the foot passengers might walk at any time. To this seat Allen gave the name which is now given to the neighborhood—'Mount Airy.' The property remained in the possession of the family until long after the Revolution."—Thompson Westcott's History of Philadelphia, chapter 217.

Chief Justice Allen lived in King street, now called Water street. "near Beck's wharf, south of High or Market street. He had been a great merchant and took a deep interest in the two expeditions fitted out by Philadelphians. which sailed from this city in 1753 and 1754 to discover the Northwest Passage. The style of his establishment may be imagined from his famous coach with its four black horses, and his English coachman, who was an accomplished whip. In this stately manner would the Chief Justice be driven to his fine country seat at Mount Airy, where all that remains of so much grandeur is his name in 'Allen's lane.'"—"North Second Street and Its Associations," by Townsend Ward. Pennsylvania Magazine of History, Vol. IV, pp. 170–1.

In Charles P. Keith's "Provincial Counsellors of Pennsylvania," pp. 140–145, we find an account of Judge Allen. He married Margaret Hamilton, daughter of Andrew Hamilton, the Councillor, in Christ Church. William Allen was born August 5th, 1704, and baptized August 17th in the First Presbyterian Church, Philadelphia. He appears to have studied law in London. Judge Huston speaks of him as a distinguished barrister in London. He owned much land in Pennsylvania. He was a Common Councilman and a member of Assembly. He united with Andrew Hamilton in making the

State House Square, advancing money for the purpose. In 1735 he was elected Mayor, and at the end of his term the new Hall of Assembly witnessed a fine collation given by him. The *Pennsylvania Gazette* said: " It was the most grand and the most elegent entertainment that has been made in these parts of America."

Allen was a partner of Joseph Turner, the Councillor. He was "perhaps the richest man in Pennsylvania, notwithstanding his charities." He often served as Judge of the Orphans' Court and Common Pleas, and was Recorder of the city. He became Chief Justice of the Supreme Court of the Province. For near a quarter of a century he was a dignified, learned and impartial Judge. He lived on King (Water) street, next his wharf and stores, having a stable and coach-house on the east side of Front street. About 1750 he took up his country seat of forty-seven acres at Mount Airy. Allentown, Pa., is on land once owned by him. It was first called Northampton. In 1767 he gave the large tract he owned in that section to his son James. Judge Allen was a man of public spirit, and gave influence, time and money to advance the colony.

He contributed largely to the Pennsylvania Hospital and to the College, of which he was one of the first trustees. He gave his salary as Chief Justice to charities, according to E. F. de Lancey's statement. In a visit to England, in 1763, his strong influence checked a bill in Parliament concerning taxation of America relating to Stamp Duty. His three eldest sons were members of the Philosophical Society. He was a friend of Benjamin West. While siding with the Colonies at first, Allen desired to maintain the union with the mother country. He freed his slaves. While it has been stated that Judge Allen died in London, it is probable, as Keith states, that he died in Philadelphia or Mount Airy. He died September 6, A. D. 1780. (Tilghman's Estate, 5 Wharton, 44.) On September 10, Jasper Yeates writes from Lancaster to Colonel Burd, speaking of a letter received from Mr. Parr, in Philadelphia, noticing Mr. Allen's death. On September 16 his will and codicil were proven in Philadelphia. These dates being so near each other show that he could not have died in London.

In Watson's Annals, Vol. II, p. 33, is this notice: " The first carriage of the coach kind they ever saw or heard of belonged to Judge Allen, who had his country seat at the present Mount Airy College. It was of the phaeton or Landau kind, having a seat in front for children, and was drawn by four black horses. He was, of course, a very opulent man, a grandee in his generation. Such phaetons cost £400. The country seats then were few." A note adds: "There were three or four earlier carriages in Philadelphia, viz.: Norris, Logan and Shippen's." It may be added that Governor Keith's carriage, when he lived at Graeme Park, near Hatborough, was a wonder to the country people.

Imagine the eager faces at doors and windows when Judge Allen's grand coach stirred the ancient country people, as the " Tantivy," now enlivens the road between New York and Philadelphia.

A portrait of Chief Justice William Allen, who was on the bench in 1754, was painted by Benjamin West. Brown describes it in the "Forum," Vol. I, pp. 248-9, and Scharf & Westcott's History of Philadelphia, Vol. II, p. 1631, quotes from his description: "He had a curled wig and ruffled sleeves, but is otherwise dressed as plainly as possible. The face is round, with rather straight features."

Horace Wemyss Smith's Life of Provost William Smith refers to a meeting called on August 10th, 1754, by the Governor, "of the trustees of the Society for Propagating Christian Knowledge among the Germans settled in Pennsylvania." The meeting was held "at the house of William Allen, Esq., in Mount Airy." James Hamilton, Richard Peters, Benjamin Franklin and William Smith were present.

James Allen, who was, I think, a son of Judge Allen, built Trout Hall, in Allentown, and resided in it. My informant thinks he also had a house in Chestnut street, Philadelphia, near Fourth street. His daughter, Mrs. Greenleaf, lived for years in the old mansion in Allentown. Her daughter, Mrs. Dale, also lived there. See Diary of James Allen, Pennsylvania Magazine of History, Vol. IX, No. II, A. D. 1885. Andrew Allen, First Lieutenant of the First City Troops of Philadelphia, was a brother of James Allen. Allentown is said to have been named after James Allen.

Mt. Airy College was located on James Gowen's place. He was the father of Franklin B. Gowen, the late President of the Reading Railroad. General Beauregard and General George G. Mead and his brother were pupils. The college building was of stone. It stood flush with the street and the second story balcony projected across the full width of the sidewalk, forming an arcade. The property belonged to the Allen family, from whom Allen's lane is named. Mr. Allen, who was an Englishman, erected the building as a private house. Mr. Constant, a Frenchman, was the head of the college at first. Afterward Augustus L. Roumfort was associated with him, and it was made a military school by him. He was a Representative in the Pennsylvania Legislature, being a Democrat. He was afterward Mayor of Harrisburg and Superintendent of the Pennsylvania Railroad, and Superintendent of Bridesburg Arsenal. He died at Harrisburg. One of the teachers was named Douglass. The pupils would march to St. Luke's Church, Germantown, to service in Colonel Roumfort's day. William Green, who has just died in Germantown, was a pupil. There were two Mexican lads, brothers, named Canedo. One of them, Cipriano, married Peter Keyser's youngest daughter. Pupils came from all sections of the country. Colonel Kober, a Prussian, taught German. One of the professors married Miss Wise on the Wissahickon. A cousin of the late William Green married a sister of this lady.

Mount Airy College was founded by Rev. Francis Xavier Brosius. He was a Frenchman by birth, and the teaching of French was made quite a point in the instruction. Benjamin Condon Constant, another Frenchman, succeeded Brosius as principal, and had quite a flourishing school. The associate principal in 1826 was August L. Roumfort, who had been the teacher of mathematics and languages. Colonel Roumfort's father was contemporary with the DuPonts, of Wilmington, Del., and perhaps came to this country with them. When Mr. Constant left, Mr. Roumfort purchased the property and had some 150 pupils, sons of gentlemen. General Quitman, of the Confedrate Army, was a teacher in this college. The scholars were mostly southerners. There were also Cubans and Mexicans. Simon F. Blount was a pupil.

The college property was bought by Mr. William Rogers, who occupied it for many years as a summer residence. After his death James Gowen, the father of Franklin B. Gowen, the former President of the Reading Railroad, purchased it, in 1846. He demolished the old building and had a fine large stone mansion erected. It is roomy, and with its piazzas presents a very pretty appearance. This was occupied by the family of James Gowen as a residence from 1849 until the death of Mr. Gowen's widow in 1874, and has recently been sold to the Lutheran Church for their Theological Seminary, which is to be moved out from the city. The old house for the present will be retained as the central part of the institution, and there will be two wings three stories in height. There will be four towers on the building. It is to be constructed of light gray stone, with red stone trimmings. The chapel will be entered from beneath the balcony. Library, reading-rooms, study and class-rooms, and students' rooms will make a fine institution of this old site of learning. The architecture will be collegiate gothic, as the seminary is a building devoted to the interests of the church. The chapel and library will be fire-proof. The seminary owns some rare and valuable books. The students' rooms will be in the wings. There will be laboratories on the first floor. The dining-room is to be in the basement of the south wing. Burd Patterson, a nephew of Dr. Burd, of Ninth and Chestnut streets, who afterward moved to, and resided for many years at Pottsville, was professor of Latin in Mount Airy College. Rev. John R. Goodwin, a Lutheran clergyman, was professor of English literature. He afterward became an Episcopal clergyman and started the church at Pottsville in 1827. After leaving the college he took charge of the Germantown Academy. Felix Merino taught Spanish. His daughter Florentine teaches in Girard College. Merino was a nobleman driven from Spain for government reasons. He was a great gentleman, and was the Spanish Consul. He died in Philadelphia. He has a son living in Philadelphia, and several of his daughters are still living.

In the *Irish Catholic Benevolent Union*, of Philadelphia, published by Martin E. J. Griffin, October 15 and November 1, '85 (double numbers), in the Library of the Historical Society of Pennsylvania, is an account by Mr. Griffin, of Mount Airy College, which I will abridge. The Seminary was opened March 16, A. D. 1807, by Rev. Francis Xavier Brosius. He had an advertisement in *The Aurora* of January 8th, stating that he had been urged to open the Seminary and would teach the languages, history, geography and mathematics, by means of proper masters. French was to be the "predominant language." Applications for information were to be made to the principal, in the city, at No. 28 Pine street, or at Mr. Stephen Sicard's, No. 130 Arch street. Rev. Dr. Carr, rector of St. Augustine's Church, commended the school, which was, I suppose, the individual work of Rev. Mr. Brosius. Mr. Sicard was a dancing master, who gave practicing balls in a large room back of the Bank of Pennsylvania. On January 29, Mr. Brosius advertises "that he has taken that beautiful house and concerns called Mount Airy * * * which for healthfulness and situation he conceives cannot be surpassed." In an advertisement on April 24, it is stated that there is an elementary class. Terms and regulations will be given on application "to Rev. Dr. Carr, Messrs. P. Byrne, S. Sicard, L. Desaque, J. Carrel, Matthew Carey."

This article states that the Allens were on the Colonial side until the Declaration of Independence, and then became loyalists, and Mount Airy was confiscated.

FATHER BROSIUS came to America in A. D. 1792, with the Priest-Prince Gallitzin, whose noble work near Altoona, Pennsylvania, is commemorated by the town which bears his worthy and honored name. He was an humble, devoted and benevolent priest, who strove at great sacrifice to guide his flock in temporal and spiritual affairs. Rev. Joseph M. Finotti, in his book "Bibliographia Catholica Americana," p. 54, states that the "venerable mother" of Gallitzin deputed Father Brosius to accompany the Prince-Priest to America, from Munster in Germany. Gallitzin called Brosius "a pious and learned priest." Brosius was in Boston a short time. Bishop Carroll sent him to Conewago. He was afterward pastor of St. John's, Baltimore. Among Brosius's pupils was George A. Carrell, of Philadelphia. He became Bishop of Covington, Ky. Years before his consecration he wrote Mark Antony Frenaye of Philadelphia of a person needing alms, "When she stated her case to me I wept, because I was so poor I could not even obtain one dollar to give her."

Father Brosius, in 1813, issued "The Elements of Natural or Experimental Philosophy," at Philadelphia. The book was by Tiberius Cavallo, F.R.S., and notes from various authors were added by Brosius. Thomas Dobson published the book "at the Stone House, No. 41 South Second street, William Fry, Printer."

In 1815 we find Brosius near Boston. In George Ticknor's Life, Vol. I, p. 11, it is said that Ticknor wanted to go to the University of Gottingen and desired instruction in German, but no one in Boston could give it. Brosius, then at Jamaica Plains, described as "a native of Strasburg" was ready to teach him, though warning him "that his pronunciation was bad, as was that of all Alsace which had become part of France."

In 1815 Brosius put out "A New and Concise Method of Finding the Latitude by Double Latitudes of the Sun." This was dedicated to the Boston Marine Society. Cambridge, Hilliard and Metcalf, p. 51, 8vo. [See Finotti, p. 54.]

Soon after this Brosius went back to Germany. He was in Cincinnati in 1816. He held his Mt. Airy Seminary until 1813. It then became "a collegiate institution" in charge of B. Constant. There were "pupils from St. Louis, New Orleans, Charleston, West Indias and other distant places. John A. Quitman, Professor of English, afterward became a general in the Mexican War and Governor of Mississippi. Admiral DuPont was a pupil. General A. L. Roumfort was Professor of mathematics from 1818 to 1826, when he succeeded Constant. Roumfort transferred it into a Military School under the title 'American Classical and Military Lyceum.' He continued it until 1834-35, when President Jackson appointed him Military Storekeeper in Philadelphia. Captain Alden Partridge, succeeded him in the Mt. Airy College." [Thompson Westcott in the *Dispatch*, November 18-25 and December 2, 1883.]

Captain Partridge, was also in charge of an establishment which was formerly Bristol College in Pennsylvania, and also of another in Norwich, Vermont.

In Thompson Westcott's History of Philadelphia, chapter DCXXVI, Scrap Book, Vol. 5, in Historical Society of Pennsylvania Library, we read, after an account of Clermont Seminary, as follows: "Rev. F. X. Brosius gave notice in 1807 that the Mount Airy Seminary, Germantown road, eight miles from Philadelphia, would open for scholars March 16th. 'The system of education laid down for the youth of the above establishment has been submitted to the Rev. Dr. Carr, Director of St. Augustine's Church, who has approved thereof, and allows reference to be made to him, to afford parents and guardians every satisfaction on so essential a point. References: Rev. Dr. Carr, P. Byrne, S. Sicard, M. Carey, J. Campbell, Lewis DeSaussere.' Dr. Brosius was a Roman Catholic Clergyman, and his school was conducted in a manner satisfactory to the authorities of that Church."

"At a later period the American Classical and Military Lyceum, at Mount Airy, was opened under the superintendence of B. Constant and of Colonel A. L. Roumfort, formerly of West Point. The latter subsequently succeeded to the control of the institution. The United States Military Academy was taken as a model for the internal government, and in the choice of authors to be studied in the different departments of science. The plan was to prepare the pupils for admission to West Point and also to teach them the elements of mathematics and a perfect knowledge of the French language, as necessary to the study of the higher branches of mathematics and engineering. A course of navigation, and the application of trigonometry to nautical astronomy were proposed to be taught to young gentlemen of the navy who intended to fit themselves for examination. The hours generally appropriated to idle recreation in other schools were devoted to field exercises and attending lectures on tactics and engineering. The school started with seven permanent instructors, the number of which was to be increased to ten as additions were made to the roll of cadets. The terms were ten dollars entrance and two hundred and fifty dollars a year, which included boarding, washing, mending, fuel and lights. The cadets were uniformed in gray, with pants of the same color in winter, and white Russia-duck sheeting for summer. The uniform cap was of black leather, with a bell-crown, seven inches high, semicircular vizor, yellow plate and band of black pompon six inches long, and a yellow cockade, with yellow eagle."

There was the old contest of "Town and Gown" between the Germantown boys and the college pupils. The Cubans and others were aristocratic and looked down on the country lads. Fights resulted and Germantown generally got the victory, according to a Germantowner's report. Samuel Keyser's shoeshop employed many boys who mixed with the Germantown crowd, and gave it strength. The shoe-shop was on the site of the Pastorious house, at Pastorius and Main streets. Shoes were made for the southern trade. Samuel Keyser was Gideon Keyser's father.

Colonel Roumfort graduated at West Point in 1819, taking high honors. He was of noble birth in France, and when seven years of age came with his parents to the United States. The family were bereft of their property by the French Revolution. The principal of Mt. Airy College was a thorough American citizen, very domestic, and gave up all titles. He was born December 10, A. D. 1796, and died August 2, 1878. He ceased teaching in 1835, and entered political life, selling his property to Mr. Rodgers. Colonel Roumfort did not add to the buildings. The main building, guard house and cells did their special work. The cells often received boys who had been disorderly. No. 7, a room above the cistern, was a private apartment for the larger pupils. No. 6 still stands as a laundry room, and the room above, as a servants' lodging room. Mr. Roumfort was an Episcopalian, and the students attended service at St. Luke's, Germantown, in the rectorship of the late Rev. John Rodney.

Professor Glass, now residing in the West, was once a teacher in Mt. Airy College.

It is pleasant to think of Constant Guillou, Esq., Admiral DuPont and General Meade as in the same military company at Mt. Airy. The future General and Admiral knew not of the glory that awaited them in military life, while the lawyer made a name in quieter pursuits, in which his son succeeds him. Professor Constant was the godfather of Constant Guillou.

In Townsend Ward's "Germantown Road," Pennsylvania Magazine of History, No. 4, Vol. VI, p. 381, I find a recommendation by Brosius of an epitome *Historiae Sacrae* published by Joseph De la Plaine and John F. Watson.

General W. H. H. Davis, editor of the *Doylestown Democrat*, writes me that Mr. Roumfort "was a large, handsome-looking man, and had a good deal of the manners of a Frenchman."

Mr. W. Y. McAllister, a former pupil at Mount Airy College, writes that "Mr. Constant died many years ago," and sends the following interesting list of pupils. When the roll is now called most of them must give Colonel Newcombe's dying answer "*adsum*" (present) in another world:—

"The following persons were at Mt. Airy School between 1826 and 1828. Part of the list is from the roll-call of 1826 or 1827, a copy of which is in my possession.

Constant Guillou, Charles Guillou, Alfred Guillou, John Andrews, Henry Andrews, William Roberts, Alexander Henry Jandon, Napoleon A. Jennings, John Ingersoll, Wilson R. Desilver, John L. Goddard, James Stokes Biddle, Edward Pease, Arnauld Thouron, Joseph C. Walsh, W. Y. McAllister, Ferdinand Stoever, Cowell, Francis Barry, Charles Duval, Robert Meade, Henry Warren, Richard Kelly, Lewis Henry Roumfort, Henry Willing, Alfred Coxe, Victor L. Godon, James West, Benjamin Ingersoll, E. H. Abadie, Erringham, Beauveau Borie, Sol. Vickers, Charles Geisse, Christian Geisse, George W. Geisse, G. W. Hunter, Gardette, George Gordon Meade, all of Philadelphia; Francisco Cepero, of Porto Rico; Robert Johnson, of Salem, New Jersey; Louis Lalande, of Louisiana; Richard Bell and Joseph Bell, of Cuba; Charles Forstall, of Louisiana; Louis Lepage, of Norfolk, Va; W. C. Brien, of Frederick, Md.; Stephen Bickham Girard, of Havre, France; Alexander Jean Jacques Planche, of Louisiana; Octavius Anthony Cazenove, of Alexandria, Va.; George W. Tyler, of Frederick, Md.; Veneron Broes, of Louisiana; William Sanvall, of Charleston, S. C.; William Offutt, of Louisiana; Charles Victor Berault, of New York; Henry DuPont, of Wilmington, Del.; Victor C. Sanchez, of Mexico; Benigno Rojas, of South America; Samuel Dickinson, of Trenton, New Jersey; Raphael Benito, of South America; Philip Horruitinal, of Cuba; Raphael Roca, of South America; John Middleton, of Charleston, S. C.; Persifor F. Myers, Chester, Pa.; William Keim, Reading, Pa.; Hoe, of Maryland; W. S. Drayton, of South Carolina; Ringgold, of Maryland, Edward Schriver, of York, Pa; Brien, of Maryland; Corall, of South America; Baker, Thomas Forrest Betton, W. Green, all of Germantown, Pa.; Snyder, of somewhere in Pennsylvania; John Henry Hobart, of Pottstown, Pa.; two brothers by the name of Fortier, from Louisiana; Herbert, of Prince George Co., Md.; Manadon, of Louisiana; McAllister, of Tennessee; Saul, of New Orleans; E. Crosby, Chester, Pa.; Gen. George Gordon Meade, Thomas F. Betton, Henry DuPont, James S. Biddle, and Constant Guillou, became prominent men. Of this list all that I know now living are: Henry Wilson Andrews, James S. Biddle, G. W. Hunter, C. V. Berault, Henry DuPont, W. Y. McAllister.

To this list of survivors should be added Charles Guillou, New York, and Henry Warren.

As teachers, Professors Manlove, Abadie, Hall (Chemistry); O'Flaherty (Elocution); Felix J. Grund and others must be added.

H. W. Andrews names Mr. Claisson, of New York, as Professor of Belles-Lettres. He married a Germantown lady. He died in London, England.

Richard Bell 2d, of Cuba, died at the school. The School once attended Presbyterian service in Germantown, under Rev. Mr. Baker, whose son died when a pupil, in 1827.

General Meade's brother, Robert, was a pupil. Rev. Dr. Ducachet, was also a scholar.

Rev. Dr. F. W. Conrad, editor of the LUTHERAN OBSERVER was a pupil at Mt. Airy. The PHILADELPHIA LEDGER gave an account of the celebration of the 50th Anniversary of his entrance to the ministry, which occurred May 30, A. D. 1889.

Col. Roumfort had a clerical appearance. He used to read the Scriptures and morning prayers for the school. He also read sermons, I suppose, on Sundays.

It is pleasant to look at the photos preserved with loving care by Wm. Y. McAllister; they must be specially interesting to the "old boys."

Dr. Edward Pease, of Philadelphia, was a pupil. He married a daughter of Richard Willing.

The mark in a former pupil's notes after Chas. Forstall's name (Louisiana), is " a right good fellow."

Mr. Henry DuPont, of Wilmington, Delaware, gave many names for Mr. McAllister's list of pupils.

The wife of the drummer or fifer " kept a little shop up the lane " where the boys' pennies went " for cranberry tarts, chestnuts, cakes and apples." Passes signed by Col. Roumfort were necessary in going out of bounds.

Mr. George W. Hunter, a former pupil at Mt. Airy in Col. Roumfort's day, speaks of Mr. Pierson, one of the instructors, as having been a good teacher of English branches of learning.

Mr. W. Y. McAllister's notes in manuscript state that Madame Williams was in charge of the house matters. Her daughter, Miss Adele, married Mr. Abadie.

There was a girls' school at Mt. Airy College before it became a boys' school. Madame Chapron kept it. Mr. McAllister's mother was a pupil.

The French people who came to this section appear to have been very industrious, and were ready to adapt themselves to their work. They had the true nobility of self-respect, but had seen better days in France.

Mr. McAllister writes thus in his reminiscences: " All that is left of the old place is a small stone tool house on the northwestern side of the lot.

" It was a military school and we had a musket and a uniform, and morning and evening parade, and were called up in the morning by the fife and drum, and the tattoo beat at night for bedtime. The uniform was gray, trimmed with black braid and round gilt buttons, one of which I now have.

Every boy's clothes and bedding were numbered. My number was sixty, and the numbers on this list are the clothes' numbers." A list of pupils follows in Constant and Roumfort's time.

The numbering was probably imported from France. A friend of mine who studied in Paris, in after years in a public conveyance, was startled to hear his number called out in French, and found the old designation came from the lips of a fellow pupil. Reviewing school life is sad, and one could wish for a poet like Gray to describe Mt. Airy instead of Eton College. The faithful list covers much territory. Porto Rico, New Jersey and Louisiana are here contiguous. Joseph Bell (Bell 1st) dies at his residence in Madrid, Spain; Stephen Bickham Girard is marked Havre, France; Victor Caledonia Sanchez is from Mexico. It was not uncommon in those days for foreigners to put sons under the care of business friends in the United States, who selected a school for them. A friend has just given me a case where his father thus chose Mt. Airy for one or two foreign wards. Raphael Benito and Raphael Roca, from the Republic of Columbia, and Phillippi Horruitinal, of Cuba, are noted together. Dr. Edward Pease, of Philadelphia, was a pupil. Benjamin Ingersoll, another scholar, died at Rome. McAllister, of Tennessee, was killed in the Texan war. Saul, of New Orleans, is noted. Could it have been the late benevolent Rev. Dr. Saul?

PHILADELPHIA, March 30, 1888.

Dear Sir.—My recollection of the Mt. Airy School, though very vivid, affords no material for interesting anecdote. It was not called a "School" or a "College," but a "Military Lyceum," and in its character, as well as name, was something of a new departure. The study of the classics was thrown into the back ground and the chief attention was given to modern languages and mathematics. All the teachers were excellent, being far better than I have ever seen elsewhere, and no pupil left there without being well grounded in French and Spanish. The discipline was strict. There was no corporal punishment whatever, but I *do* recollect having my ears boxed most unjustly by Mr. Constant for mispronouncing the French word *medicin*. I am afraid to say how many years ago this was, but I am not sure that I have forgiven him. Perhaps with this incident I may point a moral for teachers.

Col. Roumfort was a graduate of West Point, and in every way a very capable man. After the school was broken up he became Superintendent of the U. S. Arsenal at Frankford, and later, Superintendent of the Pennsylvania Railroad at Harrisburg, and Mayor of the city.

Mr. Constant, a Frenchman of good abilities, was really the founder of the school. When it closed he went to Havana and was private tutor in the Scull family, an offshoot of the Sculls of this city.

The school building was directly on the street and of large extent. It had been the residence, before the Revolution, of Chief Justice Allen. Charles Biddle, in his autobiography says: "Mr. Allen used to say 'that America was the finest country in the world;' 'Pennsylvania the garden of America'; 'Philadelphia the first city of America'; and 'his house the best situated of any in Philadelphia.'" I presume he spoke of Philadelphia county, and that our school was the home he had reference to. Not a stone of it is left, but a year ago I stood by the pump whence I had filled my wash basin on many a cold morning. There was no coddling of boys in those days.

The chief distinction of the Mt. Airy School, however, is that there our gallant fellow townsman, George G. Meade, received the first rudiments of that military training which enabled him to save his beloved Pennsylvania in her hour of danger. Every Mt. Airy boy is proud to have been a schoolmate of the hero of Gettysburg.

> "His name a great example stands to show,
> How strangely high endeavors may be blessed,
> Where piety and valor jointly go."
>
> JAMES S. BIDDLE.

Mr. W. Y. McAllister has furnished the following article from the pen of TOWNSEND WARD, which appeared in the PHILADELPHIA AGE, August 26, A. D. 1869. It is pleasant to hear again from one who started his walk on the Germantown Road, and fell by the wayside before it was finished.

"Gorgas's lane was the last point we reached, and at the northeast corner of it and the avenue is Mr. Carstair's old place; not far beyond which but on the west side and far removed from the avenue, is the Lutheran Orphans' Home, with Klincken Johnson's old stone house on the north side of the front of its lot. There are now for a time, fewer houses, but the general appearance and character of the road is preserved, and soon we come on rising ground, through which the turnpike passes by a considerable excavation. This is now called Mount Pleasant, and on the southwest side is Mr. George Garrett's house and well-kept grounds. Opposite is the mansion of Admiral Breeze, recently erected, and a little north of it, the old house once belonging to Mr. Pierce, but now quite altered from the strange looking thing which many yet remember as having been called 'The Steamboat,' because on its top was built an additional story, all windows, that had the appearance of an upper deck. It failed of its purpose, a cocoonery, but the mulberry trees which supplied the silk-worms with their food of leaves, still stand in the rear of the premises. A stone here marks eight miles from Vine street. The houses, as for some little distance past, are yet rather sparsely set along the road, but it is not very far to the house on the west side, formerly of Charles Bonsall, now living in Cincinnati, and which has become one of the boarding houses of Mrs. Miller. These are situated on the nearest part of Mount Airy, which, however, at this point, is of the same elevation, and is the same hill as Mount Pleasant. Opposite these houses is one of stone, near the roof of which is the mark '17, W. Hottenstein, 95.' The Odd Fellows' Hall is not much beyond, and opposite to it, on the west side, is the White Swan, and very near is Allen's lane. But the ground has fallen off a little, and again has risen as we reach on the east side, the commencement of Mr. James Gowen's place, with its front of five hundred feet along the road. This was once the country seat of Chief Justice Allen, the man of the greatest wealth of all of them in the colony, and whose great coach with four black horses was long remembered. On the approach of the Revolution, the Chief Justice went to England, and died there in 1780. His son Andrew Allen, successor to Judge Chew, who had succeeded the father, was a member of the Continental Congress and of the Committee of Safety; but in the dark days of 1776 he put himself under the protection of General Howe, at Trenton, and went to England, where he died in London in 1825. John also joined the British at the same time with his brother. William, another son, at first served under General St. Clair, but he, too, succumbed in 1776, and a year afterward raised a corps called the Pennsylvania Loyalists, of which he was Lieutenant-Colonel commanding. James, who died in 1777, was the only son who did not join the Royalists. Since Fort Allen no longer exists, the name of the family is almost unknown to us, except in Allen's lane and in the town on the banks of the Lehigh.

"About the beginning of the century, the place was occupied, and, perhaps, owned by a Frenchman, Mr. Tarascon, who lived there with his brother. Their town residence was the double house on the lot, where now stands the Arch Street Theatre. Not long after that time, these gentlemen went to Portland, Kentucky, where they established factories, and where, in 1825, they still remained. About the time Mr. Tarascon had left the place it was for a short time used for the school for females, established by the competent Madame Chapron. Not long afterward a noble emigrant from France assuming his wife's name of Bouchard, but subsequently resuming his own, Roumfort, instituted a school there. After a time he had for an associate, Mr. Constant, another Frenchman who had also possessed a title in France; and a little subsequent to this, Mr. Constant conducted the school by himself, and continued to do so for a number of years. In the course of time he associated with himself a son of the gentleman who first established the school. Colonel Roumfort, who is now living, is the present Mayor of Harrisburg. Under the administration of accomplished gentlemen the school justly acquired considerable celebrity. It was changed to a military school under its latter management, and among its pupils were many of the youth of the day, not a few coming from Louisiana. Mr. Forstall and General Planche, who was second in command under General Jackson at New Orleans, were there. Admiral DuPont and his brother, Henry DuPont, were pupils. General Quitman of Mississippi, well remembered for his amiable courtesy, was for a time a teacher. General George G. Meade and the Reverend Dr. Ducachet were pupils, and also Warren and Cowell, sons of the celebrated actors of those names, and John L. Goddard, Doctors Edward Peace and Thomas F. Betton, John and Benjamin Ingersoll, William Heyward Drayton, William Y. McAllister, a Walsh, a Borie and a Gardette, and Mr. Constant Guillou, for whom Mr. Constant was godfather, and to whom his name was given. This gentleman remembers, as an incident of his school days, that the boys would write their names high up in the cupola, and that above all the others, was that of Verrier, with whose children his own subsequently intermarried. In one of the nocturnal battles the opposing parties of the school, with pillows for their weapons, struggled for victory until the signal that Mr. Constant was at hand, when in another instant every boy was in bed and seemingly asleep, as boys so perfectly can feign; —all of them except Berrabi Sanchez, a Mexican, who happened to be at too great a distance to be able to reach his bed in time to avoid discovery. With perfect presence of mind he stood quite still while Mr. Constant passed his candle before his eyes, exclaiming 'Wonderful! Wonderful! He is a somnambulist.' With another striking evidence that he was not conscious that he was in the presence of a superior, Sanchez turned toward his bed and got into it; Mr. Constant carefully arranging the clothes and expressing his admiration by repeated exclamations. Years after this, in one of the many revolutions in unhappy Mexico, Sanchez was pursued by some soldiers, and for the last time got into a bed, and under a mattress where he was bayoneted to death.

"On one occasion the Latin teacher asked young Guillou whether he had studied his lesson, and to his reply 'Yes, sir,' exclaimed, 'How can you tell me such a lie? You have not studied it.' Guillou, with the courage of that day, retorted, 'How can you, sir, tell such a lie! I have studied it.' For the offense he was imprisoned in the guard house for a week, and when liberated, his young companions carried the youthful martyr on their shoulders in triumph around the grounds. It is among the early recollections of a well-known physician of French descent, that when he and Colonel Roumfort were boys and very intimate, they emulated Beaumont and Fletcher by writing and acting as a joint production, a play that rivalled Fielding's 'Tom Thumb'; for while Fielding only kills off all his characters at the end of his fifth act, they accomplished that feat in the first of their tragedy, and so had not a single character left with which to commence a second act.

"Old Moore, the drummer, and Bender, the fifer, were so recently living at Nicetown that it is probable they yet survive; but the school and many of its scholars have passed away; the house is down and in its place stands another erected by Mr. Gowen. We cannot leave the spot without remarking how many French names have been associated with it. The yellow house near the entrance and one situated in the rear of it, and of the same color, were part of the College buildings. After the military school ceased to exist, these buildings, together with one next to be mentioned, were occupied during its brief existence, by the Agricultural College under the charge of Mr. Wilkinson. On the north of the yellow buildings is the large double house of stone, built in 1792, by Joseph Miller. Mr. Joseph B. Baker lived there while Collector of the Port, but it is now occupied by Mrs. John F. Ohl. On the other side of the avenue is the pretty place of the gardener, Mr. Charles H. Miller, to whose taste Chestnut Hill is not a little indebted. Only a little further, situated, however, upon the east side, is where the old Golden Swan stood, at which the elections were held. It was torn down some fifteen years ago, and the present building, now occupied by Mrs. Latour, was erected by Mr. Gowen.

"Two or three fields of no great extent, now make us for a moment suppose we are about to leave the constant succession of houses, and give almost a farm-like appearance to the scene. But it quickly vanishes. On the west side is the house where General Michael W. Ash, Representative in Congress, once lived; then on the same side comes Mr. Shaffer's place, with its well-looking house standing in a group of fine weeping willows and other trees. Opposite to this the previously curving road, to avoid a hill, sweeps a little to the right, around some rocks, and then descends to the lower ground through which Cresheim creek passes, with old stone houses on its banks. On the rising ground a little beyond the creek, and surrounded by fine old trees which add to its attractive appearance, is the Mermaid-Inn, a name that cannot but recall that still more ancient Mermaid in Friday street, London, where, about the year 1603, Sir Walter Raleigh instituted the club of *beaux esprits*, which combined more talent and genius than ever met together before or since. The rare Ben Jonson, and sweetest Shakespeare, fancy's child, Beaumont and Fletcher, and Selden, with many others of hardly less note, regularly met there, and discovered that what Ben Jonson wants

'Is a pure cup of rich canary wine,
Which is the Mermaid's now, but shall be mine.'

"Standing at the corner of the turnpike and Mermaid lane is an old log house, nicely whitewashed and well preserved, that is a fine specimen of the style of building once almost universal, but of which the last vestiges are now rapidly disappearing. An old occupant of it, Conrad Weiss, is well remembered for his disordered reason, but whether crazed with care, or crossed in hopeless love no story tells. He was remarkable for great physical strength, and had a habit of walking daily to the end of Germantown and back again, stopping, however, before some store to deliver a long oration with considerable emphasis and gesticulation, pointing ever and anon to the paper in his hand, which, to his disturbed intellect, fully sustained the view he had taken of the subject of his discourse. Beyond Mermaid lane the houses are nearer together and not unfrequently adjoin one another. The Park avenue soon crosses the turnpike, and near it a house of an early date stands some distance from the turnpike. The Wissahickon avenue next crosses, and is being macadamized. Upon the east side, a little further on, is the large stone house, with a stone barn back of it, formerly of the Rex family.

"We are now at Hartwell avenue, and on the right hand the tower of the Chestnut Hill Water Company appears in sight. Then comes the Masonic Hall built by Hiram Lodge. The large stone house of Doctor Rex is soon passed, and not far off is the Eagle Inn, an old stone building with a front of eighty-five feet, erected long ago by Jacob Peters, and where his line of Philadelphia stages stopped. After passing a few houses we come to Summit street, the elevation of which point above ordinary high tide is four hundred and forty-three feet. Here at the gate sits the worthy and simple hearted man who for many years has taken toll from him bound for Whitemarsh, or for the further Bethlehem, to reach which place, one must keep to the right.

"On the west, or left-hand side of that road along which we are sauntering, is the place of Mr. Caleb Cope; then Presbyterian lane, on the far side of which is the church which has lent its name to the narrow road. Beyond is the house where dwells Mr. Ambrose White, who, although in the ninetieth year of his age, may be seen walking about as if but three score years were on his head, or, often he may be seen on horse-back, and not unfrequently, thus mounted, on his ride to the city. On the right hand, is Dr. Moss's house, and then at the other corner of Chestnut Hill avenue is General Owens's. The Methodist Church on the left-hand comes after Mr. White's. Then on the east side is the beautiful place and capacious mansion of Mr. Richard Norris, and opposite to it is Mr. Rex's, beyond which is Mr. Isaac Starr's, and next to it, Mr. J. Krider's. On the east side and opposite to Mr. Starr, is a place belonging to Mr. Henry Norris, next to which is that of Mr. Charles Taylor; on the north side of whose grounds stands the cottage of the late William H. Brown. On the west side, then appears the extensive and beautiful Hildeburn place, now occupied by Mr. Isaac S. Waterman. Willow avenue now leaves the turnpike by passing northeastwardly across the side of Mr. Taylor's place. That on the further side of Willow avenue belongs to Mr. Henry Norris, and is his residence; but it owes its beauty to the good taste of Mr. William Henry Trotter, who established it. The Norway firs, which line its front, were wisely and fortunately planted so far apart that their growth has not been checked.

"We are now on the descent from Chestnut Hill, and the road to Bell's mill crosses the turnpike. On the right hand side is the residence of Mr. Randolph Price, formerly of Thomas Earp, and next to it a house so old that one of Washington's many nurses might almost have been born in it, but in which, it is well known, Mr. William Stroud has lived for many years. And now we turn to the left hand and gain the elevation of an outlying hill of considerable extent, formerly called 'The Sugar Loaf,' and commanding even a finer view of the charming valley at its foot. On this hill, fine as it is, and which is even less adorned by the trees and shrubbery, and the beautiful houses of Mr. Edward H. Trotter, and Mr. John Thompson, than by the exquisitely English-like sward which they have brought to something like perfection, one may have a view from its southwestern side, of the nearer part of the wooded region through which the romantic Wissahickon breaks. The elevated hills and their sloping sides, broken into wild and charming irregularity by the winding course of the beautiful stream, are covered with a seemingly primeval forest, that shall in time allure the artist to one of his richest fields. These woods are to be preserved, and already owners have been prohibited from felling trees, for under the authority of recent legislation, the Park Commissioners wisely use their absolute power over the wood and water; and they design also, that in time, the fine drives now in progress of construction shall be extended to this point. One feature in the grounds of Mr. Trotter and Mr. Thompson, which latter place was laid out by Mr. Charles W. Trotter, is well worth mentioning. The walks are constructed of a foundation of broken stone, on which a mixture of tar and gravel is laid, over which more gravel is spread. The sides or gutter part of the carriage drives are made in the same manner. Passing over an undulating surface, they are consequently exposed to a thorough test of their capacity to resist washing, and an experience of several years, with no part impaired, would seem to show that something like a correct principle in road-making had been adopted.

"In front, lying at our feet, as it were, is the beautiful and fertile valley of Whitemarsh, over and beyond which, on a clear day, the vision may have a range of many miles, even so far as to include the distant hills of Reading. Less than a mile distant is the charming place that Mr. John C. Bullitt embellished and occupied for several years, and alongside of it, the extensive grounds of the Convent of St. Joseph. On approaching it, just as a boy mounted on a donkey passes by, its vesper bells strike upon the ear, and for a moment we are transported to Italy or Spain, and look around to see the holy friar who should be there, or the pilgrim with his scallop shell, fresh from the shrine of St. Iago de Compostella. These have not come yet, perhaps may never come. The order of the Sisters of St. Joseph have, however, established this as the Mother House, with the well-known Sister St. John, as the Superioress, to preside over it. Within its gates are eighteen sisters professed, eighteen novices, and eight postulants—the total number in the diocese being one hundred and forty-seven. At this convent, which, by the way, is not a cloistered one, the sisters have an academy, for their mission includes teaching as well as nursing, and this, their Academy of St. Joseph, as they call it, has fifty boarders and forty day scholars. The chapel is attended by the Augustinian Fathers of Chestnut Hill.

To the north of the Convent, and about a mile distant, is the farm of three hundred acres, where Mr. A. Welch has established himself in a pursuit that requires not only great resources and an unusual capacity for administration, but one that at the same time elicits the peculiar pride in the possession of a fine courser, and that tender affection for him which are such attractive features in the character of an Arabian chieftain. Pasturing in fine fields, or well cared for in capacious stables, are some scores of horses and colts of the best stock in the country. While some of them are of striking beauty, there are among them those bearing names which have become famous over the world; and it is hardly too much to say that nowhere can be found their superiors, perhaps not even their equals. The track at Buffalo, on which Dexter made his famous time, and on which recently even that has been almost rivalled, is proverbially a quick track, while that near the city of New York, on which Lady Thorne made her fast time, is well known to be a slow track. And so the time of no two tracks can very well be compared; for the ground of one may be hilly or it may be heavy, or the measurement may not be so near the pole or inside line, as may be the case with the other. An apparently trivial circumstance may, therefore, be the cause of that difference of a second or two in a mile, the declaration of which, as there is an Atlantic cable, now agitates two continents, not, however, without exciting the indignation of an old-time Pennsylvanian, whose honest heart knows the practice of no guile. No one can visit this place without a desire to see that marvel, Flora Temple, so long known, and with no blemish to indicate work or age."

CRESHEIM.

The name Cresheim was given to the stream which now forms the boundary between Chestnut Hill and Mount Airy, and empties into the Wissahickon at the romantic spot called the "Devil's Pool," which was a well-known place of resort for picnics, etc., back as far as Revolutionary times. It also designated a tract of land above Germantown. Cresheim is apparently what is now known as "Kriegsheim," which means war's home.

In response to a query about Cresheim, the following letter was kindly sent me:

When I visited Germany in 1874, I was quite anxious to *discover* the town of Kriesheim in the Palatinate, as no manual of geography, geographical dictionary or map recorded such a name. How I finally became convinced that the place now called Kriegsheim, about six miles from Worms, is identical with the old Kriesheim, and some particulars of my visit, I have related in THE FRIEND of November 28, 1874. The dealings that William Penn had with the Quaker converts of Kreisheim are very pleasantly related by him in his Journal of a visit to Holland and Germany in 1677. I have tried to supplement his account from other sources in a paper printed in the PENNSYLVANIA MAGAZINE of 1878. ("William Penn's Travels in Germany.") I have nothing further to add to the information contained in the articles mentioned, except that Rev. Mr. Keller, of Kriegsheim, in a letter received a few years ago, makes mention of further documentary confirmation as to the identity of Kriesheim and Kriegsheim.

Very respectfully yours,

OSWALD SEIDENSTICKER.

In THE FRIEND, Seventh day, Eleventh-month 28th, 1874, Prof. Oswald Seidensticker, of the University of Pennsylvania, gives an account of his search after Cresheim in Germany, which I will condense. He speaks of Cresheim street and Cresheim creek, in Germantown, as "time-honored names," witnessing to the fact that some of the early settlers came from a German Krisheim. He states that Sewel relates how William Ames, a Friend, visited that village in the Palatinate and made the acquaintance of Baptists (Mennonites?) in Kriesheim, which was not far from Worms. Some of the Germans became Friends and emigrated to Pennsylvania. Not long after the Palatinate was wasted by the French in a war. (Philadelphia edition, 1826, Vol. I, p. 260.)

In Stephen Crisp's Journal, in 1669, is a note acknowledging the preservation of the Lord who brought him to Greisheim, where divers had embraced the Friends' doctrines. (London edition, 1694, p. 23.)

William Penn, in his mission in Holland and Germany, visited and comforted these Friends. In his Journal of Twenty-third day of Sixth month, 1677, he writes that he reached Crisheim, the Paltzgrave's country, and joyfully found "a meeting of tender and faithful people." Though the Friends were in danger of governmental interference in preaching, Penn dared to speak to the meeting, declaring that he was ready to be carried to testify before the Prince. The meeting was quiet, "of which a coachful from Worms made a part." (Collections of Works of Penn, two volumes, London, 1726, Vol. I, p. 72.) On another visit he walked from Worms to Crisheim, being "about six English miles," and had a good meeting on the Lord's day. "The Vaught or chief officer himself stood at the door of the barn, where he could hear and not be seen." These "poor hearts" had mostly been "gathered by dear William Ames."

Some years later Penn was proprietor of Pennsylvania, on which the Palatinate would have made a small appearance in size. He invited the persecuted to his broad domain, and Krisheim people joined the settlement of Pastorius, the agent of the Frankfort Company at Germantown. Peter Schumacher, John Krey, Isaac Thomas Williams, John and Arnold Cassel, and a number of the Hendricks family, were among these.

In 1689 German township was laid out and its four divisions were Germantown, Krisheim, Summerhausen and Crefeld. The two last-named designations have faded away.

Prof. Seidensticker was naturally anxious to trace the Krisheim whence the Germantowners came, and to look up its traditions. He found no name with the American spelling, but Kriegsheim (meaning in German, war's home) and Griesheim were puzzlingly near Worms. The Lutheran parson at Worms could not tell him where William Penn had preached among Quakers, and did not know that there had been Quakers near him, or that Penn had made a missionary tour here, though Penn's Journal states that a predecessor of his had gone from Worms to be at Penn's meeting in August, A. D. 1677. Greisheim seemed nearer to Cresheim in spelling as G and K are interchanged. Stephen Crisp had styled the place Greisheim, but no Greisham answered to the distance from Worms given by Penn, though there were several villages so called, and they were outside the Palatinate, while Kriegsheim was within it, and "at the proper distance." So Prof. Seidensticker visited Kriegsheim, and in his half-mile walk from the railway at Monsheim pondered over Penn, the founder of a great commonwealth, who had passed through grain fields and potato patches about two centuries before to teach German peasants in divine things, near where Luther had spoken bold words before the Imperial Diet of Worms. Kriegsheim is for the most part "two rows of humble dwellings lining the road." The Professor sought the clergyman of the village for information.

The Rev. Mr. Keller, who was the parson, was surprised at the information given him. He had never heard of any Quakers in the village, nor of William Penn's visit, nor of the emigration to America of Krisheimers. The Professor gave him the names, from " Besse's Sufferings of the Quakers," of Hendricks, Jansen, Laubeck, Moret Gerritts and Schumacher as inhabitants of Krisheim, who had been fined for being Friends. There were no such family names then in Kriegsheim, except that of Jansen, and they had no traditions of a Quaker ancestry.

The clergyman had a manuscript volume noting the assessment of real estate in the middle of the last century, where the name of the German village was spelled Kreisheim, so that Kriegsheim appeared an innovation. The names did not aid a solution of the question. The books recording births, deaths and marriages, which are noted carefully in Germany were missing. The person who had had charge of them was annoyed by the queries concerning them from descendants of those who were deceased. He therefore stated that the records were missing, and a popular report states that they were burned.

The Professor was deeply annoyed at this break in a connecting link in tracing the settlers of Germantown to their old home. The schoolmaster was called on "to no purpose." The teacher knew of Penn's works in Pennsylvania, but did not know that the famous founder of Pennsylvania had walked through his village and preached in a barn. He had never heard of German Quakers.

Professor Seidensticker afterward made inquiries in Griesheim, but the old church records did not contain the names of Besse. He thinks that the distance given by Penn from Worms to Krisheim fastened the conclusion on Kriegsheim. While it is remarkable that oblivion has covered the local history, it may be probable that all the Quakers of the village became emigrants to Pennsylvania; and "the atrocious war waged by Louis the Fourteenth in the Palatinate, singed out cities and villages and scattered the inhabitants. Worms, with the surrounding country, was most severely smitten during that war."

In the *Pennsylvania Magazine of History*, A. D. 1878, Vol. II, No. 3, Prof. Seidensticker's lecture before the Historical Society of Pennsylvania on "William Penn's Travels in Holland and Germany in 1677," is given. It contains an account of the progress of the Friends, and of the relation of Penn's visit to the formation of the Frankfort Company. On page 265, we read of Penn's visit to Krisheim, where "a little congregation of German Quakers had, in spite of many tribulations, managed to hold together ever since William Ames and George Rolfe, in the year 1657, had convinced them."

At times traveling Friends visited "this distant offshoot of their brotherhood." William Carter had a pleasant visit there, and assisted in "the time of their vintage." Stephen Crisp and William Moore also visited here.

Penn also sought these "simple husbandmen and weavers" to comfort his co-religionists and preached to them.

To check the local annoyances of the inoffensive Friends, he strove to make "a personal appeal to the sovereign of the Palatine, Charles Louis." He walked to Mannheim, but the Prince had gone to Heidelberg, and, as Penn was to hold another meeting in Krisheim, he could not go after him, but wrote a strong and noble plea for liberty of conscience.

When Penn preached the second time in Krisheim in a barn, the magistrate listened behind the door and made a good report of the character of the teaching.

When it was learned that Penn had a vast estate in North America, where liberty of conscience was allowed, the Quakers and Mennonites of Krisheim determined to emigrate thither.

At Duisburg, on the Rhine, Penn became acquainted with Dr. Gerhard Mastricht, having a letter of introduction to him from a Cologne merchant. He afterward became a partner in the Frankfort Company, his share entitling him to $16666\frac{2}{3}$ acres of land in Pennsylvania. Penn's present visit however was only of a religious nature. His preaching was earnest and effective, and he was undaunted by opposition, believing that he was performing his duty. Fox spoke through an interpreter. It is thought that Penn may have preached in Dutch and German, as he could use these languages "with some fluency." His mother, Margaret Jasper, was born in Holland, her father being John Jasper, a Rotterdam merchant. Pepys says (I give the extract to which Prof. Seidensticker only refers giving but a few words from it. Diary, August 19, 1664): "To Sir W. Penn's, to see his lady the first time, who is a well-looked, fat, short old Dutch woman, but one that hath been heretofore pretty handsome, and is now very discreet, and I believe hath more wit than her husband. Here we staid talking a good while, and very well pleased I was with the old woman." Janney's "Life of Penn," narrates that when Peter the Great was in England, the Friends chose William Penn to converse with him in German and state their views. Penn's personal magnetic influence proved very great in his tour in Holland and Germany. His religion was fervent. While Penn's journey was not a business one, the friends he then made remembered him, and the Frankfort Company was started by some of them. They held five shares, being 25,000 acres of Pennsylvania land, and Quakers from Krisheim came to Germantown.

Crefeld also sent its quota, and was commemorated in the name of the region above Chestnut Hill. In the Memorable Account of Christian Experience of Stephen Crisp, London, 1694, occurs this note: "Another time he made a journey into the county of Meurs, to the town of Crevel, where a meeting was set up."

Benjamin Furly, of Rotterdam, had been a "traveling companion" of Penn, and became the agent to negotiate the sale of the land, and procure passage for emigrants. He applied to James Claypole, and secured a passage "on the *Concord*, William Jeffries, Master, a staunch vessel of five hundred tons' burthen. It was to sail on the 17th of July, but, as the Crefelders were delayed, did not leave till the 24th." James Claypole's letter-book MSS. of the Historical Society of Pennsylvania. "This pioneer guard of German emigrants to America consisted of thirty-three persons forming thirteen families." Prof. Seidensticker adds the names of the heads of families, and refers to "Germantown *Grund and Lager Buch* in the Recorder's office, Philadelphia."

The *Concord* had a long but "pleasant passage," and reached Philadelphia, October 8, A. D. 1683. James Claypole writes: "The blessing of the Lord did attend us, so that we had a very comfortable passage, and had our health all the way." Peter Bleickers was born on board the ship. (Abington Meeting Records.)

Pastorius had preceded these emigrants by a few weeks' voyaging "in the *America*, Captain Wasey." Penn received him kindly and hospitably, and doubtless the Krisheim Friends were glad to meet Penn again, on the "free soil of Pennsylvania," where no persecutor could attack them. New homes rose in the "German-town," and Penn preached at Peter Shoemaker's to the new settlers.

Penn thus "opened the gates through which Germany poured a continuous and widening stream of emigration into the new province." The armies of Louis XIV helped to drive Germans from home to more peaceful quarters. Cruelty wasted the Palatinate with "fire and rapine." "Those that could escape to Pennsylvania blessed the asylum prepared for them, and twice blessed its enlightened and kind-hearted founder." "Not only the Pennsylvania pioneers of English nationality recognize in William Penn their head and leader, the standard of religious liberty that he planted here, shone as a beacon sign also to the oppressed multitudes of Germany, and gladly they flocked to the fertile vales whither the gentle Friend invited them."

Thus does Prof. Seidensticker close the learned article which has been here only in part synopsized, and those who wish to learn more of the romantic events that accompanied this tour of Penn, and of the Labadists, and kindred subjects should read the complete article.

WAR TIMES.

While the Battle of Germantown has been described in these articles, an account of the skirmish at Mount Airy is appropriate here. In Sparks's Washington, Vol. V, pp. 468-9, is an extract from a letter written by Colonel John E. Howard to Colonel Pickering, dated Baltimore, January 29th, 1827. It says: "As we descended into the valley near Mt. Airy the sun rose, but was soon obscured. The British picket at Allen's house had two six-pounders, which were several times fired at the advance, and killing several persons. Sullivan's division in the valley left the road, and moved to the right through fields, and formed in a line running from Allen's house toward the Schuylkill; our left about two hundred yards from the house. Soon after being formed, we had orders to move on, and advance through a field to the encampment of the British light infantry in an orchard, where we found them formed to receive us. A close and sharp action commenced, and continued fifteen or twenty minutes, when the British broke and retreated. In one regiment four officers and upwards of thirty men were wounded; and to the best of my recollection several men were killed. In the advance we had inclined to the left, until we reached the road; and in the action one company, commanded by Captain Daniel Dorsey, crossed the road. It is certain that no other part of the army was up with us at that time.

"Colonel Hall who was on foot, ordered me to bring up the company that had crossed the road; but finding them engaged from behind houses with some of the enemy, whom I supposed had belonged to the picket, I judged it not proper to call them off, as it would expose our flank. I reported to Colonel Hall who then desired me to let him have my horse, and said he would bring them up himself. Riding one way, and I looking another, the horse ran with him under a cider-press, and he was so hurt that he was taken from the field. I was then left in command of the regiment, as Lieutenant Colonel Smith some time before had been detached to Fort Mifflin. The enemy by this time had given way, and I pushed on through their encampment, their tents standing, and in the road, before we came opposite to Chew's House, took two six-pounders, which I supposed were those that had been with the picket; but as the drag-ropes had been cut and taken away, we could do nothing with them."

General Sullivan wrote to Meshech Weare, President of New Hampshire, from the camp at Whitemarsh, on October 25, 1777, that the right wing of the American Army reached Chestnut Hill at break of day, and a regiment of Conway's Brigade, and one from the Second Maryland Brigade, were sent to Mount Airy to attack the pickets at Allen's house. Sullivan's Division followed Conway's, and Wayne's Division brought up the rear. The picket when attacked was reinforced by the light infantry. General Conway endeavored to repulse the brave infantry, who stood their ground, and Sullivan aided him. The English strove to flank the Americans. Sullivan ordered Ford's regiment to repulse them. Wayne's Division was formed on the east side of the road to attack the right of the enemy. There were various manœuvers in the perplexing fog. Fence walls and ditches gave the English a chance to stand, and the Americans were detained in tearing down fences. Cannon balls and bayonets were in aftertimes dug up in this section. Major Morris, the aid-de-camp of Sullivan, was ordered by his General to inform Washington when the British left wing gave way, and request his Excellency to order Wayne to advance against the right of the English force. Washington ordered Wayne to advance, which he did rapidly with his brave men to Germantown. (Sparks's Washington, Vol. V, pp. 464–5.)

I would add that at a house on the lower side of Cresheim creek was the American outpost at the battle of Germantown. The British were where a spring-house now stands, and where a log cabin originally stood. The British fired on the morning of the battle, and a picket wounded a civilian leaning against a tree. This was the first shot of the battle, and after it the British retreated towards Germantown.

THE ALLENS.

A short account of Chief Justice Allen and his sons may be found in Sabine's American Loyalists.

Trout Hall heretofore mentioned on the site of Allentown, was built "before 1755, as it is marked 'William Allen's House' on a draft of the road from Easton to Reading drawn that year." (Davis's History of Bucks County, p. 595.) "What remains of the old Hall is incorporated with the buildings of Muhlenberg College." *Ib.* Fort Allen built of logs, was on the site of Allentown, which has been named in connection with Judge Allen. Before the Revolution it saw the courage of Col. James Burd, in Indian wars. In the Revolution the bells of Christ Church, Philadelphia, were concealed in Allentown and there John Fries stirred up the "Northampton Insurrection."—(See Watson's Annals, Vol. II, pp. 149, 180 and 206.)

The main street of the town runs over the place where the fort stood. The fort was once taken by surprise by the Indians, while the garrison were skating on the Lehigh river.

Allen's lane took its name from Judge Allen, who owned property on the upper side of it. A depot on the Pennsylvania Railroad perpetuates the name. The Judge, who was quite wealthy, gave the ground where the first school house was built on that lane. The building was erected by the public, but it was a pay school, as it was before the day of free schools. William Kulp, Jacob Bockius and Mr. Thomas were teachers. I am indebted to the memory of John Bishop, an old pupil, for these notes. An old house of the Livezey family, at the end of Allen's lane on the creek, has a Revolutionary history.

In Watson's Annals (Vol. II. p. 71), we find from John Miller's diary, that on June 10, 1778, the British "came up again by different routes and joined forces at Allen's lane (now Mt. Airy), and returned before nine o'clock in the morning—effecting nothing but the plundering of gardens, etc." On June 13th they marched to Mt. Airy for the last time. So for months after the battle this country district was unquiet.

Allen township, in Northampton county, Pennsylvania, is named for Chief Justice Allen. There is also an East Allen township. See Dr. W. H. Egle's History of Pennsylvania, also Hotchkin's Pocket Gazetteer of Pennsylvania, pp. 132–3.

THE LOVETT FREE LIBRARY.

Mrs. Charlotte Bostwick has given $25,000 to endow a free library at Mt. Airy. She also bought the ground, built the library building and has put it in charge of a board of managers. Her rector, Rev. Simeon C. Hill, is the president of the board. He is in charge of Grace Episcopal Church, Mount Airy, and has given me some particulars as to the library, which I will add to this notice.

The Memorial Free Library is at the corner of Main street and Sedgwick, and is a memorial of Mr. Thomas R. Lovett, erected 1887. It is a stone building. The lot is 100 x 115—all donated by Mrs. Bostwick, a sister of T. R. Lovett. It is on a part of the ten-acre lot. The library was started in Grace Church and had a room 12 x 12 for two years. The ladies' offered their services for librarians. We have two thousand and one hundred books; seven thousand books were taken out during the year.

The houses being built on Mt. Pleasent avenue are constructed by Mr. Ashton Tourison, architect and builder.

The improvements in Mt. Airy began about three years ago. Gowen avenue was macadamized two or three years ago; the other streets are not paved.

The station houses at Mt. Pleasant and Mt. Airy are about four years old, mostly in same place as previous ones, or nearly same location.

Gowen avenue was formerly called Miller avenue.

Opposite Grace Episcopal Church, on Mt. Airy avenue, is a large building which was erected as a church by the United Brethren, and used by them for four or six years. The Presbyterians started a service in the vicinity and the building of the United Brethren was sold.

FRANCIS I. GOWEN has a pleasant modern cottage on Gowen avenue, of wood and stone. Boyer street contains some nice cottages. Charles S. Binney, Esq., resides in one of them, and Mr. Haines occupies another. Mr. DeWahle has a modern stone cottage on Gowen avenue, and John Hartman a fine brick cottage, and Jordan Roper, Esq., a stone cottage on the same avenue. Mr. Roper married a sister of F. B. Gowen, Esq. Messrs. W. H. Thorn and Schwatky occupy twin cottages on Gowen avenue. Mr. Bunford Samuels is building a new stone house on Gowen avenue. He is connected with the Ridgway Library.

The stone house next but one below the Swan Hotel, on the same side, was built by FRANCIS BOCKIUS, who came to this country from Germany. The wife was a Miss Miller. The large old stone barn on Gowen avenue, which is a striking feature, belonged to the farm. The property now belongs to the Gowen estate. Mr. Edmund Bockius, son of John M. Bockius, the eldest son of Francis, is a saddler at 5014 Main street, Germantown. In the War of 1812, John M. Bockius raised a rifle company of one hundred and twenty men in ten days, and went to the rendezvous at Marcus Hook, but after the defeat of the Battle of New Orleans, the British failed to appear. The Captain had a harness store at the corner of Manheim and Main streets, Germantown.

As we come to the bridge over Cresheim creek, we meet with the house of Mrs. Dunn. Next to this is a new house where the Guyer family reside.

Just after leaving Mt. Airy station, going toward Chestnut Mill, on the Reading Railroad, the traveler may have observed a board-walk on the right leading to a retired rustic abode. This is the

RESIDENCE OF FRANKLIN B. GOWEN, Esq.,

late President of the Reading Railroad, and known as a business man and a lawyer in the old world, as well as the new. Here, among the scenes of his boyhood, in a pretty English-looking cottage, he finds rest from the city's turmoil. The rear of the lawn looks as if it might be a country solitude, though Gowen avenue in front betokens life and advancement. This place bears appropriately the historical name "Cresheim."

On the border of Cresheim creek, on the west side of the turnpike, is a place which was formerly owned by the Riter family, who were old inhabitants. The old mansion of stone, near the road, is a story and a half high. The Schaeffer family now own the property. Its wooded grounds are a pretty feature. Levi Rex married Kate Riter, and the place passed into their hands. A later house was built, but the newer one has seen half a century.

Let us look at the bridge. The modern wall, with its brown stone coping, looks too grand for the little simple Cresheim creek, which would prefer the wild Indian days to the gay modern life that now drives over it. The old stone barn on the upper side is a relief, as it has an antique look. The hills, beautifully wooded, rise from the meadow that skirts the stream, while a weeping willow finds its home by the bridge. As we look beneath the coping of the bridge, heated by the sun so as to be warm to the touch, we read in a large square brown stone, the figures 1884, and long to see the first rude log that spanned the humble stream. Still, the passing water cart is a refreshment of civilization on this June day, and the new days are in some respects superior to the old ones.

THE GOWEN FAMILY.

JAMES GOWEN, the father of James E. Gowen and Franklin B. Gowen, was an Irishman, born at Newtownstewart, county Tyrone, Ireland, on the 17th of March, A. D. 1790. He was educated at the Academy of Strabane, after leaving school was tutor in a private family for two years, and came to America on reaching the age of twenty-one years. He entered the counting-house of the late Henry Pratt, Philadelphia, and in a short time engaged in business as a shipping merchant and made a voyage to Ireland in 1817 in a ship of which he was part owner. In 1827 he suffered during the panic then prevailing and subsequently engaged in business as a grocer, and afterward

RESIDENCE OF THE LATE JAMES GOWEN, AT MOUNT AIRY, NOW LUTHERAN THEOLOGICAL SEMINARY.

as a wine merchant, at the corner of Third and Dock streets, and was later the senior partner in the firm of Gowen, Jacobs & Co., on Dock street, near Third. Mr. Gowen, in 1827, married Mary, daughter of Joseph Miller, of Mount Airy (a descendant of Sebastian Miller, whose ancestor came to America with Pastorius), and subsequently purchased the Miller estate, which still remains in possession of his family. After his marriage, Mr. Gowen resided on Third street, opposite St. Peter's Church; but in 1834 moved to Mount Airy, and took up his residence in the old Miller house which was built in 1792 and is now occupied by the family of his son, James E. Gowen, deceased. Mr. Gowen was a Democrat in politics, but during the United States Bank struggles he ran on the Anti-Jackson ticket for Congress in 1828 and 1832, and was defeated by the regular Democratic nominee. On one of these occasions the names of the four candidates for the four Congressional districts of Philadelphia on the same ticket were Watmough, Harper, Ingersoll and Gowen, the initials spelling W H I G. Mr. Gowen retired from business in middle life, and became a well-known agriculturist. He was the first to import a herd of blooded cattle, and his well-known Durham stock was for many years celebrated over the United States, and his spring sales of blooded cattle attracted to Mount Airy a concourse of cattle breeders and agriculturists from many States. Mr. Gowen was instrumental in organizing the Pennsylvania Agricultural Society, and was second president of the association. He wrote much upon scientific agriculture and delivered many addresses upon this and other kindred subjects. Before moving to Mount Airy he took an active part in all the business and social affairs of his adopted city. He was a vestryman of St. Paul's Episcopal Church, South Third street, a member of Councils, a Director of the Bank of Pennsylvania, and a prominent member of St. Patrick and other institutions for the amelioration of the condition of his fellow countrymen, the Irish, to whom he was always warmly attached, and many of whom he aided by his means and counsel. He died at his residence "Magnolia Villa" at Mount Airy on the 8th of January, 1873, in the 83d year of his age, and is buried at St. Luke's Graveyard, Germantown, which Church he had attended for many years, the old rector, Rev. John Rodney, having been an intimate personal friend of his before Mr. Rodney came to Germantown.

"In 1848, James Gowen, a noted Philadelphia agriculturist, established a school for practical farmers, at Mount Airy, Germantown. A farm was cultivated in connection with the school. The institution was successfully conducted for several years."—Wickersham's History of Education in Pennsylvania, p. 432. The Agricultural State College followed in a few years. The Mount Airy School began in April, 1848, and continued for five years.

James E. Gowen, son of the above, was born in South Third street, Philadelphia, on the 3d of February, A. D. 1830. He was educated, and graduated with high honors, at Mount St. Mary's College, Emmittsburg, Maryland, taking the degrees of A. B., and afterward A. M., and later in life was made

LL. D., by the same institution. He studied law with the late John M. Scott of Philadelphia, and was called to the bar when 21 years of age. He was for many years the law partner of the late St. George T. Campbell, and had a large and lucrative practice, principally in equity and corporation cases. He died February 16, 1885, and is buried at St. Luke's Churchyard, Germantown. He was of great learning in and out of his profession, of studious and retiring disposition, warmly attached to his profession and was, at the time of his death, not only one of the most learned members of the bar of Philadelphia, but universally respected and beloved by the entire profession. This prominent and brilliant lawyer died at the Miller homestead in Mount Airy, in the 56th year of his age.

The old GOWEN or MILLER HOMESTEAD, a view of which, by the courtesy of F. B. Gowen, Esq., has appeared in these articles, was occupied as an Agricultural College, under the charge of John Wilkinson, from 1848 to 1853.

In the Rev. J. F. Dripp's sketch of the First Presbyterian Church in Germantown, Mr. B. F. Gowen contributes the following note about his grandfather: "Mr. Joseph Miller, my maternal grandfather, was born at Mount Airy, in the upper part of Germantown, on January 26th, 1757, and died at Mount Airy, March 27th, 1825. He married Susanna Raser, who was born January 12, 1767, and who long survived him, dying in Philadelphia, September 23, 1853. In 1792, he built the stone house at Mount Airy, in which he subsequently lived and died, in which my mother and myself were born, in which I recently lived, and which is now occupied by my brother, Mr. James E. Gowen."

Mr. Miller's father wrote his name Sebastian Müller, in German fashion. His marriage record is dated April 10th, 1754. The marriage took place in Germantown. Mr. Dripps states that the family was one of the oldest connected with the German Reformed Congregation, and that Mr. Miller was prominent in the community. He very reluctantly left the old church, when he felt that the necessities of his children and other youth for English religious services compelled his action, "as a chief founder of the new organization." Rev. Dr. Blair and Mr. Miller made the agreement for an organ of fourteen stops, to cost $1200, to be completed within a year, by Alexander Schlotman. Mr. Miller added to other duties that of organist of the new church for many years (p. 19). Mr. Miller was a great pedestrian, and a friend of the family informs me that he walked once from his own house to Norristown and back in the morning, and the same afternoon into the city and back.

I am indebted to Mr. Charles Miller, a son of Joseph Miller, who resides on Gowen avenue, for local information. He is over eighty years of age. An old cherry tree still stands in a field opposite his house from which he plucked cherries when almost an infant. When I saw the old tree its top was wearing away, but many blossoms still adorned it, and gave promise of coming fruit. Mr. Miller's son, Rev. Joseph L. Miller, is assistant minister at St. Stephen's Episcopal Church on Tenth street.

THE GOWEN HOMESTEAD AT MOUNT AIRY.

Mr. James Gowen's will, in a printed pamphlet, shows that he styled himself in that document, "formerly merchant, now farmer." He calls his mansion "Magnolia Villa."

Modern Mt. Airy looks at the reader prosperously as he glances over *The Country House*, of November '85, published by Howard M. Jenkins, and sees the last page entirely devoted to displaying the natural and artificial advantages of the Gowen estate for residences, while telegraphs and cheap fare make it a desirable suburb. A yellow colored pamphlet in my hand, with its account of a Telford road, among the old houses and their newer cousins, and the ancient and modern trees make a fine showing for antique Cresheim, modernized beyond its expectation.

Cresheim creek and Cresheim road, however, still keep up the association with Germany, and in the modern rage for change may their names be allowed to stand as monuments of two past centuries. Through the ancient German township, as the tract was called, still runs faithful Germantown avenue formerly known as "The King's Highway," or "Plymouth and North Wales Great Road." It has uncomplainingly borne the tread of provincials and the citizens of a modern republic, and cart and carriage are alike welcome to it. The Mermaid Hotel is one of the oldest in the country. It is of stone, standing a little in the rear of the pike on the east side just above Cresheim creek. A branch of Cresheim creek formerly ran near the hotel, and a pond was made there which was used for baptizing by immersion. Many years ago Mr. Webker was host here. In those days there were turkey-shooting matches. Martin Painter was another landlord who held the post for many years. Messrs. Beans, Hinkle and Clark were subsequent landlords. James Kershaw, the present owner, is the successor of Mr. Clark. At one time prize-fighters were trained here, but fortunately those days have departed.

MERMAIDS.

The "History of Sign Boards," by Jacob Larwood and John Camden Hotten observes that Shakespeare and Ben. Jonson notice this sign. Hollinshed gives an account of a merman caught in King John's day. Gervase of Tilbury, said that mermen and mermaids lived in the British ocean. The mermaids were sometimes exhibited, whatever they were. The sea-serpents are their rivals. In 1603, Sir Walter Raleigh established a literary club at the Mermaid tavern, in Bread street, London, thought to be doubtless the first in England. Shakespeare, Ben. Jonson, Beaumont, Fletcher, Selden, Carew, Martin, Donne and Cotton were members. Beaumont writes to Ben. Jonson poetically:

> "What things have we seen
> Done at the Mermaid!"

Adding an account of the wit that sparkled there.

There was another Mermaid in Cheapside. The sign was used by printers. John Rastall, brother-in-law of Sir Thomas More, "emprynted in the Cheapesyde at the sygne of the Meremayde, next to Poulysgate in 1527."

" In 1576 a translation of the " History of Lazarillo de Tormes, dedicated to Sir Thomas Gresham," was printed by Henry Binneman, the Queen's printer, in Knightrider street, at the sign of the Mermaid. A representation of this fabulous creature was generally prefixed to his books."

There was a carriers' inn in Carter lane, in 1681, called the Mermaid. One of the London mermaids could hardly have swum over to Philadelphia. If a London mermaid came to give name to this hotel she must have taken the old long route down the Thames, across sea to the Delaware river, up that river to the Schuylkill, and Wissahickon and Cresheim creeks. Her name at least abides. Mermen first grew scarce and mermaids are also vanishing, but read the following from a newspaper:

MERRY MAIDEN AND THE TAR.—If any one doubts the existence of mermaids the fishermen of Cape Breton do not, for one was seen there the other day. The North Sydney *Herald* reports that while Mr. Bagnall and several fishermen were out in a boat they saw floating on the water what they thought was a corpse. They approached for the purpose of taking it ashore for burial, when, to their great surprise, it turned around to a sitting position and looked toward them, and disappeared. A few moments after it appeared to the surface and again looked toward them, after which it disappeared altogether. The face, head, shoulders, and arms resembled those of a human being, but the lower extremities had the appearance of a fish. The back of its head was covered with long, dark hair resembling a horse's mane. The arms were exactly shaped like those of a human being, excepting that the fingers were very long. The color of the skin was not unlike that of a human being.

Oliver Wendell Holmes pays compliment to the mermaid in the " Ballad of the Oyster-man." When the fisherman's daughter swoons and never revives, and her lover, who has swum to meet her, in returning, is taken with cramp and drowned, perishing as did Leander in one of his visits to the lovely Hero, the poem closes:

> " But Fate has metamorphosed them, in pity of their woe,
> And now they keep an oyster shop for mermaids down below."

The pursuit of mermaid history is however exasperating, as Josiah Allen's wife found it to be when her irate husband, hoping to hear one sing, saw a dried mummy with horse-hairs pasted on its shell, and, according to the sketch, desired to extinguish the mariner who presented the false show at Saratoga. She closes her sad experience thus: " Truly, there is something that the boldest female pardner dassent do. Mermaids is one of the things I don't dast to bring up. No! no, fur be it from me to say 'mermaid' to Josiah Allen." A vignette of a mermaid on a rock, combing her long locks and holding a harp, appropriately ends this chapter of Miss Holly's " Samantha at Saratoga." Mt.

Airy people do not fear a mermaid, for a pretty station-house on the Reading Railroad and an avenue bear the name.

GLEN FERN AND THE LIVEZEY FAMILY.

At the foot of Allen's lane, on the Wissahickon creek, lies the old mansion of the Livezey family, styled "Glen Fern." It is a fine relic of the past and deserves better care than it has received since it became a part of the Park. The ancient stone house no doubt felt very grand when it was first built, and its old age should be rendered at least respectable. It is a fine specimen of the antique American farm house. The main part of the building is two stories in height, and a dormer window surmounts its roof. Two attic windows look benignantly from the gable over the lower section of the house. One chimney rises from the rear of the roof, while another stands between the mansion and its adjunct, and a third is seen on the lowest extension. The main house has a porch. The dwelling has three parts, rising in grades, like steps, from the ground. The second elevation has an attic and another dormer window, while the third and lowest section modestly refrains from such an adornment. Each part boasts its own front door, so that, as in the adobe houses in New Mexico, one may go in or out one portion of the house without disturbing a person in another portion. A stone wall guards the property in front. The old trees stand as sentinels on the hill in the rear, and under the winter snow, or in the summer sun, present a pretty sight to the beholder. The building has been photographed in winter with good effect. I am indebted to Mr. John Livezey, of Mount Airy, for valuable information in regard to those who dwelt in this historic mansion in past days.

There are a quantity of family papers in the possession of the family. While the family name is sometimes pronounced differently, the above is the old way of spelling it. The Livezeys belonged to the Society of Friends. The will of Thomas is dated 1695. He was the first purchaser of five hundred acres of land from William Penn. The will of his son, and that of his only grandson, Thomas, as well as the wills of others, are in the hands of Mr. John Livezey. The grandfather of John Livezey was a flour merchant and ran flour mills. He was also an importer. One invoice, dated about 1800, shows that he sent four thousand Spanish dollars on the ship *Pacific*, bound for Canton, for china, silk and tea. The tea was for private use, and to be packed in small packages, as directed. There is still a large hall-clock in the family, which was mentioned in the first will, and has been handed down by will to the present generation. It still runs and keeps good time, though the winter affects it and makes it strike as if it had a bad cold.

Several casks of wine were buried in the Wissahickon creek at the old Livezey house. Mr. John Livezey writes me that his father had some of this ancient wine, which was left him by his father. Mr. John Livezey's father died in his 85th year. The wine was placed under water to keep it from the British in Revolutionary days.

CHESTNUT HILL.

Chestnut Hill.

Summerhausen, from the German (Summerhouses), was the native place of Pastorius; as it was the old name of Chestnut Hill, it should be perpetuated in some new avenue which may be formed. Summerhausen, a village in Bavaria, in Lower Franconia, on the right bank of the Main, S. E. of Wurzburg. Population 1229, Lippincott's Gazetteer of 1866. Cresheim holds its own, and the other relics of German history should be preserved. Crefeld, which was the German name of the section above Chestnut Hill, should also give name to an avenue in that section which is being laid out and improved. Chestnut Hill was so named from the abundance of chestnut timber. The Germans called it Chestnut Barracks. In treating Chestnut Hill we desire to give everything interesting which meets us, whether it be ancient or modern. In George Greeve's translation of De Chasteleux's "Travels in North America," Vol. I, p. 291, it is written of this place: "It is called Chestnut Hill, from a little church of that name, situated on its summit." The writer speaks of the two hills and the encampment of the army, so he refers probably to the St. Thomas's church, at White Marsh, but is mistaken as to the origin of the name. About 1780 deeds note this place as "Chestnut Hill."

When good Mrs. Lydia Darrach, the wife of the Philadelphia teacher, William Darrach, by her information started Colonel Craig on his ride from Frankford to Whitemarsh, to warn Washington that the British had planned to attack him secretly did the Colonel rush along this Germantown road, where the carriages and wagons now pass so peacefully? A little glance at those days may well introduce the history of this section.

Washington on the 10th of December, 1777, writes from the Whitemarsh Camp to the President of Congress that on the preceding week General Howe had left Philadelphia with a force at night and the next morning had reached Chestnut Hill. In a skirmish the American General Irvine was wounded and captured. On a later day Colonel Morgan and his corps, and the Maryland militia under Colonel Gist, attacked the British force. The next day the English retreated to Philadelphia. Major Morris, who is styled by Washington "a brave and gallant officer," was wounded during this expedition. (Sparks's Washington, Vol. 5, pp. 180–1.)

General Washington writes Richard Henry Lee, from Valley Forge, on February 15th, A. D. 1778: "Lord Cornwallis has certainly embarked for England, but with what view is not so easy to determine. He was an eyewitness a few days before his departure to a scene, not a little disgraceful to the pride of British valor, in their manœuvre to Chestnut Hill, and precipitate return, after boasting their intentions of driving us beyond the mountains." (Sparks's Washington, Vol. 5, p. 238.)

The geology of this region is described as follows: "Rock-faced bluffs are found at Chestnut Hill, four hundred feet above tide-water mark." (Bean's History of Montgomery County, p. 3.) "The northwestern slope of these hills descends to the basin of the Plymouth valley, through which runs a belt of limestone, some two miles in width, with rich beds of hematite iron ore, white and blue marble, limestone, soapstone, and large masses of gray rock, easily quarried and largely used in heavy masonry. This limestone belt crosses the Schuylkill river between Conshohocken and Swedes' Ford and extends in a westerly direction to Howeltown, in the Schuylkill valley. The soil of this locality is very productive, and is considered by many the most valuable in the county for agricultural purposes." (Bean's History of Montgomery County, p. 3.)

I subjoin a touch of legendary love, which Judge Samuel W. Pennypacker, informs me that he furnished to Townsend Ward, and which I found among Mr. Ward's manuscript notes in the Historical Society of Pennsylvania's Library.

It is from a German book, entitled (Erschsinungen der Gester) "The appearance of Spirits." Mr. Pennypacker translated this story.

"Many years ago, the still living Christian Gunti was traveling along the road leading out of Germantown over Chestnut Hill, and he saw two Indians approaching. Since the sun had already gone down, he could not determine whether they were men or women, but still he saw that they had angry faces. The one took the other by the neck and choked him, threw him down on the ground, knelt upon him, and choked him standing on his throat. Meanwhile Christian Gunti approached (he cared less for the dead than the living, and saw such evil spirits wherever they were, so that such things were not new to him) and when he came near and looked at them, he knew that he could be of no assistance. After he had watched them awhile they both disappeared. Some time after that he had to help repair the road, and when they came to this place, a neighbor said, "Here once an Indian beat his wife to death." Christian Gunti answered, "I don't believe that he beat her, he choked her."

The writer will be deeply obliged to any one who may have any historical knowledge or any collection of newspaper clippings or other matter concerning Chestnut Hill, if he will communicate with him, and, if so disposed, add his store to the common heap which may thus accumulate, as the word indicates, cumulus, in Latin, meaning a heap. Thus did Mr. Pennypacker aid his friend Ward in the preceding note.

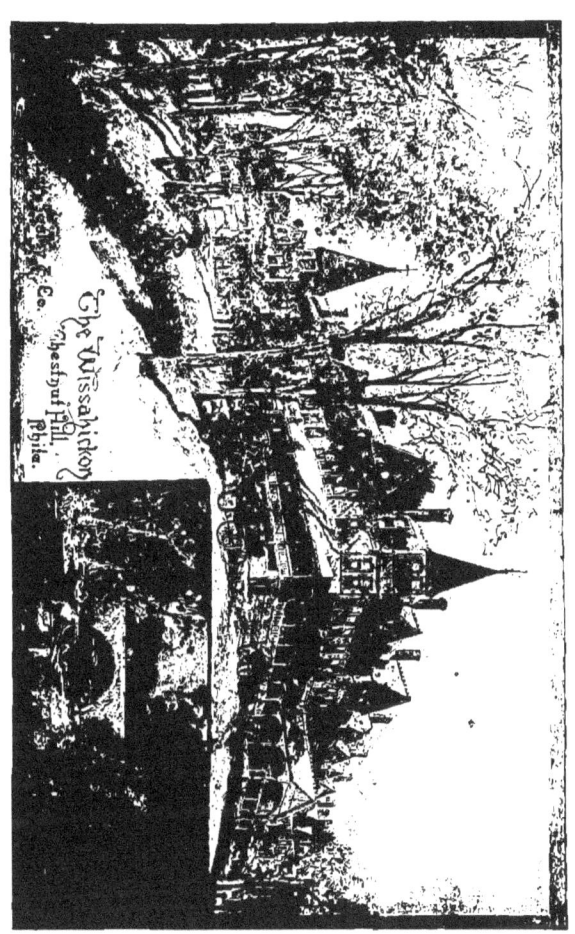

CHESTNUT HILL.

WISSAHICKON INN.

James M. Aiman, Sr., of Springfield avenue, kindly gives me information with regard to the neighborhood of the Wissahickon Inn. The Wissahickon Inn is on the site of the old Park House, which was burned on the 29th of March, A. D. 1877. The building was burned at night. It was empty at the time, and was left vacant during the winter season.

The Park Hotel was built in 1863. Previous to this there had been a small hotel at this point kept by Reuben Sands, of Indian Rock, now deceased. The new hotel was added to this building. When the Chestnut Hill Hospital was sold a part of the material was purchased and used in constructing the Park Hotel, which contained about ninety rooms. It was a summer boarding house kept by Mrs. Mary Andrew, at the time of the burning. Mrs. Field had had charge of it before 1872 for several years. George W. Hill, of Philadelphia, owned the hotel. After the fire Mr. H. H Houston bought the property, which embraced 237 acres of land, and included the cricket ground, lawn, playground and drive. The drive on which St. Martin's in-the-Fields is to be constructed belonged to Hiram Hartwell, and was sold by him to Mr. Houston. Joseph Casper Weiss owned the land where the Wissahickon station now stands. Mr. Weiss lives on Germantown road, above Mermaid lane.

The plastered stone house, owned and occupied by James M. Aiman, Sr., on Springfield avenue, was formerly the property of the Streeper family. John Streeper, who has been dead for several years, was born here. The house must be eighty or more years old. One of the old deeds recites that it once belonged to a spinster, using the word which indicated that maiden women spun when the word was coined, as the similar word in Webster means a weaver. The old Cresheim road runs from the front of this house, on Springfield avenue, to Carpenter's lane, in Germantown, where it ends. The distance is under two miles. France's Mill lies on this road. His dam has lately been named Lake Surprise, and the Wissahickon guests use it for boating. Mr. Houston has deepened and improved it. In winter it is a skating-ground. The old stone house is now a children's home.

On a lane, or a blind road without an outlet at the farther end among the hills and rocks, lies Hill's Mill, which was formerly a woolen mill, and now is being turned into a paper mill. This is a part of Mr. Houston's property. Some old houses still lie along the road. Near Carpenter's lane was the place of William Bohlen, which is now in the hands of Mr. Houston.

Mr. George Rahn lived at the southwest corner of Cresheim road and the lane leading to Hill's Mill. He died several years ago. He was a man of influence in the neighborhood, and was a highly esteemed member of the Democratic party. He was quite intelligent and a leader.

Watson, in his "Annals," Vol. II, p. 18, says: "All the settlers in Cresheim built on the Cresheim road before settling a house on the Germantown road through Cresheim. There is an old map, made in 1700, in which all their residences and barns at that time are marked." So this is the mother settlement here, and is interesting on that account to the antiquary.

Some pretty modern stone cottages meet the pedestrian as he enters Cresheim road. While the earliest settlers are said to have selected this old highway for their homes they erected simpler dwellings. A child's tent and drum, in the rear of the first cottage on the right may remind us of Revolutionary days. Beyond the cottages, a neat white house, standing back from the road, contrasts prettily with the green trees in front of it, and has a cool look on warm days. A ha-ha wall is in front, and a wall at the side of the footway bounds the road, stone steps are in front while a street lamp opposite would have astonished the old Cresheimers.

An old-fashioned, ample plastered house is on the other side of the road, almost opposite. On the right more modern stone cottages crowd the country district along the railway. France's Mill is three stories in height with an attic with dormer windows. It looks very lonesome, and as if it longed to hear again the busy noises and cheerful voices which waked the echoes in the past.

The road descends rapidly here amidst striking scenery, and runs under one of the fine bridges of the Pennsylvania Railway. Two trains have passed diverse ways almost over my head, as I write these lines, indicating how modern civilization crowds on antique life. A number of small houses are in blocks on the left and have apparently stood for some time.

A deep spring, with a well-like wall, is a pretty feature on the right. An old square tower of a spring-house, looking like a mimic foreign castle, stands near the spring.

On the opposite side of the road an old boiler pipe has been utilized to throw the sparkling water on the rocks below, and in continuous flow it keeps up a constant pleasant sound. Near by is Hayes's picker house, used for preparing carpet yarn. It is a new building. The old grist-mill called Hinkle's mill, described heretofore in these articles, stood in front of it. That mill was burned and its walls were taken down to make room for the railway, except the upper wall, which was left standing. Hayes's mill proper is near Germantown road, above the picker house at Hinkle's mill. Mr. David Hayes lives in Germantown. He owns this property. This mill and that on the Cresheim road belonged to the France family. Two brothers, John and Ervine France, built the mill on Cresheim road after selling the other one.

The woods and rocks back of Hayes's mill are pretty, and a low house in the rear of the mill has an English look. A wheel hanging on the wall added to the picturesqueness of the scene. Mr. Hayes has a stone quarry near Germantown avenue, just above Cresheim creek.

Daniel Thomas had a grist-mill on the Wissahickon, not far from Wissahickon Inn. Mr. Megargee made a paper mill of this property. Mr. Thomas's son was drowned in early manhood, and the mother, then a widow, soon moved to Philadelphia, and the property passed out of the hands of the family.

This magnificent and pleasant summer resort occupies a high position near the Pennsylvania Railroad. A continuous wood runs from the rear of the Inn to the romantic Wissahickon, so that children can find places for recreation close at hand, and adults can lose themselves among the wild beauties of nature within a few minutes' ride of the teeming and busy city. The erection of this splendid building was one of the efforts which have been made of late to give citizens and their families places of recreation and refreshment near the town. The Devon Inn on the main line of the Pennsylvania Railroad, is another instance of this kind of commendable enterprise. The Wissahickon Inn stands on the site of the old Park Hotel, which was burned. There was a race-course near by. The new building was finished on the 30th of May, A. D. 1884. It is constructed of stone and tile. It contains about two hundred and fifty rooms. William C. Mackie, of Chestnut Hill, was the contractor, and G. W. and W. D. Hewitt were the architects. The *porte cochere* and piazzas give a pleasant look to the exterior. The high position makes the building visible at a distance. Mr. H. H. Houston, who owns the Wissahickon Inn, is building many fine houses in this vicinity. The cricket ground, with its high brown fence, is near the Inn.

The Devil's Pool, a little way from the Wissahickon Inn, was the scene of an engagement in the battle of Germantown. See Charles S. Keyser's "Fairmount Park," p. 108. It is narrated that in 1776, when the soldiers left Roxborough, at the branch running into the Devil's Pool, they separated from their wives and sisters and fathers and mothers, and kneeling on the rocks the old men commended their beloved to God in prayer. It was such Christian faith and trust that gave power to the American Revolution, and this place is hallowed by such a remembrance. Mr. Keyser says that in provincial times the superstitious sought this spot, while now artists and lovers of nature resort to it. He adds: "It is certainly a wild place; rocks are thrown together in great masses, and the long trunks of hemlocks and pines jut up from the darkness around the pool into the sunshine above."

A tributary of the Wissahickon creek feeds this pool, the depth of which stirred superstitious minds to give it its name. It was also, however, called the Hermit's Pool. Its picture may be seen in art galleries. The word Devil should be avoided in naming places. Kentucky has a post office called Devil's Creek, and Dakota one styled Devil's Lake. The Hermit's Pool gives a thought of the interesting and romantic story of the hermits of the Wissahickon, and is a better appellation than the Devil's Pool. In W. M. Praed's poem, "The Red Fisherman," we see the unpleasant effect of an evil name:

> "And bold was he who thither came,
>   At midnight, man or boy;
> For the place was cursed with an evil name,
>   And that name was 'The Devil's Decoy!'"

The fearful sights which the ballad represents as passing before the eyes of the Abbot as the Devil fishes his victims from the pool justify the name, and it is a relief to hear the close, beginning:

"Oh ho! on ho!
The cock doth crow;
It is time for the Fisher to rise and go."

So the keys turn, the locks creak, and the Red Fisherman stalks away with his iron box with its strange bait.

YEAKEL COTTAGE.

The YEAKEL COTTAGE is one of the greatest antiquities on the Germantown road. It is at the upper corner of Mermaid lane and Germantown road. It is one of the few log-houses remaining in this region. It is one-story in height, but is cosy within and has a pleasant attic. It feels its years and needs repair, but it has done its work bravely for a generation. Its steep roof is broken by a chimney in the middle. The eave juts over the front door. Some friendly trees in front protect their ancient friend. The two on Mermaid avenue stand like Baucis and Philemon of mythological story. A little addition has been made to the upper side of the house. The gable end is on Germantown avenue. The Mermaid Hotel stands on the lower side, back from the street. Its white front contrasts prettily with the two guardian trees which stand before it clad in their summer verdure.

ISRAEL GILBERT, the father of Dr. F. C. Gilbert, the well-known practitioner of Chestnut Hill, lived for several years in the house now owned and occupied by Mrs. Quigg, on Main street, above Springfield avenue, on the west side. This old stone house was built by Wickard Miller in the 18th century, before the turnpike was made. Mr. Gilbert kept a store in a building adjoining this house, which has been removed, and a piazza has taken its place. After giving up merchandise, he was Justice of the Peace, and this building was his office. He improved the neighborhood by erecting buildings. He was a man of influence and standing in the community. He died in this house. His eldest son, Jonathan H. Gilbert, M. D., also died here. He had commenced practicing medicine at Fox Chase. Another son, Curtis T. Gilbert, removed to Virginia.

Maria A., a daughter, married Rev. R. F. Young, and died in Haddonfield, N. J. Her husband was the pastor of the Baptist Church there. There were two other daughters, Clementina Murray, who resides with Dr. J. C. Gilbert, and Deditnia, who married William D. Miller, a broker of Philadelphia, who died several years ago. Dr. Gilbert's father was the very first subscriber on the list of the GERMANTOWN TELEGRAPH, and was a warm friend of Major Freas. The old Gilbert house has a fine large yard on the upper side. The lady who now owns it is the mother-in-law of the present Dr. Gilbert, so that it is still in the family.

HAUNTED HOUSE.

On Stenton avenue, between Graver's lane and Willow Grove avenue, on the east side, stood a stone house belonging to Mr. Koons, who lived in it and owned it before the Revolution. He owned a tract reaching from that point to beyond Birch lane. My informant thinks that he was the English Consul. Rev. Michael Schlatter, a German Reformed minister, once lived here. A couple once came to be married on horseback, and wrapped the marriage fee in a piece of paper, which proved to be one cent instead of a gold piece. Two sons of Mr. Schlatter were in the Revolutionary army, named Michael and Claudius. He afterward owned and lived in the old stone house. He complained that his house was plundered by British troops. See Scharf & Westcott's History of Philadelphia, Vol. I, p. 386. The old building near the reservoir was called "the Spook House." It is said that the reputation of being haunted was given by those who wished to have privacy in playing cards there at night. Spook is a German word, meaning ghost. The spooks were said to walk at night in a path which ran around a certain tree. The long stone house presents a gable toward Stenton avenue, and a front toward Bethesda Home. It is two and a half stories in height, with a hipped roof. A colored man named Daniel Davis, with his family, were the last occupants. The stories of haunted houses are popular and stir the mysterious element in man's nature. Thomas Hood describes such a place:

> "O'er all there hung a shadow and a fear,
> A sense of mystery the spirit daunted,
> And said, as plain as whisper in the ear,
> The place is haunted!"

While grown people and children alike love such legends, Longfellow, in his "Haunted Houses" (Poems, Vol. I, pp. 368–9), indicates that memories of the dead hang around all old houses.

> "All houses wherein men have lived and died
> Are haunted houses. Through the open doors
> The harmless phantoms on their errands glide,
> With feet that make no sound upon the floors."
> * * * * *
> "We have no title deeds to house or lands;
> Owners and occupants of earlier dates
> From graves forgotten stretch their dusty hands,
> And hold in mortmain still their old estates."

It is said that the ghost of modern writers is more polished than the fantastic apparition of former days. See a literary article in the Philadelphia PRESS, June 6, 1888 A. D.

The first cross street in entering Chestnut Hill from Mt. Airy is Mermaid avenue. Next comes Wissahickon, now called Springfield avenue. I believe it was first styled Park avenue. It is open only on the west side of Germantown road. Hartwell avenue follows; then Southampton, open on the west side only. The Lutheran Church is on the south of this avenue. Graver's lane succeeds. Then Highland avenue, open on the west side, but about to be cut through. Evergreen avenue takes us to the junction of the Bethlehem and Reading pikes.

Enoch Rex, Sr., owned the Haas property, at the northeast corner of Willow Grove and Germantown avenues, where are the ruins of the old stone barn which belonged to the ancient farm house. The stone house was far in the rear of Mr. Walter's present house. The house was demolished, and Anthony Groves, Jr., has a dwelling on its site. The farm belonged to Abraham Rex, the father of Enoch Rex, Sr.

Abraham Rex, in Revolutionary times, had a store, lumber-yard and lime-yard in Chestnut Hill. Walter Rex informs me that the store was on Main street, near Willow Grove avenue, on the east side of the way; The dwelling is on the estate of Matthias Haas. The store has departed. The burned wall of the barn stands near the location of the store. Abraham Rex is spoken of by Watson as the man who introduced clover seed, called in German " Kastanie Hugel." Watson also speaks of Rex's store as one of the old important places of trade for farmers when the turnpike was not built, and a journey to the city in muddy times was a great task.

The tower of the Public Buildings, at Broad and Market streets, is visible from Union avenue, near Germantown avenue.

Casper Strauss, a policeman, of Highland avenue, has an old map of Chestnut Hill.

There was an old toll-gate on Main street, at the point where Evergreen avenue now joins it, on the east side. It disappeared in 1774. The turnpike was then adopted by the city.

On Miss Harriet Benson's property there stood an old stone house which was torn down a few years ago. It was on the turnpike, and was anciently owned by Rev. Michael Schlatter, who lived in it.

John Detwiler owned about seventeen acres both sides of Southampton avenue. He died sixty-eight years ago in the house of Mrs. Mary Wood, on Germantown road, where Mrs. Wood now lives. He was a butcher, and an excellent man. John Detwiler, the father of Mrs. Mary Wood, was for four years a soldier in the Revolutionary army. Mrs. Wood has kindly given me information concerning this section of Chestnut Hill. The pebble-dashed house standing second below Hartwell avenue, on the west side, was owned in olden times by the Peters family. The Detwiler family obtained it by heirship from that family. Then Henry Hallman became its owner. It now belongs to John Hobensack, who was a son-in-law of Mr. Hallman. Ezra Sands, who now dwells in it, has occupied it thirty-three years. Ezra Sands, Sr., and Eleanor, his wife, the parents of the present occupant, died here.

The double house nearly opposite was formerly a single dwelling, owned by Joseph and William Rex, two bachelors. William died first.

A wheelwright shop stood where the house above, on the same side, is now situated.

The second house below Daniel Kerper's is a double house of wood, plastered on the outside. This belonged to the widow of John Rex. It was one house. Back of the ruins of the barn was the farm of Enoch Rex, and the barn was once included in it. Now the rear is the property of Anthony Groves, and he has built a new house on it.

In this narrative I follow, for the most part, rather the order of persons giving information than of place, and different informers give various data as to the same places, as a matter of course.

CHRIST EVANGELICAL LUTHERAN CHURCH.

Rev. C. J. Hirzel, pastor, is situated at the corner of Main street and Southampton avenue. It is a pretty Gothic stone building, adorned with growing ivy, with a bell-gable, which contains the bell used in the army hospital during the last war. It stands back from the street, with a pleasant yard in front of it, and gives an attractive picture to the passengers on the Reading Railroad. It is in contemplation to erect a stone parsonage in the rear. This mission is the outgrowth of the labors of Rev. Professor Schaeffer, Rev. H. M. Bickel and Rev. G. W. Frederick.

Prof. Schaeffer, when pastor of St. Michael's, Germantown, held occasional services in the old Union Chapel at Graver's lane and Twenty-seventh street, now demolished. The building had been used by various religious bodies.

Under Rev. H. M. Bickel, who was located here as a missionary, an organization was effected on December 9th, A. D. 1860. For a time he conducted the services in the Union Chapel, and then, in 1862, removed the services to Masonic Hall, nearly opposite the present church. Mr. Heebner, the owner of the hall, kindly gave the congregation a free use of it. After Mr. Bickel left the parish, the Rev. W. Ashmead Schaeffer, son of Professor Schaeffer, then a theological student, continued the work of the Sunday School. Rev. G. W. Frederick next took charge of the work. Under his pastorship the church was built by his faithful and self-denying personal efforts. Rev. E. T. Horn next assumed charge, and found his labor lightened by the church building being completed. He carried on well the work so well begun. In July, 1876, Rev. C. J. Hirzel, the present pastor, entered on his duties. The good work has grown in extent and influence. The indebtedness has been largely decreased and the future is promising.

THE OLD FREE BURYING GROUND.

On Graver's lane and Bowery avenue is an interesting spot. It was bought by subscription. Among the bushes and birds and the weeds and the grass lie the old inhabitants and may they lie unmoved as a constant lesson of mortality to the living. Frederick Detwiler, born in 1789, here rests. Alexander Parks, who died in 1864, has on his flat tombstone a tent, cannon and flag engraved, and the inscription: "He sleeps his last sleep; he has fought his last battle." Like Napoleon, he is at rest. Modern tombs are mingled with the ancient ones. Mrs. Catharine, wife of John Jennings, who died in 1863, is shaded by kindly overhanging shrubbery as the sun rests on her grave; while a cedar shades Catharine Antieg's gravestone, who attained to seventy-three years. A touching sight is a row of children's graves from "The Sheltering Arms." They are now "safe in the arms of Jesus." May their bodies rest undisturbed in their little graves till the day of Christ's appearing.

The Chestnut Hill public school, a fine stone building of two stories, with a tin roof, is on the upper side of the graveyard, on Highland avenue. A path from Graver's lane runs through the graveyard to it, and the merry children who pass along it bring life into the place of death, while workmen have another path through it.

Graver's lane was formerly called Jacoby's lane, from Dr. Jacoby, who lives on the lane. The name was changed in regard to Mr. Andrew Graver, an old resident, who owned much land and lives on the corner of the lane and Main street.

Chestnut Hill Hotel, owned by Samuel Y. Heebner and kept by Mrs. Anna Gold, is on Main street, near Hartwell avenue, next above the Masonic Hall. The building is of stone. It is an ancient structure. It was an old stage house. The hotel was owned in olden times by Mr. Graver, Mr. Kline and H. Barndt, in succession. Then it came into possession of Charles Heebner. Mr. Eshbauch kept it before Mr. James L. Gold became its landlord. Mr. Gold's widow still conducts it. The hotel property extended back and included the Chestnut Hill Water Works. A brickyard formerly occupied the site of the Water Works.

Hartwell avenue takes its name from Hiram Hartwell, a grocer at Ninth and Spring Garden streets, who owned the land cut by the avenue, and a tract extending to the Park. He has sold much of this tract to Mr. H. H. Houston. Mr. Hartwell owned the Washington Hotel, in Chestnut street. On account of ill health, forty years ago he selected this place as a health-improving location, and was greatly benefited, and is now a hale and hearty man.

DANIEL KERPER'S REMINISCENCES.

The old-fashioned pebble-dashed house on Main street, below the open field near Hartwell avenue, on the west side, is the abode of Daniel Kerper. The house is older than the turnpike, which was constructed in 1802. Its solid walls and hall-doors have lasted many a year, having been built in 1795. The Kerper family are among the oldest settlers of Chestnut Hill. Julius Kerper and his wife came to Chestnut Hill from Germany, and about 1763 purchased the farm of 125 acres on the west side of Main street, running from Hartwell avenue southward to Willow Grove avenue. Daniel Kerper is now aged 83, and is a grandson of Julius. Julius had six sons and three daughters, a son named Jacob being Daniel's father. The family was long lived. They were a toilsome race. Julius Kerper lived in the old stone white farmhouse about two squares back of Main street, between Hartwell and Willow Grove avenues. Miss Bohien now owns the dwelling, and it is occupied by Italian workmen. The Hessians burned a former house, at the battle of Germantown, and Julius Kerper rebuilt it.

Jacob Kerper was fourteen years old at the time of the battle. He used to say that the Hessians mistook the standing corn shocks on that foggy morning for sturdy American rebels, who could not be moved. Jacob Kerper had traps set for muskrats, and going early one morning for his game was seized, and held an hour or two as a prisoner. The country suffered under English and Hessian raids.

Wickard Miller owned a large farm below the Kerper estate, on the east side of Main street. The old stone house occupied by Mrs. Wiley was the old Miller mansion. The Miller estate ran to the Wissahickon creek, at Valley Green. Next below the Miller farm was that of Cornelius Roop, which spread over both sides of the pike, and ran to Wissahickon creek. George Roop, the husband of Barbara Roop, was a son of Cornelius. The Hinkle family had land below the Roop property. Their old stone house stands on the west of the pike, near the Pennsylvania Railroad.

Hampden Place is a fine old stone mansion on a high bank among trees nearly opposite the Lutheran Christ Church, above Southampton avenue. It is now the residence of W. H. Johnstone.

The Kitty Miller house (Wistar's office) was Andrew Artman's house.

The stone house above the Lentz property was Wickard Jacoby's residence.

The old stone house on the bank, west side of Main street, first house below Southampton avenue, below the open lot, is the property of the Detwiler family. It was built about 1800, and about that time the surrounding property was divided into large lots and sold to various parties.

Mr. Daniel Kerper gives the above reliable information.

The old two-story stone house with dormer windows, on the east side of the pike, above Wissahickon avenue, was built by Melchoir Newman about 1812. A farm surrounded it. After his death, Matthias Haas bought it, and when he died Dr. Jacoby purchased it.

On the corner of Wissahickon and Germantown avenues stands an old stone house, where years ago the Rev. Dr. Roger Owen and his brother, General Joshua T. Owen, conducted the Chestnut Hill Academy. This was a temporary undertaking and was employed as a means of establishing the Presbyterian Church. Dr. Owen became pastor of that church, and Joshua Owen entered the profession of the law, and afterward served his country as a leader in the Southern War. The father-in-law of General Owen was Owen Sheridan, whose farm and country-seat are on the left of the Pennsylvania Railroad after passing Wissahickon station. Mrs. Sheridan owns the property. Mr. H. H. Houston has bought part of the farm. The Reverend Mr. McGuffin formerly owned it. The Union Chapel in Graver's lane was founded by him. Mr. Barry owned the property before Rev. Mr. McGuffin obtained it. The old style mansion is a striking object as seen from the car window.

The old stone house at the northwest corner of Hartwell avenue and Main street was enlarged by Henry Kerper, but built many years before he bought it. Mr. John Stallman lived in it before Henry Kerper. Mr. Kerper used to walk with his friends to worship at the Market Square Presbyterian Church in Germantown, as there was no church in Chestnut Hill.

JOHN STALLMAN'S REMINISCENCES.

Mr. Stallman is ninety-six years old, being the oldest resident of the neighborhood. The Eagle Hotel, on Main street, near Evergreen avenue, used to be called Cress's Hotel. It was burned in the Revolutionary War and afterward rebuilt. It was utilized by the American soldiers as a hospital before the burning. It is no longer a hotel. A part is used as a stove and tin-store. Mr. Stallman was a soldier in the War of 1812. One hundred volunteers from Chestnut Hill went out for three months, John Huston being captain. They went as far as Marcus Hook. All the company are believed to be dead except this veteran.

The house next below the Eagle Hotel, owned by Mr. McCallum, was in the possession of the Peters family; in later years it fell into Mr. Stallman's hands, who sold it to Mr. McCallum.

From Cresheim creek to Bethlehem pike, on Main street, was the oldest part of the village of Chestnut Hill.

Dr. Jacoby's old-fashioned stone house, on its high bank, east side of Main street, below Graver's lane, had been in the hands of that family from Mr. Stallman's boyhood. Mr. Johnstone now owns it.

The Cress family owned and occupied the old house just above Mr. Stallman's brick house.

The old inhabitants were the Cress, Peters, Rex, Graver, Yeakle, Lentz and Haas families.

Mr. Ardman lived where the stone-cutter's yard is.

Mrs. Uhler's boarding-house belonged to the Lentz family. Is is now the property of Mrs. Goodwin, who resides in a house just beyond it on the Bethlehem pike.

Donat's Hotel is an antique. It is of stone throughout, having some stone partitions. A date in a stone in the chimney is 1712. It belonged to the Rex family. Levi Rex, and afterward his son George, kept the hotel before Mr. Christian Donat's day. Mr. Donat has enlarged it on the lower side.

In the time of Levi Rex the farm wagons used to be stretched along the pike at night. The horses were fed in troughs at the tongue and slept in the road, not being blanketed in cold weather. The Eagle Hotel was a stopping place of the Broad Axe stages from Montgomery county. Mr. John Stallman owned and ran the stages. He has carried over forty passengers in one four-horse stage before reaching the city. Broadway busses used to take similar loads.

Donat's Hotel was also at one time a stage stopping-place, where passengers from Philadelphia breakfasted, going countryward.

Mrs. Catharine A. Miller's house, opposite the Pennsylvania Railroad depot, is an antique one. Mrs. Miller thinks that her grandfather, Martin Ardman, built the lower part of this stone house with its half door, occupied by the offices of Dr. Cheston and Wistar & Kerrigan, on the first floor. Martin Ardman came from Germany. The old part of the dwelling is considerably over a century old. The elevated part of the house, on the upper side, was added by Andrew Ardman, the father of Mrs. Miller. His wife was Sarah Edleman, of Chestnut Hill. He was a shoe dealer and lived here many years, dying in this house in 1830. His wife died in the old mansion in 1849. Mr. Adam Miller died here in 1882. He was one of the first wagoners from Philadelphia to Pittsburgh, New York and Baltimore, when the Conestoga wagon took the place of the present freight car. The house is now in possession of the third generation. The old well with its windlass has served all these generations. Two aged, magnificent pear trees bear it company.

The next house above, on the same side, now repaired and improved by the present owner, Mrs. Wharton, for the occupancy of Dr. Cheston, was formerly the property of the Kittinger family.

The residence of Mrs. Wharton on the corner of Bethlehem and Reading pikes, combines an old portion on the upper side with an addition of a later date on the lower side, the whole building being of stone, plastered. The construction of the upper section shows antiquity, the wooden window casings and mantels exhibiting the fine carpenter work of a former day.

The old stone double house, opposite Donat's Hotel was owned by John Peters and fell to his widow. John Stallman owned it for a time. It now belongs to Mr. McCallum, of Germantown.

The Bank of America, next below, was Mr. Jarrat's residence. It is a very old house, but has been altered. It became the property of his daughter, and is now owned by Andrew Goeser. He occupies the house with the exception of the front room, which has lately been taken possession of by a branch of the Bank of America, whose location in the city is at the S. W. corner of Fourth and Chestnut streets. Louis E. Pfeiffer is President, and Richard W. Cline, Cashier.

The late Dr. Edward Jacoby informed me that the property on the east side of Main street, from Gold's Hotel to Graver's lane and along that lane to the

Reading Railroad, belonged to the Jacoby and Ottinger families. The upper part of the tract belonged to the Jacoby family, and the lower one to the Ottingers. The tracts were about equal in extent. Dr. Jacoby's residence on Graver's lane is on the Jacoby tract. The stone building, with a wooden house adjoining it above and another below was built and occupied by Wickard Jacoby, the father of the doctor. He was a carpenter. An old stone building near the railroad, on the Jacoby tract, is considerably over a hundred years old. Gobl's Hotel, on the Ottinger tract, was there in ancient days, but has been altered. It was called Graver's Tavern, being kept by a John Graver. Farmers and hucksters on the way to the city spent their nights here. For a century it has entertained the wayfarer. The Water Works and Kerper's coal yard are on the Ottinger property. Springs in the meadow furnish the main part of the water. When more water is needed the supply comes from Roxborough. About thirty or forty years ago the Water Works were erected. There is an old stone quarry on the Jacoby place, where cannon balls fired by the British were found. The Ottingers and Jacobys are of German descent. William Ottinger was Dr. Jacoby's maternal grandfather. He resided in Springfield, Montgomery county, near Chestnut Hill.

The second house below Willow Grove avenue, being of stone with a porch in front, and another at the side, and a stone barn in the rear, was the property of Wickard Miller, who owned much land in this vicinity. He was a blacksmith, and his stone shop stood north of the house, but it has disappeared, having vanished about sixty years ago. Melchior Newman bought the place, and afterward Matthias Haas purchased it. He was a butcher. Dr. Jacoby bought the property from him, and James Ryan now lives on the farm.

Wickard Miller owned the Gilbert estate and the Wiley estate. His residence and shop were on the Wiley place.

The stone house next above Andrew Graver's is ancient. It belonged to Mrs. Sarah Faust, wife of Peter Faust, about sixty years ago. She was the mother of Mrs. Jacoby. Christian Dannaker and George Walton were previous successive owners.

Frederick Sleager owned the property adjoining it above, and Nicholas Uber that below, now in the hands of Andrew Graver.

The Johnstone house was built by Dr. Henry Lentz, who bought of John Jacoby. The administrators of Dr. Lentz sold to Mr. Johnstone.

The old stone house on the bank, being the second house below Graver's lane, west side, lately bought by H. H. Houston, was the property of the Weyant family. Mr. Weyant was a teamster. David Haas bought it from him. He was a stocking weaver, and stockings were woven in the house, as was the custom in ancient Germantown.

The old stone blacksmith shop below Donat's Hotel, west side, belonged to Levi Rex's estate. Christian Donat owns it. John Light was for many years the blacksmith.

CHESTNUT HILL.

The double houses next above the Lutheran Church were built by George and Jacob Kerper. George built the upper and Jacob the lower one.

Mrs. Mary H. Wood's old stone mansion on the bank, nearly opposite Gold's Hotel with high stone steps, was built by Mr. Schwenck, who sold it to William Ruff, the grandfather of Mrs. Mary Wood, who now dwells here in her ninetieth year. She and her mother were born in this house. Her mother was nearly ninety-eight years old at her death. Her mind was clear. She died July 11th, A. D. 1864. Mrs. Wood's grandmother, Mary Ruff, took her child Barbara, to Reading when she was nine years old on account of Revolutionary troubles. She was a widow, and British soldiers took her cow, and even the flour from her dough trough. The girl remained for years and the mother returned. The girl was Mrs. Wood's mother. The people then were accustomed to walk from Chestnut Hill to Reading.

The second house below, of stone, was built in 1744. The date used to be over its door. Mr. Schwenck also built this house. He owned the land from one house to the other. His daughter Elizabeth heired the upper, and another daughter, Anna, the lower place. Elizabeth was the mother of Mrs. Wood's father.

Mrs. Wood's grandmother, Elizabeth Detwiler used to walk from Flourtown to the Market Square Presbyterian Church, in Germantown, a distance of five miles, when there were muddy roads and the turnpike had not been built. This doubled the distance in wet times.

A. B. Kerper's residence, on the northwest corner of Hartwell avenue and Main street, combines an ancient and modern house.

The pebble-dashed stone house on the west side, below Hartwell avenue, was owned by John Peters seventy-five or more years ago. It is now owned by Mr. John Hobensack, a storekeeper at Broad Axe, Montgomery county.

The double house opposite was owned by the Rex family. There was a wheelwright shop there which departed over sixty years ago. John Walter's tailor shop, near by on the same side, was another property belonging to this family, having been owned by Abraham Rex. The lower part is the oldest, the upper having been added. A stone wall runs along the front of the property. The wall has a picturesque effect.

The handling of posts and rails was a business of importance in old time where hedges and walls and iron railings now rule. Mr. Daniel Kerper squared tens of thousands of posts, and made thousands of panels of rail fence. Job Walton is said to have split 3600 rails in a week, the logs being cut off for him. See History of Byberry and Moreland, by Dr. Joseph C. Martindale, p. 44. One wonders how many the strong President Lincoln could handle in early life. He had harder work to do in his last days. Now the wire fence checks this handicraft.

The figure of the psalm of Asaph (Psalm 74, 5) applies here, as Perowne translates it:

> "It seems as though one lifted up on high
> Axes against the thickets of the wood."

The making of barrels for flour mills on the Wissahickon was also an important industry. The barrels were made at the houses of the mechanics. Mr. Kerper was also a cooper. I have lately learned with regret of Mr. Kerper's death. He gave me much valuable information.

The stone plastered house at the S. E. corner of Willow Grove avenue and Germantown road, owned by Mrs. Robert Wiley and occupied by her, was built over forty years ago by Mrs. Charlotte Strows. A house on the lower side of the mansion is one hundred and twenty-five years old. It is now used as a barn. That building was Wickard Miller's abode. He died sitting in the wood fire-place of the house.

The lot above Willow Grove avenue, with a picturesque ruin of a barn, has lately been bought from the heirs of Matthias Haas by H. H. Houston.

DONAT'S HOTEL.

The rear part of this building is quaint with its one-story addition, and foreign-looking one-story outbuilding with its lean-to. Still farther back is the old stone barn with its windows with permanent blinds, and its old barn doors with strap iron hinges and the gangway leading up to them. Many a load of hay has gone into those doors for several generations of horses. Back of Donat's Hotel is the Chestnut Hill sub-station of the Philadelphia Fire Department. It is a brick building, plastered. Three horses in line stalls await the call of danger as true philanthropists. The stalls are marked with certain names, and each new horse takes the name of his stall, which is in gilt letters above his head. The stable is in the rear part of the building. In the second story of the front portion of the structure is a fine, high-ceiled bedroom for the use of the members of the Philadelphia Fire Department. P. F. D. is their short title. Six men belong to the station. The building has a sitting-room and office. The arrangement is far different from the old bucket and hose companies, but the service is more ready and systematic, though the personal interest engendered in the old companies was a pleasant one, in that they were working voluntarily for the benefit of themselves and their neighbors. Still good work is praiseworthy in the present arrangement.

Next below the old orchard which joins the Pennsylvania Railroad Depot is the house of Mr. Charles Still, with its two places of business. It was once the property of Jacob Cress, but the upper addition was made by Mr. Still.

The stone house on the east side of Main street, at the corner of Hartwell avenue, belonged to Henry Cress in Revolutionary days. It was twice plundered by the British. Daniel Cress, of North Carolina, son of Henry, was the next owner. He willed it to his nephew, Henry Cress, Jr. It has passed out of the family, who were old settlers from Germany.

Dr. William Malin's residence, which is just above Graver's lane, on the east side of Main street, belongs to George Cress. It is an old house. Dr.

CHESTNUT HILL.

Heydrick was a former owner. Mr. Henry Cress bought it of Dr. Heydrick, it then became the property of Charles Still, before George Cress obtained it by purchase. The Eagle Hotel in yellow fever days was filled with city boarders. It was kept by Henry Cress, the second, and owned by Henry Cress, the elder. Stages ran from here to the city.

Mr. Charles Still, a member of the company, states that the Congress Fire Company, of Chestnut Hill, was organized in 1816, and incorporated in 1847. It was an old-fashioned bucket company. Daniel Snyder, the school-master, Hamilton Cress, William Henry Jordan, George Weiss and Jacob Hinkle were among the founders. The first engine-house was a one-story frame building standing on Main street, on the site of Evergreen avenue, which has been opened since the demolition of that structure. The new building was erected about twenty years ago. About 1871 the Fire Department of the city took up the work, and the old organization is kept up as a social matter, without addition of members; so that, like the society of "The Last Man," it must die out. The present officers are: President, Charles C. Warrel; Treasurer, Alexander Huston; Secretary, Samuel A. Topham. The meetings are held at Gold's Hotel. The present engine-house belongs to the estate of William Henry Jordan.

The Sons of Temperance have a good hall on Highland avenue, on the corner of Twenty-seventh street. It is a stone, plastered building of two stories. The lower story is composed of two tenement houses. The upper story is used by the Knights of Pythias. There are but nine members of the Sons of Temperance left, and only occasional meetings are held. Albert B. Kerper is Secretary, and George Bessan is Treasurer. The Society was organized about 1844.

The following has been contributed:

Perseverance Lodge, No. 46, K. of P. Instituted February 19, 1868. Samuel A. Topham, Thomas B. Rayner, William B. Hart, Charles A. Graver, Jacob H. Fisher, Conrade Grebe, Jacob R. Thomas, Samuel K. Kleaver, Thomas H. Rinker, Charles Gorgas. The last three are no longer members (Kleaver, Rinker and Gorgas). Present officers: Sitting P. C., H. C. Smith; C. C., Justus D. Dickinson; V. C., J. Elmer Still; Prelate, Joseph Windolph; M. at Arms, Howard E. Finley; M. of Ex., George S. Roth; M. of F., Lewis R. Worrell; K. of R. and S., Jacob R. Heitz; Inner Guard, William L. Detwiler; Outer Guard, Moses R. Mankin; Trustees, John H. McBride, Moses R. Mankin, Samuel A. Topham; Representative to Grand Lodge, William B. Hart, since 1875. Membership 124. Value of property about $6300. The Lodge meets in Temperance Hall, Highland avenue, on Tuesday evenings.

FREE MASONS.

Hiram Lodge, at Chestnut Hill, is one of the oldest lodges in the State, having been founded in 1800. The lodge used to meet in Johnson's Hall, Franklinville. Charles Heebner built the present Masonic Hall, next to

Gold's Hotel, and rented it to the Masons, who furnished the third story rooms about twenty years ago. The Worshipful Master is William Tomlinson, and Charles A. Graver is Senior Warden, and John Robinson, Junior Warden. D. Morrell, of Chelten avenue, Germantown, is Secretary. Joshua Cozzens, John Sellers and David Cowden were early members.

The Schultz house, in front of the Pennsylvania Railroad Depot, and on the property which was bought for the station, has an old orchard yet standing just below it, which was part of the estate, and indicates a period when land was less valuable at Chestnut Hill than it is now. After Mrs. Rebecca Schultz's death about six or seven years ago, there was much excitement over a vendue which occurred. Such an old place contained an interesting collection of antiquities. An old clock brought over two hundred dollars, and was bought by Charles Yeakle, a descendant of Christopher Yeakle. The barn of the Schultz farm stood about where the Depot of the Pennsylvania Railroad now stands. British soldiers took by force liquor which was stored in this place in the Revolution. The old stone barn was pulled down about seven or eight years ago. It had served its generation, but Chestnut Hill is filling up too rapidly to leave much room for farm barns, and they do not suit the new styles of architecture in dwelling and business places. Still the contrast tells of old times, and it is pleasant occasionally to see one preserved, with its fine grass-grown ascent to the wide barn door, and its chickens and other animals collected around it.

There was an old school-house on Highland avenue where the present police station is. Prior to that the Chestnut Hill school-house was at the junction of Summit street and the Bethlehem pike, on the lower corner.

The present Consolidated public school has been under the charge of Mr. M. Murray, but lately Mr. H. C. Payne, who was the excellent principal of the Fayette Graded Public School at Bustleton, Philadelphia, has been promoted to the leadership of the Chestnut Hill School.

THE PENNSYLVANIA RAILROAD.

This fine new road was opened on the 11th day of June, 1884; on Wednesday morning, at 7:20, the first train ran into Philadelphia from Chestnut Hill, Harvey J. Smith being conductor. The Philadelphia, Germantown and Chestnut Hill Railroad runs from Chestnut Hill to Germantown Junction, being six and six-tenths miles in length. The construction began about two years before the opening. In the vicinity of Chestnut Hill the cutting was very costly. $2,000,000 was appropriated for the construction of the road, but the donations of rights of way reduced this amount to the extent of $500,000, which was expended in three months after the opening, on improvements about the stations, sodding, sidings, etc. Messrs. H. H. Houston and Henry D. Welsh were largely instrumental in the construction of the road. The fine depot of stone and brick, with its covered ways of approach, is an ornament to the town. This road has developed a fine country which will improve rapidly. G. T. DuBois is the present agent, who has given me this history. The road started with five trains a day; in the second week ten extra trains were added. On the 1st of January, 1885, ten more trains were added, and five trains were added before December 20th of that year, when two more trains were added, making thirty-two daily trains. The cutting for the road is depressed below the carriage road, so that passengers descend by covered stairs. The stations on this road are well constructed and picturesque. The natural features of the country through which it passes are beautiful. A pretty little stream, which runs along the side of the railway near Queen Lane Station, Germantown, protests against being forgotten in the onward rush of civilization.

Mr. Henry D. Welsh, the President of this Railway, has just erected a fine new mansion, with a tower to break its outline at Wissahickon Station.

If any one can give me information about an ancient place called "De-Walden," near Stenton, or places called "Bellan" and "Marks," above Germantown, it will be acceptable. Westcott names them. Scrap Book, Chapter 126.

The fine old large yellow, plastered stone house, occupied by Dr. Oliphant, next the Presbyterian manse, on the west side of Main street, was for many years the country seat of Ambrose White, an eminent Philadelphian. He made some alterations in it. Before his day the Rex family owned the property. This family owned the site of the Presbyterian Church and manse. When Mr. White bought the property, which is about the highest point on Chestnut Hill, he found a tradition that "Emlen's Folly" had been located on it. Emlen was a sea captain, who loved to look on the sails on the Delaware, and erected a tower for this purpose, which was given the name mentioned. The Delaware sails could also be seen from the tower of the Presbyterian Church. The White estate comprises quite an amount of land, running from the Presbyterian manse to the Methodist Church Grounds.

COPE'S GROTTO.

One of the prettiest features of Chestnut Hill is Mr. Caleb Cope's grotto and spring, which he generously throws open to the public. A board walk from Rex avenue leads the pedestrian to the stile which is at the head of a sunken stone walk to the clear basin of running water, surrounded by bright green ferns and overhung by willows, which love "the water courses," as they did in the days of the Psalmist. A number of seats invite to rest. The Cope lawn is extensive and in good taste. The large stone mansion faces Main street. The Pennsylvania Railroad runs just below it. As its many trains come and go let us compare the following old record with a modern time-table. In the UNITED STATES GAZETTE, of Philadelphia, published by E. Bronson, May 6, A. D. 1812, there is an advertisement of William T. Stockton & Co., of the Baltimore and New York Pilot Lines of Stages. "Through in one day.

Only seven passengers admitted." The Baltimore passengers were to breakfast at Newport and dine at Havre-de-Grace.

Opposite the "Grotto" Mr. Evelyn Smith's house stands on a high bank. Beyond the "Grotto," on the same side of Rex avenue, is the house where the venerable Rev. Dr. Richard Newton, rector of the Church of the Covenant, in the city, lately died. He passed away to Paradise full of years and honors shortly after the death of his beloved wife, and a little before that of his friend, Bishop Stevens. They had worked faithfully together as bishop and rector for many a year. In this quiet home Dr. Newton carried on his sacred and literary work. Few men have done more to instruct young and old in the ways of Christ's religion. His works have been translated into various languages and gone over the world. All honor to the toiler who worked on till death came. The house, with its ample piazza and surrounding yard, looks as if it might have been a literary retreat. It should be deemed a place of historical importance.

Miss Uhler's house, at the corner of Bethlehem and Reading pikes, was opened in the Centennial year. At this house in old times a store was kept by the firm of Thomas Bates and Mr. Yeakle. A part of the house is of Revolutionary date. This was the one store of Chestnut Hill when it was a country place. The building has been much enlarged and improved to answer its present purpose. Watson mentions Miss Uhler's house as the house of Mr. Lentz.

SAMUEL SAUER.

In delivering a lecture on Baltimore in the German language, Professor Seidensticker received notes from Chas. G. Sower, the Philadelphia publisher, who pursues the family's ancient vocation, which throw light on the life of a Chestnut Hill printer. The Professor has placed the memoranda in my hands and they will be useful in this history. His letter is explanatory:

PHILADELPHIA, June 12, 1888.
REV. S. F. HOTCHKIN:

Dear Sir:—I enclose to you the notes that Mr. Charles G. Sower gave me. He extracted them from private letters of Samuel Sower in his possession. I add that S. Sower was born in Germantown, 20th of March, 1767, and died in Baltimore, 12th of October, 1820. He commenced publishing a German weekly (*Chestnuthiller Wockenschrift*) in Chestnut Hill on the 15th of December, 1790. In 1794 he removed to Philadelphia, and in 1795 to Baltimore. I have the titles of eleven German books which he published in Chestnut Hill, of two published in Philadelphia, and of nine published in Baltimore. His weekly was continued until 1794, in Philadelphia, under the title of *Das Philadelphier Wockenblatt*. I have been assured by several gentlemen of Baltimore that they have seen a copy of a newspaper printed by Samuel Sower in

Baltimore, but they did not remember its title, nor could the paper be produced.

Very respectfully yours,
C. SEIDENSTICKER.

I add Charles G. Sower's information:

"The will of Christopher Sower (2d), bequeathed to his son Samuel 'my messuage and tenement and lot of ground in Germantown purchased of Samuel Morris, Sheriff, situated on the southwest side of the Main street, and on the northwest side of the road leading to the Falls of Schuylkill; also my other lot of ground purchased of Hannah Rawlinson, on northwest side of said road to Falls of Schuylkill, bounded by lands of Henry Hill, Esq., John Keyser and William Tustin.' Will made March 23, 1777."

"After Christopher Sower (3d) returned from England he went first to Nova Scotia, but finally returned and settled in Baltimore, where he entered business with his brother Samuel, but he soon sickened and died."

"Samuel Sower's first wife was Sarah Landis. She died February, 1791. Her sister, Catherine Seitz, died on the day of Sarah's funeral. They lived in the same house."

Baltimore, December 7, 1798, Samuel Sower writes:—I am chained down (to business) closer than ever, for I am employing the two Kempfers, a journeyman and a young learner, beside the stamp cutter and six or seven apprentices, and expect to employ one or two more journeymen. My partner will not bother himself with business, having invested between $7000 and $8000 in the business, and built for me a house costing at least $3000. I see him not more than once a month, and he leaves everything in my hands to manage, saying if he had not the utmost confidence in me he should not have gone into it."

"The business of type founding is making great strides, orders pouring in from everywhere, so that we cannot fill the half of them. We have undertaken to cast the smallest type that have yet been used in the world. You may judge of its fineness when it takes 4000 to 5000 spaces to weigh a pound. Of this type we have one order from New York for three hundred pounds for a Bible. I sent Brother David a catalogue containing about all the type we have had engraved, and you may never have looked upon a neater specimen of type. We have received an order from Albany for a note type for a book of hymns—1500 pounds for $2587. If we could get antimony enough we would have work for twelve founders. I am working night and day. We have eleven boys and six journeymen at work, and orders for 5000 pounds of type."

November 10, 1813, he writes that he has been invited to become a preacher. His only daughter, Maria, had married Mr. Richard Spalding, "a respectable, industrious, home-loving, sober and honest merchant, educated as a lawyer but preferring business to the law." The greater part of the letter relates to "religious thought and experience."

January 7, 1815, he writes of the war: "Every sound man is compelled to shoulder the musket, whether he be worth $100,000 or nothing." Some religious thoughts upon war follow, showing his adherence to the peace principles of his father. Mentions being present in Germantown, when the battle was fought in 1777, and compares it to the bombardment of the fort in Baltimore, which he describes as terrific. The type foundry was partly buried in the ground and partly sent to the country on account of the invasion of the British.

March 11, 1819, he writes to his sister, complaining of his eyes and general health, but says: "Jesus and my small chamber are a world" for him. Financially his circumstances are good."

October 19, 1819, his sister writes to him: "I think you have ruined your eyes by so much letter engraving"—probably models for new type.

February 17, 1820. He replies and speaks of his "kind and loving" daughter, who "is now and always has been 'my darling.'" As regards property, "Providence has been very lavish to me, but property has been much reduced in value." His house that rented for $350 now rents for $200. Houses that cost $5000 and $400 ground rent are now renting for $175.

He says: "I employ but one caster, and should dismiss him and close up my type foundry if it were practicable. I have from $5000 to $6000 worth of type in stock, and of $1000 or $1500 that I was quite sure of getting about newspapers I have received but $75."

Mr. Charles G. Sower has a number of books which were published by Samuel Sower. He published "Washingtoniana," a biographical sketch. Baltimore, 190 Market street, 1800. With portrait of Washington. 12mo., sheep, 300 pp. Also, "Count Roderic's Castle." Baltimore: Printed by Samuel Sower for Keating's book store, 1795. Two volumes in one. 12mo., sheep, 200 pp. Also, "Ready Reckoner." 12mo., sheep. Chestnut Hill: Samuel Sower, 1793. He also put out several German books. A German Almanac was issued at Chestnut Hill, 1792. This gives the name as Saur in German fashion. In 1796 he published "Der Psalter," in Baltimore. 24mo., 280 pp. One German book was first published in Chestnut Hill in 1791, and re-published in Baltimore in 1797. This was "Der Davidische Psalterspiel." Chestnut Hill, 1791. Sixth Edition. 12mo., sheep, 648 pp. Other German works: "Der Geschwinde Reckoner" (Ready Reckoner), erste. Auf. (i.e. Auflage [edition]), Baltimore, 1801. 24mo., sheep. "Johann Lassenin's Politische Geheimnis" (John Lessenin's Political Secret). Baltimore, 1795. For Saur & Jones, Philadelphia. 24mo., 200 pp. "Prophetische Muthmaszungen (Prophetical Conjectures) uber die Franzosische Revolution," No 51. "Ressestrasse zwischen der zwezte und dritten strasse," 1797.

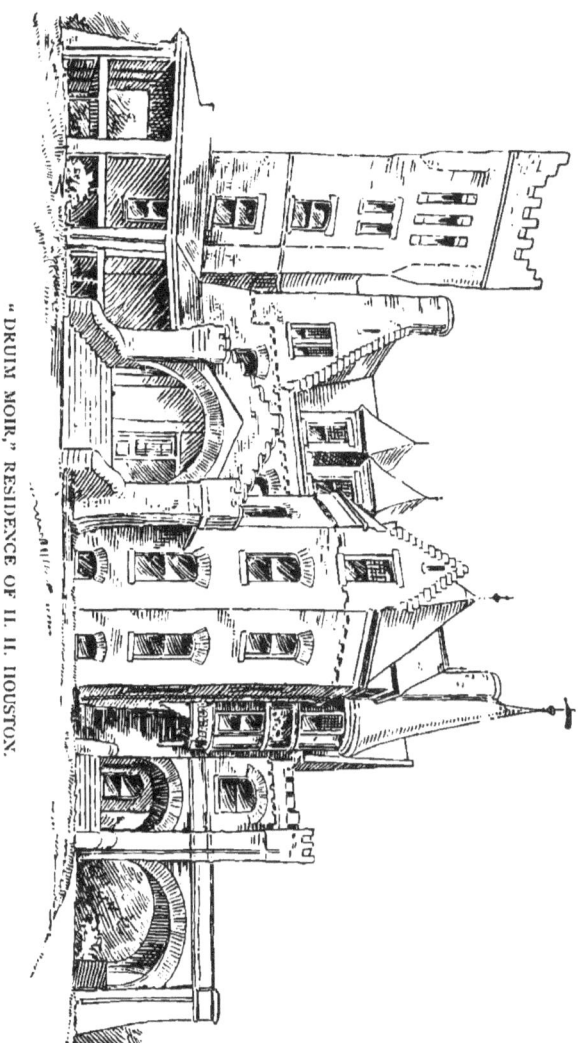

"DRUM MOIR," RESIDENCE OF H. H. HOUSTON.

I append letters received from Prof. Seidensticker and Charles G. Sower.

PHILADELPHIA, November 13, 1888.

Rev. S. F. Hotchkin:

The Almanacs, which S. Sower commenced publishing in 1792 were regularly continued in Chestnut Hill, Philadelphia and Baltimore.

In addition to the books mentioned by you, he printed a number of German books of which I have a list.

The impression that F. D. Pastorius had resided in Chestnut Hill is probably due to the fact, that for some time he owned there 200 acres of land, a gift of Wm. Penn. He sold these to Abraham Gunis and Wm. Streepers. The details as to price and time I have not at hand, but remember that Pastorious somewhere remarks, he had sold the land at a very low figure. In his will he disposed of 893 acres of land on the Perkiomen creek and 50 acres in Germantown; likewise of a claim to 107 more acres in Germantown.

By some verses he wrote in 1711, and again in 1716 it appears that Christopher Witt was his neighbor. Those of 1711 have the heading: "When anno 1711 Christopher Witt removed his flower-beds close to my fence." First comes a Latin distich:

> Floribus in propiis habet et sua gaudia Pauper
> Atque in vicinis gaudia Pauper habet.

The other poem has for its subject "Christopher Witt's Fig Tree." Pastorius threw the paper, on which it was written over the fence and received an answer, likewise in verses, by the same mode of conveyance. Pastorius expressed in his lines a fear that the fig tree would not stand the severity of the climate during winter, mentioning at the same time the manifold good uses figs could be put to. Christoper Witt answers, he would give his tree at all events a trial; may be it would, the next summer, rejoice us with its precious fruits.

(See my contribution to the DEUTSCHE PIONEER, Cincinnati, 1871, p. 183.)

Very respectfully yours,

C. SEIDENSTICKER.

PHILADELPHIA, December 17, 1888.

Rev. S. F. Hotchkin:

Dear Sir.—As may be seen by the article, "Samuel Sower did a very large business in Baltimore. Having but one child and that a daughter, the name of Sower became extinct in Baltimore although many of his descendants still live there. His third wife, mother of the daughter alluded to, was Elizabeth La Motte, who died in March, 1862, at an advanced age. Richard B. Spalding, husband of the daughter (Maria), was a member of the Roman Church and related to Arch Bishop Spalding, I am informed.

"A daughter of Richard and Maria Spalding, married Benj. P. Power, and one of their sons is now extensively engaged in the publishing business in Buffalo, N. Y.

"As all of Samuel Sower's descendants are through Richard B. Spalding, whose wife also joined the R. C. Church, they are naturally members of that church. Samuel Sower, however, remained faithful to the faith and doctrines of the Dunkards, and during all his life his correspondence shows the depth of his piety and the meekness, purity and complete resignation to his Master's will characteristic of that denomination.

CHARLES G. SOWER."

DRUIM MOIR.

Mr. H. H. Houston calls his mansion Druim Moir, which means Great Ridge. There is a place in Lancaster county bearing this name. Drumore township received its name from Dromore, Druim Moir (Great Ridge), a strongly fortified place, in County Down, Ireland, on the Lagan. The township account book has written on its headings from the year 1765 to 1800 "Dromore" and "Drummore." Since then it is written "Drumore."

In Murray's Hand Book of Ireland, is the following: "Drumore, from very early ages was the seat of an Abbey for Canons Regular, which afterward became the Cathedral for the Protestant diocese of Down, Connor, and Dromore. It fell into ruins however, and the present church was built on its site by Bishop Jeremy Taylor, who together with Dr. Percy, author of "Reliques of Ancient English Poetry," were the two most noteworthy prelates. Adjoining the town is the Palace, the grounds designed and planted by the latter bishop after the model of Shenstone's Leasowes. In the "See" House the several Bishops of the diocese resided up to 1843, when, at the death of Bishop Saurin, it was annexed to Down and Connor." Drumore is on the route from Dundalk to Belfast.

While the name of this country place reminds one of an old Irish town which was the seat of a bishop, and had the ruins of a castle near it, the Church of St. Martin-in-the-Fields, near by, takes us back to a time when green fields were seen where London streets now rule. Such associations are interesting and instructive. Mr. Houston's fine mansion is built of local stone, with granite trimmings and shingle roof. The location is at the end of the ridge on which the Wissahickon Inn lies. One of the most striking features of the building is a fine English Tower five stories in height, with a battlement surmounting it, containing a portion of the library in the lower story. The house is of a composite style of architecture. At the eastern side of the mansion a piazza commences which runs southwest round the tower and then to the end of the dining-room. An ample *porte-cochère* invites the guests to enter. The kitchen is in the rear of the carriage entrance. An embattled square-roofed erection rises in the rear of the *porte-cochère*, covering the entrance. Three gables in English fashion face the northeast while an oriel rises with its comi-

"DRUIM MOIR."

cal top, next which an exposed outer chimney gives another English touch to the exterior. Adjoining this, a dormer window prettily breaks the roof. The grounds were tastefully laid out by the owner, and winding drives and natural shrubberry which adorned the ground before the erection of the house, mingle with flower and rhododendron beds planted by Mr. Houston. The effort has been to follow nature rather than to force new ideas upon her. The road from the house to the Wissahickon drive, is specially beautiful, being lined with dogwood trees. Here nature has been left to her own sweet will, and it looks to the rider as if he were passing through the Kaaterskill drive in the Catskill Mountains. Such wildness near a city is delightful. The crows which frequent this height have always had fine views over hill, forest, and one of the deepest wooded valleys of the Wissahickon. The following is from "Appleton's Rural Homes:"

"One of the largest and most commanding suburban villas in this country is that owned by Mr. H. H. Houston, in the suburbs of Philadelphia. The walls are built and faced with Chestnut Hill gray stone, laid in coursed work, rock face, and the trimmings are of Eastern granite. Entering the building, we find the hall and stairway in oak; the parlor in butternut; the reception-room in mahogany; the library and dining-room in quartered oak; the office in cherry; the servants' quarters in white pine; and the principal bedrooms, in oak, cherry and sycamore. Particular attention may be directed to the high wainscoting of the main hall, and to the wooden ceiling on each floor; also to the dome at the top, with a centre skylight. All the columns and arches of the hall are in oak, with carved panels and caps. The wainscoting of the dining-room and library is accompanied by paneled ceilings in oak. The work was finished in July, 1886. On leaving the house one casts a respectful glance at the large red-stone mantel in the hall and the mosaic floors in the vestibule. The architects were Messrs. G. W. Hewitt and W. D. Hewitt, of Philadelphia.

"Considered in its more general aspect, this house has many manifestations of common sense in architecture. For example, in arranging the rooms connected with the kitchen, care has been taken that the servants shall be required to traverse as little space as possible in the performance of their duties; the butler's pantry has been put just where it is most convenient, without interfering in the least with the more important rooms. In this position it serves also the useful purpose of preventing the necessary odors of the kitchen from permeating the hall and library, and is of convenient size, with appropriate dresser, shelving, drawers and closet. The practice of incorporating what is known in England as a serving or sideboard-room, in the interior plan of the house, is less common here than there, although, where the house is one of any pretensions, the purpose of the sideboard-room, which serves as a means of communication between the dining-room and the kitchen, is promoted in a similar way—as in the present instance, where a simple hall answers every requirement. Furthermore, the architect has succeeded in arranging the various rooms of the first floor as to provide each with the requisite space, and to locate all as compactly as possible. The drawing-room is not so large as to rob the library. Wherever an opportunity has offered for favoring one room above another, the preference has been given to those rooms in which the family pass the most of their time; and for them special arrangements have been made in the interest of ventilation and of heating. The value of light in these apartments could not have been more thoroughly appreciated; and there is little disposition to sacrifice this luxury for the sake of adding a convenient piazza or introducing an imposing balcony. In the servants' quarters, also, this principle has been applied, on the general theory that servants can do more for their mistress when laboring under hygienic conditions—so much more, indeed, that the slight additional expense necessary to create such conditions was considered of no consequence, in view of the gain in positive comfort. It seems as if the owner had said to the architect, 'What I desire, first of all, is a comfortable place to live in'; and as if the architects, in meeting this wish, had possessed adequate apprehensions of the necessity of treating servants well, if the full measure of household comfort was to be secured. The position of the porch, in relation to the points of the compass, has been carefully considered. Some porches are so heavily built that they dwarf the impression made by the main walls themselves; and others are so large that they seem intended as places of permanent abode, or at least to serve the purpose of an entrance-hall. Nothing of this kind occurs in the house in hand; and when we come to the entrance-hall itself, we find it both artistic in its appurtenances and convenient in its dimensions, as if in memory of the fact that in our modern house it is all that remains of the old Gothic hall."

Mr. Samuel Frederic Houston, a son of H. H. Houston, has a residence on the grounds described. It lies west of Druim Moir and is built of stone and shingles in French-Norman style of architecture. The view from this dwelling is wilder, but less extensive than that from Druim Moir. The house is very appropriately named "Brinkwood," being situated on the edge of the Wissahickon forest. The interior of the dwelling is very unique, having a triangular hall in which is situated the stairway which is a beautiful feature. A house is now nearly finished for the residence of Mr. and Mrs. Charles W. Henry. Mrs. Henry is a daughter of Mr. Houston. This dwelling is on the adjoining ridge to Mr. Houston's property. Springfield avenue divides these places. It is of stone, and of Colonial style, with an ample piazza. A *porte-cochere* introduces one to the front door. There are large rooms in the house and each room commands its own beautiful view. A fine conservatory will adorn the southern side of the mansion. The whole aspect is pleasing.

ST. MARTIN-IN-THE-FIELDS.

Tuesday, the 5th of June, A. D. 1888, was a delightful summer day, and toward evening a train of surpliced choristers and clergy marched over the temporary floor of this new free church which will add one more to the various

ST. MARTIN-IN-THE-FIELDS, WISSAHICKON HEIGHTS.

CHESTNUT HILL. 425

Episcopal Churches which have risen to the glory of God in Christ, in Germantown and Chestnut Hill. The 122d Psalm, "I was glad when they said unto me: We will go into the house of the Lord," etc., was read responsively as this " new Jerusalem " was entered, and may have led some to think of the heavenly Jerusalem above, " the mother of us all." Gal. 4, 26. The corner, stone was laid by the Rev. Dr. J. De Wolf Perry, Dean of the Convocation of Germantown, and Rector of Calvary Church, Germantown. Rev. Dr. T. S. Rumney, Rector of St. Peter's Church, Germantown, assisted in the service, and the choir was from St. Peter's, Germantown.

The earnest address spoke of a time when the surrounding fields would be closely built upon, and those who were present at the laying of the cornerstone would be in another world. The following description is from the PHILADELPHIA INQUIRER of Wednesday, June 6, A. D. 1888.

Before introducing it, it should be added that the Hymn, "O Lord of Hosts, whose glory fills the bounds of the eternal hills," rang out grandly among the " hills of God " which encompass the new church, while the blue vault of heaven above showed the roof of God's great temple, the universe over-shadowing the earthly temple " made with hands."

The edifice is to be a clere-story church, with columns and aisles, and consists of a nave, two transepts, a deep chancel, organ room, vestry and choir rooms, and a carriage porch. The dimensions of the nave, including the aisles, are 46 by 80 feet, of the transepts, 10 by 22 feet : of the chancel, 25 by 28 feet ; choir and vestry rooms, 20 by 15 feet. The height from the floor to the apex of the roof will be 50 feet. The material to be used in the construction of the church is local graystone from adjoining quarries, with trimmings of Indiana limestone. The interior will be entirely faced out with brick and the general tone of the walls is to be buff, with wainscoting of red and decorated bands of different colors. The clere-story columns are of Indiana limestone and have carved caps and bases of the same. The clere-story arches are of red brick. The tracery of the windows is also of Indiana limestone. The roof will be of open timber construction so as to show all the timbers, forming a ceiling of varnished wood throughout. The pews are to be of hard wood. The chancel end of the church will be surmounted by a tower of stone 100 feet high.

The Hewitts are the architects and W. C. Mackie is the builder.

The procession was composed of the following persons :
The surpliced choir of St. Peter's Church, Germantown, Mr. Charles O. Fraser, choir master; Revs. J. De Wolf Perry, D. D., T. C. Rumney, D. D., Charles R. Bonnell, S. C. Hill, J. Andrews Harris, D. D., Charles Logan, J. T. Carpenter, J. K. Murphy, William Ely, S. Upjohn, Thomas Taylor, George Bringhurst, J. G. Furey, C. H. Hibbard, E. Weil, T. P. Ege, S. F. Hotchkin, R. E. Dennison, J. L. Miller, Joseph Miller, Jr., W. C. French, D. D., Messrs. George B. Bonnell, B. B. Comegys, H. H. Houston, E. S. Bulkley, George E. Peabody, H. H. Kingston, S. K. Kille, J. Vaughan Merrick, C. Stuart Patterson, E. A. Crenshaw, Charles Bullock, Joseph A. Shaeffer, W. W. Harding, Edwin

Bedlock, W. C. Mackie, George W. Hewitt, Peter B. Hinkle and a large number of ladies and gentlemen not only from the vicinity but from the city.

An address was made by Rev. Charles R. Bonnell, of St. Stephen's Church, Manayunk. He referred to the great helps in the worship of God. The act of worship in God's house is offering. For men whose spirits are known the worship of God involves the offering of substance. The government under which we live is acknowledged in the payment of taxes. The duty of man is in the use of what he has. God makes every man responsible for that over which His Providence has placed him. The duties of charity should be according to man's ability. The payment of tithes is not an act of charity, but a duty. Here, said he, God's house is building; God provides for spiritual wants by spiritual agents. This church now building does not come after men have been working a subscription; it comes to us as an offering, as an acknowledgment of Almighty God. Here is an altar built to God, and as this church is begun so also ought it to continue. People frequently forget that one-tenth of our substance is due to God. This is called a free church, where what God provides is offered freely to all. Here a tower of witness will be erected telling that the Almighty God is possessed of Heaven and earth. Here also is a treasure house, because here will be found the means of grace which God abundantly provided. It is manifest that that which man depends upon must influence him. There is a well of salvation open here. This church is called St. Martin-in-the-Fields. St. Martin had the characteristics of courage, of devotion and of unlimited charity. Henry VIII built St. Martin-in-the-Fields, and now it is St. Martin's, Trafalgar Square, London. Let us seek, like St. Martin, to be courageous and devoted. May this altar never fail of offerings, and may the well of salvation to be opened cleanse and refresh throughout all generations. The services concluded with the benediction by Rev. Dr. Perry, and the recessional hymn was "The Church's One Foundation."

The ground and the entire cost of the new edifice are the munificent gift of Mr. H. H. Houston, of Chestnut Hill. The church, when completed, will be quite an addition to the church architecture of the diocese.

A stone rectory and a fine parish building of stone adjoin the church.

THE PRESBYTERIAN CHURCH.

In the fall of 1850, the Rev. R. Owen came to Chestnut Hill to establish a school for boys, having been obliged to give up preaching for a season on account of his throat. The next spring, having regained his health, he was urged by the Presbyterians on the Hill to hold religious services, which he did, starting in the school house, and later in the old Union Chapel, situated on what is now Union avenue and Twenty-seventh street. This chapel was built for the use of all denominations, by Rev. Mr. Magoffin, a large land owner here in the early days, and most of the different churches held their meetings there until able to erect suitable buildings. The church was organized in May, 1852, with seventeen members, and Dr. Smith as ruling elder. The necessity of having a larger place of worship was now felt, and on the 1st of July, 1852, the corner stone was laid, and on the 16th of June, 1853, it was dedicated, having at that time a membership of forty persons, and a Sabbath school of forty pupils. In 1857 the house was built, and in 1869 the church was enlarged. In 1879, it was found that the room used by the Sabbath school was too small, and a large addition was made containing a lecture room, ladies' parlor infant class room, session room, and Sabbath school room, at a cost of $12,000. Rev. R. Owen, D. D., continued in charge until February, 1885, when, owing to ill health, he resigned all active duty, and was made pastor emeritus. In October, 1885, Rev. W. W. Hammond, D. D., was installed as pastor.

CHRISTIAN HALL LIBRARY.

David Macfarlane, librarian. An old library was kept in the ancient Snyder house, now occupied by the Johnson family, nearly opposite the present library. That library closed about 1840. This was a pay library kept by Daniel Snyder. After it ceased to exist the town was without a public library until 1870, when Henry J. Williams founded the present one. Mr. Williams built the rough-dressed stone building from a Chestnut Hill quarry and presented it to the village, appointing trustees for its care. The founder gave personal oversight to its construction. The lower story is used for library purposes, and at first was divided into two rooms, but the partition has been removed. The upper story was occupied by the Christian Association for religious services and social purposes. The Association has passed away. The Presbyterians and Methodists have used it when additions were being made to their churches. The colored people have services here in the summer, having various colored and white ministers, though they have no religious organization

The hall is also available for public entertainments and lectures. It was furnished by Mr. Williams. The bulk of the library was presented by Henry J. Williams who fitted up the room. The cases were from his own law office. He was a distinguished lawyer.

Henry D. Landis and James T. Young donated a portion of the books. Mr. Young also donated a library to the Sunday school of the Presbyterian Church, and also a parish library to that church.

The library is a fair selection of valuable books for general use. It was started as a reading room. In a few years the trustees, to extend its usefulness, made it a subscription library. About five years later it was thought useful to make it a free library. Mr. Williams left the interest of $15,000 to sustain it, and the deficiency is made up by the generous citizens of Chestnut Hill. Mr. Williams appointed fourteen trustees. Rev. Dr. Owen has been the continuous president. The Hon. John J. Macfarlane is secretary, having also held the office from the first. George Bessan, who was postmaster, was the first librarian and Andrew Fisher the second, and Mr. Macfarlane was the third. Would that every village had such a library for public improvement! Persons receiving such free books should show appreciation by a careful use of them.

A frame building in the rear was built by Mr. Williams for social purposes for the Christian Association. It was used by a literary society and afterward by the Workingmen's Club.

The librarian, Mr. Macfarlane, a brother of State Senator Macfarlane, has died since the above account was written. He kindly aided my investigations.

The report of May 1, A. D. 1886, showed the expenses of the year to have been $1360 for which Mr. Williams's fund yielded $425. The report says: "The library is used by all classes of citizens. Upwards of seven hundred take books out of the library, and twelve hundred volumes are taken out in a month." The report appeals for subscriptions to aid the good work. It is signed by R. Owen, president, and John J. Macfarlane, secretary.

A condensed history of the METHODIST EPISCOPAL CHURCH, at Chestnut Hill, Twenty-second ward, Philadelphia, taken from memoranda in possession of Robert Thomas, Esq.:

Prior to the year 1820 there was very little, if any preaching at Chestnut Hill. Occasionally a Methodist or Baptist minister would preach there—in the school house, or such other place as could be had for that purpose. In the year 1821, Mr. John Maguffin, a Presbyterian, erected a chapel on his farm on the road now known as Graver's lane, or Union avenue, southwestward from Germantown avenue, and named it "Union Chapel," desiring that all Christians, of whatever denomination they might be, should have a place in which to hold religious services. Shortly after the completion of this chapel Chestnut Hill was recognized as one of the regular appointments on what was then known as Bristol Circuit. This circuit extended from Bristol on the Delaware westward to the Schuylkill and northward from Germantown to the Blue mountains; and once in every five or six weeks there was preaching by either one of the circuit preachers or a local brother, in said chapel.

The first Methodist class was formed in the latter part of the year 1822, or early in 1823. William Hawes was the first class leader, and they met at the house of Jacob Hawes, on the Main street, just below what is now known as Highland avenue.

In the year 1831 the old Bristol Circuit was divided and Germantown Circuit formed out of a part of it. Chestnut Hill was included in Germantown Circuit, the whole circuit embracing fourteen preaching places, and having sometimes two and sometimes three circuit preachers.

During the year 1844 it was determined to build a church for the Methodists exclusively, and the lot on which the present church edifice stands was secured for that purpose. The corner-stone of the first church was laid on the second Monday in June, 1845.

It was so arranged in 1847 that the junior preacher of the circuit should reside at the Hill, in order to give more pastoral care to the congregation, the preacher in charge residing in Germantown. This arrangement continued until 1851, when Germantown was made a station and Chestnut Hill Circuit was formed.

The congregation at Chestnut Hill was incorporated by act of Assembly, approved May 18, 1847, by the name, style and title of "Wesley Chapel, Methodist Episcopal Church, of Chestnut Hill."

In the year 1877 the present parsonage was erected, while Brother S. T. Kemble was pastor, at a cost of about $5000, a large part of which he was instrumental in raising.

During 1881-82 Rev. Samuel Irwin labored hard to raise funds for the erection of a new church, and succeeded in raising about $1000.

In March, 1884, the Conference appointed the Rev. A. F. Dotterer, pastor for the purpose of building a new church edifice. With many to predict failure, and comparatively few to give encouragement, he undertook the task. His first step was to secure the removal of the bodies interred in front of the old church. In this he succeeded in so far as relates to the ground covered by the new building, and in fact all, with perhaps two or three bodies still remaining between the building and the street line. Ground was broken for the new building August 25, 1884. The corner-stone was laid September 27, 1884, by the Presiding Elder, Rev. Joseph Welch, assisted by other pastors of his own denomination and sister churches. The new building was finished and dedicated to the worship of Almighty God, free of debt, on Sunday, June 21, 1885. The entire cost of the new building and improvements was about $12,000 all of which, with the exception of the $1000 raised by Brother Irwin, and its accrued interest, was raised by the untiring efforts of Brother Dotterer, assisted by his brethren and friends.

The following is a list of the pastors serving said Church since it was set apart as a special organization, commencing with the year 1847:

1847, J. E. Meredith; 1848, Alfred Cookman; 1849, J. B. McCullough; 1850, Reuben Owen; 1851, Andrew Manship; 1852, Andrew Longacre; 1853, 1854, T. Snowden Thomas; 1855, Henry H. Bodine; 1856, J. L. Heysinger; 1857, Richard W. Humphries; 1858, Noble Frame; 1859, T. M. Griffith; 1860, S. L. Gracey; 1861, 1862, S. N. Chew; 1863, J. F. Reynolds; 1864, 1865, Isaac Mast; 1866, C. J. Little; 1867, 1868, S. Townsend; 1869, 1870, 1871, Andrew Manship; 1872, O. L. Haddock; 1873, George W. Lybrand; 1874, 1875, J. R. Merrill; 1876, 1877, 1878, S. T. Kemble; 1879, J. B. Maddox; 1880, Joseph S. Cook; 1881, 1882, Samuel Irwin; 1883, Thomas W. Simpers; 1884, 1885, 1886, A. F. Dotterer; 1887, 1888, J. P. Miller.

William B. Reed lived in Furman Shepherd's house, the second door back of the railway depot, on the upper side of the street.

At the corner of the Reading pike and Chestnut avenue is the house of Dr. Moss. The three neighboring houses here were built by a gentleman who sold them to persons who occupied them. Dr. Moss was the first occupant of the corner house. The three dwellings have been built about twenty-five years.

The tasteful and quaint tile house of Dr. Bolling was built by him six or seven years ago. It stands on the Reading turnpike, near the Library and on the same side of the street. The red color and the half door give it a foreign look, and the interior, as well as the exterior, show taste in design and execution. It is pleasant to see a return to old styles of architecture, and a variety in the color of houses gives a pleasing effect to the village. The foundation of this house is of stone, the first story of brick, and the upper part of tile. I am indebted to its owner for information about Chestnut Hill, where his daily drives make him well informed.

The yellow house of Mrs. Richard Norris is next to that of General Owen. It is on the Reading pike. This was formerly the residence of John M. Hildeburn, but it has been twice remodeled by Mr. Norris, and is now a pleasant mansion three stories high, with a bay window. He bought it about 1858 and added to it then, and made a fresh addition in 1864, making a large building. Richard Norris was an eminent engine builder.

The house of Henry Norris, son of Richard Norris, stands next beyond the one just described. Samuel Smith, Sr., formerly owned and occupied it. This old-fashioned yellow house stands among the trees, which are its ancient companions. These residences are surrounded by fine and ample grounds

The abode of Miss Harriet Benson is next in order, on the brow of the hill, with its pleasant surroundings. This was the home of Charles Taylor, and bore the name of "Norwood." The lawn above the house is remarkably fine and extensive.

The falling ground as we proceed offers a delightful view, especially in the early morning. Sunset avenue is the pretty name of the next highway, which recalls the fact that the setting, as well as the rising, sun sheds its glory here.

Beyond this avenue is the country seat of Alfred C. Harrison, the sugar refiner, of the firm of Harrison and Fraser. The next place belongs to the Shepherd family.

On the left side of the Reading pike, in going from the town, stands the three-story bluestone house belonging to the estate of George V. Rex, and now occupied by Mr. Whitaker. Walter E. Rex, son of George V. Rex, was long the Recorder of Deeds in the city. The Rex family is one of the oldest families in Chestnut Hill.

Next below this residence Richard Chapman's extensive lawn sweeps down the hill. The proprietor is the son of a physician, and is a wholesale dry goods merchant in Chestnut street.

Jesse Kneedler's beautiful place comes next in order. He is also a wholesale dry goods merchant.

The adjoining residence, with its fine grounds, is the property of Isaac Waterman. It is occupied by his son-in-law, Mr. Dwight. Next beyond this is Mrs. Penrose's place.

Mr. Page has a residence on Sunset avenue and the Reading pike. He is a son of the gentleman who has a mansion on "Sugar Loaf."

In leaving the town and going toward Barren Hill, at the hill called "Sugar Loaf," Charles W. Trotter and Joseph F. Page have beautiful mansions of stone on splended sites, which afford good views. Mr. Page's house is in front of Mr. Trotter's. "Sugar Loaf Hill" formerly constituted a part of the farm of William Stroud. Mr. Page's gently sloping lawn reaches down to the turnpike.

Beyond the house of Mr. Page is the fine country seat of Mr. Bodine. There is an observatory on the top of the mansion in the form of a cupola. The position is a good one for observation. Mr. Bodine is a broker and the partner of John F. Keen.

Christopher Yeakel owned the property which contains the sites of the Pennsylvania and Reading depots, as well as much other land in Chestnut Hill. Mr. Yeakel was from Germany, being a Shwenckfelder. He came here under persecution. The Government at home afterward invited the Shwenckfelders back, but they declined. The graveyard adjoining the Williams estate is the Yeakel family's yard. The inscriptions are largely in German.

Mrs. Thomas Bates, of Chestnut Hill, and Charles, Joseph and William Yeakel, living in Montgomery county, near Chestnut Hill, are descendants of this family.

Daniel Yeakel lives on a farm on the Bethlehem pike, on the right going northward from Chestnut Hill, just beyond the toll-gate, which was the property of Abraham Yeakel, who died in 1762, a brother of Christopher. His wife was named Maria.

The English soldiers knocked Christopher's hat from his head with a spear when at his own door. The British soldiers came out of the city to surprise Washington at Whitemarsh in the night and returned in disappointment. Some of the farmers were obliged to do their seeding at night in those troublous times.

The Schwenkfelders worshiped in Towamensing, where they still have a church, under the care of Rev. George Master. See the "Genealogical Record of Descendants of the Schwenkfelders," by Rex. Balthazar Heebner, and from other sources by Rev. Reuben Kriebel, with historical sketch by C. Heydrick.

"Christopher Yeakle was about eighteen years of age when he came to Pennsylvania with his mother in 1734. His father died in Germany. He apprenticed himself to a cooper and continued during life to follow his trade. He built the log house in 1743; yet standing in 1879; it still stands in 1888, at Cresheim, Germantown township, Philadelphia, which was his dwelling until nearly the time of the Revolution, when he purchased the property on the summit of Chestnut Hill, now owned by his granddaughter, and died there at a very advanced age. By his industrious and frugal habits he died possessed of considerable property. His descendants are quite numerous in Philadelphia, and in Montgomery county, Pennsylvania." The log house is at the northeast corner of Main street and Mermaid lane.

"Abraham Heydrick, son of Balthazar, married Susanna, daughter of Christopher Yeakle, May 4, 1767."

"After his marriage he settled and kept a store and farmed at the foot of Chestnut Hill, in Springfield township, where Charles Heydrick now lives." The store has been turned into a dwelling.

"John Schultz, son of Rev. John Schultz, married Rebecca, daughter of Christopher Yeakle, February, 1840."

"J. S. resides on Chestnut Hill, Philadelphia, late the residence of Christopher Yeakle."

"Rev. John Schultz, son of Christopher, married Regina, daughter of George Heebner. This Schwenkfelder clergyman lived in Hereford township, Berks county. He was a farmer, as well as a minister, and was highly esteemed for his earnest and impressive piety."

Dr. Christopher Heydrick studied medicine under Dr. Benjamin Say, of Philadelphia, and graduated with high honors in the University of Pennsylvania, in 1792, at twenty-two years of age. He was a physician in the Philadelphia Hospital, and a member of the Cabinet of Sciences. For a time he practiced in Chestnut Hill. He undertook farming in French Creek, Venango county where he became blind.

Governor Hartranft, is a decendant of the Schwenkfelders, and Governor Schultz is of the same name mentioned in these notes.

Edward Dowers, born in 1796, married Regina, daughter of Abraham Heydrick. He died in 1841. He lived on the Main street, near Donat's Hotel, on the same side of the way. The house is now the grocery store of Charles Still. He was a useful and respected citizen. Mr. T. L. Bates has given me information in this interesting matter.

POST OFFICE.

Chestnut Hill post office was established February 6, 1828. The first postmaster was Jacob Guyer, who was gate-keeper at the toll-gate on the east side of Main street, at Evergreen avenue, where the post office was kept. Samuel Butcher succeeded him as toll-gate keeper and postmaster. Benjamin Ewing, a druggist, succeeded him as postmaster, and the post office was then removed to the west side of Main street, to the drug store which was the room now used as Isaac Russel's grocery store. The next postmaster taking charge was George Bessan, October 21, 1863. The post office was then moved to the property which was formerly Titlow's Hotel, at the site of the present drug store of T. L. Buckman, and Miss M. Haas's trimming store.

In the summer of 1864 the office was made a sub-station of the Philadelphia office, and the postmaster was made superintendent of the sub-station. There was then one carrier and now there are three. George Bessan then became carrier. The office was removed from the last-named site, in 1865 or 1866, to Main street, below Highland avenue, in the building now used by Miss Hare as a trimming store.

During Andrew Johnson's administration, for five months and two weeks, the office was in the hands of Levi Cope as postmaster, and John D. Wood as carrier. During that period the office went back to the old Titlow Hotel site. Then George W. Bessan was replaced, removing to the site of Miss Hare's store once more, which building had been built by George Bessan for a post office, though it was his private property. The building was used exclusively for the post office. In April, 1880, the office was moved to the present central location, at the intersection of the Bethlehem and Reading pikes. The building belongs to the Jordan & Buckenhorst estate. The post office is Station H. There are six daily mails.

THE BETHESDA CHILDREN'S CHRISTIAN HOME, for girls and boys, is indeed a House of Mercy, according to its meaning in the Hebrew word which designates it. Bethesda Home was started by Miss Anna M. Clements, on the faith principle in the Park House, a deserted hotel building near the driving park, on the site of the Wissahickon Inn. It was changed from place to place until Mr. Williams gave it a local habitation. The work of the foundress is above all praise. The Home is pleasantly situated on Stenton avenue, near Wyndmoor Station, on the Reading Railroad. It was established about A. D. 1861, and was much aided by Henry J. Williams, Esq., who gave the grounds and buildings in his lifetime and left a legacy to the institution. In 1883 there were 140 inmates—This was the twenty-seventh year, and it began with 157 children at the Home.

This lengthy report shows that Christian trust is not misplaced, that charity is not dead, and that young and old hearts will respond to living appeals of want. The year closed with 174 children in the Home.

The following is a sketch of the

CHESTNUT HILL BAPTIST CHURCH,

furnished by Rev. B. F. Robb, Pastor:

"In the early part of the present century John MacGoffin, a Scotch Presbyterian, lived on what is now known as the Sheridan farm. Wishing to do something for the spiritual welfare of his neighbors he talked over the subject with Abraham Heydrick, most of whose grandchildren are now active members of the Baptist Church (one of whom, W. H. H. Heydrick, being deacon and clerk). The result of their deliberations took shape in Mr. Heydrick giving a lot of ground on Jacoby's lane, now West Union street, at the intersection of Twenty-seventh street. With a donation of three hundred dollars from Philadelphia Presbyterians, about 1825, Mr. MacGoffin built a chapel capable of seating one hundred and fifty people. This chapel was at first called 'MacGoffin's Meeting-house,' afterward 'Union Chapel.' It was free to all Christian denominations, and was used by all the churches which now have their own church edifices on the Hill. When no other services were appointed MacGoffin led in worship, and read a printed sermon.

In May, 1834, Robert F. Young, a young Baptist preacher, began a series of protracted meetings in Union Chapel, assisted by Rev. D. A. Nichols. In these meetings eleven persons were converted. In the afternoon of August 15 they were baptized in the Wissahickon by Rev. D. A. Nichols. In the evening the eleven asked the opinion of the visiting brethren as to the expediency of organizing a Baptist Church. This was recommended. A council of eleven Baptist Churches was called to meet in Union Chapel, September 6, 1834. After listening to the articles of faith and views of Christian doctrines, it recommended that the converts, now increased to sixteen, be organized into a Baptist Church. After organization the church elected Israel Gilbert, father of Dr. J. C. Gilbert, and Ezra Sands, Sr., as deacons, and they were at once ordained. They both filled this office, and were most self-sacrificing, earnest Christians till their deaths. Jonathan Gilbert was elected clerk, and Rev. Robert F. Young was invited to supply the pulpit and accepted. On March 22, 1835, he was called to and assumed the pastorate of the church, and remained in charge until October 1, 1849.

At the junction of Springfield and Reading Pike was a lot of ground, occupied as a stoneyard by Henry S. Lentz, who subsequently became deacon of the church. This lot Israel Gilbert bought and presented to the church. In January, 1835, steps were taken to erect a meeting-house on it, and in the May following the corner-stone of a building 40x45 feet was laid by Rev. H. G. Jones, of Roxborough. In August it was dedicated. On the following Sunday regular services in the new house were commenced, which have continued without intermission to the present. During the pastorate of Rev. R. F. Young, a mission station was opened at Plymouth, which, under the nourishing care of the church, has grown to be a thriving, self-supporting church. On December 6, 1849, Rev. L. Walton, of the Eleventh Baptist Church, Philadelphia, was called to the pastoral charge. He remained in charge until 1853, when, to the grief of the church, he was called to his rest. The succeeding pastors have been Rev. Mr. Barnhurst, in charge from July 14, 1853, to April, 1854. August, 1854, Rev. R. F. Young was again called and remained until March, 1859. During his second pastorate the church edifice was enlarged to its present dimensions.

In May, 1859, Rev. William B. Tolan assumed charge, remaining until November, 1864. March 7, 1865, Rev. W. W. Case, resigned November, 1868, and was recalled in September, 1870, remaining until September, 1871. Rev. I. D. King, from April, 1872, to October, 1875, and Rev. Edward McMinn, from January 1, 1876, to April 1, 1879, were in charge. The present Pastor, Rev. B. F. Robb, assumed charge, June 8, 1879. The church, after fifty years of life, is steadily increasing in membership, and has no debts and is doing a useful work in the community.

I am indebted to Mrs. Jesse Roberts for the following: John Huston lived on the farm lately bought by J. Lowber Welsh, at the first toll-gate above Chestnut Hill, on the left side going north. He was one of the oldest settlers of this neighborhood, being a surveyor and conveyancer. He was a Scotch-Irishman, who settled in Bucks county, having come to this country in early life. From Bucks county he removed to this point. The property was kept in the family, keeping also the name until within the last four years, when Mr. Welsh bought it and has improved it by laying out roads and preparing it for country-seats. The farm was in possession of the Huston family and its descendants for one hundred years lacking three days.

John Huston was a captain in the American Army in Revolutionary days. He lies buried in the Abington Presbyterian Graveyard. He married Elizabeth, daughter of Christopher Ottinger, who lived on the Heydrick farm. Mrs. Heydrick was a granddaughter of Christopher Ottinger. On one occasion during the war, when courting, he rode on horseback to visit his lady-love. The British pursued him, but he gained on them, so as to have time to put his horse into a single stable, and bury his saddle and himself under the hay in a barn. The soldiers walked over him without finding him. The Hustons are a numerous family and are still largely settled in Chestnut Hill and Montgomery county.

The Pennsylvania Railroad Depot site, of late years was in possession of Mrs. John Shultz, who was a descendant of Christopher Yeakle.

DANIEL SNYDER's old stone house, plastered, on the southwest corner of Chestnut avenue and Main street, is an interesting antique with its moss-grown roof. Daniel Snyder was the son of Adam Snyder, who lived in this neighborhood. Daniel Snyder took possession of the story-and-a-half house about sixty-two years ago, when it was smaller than it is at present, two enlargements having been made since that day. His wife was Hannah Baker, of Norriton township, Montgomery county.

Mr. Snyder taught school in this old building. He was previously usher in Charles Keyser's school. In his day several acres were connected with the house. He acted in the double capacity of teacher and farmer, and was also a magistrate and conveyancer, being known as 'Squire Snyder. A village library was kept in the antique house. He was a methodical and decided man, and took a personal interest in the advancement of his pupils. He was a fine penman. He used to begin his stories with the expression, "when I was usher for Charles Keyser," which was an important time in his life. His property was made by his own industry for the most part, and he left a valuable estate for that day. He died in the old mansion in 1858. He was a

Free Mason of high position, being secretary of the Lodge when he died. He was a very early riser. After a meeting at the Lodge he spent the night at Barbara Roop's Hotel, at Franklinville, and was found partially paralyzed the next morning, and brought home to die. Mr. Snyder was six feet two inches in height, and correspondingly broad. His descendants still occupy the house. Children of the fifth generation of this family have been entertained in it. The present residents are Mr. Joseph P. Johnson, and his wife, Mrs. Hannah Johnson, with their five children and Miss Susan Snyder. Mrs. Johnson and Miss Snyder are grandchildren of Daniel Snyder. A noted well of fine water was a feature of the place in Daniel Snyder's day. I am indebted to Mrs. Johnson and Miss Snyder for these notes.

HENRY J. WILLIAMS, Esq., a lawyer of note in Philadelphia, deserves notice as a prominent citizen of Chestnut Hill. The Rev. Dr. R. Owen, pastor emeritus of Chestnut Hill Presbyterian Church, edited his book entitled "Studies of the Epistle to the Hebrews." From Dr. Owen's Memoir prefixed to this work, we learn that Mr. Williams was born on Christmas Day, 1791. The famous Welsh preacher Christmas Evans received his name because he was born on Christmas day. Mr. Williams died in his 88th year. His social rank was high. His paternal grandfather was a Boston Puritan of wealth, and strong character. He was chairman of a meeting at Faneuil Hall, which resolved to prohibit the landing of the tea sent from England, which was a first step in the Revolution. When Boston was taken by the British, his large store of goods was burned and his property confiscated and destroyed. This gentleman was a relative of Franklin.

The father of H. J. Williams was General J. Williams, the first Superintendent of West Point Military Academy; he was a useful and educated man of decided character. The graduates of the Academy showed the good effects of his influence. The mother of the subject of this sketch, was a daughter of William Alexander, Esq., of Edinburg, Scotland, a relative of Lord Sterling.

Mr. Williams was born in Philadelphia. He received a military and collegiate education, and studied law under Horace Binney, Esq. He married Julia, the daughter of the eminent Dr. Benjamin Rush, of Philadelphia. In 1857 he bought a country place at Chestnut Hill and retired. He took great interest in the Presbyterian Church here, which was then young and weak. In old age he said: "I have been living on credit since I completed my eightieth year, for that is the utmost limit of the promise." He told his clergyman to let him know when he heard of any case of destitution. In his old age he made benevolence a business and loved to give as a privilege. The Christian Hall Library was his gift to Chestnut Hill. The Bethesda Orphan Home, with its two buildings, under the faithful care of Miss Clement, is the result of his bounty. It is, like Muller's, at Bristol, England, a Faith Home. Mr. Williams left a bequest to increase its usefulness. At the age of eighty-three he entered on the work of preparing a commentary on the Epistle to the

Hebrews. His death was felt to be a public calamity. It took place on the 12th of March, A. D. 1879.

SUMMIT STREET.

The street which runs out from the Bethlehem pike, probably takes its name from its elevated position. In passing along it, going from Bethlehem pike toward Stenton avenue, we meet with the large mansion of the Lorenz family on the right hand. There is an extensive lawn above it. The building is of a light color, and a porch in front is supported by pillars which extend to the roof of the house. This place is occupied by Thomas Potter. The next house, on the same side, is the pretty building of pointed stone belonging to Mrs. John Clayton and her place of residence. A tower with a pointed roof, and a tasteful piazza, a tiled gable and an angular bay window under it, mark this dwelling, while a pleasant lawn with trees surrounds it. This was the property of Judge Thayer before the late Mr. Clayton bought it. Next comes the estate of Charles Heebner, with its ample grounds. This is the residence of Miss Julia Heebner, daughter of Charles Heebner. Mrs. Taylor's cottage faces Summit street and the Reading Railroad. Mrs. Taylor was an heir of Stephen Girard. This property belonged to Mr. Hollingsworth.

Passing over the bridge which covers the Reading Railroad the large stone house of Spencer Janney, of a tasteful moderate architectural design, is before us. David Webster, an attorney, formerly owned this place. Mr. Watson, the carriage maker, built the house. Mr. Janney has enlarged it. We next reach Thomas Potter's estate, where his widow resides. The house was erected by S. Sanford, of the Adams Express Company. The building is a large one, and square in form with a double piazza. An arch of stone leading to the porch, and a gable with two irregular dormer windows, give variety to this mansion.

In returning, we will note on the other side of the street the beautiful place of Mrs. Richard Levick. It was built by the late Norman L. Hart. A strongly-built stone tower adorns the upper side of the mansion, and there is a bay window on its lower side, and piazzas diversify the exterior. There is a quaint roof over an upper window, and the flowers beneath it add to the picturesque air of this striking edifice.

Henry Tilge's place is next in order. This was the residence of Samuel H. Austin, Esq., and was built by him. He opened Summit street, as well as Chestnut avenue, and built a number of houses. He was a benefactor to Chestnut Hill, and a public-spirited man. A fanciful and pleasant piazza, with colored tile roof, marks the abode of Mr. Tilge, and there is a bay window on its lower side.

The massive stone mansion, with its front door welcoming the incomer, without a porch to guard it, is the residence of Miss McCall, a sister of the late General McCall. The late George Weaver, the rope manufacturer, who was a partner of Mayor Fitler, built this house, and resided in it. Next comes the place of J. B. Cowperthwaite, the publisher. A pretty addition has been made on the upper side of this house. Then follows Miss Anna E. Biddle's gray stone mansion, with two dormer windows to relieve the monotony of the roof. Miss Biddle is a daughter of Nicholas Biddle.

We now reach W. W. Harding's place, next the Reading Railroad, and just over the bridge which covers it. The front of the house is similar to that of Miss Biddle, which adjoins it. The Harding property is bounded by the Reading Railroad and Chestnut avenue, on the left side. The carriage entrance is on Chestnut avenue. There is a small lawn in the rear. The Reading Railroad Depot lies just behind it, and the location is a good one for a newspaper man, who for years has furnished the readers of the PHILADELPHIA INQUIRER their news with their breakfast. The Reading Railroad Depot is not far away, and a telephone makes the countryman who wants light and air a citizen, even in the hours after general business is closed. Few know the task of running a newspaper. I wish that all editors could have a cosy retreat when their brain work is closed for the day, and the incessant strain of criticism, and demand for novelty, had given place to the blessed quiet of the evening hour.

After crossing the bridge over the Reading Railroad, the first place on the left belongs to the Richard Levick estate. The house is of a light color, and there is a lawn about it. We now pass over Prospect avenue and come to the late Rickard Levick's former residence, which is occupied by Samuel B. Stinson. It is built of Trenton brown stone. We have now reached Township line, which divides Montgomery county from Philadelphia. It touches Springfield township in Montgomery county. This is called Stenton avenue, and runs from Germantown to Chestnut Hill

STENTON AVENUE.

This pleasant highway bears the name of James Logan's Country Place, of historic fame in Germantown, at Wayne Junction. Stenton is a town in Haddingtonshire, Scotland, where it is said that Logan or his parents had lived. Stenton avenue leaves the Bethlehem pike just about the grounds of the attractive summer resort, styled "The Eldon." The first place on the left is that of Colonel Alexander Biddle. A new wall was being constructed along the avenue when I viewed it. Pretty flower beds adorned the yard. The proprietor kindly allows strangers to share the magnificent view which stretches for many miles before the delighted eye of one who stands on the piazza of this mansion. There is a natural terrace, and the hills rise in their beauty in the distance, as Whitemarsh is spread out before the delighted beholder. St. Thomas's Episcopal Church lifts its dark stone walls and erects its tower on the same hill where its predecessor stood long years ago, when a rustic congregation assembled within its walls. May the glory of the new temple be greater than that of the old one! It is beautiful for situation, and a landmark

THE PHILADELPHIA PROTESTANT EPISCOPAL CITY MISSION.
HOME FOR CONSUMPTIVES, CHESTNUT HILL.

around the country side. The Whitemarsh valley is a charming one, and the wide prospect from this piazza is one of the finest in the region of Philadelphia.

This magnificent and extended view of God's glorious handiwork exemplifies the force of Addison's words in the Spectator (No. 412), on the Pleasure of the Imagination: "The mind of man naturally hates everything that looks like a restraint upon it, and is apt to fancy itself under a sort of confinement, when the sight is pent up in a narrow compass, and shortened on every side by the neighborhood of walls or mountains. On the contrary, a spacious horizon is an image of liberty, where the eye has room to range abroad, to expatiate at large on the immensity of his views, and to lose itself amidst the variety of objects that offer themselves to its observation. Such wide and undetermined prospects are as pleasing to the fancy, as the speculations of eternity or infinitude are to the understanding." This property formerly belonged to that good man, and public benefactor, Henry J. Williams. The family who now own it are relatives of that Christian gentleman.

A brown mansion among the trees next meets us on the left. This was once the home of William Platt. It now belongs to the estate of St. George Tucker Campbell, and is occupied by the widow.

We next reach the place of Mr. Kelsey, on the same side. The house was built by William Platt, who resided in it after he had lived in the last-named house. Then John Welsh, Jr., owned it for a number of years. Then it was purchased by Mr. Kelsey. Birch Lane runs along the side of the property. This is a sweet rustic lane, which in its wildness appears to be far away from the rush of city life, with its "madding crowd." There is a beautiful spring on this property near the lane. There are two basins to contain the water, and a country path and a miniature waterfall are striking points in the landscape, while overhanging trees add beauty to the scene. A stream runs along the base of the hill. The Kelsey mansion has a bay window on the upper side, and a stone porch adorns the front. The cattle feeding on the hillside, in the early morning, where the pasture extends along Birch lane, present a scene which would delight a painter like Rosa Bonheur. Beyond Birch lane lies the Bucknell property and residence, and the Consumptives' Home.

THE CONSUMPTIVES' HOME.

The excellent CONSUMPTIVES' HOME on Stenton avenue, due to the generosity of the Bucknell family, needs further aid, that it may be worthy of the place. Bethesda Home and this noble charity honor the Hill. The following from a newspaper shows that the "Cottage" plan has been adopted. The sufferer must find it more homelike.

Home for Consumptives, Chestnut Hill.—After the successful plan for the world-renowned Consumptives' Home, Ventnor, Isle of Wight, the "Cottage" or "Separate System" was adopted by the management of the Home for Consumptives, Chestnut Hill, and one cottage has been built and was formally opened for the reception of patients.

The grounds are ample to admit of the erection of other cottages, and it is hoped that several of these may soon be built by persons of means, as fitting monuments to departed relatives and friends. A cottage complete and ready for use will cost twelve thousand dollars, and all of which are built as memorials will be known by the name or names of those in whose memory they are erected. Donations toward the erection of cottages should be sent to William M. Runk, 1126-28 Chestnut street or Rev. Thos. J. Taylor, Supt. P. E. City Mission, 411 Spruce street, Philadelphia.

The following is from the *Standard of the Cross and the Church* of Nov. 30th, 1889:

This beautiful charity, of whose edifice we are able this week to present an engraving, is a branch of the work of the Philadelphia City Mission, Rev. H. L. Duhring, Superintendent. The City Mission was instituted May 1, 1870. One of its objects was to provide temporal and spiritual help and comfort for the poor and sick. The neediest class of applicants for relief was soon found to be persons in some stage of consumption. In 1876, the first steps were taken to provide a Home for Consumptives. That year Mr. and Mrs. Harry Ingersoll gave the Mission the house No. 411 Spruce Street for its uses. The offices of the Mission are in this building, known as the House of Mercy, and rooms are fitted up in it for a small number of female patients. Other considerable gifts for a consumptives' home were a legacy of over $100,000 from Miss Mary Shields, and a house and lot in the southwestern portion of the city from Mr. I. V. Williamson. When the Board of Council had decided to erect a home in one of the suburbs, about 1885, a noble token of approbation of the work came from one not of our communion, William Bucknell, Esq., who gave his beautiful country seat, at Chestnut Hill, with its adjacent grounds, comprising about eleven acres, and valued at $75,000, to be specially used as a Home for Consumptives. This led to the preparation of extended plans for the most comfortable and approved sort of edifice which, with the aid of modern experience and science, could be devised. The buildings now in use, and presented in this engraving, are the central building of the scheme, containing the offices, reception rooms, hall, chapel, etc., and one pavilion or separate cottage, twelve of which are intended to complete the group. The cost of these buildings was about $40,000; each of the cottages will cost about $12,000. Messrs. Furness & Evans of this city, are the architects.

A pretty descent leads the pedestrian down Birch lane, and a curve in the walk is attractive. Man loves these curves as they constantly surprise him with a new view and relieve the monotony of long straight roads. Even horses seem to have a fancy for them, and go in a lively rate around a corner as if they would see what lies beyond. The wildness of the avenue is height-

REV. SAMUEL DURBOROW,
LATE SUPERINTENDENT OF THE EPISCOPAL
CITY MISSION.

ened by the fact that the surrounding trees have been allowed to stand, and some grand forest monarchs are permitted yet to keep their place in the path, in defiance of modern so-called improvements. The woodman has wisely spared the trees, and thus this wildest avenue in Chestnut Hill retains much of its primitive beauty with its woody name. A portion of a maple trunk on the right shows departed greatness as it lies on the ground. It reminds one of the end of human life but an early morning church bell strikes as I look on it, and suggests a future life after death.

Next to the Kelsey place we find the residence of Thomas C. Price, which was built by Clayton Platt, the son of William Platt, who lived there for a long time. Birch lane ends in Montgomery avenue. This avenue is pretty, but as the Scotch would say, it is "unco' short."

The English looking house of John Lowber Welsh faces the end of Birch lane on Montgomery avenue. The position is a remarkably fine one for a dwelling. Mr. Welsh is a son of the late Hon. John Welsh, who was the United States Minister to England. The mansion which he has constructed is an architectural one of stone that would draw the attention of the passer-by for its beauty. A piazza gives the privilege of a view of uncommon extent and grandeur. Chestnut Hill abounds in piazzas, which are equal to additional rooms in a house. They are pleasant places to enjoy the pure morning air or to gaze on a beautiful sunset, and this rolling country affords so many exquisite views that a house should be arranged in such a way as to give means of enjoying them.

In passing from Stenton avenue along Birch lane, on the right where the lane joins Montgomery avenue, is a house with an ivy covered piazza, which was built by Clayton Platt. It was purchased by Lawrence Lewis, and is now occupied by Mr. Coit, of the Reading Iron Works. It is surrounded by a fine hedge.

We now return to Stenton avenue and next below Mr. Bucknell's place, after crossing Evergreen avenue, and on the left corner of the two avenues named, find Redmond Abbott's place. The ivy-covered side of the house and the ivy on the rear chimney, climbing bravely to emulate the height of the neighboring trees, make a pretty picture. There is an extended hedge on Stenton avenue bounding the lawn. Amid the fine shrubbery on the lawn a child's tent shows a mimic encampment and the longing of civilization to seek the primitive state of simplicity again. Next below this place, on the upper corner of Graver's lane and Stenton avenue, is a property belonging to Jacob Uhle.

Next on the left is Frank Alcott Allen's large place. The house was built some eight or ten years ago. It stands far in the rear of the street with an extensive lawn before it. The cottage has an abundance of windows to admit God's air and light, and suggests the Reverend Sidney Smith's bright saying: "Throw open the window and glorify the room."

Still farther on at some distance on the left is Bethesda Home. The Military Hospital was on Wyndmoor avenue, between the railroad and BETHESDA HOME, during the war. The house of Mrs. Conway, with its deep lawn, is on Springfield avenue.

THE MOWER HOSPITAL, at Chestnut Hill was the largest in the country. It contained 3500 patients. Dr. T. C. Brainerd was once in charge of it. (See Memoir of Rev. Dr. Thomas Brainerd, by his wife, p. 318.)

Dr. Robert Bolling, of Chestnut Hill, was the assistant executive officer of the hospital.

Dr. Horace Y. Evans and other physicians were interested in this good work. I hoped for a sketch of it from one of the Doctors but it failed me.

We now return along Stenton avenue and at the left hand corner, where it joins New street, which used to be called Platt street, we note the new lawn, with its growing trees, which surrounds the pretty gray stone cottage of the late William Arrott. Its gables, chimneys and piazza, with its flowers are pleasant features. Next to this place is the house of J. B. Watson, of the firm of T. Watson & Sons. The roof is broken by gables which give pleasant variety. There is a well-shaded yard and a pretty sloping lawn.

Next on Stenton avenue is William Potter's newly-built house. The architecture is quaint and striking. The tiled roof is all corners, gables and windows. The *porte-cochere* piazza, and red ornamental chimneys afford a pretty variety. Striking little windows peep at you such as Hood describes in his poem:

> "I remember, I remember
> The house where I was born,
> The little window where the sun
> Came peeping in at morn."

The upper roof of the front slopes to within a few feet of the ground. As Mr. Potter's house stands at the edge of Union avenue, we turn to the left and pass along that avenue.

On the right side is the house of Joseph Patterson, Esq., a lawyer, and the son of the late Joseph Patterson, the president of the Western Bank. This is an antique looking modern building, with shingle work on the exterior, such as may be seen on some old houses at Lewes, Delaware, near the sea. Irregular windows are set in the gable end on Stenton avenue. The studied irregularity of this kind of architecture affords a pleasing relief to the eye, tired of the monotony of a house built merely to accommodate itself to the furniture which is to be placed in it.

The next house on the same side is that of Judge C. Stuart Patterson. Yellow and brown colors on it give it individuality, and afford a contrast to the surrounding dwellings. The woodwork displays the cross-beams on the outside after the manner of Swiss and English cottages.

We now cross Prospect avenue and on the right reach the late Joseph Patterson's place, and next the abode of John C. Sims, the son-in-law of Joseph Patterson. Joseph Patterson was the president of the Western National Bank.

ST. PAUL'S CHURCH AND PARISH BUILDING, CHESTNUT HILL.

CHESTNUT HILL.

The house in which he lived is a pleasant and ample stone mansion with an extensive lawn about it. Between Judge Patterson's residence and Prospect avenue, on the corner of Union avenue, is the pretty gray stone, ivy-covered mansion of J. E. Terry. This lies on the left in going from Stenton avenue. A bay window adorns the mansion. Mr. Brown has a house on Prospect avenue. Mrs. Henrietta C. Booth has built a small village of neat and pretty houses at the eastern end of Grayer's lane.

MONTGOMERY AVENUE.

This avenue runs parallel with Stenton avenue in the rear of Mr. Bucknell's property. Next below the house of John Lowber Welsh is the residence of William Henry Trotter, the brother of E. H. Trotter, who owns the pleasantly-located mansion on Sugar Loaf. The lawn descends abruptly to a meadow-like ground below.

We next come to the place of Thomas Stewardson. A double bay window relieves the form of the exterior of the house, while the roof is broken with gables. There are woods in the rear and a ravine. The gabled front shows the woodwork above the porch. The number of stone houses in Chestnut Hill is noteworthy. It is almost the universal material used in building, but quarries are close at hand and it is natural to utilize them.

T. C. Price's place at the lower corner of Birch lane and Montgomery avenue is marked by a fine old tree at its entrance. A curve in the road makes the house and grounds prominent, as it faces Birch lane, and the ivy-clad front and gable render the sight a pleasing one. There is an abundance of ivy on the walls of the houses in Chestnut Hill, and this beautiful creeping plant adds much to the beauty of the town.

North of Mr. Coit's is the residence of Mrs. Rachel Morris. It is a neat gray stone building, with a Mansard roof and an ivy-covered porch. An old tree that evidently antedates the house shades its new neighbor on the lower side.

The place of Frederick Collins next draws the attention. The front of the house is inviting, with its second story veranda adorned with flowers as companions to the beautiful vines on the walls.

Next is the house of Henry D. Landis. The stone front of this house is relieved by much ornamental woodwork suggesting Hawthorne's "House With the Seven Gables."

ST. PAUL'S EPISCOPAL CHURCH.

The following is a sketch of St. Paul's Episcopal Church, Rev. J. Andrews Harris, D. D., rector:

Previous to 1853 services were held at rare intervals by Rev. George Hopkins, residing in Philadelphia. On July 4, A. D. 1853, it was resolved by Messrs. John Bohlen, Cephas G. Childs, Charles Platt, Charles Taylor and

Thomas Earp, Jr., to provide for the worship of the church the remainder of that summer. Services were held in the little Union Chapel on Sheridan's (now Graver's) lane at Twenty-seventh street. The opening service was held by Dr. Kingston Goddard, on the second Sunday of July, 1853. Other services during the summer were held by Dr. Richard Newton, Dudley A. Tyng, Dr. Charles D. Cooper, Charles H. Wheeler, Rev. Dr. Lounsberry, Mr. Woods, Dr. Atkins, and others. These services continued through the winter and spring. Col. Cephas G. Childs was a most efficient aid in this church work.

In 1855, on the 18th of June, a meeting was called in the hall of the Reading Railroad depot, and the parish was organized and eleven vestrymen were elected as follows: John Bohlen, Cephas G. Childs, Charles Platt, Joseph H. Hildeburn, Charles Taylor, Thomas Earp, Jr., Frederic Fairthorne, Clayton T. Platt, John C. Bullitt, William Henry Trotter and Thomas Mason. When the charter was obtained eight was fixed as the number of the vestry. Colonel Childs became rector's warden, and Frederic Fairthorne, accounting warden. The services were transferred to the hall over the railroad depot, where they were held for several months by Rev. R. W. Oliver. On November 6, 1855, Rev. Alexander Shiras was elected rector.

In 1856 a lot was procured from Messrs. Purvis and Webster, on Chestnut avenue, for $5500, for a site of a chapel. The stone chapel was consecrated in September, 1856. It has since been enlarged, and is now used as a Sunday school and parish building. It is a very pretty edifice. Mr. Shiras resigned in 1860, and Rev. William Hobart Hare, now Missionary Bishop of South Dakota, assumed the rectorship on Whitsunday, May 19, 1861. The cornerstone of the new church was laid October 25, 1861, by Bishop Alonzo Potter. Sidney & Merry were the architects and builders. It is constructed of Chestnut Hill sandstone. The church was ready for divine worship on June 15, 1862, and was then used for the first time. The building cost $6500, and a debt of $4500 remained on it.

In June, 1863, the Rev. Mr. Hare was granted six months' absence, as the physicians ordered his wife's removal from the place on account of her health, and Rev. J. A. Harris took the rector's post for the time. Mr. Hare, however, resigned the parish for the same cause which made his vacation necessary, and the resignation was reluctantly accepted. Rev. J. Andrews Harris, D. D., was elected rector and assumed the rectorship February 7, 1864. The debt of $4500 was liquidated, and on October 15, 1865, the church was consecrated by Bishop Stevens. A stone rectory was finished on the church grounds in 1868, in which year the interior of the church was modified and a new organ purchased.

In 1881, Edwin N. Benson presented the vestry with $5000 to improve the church building, coupling the gift with the request that a stained glass window, the subject of which should be "Christ Blessing Little Children," should be placed in the building. This made necessary the building of a new chancel to contain the window, which was finished so that service was held in it May 21,

1882. The architect of the chancel was James P. Sims, but his sudden death the day before the occupation of it devolved the decoration upon his successor, Wilson Eyre, of Philadelphia. The coloring was done by John Gibson, of this city. The window was made by Paine & Peyne, of Orange, N. J.

The grounds and buildings form a pleasant picture on Chestnut avenue. This valuable property is entirely free from debt. The present rector has been in charge for over twenty-five years, a pleasant fact to pastor and people. The silver communion service of the parish, now in use, is a memorial of Richard Norris, for many years, and at the time of his death, the accounting warden of the parish.

The rector of St. Paul's Parish conducted a mission between 1867 and 1872 inclusive, on Springfield or Wissahickon avenue, near Wissahickon station, on the Pennsylvania Railroad. In this work the late Miss Ellen R. Brown was a most efficient aid. A frame chapel was constructed in 1866, but on account of removals and other changes the work was dropped, of necessity, and the property was afterward sold. A new parish building has been constructed on the grounds of St. Paul's Church to advance the good work of the church.

REV. MICHAEL SCHLATTER.

The Rev. H. Harbaugh, wrote an account of the Life and Travels and Labors of this remarkable man among the Germans. Mr. Schlatter was the descendant of an excellant family of St. Gall, in Switzerland. He was born in that town, lying between two mountains "on the bank of the Steinach," in A. D. 1716. He was the first child in the family and was piously instructed. He seems to have been confirmed before he was fourteen years of age, which was the proper age among the German Reformed. He became a communicant, and was a candidate for the ministry a few days before he was fourteen years old. He taught in Holland and appears to have been admitted to the ministry there, and for a short time did clerical work in Switzerland. The cry of American emigrants for sacred services drew him to this land. He came under direction of Holland Synods to visit the scattered sheep of the German Reformed body. He had supervisory power, and sailed in 1746. He took charge of the church in Philadelphia and the one in Germantown, the aged Mr. Boehm, his predecessor, assisting somewhat. He also visited New York and organized a Synod. He visited the old country in behalf of the poor American churches, and went to Holland, Germany and Switzerland, procuring pecuniary aid and six clergymen, and seven hundred German Bibles. Mr. Schlatter published a touching account of the condition of the Pennsylvania churches in a book form. On his return this devoted man worked earnestly in his missionary and parochial tasks. The Americans were much encouraged by the sympathy of their foreign Christian brethren. Some delegates came two or three hundred miles to get Mr. Schlatter's aid for their parishes. Two men came from Virginia, and we find Mr. Schlatter visiting Maryland

and Virginia. He baptises a redeemed negro slave and his child in Germantown.

Mr. Schlatter states the need of schoolmasters, and also appeals for aid for the Indians, that they may be taught the Christian religion. The London Society for establishing schools among the Germans in Pennsylvania made Mr. Schlatter their superintendent and traveling agent, and in his travels he hoped to assist both churches and schools. He labored for a fund for the widows of deceased clergy. The project which interested the Coetus at last became a law. The King of England and the Princess Dowager of Wales subscribed to the school fund. The education, according to the good notions of olden times, was to have a religious cast. The Rev. Dr. William Smith, Provost of the College of Philadelphia, a distinguished Episcopal clergyman, was secretary. There was a feeling amongst the Germans that the schools were too much under English influence.

Mr. Schlatter was a chaplain in the French war. He was at the sieges of Halifax and Louisburg in 1757, where the British broke the French power. He was one of the chaplains whom Mr. Harbaugh, quotes Bancroft (Hist. U. S., Vol. IV, p. 300), as thus describing: "There were the chaplains who preached to the regiments of citizen soldiers, a renewal of the days when Moses, with the rod of God in his hand, sent Joshua against Amalek."

After Mr. Schlatter returned from Nova Scotia he is found at Chestnut Hill on the Coons farm, near the Reading turnpike, residing on a lane. His place was called "Sweetland." Rev. Mr. Muhlenberg and Rev. Mr. Wrangel, the Swedish Provost, spent a night with him here. Here he lived quietly until the Revolution. Many persons came to him to be married from a distance of many miles. He was popular among those entering upon matrimony. He often preached at Barren Hill and Franklinville (I suppose St. Michael's), and other places. The Halle Historical Records, in German, give notes about him. *Hal. Nachrichten*, pp. 865, 895, 896. (Hist. Soc. of Pa. Lib.) Mr. Schlatter was a British chaplain in the Revolutionary war.

When the British invaded Germantown he declined to obey orders and was taken to Philadelphia and imprisoned. His house on Chestnut Hill was entered and plundered by soldiers. His youngest daughter, Rachel, heroically, though but fourteen years old, risked her life to snatch her father's portrait from a soldier's hand and bear it away. The furniture was broken by the soldiers, and the feather beds cut open. The silverware was thrown into the well, perhaps in the hope of getting it afterward. The papers were burned. The coat of arms was rescued, and "the silver-handled knife and fork and silver spoon," used in the army, and some instruments which were possessed by his grandson, Michael Snyder, Esq., in Manayunk.

Rachel rode on horseback to the city often during her father's short imprisonment, to cheer him and convey provisions. Has the Germantown road ever witnessed a prettier sight than this damsel on her loving errand? When set free Mr. Schlatter returned to Chestnut Hill. He sympathized with the

Americans warmly. One son was a grenadier and another an adjutant. The "mob-like confiscation" destroyed much of Mr. Schlatter's property. In April, 1788, he bought "a small home for £550." The first place must have been the one named in these sketches near the water reservoir; the second was at Miss Harriet Benson's place. It is a beautiful spot. Mr. Harbaugh calls it a "summer paradise of cool shade, of trees beautiful to look upon, of fruit pleasant to the taste, of blooming flowers, and of singing birds. It was then simply rural. It is now suburban, and citizens enjoy it." The stone house on the Benson place was two stories high, and had a porch which was removed. Everything about it was antique. The old knocker remained. Some hardy poplars stood as sentinels to guard the house. This was the new Sweetland. Rev. H. M. Muhlenberg, the first Lutheran preacher in this country, sent in 1762 by the Very Reverend Court Preacher Ziegenhagen, of London, and Mr. Schlatter, were great friends. Mr. Muhlenberg was a leader in his church. The writer of Mr. Schlatter's life likens his closing days to those of a "venerable hermit sitting before his cave on the silent mountain side," with the glory of the setting sun on his face, with faith in Christ, singing: "Though I walk through the valley of the shadow of death I will fear no evil."

He was cheerful, and was loved by his neighbors, and "venerated as a patriarch by old and young." His appearance was venerable, and his countenance mild. His bushy hair was white, and hung down to his shoulders. He wore a wig, according to the custom of the day, "on public occasions," and always used it when performing marriage. In church service he wore a black gown and white bands on the neck, as his portrait shows. On a summer morning he could be seen at his door, in his dressing gown, pleasantly greeting the passer-by with kind words "and a graceful bow." He "was a great friend to children," and was loved by them. The diffident found it easy to approach him; hence bashful lovers sought him for marriage.

Governor Mifflin visited him. General Joseph Heister, afterward Governor of Pennsylvania, was his friend. He was hospitable to all. His wife, who aided his life-work, was from New York city. Her Christian name was Maria Henrika. She is buried at Barren Hill. The day of Mr. Schlatter's death is uncertain. His will is dated October 22d, A. D. 1790. It was admitted to probate on November 23d of that year. An aged man in Chestnut Hill said he died in the latter part of October. He was in his 75th year. He was buried at Franklin Square, in Philadelphia, the German Reformed burying-ground at that time. Here he sleeps among his former flock. An account of Mr. Schlatter's children is given. Elizabeth, the oldest, lived to ninety-one, and died single. With Hester and Rachel she resided at Chestnut Hill. Elizabeth and Rachel died while Rev. A. Helfenstein, Jr., was pastor of the German Reformed church of Germantown. These three daughters were buried at Barren Hill. They were highly respected. There were several other children. Mr. Schlatter displayed a charitable spirit toward other Christian bodies than his own, and was "faithful to the trusts committed to his hands." He was industrious and persevering, and his memory is blessed.

His name is met with in accounts of early times in Pennsylvania. In Watson's Annals (Vol. I, p. 452), we learn that the German Reformed Church in Race street, near Fourth street, was built about A. D. 1747, in an octagon form, with a steeple. It only stood a few years, and gave place to a larger one. It was built for the Rev. Mr. Schlatter, "who was from the Society in Holland."

Watson adds: "His old journal I have seen wherein he states, that before his coming they were preached to by a Mr. Boehm, a layman, at a hired house. When Mr. Schlatter arrived, he found 165 communicants in Philadelphia, and 115 in Germantown."

The Swedish traveler, Rev. Professor Kalm, said that the first church here named was like one near Stockholm.

When a society was formed in Europe to raise money to teach poor German children, and provide ministers for them, the nobility of Holland and England patronized it, and noted Americans were "Trustees of the charity—such as Hamilton, Allen, Franklin, Peters, etc. The Rev. Mr. Schlatter is made visiting and traveling inspector and agent, and the Rev. Dr. Smith, our provost, was charged with the publication of a German newspaper."

The states of Holland and West Friesland subscribed, and Amsterdam gave much. The General Assembly of Scotland, the King of England, the Princess of Wales, and the Proprietaries helped this missionary effort to advance the Protestant religion, and to teach the reading of the Bible, and singing Psalms and writing and casting accounts. See Watson's Annals, Vol. I, p. 257.

In Scharf and Westcott's History of Philadelphia (Vol. I, p. 386), the plundering of Rev. Michael Schlatter's house by the British is noted.

In Hotchkin's Pocket Gazetteer of Pennsylvania, under Franklin county, p. 73, it stated that: "In early times, Rev. Michael Schlatter wrote that the Indians in this region were well disposed and friendly to Christians when not under the influence of liquor."

See also the valuable History of Pennsylvania by Dr. Wm. H. Egle, the State Librarian, from which the Gazetteer is compiled.

In Rev. J. F. Dripps's Sketch of the First Presbyterian Church, Germantown, on pages 11 and 12, he speaks of the worthy and devoted Rev. John Bechtel, in whose ordination Bishop Nitschman of the Moravian Church participated, and whose people built the first German Reformed Church building in Pennsylvania. "Consecrated and fervent" pastors succeeded him, who came to this new land in a true missionary spirit. It is added: "One of them especially, Rev. Michael Schlatter, was widely honored throughout the Province for his character and work by all classes and churches. He was to this church, what his friend Muhlenberg was to the Lutheran body."

"GRAYSTOCK," THE COUNTRY-SEAT OF GEORGE C. THOMAS.

CHESTNUT HILL.
"GRAYSTOCK"—EVERGREEN AVENUE.

This avenue with its rustic name, runs at right angles with Montgomery avenue. On the lower side of Evergreen avenue is situated "Graystock," the residence of George C. Thomas, of the banking firm of Drexel & Co. The mansion is an ample one, of stone, surmounted by an observatory, which is useful in the midst of such beautiful scenery. Mr. Thomas is well known as an energetic Sunday School worker in the Episcopal Church. He bought this place, which is his country seat, of Joseph B. Dulles, a prominent Philadelphia merchant, in 1881. He had lived there for some twenty years previous to this date. Before that time the property was owned by Mr. Clayton Platt, who commenced building the house, but Mr. Dulles purchased it from him before it was completed, and finished it. Since Mr. Thomas has occupied the mansion, Ardmore avenue has been opened through the grounds, appertaining to it, and he has acquired the place on the other side of that avenue, which has the quaint and appropriate name of "The Gables." Mrs. Thomas's sister, Mrs. Caroline F. Moorhead, now resides in this house with her children. The place originally belonged to Mr. Houpt. Mr. Thomas has improved it very greatly since he bought it in 1886.

Mr. Thomas's improvements to his residence were designed by Geo. W. & W. D. Hewitt, Architects, and subsequently Wilson Brothers & Co. The first named superintended and drew plans for the tower, etc., and the last named for further additions, mostly in the rear. Mr. W. C. Mackie was the builder in both cases.

The name "Graystock" comes from a place in England, in which Mrs. Thomas's maternal ancestors, of the Gilpin family, lived for several centuries. There is something very pleasant and desirable in connecting these beautiful places among the hills of the new world with the abodes of old time in the mother country.

The magnificent and varied scenery which meets the eye at this point, and at Alexander Biddle's, and John Lowber Welsh's places, and indeed throughout Chestnut Hill, should move a thankful and devout mind to praise God who piled up the hills and hollowed out the valleys, which in their light and shade, under sun and shower, covered with green grass, or shining with a pure snow mantle, draw exclamations of delight and wonder by their exceeding beauty. When the devoted Bishop Heber saw sublime glens and forests in his Indian travels, he says: "My attention was completely strained, and my eyes filled with tears; everything around was so wild and magnificent that man appeared as nothing, and I felt myself as if climbing the steps of the altar of God's great temple."

There is another interesting feature in the history of Chestnut Hill besides its scenery, and that is its rapidly improving architecture. The architects have done much to beautify this suburb, and to construct houses which should suit their natural surroundings, and also be comfortable homes. They deserve great credit for their work, and it is a pleasant thought that as this new country advances in wealth its structures are improving. In an article on History and Geography, and their relations to each other, by James Bryce, M. P., in the *Contemporary Review*, of March, 1886, we read : " It is worth observing that you may classify countries and parts of countries according as they are stone building or brick building regions, and you will be surprised to find the difference in architecture between the two. If you travel across Italy from east to west, for instance, you constantly get out of brick into stone regions as you enter the mountains, and you will find the character of the cities alters immediately."

If Mr. Bryce were to visit Chestnut Hill he would find it in a transition state. While the Chestnut Hill quarries have built its houses, and one gentleman has sent for his home stone to build a house in Pittsburg, brick is also available, and brick and tile are crowding on the old material. What effect this change may have on the character of the future buildings we know not.

Next to Mr. Thomas's in the direction of the Bethlehem pike, is the house of Mrs. Morris, the widow of George C. Morris, Esq., who was also a man highly honored in the Episcopal Church, and a member of the Standing Committee of the diocese of Pennsylvania. The house stands with the gable to the road, which makes it the more retired, and a little back from the street, as do the residences of Chestnut Hill in general, showing good taste in its inhabitants.

On Evergreen avenue opposite the side of Mrs. Bucknell's property and next to the house of Mrs. Morris, is the stone, ivy-clad house of Mrs. Vanuxem.

THE RESIDENCE OF COL. GEORGE H. NORTH.

Mr. Stewart, who was interested in the erection of this house for Mr. Taylor, states that it was built during the year 1861. In the fall of that year it was sold to Mr. Horace Brown. Mr. Charles Taylor was the capitalist who had the house constructed. He owned a large quantity of ground in Chestnut Hill, and was a leader in improvements which adorn this beautiful suburb. Mr. Brown sold the mansion to Dr. Bolling, from whom Col. North purchased it in 1883. The building is in the Gothic style of architecture, and is perfect in construction. The angles are exact. It has been greatly admired by architects, and has been by some considered the prettiest house on the Hill. The architect of Col. North's house was Samuel Sloan, the builder and contractor was Peter Hendel. This pleasant mansion of my friend bears the cosy name, "Our Home." The children of the owner, who roam through it, find the name well given. While it has been said that the French lack homes, the Americans have an abundance of them. Originally the old word "ham," from which "home" is derived, meant an inclosed place, and how many joys centre within those four walls which make a home! It is a castle which shuts out the world, but introduces the joys of domestic life. The home-like mansion has just been re-colored and looks beautiful in its new dress of red

RESIDENCE OF COLONEL GEORGE H. NORTH, NORWOOD AVENUE.

and green. The location is at the corner of Norwood and Chestnut avenues, opposite St. Paul's Episcopal Church, on Chestnut avenue, and Mrs. Comegys's School, on Norwood avenue. The grounds cover about an acre and a half, giving room for a lawn, where children can enjoy an out-door life in summer, and also affording space to display the beauties of the mansion. There is a fine stable, and a greenhouse adds to the beauty and value of the property. The head of Norwood avenue makes a fine location, for this is one of the best avenues in any suburb of Philadelphia.

Col. George H. North is the son of the late George W. North, and the grandson of Col. Caleb North, who was an officer in the Revolutionary war. Col. North entered the army at the breaking out of the Southern war in April, 1861, as a private in the Commonwealth Artillery, served three months, and entered the service again as Lieutenant in the Fourteenth Pennsylvania Cavalry, and served during the whole war, being honorably discharged in July, 1865. He was upon the staff of many prominent Generals, including Averill and Torbert. Since the war he has taken an active interest in the National Guard of Pennsylvania, and is the Adjutant General for Major General Hartranft, the Commander of the National Guard of Pennsylvania.

CHURCH OF OUR MOTHER OF CONSOLATION.

Rev. Francis Joseph McShane, rector; assistant, Rev. John Whelan. This church was founded in the summer of 1855. The corner-stone was laid by the late Rev. Dr. Moriarty, who was in charge of the parish and then resided in Chestnut Hill. The material of the building is gray stone. The parish from the beginning has been under the care of the Fathers of the Order of St. Augustine. Dr. Moriarty was at one time the Superior of the Order in the United States. He died at Villa Nova, Pa., in July, 1875. He was noted as an orator and divine, and had been in various parts of the world in the service of the Church. Father Moriarty, held the parish until the completion of the first church, which forms the nave of the present building. He also continued as rector for some years afterward. In the summer of 1868, Father James Darragh assumed charge of the parish. He was in turn succeeded by Rev. C. A. McEvoy, in April, A. D. 1871.

The pleasant stone parsonage was erected at the beginning of Father Moriarty's rectorship. He loved to call it "The Hermitage," and the priests of the order are called the hermits of St. Augustine. A yard beautifully adorned with flowers lies between the parsonage and the church and forms a pretty feature on Chestnut avenue. The parsonage was enlarged under Father McEvoy in 1878, and the church had a transept and chancel added in 1880 in his rectorship. Apartments in the basement of the new portion were arranged for parish day school purposes.

Father McEvoy was succeeded by Father McShane in July, 1882. A fine spire was placed on the tower during his rectorship, in the fall of 1885, and the gilded cross, lifted high in air, shows the emblem of Christian faith to the surrounding country. The parish school is taught by the Sisters of St. Joseph from the Convent of St. Joseph, on the Wissahickon. The land and buildings have probably cost about $50,000.

The Convent and Female Boarding School of St. Joseph lie on the Wissahickon, at the junction of the County line and Germantown pike. This Convent was founded in 1858 by Mother St. John. The Sisters of St. Joseph conduct it. The buildings are of stone in a fine location. They have been built and enlarged at great expense. The site was the old Middleton homestead. A part of the Convent building was the Middleton mansion. I am given these facts by the courtesy of Father McShane.

Mount St. Joseph Academy was begun in McSherrystown, Pa., and moved to its present beautiful site in A. D. 1858. The academy proper was finished in 1875, having cost $100,000. There is a library of five thousand volumes. The Church in Chestnut Hill is now adding a parochial building for schools, etc., to their property.

The conformation of the rolling ground about Chestnut Hill renders it very suitable for building sites, and of late years the citizens have eagerly seized upon these points of natural beauty, and planted their residences on many a hillside. If the old residents could now look upon their former homes, they would scarcely recognize their old farms, as they are studded with bright and attractive new dwellings. I gladly acknowledge the great aid which I have received from Mr. Mackie in my researches in Chestnut Hill.

Mr. Joseph Middleton came to Chestnut Hill in 1838. He is a brother-in-law of Judge Longstreth. He has kindly added some reminiscences to my collection. On Militia Hill, are the old fire hollows which were used by the soldiers of the Revolution. One of the soldier's buttons with G. W. on it has been found in this locality. They were George Washington buttons, as the initials indicate. Indian arrows, hatchets, axes of stone and green stone pipe, of rare material, and Indian beads have been found here. Mr. Middleton discovered an arrowhead lately. At the famous Indian Rock at the Wissahickon, on Mr. Middleton's place, the last Council of the Delaware Indians was held. The Indian statue, which was a way mark for those driving by, was put upon its lofty site by Mr. Middleton. Tedyuskung, the famous Indian chief, used to visit at a house where Mr. Charles Newhall's barn now stands. Mr. Middleton named Chestnut avenue Tedyuskung, and although the name did not hold, he hopes for its renewal, as it is a thoroughfare which leads to Indian Rock. As the Inn and the Creek bear an Indian name, it seems appropriate and desirable that this avenue, or some new one, should perpetuate the memory of one who wisely used his power among those who once owned the land where the white now lives in luxury.

There are two mounds in one of the fields on this property which the owner wishes were opened, but perhaps it is as well to let the old secrets sleep, although the American is always anxious to find out everything. Not far from the house is an old barn or press-house. When it was built the corner of an Indian burial mound was struck, which contained Indian relics. The burial grounds certainly should be kept sacred, if we desire our own graves in future to be undisturbed, if a man would not like to see the new-made grave of his wife or child rifled, and if the opening of fresh graves is considered one of the most shameful acts.

I append some notes of historical interest handed me by Mr. Middleton, from the PHILADELPHIA INQUIRER of December 31, A. D. 1881, and am sorry to add the notice of his death in the same paper dated October 19, 1887:

"ECHOES FROM THE INDIAN ROCK."

To the Editor of THE INQUIRER:

SIR:—A communication in your paper, some weeks ago, under the caption of "Lo, the Poor Indian," asks for some information regarding the aborigines who once dwelt in the vicinity of the Wissahickon valley. I submit a few points about them: The monuments, or vestiges, of the Indians of the once powerful tribe (Lenni-Lenape) who formerly inhabited this eastern part of Pennsylvania, are reduced, as regards this neighborhood, to these three, viz.: First. The rocks along the Wissahickon, referred to by your correspondent, i. e., the Overhanging Rock, the Temple Rock and the Council Rock. They are about seven and a half miles from the city at Market street. The last of these, the most important, is near the hilltop skirting the northern bank of the Wissahickon creek, and opposite the Indian Rock Hotel. It is commonly called the Indian rock *par excellence*. It is arch-shaped in front, towards the south, and hollowed out like the apse of a church, with an altar-shaped projection in the centre of the apse or overhanging rock, as if to serve either for a pulpit, or perhaps the chieftain's seat in council.

This rock with the other two, was undoubtedly an object of veneration to the Indians. In the case of the first, a few years ago might have been seen covering the rough, hollowed rock many traces of Indian sign language, strange marks and figures in red clay or paint. They have been mostly obliterated by thoughtless tourists and visitors who frequent the spot in fine weather, attracted by the wild grandeur of the locality, and by the large figure of heroic size of an Indian chief which surmounts the Council Rock, sole guardian of the once sylvan home of his prototypes. By the way, this heroic Tedyuscung of word and deed, for it is a memorial of that valiant warrior, was erected about the year 1854, by Mr. Joseph Middleton and some of the citizens of Chestnut Hill, who now own the land on which it stands. The figure is seen plainly from the Wissahickon turnpike road. Relics of the aborigines are still frequently found around the rocks and its vicinity, and near by several mounds still exist and can be pointed out—one in particular near an old press house, until lately owned by the descendants of John Adam Piper, who bought it in 1705, and who was an attached friend of Tedyuscung. On this ground, adjoining the press house, a mound—*tumulus*—still exists, in which, when opened some years since, were found skeletons of human bodies, implements of warfare, hatchets, arrowheads, trinkets, beads, etc., all evidently denoting some ancient burial place of the Delawares, of which Tedyuscung was principal chief.

About four miles distant on Camp Hill, can be pointed out numerous mounds; there was also a grand camping ground for the Indians. Tradition has handed down a large amount of information of these lost races; but the facts above stated are undisputed. A word about Tedyuscung, the old hero of the place. This chief was known, after his admission among the Moravians, as "Honest John," although baptized "Gideon." He met his death from burning at Wyoming, in April, 1763. Up to 1758 he and the remnant of his tribe spent the greater part of their time around the Council Rock, on the banks of the Wissahickon, near Chestnut Hill—then called Somerhausen—frequenting the house of the venerable John Adam Piper. In 1758 the Colonial House of Congress, then sitting in Philadelphia, in consideration of safety of the Indian tribes, ordered comfortable houses built at Wyoming, whence they were all removed in 1763; but, unfortunately, in a drunken frolic, their houses were set on fire, and in the burning, among others, the noble Tedyuscung.   JOSEPH MIDDLETON.

CHESTNUT HILL.

DEATH OF A WELL-KNOWN CITIZEN.

"Mr. Joseph Middleton, died yesterday at his residence, "Wood-ide," Chestnut Hill. Mr. Middleton was in the 74th year of his age. He had long been prominent in Roman Catholic circles in the community where he resided.

His funeral is announced for 9:30 A. M. to-morrow. Services at the Church of Our Lady of Consolation, Chestnut Hill."   *Phila. Inquirer*, Oct. 19th, 1887.

Susan and Lydia Piper owned Mr. Middleton's farm before it came into his possession. Their father was a great friend of the Indians. The modern residence which now stands here was built by Mr. Middleton. There is an old house, stable and carriage house. Mr. Middleton formerly lived on the St. Joseph Convent property. In the neighborhood of Mr. Middleton's place are Mr. H. H. Houston's pretty stone cottages along Thirtieth street and Chestnut avenue. I regret to note the death of Mr. Middleton. Mr. Mitchell's neat architectural cottage is on Thirtieth street, near Chestnut avenue.

NORWOOD HALL.

Norwood Hall is located in Chestnut Hill at the end of Chestnut avenue and directly on the hill forming the northeast boundary of the Wissahickon

NORWOOD HALL near CHESTNUT HILL PENNSYLVANIA

at that point, and known as Indian Rock. It is a notable example of the Tudor style of architecture and the only one of that style strictly, in the near neighborhood. The natural *locale* greatly aids the effect produced by the large mass of the building as it rises on the tower side at the head of a quite extended knoll, and the bounteous background of fine trees gives it the *ensemble* of a well-preserved manorial estate rather than of a creation of the present time, and the extended and beautiful views of hill and vale, greensward and forest, with their ever-varying light and shade, please the eye in every direction.

The estate belongs to Mr. Chancellor C. English, who purchased it from Mr. Joseph Middleton and others, and is noted historically as being the site of Indian Rock, a council place of Indian tribes in past times and also the scene of visits from Tedyuscung, a noted chief. Certain mounds here bear witness to the spot having once been used by the Indians as a burial ground. From relics found, the near neighborhood, with this, seem to have been the haunts of the roving red men of the forest, and the principal charm of the place is that a few steps away from the new Hall and its modern life, one may enjoy the quiet of woodland scenes, now much the same as in the days of the painted savage.

The designs of the architect, Mr. Pearson, of Philadelphia, have been well interpreted by the use of a local stone, quite rough, much of it quarried from the site of the building, and with the aid of hood mouldings, battlements, large traceried windows and other characteristics of the style used, suggest pleasing possibilities for the coming years, when clinging vines will find on this rough stone a hold to aid them in adding their leafy blending of base and crest.

Entrance is made through the *porte-cochère* by a large doorway, the door of which is heavy oak, plain, with wrought iron hinges, and studded, into the Great Hall 25x45, on the right corner of the building, and extending the full height inside to the roof, the timbers of which are of oak, with arched and carved truss supports. This noble apartment abounds in wood carvings and tracery, has oak paneling on the walls 13 feet high, and an arcade on two sides of the second story forming one side of the passage-way to the apartments on that floor. At the northwest or right end of this Great Hall, the main staircase is placed, with pierced and carved tracery work, newells with long carved ends, rising from successive landings, one of which is in the square bay front, to a balcony from which steps are taken thro' an archway into the rounded tower and thence to the second story Hall from which thro' the arcade before mentioned one may get the full effect of the main Hall, with its many windows and other features of interest.

As one enters the Hall attention is at once attracted to a large Tudor fireplace on the southwest side, of carved red stone, arched, and flush with the wall. On either side of this a large opening gives access to the Drawing-room 20x23 at the Tower end, and to the Library. This Library is an impressive room, 18x23 finished in mahogany, with stationary book shelves and ample stone fire-place. The walls are wainscoted, and to the southwest a large square bay opening on a veranda, affords light and glimpses thro' the woods to the Wissahickon. On the left side of the Hall is the Dining-room, finished in oak, 26x29, with large alcove and bay, the entire apartment having high paneling on walls, and carved ceiling beams, arch-work, traceried screens, china cabinets and fire-place. Opening off the left of this room is the Morning room, 14x16, specially arranged to receive the sunlight on winter days. All of these main apartments communicate with each other by wide openings, and the large windows in each room are arranged on the same axis so that one may have a vista extending thro' the house in any direction and so comprehending the delightful scenery in which the place abounds. Immediately adjoining the entrance is an office facing front, and separated from the Great Hall by a vestibule, leading also to the Butler's room. The left end of the house is assigned solely to the domestics' use in each story. On the second main story are the principal family sleeping apartments all quite large and opening on the gallery formed behind the arcade of the great Hall. These are supplemented in part of the roof story by several guest chambers one of which in the Tower has a most superb view of near and distant scenery, and from which also a private staircase leads to the Tower roof.

No elaborate wall decorations of any kind have been used, but the walls and ceilings are in quiet plain monotints throughout. The interior as well as the exterior has been designed throughout, to be in perfect harmony with the style of the Tudor days, principally because the site was a lordly one, and such a style lends its own dignity and simplicity to supplement what nature has already so well done, and as years add their toning down processes to the walls, and the ivy creeps steadily ever higher and more broad, the walls, the trees, and the sward will give, as time wanes, new beauty to Norwood Hall.

Charles Newhall has a modern residence on Chestnut avenue, at the end of Rex avenue, near Mr. Middleton's place. There is no fence around the grounds to check the view, and this is always pleasing. The side of the house runs along parallel with the side of the avenue. The foundation is of blue stone, which extends half way up the first story, terminating in a wall around the rear of the mansion. Above there is brick work, with square-topped windows, but in the second story at the end gable there is a triplet window, with a semi-circular arch over the middle division, according to an antique style. In the rear part of the building there is woodwork above the stone. The porch in front is inclosed by a brick wall on two sides a few feet upward. An old orchard in the lawn indicates an old settlement before the building of the present house. There are trees still standing along Chestnut avenue which may have delighted the eyes of Tedyuskung in the old Indian days, which may not seem so far away when we get under the shade of the monarchs of the forest, and feel that it is good to live in the open air in hot weather, as did our savage forerunners. I believe that a plastered log house stood near that of Mr. Newhall, and that the logs were good when repairs were lately made.

THOMAS LIVEZEY AND JOSEPH GALLOWAY.

The following article, by Hon. Horatio Gates Jones was published in the *Pennsylvania Magazine of History and Biography*:

"Nearly one hundred and fifty years ago the banks of the Wissahickon creek were occupied by mills of various kinds at all available places. There were grist, fulling, oil and paper mills. The most prominent millers were the Robesons, Gorgases, Livezeys, and Rittenhouses. These mills were accessible only by cross-roads leading from the Manatawny or Reading Road, in Roxborough, and the Main street in Germantown. As early as 1745 the Livezeys had a grist mill just above where the Pipe Bridge now is, and that was only to be reached from Germantown by what is now known as Allen's lane. For many years a certain Thomas Livezey owned and resided at the mill, and cultivated a large farm, and on the hillsides had a vineyard, and, as was the custom in those days, made his own wine. No doubt it was good, for in 1768, Robert Wharton sent a dozen bottles to Dr. Franklin, who, in a letter dated February 20, 1768, wrote to Wharton as follows:

"'DEAR FRIEND,—I received your favors of November 17th and 18th, with another dozen of excellent wine, the manufacture of our friend Livezey. I thank you for the care you have taken in forwarding them, and for your good wishes that accompany them.'

"Mr. Livezey was a member of the Society of Friends, and when the British were in Philadelphia, and our troops used to wander about seeking provender, he sunk a number of barrels of wine in his dam in the Wissahickon, where it remained until the close of the war. Some of that wine was bottled and preserved by the late Mr. John Livezey, a grandson of the said Thomas Livezey, until a short time before he died, in 1878. He gave me a small bottle of this *Revolutionary Wine*, which I shall deposit in our Society.

"Mr. Livezey was a man of great prominence in his day, and for many years was a member of the Pennsylvania Assembly. Among other members of the Assembly was the celebrated Joseph Galloway, who was one of the leading lawyers of the Colony. He and Mr. Livezey were warm friends, and, being full of wit, often joked his friend Thomas for living in such a hidden place as the wilds of the Wissahickon, so far removed from the busy world and so inaccessible.

"Mr. Livezey had a large family of daughters and three sons. One daughter married John Johnson, of Germantown, and another Peter Robeson, of Roxborough. Two of his sons were named John and Joseph. He died in 1790, and in his will speaks of his copy of Blackstone's Commentaries, which shows he had some knowledge of law. The following letter to his friend Galloway shows his wit and also his appreciation of the beauties of Nature, which were to be found then as now along the banks of the picturesque Wissahickon:

"'Roxborough, 12th Mo. 14th, 1765.

"'Dear Friend,—As thou hast often concluded from the lowness of my situation that I must be nearly connected with the Lower regions or some Infernal place of abode, I have sent thee the following true description of the place of my residence in order to convince thee of that error:

"Near Wissahickon's mossy banks, where purling fountains glide
Beneath the Spruces' shady boughs and Laurel's blooming pride,
Where little fishes sport and play, diverting to the sight,
Whilst all the warbling winged race, afford my ear delight;
Here are evergreens by Nature set, on which those warblers sing,
And flowery aromatic Groves form an eternal spring;
Refreshing breezes round me move, which with the blossoms play,
And balmy odors on their wings through all my vale convey.
Those charming scenes—did'st thou dwell here—would all thy care beguile
And, in the room of anxious fear, would cause a harmless smile.
Here's innocence and harmony, which give me thoughts sublime,
Little inferior to the place call'd Eden in its prime.
Thus situated, here I dwell, where these sweet zephyrs move,
And, little rivulets from Rocks add beauty to my Grove.
I drink the wine my Hills produce; on wholesome food I dine;
My little Offspring round me are like Clusters on the Vine;
I hand in hand with second self oft walk amidst the bowers,
Whilst all our little prattling ones are gathering opening flowers.
In this low station here I'm fixed, nor envy Court nor King,
Nor crave the honors Statesmen crave, nor Cares which riches bring.
Honor's a dangerous, tempting thing, which oft leads men astray,
Riches, like insects, spread their wings and quickly flee away.
My meditations here are free from interrupting strife,
Whilst different ways, aspiring men pursue indifferent life;
I see what cunning artifice the busy men employ,
Whilst I this lonely seat of bliss unenvied here enjoy.
This is the place of my abode, when humbly here I dwell,
Which, in romantic Lawyer mood, thou has compared to Hell.
But Paradise where Adam dwelt in blissful love and ease,
A Lawyer would compare to Hell, if thence he got no fees.
Canst thou prefer thy Heaven on earth—thy fee the Root of evil—
To this my lonely harmless place,—my Hell without a Devil?"

"'Permit me from my low situation to thine of eminence, to do myself the Justice to say, I am with much respect,

"'Thy sincere friend,

"'Thomas Livezey.

"'I shall conclude with the words made use of to Zaccheus of old: "Come down—come down quickly," for I want thee to dine at my house.'"

STONECLIFFE.

In 1849 Mr. Charles Taylor, who was almost a pioneer in Chestnut Hill, purchased a few acres on the Reading pike and commenced building a stone

"STONECLIFFE," THE RESIDENCE OF MRS. CHARLES TAYLOR.

house, which was finished in 1852. It was not very large, but a beautifully designed English cottage, called "Norwood." It is now the summer residence of Miss Harriet Benson, who enlarged it, and changed the architecture. Mr. Taylor added acre after acre to the original purchase, until forty acres belonged to the Norwood estate. In 1860 Norwood avenue was opened through the place, from Sunset avenue to Chestnut avenue, and several fine houses were erected.

In 1880 and 1881 "Stonecliffe," the residence of Mrs. Charles Taylor, was erected on a commanding situation. T. P. Chandler, was the architect. The site is remarkably picturesque, the view is extensive and charming. The wide prospect embraces the Reading hills, and a spur of the Blue Mountains is visible from the piazza; while the whole White Marsh Valley, at the base of the hills, delights the eye of the beholder. This is one of the finest situations for a dwelling in Chestnut Hill, or in any suburb of Philadelphia. The massive and architectural stone house would be a beauty and ornament in any country district, and a notable feature in the landscape; but in this case the picture is enhanced by its setting, and the framework of hill and valley give it an especial charm. The view has been thought the finest one in Chestnut Hill, and amateur photographers often fasten it, that they and their friends may enjoy a recollection of it. This house affords views from the rear, as well as from the front. The grounds of "Stonecliffe" contain ten acres. The entrance from Norwood avenue, is through a stretch of wood, and its natural beauty has been much admired. Sometimes, in a rural district, each place has some particular feature which calls the attention of the passer-by, but this combines several attractions as the architectural mansion is striking, and the views grand, and the grounds so extensive as to rightly display all the attractive character of the surroundings. Mr. Charles Taylor erected "Edgcumbe," now owned by Mr. Charles B. Dunn.

THE OLD YEAKLE GRAVEYARD.

"There is a calm for those who weep,
A rest for weary pilgrims found ;
And while the mouldering ashes sleep,
    Low in the ground.

The soul, of origin divine,
God's glorious image, freed from clay,
In heaven's eternal sphere shall shine,
    A star of day."
—*James Montgomery.*

Gray's Elegy in a country churchyard has stirred the hearts of generations, and even in this new land many a country graveyard wakes similar associations. There is a poem by Rose Terry Cooke, entitled the "Two Villages," which naturally came into my mind in looking from the Eldon day by day, at the quiet old graveyard in view across Stenton avenue. The still village is under our eyes. The farmers and their faithful wives, who arose with the early morning to drive the plough or perform the duties of the house, are no longer waked by the song of the bird. The village over the hill, where the new citizens dwell is astir with its hopes and fears. The Schwenckfelders, of the primitive days of Chestnut Hill, lie within the quiet walled inclosure. A little babbling busy stream, with mimic waterfalls, runs before the cemetery. In one part the water is underlaid with stones, which add to its beauty. This water changes like the generations of men, but the stream abides, and seems to sing:

> "Men may come, and men may go,
> But I flow on forever."

In these lines from Tennyson's "Brook," does the poet allude to Horace's Latin Epistle to Lollius?—Ep. II. Bk. I:

> "Labitur, et labetur in omne volubilis aevum."

The fable referred to was that a countryman waited for the river to flow by, so that he could pass over on dry land.

In a translation of an Oriental poem, made by W. R. Alger, we see the wise Adi, with the youthful scholar and Prince Noman, walking where a river passed an ancient cemetery, and the tutor says to the pupil that the dwellers in the graves are telling the caravans that pass by that they too in time must die.

The old graveyard before us is on the slope of a hillside, surrounded by the property of Alexander Biddle. A good stone wall incloses it, and shows that the living have not forgotten the duty of piety toward the dead. Some plain, low, ancient stones still keep their places. There are two German inscriptions of Christopher and Maria Jackel. The Heydricks are relatives of the Yeakels. Here is an inscription: "Abraham Yeakel, geboren den 14 Mertz, 1752; gestorben den 17 Juni, 1841. Alt geworden 89 Jahr 3 Mo. und 3 tage." A late burial is that of Amy Yeakel, born in 1808 and died in 1883, aged 75 years. The name Jacob Neff meets us; also that of Rebecca, wife of John H. Schultz, who died in 1881, aged 85 years. We will add others: Fridrick Eshamann; Elenora, wife of Jacob Bauer, Maggie Shuman, 16 years old, and Sarah, under twenty, daughters of William and Barbara Shuman, sleep quietly side by side. There are said to be some soldiers of the War of 1812 buried here. As the Oriental poem has it in Alger's translation:

> "A furloughed soldier, here I sleep, from battle
> spent,
> And in the resurrection I shall strike my tent."

E. N. BENSON'S MANSION.

Architecture has been defined as

> "The art where most magnificent appears
> The little builder man."

CHESTNUT HILL.

The most massive and perhaps the most expensive residence that came under my close observation in Chestnut Hill was that of Mr. Benson. It has more the appearance of a castle than a private house, and as I gazed on it from my window day by day the effect was a pleasing one. It is not difficult in looking at such a structure to imagine yourself in "merrie England," or on the banks of the Rhine. This new country is rapidly acquiring the architectural beauties of the Old World.

The position of this building by reason of the slope of the hill is a good one to display the solid masonry which forms the foundation of the edifice. The quiet old Bethlehem turnpike was astonished when this mansion rose and groaned and complained over the heavy loads of stone which passed over it for its construction. It doubtless seemed to it that the ideas of Christopher Wren were invading this land, and that the poor earth which in former years had merely borne the weight of the Indian tent, or the white man's log cabin must now support a heavier load. The gray stone mansion is surmounted by a square tower, and gables and chimneys vary the exterior. So English is the scene that one almost looks to see the sentinel standing by the massive stone gate posts. There is a *porte-cochère*, with a pretty stone arch in front, and another at one side of the house. The stone gate-posts are high. The slope of the lower lawn is especially beautiful.

This property belonged to the Piper family, and afterward to Joseph Howell. Mr. Benson's first house was burned, and then he built this mansion in 1884. There is a picture of the ruins of the old house in Lippincott's Magazine, in an article on Germantown. Mrs. Charles Taylor's house, on Sunset avenue, may be compared with Mr. Benson's, as to massiveness.

Mrs. Rae, the mother-in-law of Mr. Benson, lives in the gray-stone house just below the mansion which has just been described. This property formerly belonged to Mr. Mitchell. Just below this is the winding wooded entrance to the Bohlen place. Bohlen station, in the African Mission, and the Sunday school building of Holy Trinity Chapel at Twenty-second and Spruce streets, keep green the memory of a good man. It was at the Chestnut Hill country place that the earnest clergyman, Rev. Dr. Heman Dyer, solicited and obtained aid from the Bohlen family for the work of construction of a needed building for the Episcopal Theological Seminary of Virginia, located at Alexandria, which has no doubt been the means of much good in that school of the prophets. The name of John Bohlen must be placed with that of Henry J. Williams, in Chestnut Hill, as worthy of remembrance among the faithful workers for Christ and His Church. The account of Dr. Dyer's visit of benevolence to Chestnut Hill, will be found in his "Records of an Active Life," published by Thomas Whittaker, of New York, which is an interesting narrative of his own experience in various public positions in the church.

There are several features of the country at Chestnut Hill, and the region around it, which make settlement pleasant and desirable. The ground is rolling, as is all the Pennsylvania suburbs of Philadelphia. This produces fine views and affords good drainage, so that the building sites have a double advantage. In the White Marsh region the hills rise to quite a height. The vicinity of the beautiful and romantic Wissahickon creek, with its store of traditions, adds interest to walks and drives. St. Thomas's Episcopal church, and the German Reformed and Lutheran associate church near it, and Washington's headquarters enliven the drives in the White Marsh section; though the Washington place is a little outside of White Marsh, yet it is connected with it in our historical ideas.

The winding White Marsh valley is beautiful wherever its vistas open, and such vistas are constantly presenting themselves. The history of architecture is marked plainly in the stone houses of Chestnut Hill. The two little, one-story, antique farm cottages where Stenton avenue joins the Bethlehem pike, are pictures of the early day when perhaps as happy a life was led in them as in the grander mansions which have followed—for the desires were less. The old pebble-dashed house next above the Eldon, on the same side of the way, which was for perhaps a half a century in the hands of the Streeper family, who dwelt in it, is an advance in size and dignity. But a better example of the gradual advance may be found in the good, well-built old stone houses which are found between Cresheim creek and the junction of Bethlehem and Reading pikes.

A more pretentious style of house arose when Cephas G. Childs and others began the improvement of Modern Chestnut Hill. His own former residence, and the Norris house, and others on the Reading pike, indicate this progress. Of late many fine residences described show a farther advance; and who can tell what is to come next? The opening of the Pennsylvania railroad, and the frequent trains make the city convenient of access, and if an elevated railway should ever look this way the newer residences may find themselves indeed within the city proper, and a new "*rus in urbe*" may arise farther northward. But we need not look so far; let us rather, like the Indian chief, enjoy what is before us, and cry with him "Alabama," which in his language meant. "here we rest."

A prominent citizen of Chestnut Hill has called my attention to a valuable article in the Philadelphia TIMES, by W. H. Whitty, one of its staff of writers, concerning the "WISSAHICKON REGION." It dwells on the vast and costly improvements that have followed the opening of the Pennsylvania Railroad. The McCallums are spoken of as former land owners. The writer says that it has been said that the Wissahickon exceeds Shakespeare's Avon, and Wordsworth's Wye, " in sentiment or romance." On the John Welsh property, T. P. Chandler, G. T. Pearson, and Cope and Stewardson have furnished varied architectural plans for many new structures. Mr. Baily, Mr. Swope. Mr. Littlefield, James B. Young, John B. Bell, Samuel W. Bell, President of the Farmers and Mechanics Bank, Henry N. Almy, Morris Dallett, Esq., S. Arthur Love, Judge Henry Reed, Mr. Stewart, H. F. McIntire, Mr. White,

J. W. Ogelvee, William P. Houston, Mr. Thomas, Mr. Blummer, Mr. Loper Baird, Fenton Thompson and William Henderson reside on this Welsh property.

The house of Mrs. Strawbridge on this tract is occupied by Captain Taylor, U. S. Marine Corps.

Gustavus A. Benson's fine house near Carpenter station is noted, and the "very handsome house" of Nathaniel E. Crenshaw. Opposite this Captain James Hacker has erected "a light-gray stone house so pretty, so happily conceived and so fitted to its surroundings that it has been sketched by artists, has amateur cameras pointed at it every day, and has been illustrated in a number of architectural journals. It is the first house seen from the railroad approaching Carpenter's." A "picturesque bridge" and "grassy slope" add to the effect. Deanewood is the name of the place. It is prettily wooded.

Mr. Harvey has an Oriental house near by, with "gables and bands of broken-up bricks set out from stone, giving a very rustic effect."

"Two very fine houses" near Upsal are those of Cornelius N. Weygandt, President of the Western National Bank, and J. Henry Tilge. Harvey Ellis, Mr. Mason and John W. Moffly, President of the Manufacturers' National Bank, have built very expensive and elaborate houses at Carpenter's.

Clarence White, son of the late Dr. S. S. White, has "a fine house here" standing across the lot to face the corner.

William McLean has "a very fine house close to Carpenter's." The old McCallum mill stands near. It is idle. "The Carr cotton lap factories" are mentioned, "and their quaint and once elegant adjacent homestead that now forms such a picturesque spot just below Allen's Lane station." H. H. Houston has built between eighty and a hundred houses. Henry D. Welsh's castellated, mediaeval house at Wissahickon Heights' station is properly noticed. "It is built entirely of stone and copper, with a fine stone porch and carriage entrance, and has tiled floors and all the late interior elegancies." Joseph M. Gazzam, son-in-law of John G. Reading, has a "fine new house" on Seminole avenue. Near by are "four fine separate houses, all large and very complete." At Highland avenue Frank L. Neal, William G. Audenried, Eugene Borda and Monroe W. Tingley reside.

The writer of the TIMES' article, which I have followed, runs back to Tulpehocken, and finds "four fine houses, all of stone on elevations varied in architecture, and with graded terrace and low stone walls, occupied by Mr. William Brockie, Miss Scott, Charles H. Scott and Naval Officer Henry B. Plumer.

Four more houses are "at the same pretty station, facing the woods." They are "charming houses, not so large as some of the others, but all exquisitely arranged and of stone, with decorated shingles and slate roofs." General Passenger Agent James R. Wood, of the Pennsylvania Railroad, occupies one of these houses. Twelve new houses of brick and stone on Wayne street, above Walnut lane, are in pairs in somewhat of the cottage style, and light similar houses are opposite. At the corner are two "gray stone houses, with tiled roofs, finished in mahogany, and altogether very fine. They are occupied by Mr. Davis and Mr. Grove. Beyond these are three very picturesque single houses, each different, overlooking the bluff. Several other striking new houses are close by, notably that of Edward T. Coxe, of gray stone and tiles, with terraces, porches, stained glass windows, and a fine approach, and beyond it that of Henry L. Townsend. This has a striking "*porte-cochère*, massive stone arches, terrace, porch and conservatory." This writer should renew his observant walks elsewhere.

"THE EVERGREENS."

The roomy and comfortable mansion, with its ample grounds and surrounding shrubbery, at the corner of Stenton avenue and Summit street, is the abode of Mrs. Thomas Potter. The house was built by Mr. Sanford. The brief of title shows that this land was a part of a tract conveyed by William Penn to Francis Daniel Pastorius. Mr. William Potter has a printed pamphlet containing the brief of title. This place was a portion of the tract of land sold by Judah Foulke, High Sheriff of Philadelphia, to Matthias Bush, December 20, 1771; thence in May, 1791, to James McCrawley; thence, April, 1795, to Christopher Yeakel; thence, March, 1836, to David Shultz; thence, April, 1845, to John Krieble; thence, May, 1851, to Clayton T. Platt; thence, December, 1853, to William C. Taylor; thence, in that same year, to Cephas G. Child; thence, August, 1855, to Samuel H. Austin; thence, October, 1855, to Edward S. Sanford; thence, June, 1862, to Robert H. Gratz; thence, June, 1869, to Thomas Potter. The house of Charles A. Potter was built on a portion of this land owned by Mrs. Thomas Potter. The name of her son Charles's house is "The Anglecot." It was built in the spring of 1883.

THOMAS POTTER.

THOMAS POTTER, a distinguished citizen of Philadelphia, banker and founder of the great manufacturing establishment of Thomas Potter—now conducted under the style of Thomas Potter, Sons & Co.—and prominent for many years in public affairs, was born in the County of Tyrone, Ireland, Aug. 17th, 1819, and died at Philadelphia, Sunday Sept. 29th, 1878. "The family of Potter, formerly of Potterstown, County of Fermanagh, is descended from George Potter, an officer who accompanied the army of Cromwell from England, and was compensated for his services in reducing Ireland to the rule of the Commonwealth by extensive grant of lands in the County Fermanagh. The lands thus granted were formerly the property of the Lord Marquis, Chiefton of Fermanagh, who, for his complicity in what is known as 'the Great Rebellion of 1641,' was convicted of high treason, his estate being confiscated to the English Government. Under the Act of Settlement and Plantation of 1660 (time of Charles II), as may be seen in the public records of Ireland, George Potter was

"THE EVERGREENS," RESIDENCE OF MRS. THOMAS POTTER.

confirmed in the possession of the lands of Oaghill, Mullinscarty, Carderghill, Tremern, and Cromey, all situated in the Barony of Maglierestepha, County of Fermanagh, which came thence forward to be known and designated as Potterstown and Pottersrath. This property the Potter family continued to possess for many years until, as appears from a deed of conveyance now in the possession of the Right Honorable, The Earl of Belmore, K. C. M. G., of Castlecool, County Fermanagh, Abraham Potter, son of the above-mentioned George Potter, disposed of the entire estate to James Corry, the son of a Scotch adventurer and the founder of the family of the present Earl of Belmore."

This disposition of the paternal estates was the inevitable result of the heavy mortgages, which had been placed upon them in order to meet obligations caused by improvident living, consequent upon the prevailing habits of the landed people of the period.

The Potter family although their interests in the estates originally granted to their ancestor was thus severed, continued to reside in the County. No longer members of the great landed aristocracy they, nevertheless, occupied a good position. In the year 1791, James Potter, at that time the representative head of the family, who resided in Ramaley in the County of Fermanagh, became possessed of a property at Rilaghquiness in the County of Tyrone. On his death he was succeeded by his son, George Potter, who, having decided to settle in the United States disposed of his property in Ireland, and left the County with his wife, three daughters and a son Thomas, in the year 1828.

George Potter arrived in Philadelphia with a moderate sum of money, and in a few years was taken ill and died leaving his family but a small estate and limited means.

His son Thomas had been desirous of entering the ministry, and his parents were arranging to prepare him for college, but the death of his father caused him to forego this cherished hope, and forced him at once to maintain himself, as well as contribute to the support of his family.

He learned the trade of manufacturing oil cloth with Isaac Macauley, proprietor of the Bush Hill Oil Cloth Establishment, the main building of which was the original manor house of James Hamilton, twice Colonial Governor of the Province of Pennsylvania.

Appreciating, however, the importance of a thorough education he devoted himself to diligent study at night under the tuition of his mother, and he acquired a broad and liberal framework of knowledge, the completeness and good purpose of which was shown in after life.

While devoting his leisure hours to self-improvement and study, he gave such diligent and valuable attention to his business that in a few years he was made manager by Mr. Macauley.

In 1838, though then but nineteen years of age, he founded the house of Thomas Potter—succeeded by Thomas Potter, Sons & Co.—and shortly thereafter purchased from Isaac Macaulay the Bush Hill Oil Cloth Works, in which he had served his apprenticeship. In 1870 he sold Bush Hill, and purchased the ground and erected the extensive establishment at Second and Venango streets on the New York Division of the Pennsylvania Railroad, since greatly enlarged, and where the business has so increased that it is now the most extensive of its kind in the United States.

Here the business is still carried on by his sons.

Mr. Potter married, on Oct. 2nd, 1845, Miss Adaline Coleman Bower, a granddaughter of General Jacob Bower, of Reading, Pa., who served as an officer in the Continental Army from June, 1775, to the end of the struggle for Independence, in 1783, and was one of the founders of the Pennsylvania section of the Society (or Order) of the Cincinnati, and during the War of 1812 a Brigadier-General of Pennsylvania Militia. The children of this marriage were six sons and two daughters. Four of the sons survive, and have succeeded to the business established by Mr. Potter. Mr. Potter's civic life was marked by characteristic energy and he held many positions of trust and honor in the city of his adoption. A brief list of these will strongly exhibit the esteem with which he was regarded by his fellow-citizens: In 1853 he was elected a Commissioner. Three years later after the Consolidation he was nominated by the Democratic party and elected to the City Councils, and was immediately appointed to the Chairmanship of the Committee on Schools (having been also a School Controller and School Director). Two years later he allied himself with the Republican party and was nominated and elected on that ticket to the Common Council in 1858. In 1859–60–61, he represented the People's party in the same body. During these years he was Chairman of the School Committee and a member of the Finance Committee, and he took an active and leading part in all municipal legislation. He was especially interested in the improvement of the Public School system, upon which subject he made several valuable reports, and was chiefly instrumental in organizing the paid Fire Department of Philadelphia.

In 1861 he orginated and carried through, the ordinance for the appointment of a Commission to assist in supporting the families of volunteers in the Union army from the city of Philadelphia.

He not only gave this project his untiring attention, but tendered his private office for the use of the Commission. In 1865 and 1866 he was again elected to Councils; was made Chairman of the Finance Committee, and was instrumental in passing the bill which secured to the city the eastern portion of Fairmount Park. He was also active in passing the bill which required the City Treasurer to pay City Warrants according to date and number, which had the effect of bringing them to par and strengthened the credit of the city.

The bill providing for the revising of the assessment of real estate also received his hearty and earnest support.

Mr. Potter carried through Common Council a bill, which, had it not been ultimately defeated, would have proved one of the most important ordinances ever passed in the city of Philadelphia; it was to provide for the passage of an Act of Assembly authorizing the public Squares at Broad and Market streets to be used for the erection of an Academy of Natural Sciences, and Academy of Fine Arts and other educational institutions. He had many opportunities of holding more ambitious offices and positions of public trust, but his chief pride lay in trying modestly but diligently to further the material interests of Philadelphia by every means in his power. Mr. Potter's intense devotion to his public duties and the demands of his private interests began to tell upon his strength, so that in 1868 he was obliged to resign his seat in Councils and traveled in Europe, where he spent some time vainly seeking to recover the health which he had shattered chiefly in the service of his fellow-citizens. In 1871, after his return from Europe, he was elected President of the City National Bank of Philadelphia, and held that position until his death which took place at his residence, "The Evergreens," Chestnut Hill, Philadelphia, Sunday, September 29, 1878. The value of his services to the Bank can best be recorded by giving extracts from the minutes of the Board of Directors, and from the Resolutions passed by the Philadelphia Clearing-House Association,

Mr. Potter was alike distinguished for his public and private virtues and evinced his interest in whatever cause he espoused by his zeal and devotion to it.

In private life he was a friend of the poor, a guide and counsellor to the young and dependent, a successful man of business, above all, a man of strict integrity, a sincere and earnest Christian.

He was unremitting in his attention to the interests of the Bank, and, in the conduct of its affairs, always exhibited that union of sound judgment, calm temper and courtesy of manner that marked his success through life.

He was equally true to the many public trusts with which he was honored, and in his death the city loses one of its best and purest citizens. His whole life commands admiration and should incite both old and young to emulate and imitate his many virtues.

The following is the resolution of the Clearing House Association:

"In the decease of our valued friend and associate, Mr. Thomas Potter, this Association has sustained the loss of one who, for the last seven years, has enlightened our counsels and honored our membership, and we desire to testify our appreciation of his exalted character as a man of strict integrity and high personal honor, whose mind was ever ready to meet the most difficult question presented for our consideration. He was one of our most public spirited citizens, always faithful and trusted, ever pure and true."

The following extract from the pen of Hon. Henry J. Williams, summarizes briefly and makes plainly evident the high standard of his life and character as a man:

"Mr. Potter was born in Ireland but came with his parents to this country when only ten years old and has been a resident of Philadelphia from that time to the day of his death. His activity, enterprise and sound judgment made him very successful in his business and he soon realized a large fortune which he employed with great liberality in the service of his Master. He held many positions of trust and responsibility in our municipal and financial corporations and has left behind him the character of a Christian gentleman, remarkable for his purity, uprightness and generosity; without a stain to dim its lustre. He was gentle and courteous in his manner; kind and affectionate in his disposition; earnest and indefatigable in his efforts to promote the cause of his Divine Master, and using his great wealth with great liberality for the benefit of religion.

"Like the centurion of old he built at his own expense a church for his workmen and their families, and was also a munificent contributor to almost every institution of religion and charity."

Mr. Potter was baptized in the Episcopal Church, but soon thereafter became a Presbyterian; yet all through his life, he was very catholic in his religious belief; with him the name signified but little; the life everything. In early life he connected himself with the Presbyterian Church at Seventeenth and Filbert streets (Dr. Gilbert's) and in a few years was made Ruling Elder, and Superintendent of the Sunday School; both of which positions he held for many years.

He was subsequently with M. W. Baldwin, Esq., and others, the founders of the Presbyterian Church at Broad and Green streets (Dr. Adams's).

He was always distinguished as a cheerful and earnest worker, a most liberal giver, and a man of singular purity of life.

In late years it was his custom to publicly address his workmen, and their families, in the Lyceum at Franklinville, on both moral and religious subjects. Until his death he was an active member, Ruling Elder, and Sunday School teacher in the Presbyterian Church at Chestnut Hill, Philadelphia.

(George Albert Lewis.)

The riding in the neighborhood of Chestnut Hill was not as easy in old times as to-day. An old resident of Germantown has spoken to me of the vividness with which he remembered a description of a night ride in the hills, when a lady and her companion found the horse stopping suddenly on the edge of a precipice.

Cresheim introduced a German name. A friend has handed me the following list, which may be useful to those seeking new names for places:—Kriegsheim, Home of the War or War's home; Kriegersheim, Home of the Warrior; Kreisheim, Home Circle; Greisheim, Home of the Soil (old man); Kreuzheim, Home Cross; Grenzheim, Home on the Border.

The Ottingers and Heilicks were old families who lived near Chestnut Hill.

Those wishing to locate points in Germantown can consult Hopkins's Atlas. The Atlas gives streets and plots of ground with the owners' names. It is a good-sized volume, and may be found at the Mercantile Library. If any wish to pursue the history of Germantown farther they will find "The Ghost of Chew's Wall," by Oliver Oldfellow, with the signature (G.,) in *Graham's Magazine*, Vol. XIX, p. 194, etc. It is interesting and can be seen at the library of the

Historical Society of Pennsylvania, Thirteenth and Locust streets. "The Germantown Battle Ground" is the subject of another article in the same magazine, Vol. XXV, p. 17.

In the most interesting manuscript journal of Rev. Dr. Joseph Pilmoor, at the Methodist book store in Philadelphia, there are some valuable notes about Germantown and Chestnut Hill. The writer of the journal came here with Richard Boardman, sent by Wesley as the first two Methodist preachers who came to this country. Dr. Pilmoor afterward took orders in the Episcopal Church, and was rector of old St. Paul's, in Third street, and is buried under that church. He notes that he preached on Christ Crucified at the Lutheran Church in Germantown. He afterward preached in the Presbyterian Church in the same place. He was a powerful preacher. Of Chestnut Hill he writes: "At eleven I had a vast congregation assembled at Chestnut Hill (a place about ten miles from Philadelphia), so I began immediately and discoursed to them on the words of the Baptist: 'Flee from the wrath to come.' The line spreading oaks formed a noble canopy over us and we were as happy in the grove as if we had been in the most pompous temple." He preaches again in the grove at Chestnut Hill and it was a solemn and instructive service. He preached a third time in the grove. One would like to know where the grove stood that resounded to the words of God. As Bryant writes:

"The groves were God's first temples."

The Schwenkfelders have been mentioned in connection with Chestnut Hill. They seem to have had the earliest Sunday Schools in Pennsylvania. From their first settlement here in A. D. 1734 they devoted every other Sunday to the religious instruction of children, which instruction they styled "*die Kinderlehr.*"

The Hon. Horatio Gates Jones has some books which were printed by Samuel Saur.

A branch of Tunkers settled in Creyfield. Of this society a company came with Peter Becker to Pennsylvania in 1719. They settled in Germantown, where their numbers increased. They gained accessions along the Wissahickon and in Lancaster county. In 1723, those that lived in Germantown and along the Wissahickon formed themselves into a united community, and chose Peter Becker for their official baptizer. He, with some others, visited the scattered brethren in Lancaster county in November, 1734, and collected and formed them into a distinct society near the Pecquea creek.

NEWSPAPERS.

The Chestnut Hill and Montgomery News was published weekly on Saturdays. Its first issue was in 1882. It is no longer issued. See Scharf and Westcott's Philadelphia, Vol. III, p. 2065.

The Weekly Recorder was "issued by the cyclostyle process," and "edited and published by Porter F. Cope, Harry B. Bolling, Henry Cochran," when I visited

Chestnut Hill it gave local news and church and library affairs, not omitting base ball matters, including the Eldon and Wissahickon waiters' game. The number before me, published in 1886, recommends the Debating Society of the Young Men's Christian Association in the city as helpful to mental improvement. There were a number of advertisements. The paper was the work of some earnest lads, who were getting experience in this venture which will aid them in after life. It made a very creditable appearance, and they merit praise for the publication.

The Chestnut Hill Reporter was the continuation of the *Recorder*. It is no longer published. Porter Cope was the publisher.

Edward Harding, son of W. W. Harding, editor of the Philadelphia *Inquirer*, put out a paper with the lively name of *The Squeak Hawk* in the year 1886, but it has ceased to exist.

An article in the Philadelphia *Inquirer* of August 30, A. D. 1887, gives some interesting notes on Chestnut Hill, which it styles "Philadelphia's prettiest suburb." It quotes the verdict of a traveled European gentleman, who declared as to its scenery: "I never looked upon a lovelier scene than this."

The improvements made by a gentleman who purchased of John Lowber Welsh over twenty acres of land near the Erdenheim Stock Farm are mentioned. A good part of this land is "near the Wissahickon drive." A fine mansion has been built on a part of this property by John Morris.

The White estate, containing about twenty acres, at Main street and Chestnut avenue, has been bought by Mr. Goodman to be divided into building lots.

An elegant house to be erected opposite Charles A. Newhall's, at Chestnut avenue and Thirty-first street, is noted. I think that the old Norman log house stands near this point. Mr. Samuel Y. Heebner's residence on Highland avenue is spoken of.

"The Chestnut Hill branch of the Bank of America," on Main street, had bought ground of Backenhurst & Co., joining the Pennsylvania Railroad depot, for erecting a fine building.

Mr. H. H. Houston's deer park, green-houses and his large collection of roses come in for attention.

The "Trustworthy Police Force" consists "of eleven patrolmen, under command of Police Sergeant J. S. Currier, a very capable officer," and intimately conversant with the surrounding country. The district is four and a half miles on Main street, and is three miles wide.

Among prominent residents are Hon. Richard Vaux, ex-Mayor, who used to walk into the city, eleven or twelve miles, daily; Samuel Hollingsworth, of Summit avenue; John H. Mitchener, of Township line, near Evergreen avenue; Gen. Russell Thayer, Superintendent of Fairmount Park, who lives on Twenty-ninth street, near Highland avenue; Hon. Furman Shepherd, residing on New street, near Prospect avenue; S. M. Janney, on Prospect avenue, near Summit street; Joseph Baker, Evergreen avenue; J. E. Terry, Union avenue. "Samuel Goodman, Bethlehem pike and Summit street; Alfred C. Harrison, Reading

"THE ANGLECOT," RESIDENCE OF CHARLES A. POTTER.

pike, and F. O. Allen, on Township line," are named among other prominent citizens who have already been mentioned in these sketches.

The old stone house on Evergreen avenue, not far from the Pennsylvania Railroad depot, where Washington stopped, receives attention, and the tradition is given that the bodies of dead American soldiers were carried into the house on the retreat, and that the British destroyed everything in the house excepting an old clock, which is still preserved.

CALEB COPE.

The Philadelphia *Inquirer* of May 14, A. D. 1888, had a long sketch of this good man, which I will condense. He died on May 12, 1888. Born in 1797, in Greensburg, Pa., and losing his father in infancy, he early entered a store in the town. At eighteen he came to Philadelphia to the counting house of his uncles, Isreal & Jasper Cope. A third uncle, Thomas P. Cope, came to this city in 1786. They were in the East India trade. The young man became a partner when the firm was changed to Mendenhall & Cope. In 1821 the Liverpool packet line began. The firm was very successful and various vessels were added to their trade. In 1838 Mr. Cope married Miss Abbie Ann Cope. In 1839 he was Director of the United States Bank, when Nicholas Biddle was President, and acted as President in Mr. Biddle's absence. He was one of the Managers of the Philadelphia Saving Fund, and a Director of the Academy of Fine Arts. He once owned the Spring Brook property at Holmesburg, now the Forrest Home. George H. Stuart, afterward owned it. Mr. Cope was a member of the Horticultural Society and loved flowers, and his conservatory, with its Victoria Regia, was famous. He lived at 718 Spruce street. After giving up Spring Brook he purchased the place at Chestnut Hill and exercised hospitality in his country seat. His excellent wife died in 1845. Just before 1857 the partnership of the famous "three C's" (Caleb Cope & Co.) was formed. Henry C. Howell, who became Sheriff, and Buck Johnstone, were his partners. They built an elaborate building of granite on Market street. They did the largest dry goods business of any house in the city. Mr. Cope had a wide business acquaintance in the city, and had known personally every President since Jefferson. In 1857 the panic embarrassed Mr. Cope. Samuel and William Welsh loaned him a goodly sum, and in time he paid his obligations in general. He was in the Board of Trade, the Sanitary Commission, the Pennsylvania Hospital, the Institution for the Blind, the Academy of Natural Sciences, and other institutional boards. He was very benevolent. "He was a member of St. Luke's Episcopal Church," in the city. Mr. Cope celebrated his 90th birthday at Chestnut Hill. This benevolent man was beloved and greatly respected by his country neighbors, for his many kind acts. His death at ninety-one years of age was attributed to "general debility." Inflammatory rheumatism attacked him in the February preceding his death, though he rallied and appeared "bright and cheerful."

His closing illness was not painful. "Mrs. Cope and his sons, Caleb F. and Porter F. Cope, were with him to the last." A good test of a man's character is evinced by the testimony of those employed by him. I have been much struck by the love and veneration shown by a man who was long in his employ, in speaking of him. At the time of his death Mr. Cope was the President of that old and useful institution, "The Philadelphia Saving Fund Society."

RESIDENCE OF MR. WILLIAM POTTER.

The striking architectural mansion, of which a cut is here shown, on the corner of Township line and Graver's lane, was built in the spring of 1884. The architect was George N. Pearson. It was described in a previous article of this series (See Page 444 of this volume).

"THE ANGLECOT," RESIDENCE OF MR. CHARLES A. POTTER.

> "All up and down, and here and there,
> With who knows what of round and square,
> Stuck on at random everywhere;
> Indeed a house to make one stare,
> All corners and all gables."

This poem is quoted to express the astonishment with which I greeted the very pretty, but very quaint house of Mr. Charles A. Potter, at the corner of Prospect and Evergreen avenues. The position of the house is a good one for displaying its unique beauty, at the junction of two avenues, and so arranged as to command both. A nice lawn extends itself before the mansion. The tile and shingle work on the exterior, the front gables and the quaint little balcony, and the upper front gable, and the sun dial, has each a peculiar charm of its own. One front gable bursts out from the other. There is a half-door at the front entrance, and a rustic seat in the front balcony. Any one of the peculiar features of this dwelling would give a character to a house, but in combination they are like the characteristics of a great man who excels his neighbors in many ways. This strikes me as one of the quaintest and most picturesque houses in Chestnut Hill, and it is welcome in the variety which it gives. The material is brick below and tiles and shingles above. The shingles have an ancient look. There is a hipped-roof on a side gable. The front of the second story projects over the lower one. The house stands across the front of both Evergreen and Prospect avenues. One of the front gables is finished in white color. The building is a regular antique. A long, narrow window, one pane wide, cuts the bricks and shingles of the lower side of the front of the house. The windows are square-topped with black sash, though one upper front window is curved. This house reminds us of the new house of the great Dutch artist Alma Tadema, in London. It is described in a newspaper thus: "Its exterior presents in little bits nearly all the styles of

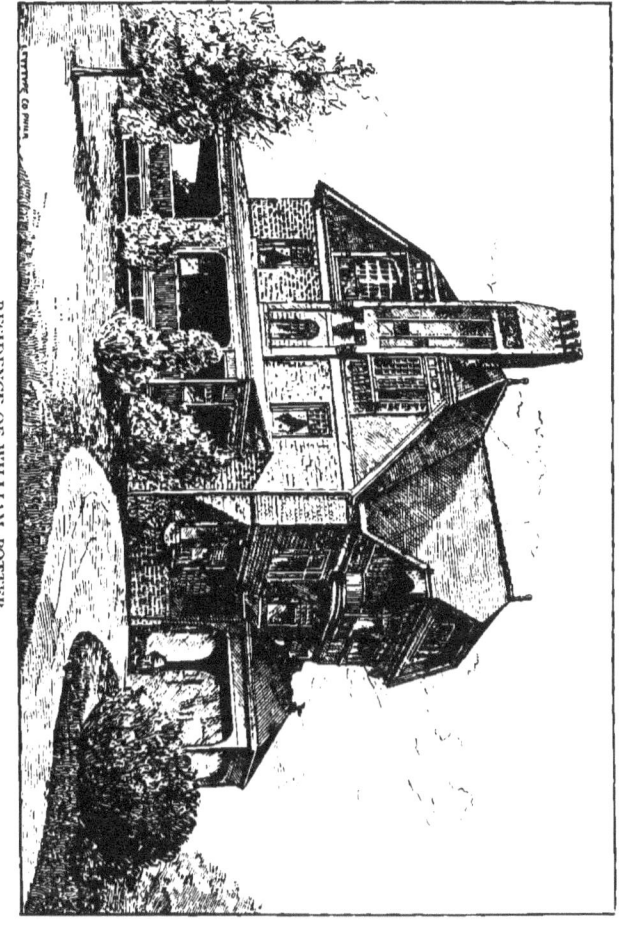
RESIDENCE OF WILLIAM POTTER.

all the ages, from the days of classic glory to the present time." Within this house the studio is beautiful and artistic, according to an illustrated volume which describes it.

The house of A. Grove, Jr., at Wyndmoor avenue, also deserves notice.

Opposite this house Mr. Bradley has a square, light colored stone house, with a Grecian pillared piazza, which gives another style of architecture. It is pleasant sometimes to see the old pillars like those of the porch, where the Stoic philosophers were wont to walk in ancient days.

A water color sketch of a view of Chestnut Hill from the Bethlehem pike in 1840, by George W. Holmes, shows an almost open country as far as the eye can reach. The original is in possession of Furman Shepherd, Esq., who presented a copy of it to Rev. Dr. Harris, in whose study I have had the pleasure of viewing it. But two or three old farm houses appear, one of which was destroyed to make way for the round-house of the Reading Railroad a year or two ago.

More than thirty years ago, William Platt came from the city to Chestnut Hill and bought the property on Stenton avenue, next above that of Colonel Biddle. Mr. Buck was about this time the owner of the Biddle place, which was afterward bought by Henry J. Williams, Esq.

Dr. Pepper, who married a daughter of Mr. Platt, built the house now occupied by Mr. Bucknell. He sold it to F. B. Gowen, who, in turn, sold it to Mr. Bucknell.

John Bohlen purchased a large tract of land on the Bethlehem pike, opposite the Eldon, and built a mansion there. The old farmhouse on that property is just below the toll-gate. William Streeper formerly owned it.

Charles Taylor built a house on the Reading pike and called it "Norwood," hence the name of the avenue. This is now Miss Harriet S. Benson's place. Mr. Charles Taylor's widow afterward built the massive stone house between Norwood avenue and the Reading pike. There were woods on the north of the old place. Did this suggest the name "Norwood?"

The site of MRS. COMEGYS'S and MISS BELL'S YOUNG LADIES' SCHOOL was occupied by Justus Donat, a brother of the inn-keeper, and was owned by Charles Taylor. A pretty old farmhouse, built of stone, well-shaded, stood on this place, but it has disappeared. Mrs. Comegys's house is a pleasant one. It is clad with vines, and the lawn contains a terrace which slopes along its lower side. The gentlemen who have been named as the builders of these houses which have been mentioned were the first city colony which settled in Chestnut Hill.

Colonel Cephas G. Childs, who lived next above the Eldon, was also an early resident, and was interested in the advancement of Chestnut Hill. The brown colored house which belonged to Colonel Childs is now owned by Mrs. Brown, and occupied by William E. Littleton, Esq. The building was erected by Colonel Childs. He obtained the land of John Nace, who lived in the house owned by John Jenks. Colonel Childs was interested in the Episcopal Church known as St. Paul's, which used to hold its services in a room over the Reading Railroad Depot. Colonel Childs was an influential and useful citizen.

Joseph Patterson built the three companion cottages which are just beyond the house of Colonel Childs, nearer to the Reading Depot. They are occupied by Messrs. Earle, Plummer and Moses Paxton. They were erected about six years ago.

J. Sargent Price, the son of Eli K. Price, Esq., remodeled the house nearly opposite the cottages just mentioned. The house belonged to John Piper. Mr. Price has had it since about 1862 or 1863.

Miss A. Piper's new house was built in 1854.

NORWOOD AVENUE.

Ex-Mayor Richard Vaux's house was built by Charles Taylor. An upper bay window in the second story overhangs the lower story. It is a fine square house with a front porch. There is a terrace above the meadow-like park, between this house and that of Mrs. Comegys. Ex-Mayor Vaux is noted for his early morning walks. I met him once in an early ramble with his faithful dog bearing him company. It is a pity that more persons do not know the value of exercise in the pure air.

E. S. Buckley built the pleasant country house next to that of ex-Mayor Vaux in 1864. There is a stone wall above the house and a hedge below it. It is a square stone mansion with ample piazzas on three sides, which afford fine views. The location is good, as the ground falls below the house as a natural terrace.

Next to the residence of Mr. Buckley, on the lower side, is that of R. C. McMurtrie. This house has been built about twenty-seven years. It is embosomed in trees, and a green-house and hedges adorn the grounds.

Mrs. Charles Taylor's place is entered by a drive, cut into the ground by reason of the conformation of the hill. The old trees have been allowed to remain. The foundations of the massive stone building are of immense size. The house is like that of Mr. E. Benson's in its grand and castle-like appearance. The roof is broken by lines that make it picturesque. A bay window varies the exterior of the house. A *porte-cochere*, with its heavy stone archway, faces Sunset avenue. The fortress-like foundations and the regular irregularity of the Taylor mansion make it a pretty and striking object in the landscape.

The spire of the Church of Our Mother of Consolation rising above the sacred edifice forms a pretty picture in looking from Norwood avenue.

"EDGCUMBE," RESIDENCE OF CHARLES B. DUNN.

CHESTNUT HILL.

"EDGCUMBE," THE RESIDENCE OF CHARLES B. DUNN.

Mr. Charles Taylor deserved great credit for his efforts to advance the new Chestnut Hill when it began to shake off its long sleep. He had the house of Charles B. Dunn erected about twenty-five years ago. Mr. Dunn's house is a very pleasant one in a beautiful position. The winding entrance road cut into the lawn introduces the way to the long house, with its piazza on the upper side and another on the lower one. Windows project from the roof. A lawn gives a view toward Barren Hill. There is a fine sloping ha-ha wall.

This pleasant mansion of gray stone was erected by Mr. Charles Taylor, about 1857, T. P. Chandler, Jr., being the architect. He was also the architect of Stonecliffe, Mrs. Charles Taylor's place.

The late Arthur H. Howell purchased the property, and resided in it until A. D. 1876, when Mr. Dunn became the owner.

In 1881 the house was greatly enlarged, and the lawn extended, by taking in the adjoining fields to the south and west.

Edgcumbe, meaning the side of a hill, is named from Mount Edgcumbe in England. Mr. Dunn is a native of St. Austell, Cornwall, England, and naturally selected an English name, from a place where his father owned a clay mine which furnished material for chinaware. The vicinity of St. Austell is famed for its china-stone, which is used in the Staffordshire potteries.

There are ample piazzas on the front and lower sides of the house, giving fine views of the surrounding beautiful scenery.

On the upper side in the music-room, is a large bay window, while the parlor and library also enjoy these cheerful adjuncts.

The house is three stories in height.

The green-house is in the rear, and also a fine stone stable.

A tower above the mansion is used as an observatory, and commands an extensive view. Some eight acres are included in this place.

A pretty winding drive, terminating in a circle, introduces to the mansion.

The four gate-posts are massively built of stone, corresponding to the house, and are adorned with flowers in the summer, brightening the entrance, and giving a pleasant welcome to the incomer.

Mr. Dunn is of the firm of Dunn Brothers, Bankers, Philadelphia and New York.

An old barn and house at the corner of Main street and Thorp's lane, represented by the amateur photo of J. W. G. Dunn, makes a striking and pretty view. The old Johnson house, lately demolished, with the Ambrose White house (also destroyed) in the background; and an old blacksmith shop, near Wheel-Pump tavern, on the Bethlehem turnpike, with a horse and several persons in front of it, as the strong sun casts their shadows on the wall, are by the same hand.

Mrs. George Whitney's house is next to that of Mr. Dunn. This was also built by Charles Taylor. It is of modern architecture, on a gentle rise of ground, inclosed by a ha-ha wall.

Next is the house of A. M. Collins, which was another Taylor house. It was formerly owned by Col. Richard Rush. The mansion has a double bay window on the upper side, and nestles among vines, with a vine-clad gable in front.

The house of Col. George North, on the corner of Norwood avenue, opposite Mrs. Comegys's School on one side and the rectory of St. Paul's Episcopal Church on the other street, is an ample stone mansion with piazzas and porch, and is surmounted by an observatory, which is desirable in the midst of such fine scenery. The lawn stretches above and below the mansion.

The bluestone mansion on the corner of Reading pike and Chestnut avenue, facing on Chestnut avenue, is the residence of the late Gen. Joshua Owen, a brother of the Rev. Dr. Owen. Samuel H. Austin formerly owned it. The open grounds on each side make it a desirable position.

GENERAL JOSHUA T. OWEN.

The PHILADELPHIA INQUIRER of November 8th and 9th, A. D. '87, contained notices of this distinguished citizen of Chestnut Hill, which give material for a brief sketch. General Owen died November 7th, 1887, at Chestnut Hill. His birth place was Caermarthen, South Wales, and the date of his birth 1825. In 1830, David Owen, his father, came to Baltimore, and established the firm of Owen & Co., for publishing books. Here Joshua learned printing. In 1840 we find him in Jefferson College. He graduated during the presidency of Dr. Robert J. Breckenridge, of Kentucky. In 1847 he was a clerk in the Philadelphia Post-Office. "In 1852 he founded the Chestnut Hill Academy." He was in the Philadelphia Common Council and in the Legislature of Pennsylvania. He practiced law till volunteers were called for in 1861. He then established the rendesvous camp at Chestnut Hill, and became Colonel of the Twenty-fourth Pennsylvania Volunteers. He was afterward in " the famous Sixty-ninth Regiment," which felt the effects of his good discipline. General Hooker complimented General Owen at Fair Oaks. In 1862 he became a brigadier-general. He was in every battle of the army of the Potomac, and was very brave and daring. After the war he was elected Recorder of Deeds by the Republicans. He founded the New York DAILY REGISTER, a legal journal. His wife was Miss Sheridan. Three daughters and a son survive him. The son continues the newspaper in New York. A son named Robert, a lawyer of promising talent died about two years before his father. The Rev. Dr. Roger T. Owen, who was long the pastor of the Presbyterian Church at Chestnut Hill, is a brother of General Owen. General Owen was courteous and genial, and his memory will be kept green. He was natural in manner and kind-hearted, a man of principle, ready to battle for the right. He was

RESIDENCE OF A. M. COLLINS.

clear-sighted, and a good lawyer. In public matters he was a leader "through force of character." He had a single aim, and a firm purpose. At the bar, in the field, and in social life, he has left an honorable name as a rich legacy to his family.

Above St. Paul's rectory was the residence of Mrs. Elias Boudinot. It is now owned by Mr. White, who has taken possession of it within four or five years.

The square house next to Mr. Whitney's was owned by Mrs. Tobias Wagner. Bishop William Hobart Hare lived in it when he was rector of St. Paul's Church. He is now the faithful Missionary Bishop of South Dakota, and resides at Sioux Falls, far away from his former parish.

Next to this house is that of James Young, who was the first one who resided in it, though it was built by another person.

At the foot of Norwood avenue is the well-shaded residence of the late May Stevenson, which was built in 1853 by Thomas Earp, Jr., who sold it to A. M. Burton, from whom Mr. Stevenson purchased it. The place has a pleasant lawn. It stands opposite Mrs. Taylor's property, on Sunset avenue, which runs along its lower border.

THE READING RAILROAD.

The officers of the Reading Railroad have settled themselves largely on the Chestnut Hill Branch. The former President, F. B. Gowen, Esq., has a delightful home, in a quiet situation, encircled by meadows, near the Mount Airy Station, far enough away from the whirl of business to give a hard driven man a little breath in the evening. The mansion is of good taste and has a comfortable look. The railway traveler may get a glimpse of it, on the right, after passing Mount Airy Station, going toward Chestnut Hill. Its red roof shows itself beyond the trees which skirt the railroad. My schoolmate, J. Lowrie Bell, the former General Traffic Manager, resided on Graver's lane, in a house belonging to Mrs. H. C. Booth, who has built several fine houses in that vicinity. Henry McKay, the Treasurer of the Philadelphia and Reading Coal and Iron Company, lives on Ivy avenue, near Mount Pleasant Station. W. A. Church, the Treasurer of the Reading Railroad, resides in Germantown, at the corner of Knox and Penn streets. C. G. Hancock lives on Duy's lane, in the same place. He is the General Passenger Agent. John W. Royer, the General Express Agent, lives on Fisher's lane, Germantown. James Colhoun, the Division General Freight Agent, is on Harvey street, Germantown, and J. Y. Humphrey, the Receiver's Assistant, and formerly the vice-President, resides on Green street, in the same place.

The Reading Depot was built in A. D. 1872. There was a previous frame building on the same site, with a hall in the second story. The present building is of stone. The railroad was completely finished and in running order and opened from Chestnut Hill to Germantown in 1857. It was opened from Philadelphia to Germantown in 1834. About 1854 the railway was in partial use. An engine then pushed the cars from Germantown to Chestnut Hill, and they returned by gravity. The rock cuttings and positions of platforms and depots on the Reading Railroad show a very wild country near a populous city. The stairs leading to the street below or the residences above the railway in Germantown have an Alpine look. In the summer of 1876 there were twenty-eight trains out of Philadelphia and twenty-seven into the city daily from Chestnut Hill on the Reading Railroad. Lincoln E. Leeds, the Station Agent, has kindly informed me as to the history of the railroad.

WISSAHICKON DRIVE.

In driving from Chestnut Hill to Barren Hill we reach Mount St. Joseph's Convent on the right of the road, which is the last property in the city limits. It joins Whitemarsh township, in Montgomery county. The buildings are of imposing size and present a striking appearance. They are of gray stone. When I passed them the large chapel was unfinished. The upper end of the "Wissahickon Drive" begins at Wissahickon avenue, near the Convent. A high hilly road soon branches from the drive on the right and goes on to Roxborough. A rustic cedar fence, with its single rail, is pretty as we see it by the roadside. A fence is generally an obstruction to the view, and if we must have it at all the less it is the better. A village like Edgewater, New Jersey, shows how much prettier places are where fences are lacking.

Let us ride along the far-famed and beautiful Wissahickon drive. A stone ruin on the left adds to the picturesqueness of the scene. The creek in its gentle beauty, creeps along below. Here is the retreat of fishermen. The road is narrow where we enter it at the upper part. There is a county bridge on the road. The constant curve of the drive, and the frequent rocks in the stream, give incessant surprise and delight. The shallow, babbling water is a lively companion. A stone double house on the left, with its little stretch of open ground about it, shows that some can find a home in this quiet retreat. A quaint old stone house stands on the far side of the creek above the Red Bridge. Thorp's lane is another landmark. The rider catches a picturesque view of dwellings on the far side of the creek, and the foliage makes them pretty. Indian Rock, and Indian Rock Hotel, and the bridge on Rex avenue with its fine wall, are passed. Some big rocks appear to give wildness to the view. There is a bridle path from Indian Rock to Falls bridge, which must lead through scenes of sylvan beauty which one longs to have the time to explore. The right side of the drive becomes precipitous. The fountains to refresh the horses are pretty, and display a laudable care for dumb animals. They are free above Valley Green. The sumac, with its red berries, gives life to the picture. It is said that France, Germany, Holland, Armenia and Persia rejoice in this same plant. The plant is of the genus Rhus; it has a number of species, and the tanner, the dyer, and the physician have found use for some of them. There is another noisy dam which should afford cheering reflections, as it sings incessantly day and night in its unfailing gladness. On the right is a neat stone Park Guard house. Such things are striking breaks in the drive. The roads or paths go climbing up the hill-sides and are lost to sight, though the imagination paints pretty scenes beyond the reach of the eye. There is a pretty waterfall on the right, and a watering-cart is preparing for its work of benevolence.

Hartwell avenue or lane has its bridge, and we pass Springfield avenue. A rustic stile and steps of stone beautify a bridle path. The work of Park improvement have been done in excellent taste. There is a cedar fence for a short distance on Hartwell avenue on the left. The wildness continues along Hartwell avenue. The "Crow's Nest," with its square tower, peers down from its height. Mr. Houston has wisely chosen a retired spot for his new home. Now comes the Wissahickon Inn, in the midst of the wild scenery at the top of the hill. Some children are playing at the little creek below with their attendants. Before reaching the Inn, we pass under the bridge over Thirty-second street and by the stone stables. Then comes the Inn, with its red tiles and gray stone and awnings.

THE READING TURNPIKE.

Just beyond Sunset avenue, on the right, in going toward Barren Hill, we meet Mr. Harrison's place. There is here a wide stretch of sloping lawn, with a ha-ha. This commands a fine reach or view on the Whitemarsh Valley. Opposite is Mr. Penrose's prettily located abode. There are two modern houses on the extension of Sunset avenue, on the other side of the pike. The more distant one has an observatory. In returning toward the town, on the right hand, in coming up from Sunset avenue, is a house with dense foliage in front of it. It is heavily built, with a square tower, and a lawn descending to Sunset avenue with a ha-ha, which has a prettier effect than a raised wall. The appropriate name of this place is "Sunset" and the evening view from this house must be charming. Still I looked at it when the morning birds were singing, and the workmen were going forth to their " labor until the evening " as the psalmist describes man's daily toil. The milk-wagon also had fallen into the line of duty, and sunrise was calling all things to work. The place described formerly belonged to Mr. Hildeburn, but is now owned by Mrs E. P. Dwight. Next above the Dwight place is Mr. Kneedler's large, three-story, brown-stone mansion, with a surrounding piazza, and an orchard in the rear. Next, on the same side, is the house of Mr. Chapman, with tall trees to guard its front. It is of a light color, and three stories in height. There is a pleasant lawn above it, and the view in the rear is a fine one. The adjoining place above this, is the Levi Rex house (now George V. Rex's estate), which was erected, A. D. 1801. It is occupied by George H. Stuart, Jr., whose honored father toiled so hard in the good work of the Christian Commission during the Southern war. This is an old-fashioned, two-story, yellow-colored house, with dormer windows. There is a lawn above it. There is an oven in the cellar said to have been used by soldiers in the war of 1812. Next comes a three-story brown house, with a piazza. The property adjoining this, on the same side, is a yellow, three-story-house, with a bay window on its upper side, and a piazza on the lower side. A lawn lies below it. This is the abode of Dr. Biddle. Next is a small house of a light color, with a plastered wall. The neat Methodist parsonage follows, and adjoining this is the pretty Methodist church, formerly under the care of Rev. Mr. Dotterer, who rebuilt it.

A gentleman of antiquarian tastes in Germantown has called my attention to a small two-story old stone house, above Allen's lane, on the Cresheim road. It is an antique, but holds its age well. It belonged to the Bolter family, as Mr. Hinkle told my informant. The building is a quaint one, with an old spring-house at its side. I found the deed in H. H. Houston's office, which recites that in the year of our Lord, 1762, while Pennsylvania was still a province, John Johnson, saddler, of German Town, as the surviving executor of Matthias Milan (alias Mallane), late of Creesam, yeoman, in the second year of the reign of George the Third, conveyed the property which Milan had received from Johannes Bleikers, in 1700, to Peter Heysler, stocking weaver of Creesam. Four rix dollars were reserved to the Frankfort Company as quit rent. Daniel Falckner was the Company's attorney. John Henry Sprogel purchased the quit rent of him and released it to Milan in A. D. 1718. A few years since the property fell into the hands of H. H. Houston. This was part of a tract of one hundred acres which has since been divided into parcels.

I believe that William Schlatter was a son of Rev. Michael Schlatter, whose biography has been given. He lived on Chestnut street, and many houses and stores now cover his old home, as he owned several acres. Horses and cows used to graze on the lot next to Thirteenth street, which ran back to Sansom street, where the stables were before the land was sold, as a friend of the family informs me.

It is sad to reflect that several aged people who have given me reminiscences have died before they appeared in print. So earthly bodies and houses vanish away. In gleaning, many golden sheaves have been kindly dropped in my way, for which I am grateful. It might be well if local history could find a new recorder every twenty-five or fifty years, and if one takes up the work in this field again may he find it as pleasant a task as it has been to the writer, who now parts from the friends who have walked with him, from Germantown to Chestnut Hill.

Lines on revisiting the Wissahickon by Miss C. H. Waterman:

> "Where thy sweetly murm'ring river,
> In its glad play,
> To the woods that round thee quiver,
> Weaves a fond lay.

"RAUHALA," THE RESIDENCE OF A. WARREN KELSEY.

CHESTNUT HILL.

> Where the wild bird loves to listen
> On its still wing,
> As thy silvery waters glisten,
> And sweetly sing."
> —*Gentleman's Magazine, Vol. III, p. 166.*

Rauhala has been described in the TELEGRAPH. (See page 439 of this volume.) The name is Swedish, and means a peaceful home, and a happy family of children enliven it. The Baroness Ispolatoff, of Helsingford, in Finland, was a particular friend of Mrs. Kelsey. She is now dead, but this American home commemorates the appellation of her residence. There are eight acres in the property, and the deeds run back to Penn and Pastorius. The land was once in the possession of a family whose five daughters all married into the Schultz family.

BARREN HILL.

The third house above Thorp's lane, on the right hand of the Reading pike in driving from Chestnut Hill, is an old farm house now remodeled and owned by Thomas Stewart. In Revolutionary days George Edleman owned the farm. When a part of the British army were returning from the unsuccessful attempt to surprise Washington at Whitemarsh, some of the soldiers drove Mrs. Edleman from her bed with her infant two or three weeks old, and burned the bed in a lot near by. There is a tradition that a soldier placed a child's red petticoat on his bayonet, and an officer told him to leave it, as they came to fight men and not children, though they were not successful in fighting the men.

Rev. Dr. Muhlenberg's Journal (Collections of Historical Society of Pennsylvania, Vol. I, p. 162) notes that on Sunday, April 13, A. D. 1777, his son Henry preached at St. Peter's, Barren Hill, and informed him that "an express had arrived in Philadelphia that the British ships of war and transports had been seen at the entrance of Delaware Bay, and that to-day alarm cannon had been fired." When I visited the quiet spot on a summer's day it seemed far from war's alarms, but then if the tidings had not disturbed the congregation they must have stirred it not long after service. Afterward came the report that the ships had disappeared.

On October 3, 1777, at midnight, good Dr. Muhlenberg heard a noise at his front door and imagined it to be the British light-horse. He struck a light and found two loose horses. There was a "report that at daylight the British outposts at Barren Hill and Germantown" would be attacked.

An old man who walked fifty miles to Barren Hill, to get a certificate of his son's baptism, saw St. Peter's Church used as a stable for the horses of the American army. The British army had a little while before taken the live stock in the neighborhood, so that little was left for the American army.

Two English women came on foot to the Doctor's house, having escaped from Philadelphia. They had waded the Skippack and Perkiomen, and were on their way to Reading, seeking their husbands.

Watson states (Vol. II, p. 26) that the Lutheran Church at Barren Hill was built by a lottery in 1761.

The Germantown and Perkiomen turnpike was finished in 1804. Length, twenty-five miles; cost, $285,000. This was a great enterprise for that day, and more notable than railway building to-day, when money is more abundant. The country stores were probably hurt by the new turnpikes, as the farmers could readily take their produce into the city over them. In 1874 this pike was made free.

ST. PETER'S LUTHERAN CHURCH, BARREN HILL.

By the courtesy of the last pastor of St. Peter's Church, J. Q. McAtee, a copy of *The Norristown Herald and Free Press*, dated April 9, A. D. 1883, is before me, containing some particulars about this old parish from the pen of the faithful local historian, the Honorable W. A. Yeakle. He refers to an old minute book, and to Dr. F. D. Schaefer, and Buck's History, and *Hallische Nachrieten*, etc., as authorities. I believe that this gentleman wrote the account of this church in Bean's History of Montgomery County.

The first election of elders noted in the minutes occurred on the 1st of April, A. D. 1766. Henrich Katz, Johannes Bauer, Andreas Koeth and Philip Lehr were then chosen to that office, while William Hiltner and Johannes Fisher were elected as deacons. Dr. Muhlenberg installed them on October 23, A. D. 1768. "Johannes Richert and Johannes Mitschele were elected elders; and on the 15th of May, 1769, Johannes Hailman (or Hallman) and Christian Stier installed by *Reverendum Pastorem* Schultze." The last election recorded in the first minute-book took place in 1775, on the 24th of September, Heinrich Katz, Andreas Coeth (Koetes), Johannes Rickert, Conrad Gerlinger (Gillinger), Andreas Bauer and Friedrich Miller received an election to the diaconate, and Leonhart Kolb and Frantz Vaaht were chosen elders, and William Linneschut held over. Rev. Dr. Muhlenberg's records end at this point.

Dr. Muhlenberg ministered over a large district of country, and was a faithful worker. Parishes often lacked pastors. The distance between churches was great, and the roads were bad. The inhabitants had been born in the old country for the most part. They owned little property, and it was difficult to support the scattered parishes. Dr. Schaefer was the pastor of St. Peter's, Barren Hill, from 1790 to 1812. He found the church and school in a poor condition. The church building had broken windows, and the roof seemed ready to fall. The pastor wrote that faith and trust would be needed, and prays "May the Kingdom of God break forth with such power that the outward affairs of the church would be better administered." The letter is dated "Germantown, the 25th of November, 1803." It is recorded in German in his own hand in the minutes.

CHESTNUT HILL.

Rev. Henry Melchior Muhlenberg, D. D., was born in Hanover, in Germany, at Eimbeck, on the 6th of September, 1711. He studied in the Universities of Gottengen and Halle. The Lutherans of Pennsylvania, sent strong appeals to those in authority at Halle for clergy, and Dr. Muhlenberg was sent in 1742. He preached his first sermon at the Swamp, in New Hanover, in Montgomery county; then it was Philadelphia county. There were then three organized Lutheran churches in the province of Pennsylvania. One was in Philadelphia, another at Trappe, and the third in Hanover. He took up his abode at Trappe, and was in charge of the three churches up to 1761, when he moved to St. Michael's, in Philadelphia, and there remained until the Revolution, when he went back to the Trappe, where he died at the age of seventy-six, on the 7th of October, A. D. 1787. His third son was the Rev. Henry Earnest Muhlenberg. He closed his studies at Halle, in 1770, and became assistant minister to St. Michael's and aided his father in his wide work. He and his father officiated at St. Peter's Church, Barren Hill, until 1777, when Howe came into Philadelphia, and young Muhlenberg went to Lancaster and took charge of a church there.

In June, 1760, John Frederick Schmidt became the pastor in Germantown, and preached alternate Sundays at Frankford and Whitpain, and occasionally officiated at Barren Hill. The Rev. Messrs. Kurtz, Voight and Buskirk preached on alternate Sundays at Barren Hill about this time, or a little subsequent to it.

In the Revolution, St. Peter's Church was on ground which was at different times occupied by both the Americans and the British. Dr. Muhlenberg notes in his journal, under date of November 8, 1777: "That it was used as a stable for horses by a portion of the American army encamped in the vicinity," and adds that a short time before the British army had taken horses and oxen, cows and sheep and hogs from the inhabitants.

Pierpont, in his poem on Washington, refers to a sad abuse of the old South Church, Boston, similar to that at Barren Hill, thus:

> "When from this gate of heaven,
> People and priest were driven
>   By fire and sword.
> And, where thy saints had pray'd,
> The harness'd war-horse neigh'd
> And horsemen's trumpet bray'd
>   In harsh accord."

> "Nor was our fathers' trust
> Thou Mighty One and Just,
>   Then put to shame
> Up to the hills for light,
> Look'd they in peril's night,
> And from yon guardian height,
>   Deliverance came."

The poet refers to Dorchester Heights, where Washington was located, and from that commanding position he forced the British to evacuate Boston.

In a short time after Mr. Schmidt became pastor at Germantown, Rev. Daniel Schroeder was, as Buck mentions, the minister at Barren Hill.

The first baptism on record at St. Peter's is that of a child of Christophel Schuppart. The name of Christian was given to it. Philip Kolb and wife were the sponsors. This was on February 10th, A. D. 1765. In this year Conrad Bischoff is named as the parish school-master. This teacher makes a note that the first church minute-book was lost, or had been mislaid. He further states that the Rev. Lewis Voight was then the pastor. Mr. Yeakle thought that it was probable that he was assisting Dr. Muhlenberg before the son of that clergyman arrived to aid his father.

La Fayette's Head-Quarters were at this church. See Lossing's Field Book of the Revolution, p. 116. An old school house and two other houses, besides the church comprised the settlement in that day. For an account of the attempt to surprise La Fayette, see p. 122. The General was in the house of a Tory Quaker,

The following quaint epitaphs in St. Peter's graveyard have been copied for this article by the Rev. Mr. McAtee:

In memory of
THOMAS TIESON,
Who departed this life Nov. 18, 1794.
Aged 24 years.

> The waves of Neptune I have conquered,
> And Borea's blasts I did not shun,
> But Jupiter with his horrible shaking,
> Soon laid me underneath the ground,
> But yet there is an Omnipotent Being
> And I know he mercy hath,
> I hope that he will show it to him,
> Who did die such a sudden death,
> If mercy he *douth* show unto me,
> Then I will set sail again,
> For God is merciful to all sinners
> Who *douth* seek his glorious name.

In memory of
PHILIP SIDNER,
Who departed this life Oct. 31, 1811.
Aged 32, 6, 21.

> Philip Sidner was my name,
> Germany was my nation,
> Plymouth was my dwelling place,
> And Christ is my salvation.
> Now I am dead and in my grave,
> And when my bones are rotten,
> When this you see remember me,
> Least I should be forgotten.

In memory of
JAMES THOMPSON,
Who departed this life July 31, 1841,
Aged 50 years.

Jesus Christ, thou amiablest, of characters, I trust thou art no impostor, and that in thee shall all the families of the earth be blessed by being connected togethar in a better world where every tie that bound heart to heart in this state of existence, shall be far beyond our present conceptions more endearing.

ST. PETER'S, BARREN HILL, PA.

BY REV. H. M. BICKEL.

The St. Peter's Lutheran congregation at Barren Hill, Montgomery county, Pa., of which Rev. J. Q. McAtee is the present pastor, and in whose midst the Philadelphia Conference of the East Pennsylvania Synod recently held their fall convention, is among the oldest organizations of the kind in Eastern Pennsylvania. We learn from the records to which we have had access that a number of Lutherans had settled in the vicinity of Barren Hill at an early day, and that in 1761 the organization of a congregation was effected. The centennial of this event was celebrated in 1861, during the pastorate of Rev. S. Sentman. One record says: "Some German families of the Protestant religion in Whitemarsh township, living destitute of school (advantages), and being without (public) divine worship, joined and agreed to erect a school-house on a place called Barren Hill. They made a small collection among themselves, and sent a schoolmaster with recommendatory letters of Henry Muhlenberg, minister, to gather charitable gifts among our German inhabitants towards the said building. The school-house, being finished and paid, served for instructing the children on week-days and for some worship on Sabbaths."

Subsequently, about 1765, a church was erected near the aforementioned school-house, and this constituted the first spiritual home of those early settlers who, being too remote from St. Michael's, at Germantown, desired a house of worship more convenient to their homes, in which they might gather and hold their public religious services. This early church was an unpretentious wooden edifice, and its completion was much hindered by reason of inadequate funds and the difficulty in securing contributions. It was in this building that some of our Revolutionary troops, under General Lafayette, were quartered about the time that General Washington wintered at Valley Forge. As the church was located upon debatable ground, it was alternately occupied by the British and American forces, and "used as a battery and a stable."

Subsequently another church was erected on the site of the first, and this in time gave way to the present Gothic structure, erected in 1849, during the pastoral incumbency of Rev. F. R. Anspach, which, being on high ground, and having a lofty spire, constitutes a prominent landmark, and may be seen for miles from almost every direction as the traveler approaches this historic spot.

CHESTNUT HILL.

The St. Peter's congregation at Barren Hill and Union congregation in Whitemarsh, of which Rev. Dr. Sheeleigh has for a number of years been pastor, were both connected with St. Michael's, in Germantown, until the period of Rev. Dr. C. W. Schaeffer's pastorate, from which time until Rev. Dr. W. M. Baum succeeded to the charge, the two country congregations constituted a separate pastorate. During Dr. Baum's incumbency, St. Peter's became a separate charge, and the Whitemarsh and Upper Dublin (or Puff's) congregations were united into a new pastorate.

Since Rev. Mr. McAtee took the oversight of St. Peter's, who has just completed the fourth year of his labors there, great changes and marked improvements have been made in the cemetery grounds and the church itself. Old sheds and unsightly structures adjacent to the church have been removed and new sheds erected; the cemetery grounds have been inclosed with a beautiful iron fence, part of which had been erected during the pastorates of former ministers; the church and tower painted; the woodwork within regrained; new chandeliers and pulpit and altar furniture provided, and the parsonage refitted, at a total cost of $2750. Besides all this an old debt has been reduced from $2800 to about $1200; and now we have at Barren Hill a commodious and beautiful church, attractive surroundings, and a congregation with a debt of $1200 and an investment at interest of about $6000, which was a legacy lately left the church. The people of St. Peter's congregation are intelligent, social, progressive, churchly and altogether constitute one of the most desirable rural pastorates in the bounds of the East Pennsylvania Synod. Brother McAtee has labored here with much success, and shown a marked degree of energy and interest in the temporal and spiritual good of his people that has greatly endeared him to them.

PASTORS.

The following constitutes the succession of pastors from 1765 to the present time: Henry E. Muhlenberg, 1765; F. David Shafer, 1791-1812; Jno. C. Baker, 1812-1828; Benj. Keller, 1828-1835; C. W. Schaeffer, 1835-1840; F. R. Anspach, 1841-1850; W. H. Smith, 1850-1852; W. M. Baum, 1852-1858; S. Sentman, 1858-1862; C. L. Keedy, 1862-1865; J. Q. Waters, 1865-1867; J. R. Dimm, 1867-1871, T. C. Pritchard, 1871-1883; J. Q. McAtee, 1883 to the present time.

It will be seen by this list, that among the pastors at St. Peter's have been some of our most honored and successful ministers, of whom the venerable Dr. C. W. Schaeffer is the senior survivor, and all of whom, beginning with Dr. W. M. Baum, are still actively engaged as pastors or professors, except brother Sentman, who has gone to his eternal rest.—*From the Lutheran Observer, December 16th, 1887.*

CHESTNUT HILL.

INSTALLATION AT BARREN HILL.

Last Lord's day, the 7th inst., Rev. A. H. F. Fischer was appropriately installed pastor of St. Peter's Lutheran Church, Barren Hill (Lafayette Hill P. O.), Montgomery county, Pa. The address to the congregation was made by Rev. M. Sheeleigh, D. D., who was substituted for Rev. T. C. Pritchard, detained at home by illness, and the charge to the pastor was delivered by Rev. H. M. Bickel, who also conducted the order of installation. A large and deeply interested audience was present, and the gratification of all was clearly seen and expressed. Brother Fischer has served St. Peter's people since the first Sunday in February, and he has already won the confidence of his parishioners, old and young, and made a most favorable and hopeful impression upon them. A new departure was inaugurated on this occasion in the manner of receiving and depositing the offerings of the congregation. The well-used baskets were substituted by silver plates, which at the proper time were received by the deacons from the hands of the pastor, and after the offerings had been gathered were brought forward in orderly manner, the bearers coming up the centre aisle, two by two, and passing the plates to the pastor who reverently placed them on the altar, after which the officers retired to their pews. Thus has prominence, solemnity and proper order been given to this act of worship. The officers and people are well pleased with the change, and are heartily disposed to pursue every course that is orderly and churchly and promotive of the good of the congregation in things temporal and spiritual.

H. M. B.

"From Hitner's mine, near Marble Hall, immense quantities of (brown hematite iron) ore have been taken. In the year 1853 about twelve thousand tons were extracted from this mine."—Bean's history of Montgomery county, pp. 13, 14. Potsdam sandstone is found in this township, p. 21. The beds of rock which underlie Whitemarsh are "Limestone, sandstone, syenite and granite rocks, mica-schist." p. 24.

It seems strange to see so much iron mining work done so near Philadelphia as in the region just above Chestnut Hill.

I am indebted to the pen of Hon. Richard Vaux for the following description, which will be of especial interest to Chestnut Hill readers:

The property situated at Chestnut Hill, between the Reading and Norristown turnpike, and what is now Chestnut avenue, or a large tract of it, was owned, fifty years ago, as a farm, by the late John R. Neff. At that day it was without any other improvements than a country, with a sparse population required for the use of agricultural land. The village of Chestnut Hill at the junction of these turnpikes was a well-known locality, by reason of the location and business transacted there by the farmers from Bucks and neighboring counties coming back and going to Philadelphia. During the last epidemic of yellow fever in Philadelphia, this village was the point where travel was curbed, and from the city came many who needed the domestic supplies that the farmers had to sell. Therefore that locality had a history which has been already noticed in the sketches heretofore published.

Mr. Neff's property was bought by Charles Taylor about 1840. He began to improve it. Mr. Samuel I. Austen, also an owner of land thereabouts, took an interest in making these improvements to meet the wants of temporary or permanent residents, on what was then regarded as a most desirable residence. In 1853, Summit street was laid out. Mr. Taylor laid out Norwood avenue in 1860. Norwood avenue began at what is now called Chestnut avenue, and terminated at the foot of the Hill. Colonel North's house is at the south corner of these streets. It has been already noticed. The next house to Colonel North's, on Norwood avenue, was built by Mr. Taylor. It was occupied in 1860 by Miss Morris. It then was bought by Colonel Richard Rush, who sold it to Mr. Collins, who now occupies it. Mr. J. S. Hodge built the next house, and it was long occupied by Col. Buck, then owned by Mr. Colesberry, and now by Mr. Disston. Mr. Taylor built the next house, and the late Mr. Arthur Howell lived in it till his death. Mr. Dunn bought it and lives there. Mr. Dunn's house is on top of the slope of the hill to the west. Mr. Thomas Stewart, who so largely aided his kinsman, Mr. Taylor, in making all the improvements on the Neff farm, built a residence to the west of Mr. Dunn's. It is a most imposing edifice. Norwood avenue turns to the west at the foot of the hill and joins the Norristown pike. At this turn Mr. Barton owned the property, and sold it to the late Mr. May Stevenson.

Opposite, or nearly so, to Mr. Dunn's houses, Mr. Edward S. Buckley bought of Mr. Taylor a piece of ground and built a residence named "Mount Stoney," which he occupies. Next east to Mr. Buckley's is "Westleigh," the home of Mr. Vaux. This house was built by Mr. Taylor and sold to the late S. Morris Waln. At his death it came to Mr. Vaux's family. Next to "Westleigh" is the school of Mrs. Comegys and Miss Bell, quite a fine building erected by these ladies for a boarding and day school, of a very high reputation, as many of the young ladies come from all parts of the United States. This description concludes Norwood avenue on both sides. This avenue is one of the most picturesque of all the rural roads near the city. It has not been dedicated as a public road, and the owners of the properties keep it in order. The trees on either side arch over the roadway and present a most striking perspective, ending in the view of the valley of Whitemarsh.

On the Reading pike from Chestnut avenue west, Mr. Piper owned a residence next to the Taylor land, then J. Sergeant Price's property and residence, and then Mr. Benson's house and land, including the Mitchell property, and then the residence of the late Mr. John Bohlen.

"WESTLEIGH," RESIDENCE OF HON. RICHARD VAUX.

On the side opposite Mrs. Bohlen's residence is "The Eldon," a large boarding-house, of which Mr. Simpson is the proprietor. Back to Chestnut avenue and the Reading Railroad depot are first the residence of the late Mr. Edward Simmons, and then other houses built by the late Mr. Joseph Patterson. The farm, as described, of Mr. Neff, and the land adjoining it, constitutes the principal plot in this section of Chestnut Hill which marks the growth of improvement for twenty-five years. Also, it is pre-eminently one of the most beautiful situations and has become the attraction for rural residences.

THE ELDON.

Those who walk and drive along the Bethlehem turnpike cannot fail to notice the pleasant, comfortable and ample building which is named above, and which each summer gives shelter to many city guests, and even in winter exercises its hospitality. Mr. George Simpson bought this place about twenty-four years ago, of James E. Mitchell, who purchased it of Daniel Streeper. A small cottage then stood at the gate, partly on the site of the present carriage drive. Mr. Simpson, who was of the firm of Homer, Colladay & Co., built a gothic cottage, of old English style in design. He carefully superintended the work of erection himself, using Chestnut Hill stone. The light colored stone in Houpt's quarry failed before the house was finished. The other stone was darker and not so good for building. The house was constructed about 16 years ago. It is named in honor of Lord Eldon. The name was given by the proprietor, and the great English jurist deserves the remembrance.

This place was opened as a summer boarding-house by Mr. Simpson, and used for one season, and then it was much enlarged, as the proprietor, at first, had merely built it for his own private residence.

The location of the Eldon is a fine one, and a current of air plays along the valley which brings refreshing coolness, and reminds one of the fact that it is a sort of mountain breeze, as the hills are not far distant.

The Eldon has been open for six seasons. Professor DaCosta and Dr. Agnew have sent patients to Chestnut Hill on account of the dryness of the air, which is remarkable, and may make the region a popular health resort. Chestnut Hill is said to be free from malaria. The Pennsylvania and Reading Railroads, with their fifty daily trains, have made the place very easy of access to the city.

The Eldon has three large parlors and also a sun-parlor, which is heated by steam. The house is more like a country home than a hotel. The surrounding views are fine. The building is four stories high and is handsomely furnished.

This elegant building is almost opposite the large mansion of Edwin N. Benson.

In vacation time it is interesting to watch the dwellers in suburban resorts and see how they manage to recreate in their various ways. Time, which lags back for the wedding of the eager bridegroom, and seems to the mourner hastening to strike the hour for the funeral, is thrown away lavishly in summer by hard-worked people who need rest and change. In the morning the waking is prolonged that the faculties may be received anew gradually, as in the growth of the child's mind. The meals break the day, and the morning newspaper, and the evening chat on the piazza, among new-made friends, and the afternoon strolls, and the glances at pretty mansions and winding roads, modestly losing themselves among the trees, make pleasant diversions.

The servants too have their pleasures. Here is a servant-girl, sitting on a fire-plug, in the street, reading, while her baby-charge is in its little coach. This shows a desirable taste for literature. One evening I noticed a party of domestics, and when a ring at the house door-bell summoned a girl from the open air to her duties, a male companion cried out in vexation that he wished that the door-bell would be let alone. The young man seemed to be in love; if so, let us hope that the smoothness of the course of his true love was not long ruffled. The colored servants at the Eldon had their base-ball nine, and their pleasant songs in the evening showed that their hearts were light.

Rev. Joseph L. Miller, of Mt. Airy, sends the following interesting account prepared by Mr. John M. Thorp, to whom he is related:

The old white house on the Wissahickon, together with the calico print mill near Thorp's lane bridge, and several hundred acres of ground, were bought by Issachar Thorp in the year 1835 from the Bell family. Mr. Thorp came to this country from England in 1809, but previous to the above purchase, carried on the calico printing business on Thorp's lane, Germantown. From his son, we have the following information concerning the old house on the Wissahickon: "It was then (1835) a wild, weird place; thickets coming close to the residence, in which roamed some shy peacocks with their large and beautiful fan tails spread proudly wide, and pheasants too were to be found in numbers amidst the laurel. A few covies of partridges could always be found in the fall, and woodcock were common on the hillsides in autumn, as also among the glades in summer. It was no uncommon thing to bag fifteen or twenty head in a morning's walk. No wealthy citizen had yet invaded the precinct with his palatial residence. It was all delightfully rural. The old white house was considered to be an old house at the time my father bought it. He renewed, I think, all the woodwork; but the walls, like the rocks around, stand firm to this day. They seemed to know in those days how to make mortar, for it was like cutting into solid stone to make a pipe hole. Whether the house was built before or after 1800 I do not know. The place was always to me singularly beautiful, a beauty no art could imitate. Standing at the front door, we could see our own hills rising on every side, tree above tree, rock above rock. The sturdy oak, the grand old chestnut and the beech interspersed to lend enchantment to the surroundings. These forest trees stretching up the hilltops made pictures as the seasons rolled round that I have never seen equalled." In later years the property was bought by William Miller, a brother-in-law of Mr. Thorp, and has been in the family ever since.

My friend Charles S. Keyser, Esq., author of "Fairmount Park," and of "Penn's Treaty," kindly allows me to insert the following from his pen:

THE RETREAT OF BARREN HILL.

Chestnut Hill terminates the northern border of Fairmount Park; the hill which rises from its foot sloping northward is Barren Hill. It is now over one hundred years ago, the 18th day of May, 1778, that Lafayette, with two thousand men, set his camp there. He was still suffering from his wound at Brandywine, and was borne to this Hill from his litter at Bethlehem. His command were shoeless and ragged men from "the mud holes" at Valley Forge. The day he camped was a day of feast and dance in Philadelphia, such as never before and never since that hour has been witnessed within its borders. The music of the Meschianza was sounding on its greater river, and in its streets; and women were reveling beneath the sombre shadow of the red cross of England waiting the fulfillment of a promise that their fete should terminate in a supper whether Lafayette should be living or dead. The night following that unholy day whose regretful memory remains, silently and very slowly, "two miles an hour," as their chroniclers write, from the city, through lines doubly set guarding the sluggish sleepers who rested after that scene of revelry, seven thousand British regulars were moving along an old road near the Delaware to make that promise sure, and along the Ridge, our pleasure ground's eastern border, another column was passing to cut his command from the Ford, while against his front was marching yet another column by the middle road to Germantown, all to reach by daylight this Hill.

These columns were set in motion to hem Lafayette in their living walls, and with him, crush his command. But the Hill stands an unstained monument among the many mounds of carnage which remain to mark that desperate war. Howe's march for all its slowness and its silence was not unnoted nor unobstructed. Lafayette's prudence broke its silence in its certain way.

There was a man in the Revolution, Allen McLane, a favorite with the army and Washington. He was a man of singular courage, genius to conceive, and daring to execute the most adventurous enterprises. On these grounds his desperate missions were undergone—along the Ridge, across these hills, to Lansdowne, to the Falls, down to the royal lines at Fairmount. His band of rangers were the moving outposts between the armies of Philadelphia and Valley Forge. Lafayette, on the morning he made his camp at Barren Hill, ordered McLane to this immediate ground, and the stealthy motion of those silent columns did not escape his restless watchfulness. In the midnight distant shots down by "the Falls" startled first the outposts of Lafayette, and in the gray dawn into his camp dashed McLane. This was McLane's work in the midnight: He had struck, he said, stragglers from Howe's advance on the further road. They reported a heavy column there and still another column on the Ridge; to Vandever's Hill he had sent Parr, of Morgan's Rifles, with his eighty men; the shots which Lafayette heard in the midnight were Parr's. Hardly was this said when a courier from Parr follows; he was holding Vandever's Hill: the head of a column of Hessians was there; and now more desperate a man from Plymouth brought these words of another, who, starting from his bed and running naked through the night had fallen at his door, that a heavy column on the further road by the Delaware was in Lafayette's rear, beyond Barren Hill, beyond Whitemarsh. The bugles sounded, the tents fell, the camp was hurried into order; and now Parr's command, marked with their work, splashes of dirt and splotches of blood, dashed into the camp and to the tent of Lafayette.

The column on the Ridge had been broken by these and were on the riverside. It was the imminence of peril, strategy alone could save them from utter destruction. Lafayette's orders met this imminence of danger. "McLane back to the Ridge, detachment to follow at once in order of battle before the British columns in his rear;" checked and bewildered the British commanders themselves fall into order of battle.

So he covered the retreat that gave him that great renown; by defiance, by courage, by prudence he made his way through inevitable slaughter; with a desperate energy yet regular and steady. Wagons and camp and arms, the whole body of his command, he swung down to Matson's ford; a bridge connecting east and west Conshohocken, now crosses at this ford. Hidden by intervening trees, along the low woody grounds, they reach the river border.

But it is from peril to peril; no bridge was here which safely reached would bear them to the further side and then broken down would leave these orderly walls of brutal iron narrowing in upon them, powerless. A swollen dangerous river only was there breast-high, neck-high, surging its waves to make their way impossible.

Lafayette's command was the flower of the army at Valley Forge, intrusted to him as Washington's outlying camp, with the most earnest admonitions for its care. Upon its preservation hung the safety of the whole Army. Behind him in order of battle he had set the body guard of Washington, behind them yet, were McLane's eighty men, fighting, baffling, masking the retreat; concentrating against himself the British Army. They must not be delayed an instant by this mass of men and horses shrinking back from the encounter with the swollen waves, for his orders to them were to hold to the last extremity. When they reach the ford they will be driven, step by step, by the heads of those three columns closing together hand to hand to the water's edge.

The men stand breast high in the water, a band of friendly Indians with them terror struck by the British Dragoons are swimming. Rough rocks lock the wagon-wheels, the danger before seems no less than the peril they leave; the moment of doubt and indecision, the supreme hour had come; in desperate emergencies it requires some act which affronts danger to inspire men, and Lafayette fails not here. He flings himself from his horse and stands or floats with the rest—strides neck deep through the water.

As in the night before he had by his prudence guarded their sleep; as in the morning he had saved them from annihilation, and even now by his couriers bringing to their succor Washington's command from Valley Forge, so by his courage, by his own equal encounter with the death before them he gives them that impulse which the hour requires. He makes himself their pathway through the perilous waters. Breast deep, neck deep, they strive against the swollen tide; the line of the soldiers lengthens toward the further shore, their heads showing like buoys in the huge nets of the fishers of the Delaware, the shouts of those who reach the opposite shore encouraging those who follow; still in the midst struggles Lafayette with the rest. Horses and wagons among the debris float down upon its swollen waters. But the further shore begins to blacken with his men, the saved increase, preponderate; Lafayette himself passes on beyond all danger; the ford is clear as McLane and the guard are borne backward to it. Close on them the red cross of England lifts above the heights, but succor had come, the peril is passed. From the opposite shore flashes and thunders against it—our own cannon from Valley Forge. The army from Valley Forge was there; its iron hail hurtles across the swollen waters as these men plunge also into the stream, and shelters their passage.

Then, writes one of the household of Washington, was presented a spectacle of memorable interest—the broad river flowing between stained and turbid. On the one shore the death emissaries of the King, paid and fed machines to do the work of death against the world's deliverance, down over them the red cross of England sullenly sinking; and on the opposite shore the clouds of the cannon of Valley Forge rising, gathering and breaking away in the sunlight, and in its golden halo the form of Washington, surrounded by his officers, encouraging by his presence and sheltering by his cannon their perilous passage.

How nobly do these two great personages of the Revolution associate here: Lafayette bringing to Washington's feet the command entrusted to him with such earnest admonitions, and saved by such consummate prudence and courage; Washington on that height, surrounded by his officers, amid the thunder of the sheltering cannon, that tried body, his own life-guard, saved; those chosen men from all the regiments of the colonies saved—saved to make from that hour the people's cause secure.

The river runs a swollen tide in the spring time, and it bears along its devastating waters rooted trees and rock, the debris sometimes of dwellings and death. So it pictures every year the dangers of that perilous passage, and the misery and desolation of that great revolution. But in these summer hours it flows in gentle sunlight and through banks of flowers. Let us not forget in this soft sunshine the darker hour of death and desolation, nor ever cease from gratitude. So forever shall our liberties endure.

WHITEMARSH AND SPRINGFIELD.

On leaving Chestnut Hill, on the Bethlehem pike, and going toward Whitemarsh, the County Line road marks the city boundary, and Springfield township, in Montgomery county, is next entered.

Two quaint little stone houses on the right, at the junction of Stenton avenue and the pike, one in the city, and the other out of it, belong to the Peterman family. Philip Peterman lived in the upper house and was succeeded by his son Jacob, who raised a large family. The family is no longer in the neighborhood. H. J. Williams purchased the houses and twenty-one acres of land of the Peterman family. Since his death they have fallen into the hands of Colonel Alexander Biddle, who resides in the brown mansion, prettily situated just above.

Passing through the toll-gate and by Thorp's lane, named from the Thorp family, who had print works on the Wissahickon, we come to the hotel with the peculiar name of Wheel-Pump, given it because of a double-acting pump, turned by a crank with a fly-wheel, making a continuous current of water. It is still in use. A little creek crosses the road here surmounted by a bridge. It is a tributary of the Wissahickon. Old deeds style the creek Gravel Run. It was sometimes called Paper Mill run, as there was a paper mill on the road leading to Roslyn Heights. A pond on the right aids by its water power the agricultural works of Wm. H. H. Heydrick. The manufactory belongs to Daniel Yeakel. The pond is on the farm of Daniel Yeakel, which consists of eighty-four acres. This farm has been in the Yeakel family over a century. Abraham, the grandfather of Daniel, owned the place during the Revolution and lived on it. Abraham was the son of Christopher, who built the old log house still standing at Cresheim creek and Germantown road, and dwelt in it, and afterward built and lived in the Schultz house, at the Pennsylvania Railroad Depot, in Chestnut Hill. Abraham's son Isaac received the property at his father's death, and from him it passed to his son Daniel, the present owner. The old stone farmhouse was built by Abraham, and an addition was made in 1787.

The Wheel-Pump tavern is owned and kept by Robert Gordon. It belonged to the Heydrick family, who leased it to various persons. The stone house on the left hand side was the Heydrick farmhouse. The long, gray stone dwelling on the right was the dwelling and store of the Heydricks. Charles Heydrick now owns and occupies it, but the store is no longer kept. The Wheel-Pump House is a name given to the hamlet.

"ROSLYN HEIGHTS."

Near by on Willow Grove road, is the Roslyn Heights Hills. Among the houses situated there is the beautiful country place built by Washington Brown, of Philadelphia, and afterward in possession of Edward Machette. It is now owned by the Gratz family and called "The Heights." Among our

"ROSLYN HEIGHTS," RESIDENCE OF STEVENSON CROTHERS, CHESTNUT HILL.

illustrations is "Roslyn Heights," lately built, the residence of Stevenson Crothers. It is one of the best-located houses at Chestnut Hill. It overlooks the Valley Forge Hills, Conshohocken, Whitemarsh Valley, Flourtown, Barren Hill and a score of little villages that dot the broad stretch of landscape to be viewed on all sides. The house is of the Modern Queen Anne style of architecture, contains twelve rooms and has all of the modern improvements. The farm consists of about sixty acres which Mr. Crothers has turned into a stock farm, which has several streams of crystal water flowing through it. He is also each year improving and adding to the natural beauty of what is already an ideal spot for a home.

Before reaching that place, the old Kerper property stretches along the road. There is an old stone farmhouse and barn. J. Lowber Welsh has bought the property for improvement.

There is a crushed stone walk from Thorp's lane on the Township line. The pedestrain leaves the street lamps, which are the tokens of city life. A stone quarry presents itself, which shows how a town like Chestnut Hill may be built, as the material is close at hand. We ride by Commodore Kittson's stock-farm and race-course, called "Erdenheim," founded by Aristides Welch, about twenty years ago. Some four or five years since he sold the property to Mr. Kittson and moved to Germantown.

In walking along the Wissahickon, we notice that it is not as wild as lower down, where the drive is so well wooded, and has made the stream so famous. Still the overhanging willows give a gentler beauty, such as is seen in pictures of English scenery, especially about Windsor Castle on the Thames. Two fishermen are patiently plying their craft in the sun, like good Izaak Walton.

The Plymouth Railroad, with its trestle work, shows that the country has felt the advance of civilization. The golden wheat, shocked or lying on the ground, forms a very pretty feature of the landscape. Some lime kilns near a bridge over the Wissahickon make a striking scene with their rude outlines, though the new bridge, built of wood, stone and iron, in A. D. 1884, gives a modern air to the spot, and affords a contrast between new and old so often found in this land. Still the bridge is a good and useful one, and let us be thankful as we walk over it that we are so well provided with a passage over the stream. This Montgomery county bridge had Ellwood Hart as its contractor; James Burnett, Hiram Burdan and William L. Rittenhouse were on the inscription as in oversight of the work. James B. Holland was the clerk. May their work long stand. A dam is just above the bridge, and sight and sound of the falling water refreshes one on a hot day. Valley Green mill stands at this point, and a country mill is always picturesque. This is now in the hands of Chalkley Ambler; it was formerly Day's mill, and still earlier Mento's mill.

The road which we have been traversing is called Valley Green road. The Hon. William A. Yeakle, a local historian of note, lives upon it, and I regretted that I did not learn that fact until I had passed his door, and it was too late to pay him a call of respect and to seek guidance in my meanderings.

On the Bethlehem pike, after leaving the Valley Green road, the Whitemarsh Union Church may be seen on a hillside. The old building is of stone and is pebble-dashed. It has been remodeled. It stands near St. Thomas's Episcopal Church, which is, however, more ancient as to parish history. The Lutherans and German Reformed use this building in common. The Lutheran minister is Rev. Dr. Sheeleigh, and Rev. Mr. Detrich is the Reformed minister. Each congregation has one service a day in the church on Sundays. Dr. Sheeleigh holds the Upper Dublin Lutheran Church also, and Mr. Detrich has another parish at North Wales. Dr. Sheeleigh resides on a cross road near the church, and Mr. Detrich lives in Flourtown. Frank Seltzer's pretty country place is quite a notable feature.

WASHINGTON'S HEADQUARTERS

Is in Upper Dublin township, at the edge of Springfield township. The farmhouse is in Upper Dublin and the springhouse in Springfield. Mr. Charles T. Aiman is the present owner of the farm, who purchased the place of the administrators of John Fitzwater, at a public sale, on November 19th, A. D. 1857. Fitzwater bought it in 1833. John Fry was the previous owner. Previous to that the Stuckart family owned it, and still previous to that George Emlen, Jr., was the possessor. It is supposed that he was the builder of the old mansion, which was styled Emlen's Folly, at Chestnut Hill, perhaps on account of its size. The fine old wood-work has lately been recolored. The parlor was the scene of the trial of General Wayne on account of the surprise at Paoli, but he was cleared. The interior and exterior have been somewhat remodeled. The windows have been filled with modern glass, but the strong old walls yet stand. Anciently there were inside shutters. A rear wing has been taken down as being in decay. Porches and piazzas have been added. In Washington's day there was a small porch on the south side and another on the west side. A long comfortable piazza now stretches the whole length of the south side, with its cedar posts in keeping with the structure. Green blinds protect the windows. The old soapstones which were under the old south porch still keep their place; and the feet of the incomer tread the stones which Washington trod. The house is long, and faces the Edge Hill and Whitemarsh road. The building is mostly of limestone to which some Camp Hill stone are added. It is two stories high with dormer windows in the roof. Two partitions are of stone. Mr. Aiman has kept the property in excellent repair and made needed improvements and added fine outbuildings. The old stone barn became decayed and was of necessity removed. Washington made this his headquarters on both of his sojourns here. The old house lies at the foot of Camp Hill. The encampment stretched from the rear of the house along beyond St. Thomas's Church toward the Limekiln pike. West of the Bethlehem pike lies Militia Hill, where the militia were encamped. The Washington house was anciently plastered with clay and cut straw, which was difficult to remove: the nails were wrought and hand made, the laths overlapped the studding and were woven together in a basket form. The present house is 80x30 feet, and the wing which has been removed was about 28x30 feet. The front stairway formerly ascended from the parlor, but has been removed by Mr. Aiman to the hall. I am indebted to Mr. Aiman for these particulars. In Lossing's Field Book of the Revolution, Vol. II, p. 114, it is stated that the farm house which Washington used was owned by the wealthy Elmer. The ruins of his springhouse are mentioned though there was a modern one. The soapstone steps of the house are also noted. The old thatched barn was said to be contemporary with the house. A large catalpa tree comes in for notice. When Lossing visited the place it was owned by John Fitzwater. The roof of the old barn was then falling in. The American camp was on the hills north of the old mansion, the right wing being on Wissahickon creek and the left on Sandy Run. Near Mather's Mill were the remains of the old redoubt. There were vestiges of the chimneys of log and stone of the huts of the army. At one time it is said that the British scouts of General Howe were killed above Chestnut Hill and the General threatened to raid the country district, if that mode of warfare was not stopped, and it ceased. The smiling country now looks as if it had never had such stern experiences.

The veteran historian, Lossing, sends the following note:

DOVER PLAINS, N. Y.,
July 1st, 1889.

My Dear Sir:—I thank you very much for your kind courtesy in sending me a copy of the GERMANTOWN TELEGRAPH, containing your valuable article on "Chestnut Hill," "Whitemarsh," etc. Your minute historical and exact details are of very great interest to readers residing in your region, nay to all, whether living far or near from these interesting localities. It would give me great pleasure to revisit them now, but it may not be. Indeed the vivid pictures in memory, of the places described in my FIELD BOOK OF THE REVOLUTION, are so changed, after the lapse of forty years, that they (the places) would not bear, in many cases, a semblance of my then delineations. Again, thanking you, I remain,

Yours most sincerely,
BENSON J. LOSSING.

REV. S. F. HOTCHKIN.

John R. Fell, son of J. Gillingham Fell, has built a beautiful stone mansion of architectural style, on the summit of Camp Hill, and Mr. Ralph of Philadelphia, has built near Camp Hill station.

WHITEMARSH.

When Washington's forces were fit to move, after the battle of Germantown, he transferred them from the Skippack to Whitemarsh, only twelve miles from Philadelphia, wishing to make further efforts to recover the American capital. His headquarters were at the "Emlen mansion," afterward the property of Charles Aiman. Some of the lines of defense then made may be seen near Fort Washington. General Howe, expecting to be attacked again, was watchful. He strove to surprise Washington. Two English officers held a conference with regard to an attack on Whitemarsh, in the house of William Darrach, about the 2d of December. One was believed to be Major Andre. The family were requested to go early to bed, but Mrs. Lydia Darrach was to let the officers out at the close of the conference. She listened at the door and heard an order for the troops to march for an attack on Washington on the evening of the 4th of December. She returned to her chamber, and when the officer knocked at her door feigned sleep, only answering the third knock. She did not dare to inform her husband, but went to Frankford apparently to buy flour, Howe having given her a pass. She met the American officer, Lieutenant Colonel Craig, who knew her, and told him her message, enjoining secrecy as to her own part in the transaction, to shield herself from danger. The Colonel informed Washington who thus baffled the attempt. Lydia returned with her flour. She heard the British troops depart at night. After their return in a few days the officer took her to his room, locked the door, and asked whether any of her family were up on the night of the conference. She said that they had gone to bed at 8 o'clock. He declared that he knew that she was asleep, as he had knocked thrice at her door before she heard him. He said that when they neared Whitemarsh the cannon were mounted and the troops ready, and he added: "We have marched back like a parcel of fools." Lydia Darrach had a son who was an officer in the army of the Americans near the city. See "Washington at Valley Forge," by Theo. W. Bean, pp. 26-28.

FRANKLIN A. COMLY.

In visiting Flourtown I had the pleasure of meeting the gentlemanly Franklin A. Comly, the first President of the North Pennsylvania Railroad Company. He died April 25th, 1887. The Philadelphia *Inquirer* states that he descended from Henry and Joan Comly, who accompanied William Penn from England in 1682. A part of the Manor of Moreland was in after years in the hands of the family. Franklin A. Comly was born at Walton's Mill, at Bethayres, as he afterward named the place for his mother, Elizabeth Ayres. The lad was in the hardware business in Philadelphia, under Robert A. Parrish. When he became of age his faithfulness caused his admission to partnership. He also became agent for a Sheffield (England) cutlery firm, and was made President of the Buck Mountain Coal Company and of the North Pennsylvania Railroad Company, which he managed with enterprise and prudence. He was a director of numerous other business companies, and was active, even in advancing years, until his health began to fail the autumn before he died, and for a few months he was much confined to his house. Mr. Comly's ample house, with its wide piazza, was once a hotel, where the passing teamsters used to sleep in the buffalo robes which they brought with them. A large barn is attached to the old-fashioned residence.

Franklin P. Seltzer's fine residence near by, with its extensive and beautiful grounds, was in 1837 the home of Judge Morris Longstreth. He died here.

ST. THOMAS'S EPISCOPAL CHURCH.

The Farmar family were the founders and principal patrons of this church. Tradition from various sources says that between A. D. 1690 and 1700, a log church was built, which was burned in 1710. We may imagine the old wooden stoves, and the dry wood around the pipe which perhaps encouraged the flames, while the country side was excited as the news of the loss was spread abroad. In the burning of a depository of religious books in New York City, a leaf of the Bible was wafted some distance by the flames, containing the words of Isaiah 64, 11: "Our holy and our beautiful house, where our fathers praised Thee, is burned up with fire; and all our pleasant things are laid waste." This may describe the feelings of the sufferers on this occasion. A new stone building was erected on land given by Edward Farmar, and the glory of the latter house was, as in Scripture prophecy, greater than that of the former. This stood 107 years. The name of the first pastor is unknown. Edward Farmar's coat-of-arms is given in Bean's History of Montgomery County, whence our information is derived. About 1695, Rev. Mr. Clayton established the services of the Church of England in Philadelphia. Rev. Evan Evans came to this country in 1700, and was rector of Christ Church, Philadelphia. He frequently went fifteen or twenty miles into the country to minister to church people who requested it. No doubt he found simple, primitive hospitality, and that the services were earnest, though infrequent. In 1718 Mr. Weyman was appointed, by the Society for Propagating the Gospel in Foreign Parts, Missionary at Oxford and Radnor. He informed the Society of the congregation at Whitemarsh, ten miles from Oxford, desiring a minister, and which had "for the decent performance of divine worship erected a goodly stone building." He resigned Radnor, and gave his labors chiefly to Oxford and Whitemarsh. In 1733, Rev. Alexander Howie succeeded him. After nine years' service, he went to the West Indies. The Rev. William Currie became rector in 1742, when the wardens were John Barge and Hugh Burk; and the vestry, Thomas Bartholomew, William Malchior, Edward Burk, Francis Colley, William Dewees, Jr., and John Burk. In 1742, it was agreed by the vestry to give James Whiley, "clark," for officiating and cleaning the church and keeping things in order, five pounds per year. The old tiles were ordered to be sold, and the roof covered with shingles. A new pew and pulpit and railing round the communion table were ordered, also a cedar fence for the graveyard, with three gates. There were some forty contributors. Samuel Gilkey repaired the roof. Jacoby Whiley and George Lawrence attended to the carpenter work.

Rev. Eneas Ross, in 1743, resigned Christ Church, Philadelphia, to take Whitemarsh and Oxford, and continued as rector till 1758. He was transferred to New Castle, Delaware. Rev. Hugh Neil succeeded him, and was rector until 1766. It is supposed that Rev. Dr. William Smith, provost of the College of Philadelphia, officiated occasionally after this date until 1779. The record books were destroyed in the Revolutionary War.

In 1768 John B. Gilpin and Andrew Redifer were elected wardens, and Edward Burk, Levi Stannard, William Hicks and Frederick Hitner, vestrymen. It was ordered that the church be repaired. Rev. Joseph Pilmore was chosen minister, and John Stewart appointed clerk. In 1797 Bishop Hobart was in charge. I suppose that this was when the Bishop of New York, in his early ministry, was rector at Oxford. Rev. Slator Clay and his son, Rev. Dr. John C. Clay, were also rectors. Rev. Bird Wilson, rector of Norristown, and Rev. Mr. Roberts did service here. Rev. John Rodney served this point with Germantown; Rev. Dr. Cruse, afterward librarian in the General Theological Seminary, New York, and Rev. John Reynolds served from 1833 to 1836; Rev. William H. Diehl to 1852; Rev. George Foote to 1855; Rev. David C. Millet from 1856 to 1864; Rev. Charles Bonnell, Rev. Peter W. Stryker, and the present rector, Rev. H. Meigs, followed.

A new church was built in 1817, but the tower and spire were not finished until between 1847 and 1857, when the parsonage and school-house were built, and additional ground bought, and a bell of 1100 pounds weight, and a communion service presented. The church was of stone. The spire was 130 feet high. A drawing of the church was made in May, 1857, perhaps the only one extant. The distance to Oxford Church does not exceed nine miles. In 1734 a road was opened between these two churches and declared public, being called "Church road." Tradition affirms that several Indian chiefs were buried at Whitemarsh churchyard. American soldiers were quartered in the church in the Revolution. The British occupied it when pursuing the Americans after the battle of Germantown, and again when they marched out to attack Washington, they stayed in it for several days. The new sandstone church was used for worship in 1877 and completed in 1881. The stone was from the neighborhood. There is a fine tower, and the beautiful location adds much to its effect. The oldest gravestone with a date in this ancient cemetery is that of James Allison, who died in 1727. This is the oldest of the Episcopal Churches in the county, the next in age being St. James's Church, Lower Providence, which dates back to 1721.

The Church road mentioned above was not properly laid out until 1811. It is pleasant to think of it in its first rude state, when the missionaries of the Propagation Society of the English Church rode along it between Oxford and

CHESTNUT HILL. 523

Whitemarsh, thinking of their dear old English homes, and the mother church which had sent them out to plant the Gospel in a new land. If one would see what kind of a life they led, let him read the most interesting history of Trinity Church, Oxford, by its former rector, the Rev. Dr. Buchanan. See also for history of St. Thomas's Church, Thompson Westcott's History of Philadelphia (Scrap Book Historical Society of Pennsylvania), Chapter 520.

William Heyward Drayton, Esq., whose beautiful place is not far from St. Thomas's Church, takes an interest in the parish. The family place of the Sheaffs is about a half a mile from the church, on the Skippack road. One of this family has been a patron of the parish school, while Mr. Bringhurst has been a good worker in church affairs, and so the old parish carries on its beneficent work through the generations.

There is a tablet to William Platt, Jr., in the church. He was the Superintendent of the Philadelphia Department of the United States Sanitary Commission, and visited the battlefield of Antietam on a mission of mercy, and was stricken by disease, and death followed. The inscription is, "Greater love hath no man than this, than a man lay down his life for his friends," St. John xv, 13.

UNION CHURCH.

UNION CHURCH, AT FLOURTOWN, is held by the Lutheran and Reformed bodies conjointly. It was built in A. D. 1818, and remodeled in 1867, when the tower was added. It is of stone, with stained glass windows; the rose window completely covered with ivy on the lower gable is beautiful. There is a large burial-ground, and its white gravestones may be seen for some distance. There is a monument to General Scheetz here. The Lutheran pastors at Barren Hill had charge of the Lutherans here until Rev. Mr. Sentman's day. Since Upper Dublin Church was built in 1857, it has been joined with that parish. Rev. Lewis Hippee was pastor until August, 1859. Rev. Edward Koons, Rev. George Sill and Rev. Matthew Sheeleigh, the present pastor, succeeded him. Rev. George Wagner was the German Reformed pastor in 1858. Rev. J. P. Dietrich, D. D., is now in charge, and he lives near the church.

THE SPRINGFIELD PRESBYTERIAN CHURCH.

A part of the German Reformed element in the Union Church, at Flourtown, wished to inaugurate new measures in advancing religion, and established a Sunday-school and carried it on for some time. The younger portion of the German Reformed Church withdrew and erected a building near Union Church, on the southeast of it, and there the Sunday-school was held, and afterward there were preaching services. This body later on removed to the lower part of Flourtown and built a church. Rev. A. J. Snyder was the first pastor, having been with the congregation at their removal. He remained about ten years, supplying also the church at Jeffersonville, above Norristown, and he passed back and fourth every Sunday, preaching alternately morning and evening at each place. There have been several pastors since. Mr. Snyder is now in New Jersey. The first building no longer stands. The church became Presbyterian, and joined the Fourth Presbytery of Philadelphia, as it then was. The Rev. A. W. Long is now the pastor.

The Cold Point Baptist Church was first called Plymouth Church, and about A. D. 1842, the place was served by Rev. Robert Young, pastor of Chestnut Hill Baptist Church. A second church was erected. Alan W. Corson, the teacher and botanist, resided near this church.

The Plymouth Friends' Meeting, on the Perkiomen turnpike, is an old institution, as well as that at Gwynedd. An Evangelical Church was dedicated in Plymouth, in A. D. 1883, Rev. H. M. Capp, pastor. Mr. Buck and the late Hon. William A. Yeakle deserve much credit in guiding the local historian in studying Montgomery county.

GENERAL HENRY SCHEETZ.

There is a portrait of this officer in the house of his great-grandson in Rex avenue, Chestnut Hill. It was painted by the deaf and dumb artist, A. Newsam, who is buried in the churchyard of St. Andrew's Episcopal Church, Wilmington, Delaware. The artist was a friend of the late Bishop Lee, the rector of that church. General Scheetz was an old-fashioned gentleman of decided character, and a leader in his neighborhood. He had a large influence in the Democratic elections. He lived in Flourtown, on the right hand in driving from Chestnut Hill. The house stands back, there being a deep yard and trees in front. It has passed out of the hands of the family. The General used to own a paper-mill at Sandy Run, near Camp Hill Station. He ran the mill for years. His son, Henry Scheetz, Jr., also conducted it afterward. The General's brother, Justus, had another paper-mill near by. General Scheetz sold the paper-mill and it became a grist-mill, which was still called Scheetz's mill. John Schaeffer bought the property. Henry Scheetz emigrated to Ohio by wagon and canal, and carried on a paper-mill at Steubenville, and died there. Most of General Scheetz's life was spent on the mill property, and in his old age he retired to the village of Flourtown. Daniel O. Hitner married the General's daughter, Catherine. Mr. Hitner owned the marble quarries at Marble Hall, and the iron furnaces which were then at Spring Mills, near Conshohocken. The Schuylkill Valley Railroad has destroyed them. D. O. Hitner, Jr., the son of Daniel O. Hitner, was the last person who conducted the furnace and marble works. His brother, Henry Scheetz Hitner, now deceased, was a partner in a portion of the business. General Scheetz was a General in the War of 1812. His son Jacob owned the stock-farm which was afterward purchased by Commodore Kittson. He farmed it. He sold it to

CHESTNUT HILL. 525

Dr. McRea, who sold to George Blight, who sold to Aristides Welch. President Buchanan was a friend of Jacob Scheetz, and visited him here when he was ex-President, about 1867. Norman W. Kittson was from St. Paul, Minnesota. The farm contained 400 acres. About 1861, Mr. Welch bought about 150 acres and increased it to 250 acres. He bred famous horses, and owned Flora Temple. In 1882, Mr. Welch sold to Mr. Kittson for $125,000. The new purchaser increased the size of the farm still further. A part of this noted farm is in Springfield township. It has been sold again lately.

John Jacob Scheetz, a minister of Crayfelt on the Rhine, was a member of the Frankfort Company. His son Henry came to this country and died in Whitemarsh. He had a paper-mill at Sandy Run, and a grist mill. He is said to have built another paper-mill in Springfield, owned by the family. General Scheetz was born in 1761, and was educated in country schools. During John Fries's rebellion, in 1798, he commanded a country brigade, but the rebellion subsided before he arrived at its scene. Governor Snyder appointed him Major General of Militia. In the war with England he marched to Marcus Hook to protect DuPont's powder works, near Wilmington. He died at Valley Green, in 1848, aged eighty-seven years. The house in which he lived, on the east side of the turnpike, became the property of Samuel Van Winkle, Jr. George Scheetz and Mrs. Sechler, of this neighborhood are relatives of the family.

The country school teacher was an important factor in early days. There was one named Patrick Menan, an Irishman, who had General Andrew Porter and David Rittenhouse as pupils, and they rapidly progressed in mathematics under him. We honor the scholars, let us not forget the teacher who helped the formation of their character. Thomas Paxson, the father of Judge Paxson, taught school in Whitemarsh. Peter Le Gaux, a meteorologist and vine grower, was a scientific man who deserves notice in this region of country, Mrs. Toland, his granddaughter, occupied his house at Spring Mill. He was a friend of the Audubons.

WISSAHICKON CREEK is a crooked stream, and it has a right to be so, for the Dutch Schuylkill and the Indian Delaware need something of its wayward disposition to enliven them, and so the grandchild stirs up both the mother and the grandmother as she pours her lively prattle into their currents. The creek rises from two small branches in Montgomery township, and flows through Gwynedd, Whitpaine, Upper Dublin, Whitemarsh and Springfield townships into the Schuylkill, nearly a mile below Manayunk. It is about nineteen miles in length and is an excellent mill stream. The principal branches are Valley Run and Sandy Run. A grist-mill was built on this creek near the beginning of the last century by Edward Farmar. On Holmes's map this is called Whitpaine's creek, after Richard Whitpaine, a large owner of land in Whitpaine township. In the Upland Court Records for 1677 it is called Wiesahitkonk, which the missionary Heckewelder says, in the Delaware Indian language, means "the catfish or yellow water stream."—From William J. Buck's account, in Bean's History of Montgomery County. The name Whitemarsh, in this same volume, is given as originally "wide marsh." I think it has also been referred to the whiteness of the marsh.

WHITEMARSH.

Madame Farmar's limestone is mentioned in a letter from Chief Justice Nicholas More, of Green Spring, to William Penn. Edward Farmar presented the lot for St. Thomas's Episcopal Church, in A. D. 1710, and took an active part in its erection and was almost its founder. A council of Indians was once held at his house. He is buried at St. Thomas's Church.

Nicholas Scull was a noted land surveyor in Whitemarsh. He was Surveyor General of Pennsylvania. Dr. Franklin's Autobiography says Scull "loved books and sometimes made verses." With George Heap he made a map of Philadelphia. He also published a map of the improved parts of Pennsylvania and Maryland. Scull could speak several Indian languages.—See Buck's History of Moreland, Pennsylvania Historical Society, Collections, Vol. I, No. 5, A. D. 1853, p. 195, note.

Silas Cleaver's mill belonged to Jonathan Robeson. The first mill was built by Edward Farmar. Peter Robeson was his son-in-law. Robeson township took its name from Judge Andrew Robeson, of this family. Nicholas Kline built the present mill and owned it. Farmar's mill, which was built in 1713, stood where the Gwynedd, North Wales and Philadelphia roads cross the Skippack. It is owned by Charles Otterson, Esq., of Philadelphia. Col. Samuel Miles organized a company of militia here in Whitemarsh for service in the Revolution.

Daniel Mentz's property, beyond St. Thomas's Church, was a camping place of the American soldiers in the Revolution, and remains of the encampment are said to be still visible. As we walk on toward Washington's headquarters we notice that the picturesque limekilns have been largely abandoned. This is because those near the Plymouth Railroad have a better chance of transportation. Lentz & Cannon's kilns are at work. The pretty arches of the old kilns are a pleasant feature, and the stone constructions at sunset may well in imagination seem like ruined towers. The furnace stack of Edge Hill, in the distance is a striking object. General Scheetz, of the War of 1812, lived in the neighborhood through which we are passing.

"BARREN HILL."

The upper part of Chestnut Hill on the Reading pike used to rejoice in the name of Pumpkintown, but perhaps the appellation is now fading away. In going to Barren Hill, here and there an old stone house of former days is seen by the roadside. There is a bridge over the Wissahickon and a fall above it. After passing the Convent, Morris Williams's place, with its water-wheel as a picturesque addition, is seen on the right hand. Hickorytown is visible in the distance beyond it, Mr. Pitcairn's house is on the brow of a hill and has a large lawn and grove around it. The village of Barren Hill has three inns, and contains some antique houses. There are two stores and a school-house. St. Peter's Lutheran Church is the main object in the town. A new building has been erected where the old church stood in La Fayette's day. The site is high and pleasant, and an ample old graveyard adjoins the edifice where the "forefathers of the hamlet sleep," as Gray expresses it in his inimitable Elegy. The parsonage is near by and was then occupied by Rev. J. S. McAtee, the pastor. The post-office here is named La Fayette Hill. There is an account of La Fayette at Barren Hill in the Pennsylvania Magazine of History, Vol. XI, p. 115. His visit to the place with De Chastellux is described by that writer in the first volume of his Reminiscences, p. 296.

In the Memoirs of the Historical Society of Pennsylvania, Vol. II, p. 76, in Joshua Francis Fisher's "Early Poets and Poetry of Pennsylvania," is an account of John Dommett, whose elegy was printed in the *Mercury*, in 1733. "He died at Whitemarsh, July 22, 1729." Dommett was, according to Mr. Fisher, "the first *Professional Poet* our country produced." He is supposed to have written panegyrical odes to Governors and others, which appeared in the *Mercury*. Some of Colonel John Parke's poems were written at Whitemarsh and Valley Forge, so the muse sang in war times, as in the case of F. S. Key, who wrote the "Star Spangled Banner" on a British vessel where he was a prisoner, having gone on board to deliver a friend from it.

Alan Corson and Mr. Middleton were the means of opening the Wissahickon turnpike. They surveyed it from Flourtown to the mouth of the Wissahickon, and pushed it in court. Its length was eight and a half miles. Mr. Middleton was the President and procured the charter. The turnpike cost $37,500. It was started as a toll road, but the city made it free. The Park owns a part of it. The Indian chief, Tedynseung, whose figure was placed on the Indian rock in the Park, belonged to the Lenni Lenape tribe. He, with forty other Indians, left this section about the time of the Revolution. The departing company consisted mostly of women, the men having gone before. See Charles S. Keyser's "Fairmount Park," p. 120.

In tracing local names one must be careful not to be guided merely by sound. For instance: Lancaster county was so named when it was formed in 1729, on account of John Wright, who was born in Lancashire, England, and so the old Roman and Saxon caster (castrum and ceaster), or camp is repeated here. On the other hand Lancasterville in the region now treated of was named in honor of a member of the Society of Friends. See Hotchkin's "Pocket Gazetteer of Pennsylvania," compiled from Dr. William H. Egle's History, p. 92.

CHESTNUT HILL.

In German days, the region above Chestnut Hill, then known as Summerhausen, was called Kerfeld or Crefeld. The town in Germany, which the emigrants, with a love of the fatherland, perpetuated, was noted for its silk and velvet manufactures. The word means Clayfield. The place has manufactories of woolen, cotton and linen goods and lace, and oilcloth. There are also potteries and tanneries. An ancient castle near by is utilized as a dye-house.

CHURCHILL HALL.

The Church Hill farm owned by Mr. Calvin Pardee is situated in Whitemarsh, Montgomery county, on Church road near where it joins the Bethlehem turnpike road. It is *vis-a-vis* on the same hill with that well-known land mark, St. Thomas's Church, and but a few paces from it eastward. It formed, in colonial days, a part of the extensive Hope Lodge Farm, and the use to which it was sometimes put is plainly shown by numerous mounds on which the tents of the American army were pitched after the battle of Germantown, in the grove between the church and farm house. This farm house, a not-pleasing three-storied building, which has for many years stood on the site, has been remodeled, from designs by Mr. Pearson, to make it in harmony with the times of historic scenes enacted in the neighborhood. To further this end, the old third story was removed and both the old part—to the left of picture—and the new addition—to the right—unified with a large hip roof, with clusters of colonial dormer windows and chimneys. The old exterior stuccoed walls, and the new, are covered with clapboards of a buff color, all the main features such as piazzas, windows, etc., being white, and the outside shutters green, the intention being to give a correct colonial treatment of line and color to the mansion on so important a site.

The main entrance is from the front piazza into a Great Hall 22 by 33 extending the full depth of the house, with windows on three sides, and all finished in white painted wood and oak floor. Paneling extends from floor to ceiling, and a cornice of colonial detail girts the room dividing it into two portions of unequal width by a colonnade continued therefrom to the floor. On the left side of this Hall is a huge fireplace of mottled brick, with high paneled mantel, and one may easily picture the great room filled with a jolly throng at holiday time, and as the fire light projects great shadows into the room, and the fire's bright chemistry unmakes the logs which nature was great years in making, recall the words of the poet:

> "Shut in from all the world without
> We sat the clean-winged hearth about,
> Content to let the north wind roar
> In baffled rage at pane and door,
> While the red logs before us beat
> The front line back with tropic heat.
> And ever when a louder blast
> Shook beam and rafter as it past,
> The merrier up its roaring draught
> The great throat of the chimney laughed."

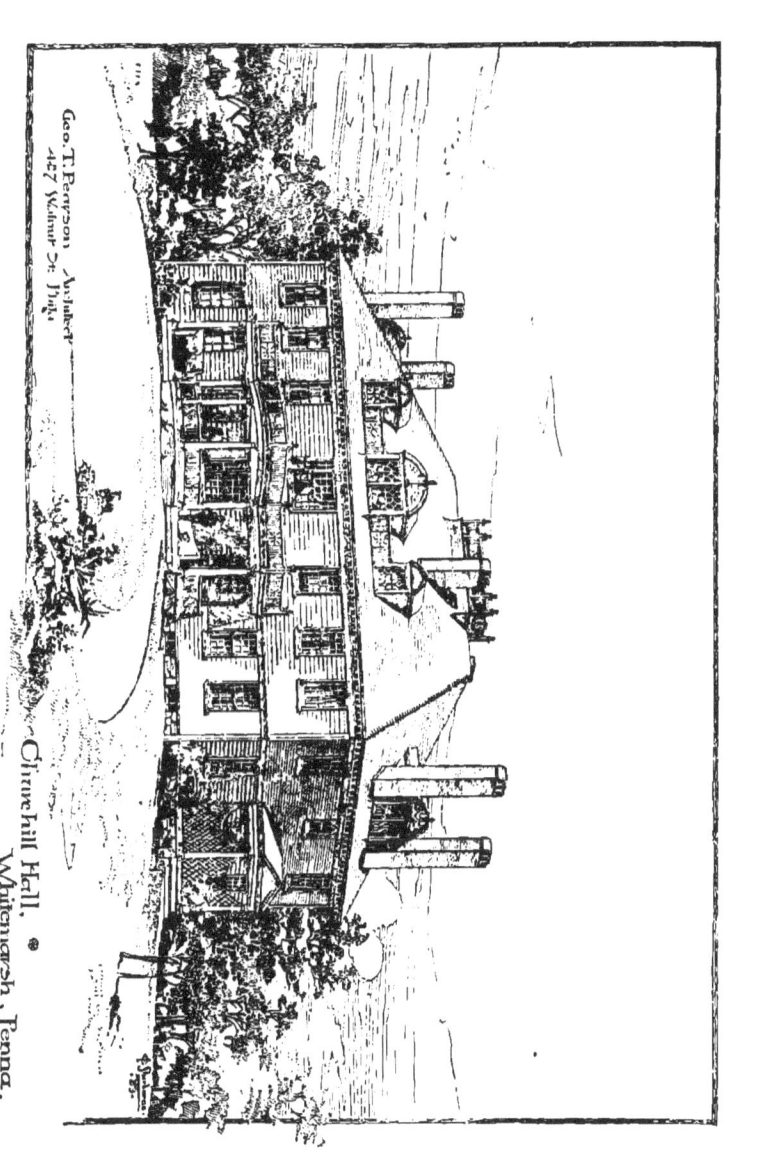

Geo. T. Pearson, Architect
427 Walnut St, Phila.

Chestnut Hall,
Whitemarsh, Penna.

At the extreme northeast end of this Hall and facing the doorway is a semi-circular bay window, through which charming views may be had of the interesting scenery. Adjoining this bay is an arched Alcove containing the main stairway of colonial and extremely simple design, with scroll sides and very plain painted wood balustrade, the rail and steps being mahogany. To the right of the Hall is the Dining Room finished in the same style in painted wood, with low-paneled wainscot, and characteristic china closets and mantel. To the rear of this room is a small Library, and the remainder of the first story is composed of kitchen and allied apartments.

The second and third stories are made up of sleeping and bath rooms all finished in white painted wood, with quiet tones of color on walls and ceilings. Most of these rooms have fire-places, the attendant mantel-pieces being of very simple forms and all suggested by sketches taken from existing old work of kindred character in New England by the architect. The interior is lighted throughout by candles in clustered wall brackets of simple antique design, there being no artificial light. The system of plumbing is complete, the supply of water for which being taken from a remarkable well 40 feet deep. The aim in this remodeling has been to combine the quaintness and simplicity of style of past times architecturally, with the comforts of the present.

The scenery which neighbors Churchill is noted for beauty, and in every direction may be seen places connected in a quiet way with historic army scenes of the revolution. But these environs bear but slight trace of this now, and in its stead one may contemplate the gentle undulation of hill and vale, the winding country roads, here a little of man, there a little of nature, and in this contemplation feel that serenity which comes to one away from the world's bustle and wrack, in such lovely spots as Churchill Hall.

Appendix.

No. 1.

Mr. Daniel K. Cassell, of Nicetown, who has written a book on the Mennonites, has corrected this sketch, and adds the following information:

A number of Mennonites came from Crefeld, a city of the lower Rhine, within a few miles of the borders of Holland. They reached Philadelphia on the 6th of October, 1682. Their first religious meeting was held in the house of Denis Kunders (Anthony Conrad), in 1683. William Rittenhouse came to Germantown from Holland, was their first minister, and in 1701 was ordained their first Bishop in America. He also built the first paper-mill in America. He died in 1708. Shortly after his death, his son Nicholas Rittenhouse and Dirk Keyser were ordained their ministers. In 1702, Jacob Godshall, a Mennonite minister, came over and settled in Germantown. On February the 10th, 1702-3, Arnold van Fossen delivered to John Neus and Henry Sellen, on behalf of the Mennonites, a deed for three square perches of land for a church, which was not built until six years later. After the death of John Neus, Henry Sellen gave a deed to the Mennonite Church of Germantown, bearing date September 6, 1714.

I have the church book from 1770 down, and I have the family records of the Funks copied. Jacob Funk, the minister, was my great-grandfather; he was ordained a minister in 1765 at the Indian Creek, Franconia, Montgomery county, and so recorded in their church book, and I have a copy of his will, also his father's will, who came from Germany and took up 150 acres of land: his patent is dated May 16, 1734.

William Rittenhouse, the first Bishop in America in the Mennonite Church, was my great-grandmother's great-grandfather, so I am a direct descendant from him. David Rittenhouse, the astronomer, was first cousin to my great-grandmother, married to Dillman Kolb. I take much interest in the history of the Germantown Church.

Mr. Cassell states that there were thirteen families of Mennonites. J. D. Rupp is the reference as to the supposed holding of service in private houses and under trees. Jacob Funk's father, also named Jacob, was the nephew of Bishop Henry Funk, of Indian Creek. Jacob Funk died the 14th of March, and not the 11th. He had exceeded 81 years but one day. "Kolp" should be Kolb. "Getter" should be Kelter. A. D. 1675, should have been 1875.

(533)

APPENDIX.

"Avenue" should be road. Jacob Funk, the minister, bought and occupied the farm in 1774. John was the oldest son of Jacob. "Febr." in the inscription, should be Febrū. The last phrase "where a building has now been erected," should be omitted. "Deacon" should be a deacon.

Mr. Cassell has Heinrich Funk's will or a copy of it.

No. 2.

MATTHIAS W. BALDWIN.

A contributor signing himself "Old Times," wrote Col. Fitzgerald, editor of the Philadelphia *Item*, a sketch of the famous builder of the engine "Old Ironsides," which we condense.

Mr. Baldwin who constructed this first American locomotive, was born in Elizabethtown, N. J., in 1795, and he died at Wissonoming, his country seat, in 1866, aged 71. His activity and purity are an example for young men of today. His father was Wm. Baldwin, and a good mother influenced his future life. His father died when he was a mere child. The faithful mother brought up the children to fear God and love their fellow men.

Mr. Baldwin was of a mechanical turn in early life, as he constructed his toys, and would take apart toys given him to observe their construction. At sixteen he was apprenticed to the Woolworth Brothers, jewelers in Frankford, and became skillful in their work. He entered the jewelry business, and made beautiful designs.

On reflection he was not content in view of the account to be given to God at last to spend his time in making ornaments. This experience however helped him in machine-building.

He and David Mason, a machinist, became partners and made bookbinders' tools, which heretofore had been imported. They also made rollers for calico-printing, and improved the old style largely.

In 1829 they brought their first steam-engine, which did not satisfy Mr. Baldwin, and he built one himself from his own plan. This was the best stationary engine then built in this country. It worked over 40 years, driving finally the entire boiler-shop at the Broad street manufactory. The engine gave the firm a reputation and they led the country in making stationary engines.

In 1830 the Camden and Amboy Railroad Company imported an engine which they strove to keep from inspection, but Baldwin and Franklin Peale, who owned the Philadelphia Museum, found a way to see it in the warehouse. Mr. Baldwin examined it and enthusiastically declared that he could make one, as his face glowed with ardor at the thought of his new work. He made a model for Mr. Peale's Museum where tracks were laid in the old Arcade in

FRANKLIN SCHOOL, GEORGE A. PERRY, HEAD-MASTER.

1831; from 4 to 8 passengers were carried. The exhibition was a success, first showing Philadelphians that steam could act as a transporter.

In 1832 Baldwin built a locomotive for the Philadelphia and Germantown railway, for $4000, the machine being made in six months, and during its construction the shop was moved from Minor street to Jayne, then styled Lodge Alley, to where the Collins & McLeester Type Foundry now stands.

Though the engine succeeded, the railway company insisted on a reduction of $500 in the price. In the *Daily Advertiser* it was stated that the engine would go daily in fair weather with passenger cars, and on rainy days horses would be used, wet rails caused too much labor for the engine.

Thus began the Baldwin Locomotive Works, now known over the world and able to produce a locomotive daily. In 1835 the shops went to Broad and Hamilton streets. Mr. Baldwin made many improvements in locomotives, being an intense student of mechanics. He was noted for industry and honest dealing. He was a practical Christian and gave much aid to the Presbyterian Church work, being generous and acknowledging his obligations to God. He gave to benevolent objects in general, and was also a good citizen and active worker in organizations to improve society. He was a friend of the colored man. He was once in the Legislature and was an Inspector of the County Prison, and one of the founders of the Franklin Institute. He belonged to several important societies.

His love of flowers is perpetuated by his family in the kindly display of the beautiful handiwork of God to the crowds who pass along Chestnut street. Music and painting charmed Mr. Baldwin, and he loved to share his pleasures. He was patient and foreseeing, and overcame discouraging obstacles, leaving a bright example to young men.

He chose his home on Chestnut street, above 11th street, as he liked to be in the busy thoroughfare and to let others see those things which delighted him.

No. 3.

FRANKLIN SCHOOL.

Franklin School was first opened in September, 1885, by Mr. George A. Perry, who for several years had been classical master of Penn Charter School of this city. Dr. William Pepper, Provost of the University of Pennsylvania, gave the school its name. Among others who first rendered it valuable assistance were Mr. Henry R. Gummey, Mr. John P. Ilsley and Rev. James De Wolf Perry, D. D.

The school could hardly have been more fortunate in buildings and in location. The fine mansion erected at a cost of $100,000 by the late Mr. Charles Magarge, on Germantown avenue, near Walnut lane, had stood unoccupied for some time and was readily secured. To enlarge the grounds, which extended from Germantown avenue to Adams street, but were too narrow to meet the requirements of the school, a large lot, 300x100 feet, was added from the adjoining estate of Mr. Shoemaker. By this addition and other improvements excellent provision has been made for out-door sports. It is scarcely necessary to state that in a building erected on a plan so massive and elegant, the rooms are exceptionally large, well ventilated and well-lighted. Seven of these have thus far been used for class rooms. The large Drawing Room on the left of the front entrance, has become the Assembly Room and Chapel, and is—like the other rooms—appropriately and tastefully furnished.

In 1887 the school was chartered. The corporation was composed of Mr. Hampton L. Carson, Mr. John G. Dunn, Mr. Henry S. Grove, Mr. Henry R. Gummey, Mr. Anson H. Hamilton, Mr. John P. Ilsley, Mr. Calvin Pardee, Dr. Thomas C. Potter, Mr. Francis Rawle, Dr. George Strawbridge, Mr. George Willing and Mr. James B. Young. Thus the school was established on a substantial and permanent basis and was enabled to carry out more perfectly the purpose for which it was founded.

This purpose contemplated a school for boys in which the highest standard of preparation for college and the schools of science should be united with extended instruction in English literature and in history, and where the association of pupils should be wholesome and elevated. Other important features are the training in articulation, expressive reading and elocution, and a system of physical culture founded upon that which was formulated by Delsarte. Vocal music and drawing are also included in the instruction given.

The present Staff of Instructors is as follows: Head-Master, George A. Perry, A. M. (Wesleyan University); Mrs. George A. Perry, A. B. (Vassar College); George P. Bacon, A. B. (Dartmouth College); John Rummell, O. M. (Monroe College of Oratory); Miss M. Margaret Fine, A. B. (Wellesley College); Miss Ethel Percy (Wellesley College, and the Sorbonne, Paris); Mr. B. Monteith (Music).

No. 4.

RESIDENCES OF G. RALSTON AYERS AND S. HUCKEL, Jr.

These new residences occupy the western half of what was formerly the Ketterlinus estate and creditably represent the new style of suburban architecture, for which this section, including School Lane, is noted. The house of G. Ralston Ayers stands directly on the corner of Wissahickon and Chelten avenues, and overlooks the century-old trees on the Strawbridge estate. From the tower of this house a view is afforded of the Wissahickon valley and Roxboro beyond and stretching away as far as Chestnut Hill. It is one of the handsomest of the new residences in this beautiful suburb, and possesses many unique points in architecture, prominent among them being the large hall and

RESIDENCES OF G. RALSTON AYERS AND S. HUCKEL.

stairway from first floor to skylight and tower, all finished in hand-carved hard woods. The draperies and ornamentation are in perfect harmony. The wall, ceiling and frieze of each room are in one color but in many different shades, and so delicately blended as to produce a most pleasing effect.

The adjoining residence of Mr. Huckel is a sample of the revival of the old colonial style, with its black-end brick, classic column and quaint shingled gables, similar to many of the historic houses herein described, and is a creditable example of the professional skill of Mr. Huckel who was the architect of both of these buildings.

No. 5.

"Philellena," No. 5510 Main Street, Germantown. The name of this beautiful place was given to it by George W. Carpenter in honor of his wife, Ellen, being a combination of a Greek syllable signifying affection with her first name. The lawn is extensive, bounding both Main and Carpenter streets. The shade and fruit trees and statuary and museum and fountain and the various buildings, including one that has an office and clock tower, diversify the scene.

Mr. George W. Carpenter's collection of minerals was extensive and well selected. Birds and shells are added to these curiosities. An old stone barn, with its openings for ventilation, and its surmounting bell, is a pretty feature on Carpenter street. It seems to protest against the widening of the street, and to envy the fine new cottages around it. The mansion stands far back from Main street, giving a good effect to the landscape. The elms and other monarchs of the wood rejoice in the ample space allowed them.

No. 6.

The following list of books, published by S. Sower, from Prof. Seidensticker, should be added to the letter on p. 421, of this volume. The Professor has the titles of other German books of this publisher.

1791. Ein ganz neu eingerichtetes Lutherisches A. B. C. Buchstabir und Namenbuch. Chestnut Hill.
1792. Die Kleine Harfe.
" Gobias Hirtes auserlesenes gemeinnütziges Handbüchlein.
" Verschiedene alte und neue Geschichten von Erscheinungen der Geister.
" Die Wege und Werke Gottes in der Seele.
" Ein Gespruch zwischen einem Pilger und Bürger.
1793. Kurzer Bericht von der Pest Ein neues auserlesenes gemeinnütziges Handbüchlein.

No. 7.

THE CUYLER ARMY HOSPITAL.

The following data concerning this hospital was furnished by Dr. James Darrach, of Germantown:

"In the year 1862 the city of Philadelphia offered the Town Hall, of Germantown, to the United States Government for hospital purposes. Under the influence of a number of patriotic ladies Dr. Darrach went to Washington and obtained from the Surgeon General an order to the Medical Director of this district, and in July of the same year the hospital was organized, with Dr. James Darrach as Surgeon-in-charge, and Drs. J. M. Leedom, W. R. Dunton, T. F. Betton, R. N. Downs, C. R. Prall, W. Darrach, Jr., Horace Y. Evans, John Ashhurst, Jr., and P. D. Keyser, as Assistant Surgeons. The capacity of the original building being too limited, additions were made which enabled the hospital to accommodate 630 beds. About this time it received the name of Cuyler Hospital in honor of John M. Cuyler, M. D., Medical Director, U. S. A. The ladies of Germantown continued to take an active interest in the hospital, and through their efforts was established a contribution room from which delicacies were daily supplied to the sick and wounded soldiers. About a year after the organization of the hospital Dr. Darrach resigned, and was followed by Dr. Josiah Curtis, U. S. Vol., and subsequently by Dr. H. S. Shell, U. S. A. The hospital continued to receive patients until the end of the war, and served a good purpose in receiving convalescent patients from the field hospitals, thus making room for those who needed prompt attention near the battle field. The hospital was closed at the end of the war, and the remaining patients were transferred to the Mower Hospital, Chestnut Hill."

Index.

A

	PAGE.
Academy, Germantown,	75
Agnew, General,	33
Allen Family,	386
America, Sons and Daughters of,	334
Antes, Henry; Rev. E. McMinn's Life of,	253
Armat, Thomas,	20
Army Hospital,	538
Ax Burying Ground,	180
Ayers, G. Ralston, Residence,	536

B

Baldwin, Matthias W.,	534
Balfour, Major,	253
Bank, Germantown Nat'onal,	337
Bank of Germantown,	101
Bardsley, John,	238
Barren Hill, 501; Retreat of, by Charles S. Keyser, Esq.,	511
Bartram, John,	178
Battle of Germantown, 192; Centennial,	203
Bayard House,	255
Bayne, John,	213
Bean, Col. Theo. W.,	202
"Beehive," Pastorius's,	258–263
Belfield,	37
Benezet, John Stephen,	230
Bensell, Dr. George,	102
Benson's (E. N.) Mansion,	468
Betton, Dr. T. F.,	54
Bentz, Jacob and John,	243
Billmeyer House,	284
Bird, Col.,	33
Black's (Wm.) Journal,	253
Blair, Rev. Dr.,	185
Bleachfield,	217
Blight, George,	296

INDEX.

	PAGE.
Bockius, Charles,	224
Born, Cornelius,	262
Bradford, William,	256
Bringhurst House,	41
Buchanan, Roberdeau,	190
Buck Hotel,	242
Burying Ground, Lower, 33, Upper. 170, 229, 241, Ax, 180, Old Tree, 407, Towamensing,	203
Butler (Ellen) Memorial,	343
Butler, E. H.,	141
Button, John,	232

C.

Carlton,	220
Carpenter, Geo. W.,	537
Channon, John C.,	135
Chestnut Hill,	399
Chew House,	192
Chew Coach,	196
Churchill Hall,	528
Church, Trinity Lutheran,	292
" Grace Episcopal, Mt. Airy,	354
" Mt. Airy Presbyterian,	356
" St. John's Episcopal,	37
" St. Stephen's M. E.,	41
" St. Luke's Episcopal,	80
" First Presbyterian,	114
" Zion Evangelical,	117
" First Baptist,	136
" St. Vincent de Paul's R. C.,	136
" St. Michael's Episcopal,	152
" St. Michael's Lutheran,	286, 291
" Mennonite,	534, 156
" St. Peter's Episcopal,	160
" Christ Episcopal,	163
" Second Baptist,	218
" Dunkard,	226
" Calvary Episcopal,	276
" Mt. Airy M. E.,	358
" Christ Lutheran, Chestnut Hill,	407
" Market Square Presbyterian,	86
" St. Martin's Episcopal, Chestnut Hill,	424
" Presbyterian, Chestnut Hill,	426
" M. E., Chestnut Hill,	428

INDEX.

	PAGE.
Church, Baptist, Chestnut Hill,	433
" St. Paul's Episcopal, Chestnut Hill,	445
" Our Mother of Consolation, R. C., Chestnut Hill,	455
" St. Peter's Lutheran, Barren Hill,	502
" St. Thomas's Episcopal, White Marsh,	521
" Springfield Presbyterian,	523
" Union,	523
" Cold Point Baptist,	524
Coach, Chew,	196
Cocoomery,	230
Collinson,	178
Comly, Franklin A.,	520
Concord School House,	169
Conrad, Dennis,	245
Consumptives' Home,	439
Cope, Caleb,	483
Cope's Grotto,	417
Cornwallis, General,	201
Corvy, The,	302
Coryell, Lewis S.,	314
Coulter, John,	223
Courts,	246, 254
Craik, Dr.,	201
Craik, Rev. Dr.,	201
Cresheim,	380
Cromwell, Oliver,	245
Cuyler Army Hospital,	538

D

Delaware River,	256
Deshler, David,	66
Devonshire Place,	296
Dispensary,	342
Donat's Hotel,	414
Dorr, Rev. Dr.,	245
Dreer, Ferdinand J.,	245
Drinker, Edward,	262
Druim Moir,	422
Dunn's (C. B.) Residence,	491
Dunton, Dr.,	155
Duplessis, Chevalier,	201
Duval, James S.,	184

E

Earthquake,	190
Eldon, The,	509

INDEX.

	PAGE.
Ely, Bishop Benjamin,	230
Engle House,	142
Evergreens, The,	472

F

Fair Hill,	262
Feeble-Minded Children,	343
Fire Insurance Company,	339
Fisher, Joshua,	34
Forrest, Col.,	180
Fountain Inn,	303
Frame, Richard,	256
Franklin School,	335
Frankfort Land Company,	229, 261
Freas, Col. Philip R.,	38
Freas, Henry,	231
Friends' Meeting-House, 62, Plymouth,	524
Friends' Home for Children,	343
Funeral Invitations,	272

G

Galloway, Joseph,	463
Germans, 253, 259, 267, Commemoration Day, 264, Characteristics,	265
Glen Fern and Livezy Family,	395
Gowen, F. B., Residence of,	388
Gowen Family,	388
Green Tree Tavern,	155
Greene, Gen.,	201
Gross, Dr. F. H.,	264

H

Hacker's (Jeremiah) House,	241
Haines, Reuben,	167
Haines, Miss,	211
Haight, Rev. Dr.,	201
Hartel, Andreas,	260
Haunted House,	405
Hazard, Willis D.,	244
Hinego, Michael,	191
Holstein, Maj. Matthias,	231
Hood, William,	31
Horticultural Society,	343
Horseback Riding,	217
Hospital, Cuyler Army,	538

INDEX.

	PAGE.
Houston, H. H.,	422
Houses, ...	240
Howe, Gen., . . .	201
Huckel, S., Jr., Residence of,	536
Hudson, Wm., . .	262

I

Indians, 246, 258, Rock, . .	457
Indian Missionary, Rev. F. Post,	307
Inn, Mt. Pleasant, .	360
Inn, King of Prussia,	105
Inquirer Phila., . .	264

J

Johnson Houses, ...	164, 165
Johnson, Justus, 231, Anthony, 231, Johnson Family,	323
Johnson, William N., M. D., . . .	173
Jones, Judge J. Righter, . .	203
Jones, Hon. Horatio Gates, .	118
Jordan, J. W., . . .	135
Junkin, Rev. Dr. George, .	185

K

Kalm, Peter, .	38
Kelpius, John, . .	178
Kelsey Place, ...	439
Kerper's (Daniel) Reminiscences,	408
Keyser, Rev. Peter, Jr., .	167, 224, 227, 237
Keyser, Dr. Peter D., .	170
Keyser, Jacob, . . .	185
Keyser, Dirk, .	271
Klinckens, .	223
Knox, General, .	201
Kulpsville, .	201

L

Land, price of, .	246
Lafayette College .	187
Laurens, John, . .	201
Lambdin, Dr. Alfred C.,	200
Levering Family, .	178
Levick, Dr. J. J., ...	175, 262
Library, Friends', 65, Association, . .	341
Library, Lovett Free, 386, Christian Hall.	427

INDEX.

	PAGE.
Lippard, George,	203, 280
Littell–Morris House,	142
Littell, Rev. Dr. T. G.,	155
Littell, C. Willing, Esq.,	143
Little, Amos R.,	280
Livezy, Thomas, 463, Family,	395
Lloyd, Governor Thomas,	262
Locke, John Engelbert,	135
Logan, James,	21
Logan, Deborah,	21, 254
Lossing's Field Book,	199
Lossing, Benson J.,	519
Lowell, E. J.,	202
Ludwig, Christopher,	288
Lutheran Home,	351

M.

Mackinett, Widow,	201
Matthias,	178
Manual Labor School,	185
Marshall, Chief Justice,	201
Marshall, Christopher,	201
Maxwell, Gen.,	201
Marriage Certificates,	271
Masons (Free),	332, 415
Martin's (St.) Church,	424
Meng Family,	315
Meehan's Nursery,	331
Mechanics, O. U. A.,	333
Mermaids,	393
Miller's (John) Diary,	211
Middleton, Joseph,	456, 458
Morris House,	66
Moravians,	122
Morris–Littell House,	142
Moyer,	230
More, Dr. Nicholas,	257
Morton's (Rob't) Diary,	253
Mount Airy,	349
Montgomery Avenue,	545
Mt. Airy College,	363
Murphy, Rev. Dr. J. K.,	175
Murdock, James E.,	231
Muhlenberg, Rev. H. M.,	254

INDEX.

	PAGE.
MacKellar, Thomas, . . .	237
McClenachan, Blair, ...	194
McCullough's (R. P.) Residence,	283

N.

Nash, Gen., .	201
Neglee's Hill, .	20
Neil, Rev. Hugh,	125
Newspapers, .	479
Norris, Isaac, .	262
Norris, Mrs. Mary,	263
Northern Liberties, . .	265
North's (George H.) Residence,	452
Norwood Hall, .	458
Norwood Avenue,	488

O

Odd Fellows, .	335, 337
Ogden, Rev. J. C.,	. 124
Orchestral Society, . .	. 345
Owen, General Joshua T., .	492
Ottinger, Douglass.	30

P

Pardee, Calvin, . .	. See Churchill Hall
Paper-Mill, . .	. 121
Paxton Boys, ...	254
Paul House, The, ...	. 255
Pastorius, Francis D., 256. Mrs. Washington,	. . 264
Pennypacker, Sam'l W., .	10, 258, 261
Peale, Charles Wilson,	. 37
Penn, William, . .	. 259
Phillips, Wm., . .	213
Philellena, .	. 537
Physicians, . .	262
Physick, Philip Syng.	230
Pickering, Col., . .	. 202
Platt, Wm., . .	. 487
Poor-House, .	167
Post, Rev. F.,	307
Pomona Grove, . . .	180
Post Office, Chestnut Hill.	. 432
Potter, Mrs. Thos.,	. 472
Potter, Thomas,	. 472

INDEX.

	PAGE.
Potter, William,	484
Potter, Charles A.,	484
Pythias, Knights of,	334

Q.

Queen Street,	219

R.

Railroad, Penna.,	416
Railroad, Reading,	495
Reminiscences,	250
Reading Turnpike,	497
Revolution,	45, 229, 253
Richards,	230
Richardson, Samuel	262
Rittenhouse Family,	118
Roads,	239
Roberdeau Family,	188
Roberdeau, Major,	231
Rochefaucault,	313
Rodney, James Duval, Esq.,	180, 229
Rodney Rev. John,	185
Rush, Dr.,	259
Rutherford, Robert,	228

S.

Sauer, Samuel,	418, 537
Saving Fund,	338
Scharf & Westcott's Philadelphia,	259, 261
Scheetz, General Henry,	524
Schlatter, Rev. Michael,	447
Schoolhouse Lane,	125
Schumacher, Sarah,	77
Schutzen Park,	223
Seidensticker, Prof. Oswald,	259, 261, 419, 421, 537
Seligius, Johannes,	178
Sener, Sven,	262
Ship House,	223
Shippen, Dr. Wm.,	189
Shoemaker, Robert,	123
Shoemaker, Samuel,	259
Smith, Aubrey H. Esq.,	211
Smith, Cornelius S.,	220
Societies,	332

INDEX.

	PAGE.
Soldiers' Monument,	211
Springfield,	, 518
Sprogell Family,	. 150
Stallman's (John) Reminiscences,	. 410
Steamboat House,	353
Stenton,	215
Stenton Avenue,	438
Stone, Frederick D.,	9
Stokes's Mill,	83
Stokes, Charles,	252
Stonecliffe,	. 464
Stuart, Edwin S.,	. 244
St. Vincent's Seminary,	. 242
Sullivan, General,	. 201
Summit Street,	437
Sweden, Holm's New,	. 256

T.

Tacitus,	259
Taylor, Charles,	464
Taylor, Enoch,	. 231
Thomas, Gabriel,	. 10-19
Thomas, Governor,	. 259
Thomas's (Geo. C.) Residence,	451
Townsend, Richard,	. 246
Toll Gate,	137
Traichel Place,	132
Tulpohocken Street,	239
Tunkens,	. 246
Tulpohocken Street,	. 320
Tustin, Rev. Dr. J. P.,	. 185
Turnpike, Reading,	. 497

U.

Ulmer, Wm. A.,	112
Unrod Family,	. 231
Unruh Houses,	. 324
Unruh Family,	. 325
Upsal,	172

V.

Valley Forge,	. 202
Vaux, Hon. Richard,	133, 507
Venable's Hist. U. S.,	. 211
Von Wurm, Col.,	. 201

INDEX.

W.

	PAGE.
Wakefield,	37
Wallace, John William,	256
War Times,	384, 247
Ward, Townsend,	9, 29, 253
Warner Family,	175
Wasey, Capt. Joseph,	262
Washington House,	66
Washington Tavern,	240
Washington Lane,	152
Washington's Piety,	201
Washington's Headquarters,	518
Water Works,	327
Watson, John F.,	76
Watson's Annals,	244
Wayne, General,	201
Well at Chew House,	281
Welsh, John,	330
West, Benjamin,	259
White Cottage,	54
Whitemarsh,	520, 526
Whittiers's Pennsylvania Pilgrim,	261
Wilkinson, General,	202
Williams, Henry J., Esq.,	436
Wilson, Alexander,	38, 191
Wissahickon Inn,	401
Wissahickon Drive,	496
Wissahickon Creek,	517
Wister (John) House,	12
Wister, C. J.,	42, 244, 253
Wister, Wm. Wynne,	302
Witherspoon, Major,	201
Witherspoon, Parson,	201
Witt, Dr.,	175, 176, 231
Women's Christian Association,	341
Woodward, Col. George A.,	132
Working Men's Club,	341
Wright, Susannah,	252
Wyck,	147

Y.

Yagers,	201
Yeakel Cottage,	404
Young Men's Christian Association,	138

www.ingramcontent.com/pod-product-compliance
Lightning Source LLC
Chambersburg PA
CBHW021226300426
44111CB00007B/442